The Waite Group's

C Primer Plus

Third Edition

Stephen Prata

A Division of Macmillan Computer Publishing
201 West 103rd St., Indianapolis, Indiana, 46290 USA

The Waite Group's C Primer Plus, Third Edition

Copyright © 1999 by Sams Publishing

International Standard Book Number: 1-57169-161-8

Library of Congress Catalog Card Number: 98-85904

Printed in the United States of America

First Printing: September 1998

00 99 98   4 3 2 1

Trademarks

Warning and Disclaimer

Executive Editor
Tracy Dunkelberger

Acquisitions Editor
Tracy Dunkelberger

Development Editor
Sean Dixon

Managing Editor
Jodi Jensen

Project/Copy Editor
Lisa M. Lord

Indexer
Tom Dinse

Technical Editor
Michael J. Tobler

Software Specialist
Dan Scherf

Cover Design
Karen Ruggles

Production
Mona Brown
Michael Dietsch
Ayanna Lacey
Heather Miller
Gene Redding

The Waite Group's C Primer Plus, Third Edition

Copyright © 1999 by Sams Publishing

International Standard Book Number: 1-57169-161-8

Library of Congress Catalog Card Number: 98-85904

Printed in the United States of America

First Printing: September 1998

00 99 98   4   3   2   1

Trademarks

Warning and Disclaimer

Executive Editor
Tracy Dunkelberger

Acquisitions Editor
Tracy Dunkelberger

Development Editor
Sean Dixon

Managing Editor
Jodi Jensen

Project/Copy Editor
Lisa M. Lord

Indexer
Tom Dinse

Technical Editor
Michael J. Tobler

Software Specialist
Dan Scherf

Cover Design
Karen Ruggles

Production
Mona Brown
Michael Dietsch
Ayanna Lacey
Heather Miller
Gene Redding

Contents at a Glance

Contents

Preface

Preface to the Third Edition

This edition of *The Waite Group's C Primer Plus* continues a tradition of aiding and encouraging those who want to learn the C programming language. The prefaces to the previous editions describe the underlying philosophy and approach of the book, so let's turn to what's new.

- Coverage of the ANSI C library has been expanded, and Appendix F, "The Standard ANSI C Library," describes the entire library.

- Now that the ANSI C standard has been around for several years, this edition devotes less space to the discussion of pre-ANSI C.

- Examples have been retested yet again using several compilers, including the latest from Microsoft and Metrowerks.

- The book discusses many of the additions to the ANSI C standard proposed by the C9X committee, some of which are already available on many compilers.

- Appendix G discusses the issues facing those wanting to compile C programs with a purely C++ compiler.

- The process of refining and improving the presentation continues.

We hope you find this newest edition enjoyable and helpful.

Preface to the Second Edition

The Waite Group's *New C Primer Plus* has, we hope, met the objectives outlined in the preface to the first edition. We were pleased to learn that the Computer Press Association recognized *New C Primer Plus* as the best how-to book of 1990, and now we're trying to improve on that book. Here's what's new this time:

- A new chapter (Chapter 17) explores the philosophy and techniques of advanced data representations. The first 16 chapters concentrate on presenting the C language to you, and this chapter focuses on introducing you to the science of programming.

- The book is ANSI-er than ever, with an earlier emphasis on following ANSI C precepts.

- Examples have been retested using the latest compilers from Microsoft and Borland.

- We pay greater attention to the Macintosh user by offering guidance on using Think C.

We hope you enjoy this book and that it helps you learn and take pleasure in C.

Preface to the First Edition

C was a relatively little-known language when we wrote *C Primer Plus* in 1984. Since then, the language has boomed. Although we don't claim that our book caused the boom, it is true that the book has helped many people learn C. Now that C is getting a new standard (ANSI C), we felt it was time for a new *C Primer Plus*. So here it is, now titled *The Waite Group's C Primer Plus*.

What's new with this edition? Here are the main changes:

- Completely revamped text to bring the book into accord with the ANSI C standard. This standard was developed by a committee of the American National Standards Institute (ANSI) in response to a need created by C's success and its spread to a variety of computer platforms. The standard is scheduled for final adoption soon.

- Revised examples, figures, and explanations.

- New order of presentation, based on reader feedback.

- Expanded coverage of C topics, including bitwise operators, enumerated types, and the C preprocessor.

- More complete discussion of functions from the C library.

We've also retained much from the earlier editions. In particular, we've kept the philosophy that the book should be a friendly, easy-to-use, self-study guide, as is reflected in the following points:

- We don't assume that you are a professional programmer. We explain programming ideas along with the C language.

- We emphasize an interactive approach. Because you learn by doing, we often use short, easily typed examples that illustrate just one or two concepts at a time.

- We clarify ideas with figures and illustrations.

- We summarize the main C features in highlighted boxes.

- We provide review questions and programming exercises so that you can test and improve your understanding of C.

Our goal in writing this introduction to C has been to make it instructive, clear, and helpful. To gain the greatest benefit, you should take as active a role as possible. Don't just read the examples. Enter them into your system and try them. C is a very portable language, but you may find differences between how a program works on your system and how it works on ours. Experiment—change part of a program to see what the effect is. Modify a program to do something slightly different. Ignore our occasional warnings and see what happens when you do the wrong thing. Try the questions and exercises. The more you do yourself, the more you will learn and remember.

We wish you good fortune in learning C. We've tried to make this book meet your needs, and we hope it helps you reach your goals.

About the Author

Stephen Prata is a professor of physics and astronomy at The College of Marin in Kentfield, California, where he teaches astronomy, physics, and programming. He received his B.S. from the California Institute of Technology and his Ph.D. from the University of California, Berkeley. His association with computers began with the computer modeling of star clusters. Stephen has authored or co-authored over a dozen books for The Waite Group, including *C++ Primer Plus* and *Certified Course in Visual Basic 4*.

Dedication

With love to Vicky and Bill Prata, who, for more than 60 years, have been showing how rewarding marriage can be.

—SP

Acknowledgments

Acknowledgments for the Third Edition

The authors wish to thank Michael J. Tobler, Sean Dixon, and especially Lisa Lord and Tracy Dunkelberger for their help.

Acknowledgments for the Second Edition

The authors wish to thank John Crudo and Scott Calamar for guiding the second edition to completion and Harry Henderson for his editorial feedback.

Acknowledgments for the First Edition

The authors wish to thank Scott Calamar of The Waite Group for guiding this book through the writing, editing, and production stages. We particularly wish to thank Bryan Costales for his useful and knowledgeable editing of the first draft.

Tell Us What You Think!

As the reader of this book, *you* are our most important critic and commentator. We value your opinion and want to know what we're doing right, what we could do better, what areas you'd like to see us publish in, and any other words of wisdom you're willing to pass our way.

As the Executive Editor for the Advanced Programming and Distributed Architectures team at Macmillan Computer Publishing, I welcome your comments. You can fax, e-mail, or write me directly to let me know what you did or didn't like about this book—as well as what we can do to make our books stronger.

Please note that I cannot help you with technical problems related to the topic of this book, and that because of the high volume of mail I receive, I might not be able to reply to every message.

When you write, please be sure to include this book's title and author as well as your name and phone or fax number. I will carefully review your comments and share them with the author and editors who worked on the book.

Fax: 317-817-7070
E-mail: `programming@mcp.com`
Mail: Tracy Dunkelberger
          Executive Editor
          Advanced Programming and Distributed Architectures
          Macmillan Computer Publishing
          201 West 103rd Street
          Indianapolis, IN 46290 USA

CHAPTER 1

GETTING READY

*I*n this chapter, you learn about C's history and features, examine the steps needed to write programs, learn a bit about compilers and linkers, and look at C standards.

Welcome to the world of C—a vigorous, professional programming language popular with amateur and commercial programmers alike. This chapter prepares you for learning and using this powerful and popular language, and it introduces you to the kinds of environments in which you will most likely develop your C-legs.

First, we look at C's origin and examine some of its features, both strengths and drawbacks. Then we examine some general principles for programming. Finally, we discuss how to run C programs on some common systems.

Whence C?

Dennis Ritchie of Bell Labs created C in 1972 as he and Ken Thompson worked on designing the UNIX operating system. C didn't spring full-grown from Ritchie's head, however. It came from Thompson's B language, which came from... but that's another story. The important point is that C was created as a tool for working programmers, so its chief goal is to be a useful language.

Most languages aim to be useful, but they often have other concerns. The main goal for Pascal, for instance, was to provide a sound basis for teaching good programming principles. BASIC, on the other hand, was developed to resemble English so that it could be learned easily by students unfamiliar with computers. These are important goals, but they are not always compatible with pragmatic, workaday usefulness. C's development as a language designed for programmers, however, has made it the modern-day language of choice.

Why C?

During the past three decades, C has become one of the most important and popular programming languages. It has grown because people try it and like it. In the past decade, many have moved from C to the more ambitious C++ language, but C is still an important language in its own right, as well a migration path to C++. As you learn C, you will recognize its many virtues (see Figure 1.1). Let's preview a few of them now.

Flexible control structures

Structured format

Compact code—small programs

Portable to other computers

Figure 1.1 The virtues of C.

Design Features

C is a modern language incorporating the control features found desirable by the theory and practice of computer science. Its design makes it natural for users to use top-down planning, structured programming, and modular design. The result is a more reliable, understandable program.

Efficiency

C is an efficient language. Its design takes advantage of the abilities of current computers. C programs tend to be compact and to run quickly. In fact, C exhibits some of the fine control usually associated with assembly language. If you choose, you can fine-tune your programs for maximum speed or most efficient use of memory.

Portability

C is a portable language. That means C programs written on one system can be run with little or no modification on other systems. If modifications are necessary, they can often be made by simply changing a few entries in a header file accompanying the main program. Of course, most languages are meant to be portable, but anyone who has converted an IBM PC BASIC program to Apple BASIC (and they are close cousins) or tried to run an IBM mainframe FORTRAN program on a UNIX system knows that porting is troublesome at best. C is a leader in portability. C compilers are available for about 40 systems, running from 8-bit microprocessors to Cray supercomputers. Note, however, that the portions of a program written specifically to access particular hardware devices—such as a VGA monitor—or special features of an operating system, such as Windows or System 7.1, typically are not portable.

You Can Take C Home

Because C is portable, you can take your UNIX C programs home to use on a personal computer. Several C compilers are available now to enable you to do that, or you can take your home-grown programs to a UNIX system.

Power and Flexibility

C is powerful and flexible (two favorite words in computer literature). For example, most of the powerful, flexible UNIX operating system is written in C. Many compilers and interpreters for other languages—such as FORTRAN, APL, Pascal, LISP, Logo, and BASIC—have been written in C. Therefore, when you use FORTRAN on a UNIX machine, ultimately a C program has done the work of producing the final executable program. C programs have been used for solving physics and engineering problems and even for animating special effects for movies such as *Return of the Jedi*.

Programmer Oriented

C is oriented toward the needs of programmers. It gives you access to hardware, and it enables you to manipulate individual bits in memory. It has a rich selection of operators that allow you to express yourself succinctly. C is less strict than, say, Pascal, in limiting what you can do. This flexibility is both an advantage and a danger. The advantage is that many tasks, such as converting forms of data, are much simpler in C. The danger is that with C, you can make mistakes that are impossible in some languages. C gives you more freedom, but it also puts more responsibility on you.

Also, most C implementations have a large library of useful C functions. These functions deal with many needs commonly facing the programmer.

Shortcomings

C does have some faults. Often, as with people, faults and virtues are opposite sides of the same feature. For example, we've mentioned that C's freedom of expression also requires added responsibility. C's use of pointers, in particular, means you can make programming errors that are very difficult to trace. As one computer preliterate once commented, the price of liberty is eternal vigilance.

C's conciseness combined with its wealth of operators make it possible to prepare code that is extremely difficult to follow. You aren't compelled to write obscure code, but the opportunity is there. After all, what other language has a yearly Obfuscated Code contest?

There are more virtues and, undoubtedly, a few more faults. Rather than delve further into the matter, let's move on to a new topic.

Whither C?

By the early 1980s, C was already a dominant language in the minicomputer world of UNIX systems. Since then, it has spread to personal computers (microcomputers) and to mainframes (the big guys). See Figure 1.2. Many software houses use C as the preferred language for producing word processing programs, spreadsheets, compilers, and other products. These companies know that C produces compact and efficient programs. More important, they know that these programs will be easy to modify and easy to adapt to new models of computers.

What's good for the companies and the C veterans is good for other users, too. More and more computer users are turning to C to secure its advantages for themselves. You don't have to be a computer professional to use C.

In the 1990s, we should point out, many software houses are turning to the C++ language for large programming projects. C++ grafts object-oriented programming tools to the C language. C++ is nearly a superset of C, meaning that any C program is, or nearly is, a valid C++ program, too. By learning C, you also learn much of C++.

In short, C is one of the most important programming languages and will continue to be so. It is used on mainframes, minicomputers, and personal computers. It is used by software companies, computer science students, and enthusiasts of all sorts. If you want a job writing software, one of the first questions you should be able to answer yes to is "Oh say, can you C?"

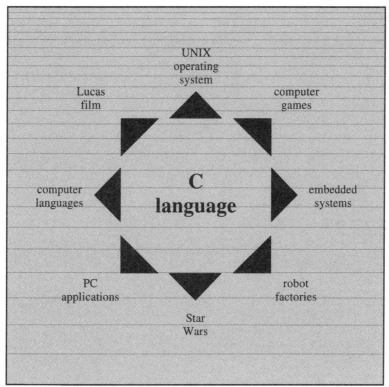

Figure 1.2 Where C is used.

Using C: Seven Steps

C is a compiled language. If you are accustomed to using a compiled language, such as Pascal or FORTRAN, you will be familiar with the basic steps in putting together a C program. If your background is in an interpreted language, however—such as BASIC or Logo—or if you have no background at all, you need to learn how to compile. We'll soon guide you through that process, and you'll see that it is straightforward and sensible. First, to give you an overview of programming, we'll break down the act of writing a C program into seven steps (see Figure 1.3).

Step 1: Define the Program Objectives

Naturally enough, you should start with a clear idea of what you want the program to do. Think in terms of the information your program needs, the feats of calculation and manipulation the program needs to do, and the information the program should report back to you. At this level of planning, you should be thinking in general terms, not in terms of some specific computer language.

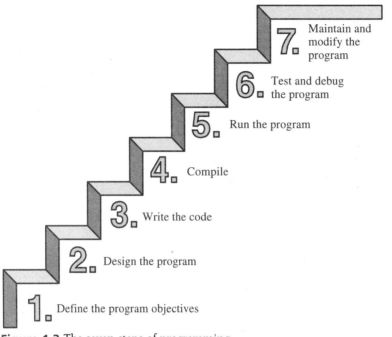

Figure 1.3 The seven steps of programming.

Step 2: Design the Program

After you have a conceptual picture of what your program ought to do, you should decide how the program will go about it. What should the user interface be like? How should the program be organized? Who will the target user be? How much time do you have to complete the program?

You also need to decide how to represent the data in the program and, possibly, in auxiliary files, and which methods to use to process the data. As you first learn programming in C, the choices will be simple, but as you deal with more complex situations, you'll find that these decisions require more thought. Choosing a good way to represent the information can often make designing the program and processing the data much easier.

Again, you should be thinking in general terms, not about specific code, but some of your decisions may be based on general characteristics of the language. For example, a C programmer has more options in data representation than, say, a BASIC programmer.

Step 3: Write the Code

Now that you have a clear design for your program, you can begin to implement it by writing the code. That is, you translate your program design into the C language. Here is where you really have to put your knowledge of C to work. You can sketch your ideas on paper, but eventually you have to get your code into the computer. The mechanics of this process depend on your programming environment. We'll present the details for some common environments soon. In general, you use a text editor to create what is called a *source code* file. This file contains the C rendition of your program design. Listing 1.1 shows an example of C source code.

Listing 1.1 An example of C source code.

```
#include <stdio.h>
int main(void)
{
  int dogs;

  printf("How many dogs do you have?\n");
  scanf("%d", &dogs);
  printf("So you have %d dog(s)!\n", dogs);
  return 0;
}
```

As part of this step, you should document your work. The simplest way is to use C's comment facility to incorporate explanations into your source code. We'll explain more about using comments in Chapter 2, "Introducing C."

Step 4: Compile

The next step is to *compile* the source code. Again, the details depend on your programming environment, and we'll look at some common environments shortly. Here, we'll take a more conceptual view of what happens.

The *compiler* is a program whose job is to convert source code into executable code. *Executable code* is code in the native, or machine, language of your computer. Different computers have different machine languages, and a C compiler translates C to a particular machine language. C compilers also incorporate code from C libraries into the final program; the libraries contain a fund of standard routines, such as `printf()` and `scanf()`, for your use. (More accurately, a program called a *linker* brings in the library routines, but on most systems the compiler runs the linker for you.) The end result is an executable file containing code that the computer understands and that you can run.

The compiler also checks that your program is valid C. If the compiler finds errors, it reports them to you and doesn't produce an executable file. Understanding a particular compiler's complaints is another skill you will pick up.

Step 5: Run the Program

Traditionally, the executable file is a runnable program. To run the program in many common environments, including UNIX and MS-DOS, just type the name of the executable file. Other environments, such as VMS on a VAX, might require a run command or some other mechanism. *Integrated development environments* (IDEs), such as those provided for Windows and Macintosh environments, let you edit and execute your C program from within the IDE by selecting choices from a menu or by pressing special keys.

Step 6: Test and Debug the Program

The fact that your program runs is a good sign, but it's possible that it could run incorrectly. Therefore, you should check to see that your program does what it is supposed to do. You'll find that some of your programs have mistakes—*bugs*, in computer jargon. *Debugging* is finding and fixing program errors. Making mistakes is a natural part of learning. It seems inherent to programming, too, so when you combine learning and programming, you had best prepare yourself to be reminded often of your fallibility. As you become a more powerful and subtle programmer, your errors, too, will become more powerful and subtle.

You have many opportunities to err. You can make a basic design error. You can implement good ideas incorrectly. You can overlook unexpected input that messes up your program. You can use C incorrectly. You can make typing errors. You can put parentheses in the wrong place, and so on. You'll find your own items to add to this list.

Fortunately, the situation isn't hopeless, although there might be times when you think it is. The compiler catches many kinds of errors, and there are things you can do to help yourself track down the ones that the compiler doesn't catch. Throughout this book, we'll give you debugging advice.

Step 7: Maintain and Modify the Program

When you create a program for yourself or for someone else, that program could see extensive use. If it does, you'll probably find reasons to make changes in it. Perhaps there is a minor bug that shows up only when someone enters a name beginning with **Zz**, or you might think of a better way to do something in the program. You could add a clever new feature. You might adapt the program so that it runs on a different computer system. All these tasks are greatly simplified if you document the program clearly and if you follow sound design practices.

Commentary

Programming is not always as linear a process as we've just described. Sometimes you have to go back and forth between steps. For instance, when you are writing code, you might find that your plan was impractical, you may see a better way of doing things, or after you see how a program runs, you might feel motivated to change the design. Documenting your work helps you move back and forth between levels.

Most learners tend to neglect steps 1 and 2 (defining program objectives and designing the program) and go directly to step 3 (writing the program). The first programs you write are simple enough that you can visualize the whole process in your head. If you make a mistake, it's easy to find. As your programs grow longer and more complex, mental visualizations begin to fail, and errors get harder to find. Eventually, those who neglect the planning steps are condemned to hours of lost time, confusion, and frustration as they produce ugly, dysfunctional, and abstruse programs.

The moral here is that you should develop the habit of planning before coding. Use the ancient but honorable pen-and-pencil technology to jot down the objectives of your program and to outline the design. If you do so, you eventually reap substantial dividends in time saved and satisfaction gained.

Programming Mechanics

The exact steps you must follow to produce a program depend on your computer environment. Because C is portable, it's available in many environments, including UNIX, MS-DOS, Windows 95, and Macintosh. We'll look at some typical examples.

First, however, let's look at some aspects shared by many C environments, including the four we just mentioned. You don't really need to know what follows to run a C program, but it is good background. It can also help you understand why you have to go through some particular steps to get a C program.

When you write a program in the C language, you store what you write in a text file called a *source code file*. Most C systems, including the ones we mentioned, require that the name of the file end in .c: for example, wordcount.c and budget.c. The part of the name before the period is called the *basename* and the part after the period is called the *extension*. Therefore, budget is a basename and c is an extension. The combination budget.c is the filename. The name should also satisfy the requirements of the particular computer operating system. For example, MS-DOS is an operating systems for IBM PCs and clones. It requires that the basename be no more than 8 characters long, so the wordcount.c name mentioned earlier would not be a valid DOS filename. Some UNIX systems place a 14-character limit on the whole name, including the extension; other UNIX systems allow longer names, up to 255 characters. Windows 95 and Macintosh also allow long names.

So that we'll have something concrete to refer to, let's assume we have a source file called concrete.c containing the C source code in Listing 1.2.

Listing 1.2   The concrete.c program.

```
#include <stdio.h>
int main(void)
{
    printf("Concrete contains gravel and cement.\n");
    return 0;
}
```

Don't worry about the details of the source code file shown in Listing 1.2; you'll learn about them in Chapter 2.

Object Code Files, Executable Files, and Libraries

The basic strategy in C programming is to use programs that convert your source code file to an *executable file*, which is a file containing ready-to-run machine language code. C implementations do this in two steps: compiling and linking. The *compiler* converts your source code to an intermediate code, and the *linker* combines this with other code to produce the executable file. C uses this two-part approach to facilitate the modularization of programs. You can compile individual modules separately and then use the linker to combine the compiled modules later. That way, if you need to change one module, you don't have to recompile the other ones.

There are several choices for the form of the intermediate files. The most prevalent choice, and the one taken by the implementations we describe, is to convert the source code to machine language code, placing the result in an *object code file*, or *object file* for short. (We are assuming that your source code consists of a single file.) Although the object file contains machine language code, it is not ready to run. The object file contains the translation of your source code, but it is not yet a complete program.

The first element missing from the object code file is something called *start-up code*, which is code that acts as an interface between your program and the operating system. For example, you can run, say, an IBM PC compatible under DOS or under Linux, a UNIX variety. The hardware is the same in either case, so the same object code would work with both, but you would need different start-up code for DOS than you would for Linux because these systems handle programs differently from one another.

The second missing element is the code for library routines. Nearly all C programs make use of routines (called *functions*) that are part of the standard C library. For example, `con-crete.c` uses the function `printf()`. The object code file does not contain the code for this function; it merely contains instructions saying to use the `printf()` function. The actual code is stored in another file, called a *library*. A library file contains object code for many functions.

The role of the linker is to bring together these three elements—your object code, the standard start-up code for your system, and the library code—and put them together into a single file, the executable file. For library code, the linker extracts only the code needed for the functions you use from the library (see Figure 1.4).

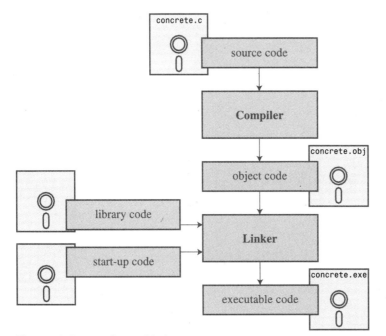

Figure 1.4 Compiler and linker.

In short, an object file and an executable file both consist of machine language instructions. The object file, however, contains the machine language translation only for the code you used, but the executable file also has machine code for the library routines you use and for the start-up code.

On some systems, you must run the compile and link programs separately. On other systems, the compiler starts the linker automatically, so that you have to give only the compile command.

Now let's look at some specific systems.

UNIX System

Because C's popularity began on UNIX systems, we will start there.

Editing on a UNIX System

Unlike BASIC, UNIX C does not have its own editor. Instead, you use one of the general-purpose UNIX editors, such as ed, ex, edit, emacs, jove or vi.

Your two main responsibilities are typing the program correctly and choosing a name for the file that will store the program. As we discussed, the name should end with .c. Note that UNIX distinguishes between uppercase and lowercase. Therefore, budget.c, BUDGET.c, and Budget.c are three distinct and valid names for C source files, but BUDGET.C is not a valid name because it uses an uppercase C instead of a lowercase c.

Here is an example. Using the vi editors, we prepared the following program and stored it in a file called inform.c.

```
#include <stdio.h>
int main(void)
{
    printf("A .c is used to end a C program filename.\n");
    return 0;
}
```

The text we just typed is the source code, and inform.c is the source file. The important point here is that the source file is the beginning of a process, not the end.

Compiling on a UNIX System

Our program, although undeniably brilliant, is still gibberish to a computer. A computer doesn't understand things like #include or printf. (At this point, you probably don't either, but you will soon learn, whereas the computer won't.) As we discussed earlier, we need the help of a compiler to translate our code (source code) to the computer's code (machine code). The result of our efforts will be the executable file, which contains all the machine code that the computer needs to get the job done.

The UNIX C compiler is called cc. To compile the inform.c program, you need to type just this:

```
cc inform.c
```

After a few seconds, the UNIX prompt will return, telling you that the deed is done. You might get warnings and error messages if you failed to write the program properly, but let's assume you did everything right. (If the compiler complains about the word **void**, your system has not yet updated to an ANSI C compiler. We'll talk more about standards soon. Meanwhile, just omit the word **void** from the example.) If you use **ls** to list your files, you will find that there is a new file called **a.out** (see Figure 1.5). This is the executable file containing the translation (or compilation) of the program. To run it, just type

```
a.out
```

and wisdom pours forth:

```
A .c is used to end a C program filename.
```

If you want to keep the executable file (**a.out**), you should rename it. Otherwise, the file is replaced by a new **a.out** the next time you compile a program.

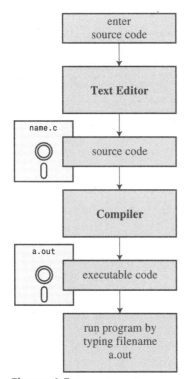

Figure 1.5 Preparing a C program using UNIX.

What about the object code? The **cc** compiler creates an object code file having the same basename as the source code, but with an **o** extension. In our example, the object code file is called **inform.o**, but you won't find it, for the linker removes it after the executable program has been completed. However, if the original program used more than one source code file, the object code files would be saved. When we discuss multiple-file programs later in the text, you will see that this is a fine idea.

Linux System

Linux is a popular public domain version of UNIX that runs on a variety of platforms, including IBM compatibles and Macintoshes. Preparing C programs on Linux is much the same as for UNIX systems, except that you would use the public domain C compiler, called gcc, that's provided by GNU. The compile command would look like this:

```
gcc inform.c
```

Note that installing gcc is optional when installing Linux, so you (or someone) might have to install gcc if it wasn't installed earlier. Typically, the installation makes cc an alias for gcc, so that you can use cc in the command line instead of gcc if you like.

Command-Line Compilers for the IBM PC

C compilers are not part of the PC operating system. They are add-ons, programs that have to be installed on the computer before you can create C programs.

The first C compilers for IBM PC compatibles were command-line compilers, which means you use them by typing commands at the DOS prompt. The usual cycle is first to run an editor program to create the source code, then exit the editor, and then run the compiler from the DOS command line. In short, the approach is much like that for UNIX. More recently, the trend has been toward integrated development environments (IDEs), which enable you to control the editing and compiling from one integrated program. In view of that, we'll make just a few general comments about using command-line compilers.

Source code files should be text files, not word processor files. (Word processor files contain a lot of additional information about fonts and formatting.) So you should use a text editor, such as the EDIT program that comes with some versions of DOS, or you can use a word processor, if you use the Save As feature to save the file in text mode. The file should have a .c extension. Some word processors automatically add a .txt extension to text files. If this happens to you, then you need to change the filename afterward, replacing txt with c.

Command-line C compilers typically, but not always, produce intermediate object code files having an .obj extension. Unlike UNIX compilers, C compilers don't remove these files when done. Some compilers produce assembly language files with .asm extensions or use some special format of their own.

Some compilers run the linker automatically after compiling; others might require that you run the linker manually. Linking results in the executable file, which appends the .exe extension to the original source code basename. For example, compiling and linking a source code file called concrete.c produces a file called concrete.exe. Some compilers provide an option to create an executable named concrete.com instead. In either case, you can run the program by typing the basename at the command line:

```
C>concrete
```

Integrated Development Environments (DOS)

The Inprise (formerly Borland) Turbo C/C++ 3.0 compiler is the most common IDE for DOS. It can run under DOS or in a DOS window under Windows. (The Borland C/C++ 3.1 compiler is similar.) After starting the program, choose File, New from the menu to create a new source code file. After entering your source code, choose File, Save from the menu to save the file. These products handle both C and C++ programs. When you save the file, use a `.c` extension to indicate that it is a C program; a `.cpp` extension indicates a C++ program.

There are a couple of paths to creating an executable file. One is to proceed step-by-step. First, choose Compile from the Compile menu. If that is successful, choose Link from the Compile menu. If that is successful, choose Run from the Run menu. Or you can just select Run as your first choice, and the Compile and Link stages are then executed first automatically.

The program runs in a DOS window, which disappears when the program finishes. However, choosing Output from the Window menu shows the results.

The IDE can have several windows open at once; for example, the editing window, the Output window, and a Message window. To compile, link, or run, make sure the editing window is the active window; you can do so by positioning the mouse cursor over the window and clicking.

Integrated Development Environments (Windows)

Quite a few vendors, including Microsoft, Inprise (formerly named Borland), Symantec, Watcom, and Metrowerks offer Windows-based IDEs. All have fast, integrated environments for putting together C programs. The key point is that each of these programs has a built-in editor you can use to write a C program. Each provides menus that enable you to name and save your source code file, as well as menus that allow you to compile and run your program without leaving the IDE. Each dumps you back into the editor if the compiler finds any errors, and each identifies the offending lines and matches them to the appropriate error messages.

The Windows IDEs are more complex than the DOS IDEs because they support a variety of *targets*, that is, a variety of environments in which the program will be used. For example, they might give you a choice of 16-bit Windows programs, 32-bit Windows programs, dynamic-link library files (DLLs), and so on. Many of the targets involve bringing in support for the Windows graphical interface. To manage these (and other) choices, you typically create a *project* to which you then add the names of the source code files you'll be using. The precise steps depend on the product you use. Typically, you first use the File menu or Project menu to create a project. What's important is choosing the correct form of project. The examples in this book are generic examples designed to run in a simple command-line environment. The various Windows IDEs provide one or more choices to match this undemanding assumption. Some earlier Microsoft compilers offered a QuickWin option, and some Borland compilers offered an EasyWin option; both are suitable. Otherwise, look for an option using terms such as *DOS e XE* or *Console* or *Character Mode executable*. These modes will run your executable program in a console-like window. When you have the correct project type, use the IDE menu to open a new source code file. For most products, you can do this by using the File menu. You may have to take additional steps to add the source file to the project.

Because the Windows IDEs typically handle both C and C++, you need to indicate that you want a C program. With some products, such as Metrowerks CodeWarrior, you use the project type to indicate that you want to use C. With other products, such as Microsoft Visual C++ 5.0, you use the `.c` file extension to indicate that you want to use C rather than C++. Some products, such as Inprise's C++Builder, do only C++. However, most C programs also work as C++ programs. Appendix G, "Differences Between C and C++," compares C and C++.

One problem you might encounter is that the window showing the program execution vanishes when the program terminates. If that is the case for you, you can make the program pause until you press the Enter key. To do that, add the following line to the end of the program, just before the `return` statement:

```
getchar();
```

This line reads a keystroke, so the program will pause until you press the Enter key. Sometimes, depending on how the program functions, there might already be a keystroke waiting. In that case, you'll have to use `getchar()` twice:

```
getchar();
getchar();
```

For example, if the last thing the program did was ask you to enter your weight, you would have typed your weight, and then pressed the Enter key to enter the data. The program would read the weight, the first `getchar()` would read the Enter key, and the second `getchar()` would cause the program to pause until you pressed Enter again. If this doesn't make a lot of sense to you now, it will after you learn more about C input.

Although the various IDEs share many broad principles in common, the details vary from product to product and, within a product line, from version to version. You'll have to do some experimenting to learn how your compiler works. You might even have to read the manual or try an online tutorial.

C on the Macintosh

The two best-known Macintosh C++ compilers are Metrowerks CodeWarrior and Symantec C++ compiler (formerly Think C) for the Macintosh. Both provide project-based IDEs similar, in basic concepts, to what you would find in a Windows compiler. (Indeed, both companies offer Windows-based versions of their compilers.) With either product, start by choosing New Project from the File menu. You'll be given a choice of project types. For CodeWarrior, select MacOS:C/C++:ANSI C Console in older versions, or MacOS:C/C++:Standard Console:Std C Console in more recent versions; for Symantec, select ANSII C. You might also have to choose between a 68KB version (for the Motorola 680X0 series of processors) or a PPC version (for the PowerPC processors).

Both products include a small source code file as part of the initial project. You can try compiling and running that program to see if you have your system set up properly. However, after you provide your own code, you should delete this file from the project by highlighting the file in the project window and then choosing Remove from the Project menu.

Next, you need to add your source code to the project. You can choose New from the File menu to create a new file or Open from the File menu to open an existing file. Use a proper suffix, such as `.cp` or `.cpp`. Use the Project menu to add this file to the project list. Some programs in this book require that you add more than one source code file. When you are ready, choose Run from the Project menu.

Why Compile?

Those of you used to BASIC might wonder about going through these steps to run a program. It might seem time-consuming, and it may even be time-consuming. After a program is compiled, however, it runs much faster than a standard BASIC program. You trade some inconvenience in getting a program running for a swifter final product. Also, if you use an integrated package, the inconvenience is much reduced.

Language Standards

Currently, many C implementations are available. Ideally, when you write a C program, it should work the same on any implementation, providing it doesn't use machine-specific programming. For this to be true in practice, different implementations need to conform to a recognized standard.

At first, there was no official standard for C. Instead, the first edition of *The C Programming Language* by Brian Kernighan and Dennis Ritchie (1978) became the accepted standard, usually referred to as *K&R C* or *classic C*. In particular, the "C Reference Manual" in the book's appendix acted as the guide to C implementors. Compilers, for example, would claim to offer a full K&R implementation. However, although this appendix defined the C language, it did not define the C library. More than most languages, C depends on its library, so there is need for a library standard, too. In the absence of any official standard, the library supplied with the UNIX implementation became a de facto standard.

The ANSI C Standard

As C evolved and became more widely used on a greater variety of systems, the C community realized it needed a more comprehensive, up-to-date, and rigorous standard. To meet this need, the American National Standards Institute (ANSI) established a committee (X3J11) in 1983 to develop a new standard, which was adopted formally in 1989. This new standard (ANSI C) defines both the language and a standard C library. The International Standards Organization adopted a C standard (ISO C) in 1990. ISO C and ANSI C are essentially the same standard. The final version of the standard is often referred to as *C90*.

The committee had several guiding principles. Perhaps the most interesting was this: Keep the spirit of C. The committee listed the following ideas as expressing part of that spirit:

Trust the programmer.

Don't prevent the programmer from doing what needs to be done.

Keep the language small and simple.

Provide only one way to do an operation.

Make it fast, even if it is not guaranteed to be portable.

By the last point, the committee meant that an implementation should define a particular operation in terms of what works best for the target computer, instead of trying to impose an abstract, uniform definition. You'll encounter examples of this philosophy as you learn the language.

For the most part, C compiler vendors for microcomputers, such as IBM PCs and Macintoshes, took an evolutionary approach to converting to ANSI C, adding features from the early ANSI drafts as it became apparent those features would be in the final version. UNIX systems, on the other hand, stuck with K&R C until the ANSI standard became official. ANSI C, therefore, came to the UNIX world later—but fully implemented—than to the PC world. The public domain **gcc** UNIX C compiler, however, switched to ANSI C earlier than the standard **cc** UNIX C compiler, so if your UNIX system has a K&R **cc** compiler, check to see whether someone has installed an ANSI C **gcc** version.

This book follows the ANSI C standard. Often, ANSI C and K&R C are much the same. However, ANSI C does support some extensions and changes. We'll mention many of them when appropriate. Because you may find yourself using implementations that lack some ANSI C features, we'll point out where there are conflicts.

The C9X Committee

In 1994, work began on revising the standard. The committee working on the revision is known as the *C9X* committee. The committee endorsed the original principles of the C90 standard, including keeping the language small and simple. Therefore, the intent is not to add new features to the language, except as needed to meet the new goals. One of the main motivations is to support international programming, such as providing ways to deal with international character sets. A second goal is to "codify existing practice to address evident deficiencies." For example, commonly available computers have moved from 8-bit processors to 16-bit processors to 32-bit processors and are moving to 64-bit processors, and C needs to respond to the increased capacities of such processors. By codifying existing practice, the committee means that it intends to meet recognized deficiencies by incorporating solutions already developed by the programming community instead of inventing solutions from scratch. This way, the committee can benefit from the experiences of those who deal with these problems in real life.

These two goals, internationalization and correcting deficiencies, are the main change-oriented goals. The remaining new goals are more conservative in nature, for example, minimizing incompatibilities with C90 and with C++ and keeping the language conceptually simple. In the committee's words, "…the committee is content to let C++ be the *big* and ambitious language."

The upshot is that C9X changes will be fairly minor and that C will remain the lean, clean, efficient language. This book points out some of the proposed C9X changes when relevant. Also, Appendix H, "The C9X Committee," summarizes many of the C9X features.

Some Conventions

We are almost ready to begin studying the C language itself. Here are some of the conventions we use in presenting material.

Typeface

For text representing programs and computer input and output, we use a type font that resembles what you might see on a screen or on printed output. We have already used it a few times. In case it slipped by you, the font looks like this:

```c
#include <stdio.h>
int main(void)
{
    printf("Concrete contains gravel and cement.\n");
    return 0;
}
```

Screen Output

Output from the computer is printed in the same format, with the exception that user input is shown in boldface type. For instance, here is program output from a Chapter 14, "Structures and Other Data Forms," example:

```
Please enter the book title.
Press [enter] at the start of a line to stop.
```
My Life as a Budgie
```
Now enter the author.
```
Mack Zackles

The lines printed in normal computer font are program output, and the boldface line is user input.

There are many ways you and a computer can communicate with each other. However, we will assume that you type in commands by using a keyboard and that you read the response on a screen.

Special Keystrokes

Usually, you send a line of instructions onward by pressing a key labeled `Enter`, `c/r`, `Return`, or some variation of these. We refer to this key in the text as the *Enter key*. When showing it as part of input in a program example, we use `[enter]`. The brackets mean that you press a single key rather than type the word `enter`.

We also refer to control characters, such as Ctrl+D. This notation means to type the D key while you are pressing the key labeled `Ctrl` (or perhaps `Control`).

Our System

Some aspects of C, such as the amount of space used to store a number, depend on the system. When we give examples and refer to "our system," we speak of a Pentium PC running under Windows 98 and using either Microsoft Visual C++ 5.0 or Borland C/C++ 3.1 (DOS). Most of the examples have also been tested using Metrowerks CodeWarrior Pro 3 on a Macintosh G3.

We occasionally refer to running programs on a UNIX system, too. The one we use is Berkeley's BSD 4.3 version of UNIX running on a VAX 11/750 computer. Also, several programs were tested on a Pentium PC running Linux.

Note

You can find the code examples from the book by going to www.mcp.com/info and typing in the ten digits of the book's ISBN (1571691618). To find out more about the Metrowerks CodeWarrior compiler, go to www.metrowerks.com.

Chapter Summary

C is a powerful, concise programming language. It is popular because it offers useful programming tools and good control over hardware and because C programs are easier than most to transport from one system to another.

C is a compiled language. C compilers and linkers are programs that convert C language source code into executable code.

Programming in C can be taxing, difficult, and frustrating, but it can also be intriguing, exciting, and satisfying. We hope you find it as enjoyable and fascinating as we do.

Review Questions

1. What does portability mean in the context of programming?

2. Explain the difference between source code file, object code file, and executable file.

3. What are the seven major steps in programming?

4. What does a compiler do?

5. What does a linker do?

Programming Exercise

We don't expect you to write C code yet, so this exercise concentrates on the earlier stages of the programming process.

1. You have just been employed by MacroMuscle, Inc. (Software for Hard Bodies). They are entering the European market and want a program that converts inches to centimeters (1" = 2.54 cm). They want the program set up so that it prompts the user to enter an inch value. Your assignment is to define the program objectives and to design the program (steps 1 and 2 of the programming process).

CHAPTER 2

INTRODUCING C

You will learn about the following in this chapter:

- Operator
  - =

- Functions
  - main(), printf()

*I*n this chapter, you learn how to put together a simple C program, how to create integer-valued variables and assign them values, and how to display those values onscreen. Also, you find out what the newline character is, how to include comments in your programs, how to create programs containing more than one function, how to find program errors, and what keywords are.

What does a C program look like? If you skim through this book, you'll see many examples. Quite likely, you'll find that C is peculiar looking, sprinkled with symbols like {, cp->tort, and *ptr++. As you read through this book, however, you will find that the appearance of these and of other characteristic C symbols grows less strange, more familiar—perhaps even welcome! In this chapter, we begin by presenting a simple sample program and explaining what it does. At the same time, we highlight some of C's basic features.

A Simple Sample of C

Let's take a look at a simple C program. (Figure 2.1 outlines a more extensive example.) This program, shown in Listing 2.1, serves to point out some of the basic features of programming in C. Before you read the upcoming line-by-line explanation of the program, read through Listing 2.1 to see if you can figure out for yourself what it will do.

Listing 2.1   A simple C program.

```
#include <stdio.h>
int main(void)                  /* a simple program          */
{
    int num;                    /* define a variable called num */
    num = 1;                    /* assign a value to num     */

    printf("I am a simple ");   /* use the printf() function */
    printf("computer.\n");
    printf("My favorite number is %d because it is first.\n",num);
    return 0;
}
```

If you think this program will print some things on your screen, you're right! Exactly what will be printed might not be apparent, so run the program and see the results. First, use your favorite editor (or your compiler's favorite editor) to create a file containing the text from Listing 2.1. Give the file a name that ends in .c and that satisfies your local system's name requirements. You can use **first.c**, for instance. Now compile and run the program. If all went well, the output should look like this:

```
I am a simple computer.
My favorite number is 1 because it is first.
```

All in all, this result is not too surprising, but what happened to the \n's and the %d in the program? And some of the lines in the program do look strange. It's time for an explanation.

The Explanation

We'll take two passes through the program's source code. The first pass highlights the meaning of each line, and the second explores specific implications and details. Figure 2.1 summarizes the parts of a C program.

Pass 1 Quick Synopsis

```
#include <stdio.h>    include another file
```

This line tells the compiler to include information found in the file **stdio.h**, which is a standard part of all C compiler packages.

```
int main(void)        a function name
```

C programs consist of one or more functions, the basic modules of a C program. This program consists of one function called **main**. The parentheses identify **main()** as a function name. The **int** indicates that the **main()** function returns an integer, and the **void** indicates that **main()** doesn't take any arguments. These are matters we'll go into later. Right now, just accept the `int` and `void` as part of the standard ANSI C way for defining `main()`. (If you have a pre-ANSI C compiler, omit the `void`.)

```
/* a simple program */     a comment
```

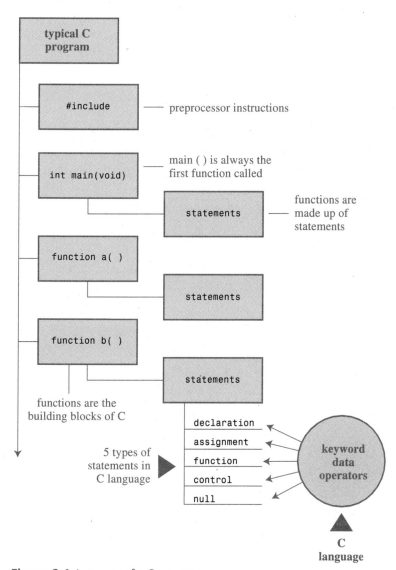

Figure 2.1 Anatomy of a C program.

The symbols /* and */ enclose comments, remarks that help clarify a program. They are intended for the reader only and are ignored by the compiler.

```
{          beginning of the body of the function
```

This opening brace marks the start of the statements that make up the function. The function definition is ended with a closing brace, }.

```
int num;        a declaration statement
```

This statement announces that you are using a variable called num and that num will be an int (integer) type.

```
num = 1;      an assignment statement
```

The statement num = 1; assigns the value 1 to the variable called num.

```
printf("I am a simple ");      a print statement
```

The first printf statement displays the phrase I am a simple on your screen, leaving the cursor on the same line.

```
printf("computer.\n");      another print statement
```

The next printf statement tacks on computer to the end of the last phrase printed. The \n is code telling the computer to start a new line, that is, to move the cursor to the beginning of the next line.

```
printf("My favorite number is %d because it is first.\n", num);
```

The last printf statement prints the value of num (which is 1) embedded in the phrase in quotes. The %d instructs the computer where and in what form to print the value of num.

```
return 0;    a return statement
```

A C function can furnish, or return, a number to the agency that used it. For the present, just regard this line as part of the ANSI C requirement for a properly written main() function.

```
}    the end
```

As promised, the program ends with a closing brace.

Pass 2 Details

Now take a closer look at the program.

#include Directives and Header Files

```
#include <stdio.h>
```

The effect of #include <stdio.h> is the same as though you had typed the entire contents of the stdio.h file into your file at the point where the #include line appears. Include files provide a convenient way to share information that is common to many programs.

The `stdio.h` file is supplied as part of all C compiler packages. It contains information about input and output functions, such as `printf()`, for the compiler to use. The name stands for **stand**ard **i**nput/**o**utput **h**eader. C programmers call a collection of information that goes at the top of a file a *header*, and C implementations typically come with several header files. ANSI C has standardized which header files must be supplied.

Some programs need to include `stdio.h`; some don't. The documentation for a particular C implementation should include a description of the functions in the C library. These function descriptions identify which header files are needed. For example, the description for `printf()` says to use `stdio.h`. Omitting the proper header file might not affect a particular program, but it is best not to rely on that. Each time this book uses library functions, it will use the `include` files specified by the ANSI standard for those functions. Because the compiler uses the information in the `stdio.h` to build a program, any information that the compiler does not use does not become part of the program. Therefore, including an unnecessary file does not make the final program any longer.

The `#include` statement is an example of a C *preprocessor directive*. In general, C compilers perform some preparatory work on source code before compiling; this is termed *preprocessing*.

Why Input and Output Are Not Built In

Perhaps you are wondering why something as basic as input and output information isn't included automatically. One answer is that not all programs use this I/O (input/output) package, and part of the C philosophy is to avoid carrying unnecessary weight. Incidentally, the `#include` line is not even a C language statement! The # symbol in column 1 identifies the line as one to be handled by the C preprocessor before the compiler takes over. You will encounter more examples of preprocessor instructions later.

The `main()` Function

```
int main(void)
```

True, `main` is a rather plain name, but it is the only choice available. A C program always begins execution with the function called `main()`. You are free to choose names for other functions you use, but `main()` must be there to start things. What about the parentheses? They identify `main()` as a function. You will learn more about functions soon. For now, just remember that functions are the basic modules of a C program.

The `int` is the `main()` function's return type. That means that the kind of value `main()` can return is an integer. Return where? To the operating system—we'll come back to this question in Chapter 6, "C Control Statements: Looping."

The parentheses following a function name generally enclose information being passed along to the function. For this simple example, nothing is being passed along, so the parentheses contain the word `void`. (Chapter 11, "Character Strings and String Functions," introduces a second format that allows information to be passed to `main()` from the operating system.)

Pre-ANSI C programs usually omitted the `int` and the `void`:

```
main()
```

ANSI C also accepts this form. It interprets the empty parentheses to mean that you decline to say anything about the kind of information `main()` requires. Omitting the `int` has no effect, for C (both K&R and ANSI) assumes that a function has an `int` return type unless you state otherwise, but explicitly using `int` more clearly documents what's going on. Also, the C9X committee proposes removing support for the implicit `int` from the next version of the ANSI standard.

Comments

```
/* a simple program */
```

Using comments makes it easier for someone (including yourself) to understand your program. One nice feature of C comments is that they can be placed anywhere, even on the same line as the material they explain. A longer comment can be placed on its own line or even spread over more than one line. Everything between the opening `/*` and the closing `*/` is ignored by the compiler. Here are some valid and invalid comment forms:

```
/* This is a C comment. */
/* This comment is spread over
   two lines. */
/*
  You can do this, too.
*/
/* But this is invalid because there is no end marker.
```

C++ has a second comment syntax that many C compilers have adopted. Also, the C9X committee proposes recognizing this common practice by adding the new syntax to the next version of the ANSI standard. The new style uses the symbols `//` to create comments that are confined to a single line:

```
// Here is a comment confined to one line.
int borg;        // Such comments can go here, too.
```

Because the end of the line marks the end of the comment, this style needs comment markers just at the beginning of the comment.

Braces, Bodies, and Blocks

```
{
...
}
```

Braces mark the beginning as well as the end of the body of a function. Their presence is mandatory. Only braces { } work for this purpose, not parentheses ( ) and not brackets [ ].

Braces can also be used to gather statements within a function into a unit or block. If you are familiar with Pascal, ADA, Modula-2, or Algol, you will recognize the braces as being similar to `begin` and `end` in those languages.

Declarations

```
int num;
```

The *declaration statement* is one of C's most important features. This particular example declares two things. First, somewhere in the function, you have a *variable* called `num`. Second, the `int` proclaims `num` as an integer, that is, a number without a decimal point or fractional part. The compiler uses this information to arrange for suitable storage space in memory for the `num` variable. The semicolon at the end of the line identifies the line as a C *statement* or instruction. The semicolon is part of the statement, not just a separator between statements as it is in Pascal.

The word `int` is a C *keyword* identifying one of the basic C data types. Keywords are the words used to express a language, and you can't usurp them for other purposes. For instance, you can't use `int` as the name of a function or a variable.

In C, *all* variables should be declared before they are used. This means that you have to provide lists of all the variables you use in a program and that you have to show which *type* each variable is. Declaring variables is considered a good programming technique, and, in C, it is mandatory.

At this point, you probably have three questions. First, what are data types? Second, what choices do you have in selecting a name? Third, why do you have to declare variables at all? Let's look at some answers.

Data Types

C deals with several kinds (or types) of data: integers, characters, and *floating point*, for example. Declaring a variable to be an integer or a character type makes it possible for the computer to store, fetch, and interpret the data properly. You'll investigate the variety of available types in the next chapter.

Name Choice

We suggest that you use meaningful names for variables. The number of characters you can use varies among implementations, but the lower limit is at least eight characters. The ANSI C standard calls for up to 31 characters, except for external identifiers (see Chapter 13, "Storage Classes and Program Development"), for which only six characters need to be recognized. (C9X raises the minimum values to 63 characters and 31 characters, respectively.) Actually, you can use more than the maximum number of characters, but the compiler won't pay attention to the extra characters. Therefore, on a system with an eight-character limit, `shakespeare` and `shakespencil` would be considered the same name because they have the same first eight characters. The characters at your disposal are the lowercase letters, the uppercase letters, the digits, and the underscore _. The first character must be a letter or an underscore. Here are some examples:

Valid Names	Invalid Names
wiggles	$Z]**
cat1	1cat
Hot_Tub	Hot-Tub
_kcab	don't

Operating systems and compilers often use identifiers with one or two initial underscore characters, so it is better to avoid that usage yourself.

C names are case sensitive, meaning an uppercase letter is considered distinct from the corresponding lowercase letter. Therefore, socks is different from Socks or SOCKS.

Four Good Reasons to Declare Variables

- Putting all the variables in one place makes it easier for a reader to grasp what the program is about. This is particularly true if you give your variables meaningful names (such as taxrate instead of r). If the name doesn't suffice, use comments to explain what the variables represent. Documenting a program in this manner is one of the basic techniques of good programming.

- Thinking about what to put into the variable declaration section encourages you to do some planning before plunging into writing a program. What information does the program need to get started? What exactly do I want the program to produce as output? What is the best way to represent the data?

- Declaring variables helps prevent one of programming's more subtle and hard-to-find bugs, that of the misspelled variable name. For example, suppose that in some language, which lacks declarations, you made the statement

```
RADIUS1 = 20.4;
```

and that elsewhere in the program you mistyped

```
CIRCUM = 6.28 * RADIUSl;
```

You unwittingly replaced the numeral *1* with the letter *l*. That other language would create a new variable called RADIUSl and use whatever value it had (perhaps zero, perhaps garbage). CIRCUM would be given the wrong value, and you might have a heck of a time trying to find out why. This can't happen in C (unless you were silly enough to declare two such similar variable names) because the compiler will complain when the undeclared RADIUSl shows up.

- Your C program will not compile if you don't declare your variables. If the preceding reasons fail to move you, you should give this one serious thought.

By the way, if you find that your compiler allows you to declare variables anywhere in a block and not just at the beginning, the compiler may be a C++ mode, for C++ does allow that behavior. (See Appendix G, "Answers to Review Questions.")

Assignment

```
num = 1;
```

The *assignment statement* is one of the basic operations in C. This particular example means "assign the value 1 to the variable num." The earlier `int num;` line allotted computer space for the variable num, and the assignment line gives it its value. You can assign num a different value later on, if you want; that is why num is termed a variable. Note that the assignment statement assigns a value from the right side to the left side. Also, the statement is completed with a semicolon, as shown in Figure 2.2.

```
num = 1;
```

assignment
operator

Figure 2.2 The assignment statement is one of the basic C operations.

The `printf()` Function

```
printf("I am a simple ");
printf("computer.\n");
printf("My favorite number is %d because it is first.\n",num);
```

These lines all use a standard C function called `printf()`. The parentheses signify that `printf` is a function name. The material enclosed in the parentheses is information passed from the `main()` function to the `printf()` function. For example, the first line passes the phrase `I am a simple` to the `printf()` function. Such information is called the *argument* or *parameter* of a function (see Figure 2.3). What does the function `printf()` do with this argument? It looks at whatever lies between the double quotation marks and prints that text on the screen.

```
printf( )
```

argument

```
printf("That's mere contrariness!\n");
```

Figure 2.3 The function `printf()` with an argument.

This first `printf()` line is an example of how you *call* or *invoke* a function in C. You need type only the name of the function, placing the desired argument(s) within the parentheses. When the program reaches this line, control is turned over to the named function (`printf()` in this case). When the function is finished with whatever it does, control is returned to the original (the *calling*) function—`main()`, in this example.

What about this next `printf()` line? It has the characters \n included in the quotes, and they didn't get printed! What's going on? The \n symbol means to start a new line. The \n combination (typed as two characters) represents a single character called the *newline character*. Its meaning is "start a new line at the far left margin." In other words, printing the newline character performs the same function as pressing the Enter key of a typical keyboard. Why not just use the Enter key when typing the `printf()` argument? Because that would be interpreted as an immediate command to your editor, not as an instruction to be stored in your source code. In other words, when you press the Enter key, the editor quits the current line on which you are working and starts a new one. The newline character, however, affects how the output of the program is displayed.

The newline character is an example of an *escape sequence*. An escape sequence is used to represent difficult- or impossible-to-type characters. Other examples are \t for tab and \b for backspace. In each case, the escape sequence begins with the backslash character, \. We'll return to this subject in Chapter 3, "Data and C."

Well, that explains why the three `printf()` statements produced only two lines: The first print instruction didn't have a newline character in it, but the second and third did.

The final `printf()` line brings up another oddity: What happened to the %d when the line was printed? As you will recall, the output for this line was

```
My favorite number is 1 because it is first.
```

Aha! The digit 1 was substituted for the symbol group %d when the line was printed, and 1 was the value of the variable num. The %d is a placeholder to show where the value of num is to be printed. This line is similar to the following BASIC statement:

```
PRINT "My favorite number is "; num; " because it is first."
```

The C version does a little more than this, actually. The % alerts the program that a variable is to be printed at that location, and the **d** tells it to print the variable as a decimal (base 10) integer. The `printf()` function allows several choices for the format of printed variables, including hexadecimal (base 16) integers and numbers with decimal points. Indeed, the **f** in `printf()` is a reminder that this is a formatting print function.

Return Statement

```
return 0;
```

The `int` in `int main(void)` means that the `main()` function is supposed to return an integer. The ANSI C standard requires that `main()` behave that way. C functions that return values do so with a return statement, which consists of the keyword `return` followed by the returned value followed by a semicolon. If you leave out the return statement for `main()`, most compilers will chide you for the omission, but still compile the program. At this point, you can regard the return statement in `main()` as something required for logical consistency, but it has a practical use with some operating systems, including DOS and UNIX. I'll return to that topic in Chapter 11, "Character Strings and String Functions."

The Structure of a Simple Program

Now that you've seen a specific example, you are ready for a few general rules about C programs. A *program* consists of a collection of one or more functions, one of which must be called `main()`. The description of a *function* consists of a header and a body. The *header* contains preprocessor statements, such as `#include`, and the function name. You can recognize a function name by the parentheses, which may be empty. The *body* is enclosed by braces { } and consists of a series of statements, each terminated by a semicolon (see Figure 2.4). The example in this chapter had a *declaration statement*, announcing the name and type of variable being used. Then it had an *assignment statement* giving the variable a value. Next, there were three *print statements*, each calling the `printf()` function. The print statements are examples of *function call statements*. Finally, `main()` ends with a *return statement*.

In short, a simple ANSI C program should follow this format:

```
#include <stdio.h>
int main(void)
{
    statements
    return 0;
}
```

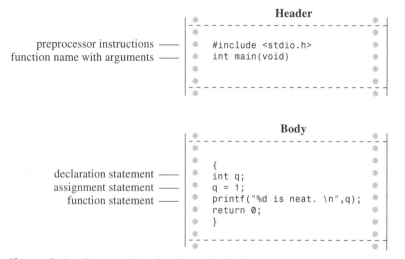

Figure 2.4 A function has a header and a body.

Tips on Making Your Programs Readable

Making your programs readable is good programming practice. A readable program is much easier to understand, and that makes it easier to correct or modify your program. The act of making a program readable also helps clarify your own concept of what the program does.

We've already mentioned two techniques for improving readability: Choose meaningful variable names and use comments. Note that these two techniques complement each other. If you give a variable the name `width`, you don't need a comment saying that this variable represents a width, but a variable called `video_routine_4` begs for an explanation of what video routine 4 does.

Another technique is using blank lines to separate one conceptual section of a function from another. For example, the simple sample program has a blank line separating the declaration section from the action section. The blank line is not required by C, but it enhances readability.

A fourth technique is to use one line per statement. Again, this is a readability convention, not a C requirement. C has a *free-form* format. You can place several statements on one line or spread one statement over several. The following is legitimate, but ugly, code:

```
int main(   void   ) { int four; four
=
4
;
```

```
printf(
      "%d\n",
four); return 0;}
```

The semicolons tell the compiler where one statement ends and the next begins, but the program logic is much clearer if you follow the conventions used in this chapter's example (see Figure 2.5).

```
int main(void) /* converts 2 fathoms to feet */ ── use comments

{
int feet, fathoms; ───────────────── pick meaningful names
                  ───────────────── use space
fathoms=2;
feet=6*fathoms; ───────────────── one statement per line
printf("There are %d feet in %d fathoms!\n", feet, fathoms);
return 0;
}
```

Figure 2.5 Making your program readable.

Taking Another Step

The first sample program was easy, and the next example, shown in Listing 2.2, isn't much harder.

Listing 2.2   The fathm_ft.c program.

```c
/* fathm_ft.c -- converts 2 fathoms to feet */
#include <stdio.h>
int main(void)
{
    int feet, fathoms;

    fathoms = 2;
    feet = 6 * fathoms;
    printf("There are %d feet in %d fathoms!\n", feet, fathoms);
    return 0;
}
```

What's new? We supplied a program description, declared multiple variables, did some multiplication, and printed the values of two variables. Let's examine these points in more detail.

Documentation

First, the program begins with a comment identifying the filename and the purpose of the program. This kind of program documentation takes but a moment to do and is helpful later on when you browse through several files or print them.

Multiple Declarations

Next, the program declares two variables instead of just one in a single declaration statement. To do this, separate the two variables (**feet** and **fathoms**) by a comma in the declaration statement. That is,

```
int feet, fathoms;
```

and

```
int feet;
int fathoms;
```

are equivalent.

Multiplication

Third, the program makes a calculation. It harnesses the tremendous computational power of a computer system to multiply 2 by 6. In C, as in many languages, the * is the symbol for multiplication. Therefore, the statement

```
feet = 6 * fathoms;
```

means "look up the value of the variable **fathoms**, multiply it by 6, and assign the result of this calculation to the variable **feet**."

Printing Multiple Values

Finally, the program makes fancier use of **printf()**. If you compile and run the example, the output should look like this:

```
There are 12 feet in 2 fathoms!
```

This time, we made *two* substitutions in **printf()**. The first **%d** in the quotes was replaced by the value of the first variable (**feet**) in the list following the quoted segment, and the second **%d** was replaced by the value of the second variable (**fathoms**) in the list. Note that the list of variables to be printed comes at the tail end of the statement after the quoted part. Also note that each item is separated from the others by a comma.

This program is limited in scope, but it could form the nucleus of a program for converting fathoms to feet. All that is needed is a way to assign additional values to **feet** interactively; we will explain how to do that in later chapters.

While You're at It...Multiple Functions

So far, these programs have used the standard `printf()` function. Listing 2.3 shows you how to incorporate a function of your own—besides `main()`—into a program.

Listing 2.3   The `two_func.c` program.

```
/* two_func.c -- a program using two functions in one file */
#include <stdio.h>
void butler(void);                  /* ANSI C function prototyping */
                    /* pre-ANSI C uses void butler(); instead */
int main(void)
{
   printf("I will summon the butler function.\n");
   butler();
   printf("Yes. Bring me some tea and writeable CD-ROMS.\n");[sr]
   return 0;
}

void butler(void)              /* start of function definition */
{
   printf("You rang, sir?\n");
}
```

The output looks like this:

```
I will summon the butler function.
You rang, sir?
Yes. Bring me some tea and writeable CD-ROMS.
```

The `butler()` function appears three times in this program. The first appearance is in the *prototype*, which informs the compiler about the functions to be used. The second appearance is in `main()` in the form of a *function call*. Finally, the program presents the *function definition*, which is the source code for the function itself. Let's look at each of these three appearances in turn.

Prototypes are an ANSI C addition, and pre-ANSI compilers might not recognize them. (We'll tell you in a moment what to do with pre-ANSI compilers.) A prototype is a form of declaration that tells the compiler you are using a particular function. It also specifies properties of the function. For example, the first `void` in the prototype for the `butler()` function indicates that `butler()` does not have a return value. (In general, a function can return a value to the calling function for its use, but `butler()` doesn't.) The second `void`, the one in `butler(void)` means that the `butler()` function has no arguments. Therefore, when the compiler reaches the point in `main()` where `butler()` is used, it can check to see whether `butler()` is used correctly. Note that `void` is used to mean "empty," not "invalid."

Pre-ANSI C supports a more limited form of function declaration in which you just specify the return type but omit describing the arguments.

```
void butler();
```

Older C code uses function declarations like the preceding one instead of function prototypes. ANSI C recognizes this older form but indicates it will be phased out in time. Later chapters in this book return to prototyping, function declarations, and return values.

Next, you invoke `butler()` in `main()` simply by giving its name, including parentheses. When `butler()` finishes its work, the program moves to the next statement in `main()`.

Finally, the function `butler()` is defined in the same manner as `main()`, with a function header and the body enclosed in braces. The header repeats the information given in the prototype: `butler()` takes no arguments and has no return value. For pre-ANSI C, omit the second `void`.

One point to note is that it is the location of the `butler()` call in `main()`—not the location of the `butler()` definition in the file—that determines when the `butler()` function is executed. You could, for instance, put the `butler()` definition above the `main()` definition in this program, and the program would still run the same, with the `butler()` function executed between the two calls to `printf()` in `main()`. Remember, all C programs begin execution with `main()`, no matter where `main()` is located in the program files. However, C practice is to list `main()` first because it normally provides the basic framework for a program.

The ANSI C standard recommends that you provide function prototypes for all functions you use. The standard include files take care of this task for the standard library functions. For example, under ANSI C, the `stdio.h` file has a function prototype for `printf()`. When we introduce defining functions with return values in Chapter 6, "C Control Statements: Looping," we'll show you how to extend prototyping to non-`void` functions.

Debugging

Now that you can write a simple C program, you are in a position to make simple errors. Listing 2.4 presents a program with some errors. See how many you can spot.

Listing 2.4   The `nogood.c` program.

```
/*  nogood.c -- a program with errors */
#include <stdio.h>
int main(void)
(
  int n, int n2, int n3;
    /* this program has several errors

  n = 5;
  n2 = n * n;
  n3 = n2 * n2;
  printf("n = %d, n squared = %d, n cubed = %d\n", n, n2, n3)
  return 0;
)
```

Syntax Errors

Listing 2.4 contains several *syntax errors*. You commit a syntax error when you don't follow C's rules. It's analogous to a grammatical error in English. For instance, consider the following sentence: *Bugs frustrate be can*. This sentence uses valid English words but doesn't follow the rules for word order, and it doesn't have quite the right words, anyway. C syntax errors use valid C symbols in the wrong places.

So what syntax errors did `nogood.c` make? First, it uses parentheses instead of braces to mark the body of the function—it uses a valid C symbol in the wrong place. Second, the declaration should have been this:

```
int n, n2, n3;
```

or perhaps this:

```
int n;
int n2;
int n3;
```

Next, the example omits the `*/` symbol pair necessary to complete a comment. Finally, it omits the mandatory semicolon that should terminate the `printf()` statement.

How do you detect syntax errors? First, before compiling, you can look through the source code and see if you spot anything obvious. Second, you can examine errors found by the compiler because part of its job is to detect syntax errors. When you compile this program, the compiler reports back any errors it finds, identifying the nature and location of each error.

However, the compiler can get confused. A true syntax error in one location might cause the compiler to mistakenly think it has found other errors. For instance, because the example does not declare **n2** and **n3** correctly, the compiler might think it has found further errors whenever those variables are used. If some of the supposed errors don't make sense to you, first correct the errors before them, recompile, and see if the compiler still complains. Continue in this way until the program works. Another common occurrence is for the error to be reported a line late. For instance, the compiler may not deduce that a semicolon is missing until it tries to compile the next line. So if the compiler complains of a missing semicolon on a line that has one, check the line before.

Semantic Errors

Semantic errors are errors in meaning. For instance, consider the following sentence: *Furry inflation thinks greenly*. The syntax is fine because adjectives, nouns, verbs, and adverbs are in the right places, but the sentence doesn't mean anything. In C, you commit a semantic error when you follow the rules of C correctly but to an incorrect end. The example has one such error:

```
n3 = n2 * n2;
```

Here, n3 is supposed to represent the cube of n, but I've set it up to be the fourth power of n.

The compiler does not detect semantic errors, for they don't violate C rules. The compiler has no way of divining your true intentions. That leaves it to you to find these kinds of errors. One way is to compare what a program does to what you expected it to do. For instance, suppose you fix the syntax errors in the example so that it now reads as shown in Listing 2.5.

Listing 2.5   The `stillbad.c` program.

```
/* stillbad.c -- a program with its syntax errors fixed */
#include <stdio.h>
int main(void)
{
  int n, n2, n3;
      /* this program has a semantic error */

  n = 5;
  n2 = n * n;
  n3 = n2 * n2;
  printf("n = %d, n squared = %d, n cubed = %d\n", n, n2, n3);
  return 0;
}
```

Its output is this:

```
n = 5, n squared = 25, n cubed = 625
```

If you are cube-wise, you'll see that 625 is the wrong value. The next stage is to track down how you wound up with this answer. For this example, you probably can spot the error by inspection. In general, however, you need to take a more systematic approach. One method is to pretend you are the computer and to follow the program steps one by one. Let's try that method now.

The body of the program starts by declaring three variables: n, n2, and n3. You can simulate this situation by drawing three boxes and labeling them with the variable names (see Figure 2.6). Next, the program assigns 5 to n. Simulate that by writing 5 into the n box. Next, the program multiplies n by n and assigns the result to n2, so look in the n box, see that the value is 5, multiply 5 by 5 to get 25, and place 25 in box n2. To duplicate the next C statement (n3 = n2 * n2;), look in n2 and find 25. You multiply 25 by 25, get 625, and place it in n3. Aha! You are squaring n2 instead of multiplying it by n.

Well, perhaps this procedure is overkill for this example, but going through a program step-by-step in this fashion is often the best way to see what's going on.

Program State

By tracing the program step-by-step, keeping track of each variable, you monitor the program state. The *program state* is simply the set of values of all the variables at a given point in program execution. It is a snapshot of the current state of computation.

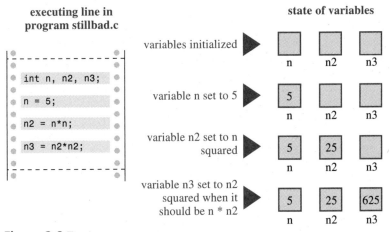

Figure 2.6 Tracing a program.

We just discussed one method of tracing the state: executing the program step-by-step yourself. In a program that makes, say, 10,000 iterations, you might not feel up to that task. Still, you can go through a few iterations to see if your program does what you intend. However, there is always the possibility that you will execute the steps as you intended them to be executed instead of as you actually wrote them, so try to be faithful to the actual code.

Another approach to locating semantic problems is to sprinkle extra `printf()` statements throughout to monitor the values of selected variables at key points in the program. Seeing how the values change can illuminate what's happening. After you have the program working to your satisfaction, you can remove the extra statements and recompile.

A third method for examining the program states is to use a debugger. A *debugger* is a program that enables you to run another program step-by-step and examine the value of that program's variables. Debuggers come in various levels of ease of use and sophistication. The more advanced debuggers show which line of source code is being executed. This is particularly handy for programs with alternative paths of execution because it is easy to see which particular paths are being followed. If your compiler comes with a debugger, take time now to learn how to use it. Try it with Listing 2.4, for example.

Keywords

Keywords are the vocabulary of C. Because they are special to C, you can't use them for variable names. Many of these keywords specify various types, such as `int`. Others, such as `if`, are used to control the order in which program statements are executed. In the following list of C keywords, boldface indicates keywords added by the ANSI C standard, and italics indicate new keywords proposed by the C9X committee for the next version of the standard.

ANSI C Keywords

auto	double	*inline*	static
break	else	int	struct
case	**enum**	long	switch
char	extern	register	typedef
complex	float	*restrict*	union
const	for	return	unsigned
continue	goto	short	**void**
default	if	signed	volatile
do	*imaginary*	sizeof	while

Chapter Summary

A C program consists of one or more C functions. Every C program must contain a function called `main()` because it is the function called when the program starts up. A simple function consists of a header followed by an opening brace, followed by the statements constituting the function body, followed by a terminating, or closing, brace.

Each C statement is an instruction to the computer and is marked by a terminating semicolon. A declaration statement creates a name for a variable and identifies the type of data to be stored in the variable. An assignment statement assigns a value to a variable or, more generally, to a storage area. A function call statement causes the named function to be executed. When the called function is done, the program returns to the next statement after the function call.

The `printf()` function can be used to print phrases and the values of variables.

The syntax of a language is the set of rules that governs the way in which valid statements in that language are put together. The semantics of a statement is its meaning. The compiler helps you detect syntax errors, but semantic errors show up in a program's behavior only after it is compiled. Detecting semantic errors may involve tracing the program state—that is, the values of all variables—after each program step.

Keywords are the vocabulary of the C language.

Review Questions

1. What are the basic modules of a C program called?

2. What is a syntax error? Give an example of one in English and of one in C.

3. What is a semantic error? Give an example of one in English and of one in C.

4. Ichabod Bodie Marfoote has prepared the following program and brought it to you for approval. Please help him out.

```
include studio.h
int main{void} /* this prints the number of weeks in a year /*
(
int s

s : = 56;
print(There are s weeks in a year.);
return 0;
```

5. Assuming that each of the following examples is part of a complete program, what will each one print?

   a. ```
   printf("Baa Baa Black Sheep.");
   printf("Have you any wool?\n");
   ```

   b. ```
   printf("Begone!\nO creature of lard!");
   ```

   c. ```
   printf("What?\nNo/nBonzo?\n");
   ```

   d. ```
   int num;

   num = 2;
   printf("%d + %d = %d", num, num, num + num);
   ```

6. Which of the following are C keywords? `main, int, function, char, =`

7. How would you print the values of `words` and `lines` in the form `There were 3020 words and 350 lines.`? Here, `3020` and `350` represent values for the two variables.

8. Consider the following program:

```
#include <stdio.h>
int main(void)
{
  int a, b;

    a = 5;
    b = 2;     /* line 7 */
    b = a;     /* line 8 */
    a = b;     /* line 9 */
    printf("%d %d\n", b, a);
    return 0;
}
```

What is the program state after line 7? line 8? line 9?

Programming Exercises

Reading about C isn't enough. You should try writing one or two simple programs to see if writing a program goes as smoothly as it looks in this chapter. Here are a few suggestions, but you should also try to think up some problems yourself.

1. Write a program that uses one `printf()` call to print your first name and last name on one line, uses a second `printf()` call to print your first and last name on two separate lines, and uses a pair of `printf()` calls to print your first and last name on one line. The output should look like this (but using your name):

Mae West	First print statement
Mae	Second print statement
West	Still the second print statement
Mae West	Third and fourth print statements

2. Write a program to print your name and address.

3. Write a program that converts your age in years to days. At this point, don't worry about fractional years and leap years.

4. Write a program that produces this output:

   ```
   For he's a jolly good fellow!
   For he's a jolly good fellow!
   For he's a jolly good fellow!
   Which nobody can deny!
   ```

   Have the program use two user-defined functions in addition to `main()`: one that prints the jolly good message once, and one that prints the final line once.

5. Write a program that creates an integer variable called `toes`. Have the program set `toes` to `10`. Also have the program calculate what twice `toes` is and what `toes` squared is. The program should print all three values, identifying them.

6. Write a program that produces this output:

   ```
   Smile!Smile!Smile!
   Smile!Smile!
   Smile!
   ```

   Have the program define a function that displays the string `Smile!` once, and have the program use the function as often as needed.

CHAPTER 3

DATA AND C

In this chapter, you learn about the basic data types that C uses and about the distinctions between integer types and floating-point types. You practice writing constants and declaring variables of those types. You begin studying how to use the `printf()` and `scanf()` functions to read and write values of different types.

Programs work with data. You feed numbers, letters, and words to the computer, and you expect it to do something with the data. For example, you might want the computer to calculate an interest payment or display a sorted list of vintners. In this chapter, you do more than just read about data; you practice manipulating data, which is much more fun.

This chapter explores the two great families of data types: integer and floating point. C offers several varieties of these types. You learn what the types are, how to declare them, how to use them, and when to use them. Also, you discover the differences between constants and variables, and as a bonus, your first interactive program is coming up shortly.

A Sample Program

Once again, you begin with a sample program. As before, you'll find some unfamiliar wrinkles that we'll soon iron out for you. The program's general intent should be clear, so try compiling and running the source code shown in Listing 3.1. To save time, you can omit typing the comments.

Listing 3.1   The goldyou.c program.

```
/* goldyou.c   -- the worth of your weight in gold */
#include <stdio.h>
int main(void)
{
    float weight;    /* user weight             */
    float value;     /* user's gold equivalent */

    printf("Are you worth your weight in gold?\n");
    printf("Let's check it out.\n");
    printf("Please enter your weight in pounds: ");

/* get input from the user                     */
    scanf("%f", &weight);
/* assume gold is $320 per ounce               */
/* 14.5833 converts pounds avd. to ounces troy */
    value = 320.0 * weight * 14.5833;
    printf("Your weight in gold is worth $%.2f.\n", value);
    printf("You are easily worth that! If gold prices drop,\n");
    printf("eat more to maintain your value.\n");
    return 0;
}
```

Errors and Warnings

If you type this program incorrectly, and, say, omit a semicolon, the compiler gives you a syntax error message. Even if you type it correctly, however, the compiler may give you a warning similar to this: "Warning—conversion from 'double' to 'float,' possible loss of data." An error message means you did something wrong and prevents the program from being compiled. A *warning*, however, means you've done something that is valid code but possibly is not what you meant to do. A warning does not stop compilation. This particular warning pertains to how C handles values like 320.0. It's not a problem for this example, and the chapter explains the warning later.

When you type this program, you might want to change the **320.0** to the current price of gold. I suggest, however, that you don't fiddle with the **14.5833**, which represents the number of ounces in a pound. (That's ounces troy, used for precious metals, and pounds avoirdupois, used for people, precious and otherwise.) Note that "entering" your weight means to type your weight and then press the Enter or Return key. (Don't just type your weight and wait.) Pressing Enter informs the computer that you have finished typing your response. Here is a sample output:

```
Are you worth your weight in gold?
Let's check it out.
Please enter your weight in pounds: 170
```

```
Your weight in gold is worth $793331.52.
You are easily worth that! If gold prices drop,
eat more to maintain your value.
```

What's New in This Program?

There are several new elements of C in this program:

- Notice that you use a new kind of variable declaration. Previously, you used only an integer variable type (int), but now you've added a floating-point variable type (float) so that you can handle a wider variety of data. The float type can hold numbers with decimal points.

- The program demonstrates some new ways of writing constants. You now have numbers with decimal points.

- To print this new kind of variable, use the %f specifier in the printf() code to handle a floating-point value. Use the .2 modifier to the %f specifier to fine-tune the appearance of the output so that it displays two places to the right of the decimal.

- To provide keyboard input to the program, use the scanf() function. The %f instructs scanf() to read a floating-point number from the keyboard, and the &weight tells scanf() to assign the input value to the variable named weight. The scanf() function uses the & notation to indicate where it can find the weight variable. The next chapter discusses & further; meanwhile, trust us that you need it here.

- Perhaps the most outstanding new feature is that this program is interactive. The computer asks you for information and then uses the number you type in. An interactive program is more interesting to use than the noninteractive types. More important, the interactive approach makes programs more flexible. For instance, the sample program can be used for any reasonable weight, not just for 170 pounds. You don't have to rewrite the program every time you want to try it on a new person. The scanf() and printf() functions make this interactivity possible. The scanf() function reads data from the keyboard and delivers that data to the program, and printf() reads data from a program and delivers that data to your screen. Together, these two functions enable you to establish a two-way communication with your computer (see Figure 3.1), and that makes using a computer much more fun.

This chapter explains the first two items in this list of new features: variables and constants of various data types. Chapter 4, "Character Strings and Formatted Input/Output," covers the last three items, but you continue to make limited use of scanf() and printf() in this chapter.

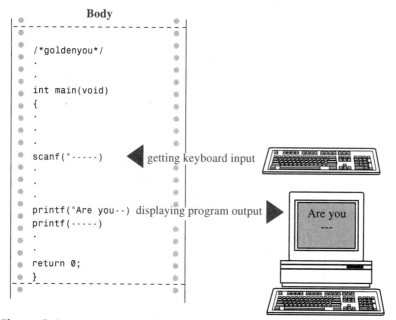

Figure 3.1 The functions `scanf()` and `printf()` at work.

Data Variables and Constants

A computer, under the guidance of a program, can do many things. It can add numbers, sort names, command the obedience of a speaker or video screen, calculate cometary orbits, prepare a mailing list, dial phone numbers, draw stick figures, draw conclusions, or anything else your imagination can create. To do these tasks, the program needs to work with *data*, the numbers and characters that bear the information you use. Some data are preset before a program is used and keep their values unchanged throughout the life of the program. These are *constants*. Other data may change or be assigned values as the program runs; these are *variables*. In the sample program, `weight` is a variable and `14.5833` is a constant. What about the `320.0`? True, the price of gold isn't a constant in real life, but this program treats it as a constant. The difference between a variable and a constant is that a variable can have its value assigned or changed while the program is running, and a constant can't.

Data: Data-Type Keywords

Beyond the distinction between variable and constant is the distinction between different *types* of data. Some data are numbers. Some are letters or, more generally, characters. The computer needs a way to identify and use these different kinds. C does this by recognizing several fundamental *data types*. If a datum is a constant, the compiler can usually tell its type just by the way it looks: 46 is an integer, and 46.100 is floating point. A variable, however, needs to have its type announced in a declaration statement. You'll learn the details of declaring variables as you move along. First, though, take a look at the fundamental types recognized by C. K&R C recognized seven keywords. ANSI C added four to the list. Two of these—void and signed—had come into general use previously (refer to Chapter 2, "Introducing C"). Here are the keywords:

Original K&R Keywords	Keywords from ANSI C
int	signed
long	void
short	const
unsigned	volatile
char	
float	
double	

We'll discuss the K&R keywords and the signed keyword here. Chapters 4 and 13, "Storage Classes and Program Development," discuss the const keyword, and Chapter 13 covers the volatile keyword.

The int keyword provides the basic class of integers used in C. The next three keywords (long, short, and unsigned) and the ANSI addition signed are used to provide variations of the basic type. Next, the char keyword designates the type used for letters of the alphabet and for other characters, such as #, $, %, and *. The char type also can be used to represent small integers. Finally, float, double, and the ANSI C combination long double are used to represent numbers with decimal points.

The types created with these keywords can be divided into two families on the basis of how they are stored in the computer. The first five keywords from the pre-ANSI C list create *integer* types, and the last two create *floating-point* types.

Bits, Bytes, and Words

The terms *bit*, *byte*, and *word* can be used to describe units of computer data or to describe units of computer memory. We'll concentrate on the second usage here.

The smallest unit of memory is called a *bit*. It can hold one of two values: 0 or 1. (Or you can say that the bit is set to "off" or "on.") You can't store much information in one bit, but a computer has a tremendous stock of them. The bit is the basic building block of computer memory.

The *byte* is the usual unit of computer memory. For nearly all machines, a byte is 8 bits, and that is the standard definition, at least when used to

continued on next page

continued from previous page

measure storage. (The C language, however, has a different definition, as discussed in the section on the `char` type.) Because each bit can be either 0 or 1, there are 256 (that's 2 times itself 8 times) possible bit patterns of 0s and 1s that can fit in a byte. These patterns can be used, for example, to represent the integers from 0 to 255 or to represent a set of characters. Representation can be accomplished with binary code, which uses (conveniently enough) just 0s and 1s to represent numbers. (Chapter 15, "Bit Fiddling," discusses binary code, but you can read through the introductory material of that chapter now if you like.)

A *word* is the natural unit of memory for a given computer design. For 8-bit microcomputers, such as the original Apples, a word is just 1 byte. IBM compatibles using the 80286 processor are 16-bit machines. This means that they have a word size of 16 bits, which is 2 bytes. Machines like the Pentium-based PCs and the Macintosh PowerPCs have 32-bit words. More powerful computers can have 64-bit words or even larger.

Integer Versus Floating-Point Types

Integer types? Floating-point types? If you find these terms disturbingly unfamiliar, relax. We are about to give you a brief rundown of their meanings. If you are unfamiliar with bits, bytes, and words, you might want to read the nearby box about them first. Do you have to learn all the details? Not really, not any more than you have to learn the principles of internal combustion engines to drive a car, but knowing a little about what goes on inside a computer or engine can help you occasionally.

For a human, the difference between integers and floating-point numbers is reflected in the way they can be written. For a computer, the difference is reflected in the way they are stored. Let's look at each of the two classes in turn.

The Integer

An *integer* is a number with no fractional part. In C, an integer is never written with a decimal point. Examples are 2, –23, and 2456. Numbers like 3.14, 0.22, and 2.000 are not integers. Integers are stored as binary numbers. The integer 7, for example, is written 111 in binary. Therefore, to store this number in a byte, just set the first 5 bits to 0 and the last 3 bits to 1 (see Figure 3.2).

The Floating-Point Number

A *floating-point* number more or less corresponds to what mathematicians call a *real number*. Real numbers include the numbers between the integers. Here are some floating-point numbers: 2.75, 3.16E7, 7.00, and 2e–8. Obviously, there is more than one way to write a floating-point number. We will discuss the E-notation more fully later. In brief, the notation 3.16E7 means to multiply 3.16 by 10 to the 7th power; that is, by 1 followed by 7 zeros. The 7 would be termed the *exponent* of 10.

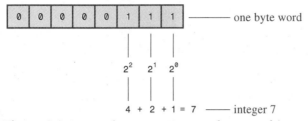

Figure 3.2 Storing the integer 7 using a binary code.

The key point here is that the scheme used to store a floating-point number is different from the one used to store an integer. Floating-point representation involves breaking up a number into a fractional part and an exponent part and storing the parts separately. Therefore, the 7.00 in this list would not be stored in the same manner as the integer 7, even though both have the same value. The decimal analogy would be to write 7.0 as 0.7E1. Here, 0.7 is the fractional part, and the 1 is the exponent part. Figure 3.3 shows another example of floating-point storage. A computer, of course, would use binary numbers and powers of two instead of powers of 10 for internal storage. You'll find more on this topic in Chapter 15. Now, let's concentrate on the practical differences, which are these:

- An integer has no fractional part; a floating-point number can have a fractional part.

- Floating-point numbers can represent a much larger range of values than integers can. See Table 3.2 near the end of this chapter.

- For some arithmetic operations, such as subtracting one large number from another, floating-point numbers are subject to greater loss of precision.

- Because there are an infinite number of real numbers in any range—for example, in the range between 1.0 and 2.0—computer floating-point numbers can't represent all the values in the range. Instead, floating-point values are often approximations of a true value.

- Floating-point operations are normally slower than integer operations. However, microprocessors developed specifically to handle floating-point operations are now available, and they are quite swift.

Figure 3.3 Storing the number pi in floating-point format (decimal version).

C Data Types

Now let's look at the specifics of the basic data types used by C. For each type, we describe how to declare a variable, how to represent a constant, and what a typical use would be. Some pre-ANSI C compilers do not support all these types, so check your manual to see which ones you have available.

The `int` Type

C offers a variety of integer types. They vary in the range of values offered and in whether negative numbers can be used. The `int` type is the basic choice, but should you need other choices to meet the requirements of a particular task or machine, they are available.

The `int` type is a signed integer. That means it must be an integer and it can be positive, negative, or zero. The range in possible values depends on the computer system. Typically, an `int` uses one machine word for storage. Therefore, older IBM PC compatibles, which have a 16-bit word, use 16 bits to store an `int`. This allows a range in values from **−32768** to **+32767**. Other machines might have different ranges. See Table 3.2 near the end of this chapter for examples. ANSI C specifies that the minimum range for type `int` should be from **−32767** to **+32767**. Typically, systems represent signed integers by using the value of a particular 1 bit to indicate the sign. Chapter 15 discusses common methods.

Declaring an `int` Variable

As you saw in Chapter 2, the keyword `int` is used to declare the basic integer variable. First comes `int`, then the chosen name of the variable, and then a semicolon. To declare more than one variable, you can declare each variable separately, or you can follow the `int` with a list of names in which each name is separated from the next by a comma. The following are valid declarations:

```
int erns;
int hogs, cows, goats;
```

You could have used a separate declaration for each variable, or you could have declared all four variables in the same statement. The effect is the same: Associate names and arrange storage space for four `int`-sized variables.

These declarations create variables but don't supply values for them. How do variables get values? You've seen two ways that they can pick up values in the program. First, there is assignment:

```
cows = 112;
```

Second, a variable can pick up a value from a function, from `scanf()`, for example. Now let's look at a third way.

Initializing a Variable

To *initialize* a variable means to assign it an initial, or starting, value. In C, this can be done as part of the declaration. Just follow the variable name with the assignment operator (=) and the value you want the variable to have. Here are some examples:

```
int hogs = 21;
int cows = 32, goats = 14;
int dogs, cats = 94;          /* valid, but poor, form */
```

In the last line, only `cats` is initialized. A quick reading might lead you to think that `dogs` is also initialized to `94`, so it is best to avoid putting initialized and noninitialized variables in the same declaration statement.

In short, these declarations create and label the storage for the variables and assign starting values to each (see Figure 3.4).

Figure 3.4 Defining and initializing a variable.

Type int Constants

The various integers (`21`, `32`, `14`, and `94`) in the last example are integer constants. When you write a number without a decimal point and without an exponent, C recognizes it as an integer. Therefore, `22` and `-44` are integer constants, but `22.0` and `2.2E1` are not. C treats most integer constants as type `int`. Very large integers may be treated differently; see the later discussion of the `long int` type in section "Type `long` and `long long` Constants."

Printing int Values

You can use the `printf()` function to print `int` types. As you saw in Chapter 2, the `%d` notation is used to indicate just where in a line the integer is to be printed. The `%d` is an example of a *format specifier*, for it indicates the form that `printf()` uses to display a value. Each `%d` in the format string must be matched by a corresponding `int` value in the list of items to be printed. That value can be an `int` variable, an `int` constant, or any other expression having an `int` value. It's your job to make sure the number of format specifiers matches the number of values; the compiler won't catch mistakes of that kind. Listing 3.2 presents a simple program that initializes a variable and prints the value of the variable, the value of a constant, and the value of a simple expression. It also shows what can happen if you are not careful.

Listing 3.2   The `print1.c` program.

```
/* print1.c--displays some properties of printf() */
#include <stdio.h>
int main(void)
{
   int ten = 10;
   printf("Doing it right: ");
   printf("%d minus %d is %d\n", ten, 2, ten - 2 );
   printf("Doing it wrong: ");
   printf("%d minus %d is %d\n", ten );   // forgot 2 arguments
   return 0;
}
```

Compiling and running the program produces this output:

```
Doing it right: 10 minus 2 is 8
Doing it wrong: 10 minus 10 is 6618680
```

Therefore, the first `%d` represents the `int` variable `ten`, the second `%d` represents the `int` constant `2`, and the third `%d` represents the value of the `int` expression `ten` - `2`. The second time, however, the program used `ten` to provide a value for the first `%d` and used whatever values happened to be lying around in memory for the next two! (The numbers you get could very well be different from those shown here.)

You might be annoyed that the compiler doesn't catch such an obvious error. Blame the unusual design of `printf()`. Most functions take a specific number of arguments, and the compiler can check to see whether you've used the correct number. However, `printf()` can have one, two, three, or more arguments, and that keeps the compiler from using its usual methods for error checking. Remember: Check to see that the number of format specifiers you give to `printf()` matches the number of values to be displayed.

Octal and Hexadecimal

Normally, C assumes that integer constants are decimal, or base 10, numbers. However, octal (base 8) and hexadecimal (base 16) numbers are popular with many programmers. Because 8 and 16 are powers of 2, and 10 is not, these number systems occasionally offer a more convenient way for expressing computer-related values. For example, the number 65536, which often pops up in 16-bit machines, is just 10000 in hexadecimal. But how can the computer tell whether 10000 is meant to be a decimal, hexadecimal, or octal value? In C, special prefixes indicate which number base you are using. A prefix of 0x or 0X (zero-exe) means that you are specifying a hexadecimal value, so 16 is written as 0x10, or 0X10, in hexadecimal. Similarly, a 0 (zero) prefix means that you are writing in octal. For example, in C the decimal value 16 is written as 020 in octal. Chapter 15 discusses these alternative number bases more fully.

Be aware that this option of using different number systems is provided as a service for your convenience. It doesn't affect how the number is stored. That is, you can write 16 or 020 or 0x10, and the number is stored exactly the same way in each case—in the binary code used internally by computers.

Incidentally, octal and hexadecimal constants are treated as unsigned values; this chapter takes up unsigned types shortly.

Displaying Octal and Hexadecimal

Just as C enables you to write a number in any one of three number systems, it also enables you to display a number in any of these three systems. To display an integer in octal notation instead of decimal, use %o instead of %d. To display an integer in hexadecimal, use %x. Listing 3.3 shows a short example.

Listing 3.3   The bases.c program.

```
/* bases.c--prints 100 in decimal, octal, and  hex */
#include <stdio.h>
int main(void)
{
    int x = 100;
    printf("dec = %d; octal = %o;  hex = %x\n" , x, x, x);
    return 0;
}
```

Compiling and running this program produces this output:

```
dec = 100; octal = 144; hex = 64
```

You see the same value displayed in three different number systems. The printf() function makes the conversions. Note that the 0 and the 0x prefixes are not displayed in the output. ANSI C provides that the specifiers %#o, %#x, and %#X generate the 0, 0x, and 0X prefixes, respectively.

Other Integer Types

When you are just learning the language, the int type will probably meet most of your integer needs. To be complete, however, we'll cover the other forms now. If you like, you can skim this section and jump to the discussion of the char type, returning here when you have a need.

C offers three adjective keywords to modify the basic integer type: short, long, and unsigned.

- The type shor t int or, more briefly, short may use less storage than int, thus saving space when only small numbers are needed. Like int, short is a signed type.

- The type long int, or long, may use more storage than int, thus enabling you to express larger integer values. Like int, long is a signed type.

- The type unsign ed int, or unsigned, is used for variables that have only nonnegative values. This type shifts the range of numbers that can be stored. For example, a 2-byte unsigned int allows a range from 0 to 65535 in value instead of from –32768 to +32767. The bit used to indicate the sign of signed numbers now becomes another binary digit, allowing the larger number.

- ANSI C and many pre-ANSI C compilers also recognize as valid types unsigned long int, or unsigned long, and unsigned short int, or unsigned short.

- Many C compilers have added the types long long int (long long, for short) and unsigned long long int (unsigned long long, for short) to provide for even larger integer values. The C9X committee proposes adding these two types to the standard.

Declaring Other Integer Types

Other integer types are declared in the same manner as the int type. The following list shows several examples. Not all pre-ANSI C compilers recognize the last three, and the final example is (at the time of this writing) part of the proposed revision of the ANSI C standard.

```
long int estine;
long johns;
short int erns;
short ribs;
unsigned int s_count;
unsigned players;
unsigned long headcount;
unsigned short yesvotes;
long long ago;
```

Why Multiple Integer Types?

Why do we say that long and short types "may" use more or less storage than int? Because C guarantees only that short is no longer than int and that long is no shorter than int. The idea is to fit the types to the machine. On an IBM PC running Windows 3.1, for example, an int and a short are both 16 bits, and a long is 32 bits. On a Windows 95 machine or a Macintosh PowerPC, however, a short is 16 bits, and both int and long are 32 bits. The natural word size on a Pentium chip or a PowerPC chip is 32 bits. Because this allows integers in excess of 2 billion (see Table 3.2 later in this chapter), the implementors of C on these processor/operating system combinations did not see a necessity for anything larger; therefore, `long` is the same as `int`. For many uses, integers of that size are not needed, so a space-saving `short` was created. The original IBM PC, on the other hand, has only a 16-bit word, which means that a larger `long` was needed.

The most common practice today is to set up `long` as 32 bits, `short` as 16 bits, and `int` to either 16 bits or 32 bits, depending on the machine's natural word size. In principle, however, these three types could represent three distinct sizes.

ANSI C provides guidelines specifying the minimum allowable size for each basic data type. The minimum range for both `short` and `int` is –32,767 to +32,767, corresponding to a 16-bit unit, and the minimum range for `long` is –2,147,483,647 to +2,147,483,647, corresponding to a 32-bit unit. (Note: For legibility, we've used commas, but C code doesn't allow that option.) For `unsigned short` and `unsigned int`, the minimum range is 0 to 65,535, and for `unsigned long`, the minimum range is 0 to 4,294,967,295. The C9X committee's proposed `long long` type is intended to support 64-bit needs. Its minimum range is a substantial –9,223,372,036,854,775,807 to 9,223,372,036,854,775,807, and the minimum range for `unsigned long long` is 0 to 18,446,744,073,709,551,615. (For those of you writing checks, that's eighteen quintillion, four hundred and forty-six quadrillion, seven hundred forty-four trillion, seventy-three billion, seven hundred nine million, five hundred fifty-one thousand, six hundred fifteen in U.S. notation, but who's counting?)

When do you use the various `int` types? First, consider `unsigned` types. It is natural to use them for counting because you don't need negative numbers, and the unsigned types enable you to reach higher positive numbers than the signed types.

Use the `long` type if you need to use numbers that `long` can handle and that `int` cannot. However, on systems for which `long` is bigger than `int`, using `long` may slow down calculations, so don't use `long` if it is not essential. One further point: If you are writing code on a machine for which `int` and `long` are the same size, and if you do need 32-bit integers, you should use `long` instead of `int` so that the program will function correctly if transferred to a 16-bit machine.

Similarly, use `long long` if you need 64-bit integer values. Some computers already use 64-bit processors, and 64-bit processing should become common in the early 2000s.

Use `short` to save storage space or if, say, you need a 16-bit value on a system where `int` is 32-bit. Usually, saving storage space is important only if your program uses arrays of integers that are large in relation to a system's available memory. Another reason to use `short` is that it may correspond in size to hardware registers used by particular components in a computer.

Integer Overflow

What happens if an integer tries to get too big for its type? Let's set an integer to its largest possible value, add to it, and see what happens. Try both signed and unsigned types. (The program uses the `%u` specifier to display `unsigned int` values.)

continued on next page

continued from previous page

```c
/* toobig.c--exceeds maximum int size on our system */
#include <stdio.h>
int main(void)
{
    int i = 2147483647;
    unsigned int j = 4294967295;
    printf("%d %d %d\n", i, i+1, i+2);
    printf("%u %u %u\n", j, j+1, j+2);
    return 0;
}
```

Here's the result for our system:

```
2147483647 -2147483648 -2147483647
4294967295 0 1
```

The unsigned integer j is acting like a car's odometer. When it reaches its maximum value, it starts over at the beginning. The integer i acts similarly. The main difference is that an odometer and the unsigned int variable j begin at 0, but the int variable i begins at –2147483648. Notice that you are not informed that i has exceeded (overflowed) its maximum value. You would have to include your own programming to keep tabs on that.

The behavior described here is mandated by the rules of C for unsigned types. The standard doesn't define how signed types should behave, but the behavior shown here is typical.

Type long and long long Constants

Normally, when you use a number like 2345 in your program code, it is stored as an int type. What if you use a number like 1000000 on a system in which int will not hold such a large number? Then the compiler treats it as a long int, assuming that type is large enough. If the number is larger than the long maximum, C treats it as unsigned long. If that is still insufficient, C treats the value as long long or unsigned long long, if those types are available.

Octal and hexadecimal constants are treated as type unsigned int unless the value is too large. Then the compiler tries unsigned long. If that doesn't work, it tries unsigned long long, if available.

Sometimes you might want the compiler to store a small number as a long integer. Programming that involves explicit use of memory addresses on an IBM PC, for instance, can create such a need. Also, some standard C functions require type long values. To cause a small constant to be treated as type long, you can append an l (lowercase L) or L as a suffix. I recommend the second form because it looks less like the digit 1. Therefore, a system with a 16-bit int and a 32-bit long treats the integer 7 as 16 bits and the integer 7L as 32 bits. The l and L suffixes can also be used with octal and hex integers, as in 020L and 0x10L.

Similarly, on those systems supporting the long long type, you can use an ll or LL suffix to indicate a long long value, as in 3LL. Add a u or U to the suffix for unsigned long long, as in 5ull or 10LLU or 6LLU or 9Ull.

Printing long, short, and unsigned Types

To print an unsigned int number, use the %u notation. To print a long value, use the %ld format specifier. If int and long are the same size on your system, just %d will suffice, but your program will not work properly when transferred to a system on which the two types are different, so use the %ld specifier. You can use the l prefix for x and o, too. Therefore, you would use %lx to print a long integer in hexadecimal format and %lo to print in octal format. Note that although C allows both uppercase and lowercase letters for constant suffixes, these format specifiers use just lowercase.

ANSI C has several additional printf() forms. First, you can use an h prefix for short types. Therefore, %hd displays a short integer in decimal form, and %ho displays a short integer in octal form. Both the h and l prefixes can be used with u for unsigned types. For instance, you would use the %lu notation for printing unsigned long types. Listing 3.4 provides an example. Systems supporting the long long types use %lld and %llu for the signed and unsigned versions.

Listing 3.4   The print2.c program.

```
/* print2.c--more printf() properties */
#include <stdio.h>
int main(void)
{
  unsigned int un = 3000000000; /* system with 32-bit int */
  short sn = 200;                /* and 16-bit short       */
  long ln = 65537;
  printf("un = %u and not %d\n", un, un);
  printf("sn = %hd and %d\n", sn, sn);
  printf("ln = %ld and not %hd\n", ln, ln);
  return 0;
}
```

Here is the output on one system:

```
un = 3000000000 and not -1294967296
sn = 200 and 200
ln = 65537 and not 1
```

This example points out that using the wrong specification can produce unexpected results. First, note that using the %d specifier for the unsigned variable un produces a negative number! The reason for this is that the unsigned value 3000000000 and the signed value -129496296 have exactly the same internal representation in memory on our system. (Chapter 15 explains this property in more detail.) So if you tell printf() that the number is unsigned, it prints one value, and if you tell it that the same number is signed, it prints the other value. This behavior shows up with values larger than the maximum signed value. Smaller positive values, such as 96, are stored and displayed the same for both signed and unsigned types.

Next, note that the `short` variable `sn` is displayed the same whether you tell `printf()` that `sn` is a `short` (the `%hd` specifier) or an `int` (the `%d` specifier). That's because C automatically expands a type `short` value to a type `int` value when it's passed as an argument to a function. This may raise two questions in your mind: Why does this conversion take place, and what's the use of the `h` modifier? The answer to the first question is that the `int` type is intended to be the integer size that the computer handles most efficiently. So, on a computer for which `short` and `int` are different sizes, it may be faster to pass the value as an `int`. The answer to the second question is that you can use the `h` modifier to show how a longer integer would look if truncated to the size of `short`. The third line of output illustrates this point. When the value 65537 is written in binary format as a 32-bit number, it looks like this: 00000000000000010000000000000001. Using the `%hd` specifier persuaded `printf()` to look at just the last 16 bits; so it displayed the value as 1.

Earlier you saw that it is your responsibility to make sure the number of specifiers matches the number of values to be displayed. Here you see that it is also your responsibility to use the correct specifier for the type of value to be displayed.

Using Characters: Type `char`

The `char` type is used for storing characters such as letters and punctuation marks, but technically it is an integer type. Why? Because the `char` type actually stores integers, not characters. To handle characters, the computer uses a numerical code in which certain integers represent certain characters. The most commonly used code is the ASCII code given in Appendix E, "ASCII Table." It is the code this book assumes. In it, for example, the integer value **65** represents an uppercase A. So to store the letter A, you actually need to store the integer **65**. (Many IBM mainframes use a different code, called EBCDIC, but the principle is the same.)

The standard ASCII code runs numerically from 0 to 127. This range is small enough that 7 bits can hold it. The `char` type is typically defined as an 8-bit unit of memory, so it is more than large enough to encompass the standard ASCII code. Many systems, such as the IBM PC and the Apple Macintosh, offer extended ASCII codes (different for the two systems) that still stay within an 8-bit limit. More generally, C guarantees that the `char` type is large enough to store the basic character set for the system on which C is implemented.

Many character sets have many more than 127 or even 255 values. For example, there is the Japanese kanji character set. The Unicode initiative has created a system to represent a variety of character sets worldwide and currently has over 40,000 characters. A platform that used one of these sets as its basic character set could use a 16-bit `char` representation. The C language defines a byte to be the number of bits used by type `char`, so a byte would be 16 bits rather than 8 bits on such systems, at least as far as C documentation goes.

Declaring Type char Variables

As you might expect, char variables are declared in the same manner as other variables. Here are some examples:

```
char response;
char itable, latan;
```

This program would create three char variables: response, itable, and latan.

Character Constants and Initialization

Suppose you want to initialize a character constant to the letter A. Computer languages are supposed to make things easy, so you shouldn't have to memorize the ASCII code, and you don't. You can assign the character A to grade with the following initialization:

```
char grade = 'A';
```

A single letter contained between single quotes is a C character constant. When the compiler sees 'A', it converts the 'A' to the proper code value. The single quotes are essential.

```
char broiled;        /* declare a char variable    */
broiled = 'T';       /* OK                          */
broiled = T;         /* NO! Thinks T is a variable  */
broiled = "T";       /* NO! Thinks "T" is a string  */
```

If you leave off the quotes, the compiler thinks that T is the name of a variable. If you use double quotes, it thinks you are using a string. We'll discuss strings in Chapter 4.

Because characters are really stored as numeric values, you can also use the numerical code to assign values:

```
char grade = 65;  /* ok for ASCII, but poor style */
```

In this example, 65 is type int, but, because the value is smaller than the maximum char size, it can be assigned to grade without any problems. Because 65 is the ASCII code for the letter A, this example assigns the value A to grade. Note, however, that this example assumes that the system is using ASCII code. Using 'A' instead of 65 produces code that works on any system. Therefore, it's better to use character constants than numeric code values.

Somewhat oddly, C treats character constants as type int rather than type char. For example, on an ASCII system with a 32-bit int and an 8-bit char, the code

```
char grade = 'B';
```

represents 'B' as the numerical value 66 stored in a 32-bit unit, but grade winds up with 66 stored in an 8-bit unit. This characteristic of character constants makes it possible to define a character constant like 'FATE', with 4 separate 8-bit ASCII codes stored in a 32-bit unit. However, attempting to assign such a character constant to a char variable results in only the last 8 bits being used, so the variable gets the value 'E'.

Nonprinting Characters

The single-quote technique is fine for characters, digits, and punctuation marks, but if you look through Appendix E, you see that some of the ASCII characters are nonprinting. For example, some represent actions such as backspacing or going to the next line or making the terminal bell ring (or speaker beep). How can these be represented?

The first way we have already mentioned: Just use the ASCII code. For example, the ASCII value for the beep character is 7, so you can do this:

```
char beep = 7;
```

The second way to represent certain awkward characters in C is to use special symbol sequences. These are called *escape sequences*. Table 3.1 shows the escape sequences and their meanings.

Table 3.1   Escape sequences.

Sequence	Meaning
\a	Alert (ANSI C)
\b	Backspace
\f	Form feed
\n	Newline
\r	Carriage return
\t	Horizontal tab
\v	Vertical tab (ANSI C)
\\	Backslash (\)
\'	Single quote (')
\"	Double quote (") (ANSI C)
\0oo	Octal value (o represents an octal digit)
\xhh	Hexadecimal value (h represents a hexadecimal digit)

Escape sequences must be enclosed in single quotes when assigned to a character variable. For example, you could make the statement

```
nerf = '\n';
```

and then print the variable **nerf** to advance the printer or screen one line.

Now take a closer look at what each escape sequence does. The alert character (\a), added by ANSI C, produces an audible or visible alert. The nature of the alert depends on the hardware, with the beep being the most common. (With many Windows implementations, the alert character has no effect.) The ANSI standard states that the alert character shall not change the *active position*. By active position, the standard means the location on the display device (screen, teletype, printer, and so forth) at which the next character would otherwise appear. In short, the active position is a generalization of the screen cursor you are probably accustomed to. Using the alert character in a program displayed on a screen should produce a beep without moving the screen cursor.

Next, the \b, \f, \n, \r, \t, and \v escape sequences are common output device control characters. They are best described in terms of how they affect the active position. A backspace (\b) moves (backspace character) the active position back one space on the current line. A form (form feed character) feed (\f) advances the active position to the start of the next page. A newline (\n) sets the active position to the beginning of the next. A carriage return (\r) moves the active position to the beginning of the current line. A horizontal tab (\t) moves the active position to the next horizontal tab stop; typically, they are found at character positions 1, 9, 17, 25, and so on. A vertical tab (\v) moves the active position to the next vertical tab position.

These escape characters do not necessarily work with all display devices. For instance, the form feed and vertical tab characters produce odd symbols on a PC screen instead of any cursor movement, but they work as described if sent to a printer instead of to the screen.

The next three escape sequences (\\, \', and \") enable you to use \, ', and " as character constants. (Because these symbols are used to define character constants as part of a `printf()` command, the situation could get confusing if you use them literally.) Suppose you want to print the following line:

```
Gramps sez, "a \ is a backslash."
```

Then use this code:

```
printf("Gramps sez, \"a \\ is a backslash.\"\n");
```

The final two forms (\0oo and \xhh) are special representations of the ASCII code. To represent a character by its octal ASCII code, precede it with a backslash (\), and enclose the whole thing in single quotes. For instance, if your compiler doesn't recognize the alert character (\a), you could use the ASCII code instead:

```
beep = '\007';
```

You can omit the leading zeros, so '\07' or even '\7' will do. This notation causes numbers to be interpreted as octal even if there is no initial 0.

ANSI C and many new implementations accept a hexadecimal form for character constants. In this case, the backslash is followed by an x or X and one to three hexadecimal digits. For example, the Control-P character has an ASCII hex code of 10 (16, in decimal), so it can be expressed as '\x10' or '\X010'. Figure 3.5 shows some representative integer types.

When you use ASCII code, note the difference between numbers and number characters. For example, the character 4 is represented by ASCII code value 52. The notation '4' represents the symbol 4, not the numerical value 4.

At this point, you may have three questions. One, why aren't the escape sequences enclosed in single quotes in the last example (`printf("Gramps sez, \"a \\ is a backslash\"\n");`)? Two, when should you use the ASCII code, and when should you use the escape sequences? Three, if you need to use numeric code, why use, say, `'\'032'` instead of `032`? Here are the answers:

1. When a character, be it an escape sequence or not, is part of a string of characters enclosed in double quotes, don't enclose it in single quotes. Notice that none of the other characters in this example (G,r,a,m,p,s, and so on) are marked off by single quotes. A string of characters enclosed in double quotes is called a *character string*. You explore strings in Chapter 4. Similarly, `printf("Hello!\007\n");` will print Hello! and beep, but `printf("Hello!7\n");` will print Hello!7. Digits not part of an escape sequence are treated as ordinary characters to be printed.

2. If you have a choice between using one of the special escape sequences, say `'\f'`, or an equivalent ASCII code, say `'\014'`, use the `'\f'`. First, the representation is more mnemonic. Second, it is more portable. If you have a system that doesn't use ASCII code, the `'\f'` will still work.

3. First, using `'\032'` instead of `032` makes it clear to someone reading the code that you intend to represent a character code. Second, an escape sequence like `\032` can be embedded in part of a C string, the way `\007` was in point #1.

Int Family Constants			
member	hex	octal	decimal
char	`'\x1A'`	`'\034'`	N.A.
short	±0x23	±043	±35
unsigned short	±0x23	043	35
Long	0x23L	±043L	±35L

Figure 3.5 Writing constants with the `int` family.

Printing Characters

The `printf()` function uses `%c` to indicate that a character should be printed. Recall that a character variable is stored as a 1-byte integer value. Therefore, if you print the value of a `char` variable with the usual `%d` specifier, you get an integer. The `%c` format specifier tells `printf()` to convert the integer to the corresponding character. Listing 3.5 shows a `char` variable both ways.

Listing 3.5   The charcode.c program.

```c
/* charcode.c--displays code number for a character */
#include <stdio.h>
int main(void)
{
    char ch;
    printf("Please enter a character.\n");
    scanf("%c", &ch);    /* user inputs character */
    printf("The code for %c is %d.\n", ch, ch);
    return 0;
}
```

Here is a sample run:

```
Please enter a character.
C
The code for C is 67.
```

When you use the program, remember to press the Enter or Return key after typing the character. The scanf() function then fetches the character you typed, and the ampersand (&) causes the character to be assigned to the variable ch. The printf() function then prints the value of ch twice, first as a character (prompted by the %c code) and then as a decimal integer (prompted by the %d code). Note that the printf() specifiers determine how data is displayed, not how it is stored (see Figure 3.6).

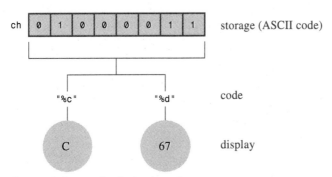

Figure 3.6 Data display versus data storage.

Signed or Unsigned?

Some C implementations make char a signed type. This means a char can hold values typically in the range −128 through +127. Other implementations make char an unsigned type, which provides a range of 0 through 255. Your compiler manual should tell you which type your char is, or you can check the **limits.h** header file, discussed in the next chapter.

ANSI C and many newer implementations enable you to use the keywords **signed** and **unsigned** with char. Then, regardless of what your default char is, **signed char** would be signed, and **unsigned char** would be unsigned.

Types `float` and `double`

The various integer types serve well for most software development projects. However, mathematically oriented programs often make use of *floating-point* numbers. In C, such numbers are called type `float`. They correspond to the **real** types of FORTRAN and Pascal. The floating-point approach, as already mentioned, enables you to represent a much greater range of numbers, including decimal fractions. Floating-point number representation is similar to *scientific notation*, a system used by scientists to express very large and very small numbers. Let's take a look.

In scientific notation, numbers are represented as decimal numbers times powers of 10. Here are some examples.

Number	Scientific Notation	Exponential Notation
1,000,000,000	$= 1.0 \times 10^9$	$= 1.0e9$
123,000	$= 1.23 \times 10^5$	$= 1.23e5$
322.56	$= 3.2256 \times 10^2$	$= 3.2256e2$
0.000056	$= 5.6 \times 10^{-5}$	$= 5.6e-5$

The first column shows the usual notation, the second column scientific notation, and the third column exponential notation, which is the way scientific notation is usually written for and by computers, with the *e* followed by the power of 10. Figure 3.7 shows more floating-point representations.

ANSI C provides that a float has to be able to represent at least six significant figures and allow a range of at least 10^{-37} to 10^{+37}. The first requirement means, for example, that a float has to represent accurately at least the first six digits in a number like 33.333333. The second requirement is handy if you like to use numbers such as the mass of the sun (2.0e30 kilograms) or the charge of a proton (1.6e–19 coulombs) or the national debt. Often, systems use 32 bits to store a floating-point number. Eight bits are used to give the exponent its value and sign, and 24 bits are used to represent the nonexponent part, called the *mantissa* or *significand*, and its sign.

C also has a `double` (for double precision) floating-point type. The `double` type has the same minimum range requirements as `float`, but it extends the minimum number of significant figures that can be represented to 10. Typical `double` representations use 64 bits instead of 32. Some systems use all 32 additional bits for the nonexponent part. This increases the number of significant figures and reduces round-off errors. Other systems use some of the bits to accommodate a larger exponent; this increases the range of numbers that can be accommodated. Either approach leads to at least 13 significant figures, more than meeting the minimum standard.

ANSI C allows for a third floating-point type: `long double`. The intent is to provide for even more precision than `double`. However, ANSI C guarantees only that `long double` is at least as precise as `double`.

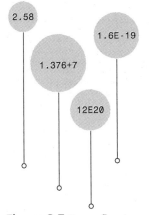

Figure 3.7 Some floating-point numbers.

Declaring Floating-Point Variables

Floating-point variables are declared and initialized in the same manner as their integer cousins. Here are some examples:

```
float noah, jonah;
double trouble;
float planck = 6.63e-34;
long double gnp;
```

Floating-Point Constants

There are many choices open to you when you write a floating-point constant. The basic form of a floating-point constant is a signed series of digits including a decimal point, followed by an **e** or **E**, followed by a signed exponent indicating the power of 10 used. Here are two examples of valid floating-point constants:

```
-1.56E+12
2.87e-3
```

You can leave out positive signs. You can do without a decimal point (2E5) or an exponential part (19.28), but not both simultaneously. You can omit a fractional part (3.E16) or an integer part (.45E–6), but not both (that wouldn't leave much!). Here are some more valid floating-point constants:

```
3.14159
.2
4e16
.8E-5
100.
```

Don't use spaces in a floating-point constant.

```
WRONG        1.56        E+12
```

By default, the compiler assumes floating-point constants are double precision. Suppose, for example, that `some` is a `float` variable, and that you have this statement:

```
some = 4.0 * 2.0;
```

Then the 4.0 and 2.0 are stored as `double`, using (typically) 64 bits for each. The product is calculated using double-precision arithmetic, and only then is the answer trimmed to regular `float` size. This ensures greater precision for your calculations, but can slow down a program.

ANSI C enables you to override this default by using an `f` or `F` suffix to make the compiler treat a floating-point constant as type `float`: examples are 2.3f and 9.11E9F. An `l` or `L` suffix makes it type `long double`; examples are 54.3l and 4.32e4L. Note that `L` is less likely to be mistaken for a 1 than is `l`. If the floating-point number has no suffix, it is type `double`.

Printing Floating-Point Values

The `printf()` function uses the `%f` format specifier to print type `float` and `double` numbers using decimal notation, and it uses `%e` to print them in exponential notation. Listing 3.6 illustrates this.

Listing 3.6   The `showfpt.c` program.

```
/* showf_pt.c--displays float value in two ways */
#include <stdio.h>
int main(void)
{
    float value = 32000.0;
    printf("%f can be written %e\n", value, value);
    return 0;
}
```

This is the output:

```
32000.000000 can be written 3.200000e+004
```

The preceding example illustrates the default output. The next chapter discusses how to control the appearance of this output by setting field widths and the number of places to the right of the decimal.

Those implementations that support the ANSI C `long double` type use the `%Lf` and `%Le` specifiers to print that type. Note, however, that both `float` and `double` use the `%f` or `%e` specifiers for output. That's because C automatically expands type `float` values to type `double` when they are passed as arguments to any function, such as `printf()`, that doesn't explicitly prototype the argument type.

Other Types

That finishes the list of fundamental data types (see Figure 3.8). For some of you, the list must seem long. Others of you might be thinking that more types are needed. What about a Boolean type or a string type? C doesn't have them, but it can still deal quite well with logical manipulations and with strings. You will take a first look at strings in Chapter 4.

Floating-Point Overflow and Underflow

What happens if you try to make a **float** variable exceed its limits? For example, suppose you multiply 1.0e38f by 1000.0f (overflow) or divide 1.0e–37f by 1.0e8f (underflow)? The result depends on the system. Either could cause the program to abort and to print a **runtime error** message. Or overflows may be replaced by a special value, such as the largest possible **float** value, underflows might be replaced by 0. Other systems may not issue warnings or may offer you a choice of responses. If this matter concerns you, check the rules for your system. If you can't find the information, don't be afraid of a little trial and error.

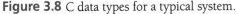

Derived Types
- arrays
- pointers
- strings
- structures
- unions

Figure 3.8 C data types for a typical system.

C does have other types derived from the basic types. These types include arrays, pointers, structures, and unions. Although they are subject matter for later chapters, we have already smuggled some pointers into this chapter's examples. (A *pointer* points to the location of a variable or other data object. The & prefix I used with the scanf() function creates a pointer telling scanf() where to place information.)

Floating-Point Round-Off Errors

Take a number, add 1 to it, and subtract the original number. What do you get? You get 1. A floating-point calculation, such as the following, may give another answer:

```
/* floaterr.c--demonstrates round-off error */
#include <stdio.h>
int main(void)
{
    float a,b;

    b = 2.0e20 + 1.0;
    a = b - 2.0e20;
    printf("%f \n", a);
    return 0;
}
```

The output is this:

```
0.000000     ¬VAX 750, UNIX
-13584010575872.000000     ¬Turbo C 1.5
4008175468544.000000     ¬Borland C 3.1, MSVC++ 5.0
```

The reason for these odd results is that the computer doesn't keep track of enough decimal places to do the operation correctly. The number 2.0e20 is 2 followed by 20 zeros, and by adding 1, you are trying to change the 21st digit. To do this correctly, the program would need to be able to store a 21-digit number. A float number is typically just 6 or 7 digits scaled to bigger or smaller numbers with an exponent. The attempt is doomed. On the other hand, if you used, say, 2.0e4 instead of 2.0e20, you would get the correct answer because you are trying to change the 5th digit, and float numbers are precise enough for that.

Summary: The Basic Data Types

Keywords:

The basic data types are set up using eight keywords—int, long, short, unsigned, char, float, double, and signed (ANSI C).

Signed Integers:

They can have positive or negative values.

`int`: The basic integer type for a given system. ANSI guarantees at least 16 bits for `int`.

`short` or `short int`: The largest `short` integer is no larger than the largest `int` and may be smaller. ANSI guarantees at least 16 bits for `short`.

`long` or `long int`: Can hold an integer at least as large as the largest `int` and possibly larger. ANSI guarantees at least 32 bits for `long`.

`long long` or `long long int`: This proposed extension can hold an integer at least as large as the largest `long` and possibly larger. The `long long` type is least 64 bits.

Typically, `long` will be bigger than `short`, and `int` will be the same as one of the two. For example, DOS-based systems for the PC provide 16-bit `short` and `int` and 32-bit `long`, and Windows 95–based systems provide 16-bit `short` and 32-bit `int` and `long`.

Unsigned Integers:

They have zero or positive values only. This extends the range of the largest possible positive number. Use the keyword `unsigned` before the desired type: `unsigned int`, `unsigned long`, `unsigned short`. A lone `unsigned` is the same as `unsigned int`.

Characters:

They are typographic symbols such as A, &, and +. By definition, the `char` type uses 1 byte of memory to represent a character. Historically, this character byte has most often been 8 bits, but it can be 16 bits or larger, if needed to represent the base character set.

`char`: The keyword for this type. Some implementations use a signed `char`, but others use an unsigned `char`. ANSI C enables you to use the keywords `signed` and `unsigned` to specify which form you want.

Floating Point:

They can have positive or negative values.

`float`: The basic floating-point type for the system; it can represent at least six significant figures accurately.

`double`: A (possibly) larger unit for holding floating-point numbers. It may allow more significant figures (at least 10, typically more) and perhaps larger exponents than `float`.

`long double`: A (possibly) even larger unit for holding floating-point numbers. It may allow more significant figures and perhaps larger exponents than `double`.

Summary: How to Declare a Simple Variable

1. Choose the type you need.

2. Choose a name for the variable.

3. Use the following format for a declaration statement:

```
type-specifier variable-name;
```

The type-specifier is formed from one or more of the type keywords; here are examples of declarations:

```
int erest;
unsigned short cash;.
```

4. You can declare more than one variable of the same type by separating the variable names with commas, for example:

```
char ch, init, ans;.
```

5. You can initialize a variable in a declaration statement:

```
float mass = 6.0E24;
```

Type Sizes

Tables 3.2 and 3.3 show type sizes for some common C environments. (In some environments, you have a choice.) What is your system like? Try running the program in Listing 3.7 to find out.

Table 3.2 Integer type sizes (bytes) for representative systems.

Type	Macintosh Metrowerks CW (default)	IBM PC Borland DOS and Windows 3.1	IBM PC Windows 98 and Windows NT	ANSI C Minimum
char	1	1	1	1
int	4	2	4	2
short	2	2	2	2
long	4	4	4	4

Table 3.3 Floating-point facts for representative systems.

Type	Macintosh Metrowerks CW (default)	IBM PC Borland 3.1 (DOS)	IBM PC Windows 98 and Windows NT	ANSI C Minimum
float	6 digits	6 digits	6 digits	6 digits
	−37 to 38	−37 to 38	−37 to 38	−37 to 37
double	18 digits	15 digits	15 digits	10 digits
	−4931 to 4932	−307 to 308	−307 to 308	−37 to 37
long double	18 digits	19 digits	18 digits	10 digits
	−4931 to 4932	−4931 to 4932	−4931 to 4932	−37 to 37

For each type, the top row is the number of significant digits and the second row is the exponent range (base 10).

Listing 3.7 The typesize.c program.

```
/* typesize.c--prints out type sizes */
#include <stdio.h>
int main(void)
{
    printf("Type int has a size of %d bytes.\n", sizeof(int));
    printf("Type char has a size of %d bytes.\n", sizeof(char));
    printf("Type long has a size of %d bytes.\n", sizeof(long));
    printf("Type double has a size of %d bytes.\n",
            sizeof(double));
    return 0;
}
```

C has a built-in operator called sizeof that gives sizes in bytes. (Some compilers, such as Think C for the Macintosh, require %ld instead of %d for printing sizeof quantities. That's because C leaves some latitude as to the actual integer type that sizeof uses to report its findings.) The output from this program is as follows:

```
Type int has a size of 4 bytes.
Type char has a size of 1 bytes.
Type long has a size of 4 bytes.
Type double has a size of 8 bytes.
```

This program found the size of only four types, but you can easily modify it to find the size of any other type that interests you. Note that the size of char is necessarily 1 byte because C defines the size of one byte in terms of char. So, on a system with a 16-bit char and a 64-bit double, sizeof will report double as having a size of 4 bytes. If you have an ANSI C compiler, you can check the limits.h and float.h header files for more detailed information on type limits. (The next chapter discusses these two files further.)

Incidentally, notice in the last line how the `printf()` statement is spread over two lines. You can do this as long as the break does not occur in the quoted section or in the middle of a word.

Using Data Types

When you develop a program, note the variables you need and which type they should be. Most likely you can use `int` or possibly `float` for the numbers and `char` for the characters. Declare them at the beginning of the function that uses them. Choose a name for the variable that suggests its meaning. When you initialize a variable, match the constant type to the variable type.

```
int apples = 3;         /* RIGHT */
int oranges = 3.0;      /* WRONG */
```

C is more forgiving about type mismatches than, say, Pascal. C compilers allow the second initialization, but they might complain, particularly if you have activated a higher warning level. It is best not to develop sloppy habits.

When you initialize a variable of one numeric type to a value of a different type, C converts the value to match the variable. This means you may lose some data. For example, consider the following initializations:

```
int cost = 12.99;           /* initializing an int to a double  */
float pi = 3.1415926536;    /* initializing a float to a double */
```

The first declaration assigns 12 to `cost`; when converting floating-point values to integers, C simply throws away the decimal part (*truncation*), instead of rounding. The second declaration loses some precision, as a `float` is guaranteed to represent only the first six digits accurately. Compilers may issue a warning (but don't have to) if you make such initializations. You might have run into this when compiling Listing 3.1.

Arguments and Pitfalls

It's worth repeating and amplifying a caution made earlier in this chapter about using `printf()`. The items of information passed to a function, as you may recall, are termed *arguments* or *parameters*. For instance, the function call `printf("Hello, pal.")` has one argument, `"Hello, pal."`. A series of characters in quotes, such as `"Hello, pal."`, is called a *string*. We'll discuss strings in Chapter 4. For now, the important point is that one string, even one containing several words and punctuation marks, counts as one argument.

Similarly, the function call `scanf("%d", &weight)` has two arguments, `"%d"` and `&weight`. C uses commas to separate arguments to a function. The `printf()` and `scanf()` functions are unusual in that they aren't limited to a particular number of arguments. For example, we've used calls to `printf()` with one, two, and even three arguments. For a program to work properly, it needs to know how many arguments there are. The `printf()` and `scanf()` functions use the first argument to indicate how many additional arguments are coming. The trick is that each format specification in the initial string indicates an additional argument. For instance, the following statement has two format specifiers, %d and %d:

```
printf("%d cats ate %d cans of tuna\n", cats, cans);
```

This tells the program to expect two more arguments, and indeed, there are two more: cats and cans.

Your responsibility as a programmer is to make sure that the number of format specifications matches the number of additional arguments and that the specifier type matches the value type. The new ANSI C function-prototyping mechanism checks to see whether a function call has the correct number and correct kind of arguments, but it doesn't work with printf() and scanf() because they take a variable number of arguments. What happens if you don't live up to the programmer's burden? Suppose, for example, you write a program like that in Listing 3.8.

Listing 3.8 The badcount.c program.

```
/* badcount.c--incorrect argument counts */
#include <stdio.h>
int main(void)
{
    int f = 4;
    int g = 5;
    float h = 5.0f;

    printf("%d\n", f, g);      /* too many arguments    */
    printf("%d %d\n",f);       /* too few arguments     */
    printf("%d %f\n", h, g); /* wrong kind of values */
    return 0;
}
```

Here's the output from Microsoft Visual C++ 5.0 (Windows 95 PC):

```
4

4 1084227584
0.000000 1075052544
```

Next, here's the output from Borland 3.1 (DOS PC):

```
4

4 -28792
0.000000 16404
```

And here's the output from Metrowerks CodeWarrior Pro 3 (Macintosh):

```
4

4 2
0.000000 0
```

Note that using %d to display a float value doesn't convert the float value to the nearest int; instead, it displays what appears to be garbage. Similarly, using %f to display an int value doesn't convert an integer value to a floating-point value. Also, the results you get for too few arguments or the wrong kind of argument differ from platform to platform.

None of the five compilers we tried raised any objections to this code. Nor were there any complaints when we ran the program. As you can see, the computer doesn't catch this kind of error during runtime, and because the program may otherwise run correctly, you might not notice the errors, either. If a program doesn't print the expected number of values or if it prints unexpected values, check to see whether you've used the correct number of printf() arguments. (Incidentally, the UNIX syntax-checking program lint, which is much pickier than the UNIX compiler, does mention erroneous printf() arguments.)

One More Example

Let's run one more printing example, one that makes use of some of C's special escape characters. In particular, the program in Listing 3.9 shows how backspace (\b), tab (\t), and carriage return (\r) work. These concepts date from when computers used teletype machines for output and they don't always translate successfully to contemporary graphical interfaces. For example, this listing doesn't work as described on some Macintosh implementations.

Listing 3.9   The escape.c program.

```
/* escape.c--uses escape characters */
#include <stdio.h>
int main(void)
{
    float salary;
    printf("Enter your desired monthly salary:");  /* 1 */
    printf(" $_____\b\b\b\b\b\b\b");              /* 2 */
    scanf("%f", &salary);
    printf("\n\t$%.2f a month is $%.2f a year.", salary,
            salary * 12.0);                          /* 3 */
    printf("\rGee!\n");                              /* 4 */
    return 0;
}
```

What Happens

Let's walk through this program step by step as it would work under an ANSI C implementation. The first printf() statement (the one numbered 1) prints the following:

Enter your desired monthly salary:

Because there is no \n at the end of the string, the cursor is left positioned after the colon.

The second printf() statement picks up where the first one stops, so after it is finished, the screen looks like this:

Enter your desired monthly salary: $_____

The space between the colon and the dollar sign is there because the string in the second `printf()` statement starts with a space. The effect of the seven backspace characters is to move the cursor seven positions to the left. This backs the cursor over the seven underline characters, placing the cursor directly after the dollar sign. Usually, backspacing does not erase the characters that are backed over, but some implementations may use destructive backspacing, negating the point of this little exercise.

At this point, you type your response, say **2000.00**. Now the line looks like this:

```
Enter your desired monthly salary: $2000.00
```

The characters you type replace the underline characters, and when you press Enter (or Return) to enter your response, the cursor moves to the beginning of the next line.

The third `printf()` statement output begins with `\n\t`. The newline character moves the cursor to the beginning of the next line. The tab character moves the cursor to the next tab stop on that line, typically to column 9. Then the rest of the string is printed. After this statement, the screen looks like this:

```
Enter your desired monthly salary: $2000.00
        $2000.00 a month is $24000.00 a year.
```

Because the `printf()` statement doesn't use the newline character, the cursor remains just after the final period.

The fourth `printf()` statement begins with `\r`. This positions the cursor at the beginning of the current line. Then `Gee!` is displayed there, and the `\n` moves the cursor to the next line. The final appearance of the screen is this:

```
Enter your desired monthly salary: $2000.00
Gee!    $2000.00 a month is $24000.00 a year.
```

A Possible Problem

Some older C implementations do not work as we've just described. The problem lies in when `printf()` actually sends output to the screen. In general, `printf()` statements send output to an intermediate storage area called a *buffer*. Every now and then, the material in the buffer is sent to the screen. Under ANSI C, the rules for when output is sent from the buffer to the screen are clear. It is sent when the buffer gets full or when a newline character is encountered or when there is impending input. (This is called *flushing the buffer*.) For instance, the first two `printf()` statements don't fill the buffer and don't contain a newline, but they are immediately followed by a `scanf()` statement asking for input. That forces the `printf()` output to be sent to the screen.

Some older C implementations, however, do not invoke the third condition (impending input) for flushing the buffer. If you run Listing 3.9 with one of these compilers, the output of the first two `printf()` statements remains in the buffer. If you type a response anyway and then press Enter, the newline generated by the Enter key flushes the buffer. You have to type your answer before you see the question! One solution to this awkward situation is to use a newline at the end of the `printf()` statement preceding the input. That newline will flush the buffer. The code can be changed to look like this:

```
printf("Enter your desired monthly salary:\n");
scanf("%f", &salary);
```

This code works whether or not impending input flushes the buffer. However, it also puts the cursor on the next line, preventing you from entering data on the same line as the prompting string. A sample run would look like this:

```
Enter your desired monthly salary:
2000.00
```

To maintain greater portability, we'll follow this model (with the response on the line following the prompt) for the rest of this book. Another solution is to use the `fflush()` function described in Chapter 12, "File Input/Output."

Chapter Summary

C has a variety of data types. The basic types fall into two categories: integer types and floating-point types. The two distinguishing features for integer types are the amount of storage allotted to a type and whether it is signed or unsigned. The smallest integer type is `char`, which can be either signed or unsigned, depending on the implementation. ANSI C enables you to use `signed char` and `unsigned char` to explicitly specify which you want. The other integer types include `short`, `int`, `long`, and the C9X-proposed `long long` type. C guarantees that each of these types is at least as large as the preceding type. Each of them is a signed type, but with ANSI C you can use the `unsigned` keyword to create the corresponding unsigned types: `unsigned short`, `unsigned int`, and `unsigned long`. K&R C recognizes only `unsigned int` from this trio. The C9X committee proposes adding `unsigned long long` to the list.

The three floating-point types are `float`, `double`, and, new with ANSI C, `long double`. Each is at least as large as the preceding type.

Integers can be expressed in decimal, octal, or hexadecimal form. A leading `0` indicates an octal number, and a leading `0x` or `0X` indicates a hexadecimal number. For example, `32`, `040`, and `0x20` are decimal, octal, and hexadecimal representations of the same value. An `l` or `L` suffix indicates a `long` value.

Character constants are represented by placing the character in single quotes: `'Q'`, `'8'`, and `'$'`, for example. C escape sequences, such as `'\n'`, represent certain nonprinting characters. You can use the form `'\007'` to represent a character by its ASCII code.

Floating-point numbers can be written with a fixed decimal point, as in `9393.912`, or in exponential notation, as in `7.38E10`.

The `printf()` function enables you to print various types of values by using conversion specifiers, which, in their simplest form, consist of a percent sign and a letter indicating the type, as in `%d` or `%f`.

Review Questions

1. Which data type would you use for each of the following kinds of data?

    a. The population of Rio Frito.

    b. The average weight of a Rembrandt painting.

    c. The most common letter in this chapter.

    d. The number of times that the letter occurs in this chapter.

2. Why would you use a type `long` variable instead of type `int`?

3. Identify the type and meaning, if any, of each of the following constants:

    a. `'\b'`

    b. `1066`

    c. `99.44`

    d. `0XAA`

    e. `2.0e30`

4. Virgila Ann Xenopod has concocted an error-laden program. Help her find the mistakes.

```
include <stdio.h>
main
(
 float g; h;
 float tax, rate;

 g = e21;
 tax = rate*g;
)
```

5. Identify the data type (as used in declaration statements) and the `printf()` format specifier for each of the following constants:

Constant		Type	Specifier
a.	12		
b.	0X3		
c.	'C'		
d.	2.34E07		
e.	'\040'		
f.	7.0		

Constant	Type	Specifier
g. 6L		
h. 6.0f		

6. Identify the data type (as used in declaration statements) and the
   printf() format specifier for each of the following constants (assume a
   16-bit int):

Constant	Type	Specifier
a. 012		
b. 2.9e05L		
c. 's'		
d. 100000		
e. '\n'		
f. 20.0f		
g. 0x44		

7. Suppose a program begins with these declarations:

```
int imate = 2;
long shot = 53456;
char grade = 'A';
float log = 2.71828;
```

Fill in the proper type specifiers in the following printf() statements:

```
printf("The odds against the %__ were %__ to 1.\n", imate, shot);
printf("A score of %__ is not an %__ grade.\n", log, grade);
```

8. Suppose that ch is a type char variable. Show how to assign the carriage-
   return character to ch by using an escape sequence, a decimal value, an
   octal character constant, and a hex character constant. (Assume ASCII
   code values.)

9. Correct this silly program. (The / in C means division.)

```
void main(int) / this program is perfect /
{
 cows, legs integer;
```

```
printf("How many cow legs did you count?\n);
scanf("%c", legs);
cows = legs / 4;
printf("That implies there are %f cows.\n", cows)
}
```

10. Identify what each of the following escape sequences represents:

    a. \n

    b. \\

    c. \"

    d. \t

Programming Exercises

1. Find out what your system does with integer overflow, floating-point overflow, and floating-point underflow by using the experimental approach; that is, write programs having these problems.

2. Write a program that asks you to enter an ASCII code value, such as 66, and then prints the character having that ASCII code.

3. Write a program that sounds the alert and then prints the following text:

   `Startled by the sudden sound, Sally shouted, "By the Great Pumpkin, what was that!"`

4. Write a program that reads in a floating-point number and prints it first in decimal-point notation and then in exponential notation. Have the output use the following format:

   The input is 21.290000 or 2.129000e+001.

5. There are approximately 3.156×10^7 seconds in a year. Write a program that requests your age in years and then displays the equivalent number of seconds.

6. The mass of a single molecule of water is about 3.0×10^{-23} grams. A quart of water is about 950 grams. Write a program that requests an amount of water, in quarts, and displays the number of water molecules in that amount.

CHAPTER 4

CHARACTER STRINGS AND FORMATTED INPUT/OUTPUT

You will learn about the following in this chapter:

- Functions
  strlen(), printf(), scanf()

- Modifiers
  const, *

This chapter introduces you to character strings. You see how they are created and stored and how you can use `scanf()` and `printf()` to read and display them. Also, you learn how to use the `strlen()` function to measure string lengths. You examine the C preprocessor's `#define` directive and ANSI C's `const` modifier for creating symbolic constants.

This chapter concentrates on input and output. You'll add personality to your programs by making them interactive and using character strings. You will also take a more detailed look at those two handy C input/output functions, `printf()` and `scanf()`. With these two functions, you have the program tools you need to communicate with users and to format output to meet your needs and tastes. Finally, you'll take a quick look at an important C facility, the C preprocessor, and learn how to define and use symbolic constants.

Introductory Program

By now, you probably expect a sample program at the beginning of each chapter, and I won't disappoint you. Listing 4.1 presents a program that engages in a dialogue with the user.

Listing 4.1   The `talkback.c` program.

```c
/* talkback.c -- nosy, informative program */
#include <stdio.h>
#include <string.h>       /* for strlen() prototype       */
#define DENSITY 62.4      /* human density in lbs per cu ft */
int main(void)
{
  float weight, volume;
  int size, letters;
  char name[40];          /* name is an array of 40 chars   */

  printf("Hi! What's your first name?\n");
  scanf("%s", name);
  printf("%s, what's your weight in pounds?\n", name);
  scanf("%f", &weight);
  size = sizeof name;
  letters = strlen(name);
  volume = weight / DENSITY;
  printf("Well, %s, your volume is %2.2f cubic feet.\n",
      name, volume);
  printf("Also, your first name has %d letters,\n",
      letters);
  printf("and we have %d bytes to store it in.\n", size);
  return 0;
}
```

(Recall that some compilers, such as Think C for the Macintosh, require `%ld` for printing `sizeof` quantities.) Running `talkback` produces results such as the following:

```
Hi! what's your first name?
Angelica
Angelica, what's your weight in pounds?
132.5
Well, Angelica, your volume is 2.12 cubic feet.
Also, your first name has 8 letters,
and we have 40 bytes to store it in.
```

Here are the main new features of this program:

- It uses an *array* to hold a *character string*. Here, someone's name is read into the array, which, in this case, is a series of 40 consecutive bytes in memory, each able to hold a single character value.

- It uses the `%s` *conversion specification* to handle the input and output of the string. Note that `name`, unlike `weight`, does not use the & prefix when used with `scanf()`. (As you'll see later, both `&weight` and `name` are addresses.)

- It uses the C preprocessor to define the symbolic constant `DENSITY` to represent the value `62.4`.

- It uses the C function `strlen()` to find the length of a string.

The C approach might seem a little complex compared with the input/output of, say, BASIC. However, this complexity buys a finer control of I/O and a greater program efficiency. It is surprisingly easy once you get used to it.

Let's investigate these new ideas.

Character Strings: An Introduction

A *character string* is a series of one or more characters. Here is an example of a string:

```
"Zing went the strings of my heart!"
```

The double quotation marks are not part of the string. They inform the compiler that they enclose a string, just as single quotation marks identify a character.

Type `char` Arrays and the Null Character

C has no special variable type for strings. Instead, strings are stored in an array of type `char`. Characters in a string are stored in adjacent memory cells, one character per cell, and an array consists of adjacent memory locations, so placing a string in an array is quite natural (see Figure 4.1).

| Z | i | n | g | | w | e | n | t | | t | h | e | | s | t | r | i | n | g | s | | o | f | | m | y | | h | e | a | r | t | ! | \0 |

▲ each cell is one byte   ▲ null character

Figure 4.1 A string in an array.

Note that Figure 4.1 shows the character \0 in the last array position. This is the *null character*, and C uses it to mark the end of a string. The null character is not the digit zero; it is the nonprinting character whose ASCII code value (or equivalent) is **0**. Strings in C are always stored with this terminating null character. The presence of the null character means that the array must have at least one more cell than the number of characters to be stored.

Now just what is an array? You can think of an array as several memory cells in a row. If you prefer more formal and exact language, an array is an ordered sequence of data elements of one type. This example creates an array of 40 memory cells, or elements, each of which can store one `char`-type value, by using this declaration:

```
char name[40];
```

The brackets after `name` identify it as an array. The **40** within the brackets indicates the number of elements in the array. The `char` identifies the type of each element (see Figure 4.2).

Figure 4.2 Declaring an array name of type `char`.

Using a character string is beginning to sound complicated! You have to create an array, place the characters of a string into an array one by one, and remember to add a \0 at the end. Fortunately, the computer can take care of most of the details itself.

Using Strings

Try the program in Listing 4.2 to see how easy it really is to use strings.

Listing 4.2   The praise1.c program.

```
/* praise1.c -- uses an assortment of strings */
#include <stdio.h>
#define PRAISE "My sakes, that's a grand name!"
int main(void)
{
  char name[40];

  printf("What's your name?\n");
  scanf("%s", name);
  printf("Hello, %s. %s\n", name, PRAISE);
  return 0;
}
```

The %s tells printf() to print a string. The %s appears twice because the program prints two strings: the one stored in the name array and the one represented by PRAISE. Running praise1.c should produce an output similar to this:

```
What's your name?
Snippy Coredump
Hello, Snippy. My sakes, that's a grand name!
```

You do not have to put the null character into the array **name** yourself. That task is done for you by scanf() when it reads the input. Nor do you include a null character in the character string constant PRAISE. We'll explain the #define statement soon; for now, simply note that the double quotation marks that enclose the text following PRAISE identify the text as a string. The compiler takes care of putting in the null character.

Note (and this is important) that scanf() just reads Snippy Coredump's first name. After scanf() starts to read input, it stops reading at the first *whitespace* (blank, tab, or newline) it encounters. Therefore, it stops scanning for **name** when it reaches the blank between Snippy and Coredump. In general, scanf() is used with %s to read only a single word, not a whole phrase, as a string. C has other input-reading functions, such as gets(), for handling general strings. Later chapters will explore string functions more fully.

Strings Versus Characters

The string constant `"x"` is not the same as the character constant `'x'`. One difference is that `'x'` is a basic type (`char`), but `"x"` is a derived type, an array of `char`. A second difference is that `"x"` really consists of two characters, `'x'` and `'\0'`, the null character (see Figure 4.3).

Figure 4.3 The character `'x'` and the string `"x"`.

The `strlen()` Function

The previous chapter unleashed the `sizeof` operator, which gives the size of things in bytes. The `strlen()` function gives the length of a string in characters. Because it takes 1 byte to hold 1 character, you might suppose that both would give the same result when applied to a string, but they don't. Add a few lines to the example, as shown in Listing 4.3, and see why.

Listing 4.3   The `praise2.c` program.

```
/* praise2.c */
#include <stdio.h>
#include <string.h>        /* provides strlen() prototype */
#define PRAISE "My sakes, that's a grand name!"
int main(void)
{
  char name[40];

  printf("What's your name?\n");
  scanf("%s", name);
  printf("Hello, %s. %s\n", name, PRAISE);
  printf("Your name of %d letters occupies %d memory cells.\n",
         strlen(name), sizeof name);
  printf("The phrase of praise has %d letters ",
         strlen(PRAISE));
  printf("and occupies %d memory cells.\n", sizeof PRAISE);
  return 0;
}
```

If you are using a pre-ANSI C compiler, you might have to remove the following line:

```
#include <string.h>
```

The `string.h` file contains function prototypes for several string-related functions. Although not necessary for this particular example, this addition makes the program more harmonious with the ANSI spirit. I'll discuss this file in Chapter 12, "File Input/Output." (By the way, some pre-ANSI UNIX systems use `strings.h` instead of `string.h` to contain declarations for string functions.)

More generally, ANSI C divides the C function library into families of related functions and provides a header file for each family. For example, `printf()` and `scanf()` belong to a family of standard input and output functions and use the `stdio.h` header file. The `strlen()` function joins several other string-related functions, such as functions to copy strings and to search through strings, in a family served by the `string.h` header.

Notice that Listing 4.3 uses two methods to handle long `printf()` statements. The first method spreads one `printf()` statement over two lines. (You can break a line between arguments but not in the middle of a string; for example, not between the quotation marks.) The second method uses two `printf()` statements to print just one line. The newline character (\n) appears only in the second statement. Running the program could produce this interchange:

```
What's your name?
Tuffy
Hello, Tuffy. My sakes, that's a grand name!
Your name of 5 letters occupies 40 memory cells.
The phrase of praise has 30 letters and occupies 31 memory cells.
```

See what happens? The array `name` has 40 memory cells, and that is what the `sizeof` operator reports. Only the first five cells are needed to hold Tuffy, however, and that is what `strlen()` reports. The sixth cell in the array `name` contains the null character, and its presence tells `strlen()` when to stop counting. Figure 4.4 illustrates this concept.

Figure 4.4 The `strlen()` function knows when to stop.

When you get to PRAISE, you find that `strlen()` again gives you the exact number of characters (including spaces and punctuation) in the string. The `sizeof` operator gives you a number one larger because it also counts the invisible null character used to end the string. You didn't tell the computer how much memory to set aside to store the phrase. It had to count the number of characters between the double quotes itself.

One other point: The preceding chapter used `sizeof` with parentheses, but this chapter doesn't. Whether you use parentheses depends on whether you want the size of a type or the size of a particular quantity. Parentheses are required for types, but are optional for particular quantities. That is, you would use `sizeof(char)` or `sizeof(float)`, but can use `sizeof name` or `sizeof 6.28`.

The last example used `strlen()` and `sizeof` for rather a rather trivial purpose of satisfying a user's potential curiosity. Actually, however, `strlen()` and `sizeof` are important programming tools. For example, `strlen()` is useful in all sorts of character-string programs, as you'll see in Chapter 11, "Character Strings and String Functions."

Let's move on to the `#define` statement.

Constants and the C Preprocessor

Sometimes you need to use a constant in a program. For example, you could give the circumference of a circle as this:

```
circumference = 3.14159 * diameter;
```

Here, the constant 3.14159 represents the world-famous constant pi (π). To use a constant, just type in the actual value, as in the example. However, there are good reasons to use a *symbolic constant* instead. That is, you could use a statement like the following and have the computer substitute in the actual value later:

```
circumference = pi * diameter;
```

Why is it better to use a symbolic constant? First, a name tells you more than a number does. Compare these two statements:

```
owed = 0.015 * housevalue;
owed = taxrate * housevalue;
```

If you read through a long program, the meaning of the second version is more plain than the first.

Second, suppose you have used a constant in several places, and it becomes necessary to change its value. After all, tax rates do change. Then you need merely to alter the definition of the symbolic constant, rather than find and change every occurrence of the constant in the program.

Okay, how do you set up a symbolic constant? One way is to declare a variable and set it equal to the desired constant. You could write this:

```
float taxrate;
taxrate = 0.015;
```

This way is all right for a small program, but it is somewhat wasteful because the computer has to peek into the `taxrate` memory location every time `taxrate` is used. This is an example of *execution time* substitution because the substitution takes place while the program is running. Fortunately, C has a couple of better ideas.

The original better idea is the C preprocessor. In Chapter 2, "Introducing C," you saw how the preprocessor uses `#include` to incorporate information from another file.

The preprocessor also lets you define constants. Just add a line like this at the top of the file containing your program:

```
#define TAXRATE 0.015
```

When your program is compiled, the value **0.015** will be substituted everywhere you have used **TAXRATE**. This is called a *compile time* substitution. By the time you run the program, all the substitutions have already been made (see Figure 4.5). Such defined constants are often termed *manifest constants*.

Note the format. First comes **#define**. In older implementations, the **#** sign should be in the leftmost column; ANSI C removes this restriction. Next comes the symbolic name (**TAXRATE**) for the constant and then the value (**0.015**) for the constant. So the general form is as follows:

```
#define NAME value
```

You would substitute the symbolic name of your choice for *NAME* and the appropriate value for *value*. No semicolon is used because this is a substitution mechanism, not a C statement. Why is **TAXRATE** capitalized? It is a sensible C tradition to type constants in uppercase. Then, when you encounter one in the depths of a program, you know immediately that it is a constant, not a variable. Capitalizing constants is just another technique to make programs more readable. Your programs will still work if you don't capitalize the constants, but capitalizing them is a good habit to cultivate.

The names you use for symbolic constants must satisfy the same rules that the names of variables do. You can use uppercase and lowercase letters, digits, and the underscore character. The first character cannot be a digit. Listing 4.4 shows a simple example.

Listing 4.4   The `pizza.c` program.

```
/* pizza.c -- uses defined constants in a pizza context */
#include <stdio.h>
#define PI 3.14159
int main(void)
{
  float area, circum, radius;

  printf("What is the radius of your pizza?\n");
  scanf("%f", &radius);
  area = PI * radius * radius;
  circum = 2.0 * PI *radius;
  printf("Your basic pizza parameters are as follows:\n");
  printf("circumference = %1.2f, area = %1.2f\n", circum,
         area);
  return 0;
}
```

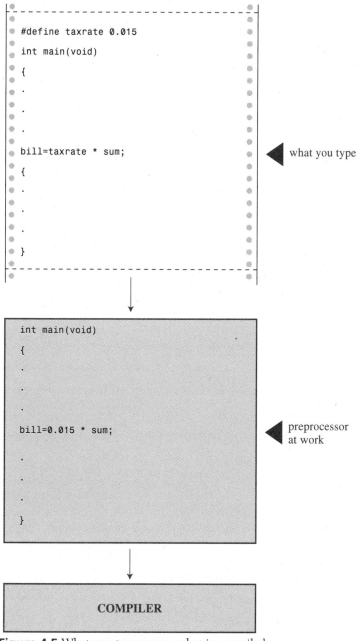

```
#define taxrate 0.015
int main(void)
{
    .

    .

    .

bill=taxrate * sum;
{
    .

    .

    .

}
```
what you type

```
int main(void)
{
    .

    .

    .

bill=0.015 * sum;

    .

    .

    .

}
```
preprocessor
at work

COMPILER

Figure 4.5 What you type versus what is compiled.

The `%1.2f` in the `printf()` statement causes the printout to be rounded to two decimal places. Of course, this program may not reflect your major pizza concerns, but it does fill a small niche in the world of pizza programs. Here is a sample run:

```
What is the radius of your pizza?
6.0
Your basic pizza parameters are as follows:
circumference = 37.70, area = 113.10
```

The `#define` statement can be used for character and string constants, too. Just use single quotes for the former and double quotes for the latter. The following examples are valid:

```
#define BEEP '\a'
#define TEE 'T'
#define ESC '\033'
#define OOPS "Now you have done it!"
```

Remember that everything following the symbolic name is substituted for it. Don't make this common error:

```
/* the following is wrong */
#define TOES = 20
```

If you do this, `TOES` is replaced by `= 20`, not just `20`. In that case, a statement like

```
digits = fingers + TOES;
```

is converted to the following misrepresentation:

```
digits = fingers + = 20;
```

The `const` Modifier

ANSI C adds a second way to create symbolic constants—using the `const` keyword to modify a variable declaration:

```
const int MONTHS = 12;    // MONTHS a symbolic constant for 12
```

This makes `MONTHS` into a read-only value. That is, you can display `MONTHS` and use it in calculations, but you cannot alter the value of `MONTHS`. This newer approach is more flexible than using `#define`; Chapter 13, "Storage Classes and Program Development," discusses this and other uses of `const`.

Actually, ANSI C has yet a third way to create symbolic constants, and that is the `enum` facility discussed in Chapter 16, "The C Preprocessor and the C Library."

Using `#define` and `#include` Together

Here is a special treat for the lazy. Suppose you develop a whole packet of programs that use the same set of constants. You can do the following:

• Collect all your `#define` statements in one file; call it, say, `const.h`.

- At the head of each source code file of your program, insert the following statement:

```
#include "const.h"
```

Then, when you run the program, the preprocessor will read the file const.h and use all the #define statements there for your program. Incidentally, the .h at the end of the filename is a reminder to you that the file is a header, that is, full of information to be placed at the head of your program. The preprocessor itself doesn't care whether you use a .h in the name.

Note that we used "const.h", not <const.h>. The difference lies in where the compiler first looks for the include file, and it is implementation dependent. On UNIX systems, placing the filename in angle brackets causes the preprocessor to look in specific system directories for the files. Placing the filename in quotes causes the preprocessor to look in the current directory first and then in the system directories. Or you can specify a full pathname, as in "/usr/tiger/myincludes/bar.h", in which case just the indicated directory (/usr/tiger/myincludes) is searched. Many IDEs have menu choices to select the standard include directory. Again, angle brackets mean to search only the standard include directory, and quotes mean to search the current directory first. Incidentally, although UNIX uses the slash (/) in pathnames, the DOS environment uses the backslash (\) for the same purpose.

C, A Master of Disguise: Creating Aliases

The capabilities of #define go beyond the symbolic representation of constants. Consider, for instance, the program in Listing 4.5. (By the way, this example is meant to be a mildly entertaining illustration of how the preprocessor works; it most definitely is not intended to be a model to emulate.)

Listing 4.5 The alias.c program.

```
/* alias.c -- uses preprocessor frivously */
#include <stdio.h>
#include "alias.h"   /* see text for more on this file */
program
  begin
    whole yours, mine then
    spitout("Give me an integer, please.\n") then
    takein("%d", &yours) then
    mine = yours times TWO then
    spitout("%d is twice your number!\n", mine) then
  end
```

Hmmm, Listing 4.5 looks vaguely familiar, a little like Pascal, but it doesn't seem to be C. The secret, of course, is in the file alias.h. What's in it? Read on.

```
/* alias.h -- a silly abuse of preprocessing power */
#define program int main(void)
#define begin    {
```

```
#define end      return 0;}
#define then     ;
#define takein   scanf
#define spitout  printf
#define TWO      2
#define times    *
#define whole    int
```

This example illustrates how the preprocessor works. Your program is searched for items defined by #define statements, and all finds are then replaced. In this example, all thens are rendered into semicolons at compilation. The resulting program is identical to what you would have received by typing in the usual C terms at the start.

This powerful defining facility can also be used to define a macro, which is sort of a poor man's function. I will return to this topic in Chapter 16.

The #define feature has limitations. For example, parts of a program within double quotes are immune to substitution. The following combination wouldn't work:

```
#define MN "minimifidianism"
printf("He was a strong believer in MN.\n");
```

The printout would read simply:

```
He was a strong believer in MN.
```

This is because MN is enclosed in double quotes in the printf() statement. However, the statement

```
printf("He was a strong believer in %s.\n", MN);
```

would produce

```
He was a strong believer in minimifidianism.
```

In this case, the MN was outside the double quotes, so it was replaced by its definition. (*Minimifidianism*, by the way, means having almost no belief.)

Manifest Constants on the Job

The ANSI C header files limits.h and float.h supply detailed information about the size limits of integer types and floating types, respectively. Each file defines a series of manifest constants that apply to your implementation. For instance, the limits.h file contains lines similar to the following:

```
#define INT_MAX    +32767
#define INT_MIN    -32768
```

These constants represent the largest and smallest possible values for the int type. If your system used a 32-bit int, the file would provide different values for these symbolic constants. The file defines minimum and maximum values for all the integer types. If you include the limits.h file, you can use code like the following:

```
printf("Maximum int value on this system = %d\n", INT_MAX);
```

If your system used a four-byte `int`, the `limits.h` file that came with that system would provide definitions for `INT_MAX` and `INT_MIN` that matched the limits of a four-byte `int`. Table 4.1 lists some of the constants found in `limits.h`.

Table 4.1   Some symbolic constants from `limits.h`.

Symbolic Constant	Represents
CHAR_BIT	Number of bits in a char
CHAR_MAX	Maximum char value
CHAR_MIN	Minimum char value
SCHAR_MAX	Maximum signed char value
SCHAR_MIN	Minimum signed char value
UCHAR_MAX	Maximum unsigned char value
SHRT_MAX	Maximum short value
SHRT_MIN	Minimum short value
USHRT_MAX	Maximum unsigned short value
INT_MAX	Maximum int value
INT_MIN	Minimum int value
UINT_MAX	Maximum unsigned int value
LONG_MAX	Maximum long value
LONG_MIN	Minimum long value
ULONG_MAX	Maximum unsigned long value

Similarly, the `float.h` file defines constants such as `FLT_DIG` and `DBL_DIG`, which represent the number of significant figures supported by the **float** type and the **double** type. Table 4.2 lists some of the constants found in `float.h`. This sample relates to the **float** type. Equivalent constants are defined for types **double** and **long** double, with **DBL** and **LDBL** substituted for **FLT** in the name. (The table assumes the system represents floating-point numbers in terms of powers of 2.)

Table 4.2 Some symbolic constants from `limits.h`.

Symbolic Constant	Represents
FLT_MANT_DIG	Number of bits in the mantissa of a `float`
FLT_DIG	Minimum number of significant decimal digits for a `float`
FLT_MIN_10_EXP	Minimum base-10 negative exponent for a `float` with full set of significant figures
FLT_MAX_10_EXP	Maximum base-10 positive exponent for a `float`
FLT_MIN	Minimum value for a positive `float`
FLT_MIN	Maximum value for a positive `float`
FLT_EPSILON	Difference between `1.00` and the least float value greater than `1.00`

The C preprocessor is a useful, helpful tool, so take advantage of it when you can. We'll show you more applications as you move along through this book.

Exploring and Exploiting `printf()` and `scanf()`

The functions `printf()` and `scanf()` enable you to communicate with a program. They are called *input/output functions*, or *I/O functions* for short. They are not the only I/O functions you can use with C, but they are the most versatile. Historically, these functions, like all other functions in the C library, were *not* part of the definition of C. C originally left the implementation of I/O up to the compiler writers; this made it possible to better match I/O to specific machines. In the interests of compatibility, various implementations all came with versions of `scanf()` and `printf()`. However, there were occasional discrepancies between implementations. The ANSI C standard describes standard versions of these functions, and we'll follow that standard. The discrepancies should disappear as the standard is implemented.

Although `printf()` is an output function and `scanf()` is an input function, both work much the same, each using a control string and a list of arguments. We will show you how these work, first with `printf()` and then with `scanf()`.

The `printf()` Function

The instructions you give `printf()` when you ask it to print a variable depend on the variable type. For instance, we have used the `%d` notation when printing an integer and the `%c` notation when printing a character. These notations are called *conversion specifications* because they specify how the data is to be converted into displayable form. We'll list the conversion specifications that the ANSI C standard provides for `printf()`, and then show how to use the more common ones. Table 4.3 presents the conversion specifiers and the type of output they cause to be printed.

Table 4.3   Conversion specifiers and the resulting printed output.

Conversion Specification	Output
%c	Single character
%d	Signed decimal integer
%e	Floating-point number, e-notation
%E	Floating-point number, E-notation
%f	Floating-point number, decimal notation
%g	Use %f or %e, depending on value. The %e style is used if the exponent is less than -4 or greater than or equal to the precision.
%G	Use %f or %E, depending on value. The %E style is used if the exponent is less than -4 or greater than or equal to the precision.
%i	Signed decimal integer
%o	Unsigned octal integer
%p	A pointer
%s	Character string
%u	Unsigned decimal integer
%x	Unsigned hexadecimal integer, using hex digits 0f
%X	Unsigned hexadecimal integer, using hex digits 0F
%%	Print a percent sign

Note

The conversion specifiers %E, %G, %i, %p, and %X did not appear in the first edition of Kernighan and Ritchie, and they are not yet commonly found in all non-ANSI implementations.

Using `printf()`

Listing 4.6 contains a program that uses some of the conversion-specification examples I discuss.

Listing 4.6   The `printout.c` program.

```c
/* printout.c -- uses conversion specifiers */
#include <stdio.h>
#define PI 3.141593
int main(void)
{
   int number = 5;
   float ouzo = 13.5;
   int cost = 3100;

   printf("The %d women drank %f glasses of ouzo.\n", number,
          ouzo);
   printf("The value of pi is %f.\n", PI);
   printf("Farewell! thou art too dear for my possessing,\n");
   printf("%c%d\n", '$', 2 * cost);
   return 0;
}
```

The output, of course, is this:

```
The 5 women drank 13.500000 glasses of ouzo.
The value of pi is 3.141593.
Farewell! thou art too dear for my possessing,
$6200
```

This is the format for using `printf()`:

```
printf(control-string, item1, item2,...);
```

`Item1`, `item2`, and so on, are the items to be printed. They can be variables or constants, or even expressions that are evaluated before the value is printed. `control-string` is a character string describing how the items are to be printed. As mentioned in Chapter 3, "Data and C," the control string should contain a conversion specifier for each item to be printed. For example, consider this statement:

```
printf("The %d women drank %f glasses of ouzo.\n", number, ouzo);
```

The control string is the phrase in double quotes. It contains two conversion specifiers corresponding to `number` and `ouzo`—the two items to be displayed. Figure 4.6 shows another example of a `printf()` statement.

Figure 4.6 Arguments for `printf()`.

Here is another line from the example:

```
printf("The value of pi is %f.\n", PI);
```

This time, the list of items has just one member—the symbolic constant PI.

As you can see in Figure 4.7, a control string contains two distinct forms of information:

- Characters that are actually printed.

- Conversion specifications.

Don't forget to use one conversion specification for each item in the list following a control string. Woe unto you should you forget this basic requirement! Don't do this:

```
printf("The score was Squids %d, Slugs %d.\n", score1);
```

Here, there is no value for the second %d. The result of this faux pas depends on your system, but at best you will get nonsense.

literal characters   literal characters

conversion specifications

Figure 4.7 Anatomy of a control string.

If you want to print only a phrase, you don't need any conversion specifications. If you just want to print data, you can dispense with the running commentary. Each of the following statements from Listing 4.6 is quite acceptable:

```
printf("Farewell! thou art too dear for my possessing,\n");
printf("%c%d\n", '$', 2 * cost);
```

In the second statement, note that the first item on the print list was a character constant rather than a variable and that the second item is a multiplication. This illustrates that printf() uses values, be they variables, constants, or expressions.

Because the printf() function uses the % symbol to identify the conversion specifications, there is a slight problem if you want to print the % sign itself. If you simply use a lone % sign, the compiler thinks you have bungled a conversion specification. The way out is simple. Just use two % symbols.

```
pc = 2*6;
printf("Only %d%% of Sally's gribbles were edible.\n", pc);
```

The following output would result:

```
Only 12% of Sally's gribbles were edible.
```

Conversion Specification Modifiers for printf()

You can modify a basic conversion specification by inserting modifiers between the % and the defining conversion character. Tables 4.4 and 4.5 list the characters you can place there legally. If you use more than one modifier, they should be in the same order as they appear in Table 4.4. Not all combinations are possible. The tables reflect the ANSI C standard; your implementation may not yet support all the options shown here. The C9X committee proposes adding an ll modifier to indicate long long values and an hh modifier to indicate that an integer value is to be displayed as signed char or unsigned char, depending on whether the original value is signed or unsigned.

Table 4.4   The printf() modifiers.

Modifier	Meaning
flag	The five flags (-, +, space, #, and 0) are described in Table 4.5. Zero or more flags may be present. Example: "%-10d"
digit(s)	The minimum field width. A wider field will be used if the printed number or string won't fit in the field. Example: "%4d"
.digit(s)	Precision. For %e, %E, and %f conversions, the number of digits to be printed to the right of the decimal. For %g and %G conversions, the maximum number of significant digits. For %s conversions, the maximum number of characters to be printed. For integer conversions, the minimum number of digits to appear; leading zeros are used if necessary to meet this minimum. Using only . implies a following zero, so %.f is the same as %.0f. Example: "%5.2f" prints a float in a field five characters wide with two digits after the decimal point.
h	Used with an integer conversion to indicate a short int or unsigned short int value. Examples: "%hu", "%hx", and "%6.4hd"
l	Used with an integer conversion to indicate a long int or unsigned long int. Examples: "%ld" and "%8lu"
L	Used with a floating-point conversion to indicate a long double value. Examples: "%Lf" and "%10.4Le"

Conversion of float Arguments

There are conversion specifiers to print floating types `double` and `long double`. However, there is no specifier for `float`. The reason is that, under K&R C, `float` values were automatically converted to type `double` before being used in an expression or as an argument. ANSI C, in general, does not automatically convert `float` to `double`. To protect the enormous number of existing programs that assume `float` arguments are converted to `double`, however, all `float` arguments to `printf()`—as well as to any other C function not using an explicit prototype—are still automatically converted to `double`. Therefore, under either K&R C or ANSI C, no special conversion specifier is needed for displaying type `float`.

Table 4.5   The `printf()` flags.

Flag	Meaning
-	The item is left-justified; that is, it is printed beginning at the left of the field. Example: `"%-20s"`
+	Signed values are displayed with a plus sign, if positive, and with a minus sign, if negative. Example: `"%+6.2f"`
space	Signed values are displayed with a leading space (but no sign) if positive and with a minus sign if negative. A + flag overrides a space. Example: `"% 6.2f"`
flagprintf() functions#	Use an alternative form for the conversion specification. Produces an initial `0` for the `%o` form and an initial `0x` or `0X` for the `%x` and `%X` forms. For all floating-point forms, # guarantees that a decimal-point character is printed, even if no digits follow. For `%g` and `%G` forms, it prevents trailing zeros from being removed. Examples: `"%#o"`, `"%#8.0f"`, and `"%+#10.3E"`
0	For numeric forms, pad the field width with leading zeros instead of with spaces. This flag is ignored if a - flag is present or if, for an integer form, a precision is specified. Examples: `"%010d"` and `"%08.3f"`

Examples

Let's put these modifiers to work, beginning with looking at the effect of the field width modifier on printing an integer. Consider the program in Listing 4.7.

Listing 4.7   The width.c program.

```
/* width.c -- field widths */
#include <stdio.h>
#define PAGES 732
int main(void)
{
  printf("*%d*\n", PAGES);
  printf("*%2d*\n", PAGES);
  printf("*%10d*\n", PAGES);
  printf("*%-10d*\n", PAGES);
  return 0;
}
```

Listing 4.7 prints the same quantity four times—but using four different conversion specifications. I used a slash (/) to show you where each field begins and ends. The output looks like this:

```
*732*
*732*
*       732*
*732       *
```

The first conversion specification is %d with no modifiers. It produces a field with the same width as the integer being printed. This is the default option; that is, what's printed if you don't give further instructions. The second conversion specification is %2d. This should produce a field width of 2, but because the integer is three digits long, the field is expanded automatically to fit the number. The next conversion specification is %10d. This produces a field 10 spaces wide, and, indeed, there are seven blanks and three digits between the asterisks, with the number tucked into the right end of the field. The final specification is %-10d. It also produces a field 10 spaces wide, and the - puts the number at the left end, just as advertised. After you get used to it, this system is easy to use and gives you nice control over the appearance of your output. Try altering the value for **PAGES** to see how different numbers of digits are printed.

Now look at some floating-point formats. Enter, compile, and run the program in Listing 4.8.

Listing 4.8   The floats.c program.

```
/* floats.c -- some floating-point combinations */
#include <stdio.h>

int main(void)
{
  const double RENT = 2345.67;  /* const-style constant */
  printf("*%f*\n", RENT);
```

```
    printf("*%e*\n", RENT);
    printf("*%4.2f*\n", RENT);
    printf("*%3.1f*\n", RENT);
    printf("*%10.3f*\n", RENT);
    printf("*%10.3e*\n", RENT);
    printf("*%+4.2f*\n", RENT);
    printf("*%010.2f*\n", RENT);
    return 0;
}
```

This time, the program uses the keyword **const** to create a symbolic constant. Here is
the output:

```
*2345.670000*
*2.345670e+003*
*2345.67*
*2345.7*
*   2345.670*
*2.346e+003*
*+2345.67*
*0002345.67*
```

Again, begin with the default version, %f. In this case, there are two defaults: the field
width and the number of digits to the right of the decimal. The second default is six digits, and the field width is whatever it takes to hold the number.

Next is the default for %e. It prints one digit to the left of the decimal point and six places
to the right. You seem to be getting a lot of digits! The cure is to specify the number of decimal places to the right of the decimal, and the next four examples in this segment do that.
Notice how the fourth and the sixth examples cause the output to be rounded off.

Finally, the + flag causes the result to be printed with its algebraic sign, which is a plus
sign in this case, and the 0 flag produces leading zeros to pad the result to the full field width.
Note that in the specifier %010 the first 0 is a flag, and the remaining digits (10) specify the
field width.

You can modify the **RENT** value to see how variously sized values are printed. Listing
4.9 demonstrates a few more combinations.

Listing 4.9   The flags.c program.

```
/* flags.c -- illustrates some formatting flags */
#include <stdio.h>
int main(void)
{
  printf("%x %X %#x\n", 31, 31, 31);
  printf("**%d**% d**% d**\n", 42, 42, -42);
  printf("**%5d**%5.3d**%05d**%05.3d**\n", 6, 6, 6, 6);
  return 0;
}
```

On a system that conforms to the ANSI C standard, the output looks like this:

```
1f 1F 0x1f
**42** 42**-42**
**    6**  006**00006**  006**
```

First, 1f is the hex equivalent of 31. The x specifier yields a 1f, and the X specifier yields 1F. Using the # flag provides an initial 0x.

The second line illustrates how using a space in the specifier produces a leading space for positive values, but not for negative values. This can produce a pleasing output because positive and negative values with the same number of significant digits are printed with the same field widths.

The third line illustrates how using a precision specifier (%5.3d) with an integer form produces enough leading zeros to pad the number to the minimum value of digits (three, in this case). Using the 0 flag, however, pads the number with enough leading zeros to fill the whole field width. Finally, if you provide both the 0 flag and the precision specifier, the 0 flag is ignored.

Now let's examine some of the string options. Consider the example in Listing 4.10.

Listing 4.10   The strings.c program.

```
/* strings.c -- string formatting */
#include <stdio.h>
#define BLURB "Outstanding acting!"
int main(void)
{
    printf("/%2s/\n", BLURB);
    printf("/%22s/\n", BLURB);
    printf("/%22.5s/\n", BLURB);
    printf("/%-22.5s/\n", BLURB);
    return 0;
}
```

Here is the output:

```
/Outstanding acting!/
/   Outstanding acting!/
/                 Outst/
/Outst                 /
```

Notice how the field is expanded to contain all the specified characters. Also notice how the precision specification limits the number of characters printed. The .5 in the format specifier tells printf() to print just five characters. Again, the - modifier left-justifies the text.

Applying Your Knowledge

Okay, you've seen some examples. Now how would you set up a statement to print something having the following form?

```
The NAME family just may be $XXX.XX dollars richer!
```

Here, NAME and XXX.XX represent values that will be supplied by variables in the program, say, name[40] and cash.

Here is one solution:

```
printf("The %s family just may be $%.2f richer!\n",name,cash);
```

The Meaning of Conversion

Let's take a closer look at what a conversion specification converts. It converts a value stored in the computer in some binary format to a series of characters (a string) to be displayed. For example, the number 76 may be stored internally as binary 01001100. The %d conversion specifier converts this to the characters 7 and 6, displaying 76. The %x conversion converts the same value (01001100) to the hexadecimal representation 4c. The %c converts the same value to the character representation L.

The term *conversion* is probably somewhat misleading because it wrongly suggests that the original value is replaced with a converted value. Conversion specifications are really translation specifications; %d means "translate the given value to a decimal integer text representation and print the representation."

Mismatched Conversions

Naturally, you should match the conversion specification to the type of value being printed. Often, you have choices. For instance, if you want to print a type int value, you can use %d or %x or %o. All these specifiers assume that you are printing a type int value; they merely provide different representations of the value. Similarly, you can use %f, %e, or %g to represent a type double value.

What if you mismatch the conversion specification to the type? You've seen in the preceding chapter that mismatches can cause problems. This is a very important point to keep in mind, so Listing 4.11 shows some more examples of mismatches within the integer family.

Listing 4.11   The intconv.c program.

```
/* intconv.c -- some mismatched integer conversions */
#include <stdio.h>
#define PAGES 336
#define WORDS 65616
int main(void)
{
    short num = PAGES;
    short mnum = -PAGES;

    printf("%hd %hu %hd %hu\n", num, num, mnum, mnum);
    printf("%d %c\n", num, num);
    printf("%d %hd\n", WORDS, WORDS);
    return 0;
}
```

Our system produces the following results:

```
336 336 -336 65200
336 P
65616 80
```

Looking at the first line, you can see that both %hd and %hu produce **336** as output for the variable num; no problem there. The %u (unsigned) version of mnum came out as **65200**, however, not as the 336 you might have expected. This results from the way that signed short int values are represented on your reference system. First, they are 2 bytes in size. Second, the system uses a method called the *two's complement* to represent signed integers. In this method, the numbers 0 to 32767 represent themselves, and the numbers 32768 to 65535 represent negative numbers, with 65535 being –1, 65534 being –2, and so forth. Therefore, **-336** is represented by **65536** - **336**, or **65200**. So 65200 represents –336 when interpreted as a signed int and represents 65200 when interpreted as an unsigned int. Be wary! One number can be interpreted as two different values. Not all systems use this method to represent negative integers. Nonetheless, there is a moral: Don't expect a %u conversion to simply strip the sign from a number.

The second line shows what happens if you try to convert a value greater than 255 to a character. On this system, a short int is 2 bytes and a char is 1 byte. When printf() prints 336 using %c, it looks at only 1 byte out of the 2 used to hold 336. This truncation (see Figure 4.8) amounts to dividing the integer by 256 and keeping just the remainder. In this case, the remainder is 80, which is the ASCII value for the character **P**. More technically, you can say that the number is interpreted *modulo 256*, which means using the remainder when the number is divided by 256.

Figure 4.8 Reading 336 as a character.

Finally, we tried printing an integer (65616) larger than the maximum short int (32767) allowed on our system. Again, the computer does its modulo thing. The number 65616, because of its size, is stored as a 4-byte int value on our system. When we print it using the %hd specification, printf() uses only the last 2 bytes. This corresponds to using the remainder after dividing by 65536. In this case, the remainder is 80. A remainder between 32767 and 65536 would be printed as a negative number because of the way negative numbers are stored. Systems with different integer sizes would have the same general behavior, but with different numerical values.

When you start mixing integer and floating types, the results are more bizarre. Consider, for example, Listing 4.12.

Listing 4.12   The floatcnv.c program.

```
/* floatcnv.c -- mismatched floating-point conversions */
#include <stdio.h>
int main(void)
{
```

```
    float n1 = 3.0;
    double n2 = 3.0;
    long n3 = 2000000000;
    long n4 = 1234567890;

    printf("%.1e %.1e %.1e %.1e\n", n1, n2, n3, n4);
    printf("%ld %ld\n", n3, n4);
    printf("%ld %ld %ld %ld\n", n1, n2, n3, n4);
    return 0;
}
```

On this system, Listing 4.12 produces the following output:

```
3.0e+000 3.0e+000 3.1e+046 3.1e+046
2000000000 1234567890
0 1074266112 0 1074266112
```

The first line of output shows that using a `%e` specifier does not convert an integer to a floating-point number. Consider, for example, what happens when you try to print `n3` (type `long`) using the `%e` specifier. First, the `%e` specifier causes `printf()` to expect a type `double` value, which is an 8-byte value on this system. When `printf()` looks at `n3`, which is a 4-byte value on this system, it also looks at the adjacent 4 bytes. Therefore, it looks at an 8-byte unit in which the actual `n3` is embedded. Second, it interprets the bits in this unit as a floating-point number. Some bits, for example, would be interpreted as an exponent. So even if `n3` had the correct number of bits, they would be interpreted differently under `%e` than under `%ld`. The net result is nonsense.

The first line also illustrates what we mentioned earlier: that `float` is converted to `double` when used as arguments to `printf()`. On this system, `float` is 4 bytes, but `n1` was expanded to 8 bytes so that `printf()` would display it correctly.

The second line of output shows that `printf()` can print `n3` and `n4` correctly if the correct specifier is used.

The third line of output shows that even the correct specifier can produce phony results if the `printf()` statement has mismatches elsewhere. As you might expect, trying to print a floating-point value with a `%ld` specifier fails, but here, trying to print a type `long` using `%ld` fails! The problem lies in how C passes information to a function. The exact details of this failure are implementation dependent, but the next box discusses a representative system.

Passing Arguments

The mechanics of argument passing depend on the implementation. This is how argument passing works on our system. The function call looks like this:

```
printf("%ld %ld %ld %ld\n", n1, n2, n3, n4);
```

This call tells the computer to hand over the values of the variables n1, n2, n3, and n4 to the computer. It does so by placing them in an area of memory called the *stack*. When the computer puts these values on the stack, it is guided by the types of the variables, not by the conversion specifiers, so for

continued on next page

continued from previous page

n1, it places 8 bytes on the stack (`float` is converted to `double`). Similarly, it places 8 more bytes for n2, followed by 4 bytes each for n3 and n4. Then control shifts to the `printf()` function. This function reads the values off the stack, but when it does so, it reads them according to the conversion specifiers. The `%ld` specifier indicates that `printf()` should read 4 bytes, so `printf()` reads the first 4 bytes in the stack as its first value. This is just the first half of n1, and it is interpreted as a `long` integer. The next `%ld` specifier reads 4 more bytes; this is just the second half of n1 and is interpreted as a second `long` integer (see Figure 4.9). Similarly, the third and fourth instances of `%ld` cause the first and second halves of n2 to be read and to be interpreted as two more `long` integers, so although we have the correct specifiers for n3 and n4, `printf()` is reading the wrong bytes.

```
float n1;   /* passed as type double */
double n2;
long n3, n4;
...
printf("%ld %ld %ld %ld\n", n1, n2, n3, n4);
```

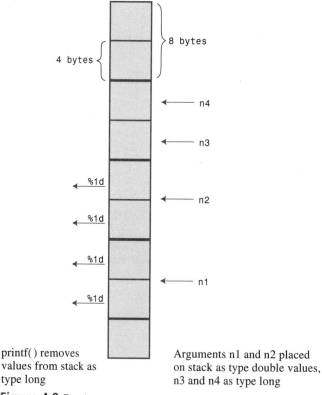

printf( ) removes values from stack as type long

Arguments n1 and n2 placed on stack as type double values, n3 and n4 as type long

Figure 4.9 Passing arguments.

The Return Value of `printf()`

As mentioned in Chapter 2, a C function generally has a return value. This is a value that the function computes and returns to the calling program. For example, the C library contains a `sqrt()` function that takes a number as an argument and returns its square root. The return value can be assigned to a variable, can be used in a computation, can be passed as an argument—in short, it can be used like any other value. The `printf()` function also has a return value: Under ANSI C, it returns the number of characters it printed. If there is an output error, `printf()` returns a negative value. (Some pre-ANSI versions of `printf()` have different return values.)

The return value for `printf()` is incidental to its main purpose of printing output, and it usually isn't used. One reason you might use the return value is to check for output errors. This is more commonly done when writing to a file rather than to a screen. If a full floppy disk prevented writing from taking place, you could then have the program take some appropriate action, such as beeping the terminal for 30 seconds. However, you have to know about the `if` statement before doing that sort of thing. The simple example in Listing 4.13 shows how you can determine the return value.

Listing 4.13 The `prntval.c` program.

```
/* prntval.c -- finding printf()'s return value */
#include <stdio.h>
int main(void)
{
  int n = 212;
  int rv;

  rv = printf("%d F is water's boiling point.\n", n);
  printf("The printf() function printed %d characters.\n",
          rv);
  return 0;
}
```

The output is as follows:

```
212 F is water's boiling point.
The printf() function printed 32 characters.
```

First, the program used the form `rv = printf(...);` to assign the return value to `rv`. This statement thus performs two tasks: printing information and assigning a value to a variable. Second, note that the count includes all the printed characters, including the spaces and the unseen newline character.

Printing Long Strings

Occasionally, `printf()` statements are too long to put on one line. Because C ignores whitespace (spaces, tabs, newlines) except when used to separate elements, you can spread a statement over several lines, as long as you put your line breaks between elements. For instance, Listing 4.13 used two lines for a statement.

```
printf("The printf() function printed %d characters.\n",
        rv);
```

The line is broken between the comma element and `rv`. To show a reader that the line was being continued, the example indents the `rv`. C ignores the extra spaces.

However, you cannot break a quoted string in the middle. Suppose you try something like this:

```
printf("The printf() function printed %d
        characters.\n", rv);
```

C will complain that you have an illegal character in a string constant. You can use `\n` in a string to symbolize the newline character, but you can't have the actual newline character generated by the Enter (or Return) key in a string.

If you do have to split a string, you have three choices, as shown in Listing 4.14.

Listing 4.14   The `longstrg.c` program.

```
/* longstrg.c -- printing long strings */
#include <stdio.h>
int main(void)
{
    printf("Here's one way to print a ");
    printf("long string.\n");
    printf("Here's another way to print a \
long string.\n");
    printf("Here's the newest way to print a "
            "long string.\n");        /* ANSI C */
    return 0;
}
```

Here is the output:

```
Here's one way to print a long string.
Here's another way to print a long string.
Here's the newest way to print a long string.
```

Method 1 is to use more than one `printf()` statement. Because the first string printed doesn't end with a `\n` character, the second string continues where the first ends.

Method 2 is to terminate the end of the first line with a backslash-return combination. This causes the text on the screen to start a new line, but without including a newline character in the string. The effect is to continue the string over to the next line. However, the next line has to start at the far left, as shown. If you indent that line, say, five spaces, then those five spaces become part of the string.

Method 3, new with ANSI C, is string concatenation. If you follow one quoted string constant with another, separated only by whitespace, C treats the combination as a single string, so the following three forms are equivalent:

```
printf("Hello, young lovers, wherever you are.");
printf("Hello, young "    "lovers" ", wherever you are.");
printf("Hello, young lovers"
        ", wherever you are.");
```

With all these methods, you should include any required spaces in the strings: `"Jim"` `"Smith"` becomes `"JimSmith"`, but the combination `"Jim "` `"Smith"` is `"Jim Smith"`.

Using `scanf()`

Now let's go from output to input and examine the `scanf()` function. The C library contains several input functions, and `scanf()` is the most general of them, for it can read a variety of formats. Of course, input from the keyboard is text because the keys generate text characters: letters, digits, and punctuation. When you want to enter, say, the integer 2002, you type the characters **2 0 0** and **2**. If you want to store that as a numerical value rather than a string, your program has to convert the string character-by-character to a numerical value, and that is what `scanf()` does! It converts string input into various forms: integers, floating-point numbers, characters, and C strings. It is the inverse of `printf()`, which converts integers, floating-point numbers, characters, and C strings to text that is to be displayed on the screen.

Like `printf()`, `scanf()` uses a control string followed by a list of arguments. The control string indicates into which formats the input is to be converted. The chief difference is in the argument list. The `printf()` function uses variable names, constants, and expressions. The `scanf()` function uses pointers to variables. Fortunately, you don't have to know anything about pointers to use the function. Just remember these two simple rules:

- If you use `scanf()` to read a value for one of the basic variable types we've discussed, precede the variable name with an **&**.

- If you use `scanf()` to read a string into a character array, don't use an **&**.

Listing 14.15 presents a short program illustrating these rules.

Listing 4.15   The `input.c` program.

```
/* input.c -- when to use & */
#include <stdio.h>
int main(void)
{
    int age;              /* variable */
    float assets;         /* variable */
    char pet[30];         /* string   */

    printf("Enter your age, assets, and favorite pet.\n");
    scanf("%d %f", &age, &assets); /* use the & here     */
    scanf("%s", pet);              /* no & for char array */
    printf("%d $%.0f %s\n", age, assets, pet);
    return 0;
}
```

Here is a sample exchange:

```
Enter your age, assets, and favorite pet.
12
144.15 hedgehog
12 $144 hedgehog
```

The `scanf()` function uses whitespace (newlines, tabs, and spaces) to decide how to divide the input into separate fields. It matches up consecutive conversion specifications to consecutive fields, skipping over the whitespace in between. Note how the input is spread over two lines. You could just as well have used one or five lines, as long as you had at least one newline, space, or tab between each entry. The only exception to this is the `%c` specification, which reads the very next character, even if that character is whitespace. We'll return to this topic in a moment.

The `scanf()` function uses pretty much the same set of conversion-specification characters as `printf()` does. The main difference is that `printf()` uses `%f`, `%e`, `%E`, `%g` and `%G` for both type `float` and type `double`, whereas `scanf()` uses them just for type `float`, requiring the `l` modifier for `double`. Table 4.6 lists the main conversion specifiers as described in ANSI C.

Table 4.6   ANSI C conversion specifiers for `scanf()`.

Conversion Specifier	Meaning
%c	Interpret input as a character.
%d	Interpret input as a signed decimal integer.
%e, %f, %g	Interpret input as a floating-point number.
%E, %G	Interpret input as a floating-point number.
%i	Interpret input as a signed decimal integer.
%o	Interpret input as a signed octal integer.
%p	Interpret input as a pointer (an address).
%s	Interpret input as a string; input begins with the first non-whitespace character and includes everything up to the next whitespace character.
%u	Interpret input as an unsigned decimal integer.
%x, %X	Interpret input as a signed hexadecimal integer.

You also can use modifiers in the conversion specifiers shown in Table 4.6. The modifiers go between the percent sign and the conversion letter. If you use more than one in a specifier, they should appear in the same order as shown in Table 4.7. The C9X committee proposes adding an `hh` modifier to indicate `signed char` or `unsigned char` and an `ll` modifier to indicate `long long` or `unsigned long long`.

Table 4.7 Conversion modifiers for `scanf()`.

Modifier	Meaning
*	Suppress assignment (see text). Example: `"%*d"`
digit(s)	Maximum field width; input stops when the maximum field width is reached or when the first whitespace character is encountered, whichever comes first. Example: `"%10s"`
h, l, or L	`"%hd"` and `"%hi"` indicate that the value will be stored in a `short int`. `"%ho"`, `"%hx"`, and `"%hu"` indicate that the value will be stored in an `unsigned short int`. `"%ld"` and `"%li"` indicate that the value will be stored in a `long`. `"%lo"`, `"%lx"`, and `"%lu"` indicate that the value will be stored in `unsigned long`. `"%le"`, `"%lf"`, and `"%lg"` indicate that the value will be stored in type `double`. Using `L` instead of `l` with `e`, `f`, and `g` indicates that the value will be stored in type `long double`. In the absence of these modifiers, `d`, `i`, `o`, and `x` indicate type `int`, and `e`, `f`, and `g` indicate type `float`.

As you can see, using conversion specifiers can be involved, and there are features that I have omitted. These omitted features primarily facilitate reading selected data from highly formatted sources, such as punched cards or other data records. Because you will be using `scanf()` primarily as a convenient means for feeding data to a program interactively, I won't discuss the more esoteric features.

The `scanf()` View of Input

Let's look in more detail at how `scanf()` reads input. Suppose you use a `%d` specifier to read an integer. `Scanf()` begins reading input a character at a time. It skips over whitespace characters (spaces, tabs, and newlines) until it finds a non-whitespace character. Because it is attempting to read an integer, `scanf()` expects to find a digit character or, perhaps, a sign (+ or -). If it finds a digit or a sign, it saves the sign and then reads the next character. If that is a digit, it saves the digit and reads the next character. `Scanf()` continues reading and saving characters until it encounters a nondigit. It then concludes that it has reached the end of the integer. `Scanf()` places the nondigit back in the input. This means that the next time the program goes to read input, it starts at the previously rejected, nondigit character. Finally, `scanf()` computes the numerical value corresponding to the digits it read and places that value in the specified variable.

If you use a field width, `scanf()` halts at the field end or at the first whitespace, whichever comes first.

What if the first non-whitespace character is, say, an A instead of a digit? Then `scanf()` stops right there and places the A (or whatever) back in the input. No value is assigned to the specified variable, and the next time the program reads input, it starts at the A again. If your program has only `%d` specifiers, `scanf()` will never get past that A. Also, if you use a `scanf()` statement with several specifiers, ANSI C requires the function to stop reading input at the first failure.

Reading input using the other numeric specifiers works much the same as the %d case. The main difference is that scanf() may recognize more characters as being part of the number. For instance, the %x specifier requires that scanf() recognize the hexadecimal digits a–f and A–F. Floating-point specifiers require scanf() to recognize decimal points and E-notation.

If you use a %s specifier, any character other than whitespace is acceptable, so scanf() skips whitespace to the first non-whitespace character and then saves up non-whitespace characters until hitting whitespace again. This means that %s results in scanf() reading a single word, that is, a string with no whitespace in it. If you use a field width, scanf() stops at the end of the field or at the first whitespace. You can't use the field width to make scanf() read more than one word for one %s specifier. A final point: When scanf() places the string in the designated array, it adds the terminating '\0' to make the array contents a C string.

If you use a %c specifier, all input characters are fair game. If the next input character is a space or a newline, then a space or a newline is assigned to the indicated variable; white-space is not skipped.

Actually, scanf() is not the most commonly used input function in C. It is featured here because of its versatility (it can read all the different data types), but C has several other input functions, such as getchar() and gets() that are better suited for specific tasks, such as reading single characters or reading strings containing spaces. We will cover some of these functions in Chapters 7, "C Control Statements: Branching and Jumps," 11, "Character Strings and String Functions," and 12, "File Input/Output." In the meantime, if you need an integer or decimal fraction or a character or a string, you can use scanf().

Regular Characters in the Format String

The scanf() function does enable you to place ordinary characters in the format string. Ordinary characters other than the space character must be matched exactly by the input string. For instance, suppose you accidentally place a comma between two specifiers:

```
scanf("%d,%d", &n, &m);
```

The scanf() function interprets this to mean that you will type a number, then type a comma, and then type a second number. That is, you would have to enter two integers this way:

```
88,121
```

Because the comma comes immediately after the %d in the format string, you would have to type it immediately after the 88. However, because scanf() skips over whitespace pre-ceding an integer, you could type a space or newline after the comma when entering the input. That is,

```
88, 121
```

and

```
88,
121
```

also would be accepted.

A space in the format string means to skip over any whitespace before the next input item. For instance, the statement

```
scanf("%d ,%d", &n, &m);
```

would accept any of the following input lines:

```
88,121
88  ,121
88 ,  121
```

Note that the concept of "any whitespace" includes the special cases of no whitespace.

Except for %c, the specifiers automatically skip over whitespace preceding an input value, so scanf("%d%d", &n, &m) behaves the same as scanf("%d %d", &n, &m). For %c, adding a space character to the format string does make a difference. For example, if %c is preceded by a space in the format string, scanf() does skip to the first non-whitespace character. That is, the command scanf("%c", &ch) reads the first character encountered in input, and scanf(" %c", &ch) reads the first non-whitespace character encountered.

The scanf() Return Value

The scanf() function returns the number of items that it successfully reads. If it reads no items, which happens if you type a non-numeric string when it expects a number, scanf() returns the value 0. It returns EOF when it detects the condition known as "end of file." (EOF is a special value defined in the stdio.h file. Typically, a #define directive gives EOF the value –1.) We'll discuss end of file in Chapter 6, "C Control Statements: Looping," and make use of scanf()'s return value later in the book. After you learn about if statements and while statements, you can use the scanf() return value to detect and handle mismatched input.

The * Modifier with printf() and scanf()

Both printf() and scanf()can use the * modifier to modify the meaning of a specifier, but they do so in dissimilar fashions. First, let's see what the * modifier can do for printf().

Suppose that you don't want to commit yourself to a field width in advance, but that you want the program to specify it. You can do this by using * instead of a number for the field width, but you also have to use an argument to tell what the field width should be. That is, if you have the conversion specifier %*d, the argument list should include a value for * *and* a value for d. The technique also can be used with floating-point values to specify the precision as well as the field width. Listing 4.16 is a short example showing how this works.

Listing 4.16   The `varwid.c` program.

```
/* varwid.c -- uses variable-width output field */
#include <stdio.h>
int main(void)
{
  unsigned width, precision;
  int number = 256;
  double weight = 242.5;

  printf("What field width?\n");
  scanf("%d", &width);
  printf("The number is :%*d:\n", width, number);
  printf("Now enter a width and a precision:\n");
  scanf("%d %d", &width, &precision);
  printf("Weight = %*.*f\n", width, precision, weight);
  return 0;
}
```

The variable `width` provides the `field width`, and `number` is the number to be print-ed. Because the `*` precedes the `d` in the specifier, `width` comes before `number` in `printf()`'s argument list. Similarly, `width` and `precision` provide the formatting information for print-ing `weight`. Here is a sample run:

```
What field width?
6
The number is :    256:
Now enter a width and a precision:
8 3
Weight =  242.500
```

Here the reply to the first question was **6**, so **6** was the field width used. Similarly, the second reply produced a width of **8** with **3** digits to the right of the decimal. More gener-ally, a program could decide on values for these variables after looking at the value of `weight`.

The `*` serves quite a different purpose for `scanf()`. When placed between the `%` and the specifier letter, it causes that function to skip over corresponding input. Listing 4.17 pro-vides an example.

Listing 4.17   The `skip2.c` program.

```
/* skip2.c -- skips over first two integers of input */
#include <stdio.h>
int main(void)
{
  int n;

  printf("Please enter three integers:\n");
  scanf("%*d %*d %d", &n);
  printf("The last integer was %d\n", n);
  return 0;
}
```

The scanf() instruction in Listing 4.17 says, "Skip two integers and copy the third into n." Here is a sample run:

```
Please enter three integers
1976 1992 1996
The last integer was 1996
```

This skipping facility is useful if, for example, a program needs to read a particular column of a file that has data arranged in uniform columns.

Usage Tips

Specifying fixed field widths is useful when you want to print columns of data. Because the default field width is just the width of the number, the repeated use of, say,

```
printf("%d %d %d\n", val1, val2, val3);
```

would produce ragged columns if the numbers in a column had different sizes. For example, the output could look like this:

```
12 234 1222
4 5 23
22334 2322 10001
```

(This assumes that the value of the variables has been changed between print statements.)

The output can be cleaned up by using a sufficiently large fixed field width. For example, using

```
printf("%9d %9d %9d\n", val1, val2, val3);
```

would yield

```
   12       234      1222
    4         5        23
22334      2322     10001
```

Leaving a blank between one conversion specification and the next ensures that one number never runs into the next, even if it overflows its own field. This is so because the regular characters in the control string, including spaces, are printed.

On the other hand, if a number is to be embedded in a phrase, it is often convenient to specify a field as small as or smaller than the expected number width. This makes the number fit in without unnecessary blanks. For example,

```
printf("Count Beppo ran %.2f miles in 3 hours.\n", distance);
```

might produce

```
Count Beppo ran 10.22 miles in 3 hours.
```

Changing the conversion specification to %10.2f would give you this:

```
Count Beppo ran      10.22 miles in 3 hours.
```

Chapter Summary

A string is a series of characters treated as a unit. In C, strings are represented by a series of characters terminated by the null character, which is the character whose ASCII code is 0. Strings can be stored in character arrays. An array is a series of items, or elements, all of the same type. To declare an array called `name` and having 30 elements of type `char`, do this:

```
char name[30];
```

Be sure to allot a number of elements sufficient to hold the entire string, including the null character.

String constants are represented by enclosing the string in double quotes: `"This is an example of a string"`.

The `strlen()` function can be used to find the length of a string (not counting the terminating null character). The `scanf()` function, when used with the `%s` specifier, can be used to read in single-word strings.

The C preprocessor searches a source code program for preprocessor directives, which begin with the # symbol, and acts upon them before the program is compiled. The `#include` directive causes the processor to add the contents of another file to your file at the location of the directive. The `#define` directive lets you establish manifest constants, that is, symbolic representations for constants. The `limits.h` and `float.h` header files use `#define` to define a set of constants representing various properties of integer and floating-point types. You also can use the `const` modify to create symbolic constants.

The `printf()` and `scanf()` functions provide versatile support for input and output. Each uses a control string containing embedded conversion specifiers, which indicate the number and type of data items to be read or printed. Also, you can use the conversion specifiers to control the appearance of the output: field widths, decimal places, and placement within a field.

Review Questions

1. Run Listing 4.1 again, but this time give your first and last name when it asks you for your first name. What happens? Why?

2. Assuming that each of the following examples is part of a complete program, what will each one print?

   a. `printf("He sold the painting for $%2.2f.\n", 2.345e2);`

   b. `printf("%c%c%c\n", 'H', 105, '\41');`

   c. `#define Q "His Hamlet was funny without being vulgar."`
      `printf("%s\nhas %d characters.\n", Q, strlen(Q));`

   d. `printf("Is %2.2e the same as %2.2f?\n", 1201.0, 1201.0);`

3. In Question 2.c., what changes could you make so that string Q is printed out enclosed in quotes?

4. It's find the error time!

```
define B booboo
define X 10
main(int)
{
    int age;
    char name;

    printf("Please enter your first name.");
    scanf("%s", name);
    printf("All right, %c, what's your age?\n", name);
    scanf("%f", age);
    xp = age + X;
    printf("That's a %s! You must be at least %d.\n", B, xp);
    rerun 0;
}
```

5. Suppose a program starts like this:

```
#define BOOK "War and Peace"
int main(void)
{
    float cost =12.99;
    float percent = 80.0;
```

Construct a printf() statement that uses BOOK, cost, and percent to print the following:

```
This copy of "War and Peace" sells for $12.99.
That is 80% of list.
```

6. What conversion specification would you use to print each of the following?

   a. A decimal integer with a field width equal to the number of digits

   _____

   b. A hexadecimal integer in the form 8A in a field width of 4 _____

   c. A floating-point number in the form of 232.346 with a field width of 10 _____

   d. A floating-point number in the form 2.33e+002 with a field width of 12 _____

   e. A string left-justified in a field of width 30 _____

7. Which conversion specification would you use to print each of the following?

   a. An `unsigned long` integer in a field width of 15.

   b. A hexadecimal integer in the form 0x8a in a field width of 4.

   c. A floating-point number in the form 2.33E+02 that is left-justified in a field width of 12.

   d. A floating-point number in the form +232.346 in a field width of 10.

   e. The first 8 characters of a string in a field 8 characters wide.

8. What conversion specification would you use to print each of the following?

   a. A decimal integer having a minimum of 4 digits in a field width of 6 _____

   b. An octal integer in a field whose width will be given in the argument list _____

   c. A character in a field width of 2 _____

   d. A floating-point number in the form +3.13 in a field width equal to the number of characters in the number.

   e. The first 5 characters in a string left-justified in a field of width 7_____

9. For each of the following input lines, provide a `scanf()` statement to read it. Also declare any variables or arrays used in the statement.

   a. 101

   b. 22.32 and 8.34E-09

   c. Chelsea

   d. catch 22

   e. catch 22 (but skip over catch)

10. What is whitespace?

11. Suppose that you would rather use parentheses than braces in your programs. How well would the following work?

```
#define ( {
#define ) }
```

Programming Exercises

1. Write a program that asks for your first name and then your last name, and then prints the names in the format last, first.

2. Write a program that requests your first name and does the following with it:

   a. Prints it enclosed in double quotation marks.

   b. Prints it in a field 20 characters wide, with the whole field in quotes.

   c. Prints it at the left end of a field 20 characters wide, with the whole field enclosed in quotes.

   d. Prints it in a field three characters wider than the name.

3. Write a program that reads in a floating-point number and prints it first in decimal-point notation and then in exponential notation. Have the output use the following formats:

   a. The input is 21.3 or 2.1e+001.

   b. The input is +21.290 or 2.129E+001.

4. Write a program that requests your height in inches and your name, and then displays the information in the following form:

   `Dabney, you are 6.208 feet tall`

   Use type **float**, and use / for division.

5. Write a program that requests the user's first name and then the user's last name. Have it print the entered names on one line and the number of letters in each name on the following line. Align each letter count with the end of the corresponding name, as in the following:

   ```
   Melissa Honeybee
         7        8
   ```

   Next have it print the same information, but with the counts aligned with the beginning of each name.

   ```
   Melissa Honeybee
   7       8
   ```

## CHAPTER 5

OPERATORS, EXPRESSIONS, AND STATEMENTS

> **You will learn about the following in this chapter:**
>
> - Keyword
>   while
>
> - Operators
>   = - * /
>   % ++ -- (type)

This chapter introduces you to C's multitudinous operators, including those used for common arithmetic operations. You learn about operator precedence and the meanings of the terms *statement* and *expression*. Then you encounter the handy while loop. Compound statements, automatic type conversions, and type casts are next. Finally, you see how to write functions that use arguments.

Now that you've looked at ways to represent data, let's explore ways to process data. C offers a wealth of operations for that purpose. You can do arithmetic, compare values, modify variables, combine relationships logically, and more. Let's start with basic arithmetic: addition, subtraction, multiplication, and division.

Another aspect of processing data is organizing your programs so that they take the right steps in the right order. C has several language features to help you with that task. One of these features is the loop, and in this chapter you take a first look at it. A loop enables you to repeat actions and makes your programs more interesting and powerful.

Introducing Loops

Listing 5.1 shows a sample program that does a little arithmetic to calculate the length in inches of a foot that wears a size 9 (men's) shoe. This first version doesn't use loops.

Listing 5.1 The shoes1.c program.

```
/* shoes1.c -- converts a shoe size to inches */
#include <stdio.h>
#define ADJUST 7.64
#define SCALE 0.325
int main(void)
{
  double shoe, foot;

  shoe = 9.0;
  foot = SCALE * shoe + ADJUST;
  printf("Shoe size (men's)    foot length\n");
  printf("%10.1f %15.2f inches\n", shoe, foot);
  return 0;
}
```

Here is a program with multiplication and addition. It takes your shoe size (if you wear a size 9) and tells you how long your foot is in inches. "But," you say, "I could solve this problem by hand more quickly than you could type the program." That's a good point. A one-shot program that does just one shoe size is a waste of time and effort. You could make the program more useful by writing it as an interactive program, but that still barely taps the potential of a computer.

What you need is some way to have a computer do repetitive calculations for a succession of shoe sizes. After all, that's one of the main reasons for using a computer to do arithmetic. C offers several methods for doing repetitive calculations, and we will outline one here. This method, called a while loop, will enable you to make a more interesting exploration of operators. Listing 5.2 presents the improved shoe-sizing program.

Listing 5.2 The shoe2.c program.

```
/* shoe2.c -- calculates foot lengths for several sizes */
#include <stdio.h>
#define ADJUST 7.64
#define SCALE 0.325
int main(void)
{
  double shoe, foot;

  printf("Shoe size (men's)    foot length\n");
  shoe = 3.0;
  while (shoe < 18.5)              /* starting the while loop */
    {                             /* start of block          */
      foot = SCALE*shoe + ADJUST;
      printf("%10.1f %15.2f inches\n", shoe, foot);
      shoe = shoe + 1.0;
    }                             /* end of block            */
  printf("If the shoe fits, wear it.\n");
  return 0;
}
```

Here is a condensed version of **shoe2.c**'s output:

```
Shoe size (men's)     foot length
      3.0                8.62 inches
      4.0                8.94 inches
      ...                ...
     17.0               13.16 inches
     18.0               13.49 inches
If the shoe fits, wear it.
```

(Incidentally, the constants for this conversion were obtained during an incognito visit to a shoe store. The only shoe-sizer left lying around was for men's sizes. Those of you interested in women's sizes will have to make your own visit to a shoe store.)

Here is how the `while` loop works. When the program first reaches the `while` statement, it checks to see whether the condition within parentheses is true. In this case, the expression is as follows:

```
shoe < 18.5
```

Here, the < symbol means "is less than." The variable `shoe` was initialized to `3.0`, which certainly is less than `18.5`. Therefore, the condition is true and the program proceeds to the next statement, which converts the size to inches. Then it prints the results. The next statement increases `shoe` by 1.0, making it 4.0:

```
shoe = shoe + 1.0;
```

At this point, the program returns to the `while` portion to check the condition. Why at this point? Because the next line is a closing brace (`}`), and you have used a set of braces (`{ }`) to mark the extent of the `while` loop. The statements between the two braces are the ones that are repeated. The section of program between and including the braces is called a *block*. Now back to your program. The value `4` is less than `18.5`, so the whole cycle of embraced commands (the block) following the `while` is repeated. (In computerese, the program is said to "loop" through these statements.) This continues until `shoe` reaches a value of `19.0`. Now the condition

```
shoe < 18.5
```

becomes false because `19.0` is not less than `18.5`. When this happens, control passes to the first statement following the `while` loop. In this case, that is the final `printf()` statement.

You can easily modify this program to do other conversions. For example, change `SCALE` to `1.8` and `ADJUST` to `32.0`, and you have a program that converts Centigrade to Fahrenheit. Change `SCALE` to `0.6214` and `ADJUST` to `0`, and you convert kilometers to miles. If you make these changes, you should change the printed messages, too, to prevent confusion.

The `while` loop provides a convenient, flexible means of controlling a program. Now let's turn to the fundamental operators that you can use in your programs.

Fundamental Operators

C uses *operators* to represent arithmetic operations. For example, the + operator causes the two values flanking it to be added together. If the term "operator" seems odd to you, please keep in mind that those things had to be called something. "Operator" does seem to be a better choice than, say, "those things" or "arithmetical transactors." Now take a look at the operators used for basic arithmetic: =, +, -, *, and /. (C does not have an exponentiating operator. The standard C math library, however, provides a `pow()` function for that purpose. For example, `pow(3.5, 2.2)` returns 3.5 raised to the 2.2 power.)

Assignment Operator: =

In C, the equal sign does not mean "equals." Rather, it is a value-assigning operator. The statement

```
bmw = 2002;
```

assigns the value **2002** to the variable named **bmw**. That is, the item to the left of the = sign is the *name* of a variable, and the item on the right is the *value* assigned to the variable. The = symbol is called the *assignment operator*. Again, don't think of the line as saying, "**bmw** equals **2002**." Instead, read it as "assign the value **2002** to the variable **bmw**." The action goes from right to left for this operator.

Perhaps this distinction between the name of a variable and the value of a variable seems like hair-splitting, but consider the following common type of computer statement:

```
i = i + 1;
```

As mathematics, this statement makes no sense. If you add 1 to a finite number, the result isn't "equal to" the number you started with, but as a computer assignment statement, it is perfectly reasonable. It means "find the value of the variable named **i**; to that value, add **1**, and then assign this new value to the variable named **i**" (see Figure 5.1).

Figure 5.1 The statement `i = i + 1;`.

A statement such as

```
2002 = bmw;
```

makes no sense in C (and, indeed, is invalid) because **2002** is just a constant. You can't assign a value to a constant; it already *is* its value. When you sit down at the keyboard, therefore, remember that the item to the left of the = sign must be the name of a variable. Actually, the left side must refer to a storage location. The simplest way is to use the name of a variable, but, as you will see later, a "pointer" can be used to point to a location. More generally, ANSI C uses the term *modifiable lvalue* to label those entities to which you can assign values. "Modifiable lvalue" is not, perhaps, the most intuitive phrase you've encountered, so let's look at some definitions.

Some Terminology: Data Objects, Lvalues, Rvalues, and Operands

A *data object* is a general term for a region of data storage that can be used to hold values. The data storage used to hold a variable or an array is a data object, for instance. ANSI C uses the term *lvalue* to mean a name or expression that identifies a particular object. The name of a variable, for instance, is an lvalue, so *object* refers to the actual data storage, but lvalue is a label used to identify, or locate, that storage.

Not all objects can have their values changed, so ANSI C uses the term *modifiable lvalue* to identify objects whose values can be changed. Therefore, the left side of an assignment operator should be a modifiable lvalue. Indeed, the *l* in *lvalue* comes from *left* because modifiable lvalues can be used on the left side of assignment operators.

The term *rvalue* refers to quantities that can be assigned to modifiable lvalues. For instance, consider this statement:

```
bmw = 2002;
```

Here, `bmw` is a modifiable lvalue, and `2002` is an rvalue. As you probably guessed, the *r* in *rvalue* comes from *right*. Rvalues can be constants, variables, or any other expression that yields a value.

As long as you are learning the names of things, the proper term for what we have called an "item" (as in "the item to the left of the =") is *operand*. Operands are what operators operate on. For example, you can describe eating a hamburger as applying the "eat" operator to the "hamburger" operand, or you can say that the left operand of the = operator shall be a modifiable lvalue.

The basic C assignment operator is a little flashier than most. Try the short program in Listing 5.3.

Listing 5.3   The `golf.c` program.

```
/* golf.c -- golf tournament scorecard */
#include <stdio.h>
int main(void)
{
  int jane, tarzan, cheeta;

  cheeta = tarzan = jane = 68;
  printf("                cheeta    tarzan    jane\n");
  printf("First round score %4d %8d %8d\n",cheeta,tarzan,jane);
  return 0;
}
```

Many languages would balk at the triple assignment made in this program, but C accepts it routinely. The assignments are made right to left: First `jane` gets the value 68, then `tarzan` does, and finally `cheeta` does. Therefore, the output is as follows:

```
                  cheeta    tarzan    jane
First round score   68        68       68
```

Addition Operator: +

The *addition operator* causes the two values on either side of it to be added together. For example, the statement

```
printf("%d", 4 + 20);
```

causes the number **24** to be printed, not the expression

```
4 + 20
```

The values (operands) to be added can be variables as well as constants. Therefore, the statement

```
income = salary + bribes;
```

causes the computer to look up the values of the two variables on the right, add them, and assign this total to the variable `income`.

Subtraction Operator: –

The *subtraction operator* causes the number after the – sign to be subtracted from the number before the sign. The statement

```
takehome = 224.00 - 24.00;
```

assigns the value 200.0 to `takehome`.

The + and - operators are termed *binary*, or *dyadic,* operators, meaning that they require *two* operands.

Sign Operators: – and +

The minus sign can also be used to indicate or to change the algebraic sign of a value. For instance, the sequence

```
rocky = -12;
smokey = -rocky;
```

gives `smokey` the value **12**.

When the minus sign is used in this way, it is called a *unary operator*, meaning that it takes just one operand (see Figure 5.2).

The ANSI standard adds a unary + operator to C. It doesn't alter the value or sign of its operand; it just enables you to use statements like

```
dozen = +12;
```

without getting a compiler complaint. Formerly, this construction was not allowed.

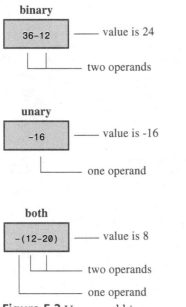

Figure 5.2 Unary and binary operators.

Multiplication Operator: *

Multiplication is indicated by the * symbol. The statement

```
cm = 2.54 * in;
```

multiplies the variable in by 2.54 and assigns the answer to cm.

By any chance, do you want a table of squares? C doesn't have a squaring function, but, as shown in Listing 5.4, you can use multiplication to calculate squares.

Listing 5.4 The squares.c program.

```
/* squares.c -- produces a table of first 20 squares */
#include <stdio.h>
int main(void)
{
    int num = 1;

    while (num < 21)
    {
        printf("%10d %10d\n", num, num * num);
        num = num + 1;
    }
    return 0;
}
```

This program prints the first 20 integers and their squares, as you can verify for yourself. Let's look at a more interesting example.

Exponential Growth

You have probably heard the story of the powerful ruler who seeks to reward a scholar who has done him a great service. When the scholar is asked what he would like, he points to a chessboard and says, just one grain of wheat on the first square, two on the second, four on the third, eight on the next, and so on. The ruler, lacking mathematical erudition, is astounded at the modesty of this request, for he had been prepared to offer great riches. The joke, of course, is on the ruler, as the program in Listing 5.5 shows. It calculates how many grains go on each square and keeps a running total. Because you might not be up to date on wheat crops, the program also compares the running total to a rough estimate of the annual wheat crop in the United States.

Listing 5.5   The wheat.c program.

```
/* wheat.c -- exponential growth */
#include <stdio.h>
#define SQUARES 64      /* squares on a checkerboard   */
#define CROP 9E14       /* US wheat crop in grains     */
int main(void)
{
    double current, total;
    int count = 1;

    printf("square   grains added   total grains   ");
    printf("fraction of \n");
    printf("                                        ");
    printf("US total\n");
    total = current = 1.0;    /* start with one grain    */
    printf("%4d %15.2e %13.2e %13.2e\n", count, current,
            total, total/CROP);
    while (count < SQUARES)
    {
        count = count + 1;
        current = 2.0 * current;
                            /* double grains on next square */
        total = total + current;        /* update total */
        printf("%4d %15.2e %13.2e %13.2e\n", count, current,
                total, total/CROP);
    }
    return 0;
}
```

The output begins innocuously enough:

square	grains added	total grains	fraction of US total
1	1.00e+000	1.00e+000	1.11e-015
2	2.00e+000	3.00e+000	3.33e-015
3	4.00e+000	7.00e+000	7.78e-015

4	8.00e+000	1.50e+001	1.67e-014
5	1.60e+001	3.10e+001	3.44e-014
6	3.20e+001	6.30e+001	7.00e-014
7	6.40e+001	1.27e+002	1.41e-013
8	1.28e+002	2.55e+002	2.83e-013
9	2.56e+002	5.11e+002	5.68e-013
10	5.12e+002	1.02e+003	1.14e-012

After ten squares, the scholar has acquired just a little over a thousand grains of wheat, but look what has happened by square 50!

50	5.63e+014	1.13e+015	1.25e+000

The haul has exceeded the total U.S. annual output! If you want to see what happens by the 64th square, you will have to run the program yourself.

This example illustrates the phenomenon of exponential growth. The world population growth and our use of energy resources have followed the same pattern.

Division Operator: /

C uses the / symbol to represent division. The value to the left of the / is divided by the value to the right. For example, the following gives four the value of 4.0:

```
four = 12.0/3.0;
```

Division works differently for integer types than it does for floating types. Floating-type division gives a floating-point answer, but integer division yields an integer answer. An integer has to be a whole number, which makes dividing 5 by 3 awkward, because the answer isn't a whole number. In C, any fraction resulting from integer division is discarded. This process is called *truncation*.

Try the program in Listing 5.6 to see how truncation works and how integer division differs from floating-point division.

Listing 5.6   The divide.c program.

```
/* divide.c -- divisions we have known */
#include <stdio.h>
int main(void)
{

    printf("integer division:  5/4   is %d \n", 5/4);
    printf("integer division:  6/3   is %d \n", 6/3);
    printf("integer division:  7/4   is %d \n", 7/4);
    printf("floating division: 7./4. is %1.2f \n", 7./4.);
    printf("mixed division:    7./4  is %1.2f \n", 7./4);
    return 0;
}
```

Listing 5.6 includes a case of "mixed types" by having a floating-point value divided by an integer. C is a more forgiving language than some and will let you get away with this, but normally you should avoid mixing types. Now for the results:

```
integer division:  5/4   is 1
integer division:  6/3   is 2
integer division:  7/4   is 1
floating division: 7./4. is 1.75
mixed division:    7./4  is 1.75
```

Notice how integer division does not round to the nearest integer, but always truncates, that is, discards the entire fractional part. When you mixed integers with floating point, the answer came out the same as floating point. When a calculation uses both types, the integer is converted to floating point before division.

The properties of integer division turn out to be handy for some problems, and we will give an example fairly soon. First, there is another important matter: What happens when you combine more than one operation into one statement? That is the next topic.

Operator Precedence

Consider the following line of code:

```
butter = 25.0 + 60.0 * n / SCALE;
```

This statement has an addition, a multiplication, and a division. Which operation takes place first? Is **25.0** added to **60.0**, the result of **85.0** then multiplied by n, and that result then divided by **SCALE**? Is **60.0** multiplied by n, the result added to **25.0**, and that answer then divided by **SCALE**? Is it some other order? Let's take n to be 6.0 and **SCALE** to be 2.0. If you work through the statement using these values, you will find that the first approach yields a value of 255. The second approach yields 192.5. A C program must have some other order in mind, for it would give a value of 205.0 for **butter**.

Clearly, the order of executing the various operations can make a difference, so C needs unambiguous rules for choosing what to do first. C does this by setting up an operator pecking order. Each operator is assigned a *precedence* level. As in ordinary arithmetic, multiplication and division have a higher precedence than addition and subtraction, so they are performed first. What if two operators have the same precedence? If they share an operand, they are executed according to the order in which they occur in the statement. For most operators, the order is from left to right. (The = operator was an exception to this.) Therefore, in the statement

```
butter = 25.0 + 60.0 * n / SCALE;
```

the order of operations is as follows:

60.0 * n	The first * or / in the expression (assuming n is 6 so that 60.0 * n is 360.0)
360.0 / SCALE	Then the second * or / in the expression
25.0 + 180	Finally (because SCALE is 2.0), the first + or - in the expression to yield 205.0

Many people like to represent the order of evaluation with a type of diagram called an *expression tree*. Figure 5.3 is an example of such a diagram. The diagram shows how the original expression is reduced by steps to a single value.

What if you want, say, an addition to take place before a division? Then you can do as we have done in this line:

```
flour = (25.0 + 60.0 * n) / SCALE;
```

Whatever is enclosed in parentheses is executed first. Within the parentheses, the usual rules hold. For this example, first the multiplication takes place and then the addition. That completes the expression in the parentheses. Now the result can be divided by SCALE.

Table 5.1 summarizes the rules for the operators used so far. (Appendix B, "C Operators," contains a table covering all operators.)

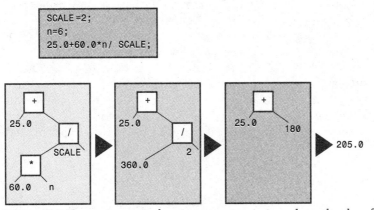

Figure 5.3 Expression trees showing operators, operands, and order of evaluation.

Table 5.1   Operators in order of decreasing precedence.

Operators	Associativity
( )	Left to right
+ - (unary)	Right to left
* /	Left to right
+ - (binary)	Left to right
=	Right to left

Notice that the two uses of the minus sign have different precedences, as do the two uses of the plus sign. The associativity column tells you how an operator associates with its operands. For example, the unary minus sign associates with the quantity to its right, and in division the left operand is divided by the right.

Precedence and the Order of Evaluation

Operator precedence provides vital rules for determining the order of evaluation in an expression, but it doesn't necessarily determine the complete order. C leaves some choices up to the implementor. Consider this statement:

```
y = 6 * 12 + 5 * 20;
```

Precedence dictates the order of evaluation when two operators share an operand. For example, the 12 is an operand for both the * and the + operators, and precedence says that multiplication comes first. Similarly, precedence says that the 5 is to be multiplied, not added. In short, the multiplications 6 * 12 and 5 * 20 take place before any addition. What precedence does not establish is which of these two multiplications occurs first. C leaves that choice to the implementor because one choice might be more efficient for one kind of hardware, but the other choice might work better on another kind of hardware. In either case, the expression reduces to 72 + 100, so the choice doesn't affect the final value for this particular example. "But," you say, "multiplication associates from left to right. Doesn't that mean the leftmost multiplication is performed first?" (Well, maybe you don't say that, but somewhere someone does.) The association rule applies for operators that *share* an operand. For instance, in the expression 12 / 3 * 2, the / and * operators, which have the same precedence, share the operand 3. Therefore, the left-to-right rule applies in this case, and the expression reduces to 4 * 2, or 8. (Going from right to left would give 12 / 6, or 2. Here the choice does matter.) In the previous example, the two * operators did not share a common operand, so the left-to-right rule did not apply.

Trying the Rules

Let's try these rules on a more complex example (see Listing 5.7).

Listing 5.7 The `rules.c` program.

```
/* rules.c -- precedence test */
#include <stdio.h>
int main(void)
{
  int top, score;
  top = score = -(2 + 5) * 6 + (4 + 3 * (2 + 3));
  printf("top = %d \n", top);
  return 0;
}
```

What value will this program print? Figure it out; then run the program or read the following description to check your answer.

First, parentheses have the highest precedence. Whether the parentheses in -(2 + 5) * 6 or in (4 + 3 * (2 + 3)) are evaluated first depends on the implementation, as we just discussed. Either choice will lead to the same result for this example, so let's take the left one first. The high precedence of parentheses means that in the subexpression -(2 + 5) * 6, you evaluate (2 + 5) first, getting 7. Next, you apply the unary minus operator to 7 to get -7. Now the expression is this:

```
top = score = -7 * 6 + (4 + 3 * (2 + 3))
```

The next step is to evaluate **2** + **3**. The expression becomes

```
top = score = -7 * 6 + (4 + 3 * 5)
```

Next, because the * in the parentheses has priority over +, the expression becomes

```
top = score = -7 * 6 + (4 + 15)
```

and then

```
top = score = -7 * 6 + 19
```

Multiply **-7** by **6** and get this expression:

```
top = score = -42 + 19
```

Then addition makes it

```
top = score = -23
```

Now **score** is assigned the value **-23**, and, finally, **top** gets the value **-23**. Remember that the = operator associates from right to left.

Some Additional Operators

C has about 40 operators, but some are used much more than others. The ones just covered are the most common, but let's add four more useful operators to the list.

The `sizeof` Operator

You used the **sizeof** operator in Chapter 3, "Data and C." To review, the **sizeof** operator returns the size, in bytes, of its operand. (Recall that a C byte is defined as the size used by the **char** type. In the past, this has most often been 8 bits, but some character sets may use larger bytes.) The operand can be a specific data object, such as the name of a variable, or it can be a type. If it is a type, such as **float**, the operand must be enclosed in parentheses. For instance, the example in Listing 5.8 shows both forms. (Some users may need to replace **%d** with **%ld**.)

Listing 5.8   The `sizeof.c` program.

```
/* sizeof.c -- uses sizeof operator */
#include <stdio.h>
int main(void)
{
  int n = 0;

  printf("n = %d, n has %d bytes; all ints have %d bytes.\n",
      n, sizeof n, sizeof (int) );
  return 0;
}
```

Modulus Operator: %

The *modulus operator* is used in integer arithmetic. It gives the *remainder* that results when the integer to its left is divided by the integer to its right. For example, `13 % 5` (read as "13 modulo 5") has the value 3, because 5 goes into 13 twice, with a remainder of 3. Don't bother trying to use this operator with floating-point numbers. It just won't work.

At first glance, this operator might strike you as an esoteric tool for mathematicians, but actually it is rather practical and helpful. One common use is to help you control the flow of a program. Suppose, for example, you are working on a bill-preparing program designed to add in an extra charge every third month. Just have the program evaluate the month number modulo 3 (that is, `month % 3`) and check to see whether the result is 0. If it is, the program adds in the extra charge. After you learn about "if statements" in Chapter 7, "C Control Statements: Branching and Jumps," you'll understand this better.

Listing 5.9 shows another use for the `%` operator.

Listing 5.9   The `min_sec.c` program.

```
/* min_sec.c -- converts seconds to minutes and seconds */
#include <stdio.h>
#define SEC_PER_MIN 60       /* seconds in a minute          */
int main(void)
{
    int sec, min, left;

    printf("Convert seconds to minutes and seconds!\n");
    printf("Enter the number of seconds you wish to convert.\n");
    scanf("%d", &sec);        /* number of seconds is read in */
    min = sec / SEC_PER_MIN;  /* truncated number of minutes  */
    left = sec % SEC_PER_MIN; /* number of seconds left over  */
    printf("%d seconds is %d minutes, %d seconds.\n", sec, min,
           left);
    return 0;
}
```

Here is a sample output:

```
Convert seconds to minutes and seconds!
Enter the number of seconds you wish to convert.
234
234 seconds is 3 minutes, 54 seconds.
```

One problem with this interactive program is that it processes just one input value. Can you figure out a way to have the program prompt you repeatedly for new input values? We will return to this problem later in the "Review Questions," but if you can work out a solution first, congratulations.

One matter the language leaves open is the result of using integer division and the modulus operator when one of the operands is negative. One way of interpreting truncating a result is tossing away the fractional part, so 11/5 is 2 and -11/5 is -2. In this case, 11%5 is 1 and -11%5 is -1. This is the most common implementation. However, you could interpret truncation as resulting in the largest integer less or equal to the result. This definition gives the same behavior for positive numbers, but results in -11/5 being -3 because -3 is the largest integer less than -2.2. In this case, -11%5 would be +4 because you would add 4/5 to -3 to get to -2.2.

To put the two options another way, suppose you entered a value of -234 when running Listing 5.9. The first way of handling negative numbers would report the result as being -3 minutes, -54 seconds, but the second would report the result as being -4 minutes, 6 seconds. The ANSI committee felt it was important to provide a portable solution that would work on all systems, but it did not want to disrupt existing code that already assumed one or the other method. So they added the `div()` function, which uses the first method. This method involves using structures, so we'll defer futher mention until Appendix F, "The ANSI Standard C Library."

Increment and Decrement Operators: ++ and --

The *increment operator* performs a simple task; it increments (increases) the value of its operand by 1. This operator comes in two varieties. The first variety has the ++ come before the affected variable; this is the *prefix* mode. The second variety has the ++ after the affected variable; this is the *postfix* mode. The two modes differ with regard to the precise time that the incrementing takes place. We'll explain the similarities first and then return to that difference. The short example in Listing 5.10 shows how the increment operators work.

Listing 5.10   The `add_one.c` program.

```
/* add_one.c -- incrementing: prefix and postfix */
#include <stdio.h>
int main(void)
{
    int ultra = 0, super = 0;

    while (super < 5)
    {
        super++;
        ++ultra;
        printf("super = %d, ultra = %d \n", super, ultra);
    }
    return 0;
}
```

Running `add_one.c` produces this output:

```
super = 1, ultra = 1
super = 2, ultra = 2
super = 3, ultra = 3
super = 4, ultra = 4
super = 5, ultra = 5
```

The program counted to 5 twice and simultaneously. I confess that the same results could have been achieved by replacing the two increment statements with this:

```
super = super + 1;
ultra = ultra + 1;
```

These are simple enough statements. Why bother creating one, let alone two, abbreviations? One reason is that the compact form makes your programs neater and easier to follow. These operators give your programs an elegant gloss that cannot fail to please the eye. For instance, you can rewrite part of shoe2.c (refer to Listing 5.2) this way:

```
shoe = 3.0;
while (shoe < 18.5)
{
    foot = SCALE*size + ADJUST;
    printf("%10.1f %20.2f inches\n", shoe, foot);
    ++shoe;
}
```

However, you still haven't taken full advantage of the increment operator. You can shorten the fragment this way:

```
shoe = 2.0;
while (++shoe < 18.5)
{
    foot = SCALE*shoe + ADJUST;
    printf("%10.1f %20.2f inches\n", shoe, foot);
}
```

Here you have combined the incrementing process and the while comparison into one expression. This type of construction is so common in C that it merits a closer look.

First, how does this construction work? Simply. The value of shoe is increased by 1 and then compared to 18.5. If it is less than 18.5, the statements between the braces are executed once. Then shoe is increased by 1 again, and the cycle is repeated until shoe gets too big. You changed the initial value of shoe from 3.0 to 2.0 to compensate for shoe being incremented before the first evaluation of foot (see Figure 5.4).

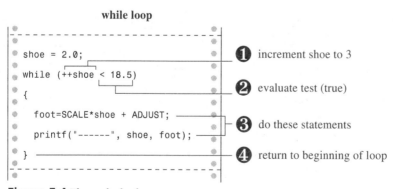

Figure 5.4 Through the loop once.

Second, what's so good about this approach? It is more compact. More important, it gathers in one place the two processes that control the loop. The primary process is the test: Do you continue or not? In this case, the test is checking to see whether the shoe size is less than 18.5. The secondary process changes an element of the test; in this case, the shoe size is increased.

Suppose you forgot to change the shoe size. Then shoe would *always* be less than **18.5**, and the loop would never end. The computer would churn out line after identical line, caught in a dreaded "infinite loop." Eventually, you would lose interest in the output and have to kill the program somehow. Having the loop test and the loop change at one place, instead of at separate locations, helps you to remember to update the loop.

A disadvantage is that combining two operations in a single expression can make the code harder to follow and can make it easier to make counting errors.

Another advantage of the increment operator is that it usually produces slightly more efficient machine language code because it is similar to actual machine language instructions. However, as implementors produce better C compilers, this advantage may disappear. A smart compiler recognizes that x = x + 1 can be treated the same as ++x.

Finally, these operators have an additional feature that can be useful in certain delicate situations. To find out what this feature is, try running the program in Listing 5.11.

Listing 5.11   The post_pre.c program.

```
/* post_pre.c -- postfix vs prefix */
#include <stdio.h>
int main(void)
{
   int a = 1, b = 1;
   int aplus, plusb;

   aplus = a++;        /* postfix */
   plusb = ++b;        /* prefix */
   printf("a    aplus    b    plusb \n");
   printf("%1d %5d %5d %5d\n", a, aplus, b, plusb);
   return 0;
}
```

If you and your compiler do everything correctly, you should get this result:

```
a    aplus    b    plusb
2     1       2     2
```

Both a and b were increased by 1, as promised. However, **aplus** has the value of a *before* a changed, but **plusb** has the value of b *after* b changed. This is the difference between the prefix form and the postfix form (see Figure 5.5).

```
aplus = a++;  /* postfix: a is changed after its value is used */
plusb = ++b;  /* prefix: b is changed before its value is used */
```

When one of these increment operators is used by itself, as in a solitary **ego++;** statement, it doesn't matter which form you use. The choice does matter, however, when the operator and its operand are part of a larger expression, as in the assignment statements you just saw. In this kind of situation, you must give some thought to the result you want. For instance, recall that we suggested using the following:

```
while (++shoe < 18.5)
```

prefix

q = 2*++a;

first, increment a by 1;
then, multiply a by 2 and assign to q

postfix

q = 2*a++;

first, multiply a by 2, assign to q
then, increment a by 1

Figure 5.5 Prefix and postfix.

This test condition provided a table up to size 18. If you use shoe++ instead of ++shoe, the table will go to size 19 because shoe will be increased after the comparison instead of before.

Of course, you could fall back on the less subtle form,

```
shoe = shoe + 1;
```

but then no one will believe you are a true C programmer.

We suggest you pay special attention to the examples of increment operators as you read through this book. Ask yourself if you could have used the prefix and the suffix forms interchangeably or if circumstances dictated a particular choice.

Decrementing: --

For each form of increment operator, there is a corresponding form of *decrement operator*. Instead of ++, use --:

```
-- count;    /* prefix form of decrement operator  */
count --;    /* postfix form of decrement operator */
```

Listing 5.12 illustrates that computers can be accomplished lyricists.

Listing 5.12   The bottles.c program.

```
/* bottles.c -- counting down */
#include <stdio.h>
#define MAX 100
int main(void)
{
  int count = MAX + 1;
```

```
  while (--count > 0) {
     printf("%d bottles of beer on the wall, "
            "%d bottles of beer!\n", count, count);
     printf("Take one down and pass it around,\n");
     printf("%d bottles of beer!\n\n", count - 1);
  }
  return 0;
}
```

The output starts like this:

```
100 bottles of beer on the wall, 100 bottles of beer!
Take one down and pass it around,
99 bottles of beer!
99 bottles of beer on the wall, 99 bottles of beer!
Take one down and pass it around,
98 bottles of beer!
```

It goes on a bit and ends this way:

```
1 bottles of beer on the wall, 1 bottles of beer!
Take one down and pass it around,
0 bottles of beer!
```

Apparently the accomplished lyricist has a problem with plurals, but that could be fixed by using the conditional operators of Chapter 8, "Character Input/Output and Redirection."

Incidentally, the > operator stands for "is greater than." Like < ("is less than"), it is a *relational operator*. You will take a longer look at relational operators in Chapter 6, "C Control Statements: Looping."

Precedence

The increment and decrement operators have a very high precedence of association; only parentheses are higher. Therefore, x*y++ means (x)*(y++), not (x*y)++, which is fortunate because the latter is invalid. The increment and decrement operators affect a *variable* (or, more generally, a modifiable lvalue), and the combination x*y is not itself a variable, although its parts are.

Don't confuse precedence of these two operators with the order of evaluation. Suppose you have the following:

```
y = 2;
n = 3;
nextnum = (y + n++)*6;
```

What value does nextnum get? Substituting in values yields this:

```
nextnum = (2 + 3)*6 = 5*6 = 30
```

Only after n is used is it increased to 4. Precedence tells us that the ++ is attached only to the n, not to 2 + n. It also tells us when the value of n is used for evaluating the expression, but the nature of the increment operator determines when the value of n is changed.

When n++ is part of an expression, you can think of it as meaning "use n; then increment it." On the other hand, ++n means "increment n; then use it."

Don't Be Too Clever

You can get fooled if you try to do too much at once with the increment operators. For example, you might think that you could improve on the **squares.c** program (refer to Listing 5.4) to print integers and their squares by replacing the **while** loop with this one:

```
while (num < 21)
    {
    printf("%10d %10d\n", num, num*num++);
    }
```

This looks reasonable. You print the number **num**, multiply it by itself to get the square, and then increase **num** by 1. In fact, this program may even work on some systems, but not all. The problem is that when **printf()** goes to get the values for printing, it might evaluate the last argument first and increment **num** before getting to the other argument. Therefore, instead of printing, say,

5   25

it may print

6   25

In C, the compiler can choose which arguments in a function to evaluate first. This freedom increases compiler efficiency, but can cause trouble if you use an increment operator on a function argument.

Another possible source of trouble is a statement like this one:

```
ans = num/2 + 5*(1 + num++);
```

Again, the problem is that the compiler may not do things in the same order you have in mind. You would think that it would find **num/2** first and then move on, but it might do the last term first, increase **num**, and use the new value in **num/2**. There is no guarantee.

Yet another troublesome case is this:

```
n = 3;
y = n++ + n++;
```

Certainly, **n** winds up larger by 2 after the statement is executed, but the value for **y** is ambiguous. A compiler can use the old value of **n** twice in evaluating **y** and then increment **n** twice. This gives **y** the value **6**, and **n** the value **5**, or it can use the old value once, increment **n** once, use that value for the second **n** in the expression, and then increment **n** a second time. This gives **y** the value **7**, and **n** the value **5**. Either choice is allowable. More exactly, the result is undefined, which means the C standard fails to define what the result should be.

You can easily avoid these problems:

- Don't use increment or decrement operators on a variable that is part of more than one argument of a function.

- Don't use increment or decrement operators on a variable that appears more than once in an expression.

On the other hand, C does have some guarantees about when incrementation takes place. We'll return to this subject when we discuss sequence points.

Expressions and Statements

We have been using the terms *expression* and *statement* throughout these first few chapters, and now the time has come to study their meanings more closely. Statements form the basic program steps of C, and most statements are constructed from expressions. This suggests that you look at expressions first.

Expressions

An *expression* consists of a combination of operators and operands. (An *operand*, recall, is what an operator operates on.) The simplest expression is a lone operand, and you can build in complexity from there. Here are some expressions:

```
4
-6
4+21
a*(b + c/d)/20
q = 5*2
x = ++q % 3
q > 3
```

As you can see, the operands can be constants, variables, or combinations of the two. Some expressions are combinations of smaller expressions, called *subexpressions*. For instance, c/d is a subexpression of the fourth example.

Every Expression Has a Value

An important property of C is that every C expression has a value. To find the value, you perform the operations in the order dictated by operator precedence. The value of the first few expressions we just listed is clear, but what about the ones with = signs? Those expressions simply have the same value that the variable to the left of the = sign receives. Therefore, the expression q=5*2 as a whole has the value 10. What about the expression q > 3? Such relational expressions have the value 1 if true and 0 if false. Here are some expressions and their values:

Expression	Value
-4 + 6	2
c = 3 + 8	11
5 > 3	1
6 + (c = 3 + 8)	17

The last expression looks strange! However, it is perfectly legal in C because it is the sum of two subexpressions, each of which has a value.

Statements

Statements are the primary building blocks of a program. A *program* is a series of statements with some necessary punctuation thrown in. A statement is a complete instruction to the computer. In C, statements are indicated by a semicolon at the end. Therefore,

```
legs = 4
```

is just an expression (which could be part of a larger expression), but

```
legs = 4;
```

is a statement.

What makes a complete instruction? First, C considers any expression to be a statement if you append a semicolon. (These are called *expression statements*.) Therefore, C won't object to lines such as the following:

```
8;
3 + 4;
```

However, these statements do nothing for your program and can't really be considered sensible statements. More typically, statements change values and call functions:

```
x = 25;
++x;
printf("x = %d\n", x);
```

Although a statement (or, at least, a sensible statement) is a complete instruction, not all complete instructions are statements. Consider the following statement:

```
x = 6 + (y = 5);
```

In it, the subexpression y = 5 is a complete instruction, but it is only part of the statement. Because a complete instruction is not necessarily a statement, a semicolon is needed to identify instructions that truly are statements.

So far you have encountered four kinds of statements. Listing 5.13 gives a short sample that uses all four.

Listing 5.13   The addemup.c program.

```
/* addemup.c -- four kinds of statements */
#include <stdio.h>
int main(void)              /* finds sum of first 20 integers */
{
  int count, sum;           /* declaration statement          */

  count = 0;                /* assignment statement           */
  sum = 0;                  /* ditto                          */
  while (count++ < 20)      /* while                          */
    sum = sum + count;      /*      statement                 */
  printf("sum = %d\n", sum);  /* function statement           */
  return 0;
}
```

Let's discuss Listing 5.13. By now, you must be pretty familiar with the *declaration statement*. Nonetheless, we will remind you that it establishes the names and type of variables and causes memory locations to be set aside for them. Note that a declaration statement is not an expression statement. That is, if you remove the semicolon from a declaration, you get something that is not an expression and that does not have a value:

```
int port                         /* not an expression, has no value */
```

The *assignment statement* is the workhorse of most programs; it assigns a value to a variable. It consists of a variable name followed by the assignment operator (=) followed by an expression followed by a semicolon. Note that the `while` statement includes an assignment statement within it. An assignment statement is an example of an expression statement.

A *function statement* causes the function to do whatever it does. In this example, the `printf()` function is invoked to print some results. A `while` statement has three distinct parts (see Figure 5.6). First is the keyword `while`. Then, in parentheses, is a test condition. Last is the statement that is performed if the test is met. Only one statement is included in the loop. It can be a simple statement, as in this example, in which case no braces are needed to mark it off, or the statement can be a compound statement, like some of the earlier examples, in which case braces are required. Read about compound statements just ahead.

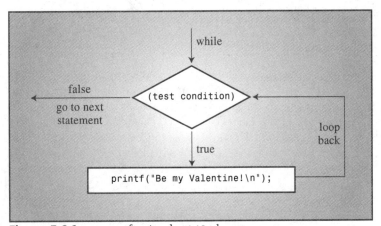

Figure 5.6 Structure of a simple `while` loop.

The `while` statement belongs to a class of statements sometimes called *structured statements* because they possess a structure more complex than that of a simple assignment statement. In later chapters, you will encounter many other kinds of structured statements.

Side Effects and Sequence Points

Now for a little more C terminology. A *side effect* is the modification of a data object or file. For instance, the side effect of the statement

```
states = 50;
```

is to set the states variable to 50. Side effect? This looks more like the main intent! From the standpoint of C, however, the main intent is evaluating expressions. Show C the expression 4 + 6, and C evaluates it to 10. Show it the expression states = 50, and C evaluates it to 50. Evaluating that expression has the side effect of changing the states variable to 50. The increment and decrement operators, like the assignment operator, have side effects and are used primarily because of their side effects.

A *sequence point* is a point in program execution at which all side effects are evaluated before going on to the next step. In C, the semicolon in a statement marks a sequence point. That means all changes made by assignment operators, increment operators, and decrement operators in a statement must take place before a program proceeds to the next statement. Some operators that we'll discuss in later chapters have sequence points. Also, the end of any *full expression* is a sequence point.

What's a full expression? It's one that's not a subexpression of a larger expression. Examples of full expressions include the expression in an expression statement and the expression serving as a test condition for a while loop.

Sequence points help clarify when postfix incrementation takes place. Consider, for instance, the following code:

```
while (guests++ < 10)
    printf("%d \n", guests);
```

Sometimes C newcomers assume that "use the value, then increment it" means, in this context, to increment guests after it's used in the printf() statement. However, the guests++ < 10 expression is a full expression because it is a while loop test condition, so the end of this expression is a sequence point. Therefore, C guarantees that the side effect (incrementing guests) takes place before the program moves on to printf(). Using the postfix form, however, guarantees that guests will be incremented after the comparison to 10 is made.

Now consider this statement:

```
y = (4 + x++) + (6 + x++);
```

The expression 4 + x++ is not a full expression, so C does not guarantee that x will be incremented immediately after the subexpression 4 + x++ is evaluated. Here, the full expression is the entire assignment statement, and the semicolon marks the sequence point, so all that C guarantees is that x will have been incremented twice by the time the program moves to the following statement. C does not specify whether x is incremented after each subexpression is evaluated or only after all the expressions have been evaluated, which is why you should avoid statements of this kind.

Compound Statements (Blocks)

A *compound statement* is two or more statements grouped together by enclosing them in braces; it is also called a *block*. The shoe2.c program used a block to let the while statement encompass several statements. Compare the following program fragments:

```
/* fragment 1 */
index = 0;
while (index++ < 10)
  sam = 10 * index + 2;
printf("sam = %d\n", sam);

/* fragment 2 */
index = 0;
while (index++ < 10)
{
  sam = 10 * index + 2;
  printf("sam = %d\n", sam);
}
```

In fragment 1, only the assignment statement is included in the while loop. In the absence of braces, a while statement runs from the while to the next semicolon. The printf() function will be called just once, after the loop has been completed.

In fragment 2, the braces ensure that both statements are part of the while loop, and printf() is called each time the loop is executed. The entire compound statement is considered to be the single statement in terms of the structure of a while statement (see Figure 5.7).

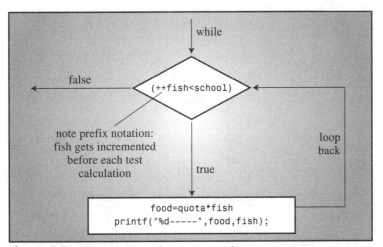

Figure 5.7 A while loop with a compound statement.

Style Tips

Look again at the two `while` fragments and notice how an indentation marks off the body of each loop. The indentation makes no difference to the compiler; it uses the braces and its knowledge of the structure of `while` loops to decide how to interpret your instructions. The indentation is there for you, so that you can see at a glance how the program is organized.

I have shown one popular style for positioning the braces for a block, or compound, statement. Another very common style is this:

```
while (index++ < 10) {
  sam = 10*index + 2;
  printf("sam = %d \n", sam);
}
```

This style highlights the attachment of the block to the `while` loop. The other style emphasizes that the statements form a block. Again, as far as the compiler is concerned, both forms are identical.

To sum up, use indentation as a tool to point out the structure of a program to the reader.

Summary: Expressions and Statements

Expressions:

An *expression* is a combination of operators and operands. The simplest expression is just a constant or a variable with no operator, such as **22** or **beebop**. More complex examples are **55 + 22** and **vap = 2 * (vip + (vup = 4))**.

Statements:

A *statement* is a command to the computer. There are simple statements and compound statements. *Simple statements* terminate in a semicolon, as in these examples:

Declaration statement:	`int toes;`
Assignment statement:	`toes = 12;`
Function call statement:	`printf("%d\n", toes);`
Structured statement:	`while (toes < 20) toes = toes + 2;`
NULL statement:	`; /* does nothing */`

Compound statements, or *blocks*, consist of one or more statements (which themselves can be compound) enclosed in braces. The following `while` statement contains an example:

```
while (years < 100)
{
    wisdom = wisdom + 1;
    printf("%d %d\n", years, wisdom);
    years = years + 1;
}
```

Type Conversions

Statements and expressions should normally use variables and constants of just one type. If, however, you mix types, C doesn't stop dead in its tracks the way, say, Pascal does. Instead, it uses a set of rules to make type conversions automatically. This can be a convenience, but it can also be a danger, especially if you are mixing types inadvertently. (The `lint` program, found on many UNIX systems, checks for type "clashes." Many non-UNIX C compilers report possible type problems if you select a higher error level.) It is a good idea to have at least some knowledge of the type conversion rules.

The basic rules are these:

1. When appearing in an expression, `char` and `short`, both `signed` and `unsigned`, are automatically converted to `int` or, if necessary, to `unsigned int`. (If `short` is the same size as `int`, then `unsigned short` is larger than `int`; in that case, `unsigned short` is converted to `unsigned int`.) Under K&R C, but not under ANSI C, `float` is automatically converted to `double`. Because they are conversions to larger types, they are called *promotions*.

2. In any operation involving two types, both values are converted to the higher ranking of the two types.

3. The ranking of types, from highest to lowest, is `long double`, `double`, `float`, `unsigned long`, `long`, `unsigned int`, and `int`. One possible exception is when `long` and `int` are the same size, in which case `unsigned int` outranks `long`. The `short` and `char` types don't appear in this list because they would have been already promoted to `int` or perhaps `unsigned int`.

4. In an assignment statement, the final result of the calculations is converted to the type of the variable being assigned a value. This process can result in promotion, as described in Rule 1, or *demotion*, in which a value is converted to a lower-ranking type.

5. When passed as function arguments, `char` and `short` are converted to `int`, and `float` is converted to `double`. This automatic promotion can be overridden by function prototyping, as discussed in Chapter 9, "Functions."

Promotion is usually a smooth, uneventful process, but demotion can lead to real trouble. The reason is simple: The lower-ranking type may not be big enough to hold the complete number. A `char` variable can hold the integer `101` but not the integer `22334`. When floating types are demoted to integer types, they are truncated, or rounded toward zero. That means `23.12` and `23.99` both are truncated to `23` and that `-23.5` is truncated to `-23`. Listing 5.14 illustrates the working of these rules.

Listing 5.14   The `convert.c` program.

```
/* convert.c -- automatic type conversions */
#include <stdio.h>
int main(void)
{
    char ch;
    int i;
    float fl;

    fl = i = ch = 'A';                          /* line 8  */
    printf("ch = %c, i = %d, fl = %2.2f\n", ch, i, fl);
    ch = ch + 1;                                /* line 10 */
    i = fl + 2 * ch;                            /* line 11 */
    fl = 2.0 * ch + i;                          /* line 12 */
    printf("ch = %c, i = %d, fl = %2.2f\n", ch, i, fl);
    ch = 5212205.17;                            /* line 14 */
    printf("Now ch = %c\n", ch);
    return 0;
}
```

Running `convert.c` produces the following:

```
ch = A, i = 65, fl = 65.00
ch = B, i = 197, fl = 329.00
Now ch = -
```

On this system, which has an 8-bit `char` and a 32-bit `int`, here is what happened:

Lines 8 and 9: The character `'A'` is stored as a 1-byte ASCII value in `ch`. The integer variable `i` receives the integer conversion of `'A'`, which is **65** stored as 4 bytes. Finally, `fl` receives the floating conversion of **65**, which is **65.00**. *Lines 10 and 13*: The character variable `'A'` is converted to the integer **65**, which is then added to the **1**. The resulting 2-byte integer **66** is truncated to 1 byte and stored in `ch`. When printed using the `%c` specifier, **66** is interpreted as the ASCII code for `'B'`.

Lines 11 and 13: The value of `ch` is converted to a 4-byte integer (**66**) for the multiplication by **2**. The resulting integer (**132**) is converted to floating point in order to be added to `fl`. The result (**197.00f**) is converted to `int` and stored in `i`. *Lines 12 and 13*: The value of `ch` (`'B'`, or **66**) is converted to floating point for multiplication by **2.0**. The value of `i` (**197**) is converted to floating point for the addition, and the result (**329.00**) is stored in `fl`. *Lines 14 and 15*: Here the example tries a case of demotion, setting `ch` equal to a rather large number. After truncation takes place, `ch` winds up with the ASCII code for the hyphen character.

The Cast Operator

You should usually steer clear of automatic type conversions, especially of demotions, but sometimes it is convenient to make conversions, providing you exercise care. The type conversions we've discussed so far are done automatically. However, it is possible for you to demand the precise type conversion that you want. The method for doing this is called a *cast* and consists of preceding the quantity with the name of the desired type in parentheses.

The parentheses and type name together constitute a *cast operator*. This is the general form of a cast operator:

`(type)`

The actual type desired, such as `long`, is substituted for the word *type*.

Consider these two lines, in which `mice` is an `int` variable. The second line contains two casts to type `int`.

```
mice = 1.6 + 1.7;
mice = (int) 1.6 + (int) 1.7;
```

The first example uses automatic conversion. First, `1.6` and `1.7` are added to yield `3.3`. This number is then converted through truncation to the integer `3` to match the `int` variable. In the second example, `1.6` is converted to an integer (`1`) before addition, as is `1.7`, so that `mice` is assigned the value 1+1, or `2`. Neither form is intrinsically more correct than the other; you have to consider the context of the programming problem to see which makes more sense.

Normally, you shouldn't mix types; that is why some languages don't allow it, but there are occasions when it is useful. The C philosophy is to avoid putting barriers in your way and to give you the responsibility of not abusing that freedom.

Summary: Operating in C

Here are the operators we have discussed so far:

Assignment Operator:

=	Assigns the value at its right to the variable at its left.

Arithmetic Operators:

+	Adds the value at its right to the value at its left.
−	Subtracts the value at its right from the value at its left.
−	As a unary operator, changes the sign of the value at its right.
*	Multiplies the value at its right by the value at its left.
/	Divides the value at its left by the value at its right. Answer is truncated if both operands are integers.
%	Yields the remainder when the value at its left is divided by the value to its right (integers only).
++	Adds 1 to the value of the variable to its right (prefix mode) or to the value of the variable to its left (postfix mode).
−−	Like ++, but subtracts 1.

Miscellaneous Operators:

sizeof	Yields the size, in bytes, of the operand to its right. The operand can be a type-specifier in parentheses, as in `sizeof (float)`, or it can be the name of a particular variable, array, and so forth, as in `sizeof foo`.

(type)   As the cast operator, converts the following value to the type speci-
                fied by the enclosed keyword(s). For example, (float) 9 converts
                the integer 9 to the floating-point number 9.0.

Function with Arguments

By now, you're familiar with using function arguments. The next step along the road to function mastery is learning how to write your own functions that use arguments. Let's
preview that skill now. (At this point, you might want to review the butler() function example near the end of Chapter 2, "Introducing C;" it shows how to write a function without
an argument.) Listing 5.15 includes a pound() function that prints a specified number of
pound signs (#). The example also illustrates some points about type conversion.

Listing 5.15   The pound.c program.

```
/* pound.c -- defines a function with an argument      */
#include <stdio.h>
void pound(int n);        /* ANSI prototype             */

int main(void)
{
  int times = 5;
  char ch = '!';          /* ASCII code is 33           */
  float f = 6.0;

  pound(times);           /* int argument               */
  pound(ch);              /* char automatically -> int  */
  pound((int) f);         /* cast forces f -> int       */
  return 0;
}

void pound(int n)         /* ANSI-style function header  */
{                         /* says takes one int argument */
  while (n-- > 0)
      printf("#");
  printf("\n");
}
```

Running the program produces this output:

```
#####
#################################
######
```

First, let's examine the function heading:

```
void pound(int n)
```

If the function took no arguments, the parentheses would be empty. Because the function takes one argument, you include one variable name, n, and indicate that this variable
is type int. You can use any name consistent with C's naming rules.

Declaring an argument creates a variable called the *formal argument* or the *formal parameter*. In this case, you've created a type int variable called n. Making a function call like pound(10) acts to assign the value 10 to n. In this program, the call pound(times) assigns the value of times (5) to n. You say that the function call *passes* a value, and this value is called the *actual argument* or the *actual parameter*, so the function call pound(10) passes the actual argument 10 to the function, where 10 is assigned to the formal argument (the variable n). That is, the value of the times variable in main() is copied to the new variable n in pound().

Variable names are private to the function. This means that a name defined in one function doesn't conflict with the same name defined elsewhere. If you used times instead of n in pound(), that would create a variable distinct from the times in main(). That is, you would have two variables with the same name, but the program keeps track of which is which.

Now let's look at the function calls. The first one is pound(times), and, as we said, it causes the times value of 5 to be assigned to n. This causes the function to print five pound signs and a newline. The second call is pound(ch). Here, ch is type char. It is initialized to the ! character, which, on ASCII systems, means that ch has the numerical value 33. The automatic promotion of char to int converts this, on this system, from 33 stored in 1 byte to 33 stored in 4 bytes, so the value 33 is now in the correct form to be used as an argument to this function. The last call, pound ((int) f), uses a type cast to convert the type float variable f to the proper type for this argument.

Suppose you omit the type cast. With ANSI C, the program will make the type cast automatically for you. That's because of the ANSI prototype near the top of the file:

```
void pound(int n);        /* ANSI prototype                   */
```

A *prototype* is a function declaration that describes a function's return value and its arguments. This prototype says two things about the pound() function:

The function has no return value

The function takes one argument, which is a type int value

Because the compiler sees this prototype before pound() is used in main(), the compiler knows what sort of argument pound() should have, and it inserts a type cast if one is needed to make the actual argument agree in type with the prototype. For instance, the call pound(3.859) will be converted to pound(3).

K&R Function Declarations and Headings

K&R C uses a different syntax for function declarations and headings. The K&R function declaration specifies just the return type and is silent about arguments:

```
void pound(int n);        /* ANSI prototype                   */
void pound();             /* K&R function declaration         */
```

Also, the K&R function heading looks different:

```
void pound(int n)        /* ANSI C */
{
   ...

void pound(n)            /* K&R C  */
int n;
{
   ...
```

Note that function arguments, such as `n`, are declared before the opening brace. Variables defined inside the function are declared after the opening brace. ANSI C recognizes both forms but will phase out the older form someday. Chapter 9 examines prototyping in more detail.

About the only reason to use the K&R forms is if your compiler doesn't support ANSI C. The ANSI C function prototype is a major improvement because it enables the compiler to check argument types. To see what prototypes do for you, consider how C behaves without them. Suppose, for example, you replace the ANSI prototype in Listing 15.15 with a K&R declaration and that you eliminate the type cast. Then, when the compiler reaches the `pound()` calls in `main()`, it knows that `pound()` has no return value, but it doesn't know what sort of argument `pound()` takes. In the absence of that knowledge, the compiler follows the usual default rules. Suppose you have this call:

```
pound(f);
```

First, the default promotion converts `f` to type `double`. On this system, that results in the function call putting an 8-byte value into the *stack,* a temporary storage area. Then the `pound()` function, expecting type `int`, reads just 4 of those bytes. The result bears little resemblance to the original value. In short, using a `float` or `double` argument when a function expects type `int` does not lead to an automatic type conversion; it leads to garbage. You can avoid that problem in K&R C by using an explicit type cast. With ANSI C, the problem is handled automatically.

A Sample Program

Listing 5.16 is a useful program (if you're a runner or know one) that illustrates several of the ideas in this chapter. It looks long, but all the calculations are done in six lines near the end. The bulk of the program relays information between the computer and the user. We've tried using enough comments to make it nearly self-explanatory. Read through it, and when you are done, we'll clear up a few points.

Listing 5.16   The `running.c` program.

```
/* running.c -- A useful program for runners */
#include <stdio.h>
#define S_PER_M      60   /* seconds in a minute  */
#define S_PER_H    3600   /* seconds in an hour   */
#define M_PER_K 0.62137   /* miles in a kilometer */
```

```
int main(void)
{
   double distk, distm;   /* distance run in km and in miles    */
   double rate;           /* average speed in mph               */
   int min, sec;          /* minutes and seconds of running time */
   int time;              /* running time in seconds only       */
   double mtime;          /* time in seconds for one mile        */
   int mmin, msec;        /* minutes and seconds for one mile   */

   printf("This program converts your time for a metric race\n");
   printf("to a time for running a mile and to your average\n");
   printf("speed in miles per hour.\n");
   printf("Please enter, in kilometers, the distance run.\n");
   scanf("%lf", &distk);  /* %lf for type double                */
   printf("Next enter the time in minutes and seconds.\n");
   printf("Begin by entering the minutes.\n");
   scanf("%d", &min);
   printf("Now enter the seconds.\n");
   scanf("%d", &sec);
   time = S_PER_M * min + sec;
                         /* converts time to pure seconds        */
   distm = M_PER_K * distk;
                         /* converts kilometers to miles          */
   rate = distm / time * S_PER_H;
                         /* miles per sec x sec per hour = mph   */
   mtime = (double) time / distm;
                         /* time/distance = time per mile        */
   mmin = (int) mtime / S_PER_M; /* find whole minutes          */
   msec = (int) mtime % S_PER_M; /* find remaining seconds      */
   printf("You ran %1.2f km (%1.2f miles) in %d min, %d sec.\n",
       distk, distm, min, sec);
   printf("That pace corresponds to running a mile in %d min, ",
       mmin);
   printf("%d sec.\nYour average speed was %1.2f mph.\n",msec,
       rate);
   return 0;
}
```

Listing 5.16 uses the same approach used earlier in min_sec to convert the final time to minutes and seconds, but it also makes type conversions. Why? Because you need integer arguments for the seconds-to-minutes part of the program, but the metric-to-mile conversion involves floating-point numbers. We have used the cast operator to make these conversions explicit.

To tell the truth, it should be possible to write the program using just automatic conversions. In fact, we did so, using mtime of type int to force the time calculation to be converted to integer form. However, that version failed to run on one of the seven systems we tried. That compiler (a somewhat obsolete version) failed to follow the C rules. Using type casts makes your intent clearer not only to the reader, but perhaps to the compiler as well.

Here's a sample output:

```
This program converts your time for a metric race
to a time for running a mile and to your average
speed in miles per hour.
```

```
Please enter, in kilometers, the distance run.
10.0
Next enter the time in minutes and seconds.
Begin by entering the minutes.
36
Now enter the seconds.
23
You ran 10.00 km (6.21 miles) in 36 min, 23 sec.
That pace corresponds to running a mile in 5 min, 51 sec.
Your average speed was 10.25 mph.
```

Chapter Summary

C has many operators, such as the assignment and arithmetic operators discussed in this chapter. In general, an *operator* operates on one or more operands to produce a value. Operators, such as the minus sign and `sizeof`, that take one operand, are termed *unary operators*. Operators requiring two operands, such as the addition and the multiplication operators, are called *binary operators*.

Expressions are combinations of operators and operands. In C, every expression has a value, including assignment expressions and comparison expressions. Rules of *operator precedence* help determine how terms are grouped when expressions are evaluated.

Statements are complete instructions to the computer and are indicated in C by a terminating semicolon. So far, you have worked with declaration statements, assignment statements, function call statements, and control statements. Statements included within a pair of braces constitute a *compound statement*, or *block*. One particular control statement is the `while` loop, which repeats statements as long as a test condition remains true.

In C, many *type conversions* take place automatically. The `char` and `short` types are promoted to type `int` whenever they appear in expressions or as function arguments. The `float` type is promoted to type `double` when used as a function argument. Under K&R C (but not ANSI C), `float` is also promoted to `double` when used in an expression. When a value of one type is assigned to a variable of a second type, the value is converted to the same type as the variable. When larger types are converted to smaller types (`long` to `short` or `double` to `float`, for example), there might be a loss of data. In cases of mixed arithmetic, smaller types are converted to larger types following the rules outlined in this chapter.

When you define a function that takes an argument, you declare a *variable*, or *formal argument*, in the function definition. Then the value passed in a function call is assigned to this variable, which can now be used in the function.

Review Questions

1. Assume all variables are of type `int`. Find the value of each of the following variables:

    a. x = (2 + 3) * 6;

    b. x = (12 + 6)/2*3;

    c. `y = x = (2 + 3)/4;`

    d. `y = 3 + 2*(x = 7/2);`

2. Assume all variables are of type int. Find the value of each of the following variables:

    a. `x = (int) 3.8 + 3.3;`

    b. `x = (2 + 3) * 10.5;`

    c. `x = 3 / 5 * 22.0;`

    d. `x = 22.0 * 3 / 5;`

3. You suspect that there are some errors in the next program. Can you find
   them?

```
int main(void)
{
  int i = 1,
  float n;
  printf("Watch out! Here come a bunch of fractions!\n");
  while (i < 30)
    n = 1/i;
    printf(" %f", n);
  printf("That's all, folks!\n");
  return;
}
```

4. Here's a first attempt at making min_sec interactive, but the program is
   not satisfactory. Why not? How can it be improved?

```
#include <stdio.h>
#define S_TO_M 60
int main(void)
{
  int sec, min, left;

  printf("This program converts seconds to minutes and ");
  printf("seconds.\n");
  printf("Just enter the number of seconds.\n");
  printf("Enter 0 to end the program.\n");
  while (sec > 0) {
    scanf("%d", &sec);
    min = sec/S_TO_M;
    left = sec % S_TO_M;
    printf("%d sec is %d min, %d sec. \n", sec, min, left);
    printf("Next input?\n");
  }
  printf("Bye!\n");
  return 0;
}
```

5. What will this program print?

```
#include <stdio.h>
#define FORMAT "%s is a string\n"
int main(void)
{
    int num = 0;

    printf(FORMAT,FORMAT);
    printf("%d\n", ++num);
    printf("%d\n", num++);
    printf("%d\n", num--);
    printf("%d\n", num);
    return 0;
}
```

6. What will this program print?

```
#include <stdio.h>
int main(void)
{
    char c1, c2;
    int diff;
    float num;

    c1 = 'D';
    c2 = 'A';
    diff = c1 - c2;
    num = diff;
    printf("%c%c%c:%d %3.2f\n", c1, c2, c1, diff, num);
    return 0;
}
```

7. What will this program print?

```
#include <stdio.h>
#define TEN 10
int main(void)
{
    int n = 0;

    while (n++ < TEN)
        printf("%5d", n);
    printf("\n");
    return 0;
}
```

8. Modify the last program so that it prints the letters **a** through **g** instead.

9. If the following fragments were part of a complete program, what would they print?

a.

```
int x = 0;
while (++x < 3)
    printf("%4d", x);
```

b.

```
int x = 100;

while (x++ < 103)
    printf("%4d\n",x);
    printf("%4d\n",x);
```

c.

```
char ch = 's';

while (ch < 'w')
{
    printf("%c", ch);
    ch++;
}
printf("%c\n",ch);
```

10. What will the following program print?

```
#define MESG "COMPUTER BYTES DOG"
#include <stdio.h>
int main(void)
{
    int n = 0;

    while ( n < 5 )
        printf("%s\n", MESG);
        n++;
    printf("That's all.\n");
    return 0;
}
```

11. Construct statements that do the following (or, in other terms, have the following side effects):

   a. Increase the variable x by 10.

   b. Increase the variable x by 1.

   c. Assign twice the sum of a and b to c.

   d. Assign a plus twice b to c.

12. Construct statements that do the following:

   a. Decrease the variable x by 1.

   b. Assigns to m the remainder of n divided by k.

   c. Divide q by b minus a and assign the result to p.

   d. Assign to x the result of dividing the sum of a and b by the product of c and d.

Programming Exercises

1. Use a `while` loop to convert time in minutes to time in hours and minutes. Use `#define` or `const` to create a symbolic constant for 60, and provide a sensible method of ending the loop.

2. Write a program that asks for an integer and then prints all the integers from (and including) that value up to (and including) a value larger by 10. (That is, if the input is 5, the output runs from 5 to 15.)

3. Write a program that asks you to enter the number of days and then converts that value to weeks and days. For example, it would convert 18 days to 2 weeks, 4 days.

4. Change the program `addemup.c` (refer to Listing 5.13) that found the sum of the first 20 integers. (If you prefer, you can think of `addemup.c` as a program that calculates how much money you get in 20 days if you receive $1 the first day, $2 the second day, $3 the third day, and so on.) Modify the program so that you can tell it interactively how far the calculation should proceed. That is, replace the `20` with a variable that is read in.

5. Now modify the program so that it computes the sum of the squares of the integers. (If you prefer, how much money you receive if you get $1 the first day, $4 the second day, $9 the third day, and so on. This looks like a much better deal!) C doesn't have a squaring function, but you can use the fact that the square of n is n * n.

6. Write a program that requests a floating-point number and prints the value of the number cubed. Use a function of your own design to cube the value and print it. The `main()` program should pass the entered value to this function.

CHAPTER 6

C CONTROL STATEMENTS: LOOPING

You will learn about the following in this chapter:	
• Keywords	• Operators

`for`
`while`
`do while`
	`< > >=`
	`<= != == +=`
	`*= -= /= %=`

*I*n this chapter, you learn about C's three loop structures: `while`, `for`, and `do while`. You use relational operators to construct expressions to control these loops, and you learn about several other operators, too. Arrays, which are often used with loops, are introduced. Finally, you take a first look at writing functions that have return values.

Powerful, intelligent, versatile, and useful! Most of us wouldn't mind being described that way. We're not going to tell you how to earn these accolades for yourself, but, with the help of C, your programs can earn them. The trick is controlling the *flow* of a program. According to computer science (which is the science of computers and not science by computers. . .yet), a good language should provide these three forms of program flow:

- Executing a sequence of statements.

- Repeating a sequence of statements until some condition is met (looping).

- Using a test to decide between alternative sequences (branching).

The first form you know well; all the previous programs have consisted of a sequence of statements. The `while` loop is one example of the second form. In this chapter, you'll take a closer look at the `while` loop along with two other loop structures: `for` and `do while`. The final form, choosing between different possible courses of action, makes a program much more "intelligent" and increases the usefulness of a computer enormously. Sadly, you'll have to wait a chapter before being entrusted with such power. Let's begin by reviewing the `while` loop.

An Initial Example

You are already somewhat familiar with the `while` loop, but let's review it with a program (see Listing 6.1) that sums integers entered from the keyboard. This example makes use of the return value of `scanf()` to terminate input.

Listing 6.1   The `summing.c` program.

```
/* summing.c -- sums integers entered interactively */
#include <stdio.h>
int main(void)
{
  long num;
  long sum = 0L;          /* initialize sum to zero     */
  int status;

  printf("Please enter an integer to be summed. ");
  printf("Enter q to quit.\n");
  status = scanf("%ld", &num);
  while (status == 1)   /* == means "is equal to"      */
  {
      sum = sum + num;
      printf("Please enter next integer to be summed. ");
      printf("Enter q to quit.\n");
      status = scanf("%ld", &num);
  }
  printf("Those integers sum to %ld.\n", sum);
  return 0;
}
```

Listing 6.1 uses type `long` to allow for larger numbers. For consistency, you initialize `sum` to `0L` (type `long` zero) rather than to `0` (type `int` zero), even though C's automatic conversions enable you to use a plain `0`.

Here is a sample run:

```
Please enter an integer to be summed. Enter q to quit.
20
Please enter next integer to be summed. Enter q to quit.
5
Please enter next integer to be summed. Enter q to quit.
30
Please enter next integer to be summed. Enter q to quit.
q
Those integers sum to 55.
```

Program Comments

Because you are reviewing the `while` loop, let's look at it first. The test condition for this loop is the following expression:

```
status == 1
```

The == operator is C's *equality operator*; that is, this expression tests whether status is equal to 1. Don't confuse it with status = 1, which *assigns* 1 to status. With the status == 1 test condition, the loop repeats as long as status is 1. For each cycle, the loop adds the current value of num to sum, so that sum maintains a running total. When status gets a value other than 1, the loop terminates, and the program reports the final value of sum.

For the program to work properly, it should get a new value for num on each loop cycle, and it should reset status on each cycle. The program accomplishes this by using two distinct features of scanf(). First, it uses scanf() to attempt to read a new value for num. Second, it uses the scanf() return value to report on the success of that attempt. Recall from Chapter 4, "Character Strings and Formatted Input/Output," that scanf() returns the number of items successfully read. If scanf() succeeds in reading an integer, it places the integer into num and returns the value 1, which is assigned to status. (Note that the input value goes to num, not to status.) This updates both num and the value of status, and the while loop goes through another cycle. If you respond with non-numeric input, such as q, scanf() fails to find an integer to read, so its return value and status will be 0. That terminates the loop. The input character q, by the way, because it wasn't a number, is placed back into the input queue; it does not get read. (Actually, any non-numeric input, not just q, terminates the loop, but asking the user to enter a q is a simpler instruction than asking the user to enter non-numeric input.)

This dual use of scanf() gets around a troublesome aspect of interactive input to a loop: How do you tell the loop when to stop? Suppose, for instance, that scanf() did not have a return value. Then the only thing that would change on each loop is the value of num. You could use the value of num to terminate the loop, using, say, num > 0 (num greater than 0) or num != 0 (num not equal to 0) as a test condition, but this prevents you from entering certain values, such as -3 or 0, as input. Instead, you could add new code to the loop, such as asking "Do you wish to continue? <y/n>" at each cycle and then testing to see whether the user entered a y. This is a bit clunky and slows down input. Using the return value of scanf() avoids these problems.

Now let's take a closer look at the program structure. You can summarize it as follows:

```
initialize sum to 0
prompt user
read input
while the input is an integer,
    add the input to sum,
    prompt user,
    then read next input
after input completes, print sum
```

This, incidentally, is an example of *pseudocode*, which is the art of expressing a program in simple English that parallels the forms of a computer language. Pseudocode is useful for working out the logic of a program. After the logic seems right, you can translate the pseudocode to the actual programming code. One advantage of pseudocode is that it enables you to concentrate on the logic and organization of a program and spares you from simultaneously worrying about how to express the ideas in a computer language. Here, for example, you can use indentation to indicate a block of code and not worry about C syntax requiring braces. Another advantage is that pseudocode is not tied to a particular language, so the same pseudocode can be translated into different computer languages.

Anyway, because the `while` loop is an entry-condition loop, the program must get the input and check the value of **status** *before* it goes to the body of the loop. That is why you have a `scanf()` before the `while`. For the loop to continue, you need a read statement inside the loop so that it can find out the status of the next input. That is why you also have a `scanf()` statement at the end of the `while` loop; it readies the loop for its next iteration. You can think of the following as a standard format for a loop:

```
get first value to be tested
while the test is successful
      process value
      get next value
```

C-Style Reading Loop

Listing 6.1 could be written in Pascal or BASIC or FORTRAN along the same design displayed in the pseudocode. C, however, offers a shortcut. The construction

```
status = scanf("%ld", &num);
while (status == 1)
{
      /* loop actions */
      status = scanf("%ld", &num);
}
```

can be replaced by the following:

```
while (scanf("%ld", &num) == 1)
{
      /* loop actions */
}
```

The second form uses `scanf()` in two different ways simultaneously. First, the function call, if successful, places a value in **num**. Second, the function's return value (which is **1** or **0** and not the value of **num**) controls the loop. Because the loop condition is tested at each iteration, `scanf()` is called at each iteration, providing a new **num** and a new test. In other words, C's syntax features let you replace the standard loop format with the following condensed version:

```
while getting and testing the value succeeds
    process the value
```

Now let's take a more formal look at the `while` statement.

The `while` Statement

This is the general form of the `while` loop:

```
while (expression)
      statement
```

The *statement* part can be a simple statement with a terminating semicolon, or it can be a compound statement enclosed in braces.

The examples so far have used *relational* expressions for the expression part; that is, *expression* has been a comparison of values. More generally, you can use any expression. If *expression* is true (or, more generally, nonzero), the statement is executed once, and then the expression is tested again. This cycle of test and execution is repeated until *expression* becomes false (zero). Each cycle is called an *iteration* (see Figure 6.1).

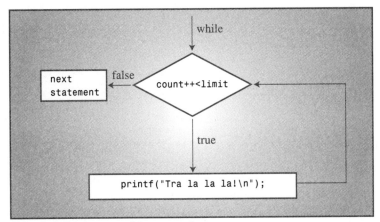

Figure 6.1 Structure of the `while` loop.

Terminating a `while` Loop

Here is a *crucial* point about `while` loops: When you construct a `while` loop, it must include something that changes the value of the test expression so that the expression eventually becomes false. Otherwise, the loop never terminates. (Actually, you can use **break** and an **if** statement to terminate a loop, but you haven't learned about them yet.) Consider this example:

```
index = 1;
while (index < 5)
   printf("Good morning!\n");
```

The preceding fragment prints its cheerful message indefinitely. Why? Because nothing within the loop changes the value of **index** from its initial value of 1. Now consider this:

```
index = 1;
while (--index < 5)
   printf("Good morning!\n");
```

This last fragment isn't much better. It changes the value of **index**, but in the wrong direction! At least this version will terminate eventually when **index** drops below the most negative number that the system can handle.

When a Loop Terminates

It is important to realize that the decision to terminate the loop or to continue takes place only when the test condition is evaluated. For instance, consider the program shown in Listing 6.2.

Listing 6.2   The when.c program.

```c
/* when.c -- when a loop quits */
#include <stdio.h>
int main(void)
{
  int n = 5;

  while (n < 7)                          /* line 7  */
  {
      printf("n = %d\n", n);
      n++;                               /* line 10 */
      printf("Now n = %d\n", n);         /* line 11 */
  }
  return 0;
}
```

Running Listing 6.2 produces the following output:

```
n = 5
Now n = 6
n = 6
Now n = 7
```

The variable n first acquires the value **7** on line 10 during the second cycle of the loop. The program doesn't quit then, however. Instead, it completes the loop (line 11) and quits the loop only when the test condition on line 7 is evaluated for the third time. (The variable n was **5** for the first test and **6** for the second test.)

while: An Entry-Condition Loop

The while loop is a *conditional* loop using an *entry condition*. It is called conditional because the execution of the statement portion depends on the condition described by the test expression, such as (index < 5). The expression is an entry condition because the condition must be met before the body of the loop is entered. In a situation like the following, the body of the loop is never entered because the condition is false to begin with:

```c
index = 10;
while (index++ < 5)
    printf("Have a fair day or better.\n");
```

Change the first line to

```c
index = 3;
```

and the loop will execute.

Syntax Points

One point to keep in mind when using `while` is that only the single statement, simple or compound, following the test condition is part of the loop. Indentation is an aid to the reader, not the computer. Listing 6.3 shows what can happen if you forget this.

Listing 6.3   The `while1.c` program.

```
/* while1.c -- watch your braces */
#include <stdio.h>
int main(void)
{
   int n = 0;

   while (n < 3)
        printf("n is %d\n", n);
        n++;
   printf("That's all this program does\n");
   return 0;
}
```

Running this program produces the following output:

```
n is 0
n is 0
n is 0
n is 0
n is 0
```

(And so on until you kill the program.)

Although this example indents the `n++;` statement, it doesn't enclose it and the preceding statement within braces. Therefore, only the single print statement immediately following the test condition is part of the loop. The variable `n` is never updated, the condition `n < 3` remains eternally true, and you get a loop that goes on printing `n is 0` until you kill the program. This is an example of an *infinite loop*, one that does not quit without outside intervention.

Always remember that the `while` statement itself, even if it uses compound statements, counts syntactically as a single statement. The statement runs from the `while` to the first semicolon or, in the case of using a compound statement, to the terminating brace.

Be careful where you place your semicolons. For instance, consider the program in Listing 6.4.

Listing 6.4   The `while2.c` program.

```
/* while2.c -- watch your semicolons */
#include <stdio.h>
int main(void)
{
   int n = 0;
```

```
    while (n++ < 3);                /* line 7 */
        printf("n is %d\n", n);     /* line 8 */
    printf("That's all this program does.\n");
    return 0;
}
```

This program has the following output:

```
n is 4
That's all this program does.
```

As we said earlier, the loop ends with the first statement, simple or compound, following the test condition. Because there is a semicolon immediately after the test condition on line 7, the loop ends there, because a lone semicolon counts as a statement. The print statement on line 8 is not part of the loop, so n is incremented on each loop, but it is printed only after the loop is exited.

In this example, the test condition is followed with the *null statement*, one that does nothing. In C, the lone semicolon represents the null statement. Occasionally, programmers intentionally use the while statement with a null statement, either to create a time delay or because all the work gets done in the test. For example, suppose you want to skip over input to the first character that isn't whitespace or a digit. You can use a loop like this:

```
while (scanf("%d", &num) == 1)
    ;    /* skip integer input */
```

As long as scanf() reads an integer, it returns 1, and the loop continues. Note that for clarity you put the semicolon (the null statement) on the line below instead of on the same line. This makes it easier to see the null statement when you read a program and also reminds you that the null statement is there deliberately. Even better, use the continue statement discussed in the next chapter.

Which Is Bigger: Using Relational Operators and Expressions

Because while loops often rely on test expressions that make comparisons, comparison expressions merit a closer look. Such expressions are termed *relational expressions*, and the operators that appear in them are called *relational operators*. You have used several already, and Table 6.1 gives a complete list of C relational operators. This table pretty much covers all the possibilities for numerical relationships. (Numbers, even complex ones, are less complex than humans.)

Table 6.1   Relational operators.

Operator	Meaning
<	Is less than
<=	Is less than or equal to
==	Is equal to
>=	Is greater than or equal to
>	Is greater than
!=	Is not equal to

The relational operators are used to form the relational expressions used in `while` statements and in other C statements that we'll discuss later. These statements check to see whether the expression is true or false. Here are three unrelated statements containing examples of relational expressions. The meaning, we hope, is clear.

```
while (number < 6)
{
    printf("Your number is too small.\n");
    scanf("%d", &number);
}

while (ch != '$')
{
    count++;
    scanf("%c", &ch);
}

while (scanf("%f", &num) == 1)
    sum = sum + num;
```

Note in the second example that the relational expressions can be used with characters, too. The machine code (which we have been assuming is ASCII) is used for the comparison. However, you can't use the relational operators to compare strings. Chapter 11, "Character Strings and String Functions," will show you what to use for strings.

The relational operators can be used with floating-point numbers, too. Beware, though; you should limit yourself to using only < and > in floating-point comparisons. The reason is that round-off errors can prevent two numbers from being equal, even though logically they should be. For example, certainly the product of 3 and 1/3 is 1.0. If you express 1/3 as a six-place decimal fraction, the product is .999999, which is not quite equal to 1. The `fabs()` function, declared in the `math.h` header file, can be handy for floating-point tests. This function returns the absolute value of a floating-point value, that is, the value without the algebraic sign. For example, you could test whether a number was close to a desired result with something like this:

```
#include <math.h>
#include <stdio.h>
...
const double ANSWER = 3.14159;
double response;
printf("What is the value of pi?\n");
scanf("%lf", &response);
while (fabs(response - ANSWER) > 0.0001)
{
    printf("Try again!\n");
    scanf("%lf", &response);
}
```

This loop continues to elicit a response until the user gets within 0.0001 of the correct value.

Each relational expression is judged to be "true" or "false" (but never "maybe"). This raises an interesting question.

What Is Truth?

You can answer this age-old question, at least as far as C is concerned. Recall that an expression in C always has a value. This is true even for relational expressions, as the example in Listing 6.5 shows. In it, you print the values of two relational expressions, one true and one false.

Listing 6.5   The t_and_f.c program.

```
/* t_and_f.c -- true and false values in C */
#include <stdio.h>
int main(void)
{
  int true, false;

  true = (10 > 2);    /* value of a true relationship  */
  false = (10 == 2);  /* value of a false relationship */
  printf("true = %d; false = %d \n", true, false);
  return 0;
}
```

Listing 6.5 assigns the values of two relational expressions to two variables. Being straightforward, it assigns **true** the value of a true expression, and **false** the value of a false expression. Running the program produces the following simple output:

```
true = 1; false = 0
```

Aha! For C, a true expression has the value 1, and a false expression has the value 0. Indeed, some C programs use the following construction for loops that are meant to run forever because 1 always is true:

```
while (1)
{
   ...
}
```

What Else Is True?

If you can use a 1 or a 0 as a while statement test expression, can you use other numbers? If so, what happens? Let's experiment by trying the program in Listing 6.6.

Listing 6.6 The truth.c program.

```
/* truth.c -- what values are true? */
#include <stdio.h>
int main(void)
{
  int n = 3;

  while (n)
        printf("%d\n", n--);
  n = -3;
  while (n)
        printf("%2d\n", n++);
  return 0;
}
```

Here are the results:

```
3
2
1
-3
-2
-1
```

The first loop executes when n is 3, 2, and 1, but terminates when n is 0. Similarly, the second loop executes when n is -3, -2, and -1, but terminates when n is 0. More generally, all nonzero values are regarded as "true," and only 0 is recognized as "false." C has a very tolerant notion of truth!

Alternatively, you can say that a while loop executes as long as its test condition evaluates to nonzero. This puts test conditions on a numeric basis instead of a true-false basis. Keep in mind that relational expressions evaluate to 1 if true and to 0 if false, so such expressions really are numeric.

Many programmers make use of this property of test conditions. For example, the phrase while (goats != 0) can be replaced by while (goats) because the expression (goats != 0) and the expression (goats) both become 0, or false, only when goats has the value 0. We think that the second form is not as clear in meaning as the first, but many C programmers prefer the second form. The popular thought has been that the second form is more efficient because it requires fewer computer processing operations when the program runs, but some compilers are clever enough to use the same efficient code for either form. The current tendency is to try for clear code and leave it to clever compilers to maximize the efficiency.

Troubles with Truth

C's tolerant notion of truth can lead to trouble. For example, let's make one subtle change in Listing 6.1, producing the program shown in Listing 6.7.

Listing 6.7   The `trouble.c` program.

```
/* trouble.c -- misuse of = */
#include <stdio.h>
int main(void)
{
  long num;
  long sum = 0L;
  int status;

  printf("Please enter an integer to be summed. ");
  printf("Enter q to quit.\n");
  status = scanf("%ld", &num);
  while (status = 1)
  {
      sum = sum + num;
      printf("Please enter next integer to be summed. ");
      printf("Enter q to quit.\n");
      status = scanf("%ld", &num);
  }
  printf("Those integers sum to %ld\n", sum);
  return 0;
}
```

Running Listing 6.7 produces output like the following:

```
Please enter an integer to be summed. Enter q to quit.
20
Please enter next integer to be summed. Enter q to quit.
5
Please enter next integer to be summed. Enter q to quit.
30
Please enter next integer to be summed. Enter q to quit.
q
Please enter next integer to be summed. Enter q to quit.
Please enter next integer to be summed. Enter q to quit.
Please enter next integer to be summed. Enter q to quit.
Please enter next integer to be summed. Enter q to quit.
```

(And so on until you kill the program.)

This troublesome example made a change in the `while` test condition, replacing `status == 1` with `status = 1`. The second statement is an assignment statement, so it gives `status` the value 1. Furthermore, the value of an assignment statement is the value of the left side, so `status = 1` has the same numerical value of 1. So for all practical purposes, the `while` loop is the same as using `while (1)`; that is, it is a loop that never quits. You enter q, and `status` is set to 0, but the loop test resets `status` to 1 and starts another cycle.

You might wonder why, because the program keeps looping, the user doesn't get a chance to type in any more input after entering q. When scanf() fails to read the specified form of input, it leaves the nonconforming input in place to be read the next time. When scanf() tries to read the q as an integer and fails, therefore, it leaves the q there. During the next loop cycle, scanf() attempts to read where it left off the last time: at the q once again. Once again, scanf() fails to read the q as an integer, so not only does this example set up an infinite loop, it also creates a loop of infinite failure, a daunting concept. It is fortunate that computers, as yet, lack feelings. Following stupid instructions eternally is no better or worse to a computer than successfully predicting the stock market for the next ten years.

Don't use = for ==. Some computer languages (BASIC, for example) do use the same symbol for both the assignment operator and the relational equality operator, but the two operations are quite different (see Figure 6.2). The assignment operator assigns a value to the left-hand variable. The relational equality operator, however, checks to see whether the left-hand and right-hand sides are already equal. It doesn't change the value of the left-hand variable, if one is present.

canoes = 5	←Assigns the value 5 to canoes
canoes == 5	←Checks to see whether canoes has the value 5

Be careful about using the correct operator. A compiler will let you use the wrong form, yielding results other than what you expect.

comparison

```
canoes == 5
```
== checks to see if the
value of canoes is 5

assignment

```
canoes = 5
```
= gives canoes
the value of 5

Figure 6.2 The relational operator == and the assignment operator =.

To sum up, the relational operators are used to form relational expressions. Relational expressions have the value 1 if true and 0 if false. Statements (such as while and if) that normally use relational expressions as tests can use any expression as a test, with non-zero values recognized as "true" and zero values as "false."

Precedence of Relational Operators

The precedence of the relational operators is less than that of the arithmetic operators, including + and -, and greater than that of assignment operators. This means, for example, that

```
x > y + 2
```

means the same as

```
x > (y + 2)
```

and that

```
x = y > 2
```

means

```
x = (y > 2)
```

That is, x is assigned 1 if y is greater than 2 and is 0 otherwise; x is not assigned the value of y.

The relational operators are themselves organized into two different priorities.

Higher-priority group: <   <=   >   >=
Lower-priority group: ==   !=

Like most other operators, the relational operators associate from left to right. Therefore,

```
ex != wye == zee
```

is the same as

```
(ex != wye) == zee
```

First, C checks to see if ex and wye are unequal. Then the resulting value of 1 or 0 (true or false) is compared to the value of zee. We don't anticipate using this sort of construction, but we feel it is our duty to point out such sidelights.

Table 6.2 shows the priorities of the operators introduced so far, and Appendix B, "C Operators," has a complete precedence ranking of all operators.

Table 6.2 Operator precedence.

Operators (From High to Low Precedence)	Associativity
( )	L–R
- + ++ -- sizeof (type) (all unary)	R–L
* / %	L–R

Operators (From High to Low Precedence)	Associativity
+ -	L–R
< > <= >=	L–R
== !=	L–R
=	R–L

Summary: The `while` Statement

Keyword:

`while`

General Comments:

The `while` statement creates a loop that repeats until the test expression becomes false, or zero. The `while` statement is an entry-condition loop; that is, the decision to go through one more pass of the loop is made before the loop is traversed. Therefore, it is possible that the loop is never traversed. The statement part of the form can be a simple statement or a compound statement.

Form:

```
while (expression)
        statement
```

The *statement* portion is repeated until the *expression* becomes false or zero.

Examples:

```
while (n++ < 100)
    printf(" %d %d\n",n, 2 * n + 1); /* single statement */

while (fargo < 1000)
{                                    /* compound statement */
    fargo = fargo + step;
    step = 2 * step;
}
```

Summary:
Relational Operators and Expressions

Relational Operators:

Each relational operator compares the value at its left to the value at its right.

    <   Is less than

    <=   Is less than or equal to

==	Is equal to
>=	Is greater than or equal to
>	Is greater than
!=	Is unequal to

Relational Expressions:

A simple relational expression consists of a relational operator with an operand on each side. If the relation is true, the relational expression has the value 1. If the relation is false, the relational expression has the value 0.

Examples:

5 > 2 is true and has the value 1.

(2 + a) == a is false and has the value 0.

Indefinite Loops and Counting Loops

Some of the while loop examples have been *indefinite* loops. That means you don't know in advance how many times the loop will be executed before the expression becomes false. For instance, when Listing 6.1 used an interactive loop to sum integers, you didn't know beforehand how many integers would be entered. Other examples, however, have been *counting* loops. They execute a predetermined number of repetitions. Listing 6.8 is a short example of a while counting loop.

Listing 6.8   The sweetie1.c program.

```
/* sweetie1.c -- a counting loop */
#include <stdio.h>
#define NUMBER 22
int main(void)
{
  int count = 1;                      /* initialization  */

  while (count <= NUMBER)             /* test           */
  {
     printf("Be my Valentine!\n");    /* action         */
     count++;                         /* update count   */
  }
  return 0;
}
```

Although the form used in Listing 6.8 works fine, it is not the best choice for this situation because the actions defining the loop are not all gathered together. Let's elaborate on that point.

Three actions are involved in setting up a loop that is to be repeated a fixed number of times:

1. A counter must be initialized.

2. The counter is compared with some limiting value.

3. The counter is incremented each time the loop is traversed.

The `while` loop condition takes care of the comparison. The increment operator takes care of the incrementing. In Listing 6.8, the incrementing is done at the end of the loop. This choice makes it possible to omit the incrementing accidentally. So it would be better to combine the test and update actions into one expression by using `count++ <= NUMBER`, but the initialization of the counter is still done outside the loop, making it possible to forget to initialize a counter. Experience teaches us that what might happen, will happen eventually, so let's look at a control statement that avoids these problems.

The `for` Loop

The `for` loop gathers all three actions into one place. By using a `for` loop, you can replace the preceding program with the one shown in Listing 6.9.

Listing 6.9 The `sweetie2.c` program.

```
/* sweetie2.c -- a counting loop using for */
#include <stdio.h>
#define NUMBER 22
int main(void)
{
  int count;

  for (count = 1; count <= NUMBER; count++)
      printf("Be my Valentine!\n");
  return 0;
}
```

The parentheses following the keyword `for` contain three expressions separated by two semicolons. The first expression is the initialization. It is done just once, when the `for` loop first starts. The second expression is the test condition; it is evaluated before each potential execution of a loop. When the expression is false (when `count` is greater than `NUMBER`), the loop is terminated. The third expression, the change or update, is evaluated at the end of each loop. Listing 6.9 uses it to increment the value of `count`, but it needn't be restricted to that use. The `for` statement is completed by following it with one simple or compound statement. Each of the three control expressions is a full expression, so any side effects in a control expression, such as incrementing a variable, take place before the program evaluates another expression. Figure 6.3 summarizes the structure of a `for` loop.

To show another example, Listing 6.10 uses the `for` loop in a program that prints a table of cubes.

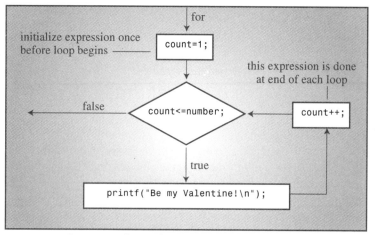

Figure 6.3 Structure of a for loop.

Listing 6.10   The `for_cube.c` program.

```
/* for_cube.c -- using a for loop to make a table of cubes */
#include <stdio.h>
int main(void)
{
  int num;

  printf("    n    n cubed\n");
  for (num = 1; num <= 6; num++)
     printf("%5d %5d\n", num, num*num*num);
  return 0;
}
```

Listing 6.10 prints the integers 1 through 6 and their cubes.

```
 n    n cubed
 1      1
 2      8
 3     27
 4     64
 5    125
 6    216
```

The first line of the **for** loop tells us immediately all the information about the loop parameters: the starting value of **num**, the final value of **num**, and the amount that **num** increases on each looping.

Using for for Flexibility!

Although the **for** loop looks similar to the FORTRAN **DO** loop, the Pascal **FOR** loop, and the BASIC **FOR...NEXT** loop, it is much more flexible than any of them. This flexibility stems from how the three expressions in a **for** specification can be used. So far, you have used the first expression to initialize a counter, the second expression to express the limit for the counter, and the third expression to increase the value of the counter by 1. When used this way, the C for statement is very much like the others we have mentioned, but there are many more possibilities. Here are nine variations:

1. You can use the decrement operator to count down instead of up.

```c
#include <stdio.h>
int main(void)
 {
   int secs;

   for (secs = 5; secs > 0; secs--)
        printf("%d seconds!\n", secs);
   printf("We have ignition!\n");
   return 0;
 }
```

Here is the output:

```
5 seconds!
4 seconds!
3 seconds!
2 seconds!
1 seconds!
We have ignition!
```

2. You can count by twos, tens, and so on, if you want:

```c
#include <stdio.h>
int main(void)
 {
   int n;              /* count by 13s */

   for (n = 2;  n < 60; n = n + 13)
        printf("%d \n", n);
   return 0;
 }
```

This would increase n by 13 during each cycle, printing the following:

```
 2
15
28
41
54
```

3. You can count by characters instead of by numbers:

```c
#include <stdio.h>
int main(void)
{
   char ch;
```

```
    for (ch = 'a'; ch <= 'z'; ch++)
        printf("The ASCII value for %c is %d.\n", ch, ch);
    return 0;
}
```

An abridged output looks like this:

```
The ASCII value for a is 97.
The ASCII value for b is 98.
...
The ASCII value for x is 120.
The ASCII value for y is 121.
The ASCII value for z is 122.
```

The program works because characters are stored as integers, so this loop really counts by integers anyway.

4. You can test some condition other than the number of iterations. In the for_cube program, you can replace

```
for (num = 1; num <= 6; num++)
```

with

```
for (num = 1; num*num*num <= 216; num++)
```

You would use this test condition if you were more concerned with limiting the size of the cube than with limiting the number of iterations.

5. You can let a quantity increase geometrically instead of arithmetically; that is, instead of adding a fixed amount each time, you can multiply by a fixed amount:

```
#include <stdio.h>
int main(void)
  {
   double debt;

   for (debt = 100.0; debt < 150.0; debt = debt * 1.1)
        printf("Your debt is now $%.2f.\n", debt);
    return 0;
}
```

This program fragment multiplies **debt** by 1.1 for each cycle, increasing it by 10% each time. The output looks like this:

```
Your debt is now $100.00.
Your debt is now $110.00.
Your debt is now $121.00.
Your debt is now $133.10.
Your debt is now $146.41.
```

6. You can use any legal expression you want for the third expression. Whatever you put in will be updated for each iteration.

```
#include <stdio.h>
int main(void)
{
    int x;
    int y = 55;

    for (x = 1; y <= 75; y = (++x * 5) + 50)
        printf("%10d %10d\n", x, y);
    return 0;
}
```

This loop prints the values of x and of the algebraic expression ++x * 5
+ 50. The output looks like this:

```
        1          55
        2          60
        3          65
        4          70
        5          75
```

Notice that the test involved y, not x. Each of the three expressions in the
for loop control can use different variables. (Note that although this
example is valid, it does not show good style. The program would have
been clearer if we hadn't mixed the updating process with an algebraic
calculation.)

7. You can even leave one or more expressions blank (but don't omit the
    semicolons). Just be sure to include within the loop itself some statement
    that eventually causes the loop to terminate.

```
#include <stdio.h>
int main(void)
 {
   int ans, n;

   ans = 2;
   for (n = 3; ans <= 25; )
        ans = ans * n;
   printf("n = %d; ans = %d.\n", n, ans);
   return 0;
}
```

Here is the output:

n = 3; ans = 54.

The loop keeps the value of n at 3. The variable ans starts with the value
2, then increases to 6 and 18, and obtains a final value of 54. (The value
18 is less than 25, so the for loop goes through one more iteration, multiplying 18 by 3 to get 54.) Incidentally, an empty middle control expression is considered to be true, so the following loop goes on forever:

```
for (; ; )
    printf("I want some action\n");
```

8. The first expression need not initialize a variable. It could, instead, be a `printf()` statement of some sort. Just remember that the first expression is evaluated or executed only once, before any other parts of the loop are executed.

```
#include <stdio.h>
int main(void)
{
    int num;

    for (printf("Keep entering numbers!\n"); num != 6;  )
          scanf("%d", &num);
    printf("That's the one I want!\n");
    return 0;
}
```

This fragment prints the first message once and then keeps accepting numbers until you enter a 6:

```
Keep entering numbers!
3
5
8
6
That's the one I want!
```

9. The parameters of the loop expressions can be altered by actions within the loop. For example, suppose you have the loop set up like this:

```
for (n = 1; n < 10000; n = n + delta)
```

If, after a few iterations, your program decides that `delta` is too small or too large, an `if` statement (refer to Chapter 7, "C Control Statements: Branching and Jumps") inside the loop can change the size of `delta`. In an interactive program, `delta` can be changed by the user as the loop runs.

In short, the freedom you have in selecting the expressions that control a `for` loop makes this loop able to do much more than just perform a fixed number of iterations. The power of the `for` loop is enhanced further by the operators we will discuss shortly.

Summary: The for Statement

Keyword:

for

General Comments:

The `for` statement uses three control expressions, separated by semicolons, to control a looping process. The `initialize` expression is executed once, before any of the loop statements are executed. Then the `test` expression is evaluated, and if it is true (or nonzero), the loop is cycled through once.

Then the `update` expression is evaluated, and it is time to check the `test` expression again. The `for` statement is an entry-condition loop—the decision to go through one more pass of the loop is made before the loop is traversed. Therefore, it is possible that the loop is never traversed. The `state-ment` part of the form can be a simple statement or a compound statement.

Form:

```
for (initialize ; test ; update)
     statement
```

The loop is repeated until `test` becomes false or zero.

Example:

```
for (n = 0;  n < 10 ; n++)
     printf(" %d %d\n", n, 2 * n + 1);
```

More Assignment Operators: +=, -=, *=, /=, %=

C has several assignment operators. The most basic one, of course, is =, which simply assigns the value of the expression at its right to the variable at its left. The other assignment operators update variables. Each is used with a variable name to its left and an expression to its right. The variable is assigned a new value equal to its old value adjusted by the value of the expression at the right. The exact adjustment depends on the operator, for example,

`scores += 20`	is the same as	`scores = scores + 20`
`dimes -= 2`	is the same as	`dimes = dimes - 2`
`bunnies *= 2`	is the same as	`bunnies = bunnies * 2`
`time /= 2.73`	is the same as	`time = time / 2.73`
`reduce %= 3`	is the same as	`reduce = reduce % 3`

In the preceding list, we used simple numbers on the right, but we could have used more elaborate expressions:

`x *= 3 * y + 12`   is the same as   `x = x * (3 * y + 12)`

The assignment operators we've just discussed have the same low priority that = does, that is, less than that of + or *. This low priority is reflected in the last example, in which 12 is added to 3 * y before multiplying the result by x.

You are not required to use these forms. They are, however, more compact, and they may produce more efficient machine code than the longer form. The combination assignment operators are particularly useful when you are trying to squeeze something complex into a `for` loop specification.

The Comma Operator

The comma operator extends the flexibility of the `for` loop by enabling you to include more than one initialization or update expression in a single `for` loop specification. For example, Listing 6.11 shows a program that prints first-class postage rates. (At the time of this writing, the rate is 32 cents for the first ounce and 23 cents for each additional ounce. You can check www.usps.gov for the current rates.)

Listing 6.11   The `postage.c` program.

```
/* postage.c -- first-class postage rates */
#include <stdio.h>
#define FIRST 32
#define NEXT  23
int main(void)
{
    int ounces, cost;

    printf(" ounces   cost\n");
    for(ounces=1, cost=FIRST; ounces<= 16; ounces++,
            cost += NEXT)
        printf("%5d %7d\n", ounces, cost);
    return 0;
}
```

The first four lines of output look like this:

```
ounces   cost
   1      32
   2      55
   3      78
```

The program uses the comma operator in the initialize and the update expressions. Its presence in the first expression causes `ounces` and `cost` to be initialized. Its second occurrence causes `ounces` to be increased by 1 and `cost` to be increased by 23 (the value of `NEXT`) for each iteration. All the calculations are done in the `for` loop specifications (see Figure 6.4)!

The comma operator is not restricted to `for` loops, but that's where it is most often used. The operator has two further properties. First, it guarantees that the expressions it separates are evaluated in a left-to-right order. (In other words, the comma is a sequence point, so all side effects to the left of the comma take place before the program moves to the right of the comma.) Therefore, `ounces` is initialized before `cost`. The order is not important for this example, but it would be important if the expression for `cost` contained `ounces`. Suppose, for instance, that you had this expression:

```
ounces++, cost = ounces * FIRST
```

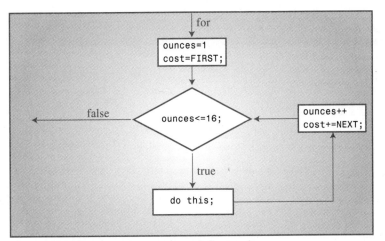

Figure 6.4 The comma operator and the `for` loop.

This would increment **ounces**, and then use the new value for **ounces** in the second subexpression. The comma being a sequence point guarantees that the side effects of the left subexpression occur before the right subexpression is evaluated.

Second, the value of the whole comma expression is the value of the right-hand member. The effect of the statement

```
x = (y = 3, (z = ++y + 2) + 5);
```

is to first assign **3** to **y**, increment **y** to **4**, then add **2** to **4** and assign the resulting value of **6** to **z**, next add **5** to **z**, and finally assign the resulting value of **11** to **x**. Why anyone would do this is beyond the scope of this book. On the other hand, suppose you get careless and use comma notation in writing a number:

```
houseprice = 249,500;
```

This is not a syntax error! Instead, C interprets the right-hand side as a comma expression, with **houseprice = 249** being the left subexpression and **500** the right subexpression. Therefore, the value of the whole comma expression is the value of the right-hand expression, and the left substatement assigns the value **249** to the **houseprice** variable. On the other hand, the statement

```
houseprice = (249,500);
```

assigns 500, the value of the right subexpression to **houseprice**.

The comma also is used as a separator, so the commas in

```
char ch, date;
```

```
andprintf("%d %d\n", chimps, chumps);
```

are separators, not comma operators.

Assignment Operators:
Each of these operators updates the variable at its left by the value at its right, using the indicated operation. The abbreviations *R—H* and *L—H* stand for right-hand for left-hand.

+=	Adds the R–H quantity to the L–H variable
-=	Subtracts the R–H quantity from the L–H variable
*=	Multiplies the L–H variable by the R–H quantity
/=	Divides the L–H variable by the R–H quantity
%=	Gives the remainder obtained from dividing the L–H variable by the R–H quantity

Example:

```
rabbits *= 1.6;    is the same as    rabbits = rabbits * 1.6;
```

The Comma Operator:
The comma operator links two expressions into one and guarantees that the leftmost expression is evaluated first. It is typically used to include more information in a **for** loop control expression. The value of the whole expression is the value of the right-hand expression.

Example:

```
for (step = 2, fargo = 0; fargo < 1000; step *= 2)
        fargo += step;
```

Zeno Meets the `for` Loop

Let's see how the **for** loop and the comma operator can help solve an old paradox. The Greek philosopher Zeno once argued that an arrow will never reach its target. First, he said, the arrow covers half the distance to the target. Then it has to cover half of the remaining distance. Then it still has half of what's left to cover, ad infinitum. Because the journey has an infinite number of parts, Zeno argued, it would take the arrow an infinite amount of time to reach its journey's end. We doubt, however, that Zeno would have volunteered to be a target just on the strength of this argument.

Let's take a quantitative approach and suppose that it takes the arrow 1 second to travel the first half. Then it would take 1/2 second to travel half of what was left, 1/4 second to travel half of what was left next, and so on. You can represent the total time by the following infinite series:

```
1 + 1/2 + 1/4 + 1/8 + 1/16 +....
```

The short program in Listing 6.12 finds the sum of the first few terms.

Listing 6.12   The zeno.c program.

```c
/* zeno.c -- series sum */
#include <stdio.h>

int main(void)
{
 int count;
 double time, x;
 int limit;
 printf("How many terms do you want?\n");
 scanf("%d", &limit);

 for (time=0, x=1, count=1; count <= limit; count++, x *= 2.0)
 {
    time += 1.0/x;
    printf("time = %f when count = %d.\n", time, count);
 }
 return 0;
}
```

Here is the output for 15 terms:

```
How many terms do you want?
15
time = 1.000000 when count = 1.
time = 1.500000 when count = 2.
time = 1.750000 when count = 3.
time = 1.875000 when count = 4.
time = 1.937500 when count = 5.
time = 1.968750 when count = 6.
time = 1.984375 when count = 7.
time = 1.992188 when count = 8.
time = 1.996094 when count = 9.
time = 1.998047 when count = 10.
time = 1.999023 when count = 11.
time = 1.999512 when count = 12.
time = 1.999756 when count = 13.
time = 1.999878 when count = 14.
time = 1.999939 when count = 15.
```

You can see that although you keep adding more terms, the total seems to level out. Indeed, mathematicians have proven that the total approaches 2.0 as the number of terms approaches infinity, just as this program suggests. Here's one demonstration. Suppose you let S represent the sum:

$$S = 1 + 1/2 + 1/4 + 1/8 + ...$$

Here the ellipses mean "and so on." Then dividing by 2 gives

$$S/2 = 1/2 + 1/4 + 1/8 + 1/16 + ...$$

Subtracting the second expression from the first gives

$$S - S/2 = 1 + 1/2 - 1/2 + 1/4 - 1/4 + ...$$

Except for the initial value of 1, each other value occurs in pairs, one positive and one negative, so those terms cancel each, leaving

```
S/2 = 1.
```

Then, multiplying both sides by 2 gives

```
S = 2.
```

What about the program itself? It shows that you can use more than one comma operator in an expression. You initialized time, x, and count. After you set up the conditions for the loop, the program itself is extremely brief.

An Exit-Condition Loop: do while

The while loop and the for loop are both entry-condition loops. The test condition is checked *before* each iteration of the loop, so it is possible for the statements in the loop to never execute. C also has an *exit-condition* loop in which the condition is checked *after* each iteration of the loop, guaranteeing that statements are executed at least once. This variety is called a do while loop. Listing 6.13 shows an example.

Listing 6.13   The dowhile.c program.

```
/* dowhile.c -- exit condition loop */
#include <stdio.h>
int main(void)
{
    char ch;

    do
    {
        scanf("%c", &ch);
        printf("%c", ch);
    } while (ch != '#');
    return 0;
}
```

The program in Listing 6.13 reads input characters and reprints them until the # character shows up. Here is a sample run:

I choose door #3!
I choose door #

How is this program different from a while loop version such as that in Listing 6.14?

Listing 6.14   The entry.c program.

```
/* entry.c -- entry condition loop */
#include <stdio.h>
int main(void)
```

```
{
   char ch;

   scanf("%c", &ch);
   while (ch != '#')
   {
        printf("%c", ch);
        scanf("%c", &ch);
   }
   return 0;
}
```

The behavioral difference appears when the # character is read. The `while` loop prints all the characters *up to* the first # character:

I choose door #3!
I choose door

The `do while` loop, however, printed all the characters *up to and including* the # character. Only after it has printed the # character does the `do while` loop check to see if a # character has shown up. In a `do while` loop, that action comes before the test condition.

This is the general form of the `do while` loop:

```
do
     statement
while ( expression );
```

The statement can be simple or compound. Note that the `do while` loop itself counts as a statement and therefore requires a terminating semicolon. Also see Figure 6.5.

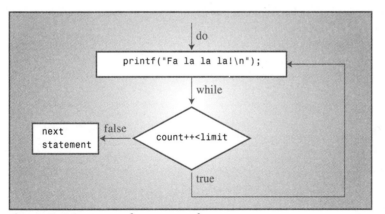

Figure 6.5 Structure of a `do while` loop.

A `do while` loop is always executed at least once because the test is made after the body of the loop has been executed. A `for` loop or a `while` loop, on the other hand, may be executed zero times because the test is made before execution. You should restrict the use of `do while` loops to cases that require at least one iteration. For example, a password program could include a loop along these pseudocode lines:

```
do
{
    prompt for password
    read user input
} while (input not equal to password) ;
```

Avoid a `do while` structure of the type shown in the following pseudocode:
```
ask user if he or she wants to continue

do
some clever stuff
while (answer is yes)
```

Here, after the user answers "no," some clever stuff gets done anyway because the test comes too late.

Summary: The `do while` Statement

Keywords:

do, while

General Comments:

The `do while` statement creates a loop that repeats until the test `expression` becomes false or zero. The `do while` statement is an exit-condition loop—the decision to go through one more pass of the loop is made after the loop has been traversed. Therefore, the loop must be executed at least once. The `statement` part of the form can be a simple statement or a compound statement.

Form:

```
do
    statement
while (expression);
```

The `statement` portion is repeated until the `expression` becomes false or zero.

Example:

```
do
    scanf("%d", &number);
while (number != 20);
```

Which Loop?

When you decide you need a loop, which one should you use? First, decide whether you need an entry-condition loop or an exit-condition loop. Your answer should usually be an entry-condition loop. There are several reasons computer scientists consider an entry-condition loop superior. One is the general principle that it is better to look before you leap (or loop) than after. A second is that a program is easier to read if the loop test is found at the beginning of the loop. Finally, in many uses, it is important that the loop be skipped entirely if the test is not initially met.

Assume you need an entry-condition loop. Should it be a `for` or a `while`? This is partly a matter of taste, because what you can do with one, you can do with the other. To make a `for` loop like a `while`, you can omit the first and third expressions. For example,

```
for ( ;test; )
```

is the same as

```
while (test)
```

To make a `while` like a `for`, preface it with an initialization and include update statements. For example,

```
initialize;
while (test)
{
  body;
  update;
}
```

is the same as

```
for (initialize; test; update)
    body;
```

In terms of style, a `for` loop is appropriate when the loop involves initializing and updating a variable, and a `while` loop is better when the conditions are otherwise. A `while` loop is natural for the following condition:

```
while (scanf("%ld", &num) == 1)
```

The `for` loop is a more natural choice for loops involving counting with an index:

```
for (count = 1; count <= 100; count++)
```

Nested Loops

A *nested loop* is one loop inside another loop. A common use for nested loops is to display data in rows and columns. One loop can handle, say, all the columns in a row, and the second loop handles the rows. Listing 6.15 shows a simple example.

Listing 6.15   The rows1.c program.

```
/* rows1.c -- uses nested loops */
#include <stdio.h>
#define ROWS  6
#define CHARS 10
int main(void)
{
    int row;
    char ch;

    for (row = 0; row < ROWS; row++)              /* line 10 */
    {
        for (ch = 'A'; ch < ('A' + CHARS); ch++)  /* line 12 */
            printf("%c", ch);
        printf("\n");
    }
    return 0;
}
```

Running the program produces this output:

```
ABCDEFGHIJ
ABCDEFGHIJ
ABCDEFGHIJ
ABCDEFGHIJ
ABCDEFGHIJ
ABCDEFGHIJ
```

Discussion

The for loop beginning on line 10 is called an *outer* loop, and the loop beginning on line 12 is called an *inner* loop because it is inside the other loop. The outer loop starts with row having a value of 0 and terminates when row reaches 6. Therefore, the outer loop goes through six cycles, with row having the values 0 through 5. The first statement in each cycle is the inner for loop. This loop goes through ten cycles, printing the characters A through J on the same line. The second statement of the outer loop is printf("\n");. This statement starts a new line so that the next time the inner loop is run, the output is on a new line.

Note that, with a nested loop, the inner loop runs through its full range of iterations for each single iteration of the outer loop. In the last example, the inner loop prints ten characters to a row, and the outer loop creates six rows.

A Nested Variation

In the preceding example, the inner loop did the same thing for each cycle of the outer loop. You can make the inner loop behave differently each cycle by making part of the inner loop depend on the outer loop. Listing 6.16, for example, alters the last program slightly by making the starting character of the inner loop depend on the cycle number of the outer loop.

Listing 6.16   The rows2.c program.

```
/* rows2.c -- using dependent nested loops */
#include <stdio.h>
#define ROWS  6
#define CHARS 6
int main(void)
{
    int row;
    char ch;

    for (row = 0; row < ROWS; row++)
    {
        for (ch = ('A' + row);  ch < ('A' + CHARS); ch++)
            printf("%c", ch);
        printf("\n");
    }
     return 0;
}
```

This time the output is as follows:

```
ABCDEF
BCDEF
CDEF
DEF
EF
F
```

Because row is added to 'A' during each cycle of the outer loop, ch is initialized in each row to one character later in the alphabet. The test condition, however, is unaltered, so each row still ends on F. This results in one fewer character being printed in each row.

Arrays

Arrays are important features in many programs. They enable you to store several items of related information in a convenient fashion. We will devote all of Chapter 10, "Arrays and Pointers," to arrays, but because arrays often are used with loops, we want to introduce them now.

An array is a series of values of the same type, such as 10 chars or 15 ints, stored sequentially. The whole array bears a single name, and the individual items, or elements, are accessed by using an integer index. For instance, the declaration

```
float debts[20];
```

announces that debts is an array with 20 elements, each of which can hold a type float value. The first element of the array is called debts[0], the second element is called debts[1], and so on, up to debts[19]. Note that the numbering of array elements starts with 0, not 1. Each element can be assigned a float value. For example, you can have the following:

```
debts[5] = 32.54;
debts[6] = 1.2e+21;
```

An array can be of any data type.

```
int nannies[22];    /* an array to hold 22 integers      */
char actors[26];    /* an array to hold 26 characters     */
long big[500];      /* an array to hold 500 long integers */
```

Earlier, for example, we talked about strings, which are a special case of `char` arrays. (A `char` array, in general, is one whose elements are assigned `char` values. A string is a `char` array in which the null character, \0, is used to mark the end of the string. See Figure 6.6.)

character array but not a string

character array and a string

null character

Figure 6.6 Character arrays and strings.

The numbers used to identify the array elements are called subscripts, indices, or offsets. The subscripts must be integers, and, as mentioned, the subscripting begins with 0. The array elements are stored next to each other in memory, as shown in Figure 6.7.

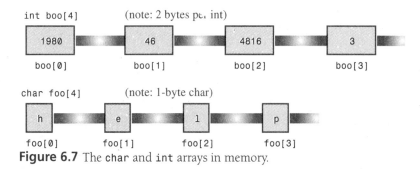

Figure 6.7 The `char` and `int` arrays in memory.

Using a `for` Loop with an Array

There are many, many uses for arrays. Listing 6.17 is a relatively simple one. It's a program that reads in ten golf scores, which will be processed later on. By using an array, you avoid inventing ten different variable names, one for each score. Also, you can use a `for` loop to do the reading. The program goes on to report the sum of the scores and their average and a handicap, which is the difference between the average and a standard score, or par.

Listing 6.17 The scores_in.c program.

```c
/* scores_in.c -- uses loops for array processing */
#include <stdio.h>
#define SIZE 10
#define PAR 72
int main(void)
{
  int index, score[SIZE];
  int sum = 0;
  float average;

  printf("Enter %d golf scores:\n", SIZE);
  for (index = 0; index < SIZE; index++)
    scanf("%d", &score[index]);  /* read in the ten scores */
  printf("The scores read in are as follows:\n");
  for (index = 0; index < SIZE; index++)
    printf("%5d", score[index]); /* verify input            */
  printf("\n");
  for (index = 0; index < SIZE; index++)
    sum += score[index];         /* add them up             */
  average = (float) sum / SIZE;   /* time-honored method     */
  printf("Sum of scores = %d, average = %.2f\n", sum, average);
  printf("That's a handicap of %.0f.\n", average - PAR);
  return 0;
}
```

Let's see if Listing 6.17 works; then we can make a few comments. Here is the output:

```
Enter 10 scores:
Enter 10 golf scores:
102  98  112  108  105  103
99  101  96  102 100
The scores read in are as follows:
  102   98  112  108  105  103   99  101   96  102
Sum of scores = 1026, average = 102.60
That's a handicap of 31.
```

It works, so let's check out some of the details. First, note that although you typed 11 numbers, only 10 were read because the reading loop reads just 10 values. Because scanf() skips over whitespace, you can type all 10 numbers on one line or place each number on its own line, or, as in this case, use a mixture of newlines and spaces to separate the input. (Because input is buffered, the numbers are sent to the program only when you press the Enter key.)

Next, using arrays and loops is much more convenient than using 10 separate scanf() statements and 10 separate printf() statements to read in and verify the 10 scores. The for loop offers a simple and direct way to use the array subscripts. Notice that an element of a int array is handled like an int variable. To read the int variable fue, you would use scanf("%d", &fue). Listing 6.17 is reading the int element score[index], so it uses scanf("%d", &score[index]).

This example illustrates several style points. First, it's a good idea to use a #define directive to create a manifest constant (SIZE) to specify the size of the array. You use this constant in defining the array and in setting the loop limits. If you later need to expand the program to handle 20 scores, simply redefine `SIZE` to be 20. You don't have to change every part of the program that uses the array size.

Second, the idiom

```
for (index = 0; index < SIZE; index++)
```

is a handy one for processing an array of size `SIZE`. It's important to get the right array limits. The first element has index `0`, and the loop starts by setting `index` to `0`. Because the numbering starts with `0`, the element index for the last element is `SIZE - 1`. That is, the tenth element is `score[9]`. Using the test condition `index < SIZE` accomplishes this, making the last value of `index` used in the loop `SIZE - 1`.

Third, a good practice is to have a program repeat or "echo" the values it has just read in. This helps ensure that the program is processing the data you think it is.

Finally, note that Listing 6.17 uses three separate `for` loops. You might wonder if this is really necessary. Could you have combined some of the operations in one loop? The answer is yes, you could have done so. That would have made the program more compact. However, you should be swayed by the principle of *modularity*. The idea behind this term is that a program should be broken into separate units, with each unit having one task to perform. This makes a program easier to read. Perhaps even more important, modularity makes it much easier to update or modify a program if different parts of the program are not intermingled. When you know enough about functions, you could make each unit into a function, enhancing the modularity of the program.

A Loop Example Using a Function Return Value

For the last example in this chapter, you'll design a function that calculates the result of raising a number to an integer power. (For the serious number-cruncher, the `math.h` library provides a more powerful power function called `pow()` that allows floating-point exponents.) The three main tasks in this exercise are devising the algorithm for calculating the answer, expressing the algorithm in a function that returns the answer, and providing a convenient way of testing the function.

First, let's look at an algorithm. Keep the function simple by restricting it to positive integer powers. Then, if you want to raise **a** to the **b** power, you have to multiply **a** times itself **b** times. This is a natural task for a loop. You can set a variable **pow** to 1 and then multiply it by **a** repeatedly:

```
for(i = 1; i <= b; i++)
    pow *= a;
```

Recall that the `*=` operator multiplies the left side by the right side. After the first loop cycle, **pow** is 1 times **a**, or **a**. After the second cycle, **pow** is its previous value (a) times **a**, or **a** squared, and so on. The `for` loop is natural in this context because the loop is executed a predetermined (after **b** is known) number of times.

Now that you have an algorithm, you should decide which data types to use. The exponent b, being an integer, should be type int. To allow maximum range in values for a and its power, make a and pow type double.

Next, let's consider how to put the function together. You need to give the function two values, and the function should give back one. To get information to the function, you can use two arguments, one double and one int, specifying which number to raise to what power. How do you arrange for the function to return a value to the calling program? To write a function with a return value, do the following:

1. When you define a function, state the type of value it returns.

2. Use the keyword return to indicate the value to be returned.

For example, you can do this:

```
double power(double a, int b)   /* power() returns type double */
{
  double pow = 1.0;
  int i;

  for(i = 1; i <= b; i++)
      pow *= a;
  return pow;                    /* return the value of pow    */
}
```

To declare the function type, preface the function name with the type, just as you do when declaring a variable. The keyword return causes the function to return the following value to the calling function. Here you return the value of a variable, but you can return the value of expressions, too. For instance, the following is a valid statement:

```
return 2 * x + b;
```

The function would compute the value of the expression and return it. In the calling function, the return value can be assigned to another variable, can be used as a value in an expression, can be used as an argument to another function, as in printf("%f", power(6.28, 3)), or can be ignored.

Now let's use the function in a program. To test the function, it would be convenient to be able to feed several values to the function to see how the function reacts. This suggests setting up an input loop. The natural choice is the while loop. You can use scanf() to read in two values at a time. If successful in reading two values, scanf() returns the value 2, so you can control the loop by comparing the scanf() return value to 2. One more point: To use the power() function in your program, you need to declare it, just as you declare variables that the program uses. Listing 6.18 shows the program.

Listing 6.18   The power.c program.

```
/* power.c -- raises numbers to integer powers */
#include <stdio.h>
double power(double a, int b);  /* ANSI prototype */
int main(void)
```

```
{
  double x, xpow;
  int n;

  printf("Enter a number and the positive integer power");
  printf(" to which\nthe number will be raised. Enter q");
  printf(" to quit.\n");
  while (scanf("%lf%d", &x, &n) == 2)
  {
      xpow = power(x,n);        /* function call          */
      printf("%.3g to the power %d is %.5g\n", x, n, xpow);
      printf("Enter next pair of numbers or q to quit.\n");
  }
  printf("Hope you enjoyed this power trip — bye!\n");
  return 0;
}
double power(double a, int b)   /* function definition    */
{
  double pow = 1;
  int i;

  for(i = 1; i <= b; i++)
      pow *= a;
  return pow;                   /* return the value of pow */
}
```

If your compiler doesn't recognize the ANSI forms, you can use the following declaration and function header:

```
double power();          /* declaration */

double power(a,b);       /* header      */
double a;
int b;
```

Here is a sample run:

```
Enter a number and the positive integer power to which
the number will be raised. Enter q to quit.
1.2 12
1.2 to the power 12 is 8.9161
Enter next pair of numbers or q to quit.
2
16
2 to the power 16 is 65536
Enter next pair of numbers or q to quit.
q
Hope you enjoyed this power trip — bye!
```

Program Discussion

The main() program is an example of a *driver*, a short program designed to test a function.

The while loop is a generalization of a form you've used before. Entering 1.2 12 causes scanf() to read two values successfully and to return 2, and the loop continues.

Because `scanf()` skips over whitespace, input can be spread over more than one line, as the sample output shows, but entering q produces a return value of 0 because q can't be read using the `%lf` specifier; this causes `scanf()` to return 0, terminating the loop. Similarly, entering 2.8 q would produce a return value of 1; that, too, would terminate the loop.

Now let's look at the function-related matters. The `power()` function appears three times in this program. The first appearance is this:

```
double power(double a, int b);     /* ANSI prototype */
```

This statement announces, or declares, that the program will be using a function called `power()`. The initial keyword `double` indicates that the `power()` function returns a type `double` value. The compiler needs to know what kind of value `power()` returns so that it will know how many bytes of data to expect and how to interpret them; this is why you have to declare the function. The `double a, int b` within the parentheses means that `power()` takes two arguments. The first should be a type `double` value, and the second should be type `int`.

The second appearance is this:

```
xpow = power(x,n);   /* function call */
```

Here you call the function, passing it two values. The function calculates the nth power of x and returns it to the calling program, where the return value is assigned to the variable xpow.

The third appearance is in the head of the function definition:

```
double power(double a, int b)   /* function definition */
```

Here `power()` takes two arguments: a `double` and an `int`, represented by the variables a and b. Note that `power()` is not followed by a semicolon when it appears in a function definition, but is followed by a semicolon when in a function declaration. After the function heading comes the code that specifies what `power()` does.

Recall that the function uses a `for` loop to calculate the value of a to the b power and assign it to pow. The following line makes the value of pow the function return value:

```
return pow;        /* return the value of pow */
```

Using Functions with Return Values

Declaring the function, calling the function, defining the function, using the `return` keyword: These are the basic elements in defining and using a function with a return value.

At this point, you might have some questions. For example, if you are supposed to declare functions before you use their return values, how come you used the return value of `scanf()` without declaring `scanf()`? Why do you have to declare `power()` separately when your definition of it says it is type `double`?

Let's take the second question first. The compiler needs to know what type `power()` is when it first encounters `power()` in the program. At this point, the compiler has not yet encountered the definition of `power()`, so it doesn't know that the definition says the return type is `double`. To help out the compiler, you preview what is to come by using a *forward declaration*. This declaration informs the compiler that `power()` is defined elsewhere and that it will return type `double`. If you place the `power()` function definition ahead of `main()` in the file, you can omit the forward declaration because the compiler would have known all about `power()` before reaching `main()`. However, that is not standard C style. Because `main()` usually provides the overall framework for a program, it's best to show `main()` first. Also, functions often are kept in separate files, so a forward declaration is essential.

Next, why didn't you declare `scanf()`? Well, you did. The `stdio.h` header file has function declarations for `scanf()`, `printf()`, and several other I/O functions. The `scanf()` declaration states that it returns type `int`. However, if you forget to include `stdio.h`, the program still works. That's because C assumes that if you don't declare the type for a function, it is type `int`. Early C programming often relied heavily on this assumption, but modern practice is to declare the function type even if it is `int`. Future practice, as proposed by the C9X committee, drops the automatic assumption of type `int`, so that is an even stronger reason to be explicit.

Chapter Summary

The main topic of this chapter has been program control. C offers you many aids for structuring your programs. The `while` and the `for` statements provide entry-condition loops. The `for` statements are particularly suited for loops that involve initialization and updating. The comma operator enables you to initialize and update more than one variable in a `for` loop. For the rare occasion when an exit-condition loop is needed, C has the `do while` statement.

All these loops use a test condition to determine whether another loop cycle is to be executed. In general, the loop continues if the test expression evaluates to a nonzero value, and terminates otherwise. Often, the test condition is a relational expression, which is an expression formed by using a relational operator. Such an expression has a value of 1 if the relation is true and a value of 0 otherwise.

In addition to relational operators, this chapter looked at several of C's arithmetic assignment operators, such as `+=` and `*=`. These operators modify the value of the left-hand operand by performing an arithmetic operation on it.

Arrays were the next subject. Arrays are declared in the same fashion as ordinary variables, but they have a number enclosed in brackets to indicate the number of elements. The first element of an array is numbered 0; the second is numbered 1, and so forth. The subscripts used to number arrays can be manipulated conveniently by using loops.

Finally, the chapter showed how to write and use a function with a return value.

Review Questions

1. Find the value of `quack` after each line.

```
int quack = 2;
quack += 5;
quack *= 10;
quack -= 6;
quack /= 8;
quack %= 3;
```

2. What output would the following loop produce?

```
for ( value = 36; value > 0; value /= 2)
      printf("%3d", value);
```

3. Represent each of the following test conditions:

    a. x is greater than 5.

    b. scanf() attempts to read a single double (called x) and fails.

    c. x has the value 5.

4. Represent each of the following test conditions:

    a. scanf() succeeds in reading a single integer
    _____

    b. x is not 5 _____

    c. x is 20 or greater _____

5. You suspect that the following program is not perfect. What errors can you find?

```
#include <stdio.h>
int main(void)
{                                       /* line 3  */
    int i, j, list(10);                 /* line 4  */

    for (i = 1, i <= 10,  i++)          /* line 6  */
    {                                   /* line 7  */
        list[i] = 2*i + 3;              /* line 8  */
        for (j = 1, j > = i, j++)       /* line 9  */
            printf(" %d", list[j]);     /* line 10 */
        printf("\n");                   /* line 11 */
    }                                   /* line 12 */
}
```

6. Use nested loops to write a program that produces this pattern:

```
$$$$$$$$
$$$$$$$$
$$$$$$$$
$$$$$$$$
```

7. What will each of the following programs print?

    a.
```
#include <stdio.h>
int main(void)
{
    int i = 0;
```

```
        while (++i < 4)
            printf("Hi! ");
        do
            printf("Bye! ");
        while (i++ < 8);
        return 0;
    }
```

b.

```
#include <stdio.h>
int main(void)
{
        int i;
        char ch;

        for (i = 0, ch = 'A'; i < 4; i++, ch += 2 * i)
                printf("%c", ch);
        return 0;
}
```

8. Given the input "Saddle up my charger!", what would each of the following programs produce for output? (The ! follows the space character in the ASCII sequence.)

a.

```
#include <stdio.h>
int main(void)
{
    char ch;

    scanf("%c", &ch);
    while ( ch != 'g' )
    {
            printf("%c", ch);
            scanf("%c", &ch);
    }
    return 0;
}
```

b.

```
#include <stdio.h>
int main(void)
{
    char ch;

    scanf("%c", &ch);
    while ( ch != 'g' )
```

```
    {
        printf("%c", ++ch);
        scanf("%c", &ch);
    }
    return 0;
}
```

c.

```
#include <stdio.h>
int main(void)
{
    char ch;

    do {
        scanf("%c", &ch);
        printf("%c", ch);
    } while ( ch != 'g' );
    return 0;
}
```

d.

```
#include <stdio.h>
int main(void)
{
    char ch;

    scanf("%c", &ch);
    for ( ch = '$'; ch != 'g'; scanf("%c", &ch) )
        putchar(ch);
    return 0;
}
```

9. What will the following program print?

```
#include <stdio.h>
int main(void)
{
    int n, m;

    n = 10;
    while (++n <= 13)
        printf("%d",n);
    do
        printf("%d",n);
    while (++n <= 12);

    printf("\n***\n");

    for (n = 1; n*n < 60; n +=3)
        printf("%d\n", n);

    printf("\n***\n");
```

```
    for (n = 1, m = 5; n < m; n *= 2, m+= 2)
        printf("%d %d\n", n, m);

    printf("\n***\n");

    for (n = 4; n > 0; n—)
    {
        for (m = 0; m <= n; m++)
            printf("+");
        printf("\n");
    }
    return 0;
}
```

10. Consider the following declaration:

    ```
    double mint[10];
    ```

    a. What is the array name? _____

    b. How many elements does the array have? _____

    c. What kind of value can be stored in each element? _____

    d. Which of the following is a correct usage of scanf() with this
       array?

       ```
       i.   scanf("%lf", mint)
       ii.  scanf("%lf", mint[2])
       iii. scanf("%lf", &mint[2])
       iv.  scanf("%lf", &mint)
       ```

11. Mr. Noah likes counting by twos, so he's written the following program to
    create an array and to fill it with the integers 2, 4, 6, 8, and so on. What,
    if anything, is wrong with this program?

    ```
    #include <stdio.h>
    #define SIZE 8
    int main(void)
    {
      int by_twos[SIZE];
      int index;

      for (index = 1; index <= SIZE; index++)
          by_twos[index] = 2 * index;
      for (index = 1; index <= SIZE; index++)
          printf("%d ", by_twos);
      printf("\n");
      return 0;
    }
    ```

12. You want to write a function that returns a long value. What should your
    definition of the function include?

13. Define a function that takes an int argument and that returns, as a long, the square of that value.

14. What will the following program print?

```c
#include <stdio.h>
int main(void)
{
    int k;

    for(k = 1, printf("%d: Hi!\n", k); printf("k = %d\n",k),
        k*k < 26; k+=2, printf("Now k is %d\n", k) )
            printf("k is %d in the loop\n",k);
    return 0;
}
```

Programming Exercises

1. Write a program that creates an array with 26 elements and stores the 26 lowercase letters in it. Also have it show the array contents.

2. Use nested loops to produce the following pattern:

```
$
$$
$$$
$$$$
$$$$$
```

3. Use nested loops to produce the following pattern:

```
F
FE
FED
FEDC
FEDCB
FEDCBA
```

4. Have a program request the user enter an uppercase letter. Use nested loops to produce a pyramid pattern like this:

```
    A
   ABA
  ABCBA
 ABCDCDA
ABCDEDCBA
```

The pattern should extend to the character entered. For instance, the preceding pattern would result from an input value of E. Hint: Use an outer loop to handle the rows. Use three inner loops in a row, one to handle the spaces, one for printing letters in ascending order, and one for printing letters in descending order.

5. Write a program that prints a table with each line giving an integer, its square, and its cube. Ask the user to input the lower and upper limits for the table. Use a `for` loop.

6. Write a program that reads a single word into a character array and then prints the word backward. Hint: Use `strlen()` to compute the index of the last character in the array (refer to Chapter 4, "Character Strings and Formatted Input/Output").

7. Write a program that requests two floating-point numbers and prints the value of their difference divided by their product. Have the program loop through pairs of input values until the user enters non-numeric input.

8. Modify Exercise 7 so that it uses a function to return the value of the calculation.

9. Write a program that reads eight integers into an array and then prints them in reverse order.

10. Consider these two infinite series:

    ```
    1.0 + 1.0/2.0 + 1.0/3.0 + 1.0/4.0 + ...
    1.0 - 1.0/2.0 + 1.0/3.0 - 1.0/4.0 + ...
    ```

    Write a program that evaluates running totals of these two series up to some limit of number of terms. Have the user enter the limit interactively. Look at the running totals after 20 terms, 100 terms, 500 terms. Does either series appear to be converging to some value? Hint: -1 times itself an odd number of times is -1, and -1 times itself an even number of times is 1.

11. Write a program that creates an eight-element array of `int` and sets the elements to the first eight powers of 2 and then prints the values out. Use a `for` loop to set the values, and, for variety, use a `do while` loop to display the values.

12. Write a program that reads in a line of input and then prints the line out in reverse order. Recall that you can use `scanf()` with the `%c` specifier to read one character at a time from input and that the newline character (`\n`) is generated when you press the Enter key.

13. Daphne invests $100 at 10% simple interest. (That is, every year, the investment earns an interest equal to 10% of the original investment.) Deirdre invests $100 at 5% interest compounded annually. (That is, interest is 5% of the current balance, including previous addition of interest.) Write a program that finds how many years it takes for the value of Deirdre's investment to exceed the value of Daphne's investment. Also show the two values at that time.

14. Chuckie Lucky won a million dollars, which he places in an account that earns 8% a year. On the last day of each year, Chuckie withdraws $100,000. Write a program that finds out how many years it takes for Chuckie to empty his account.

CHAPTER 7

C CONTROL STATEMENTS: BRANCHING AND JUMPS

You will learn about the following in this chapter:

- Keywords

  if, else, switch, continue
  break, case, default, goto

- Operators

  && ¦¦ ?:

- Functions

  getchar(), putchar(),
  the ctype.h family

*I*n this chapter, you learn how to use the `if` and `if else` statements and how to nest them. You use logical operators to combine relational expressions into more involved test expressions. You encounter C's conditional operator; study the `switch` statement; learn about the `break`, `continue`, and `goto` jumps; and use C's character I/O functions—getchar() and putchar(). You also learn about the family of character-analysis functions provided by the `ctype.h` header file.

As you grow more comfortable with C, you will probably want to tackle more complex tasks. When you do, you'll need ways to control and organize these projects. C has the tools to meet these needs. Already, you've learned to use loops to program repetitive tasks. In this chapter, you'll learn about branching structures, such as `if` and `switch`, that allow a program to base its actions on conditions it checks. Also, you are introduced to C's logical operators, which enable you to test for more than one relationship in a `while` or `if` condition, and you look at C's jump statements, which shift the program flow to another part of a program. By the end of this chapter, you'll have all the basic information you need to design a program that behaves the way you want.

The `if` Statement

Let's start with a simple example of an `if` statement shown in Listing 7.1. This program reads in a list of daily low temperatures (in Celsius) and reports the total number of entries and the percentage that were below freezing. It uses scanf() in a loop to read in the values.

Once during each loop cycle, it increments a counter to keep track of the number of entries. An if statement detects temperatures below freezing and keeps track of their number separately.

Listing 7.1   The `colddays.c` program.

```
/* colddays.c -- finds percentage of days below freezing */
#include <stdio.h>
#define SCALE "Celsius"
#define FREEZING 0
int main(void)
{
  float temperature;
  int cold_days = 0;
  int all_days = 0;

  printf("Enter the list of daily low temperatures.\n");
  printf("Use %s, and enter q to quit.\n", SCALE);
  while (scanf("%f", &temperature) == 1)
  {
      all_days++;
      if (temperature < FREEZING)
          cold_days++;
  }
  if (all_days != 0)
      printf("%d days total: %.1f%% were below freezing.\n",
              all_days, 100.0 * (float) cold_days / all_days);
  if (all_days == 0)
      printf("No data entered!\n");
  return 0;
}
```

Here is a sample run:

```
Enter the list of daily low temperatures.
Use Celsius, and enter q to quit.
12 5 -2.5 0 6 8 -3 -10 5 10 q
10 days total: 30.0% were below freezing.
```

The `while` loop test condition uses the return value of `scanf()` to terminate the loop when `scanf()` encounters non-numeric input. By using `float` instead of `int` for `temperature`, the program is able to accept input like `-2.5` as well as `8`.

The new statement in the `while` block is this:

```
if (temperature < FREEZING)
  cold_days++;
```

This `if` statement instructs the computer to increase `freezing` by 1 *if* the value just read (`temperature`) is less than zero. What happens if `temperature` is not less than zero? Then the `cold_days++;` statement is skipped, and the `while` loop moves on to read the next temperature value.

The program uses the `if` statement two more times to control the output. If there is data, the program prints the results. If there is no data, the program reports that fact. (Soon you'll see a more elegant way to handle this part of the program.)

To avoid integer division, the example uses the cast to `float` when the percentage is being calculated. You don't really need the type cast, for in the expression `100.0 * cold_days / all_days`, the subexpression `100.0 * cold_days` is evaluated first and is forced into floating point by the automatic type conversion rules. Using the type cast documents your intent, however, and protects the program from faulty compilers.

if Basics

The `if` statement is called a *branching statement* because it provides a junction where the program has to select which of two paths to follow. The general form is this:

```
if (expression)
      statement
```

If *expression* evaluates to true (nonzero), the *statement* is executed. Otherwise, it is skipped. As with a `while` loop, *statement* can be a single statement or a single block or compound statement. The structure is very similar to that of a `while` statement. The chief difference is that in an `if` statement, the test and (possibly) the execution are done just once, but in the `while` loop, the test and execution can be repeated several times.

Normally, *expression* is a relational expression; that is, it compares the magnitude of two quantities, as in the expressions `x > y` and `c == 6`. If *expression* is true (x is greater than y, or c does equal 6), then the statement is executed. Otherwise, the statement is ignored. More generally, any expression can be used, and an expression with a `0` value is taken to be false.

The statement portion can be a simple statement, as in the example, or it can be a compound statement or block, marked off by braces.

```
if (score > big)
    printf("Jackpot!\n");  /* simple statement   */

if (joe > ron)
{                          /* compound statement */
    joecash++;
    printf("You lose, Ron.\n");
}
```

Note that the entire `if` structure counts as a single statement, even when it uses a compound statement.

Adding else to the if Statement

The simple form of an `if` statement gives you the choice of executing a statement (possibly compound) or skipping it. C also enables you to choose between two statements by using the `if else` form. Let's use the `if else` form to fix an awkward segment from Listing 7.1.

```
if (all_days != 0)
  printf("%d days total: %.1f%% were below freezing.\n",
         all_days, 100.0 * (float) cold_days / all_days);
if (all_days == 0)
  printf("No data entered!\n");
```

If the program finds that days is not equal to 0, it should know that days must be 0 without retesting, and it does. With if else you can take advantage of that knowledge by rewriting the fragment this way:

```
if (all_days!= 0)
  printf("%d days total: %.1f%% were below freezing.\n",
         all_days, 100.0 * (float) cold_days / all_days);
else
  printf("No data entered!\n");
```

Only one test is made. If the if test expression is true, the temperature data is printed. If it's false, the warning message is printed.

Note the general form of the if else statement:

```
if (expression)
    statement1
else
    statement2
```

If expression is true (nonzero), statement1 is executed. If expression is false or zero, the single statement following the else is executed. The statements can be simple or compound. The indentation is not required by C, but it is the standard style. It shows at a glance the statements that depend on a test for execution.

If you want more than one statement between the if and the else, you must use braces to create a single block. The following construction violates C syntax, for the compiler expects just one statement (single or compound) between the if and the else:

```
if (x > 0)
  printf("Incrementing x:\n");
  x++;
else
  printf("x <= 0 \n");
```

Instead, use this:

```
if (x > 0)
{
  printf("Incrementing x:\n");
  x++;
}
else
  printf("x <= 0 \n");
```

The if statement enables you to choose whether to do one action. The if else statement enables you to choose between two actions. Figure 7.1 compares the two statements.

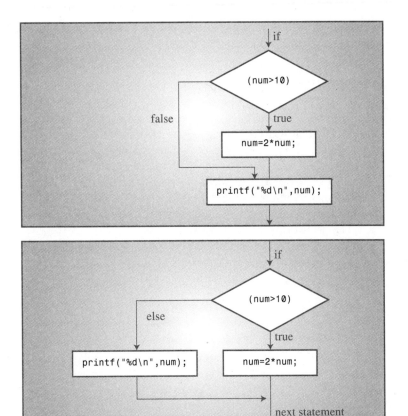

Figure 7.1 `if` versus `if else`.

Another Example: Introducing `getchar()` and `putchar()`

Most of the examples have used numeric input. To give you practice with other types, let's look at a character-oriented example. You already know how use `scanf()` and `printf()` with the `%c` specifier to read and write characters; but now you'll meet a pair of C functions specifically designed for character-oriented I/O: `getchar()` and `putchar()`.

The `getchar()` function takes no arguments, and it returns the next character from input. For instance, the following statement reads the next input character and assigns its value to the variable `ch`:

```
ch = getchar();
```

This statement has the same effect as the following statement:

```
scanf("%c", &ch);
```

The putchar() function prints its argument. For example, the next statement prints as a character the value previously assigned to ch:

```
putchar(ch); ·
```

This statement has the same effect as the following:

```
printf("%c", ch);
```

Because these functions deal only with characters, they are faster and more compact than the more general scanf() and printf() functions. Also, note that they don't need format specifiers; that's because they work with characters only. Both functions are typically defined in the stdio.h file. (Also, typically, they are preprocessor *macros* rather than true functions; we'll talk about function-like macros in Chapter 16, "The C Preprocessor and the C Library.")

Let's see how these functions work by writing a program that repeats an input line but replaces each nonspace character with the character that follows it in the ASCII code sequence. Spaces will be reproduced as spaces. You can state the desired response this way: If the character is a space, print it; otherwise, print the next character in the ASCII sequence. The C code looks much like this statement, as you can see in Listing 7.2.

Listing 7.2 The cypher1.c program.

```
/* cypher1.c -- alters input, preserving spaces */
#include <stdio.h>
#define SPACE ' '               /* that's quote-space-quote */
int main(void)
{
   char ch;

   ch = getchar();              /* read a character         */
   while (ch != '\n')           /* while not end of line    */
   {
       if (ch == SPACE)         /* leave the space          */
           putchar(ch);         /* character unchanged      */
       else
           putchar(ch + 1);     /* change other characters  */
       ch = getchar();          /* get next character       */
   }
   putchar(ch);                 /* print the newline        */
   return 0;
}
```

Here's a sample run:

```
CALL ME HAL.
DBMM NF IBM/
```

Compare this loop to the one from Listing 7.1, which uses the status returned by scanf() instead of the value of the input item to determine when to terminate the loop. Listing 7.2, however, uses the value of the input item itself to decide when to terminate the loop. This difference results in a slightly different loop structure, with one read statement before the loop and one read statement at the end of each loop. C's flexible syntax, however, enables you to emulate Listing 7.1 by combining reading and testing into a single expression. That is, you can replace a loop of the form

```
ch = getchar();          /* read a character        */
while (ch != '\n')        /* while not end of line   */
{
    ...                   /* process character       */
    ch = getchar();       /* get next character      */
}
```

with one that looks like this:

```
while ((ch = getchar()) != '\n')
{
    ...                   /* process character       */
}
```

The critical line is this:

```
while ((ch = getchar()) != '\n')
```

It demonstrates a characteristic C programming style: combining two actions in one expression. The actions are assigning a value to ch and comparing this value to the newline character. The parentheses around ch = getchar() make it the left operand of the != operator. To evaluate this expression, the computer must first call the getchar() function and then assign its return value to ch. Because the value of an assignment expression is the value of the left member, the value of ch = getchar() is just the new value of ch. Therefore, after ch is read, the test condition boils down to ch != '\n', that is, to ch not being the newline character.

This particular idiom is very common in C programming. All the parentheses are necessary. Suppose you mistakenly used this:

```
while (ch = getchar() != '\n')
```

The != operator has higher precedence than =, so the first expression to be evaluated is getchar() != '\n'. Because this is a relational expression, its value is 1 or 0 (true or false). Then this value is assigned to ch. Omitting the parentheses means that ch is assigned 0 or 1 rather than the return value of getchar(); this is not desirable.

The ctype.h Family of Character Functions

Notice that the output for Listing 7.2 shows a period being converted to a slash; that's because the ASCII code for the slash character is one greater than the code for the period character. But if the point of the program is to convert only letters, it would be nice to leave all non-letters, not just spaces, unaltered. The logical operators, discussed later in this chapter, provide a way to test whether a character is not a space and not a comma, and so on, but it would be rather cumbersome to list all the possibilities. Fortunately, ANSI C has a standard set of functions for analyzing characters; the ctype.h header file contains the prototypes. These functions take a character as an argument and return nonzero (true) if the character belongs to a particular category and false otherwise. For example, the isalpha()

function returns **true** if its argument is a letter. Listing 7.3 generalizes Listing 7.2 by using this function; it also incorporates the shortened loop structure we just discussed.

Listing 7.3   The `cypher2.c` program.

```
/* cypher2.c -- alters input, preserving non-letters   */
#include <stdio.h>
#include <ctype.h>              /* for isalpha()        */
int main(void)
{
   char ch;

   while ((ch = getchar()) != '\n')
   {
       if (isalpha(ch))        /* if a letter,         */
           putchar(ch + 1);    /* change it            */
       else
           putchar(ch);        /* otherwise print as is */
   }
   putchar(ch);                /* print the newline    */
   return 0;
}
```

Here is a sample run; note how both lowercase and uppercase letters are encyphered, but spaces and punctuation aren't:

See, it's a programmer!
Tff, ju't b qsphsbnnfs!

Tables 7.1 and 7.2 list several functions provided when you include the `ctype.h` header file. Note that the mapping functions don't modify the original argument; instead, they return the modified value. That is,

```
tolower(ch);        // no effect on ch
```

doesn't change `ch`. To change `ch` do this:

```
ch = tolower(ch);  // convert ch to lowercase
```

Table 7.1   `ctype.h` character-testing functions.

Name	True If Argument Is
isalnum()	Alphanumeric (alphabetic or numeric)
isalpha()	Alphabetic
iscntrl()	A control character, such as Ctrl+B

Name	True If Argument Is
isdigit()	A digit
isgraph()	Any printing character other than a space
islower()	A lowercase character
isprint()	A printing character
ispunct()	A punctuation character (any printing character other than a space or an alphanumeric character)
isspace()	A whitespace character: space, newline, formfeed, carriage return, vertical tab, horizontal tab, or, possibly, other implementation-defined characters
isupper()	An uppercase character
isxdigit()	A hexadecimal-digit character

Table 7.2 ctype.h character-mapping functions.

Name	Action
tolower()	If the argument is an uppercase character, returns the lowercase version; otherwise, just returns the original argument
toupper()	If the argument is a lowercase character, returns the uppercase version; otherwise, just returns the original argument

Multiple Choice else if

Life often offers us more than two choices. You can extend the if else structure with else if to accommodate this fact. Let's look at a particular example. Utility companies often have charges that depend on the amount of energy the customer uses. Here are the rates one company charges for electricity, based on kilowatt-hours (kWh):

first 240 kWh:	$0.11439 per kWh
next 300 kWh:	$0.13290 per kWh
over 540 kWh:	$0.14022 per kWh

If you worry about your energy management, you might want to prepare a program to calculate your energy costs. The program in Listing 7.4 is a first step in that direction.

Listing 7.4   The electric.c program.

```c
/* electric.c -- calculates electric bill */
#include <stdio.h>
#define RATE1 0.11439        /* rate for first 240 kwh    */
#define RATE2 0.12032        /* rate for next 300 kwh     */
#define RATE3 0.14022        /* rate for over 540 kwh     */
#define BREAK1 240.0         /* first breakpoint for rates */
#define BREAK2 540.0         /* second breakpoint for rates */
#define BASE1 (RATE1 * BREAK1)
                             /* cost for 240 kwh          */
#define BASE2 (BASE1 + (RATE2 * (BREAK2 - BREAK1)))
                             /* cost for 540 kwh          */
int main(void)
{
  double kwh;                /* kilowatt-hours used       */
  double bill;              /* charges                   */

  printf("Please enter the kwh used.\n");
  scanf("%lf", &kwh);        /* %lf for type double       */
  if (kwh <= BREAK1)
      bill = RATE1 * kwh;
  else if (kwh <= BREAK2)    /* kwh between 240 and 540   */
      bill = BASE1 + (RATE2 * (kwh - BREAK1));
  else                       /* kwh above 540             */
      bill = BASE2 + (RATE3 * (kwh - BREAK2));
  printf("The charge for %.1f kwh is $%1.2f.\n", kwh, bill);
  return 0;
}
```

Here's sample output:

```
Please enter the kwh used.
438
The charge for 438.0 kwh is $51.28.
```

Listing 7.4 uses symbolic constants for the rates so that the constants are conveniently gathered in one place. If the power company changes its rates (it's possible), having the rates in one place makes it easy to update them. The listing also expresses the rate breakpoints symbolically. They, too, are subject to change. BASE1 and BASE2 are expressed in terms of the rates and breakpoints. Then, if the rates or breakpoints change, the bases are updated automatically. You may recall that the preprocessor does not do calculations. Where BASE1 appears in the program, it will be replaced by 0.11439 * 240.0. Don't worry; the compiler does evaluate this expression to its numerical value (27.4536) so that the final program code uses 27.4536 rather than a calculation.

The flow of the program is straightforward. The program selects one of three formulas, depending on the value of kwh. Figure 7.2 illustrates this flow. We should point out that the only way the program can reach the first else is if kwh is equal to or greater than 240. Therefore, the else if (kwh <= BREAK2) line really is equivalent to demanding that kwh be between 240 and 540, as we noted in the program comment. Similarly, the final else can be reached only if kwh exceeds 540. Finally, note that BASE1 and BASE2 represent the total charges for the first 240 and 540 kilowatt-hours, respectively. Therefore, you need add on only the additional charges for electricity in excess of those amounts.

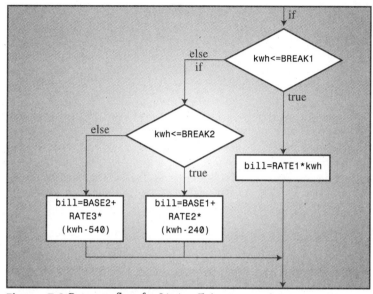

Figure 7.2 Program flow for Listing 7.4, `electric.c`.

Actually, the `else if` is a variation on what you already knew. For example, the core of the program is just another way of writing

```
if (kwh <=BREAK1)
      bill = RATE1 * kwh;
else
    if (kwh <=BREAK2)
        bill = BASE1 + RATE2 * (kwh - BREAK1);
    else
        bill = BASE2 + RATE3 * (kwh - BREAK2);
```

That is, the program consists of an `if else` statement for which the statement part of the `else` is another `if else` statement. The second `if else` statement is said to be *nested* inside the first. Recall that the entire `if else` structure counts as a single statement, which is why we didn't have to enclose the nested `if else` in braces. However, using braces would clarify the intent of this particular format.

These two forms are perfectly equivalent. The only differences are in where you put spaces and newlines, and these differences are ignored by the compiler. Nonetheless, the first form is better because it shows more clearly that you are making a three-way choice. This form makes it easier to skim the program and see what the choices are. Save the nested forms of indentation for when they are needed, for instance, when you must test two separate quantities. An example of such a situation is having a 10% surcharge for kilowatt-hours in excess of 540 during the summer only.

You can string together as many `else if` statements as you need (within compiler limits, of course), as illustrated by this fragment:

```
if (score < 1000)
    bonus = 0;
```

```
else if (score < 1500)
    bonus = 1;
else if (score < 2000)
    bonus = 2;
else if (score < 2500)
    bonus = 4;
else
    bonus = 6;
```

(This might be part of a game program, in which **bonus** represents how many additional photon bombs or food pellets you get for the next round.)

Speaking of compiler limits, the ANSI C standard requires that a compiler support a minimum of 15 levels of nesting, and the C9X draft extends the minimum requirement to 127 levels.

Pairing `else` with `if`

When you have a lot of `if`s and `else`s, how does the computer decide which `if` goes with which `else`? For example, consider the following program fragment:

```
if (number > 6)
    if (number < 12)
        printf("You're close!\n");
else
    printf("Sorry, you lose a turn!\n");
```

When is `Sorry, you lose a turn!` printed? When `number` is less than or equal to **6**, or when `number` is greater than 12? In other words, does the `else` go with the first `if` or the second? The answer is, the `else` goes with the second `if`. That is, you would get these responses:

Number	Response
5	none
10	You're close!
15	Sorry, you lose a turn!

The rule is that an `else` goes with the most recent `if` unless braces indicate otherwise (see Figure 7.3).

We indented the example to make it look as though the `else` goes with the first `if`, but remember that the compiler ignores indentation. If you really want the `else` to go with the first `if`, you could write the fragment this way:

```
if (number > 6)
{
    if (number < 12)
        printf("You're close!\n");
}
else
    printf("Sorry, you lose a turn!\n");
```

Now you would get these responses:

Number	Response
5	Sorry, you lose a turn!
10	You're close!
15	none

Figure 7.3 The rule for if else pairings.

More Nested ifs

You've already seen that the if...else if...else sequence is a form of nested if, one that selects from a series of alternatives. Another kind of nested if is used when choosing a particular selection leads to an additional choice. For example, a program could use an if else to select between males and females. Each branch within the if else then could contain another if else to distinguish between different income groups.

Let's apply this form of nested if to the following problem. Given an integer, print all the integers that divide into it evenly; if there are no divisors, report that the number is prime.

This problem requires some forethought before you whip out the code. First, you need an overall design for the program. For convenience, the program should use a loop to enable you to input numbers to be tested. That way, you don't have to run the program again each time you want to examine a new number. We've already developed a model for this kind of loop:

```
prompt user
while the scanf() return value is 1
    analyze the number and report results
    prompt user
```

Recall that by using scanf() in the loop test condition, the program attempts both to read a number and to check to see whether the loop should be terminated.

Next, you need a plan for finding divisors. Perhaps the most obvious approach is something like this:

```
for (div = 2; div < num; div++)
  if (num % div == 0)
      printf("%d is divisible by %d\n", num, div);
```

The loop checks all the numbers between 2 and num to see whether they divide evenly into num. Unfortunately, this approach wastes computer time. You can do much better. Consider, for example, finding the divisors of 144. You find that 144 % 2 is 0, meaning 2 goes into 144 evenly. If you then actually divide 2 into 144, you get 72, which also is a divisor, so you can get two divisors instead of one divisor out of a successful num % div test. The real payoff, however, comes in changing the limits of the loop test. To see how this works, look at the pairs of divisors you get as the loop continues: 2,72; 3,48; 4,36; 6,24; 8,18; 9,16; 12,12; 16,9; 18,8;. . .. Ah! After you get past the 12,12 pair, you start getting the same divisors (in reverse order) you already found. Instead of running the loop to 143, you can stop after reaching 12. That saves a lot of cycles!

Generalizing this discovery, you see that you have to test only up to the square root of num instead of to num. For numbers like 9, this is not a big savings, but the difference is enormous for a number like 10,000. Instead of messing with square roots, however, you can express the test condition as follows:

```
for (div = 2; (div * div) <= num; div++)
  if (num % div == 0)
        printf("%d is divisible by %d and %d.\n",
                num, div, num / div);
```

If num is 144, the loop runs through div = 12. If num is 145, the loop runs through div = 13.

There are two reasons for using this test rather than a square root test. First, integer multiplication is much faster than extracting a square root. Second, the square root function hasn't been formally introduced yet.

We need to address just two more problems, and then you'll be ready to program. First, what if the test number is a perfect square? Reporting that 144 is divisible by 12 and 12 is a little clumsy, but you can use a nested if statement to test whether div equals num / div. If so, the program will print just one divisor instead of two.

```
for (div = 2; (div * div) <= num; div++)
{
    if (num % div == 0)
    {
        if (div * div != num)
            printf("%d is divisible by %d and %d.\n",
                num, div, num / div);
        else
            printf("%d is divisible by %d.\n", num, div);
    }
}
```

Note

Technically, the if else statement counts as a single statement, so the braces around it are not needed. The outer if is a single statement also, so the braces around it are not needed. However, when statements get long, the braces make it easier to see what is happening, and they offer protection if later you add another statement to an if or to the loop.

Second, how do you know if a number is prime? If num is prime, then program flow never gets inside the if statement. To solve this problem, you can set a variable to some value, say 1, outside the loop and reset the variable to 0 inside the if statement. Then, after the loop is completed, you can check to see whether the variable is still 1. If it is, the if statement was never entered, and the number is prime. Such a variable is often called a *flag*.

Listing 7.5 incorporates all the ideas we've discussed. To extend the range, we've switched to type long.

Listing 7.5 The divisors.c program.

```
/* divisors.c -- nested ifs display divisors of a number */
#include <stdio.h>
#define NO 0
#define YES 1
int main(void)
{
    long num;                      /* number to be checked */
    long div;                      /* potential divisors    */
    int prime;

    printf("Please enter an integer for analysis; ");
    printf("Enter q to quit.\n");
    while (scanf("%ld", &num) == 1)
    {
        for (div = 2, prime = YES; (div * div) <= num; div++)
        {
            if (num % div == 0)
```

```
         {
            if ((div * div) != num)
               printf("%ld is divisible by %ld and %ld.\n",
                  num, div, num / div);
            else
               printf("%ld is divisible by %ld.\n", num, div);
            prime = NO;            /* number is not prime  */
         }
      }
      if (prime == YES)
         printf("%ld is prime.\n", num);
      printf("Please enter another integer for analysis; ");
      printf("Enter q to quit.\n");
   }
   return 0;
}
```

Note that the program uses the comma operator in the **for** loop control expression to enable you to initialize **prime** to **YES** for each new input number.

Here's a sample run:

```
Please enter an integer for analysis; Enter q to quit.
36
36 is divisible by 2 and 18.
36 is divisible by 3 and 12.
36 is divisible by 4 and 9.
36 is divisible by 6.
Please enter another integer for analysis; Enter q to quit.
149
149 is prime.
Please enter another integer for analysis; Enter q to quit.
30077
30077 is divisible by 19 and 1583.
Please enter another integer for analysis; Enter q to quit.
q
```

Summary: Using if Statements for Making Choices

Keywords:

if, else

General Comments:

In each of the following forms, the statement can be either a simple statement or a compound statement. A "true" expression means one with a nonzero value.

Form 1:

```
if (expression)
     statement
```

The *statement* is executed if the *expression* is true.

Form 2:

```
if (expression)
    statement1
  else
    statement2
```

If the *expression* is true, *statement1* is executed. Otherwise, *statement2* is executed.

Form 3:

```
if (expression1)
    statement1
else if (expression2)
    statement2
  else
    statement3
```

If *expression1* is true, then *statement1* is executed. If *expression1* is false but *expression2* is true, *statement2* is executed. Otherwise, if both expressions are false, *statement3* is executed.

Example:

```
if (legs == 4)
    printf("It might be a horse.\n");
else if (legs > 4)
    printf("It is not a horse.\n");
else    /* case of legs < 4 */
{
    legs++;
    printf("Now it has one more leg.\n")
}
```

Let's Get Logical

You've seen how `if` and `while` statements often use relational expressions as tests. Sometimes you will find it useful to combine two or more relational expressions. For instance, suppose you want a program that counts how many times the characters other than single or double quotes appear in an input sentence. You can use *logical operators* to meet this need, and you can use the period character (.) to identify the end of a sentence. Listing 7.6 presents a short program illustrating the method.

Listing 7.6 The `chcount.c` program.

```
#include <stdio.h>
#define PERIOD '.'
int main(void)
{
   int ch;
   int charcount = 0;
```

continued on next page

continued from previous page

```
    while ((ch = getchar()) != PERIOD)
    {
        if (ch != '"' && ch != '\'')
            charcount++;
    }
    printf("There are %d non-quote characters.\n", charcount);

    return 0;
}
```

Here's a sample run:

I didn't read the "I'm a Programming Fool" best seller.
```
There are 50 non-quote characters.
```

The action begins as the program reads a character and checks to see whether it is a period, because the period marks the end of a sentence. Next comes something new, a statement using the logical AND operator &&. You can translate the if statement thus: If the character is not a double quote AND if it is not a single quote, then increase charcount by 1.

Both conditions must be true if the whole expression is to be true. The logical operators have a lower precedence than the relational operators, so it was not necessary to use additional parentheses to group the subexpressions.

C has three logical operators:

Operator	Meaning
&&	and
¦¦	or
!	not

Suppose exp1 and exp2 are two simple relational expressions, such as cat > rat or debt == 1000. Then you can state the following:

1. exp1 && exp2 is true only if both exp1 and exp2 are true.

2. exp1 ¦¦ exp2 is true if either exp1 or exp2 is true or if both are true.

3. !exp1 is true if exp1 is false and is false if exp1 is true.

   Here are some concrete examples:

   5 > 2 && 4 > 7 is false because only one subexpression is true.

   5 > 2 ¦¦ 4 > 7 is true because at least one of the subexpressions is true.

   !(4 > 7) is true because 4 is not greater than 7.

   The last expression, incidentally, is equivalent to the following:

   4 <= 7

If you are unfamiliar or uncomfortable with logical operators, remember that

(practice && time) == perfection

Precedence

The ! operator has a very high precedence, higher than multiplication, the same as the increment operators, and just below that of parentheses. The && operator has higher precedence than ¦¦, and both rank below the relational operators and above assignment in precedence. Therefore, the expression

```
a > b && b > c ¦¦ b > d
```

would be interpreted as

```
((a > b) && (b > c)) ¦¦ (b > d)
```

That is, b is between a and c, or b is greater than d.

Order of Evaluation

Aside from those cases in which two operators share an operand, C ordinarily does not guarantee which parts of a complex expression are evaluated first. For example, in the following statement, the expression 5 + 3 might be evaluated before 9 + 6, or it might be evaluated afterward:

```
apples = (5 + 3) * (9 + 6);
```

This ambiguity was left in the language so that compiler designers could make the most efficient choice for a particular system. One exception to this rule (or lack of rule) is the treatment of logical operators. C guarantees that logical expressions are evaluated from left to right. The && and ¦¦ operators are sequence points, so all side effects take place before a program moves from one operand to the next. Furthermore, it guarantees that as soon as an element is found that invalidates the expression as a whole, the evaluation stops. These guarantees make it possible to use constructions such as the following:

```
while ((c = getchar()) != ' ' && c != '\n')
```

This construction sets up a loop that reads characters up to the first space or newline character. The first subexpression gives a value to c, which then is used in the second subexpression. Without the order guarantee, the computer might try to test the second expression before finding out what value c had.

Here is another example:

```
if (number != 0 && 12/number == 2)
    printf("The number is 5 or 6.\n");
```

If number has the value 0, the first subexpression is false, and the relational expression is not evaluated any further. This spares the computer the trauma of trying to divide by zero. Many languages do not have this feature. After seeing that number is 0, they still plunge ahead to check the next condition.

Finally, consider this example:

```
while ( x++ < 10 && x + y < 20)
```

The fact that the && operator is a sequence point guarantees that x is incremented before the expression on the right is evaluated.

Summary: Logical Operators and Expressions

Logical Operators:

Logical operators normally take relational expressions as operands. The ! operator takes one operand. The rest take two—one to the left, one to the right.

Operator	Meaning
&&	and
¦¦	or
!	not

Logical Expressions:

expression1 && expression2 is true if and only if both expressions are true. expression1 ¦¦ expression2 is true if either one or both expressions are true. !expression is true if the expression is false, and vice versa.

Order of Evaluation: ·

Logical expressions are evaluated from left to right. Evaluation stops as soon as something is discovered that renders the expression false.

Examples:

6 > 2 && 3 == 3 is true.

! (6 > 2 && 3 == 3) is false.

x != 0 && (20 / x) < 5 The second expression is evaluated only if x is nonzero.

Ranges

You can use the **&&** operator to test for ranges. For example, to test for **score** being in the range 90 to 100, you can do this:

```
if (range >= 90 && range <= 100)
    printf("Good show!\n");
```

It's important to avoid imitating common mathematical notation, as in the following:

```
if (90 <= range <= 100)     /* NO! Don't do it! */
    printf("Good show!\n");
```

The problem is that the code is a semantic error, not a syntax error, so the compiler will not catch it (although it might issue a warning). Because the order of evaluation for the <= operator is left-to-right, the test expression is interpreted as follows:

```
(90 <= range) <= 100
```

The subexpression `90 <= range` either has the value `1` (for true) or `0` (for false). Either value is less than 100, so the whole expression is always true, regardless of the value of `range`. So use `&&` for testing for ranges.

A lot of existing code uses range tests to see whether a character is, say, a lowercase letter. For instance, suppose `ch` is a `char` variable:

```
if (ch >= 'a' && ch <= 'z')
    printf("That's a lowercase character.\n");
```

This works for character codes such as ASCII, in which the codes for consecutive letters are consecutive numbers. However, this is not true for some codes, including EBCDIC. The more portable way of doing this test is to use the `islower()` function from the `ctype.h` family (refer to Table 7.1):

```
if (islower(ch))
    printf("That's a lowercase character.\n");
```

The `islower()` function works regardless of the particular character code used. (However, some pre-ANSI implementations lack the `ctype.h` family.)

A Word-Count Program

Now you have the tools to make a word-counting program, that is, a program that reads input and reports the number of words it finds. You may as well count characters and lines while you are at it. Let's see what such a program involves.

First, the program should read input character-by-character, and it should have some way of knowing when to stop. Second, it should be able to recognize and count the following units: characters, lines, words. Here's a pseudocode representation:

```
read a character
while there is more input
    increment character count
    if a line has been read, increment line count
    if a word has been read, increment word count
    read next character
```

You already have a model for the input loop:

```
while ((ch = getchar()) != STOP)
{
    ...
}
```

Here, `STOP` represents some value for `ch` that signals the end of the input. So far you have used the newline character and a period for this purpose, but neither is satisfactory for a general word-counting program. For the present, choose a character (|) that is not common in text. In Chapter 8, "Character Input/Output and Redirection," we'll present a better solution that also allows the program to be used with text files as well as keyboard input.

Now let's consider the body of the loop. Because the program uses `getchar()` for input, it can count characters by incrementing a counter during each loop cycle. To count lines, the program can check for newline characters. If a character is a newline, then the program should increment the line count.

The trickiest part is identifying words. First, you have to define what you mean by a word. Let's take a relatively simple approach and define a word as a sequence of characters that contains no whitespace (that is, no spaces, tabs, or newlines). Therefore, "glymxck" and "r2d2" are words. A word starts, then, when a program first encounters non-whitespace, and it ends when the next whitespace character shows up. The most straightforward test expression for detecting non-whitespace is this:

```
c != ' ' && c != '\n' && c != '\t'    /* true if c is not whitespace */
```

And the most straightforward test for detecting whitespace is this:

```
c == ' ' || c == '\n' || c == '\t'    /* true if c is whitespace */
```

However, it is simpler to use the `ctype.h` function `isspace()`, which returns true if its argument is a whitespace character. So `isspace(c)` is true if c is whitespace, and `!isspace(c)` is true if c isn't whitespace.

To keep track of whether a character is in a word, you can set a flag (call it `wordflag`) to 1 when the first character in a word is read. You can also increment the word count at that point. Then, as long as `wordflag` remains 1, subsequent non-whitespace characters don't mark the beginning of a word. At the next whitespace character, you must reset the flag to 0, and the program will be ready to find the next word. Let's put that into pseudocode:

```
if c is not whitespace and wordflag is 0
    set wordflag to 1 and count the word
if c is whitespace and wordflag is 1
    set wordflag to 0
```

This approach sets `wordflag` to 1 at the beginning of each word and to 0 at the end of each word. Words are counted only at the time the flag setting is changed from 0 to 1. Listing 7.7 translates these ideas into C.

Listing 7.7   The `wordcnt.c` program.

```
/* wordcnt.c -- counts characters, words, lines */
#include <stdio.h>
#include <ctype.h>        /* for isspace()              */
#define STOP '|'
#define YES 1
#define NO 0
int main(void)
{
    char c;                /* read in character          */
    long n_chars = 0L;     /* number of characters       */
    int n_lines = 0;       /* number of lines            */
    int n_words = 0;       /* number of words            */
    int wordflag = NO;     /* ==YES if c is in a word     */
```

```
    printf("Enter text to be analyzed (¦ to terminate):\n");
    while ((c = getchar()) != STOP)
    {
        n_chars++;                  /* count characters    */
        if (c == '\n')
            n_lines++;              /* count lines         */
        if (!isspace(c) && wordflag == NO)
        {
            wordflag = YES;         /* starting a new word */
            n_words++;              /* count word          */
        }
        if (isspace(c) && wordflag == YES)
            wordflag = NO;          /* reached end of word */
    }
    printf("characters = %ld, words = %d, lines = %d\n",
           n_chars, n_words, n_lines);
    return 0;
}
```

Here is a sample run:

```
Enter text to be analyzed (¦ to terminate):
Reason is a
powerful servant but
an inadequate master.
¦
characters = 55, words = 9, lines = 3
```

The program uses logical operators to translate the pseudocode to C. For example,

```
if c is not whitespace and wordflag is 0
```

gets translated to the following:

```
if (!isspace(c) && wordflag == NO)
```

This certainly is more readable than testing for each whitespace character individually:

```
if (c != ' ' && c != '\n' && c != '\t' && wordflag == NO)
```

Either form says, "If c is *not* whitespace, *and* if you are *not* in a word." If both conditions are met, then you must be starting a new word, and n_words is incremented. If you are in the middle of a word, then the first condition holds, but wordflag will be YES, and n_words is not incremented. When you reach the next whitespace character, you set wordflag equal to NO again. Check the coding to see whether the program gets confused when there are several spaces between one word and the next. In Chapter 8, we'll show how to modify this program to count words in a file.

The Conditional Operator: ?

C offers a shorthand way to express one form of the if else statement. It is called a *conditional expression* and uses the ?: conditional operator. This is a two-part operator that has three operands. Here is an example that yields the absolute value of a number:

```
x = (y < 0) ? -y : y;
```

Everything between the = and the semicolon is the conditional expression. The meaning of the statement is this: If y is less than zero, then x = -y; otherwise, x = y. In if else terms, the meaning can be expressed as follows:

```
if (y < 0)
    x = -y;
else
    x = y;
```

This is the general form of the conditional expression:

expression1 ? *expression2* : *expression3*

If *expression1* is true (nonzero), then the whole conditional expression has the same value as *expression2*. If *expression1* is false (zero), the whole conditional expression has the same value as *expression3*.

You can use the conditional expression when you have a variable to which you want to assign one of two possible values. A typical example is setting a variable equal to the maximum of two values:

```
max = (a > b) ? a : b;
```

This sets max to a if it is greater than b, and to b otherwise.

Usually, an if else statement can accomplish the same end as the conditional operator. The conditional operator version, however, is more compact and, depending on the compiler, may result in more compact program code.

Let's look at a paint program example, shown in Listing 7.8. The program calculates how many cans of paint are needed to paint a given number of square feet. The basic algorithm is simple: Divide the square footage by the number of square feet covered per can. Suppose the answer is 1.7 cans, however. Stores sell whole cans, not fractional cans, so you would have to buy two cans. Therefore, the program should round up to the next integer when a fractional paint can is involved. The conditional operator is used to handle that situation, and is also used to print cans or can, as appropriate.

Listing 7.8   The paint.c program.

```
/* paint.c -- uses conditional operator */
#include <stdio.h>
#define COVERAGE 200        /* square feet per paint can */
int main(void)
{
    int sq_feet;
    int cans;

    printf("Enter number of square feet to be painted:\n");
    while (scanf("%d", &sq_feet) == 1)
    {
        cans = sq_feet / COVERAGE;
        cans += ((sq_feet % COVERAGE == 0)) ? 0 : 1;
        printf("You need %d %s of paint.\n", cans,
            cans == 1 ? "can" : "cans");
```

```
        printf("Enter next value (q to quit):\n");
  }
  return 0;
}
```

Here's a sample run:

```
Enter number of square feet to be painted:
200
You need 1 can of paint.
Enter next value (q to quit):
215
You need 2 cans of paint.
Enter next value (q to quit):
q
```

Because the program is using type int, the division is truncated; that is, 215/200 becomes 1. Therefore, cans is rounded down to the integer part. If sq_feet % COVERAGE is 0, then COVERAGE divides evenly into sq_feet and cans is left unchanged. Otherwise, there is a remainder, so 1 is added. This is accomplished with the following statement:

```
cans += ((sq_feet % COVERAGE == 0)) ? 0 : 1;
```

It adds the value of the expression to the right of += to cans. The expression to the right is a conditional expression having the value 0 or 1, depending on whether COVERAGE divides evenly into sq_feet.

The final argument to the printf() function is also a conditional expression:

```
cans == 1 ? "can" : "cans");
```

If the value of cans is 1, then the string "can" is used. Otherwise, "cans" is used. This demonstrates that the conditional operator can use strings for its second and third operands.

Summary: The Conditional Operator

The Conditional Operator:

?:

General Comments:

This operator takes three operands, each of which is an expression. They are arranged as follows:

expression1 ? expression2 : expression3

The value of the whole expression equals the value of *expression2* if *expression1* is true. Otherwise, it equals the value of *expression3*.

Examples:

(5 > 3) ? 1 : 2 has the value 1.

(3 > 5) ? 1 : 2 has the value 2.

(a > b) ? a : b has the value of the larger of a or b.

Loop Aids: continue and break

Normally, after the body of a loop has been entered, a program executes all the statements in the body before doing the next loop test. The continue and break statements enable you to skip part of a loop or even terminate it, depending on tests made in the body of the loop.

The continue Statement

This statement can be used in the three loop forms. When encountered, it causes the rest of an iteration to be skipped and the next iteration to be started. If the continue statement is inside nested structures, it affects only the innermost structure containing it. Let's try continue in the short program in Listing 7.9.

Listing 7.9   The skip.c program.

```
/* skip.c  -- uses continue to skip part of loop */
#include <stdio.h>
#define MIN 0.0f        /* type float constant */
#define MAX 100.0f
int main(void)
{
    float score;
    float total = 0.0f;
    int n = 0;
    float min = MAX;
    float max = MIN;

    printf("Enter the scores:\n");
    while (scanf("%f", &score) == 1)
    {
        if (score < MIN || score > MAX)
        {
            printf("%0.1f is an invalid value.\n", score);
            continue;
        }
        printf("Accepting %0.1f:\n", score);
        min = (score < min)? score: min;
        max = (score > max)? score: max;
        total += score;
        n++;
    }
    if (n > 0)
    {
        printf("Average of %d scores is %0.1f.\n", n, total / n);
        printf("Low = %0.1f, high = %0.1f\n", min, max);
    }
```

```
    else
        printf("No valid scores were entered.\n");
    return 0;
}
```

In Listing 7.9, the `while` loop reads input until you enter non-numeric data. The `if` statement within the loop screens out invalid score values. If, say, you enter 188, the program tells you that `188 is an invalid score`. Then the `continue` statement causes the program to skip over the rest of the loop, which is devoted to processing valid input. Instead, the program starts the next loop cycle by attempting to read the next input value.

Note that there are two ways you could have avoided using `continue`. One way is omitting the `continue` and making the remaining part of the loop an `else` block:

```
if (score < 0 || score > 100)
    /* printf() statement */
else
{
    /* statements */
}
```

Or you could have used this format instead:

```
if (score >= 0 && score <= 100)
{
    /* statements */
}
```

An advantage of using `continue` in this case is that you can eliminate one level of indentation in the main group of statements. This conciseness can be important for readability when the statements are long or are deeply nested already.

Another use for `continue` is as a placeholder. For example, the following loop reads and discards input up to, and including, the end of a line:

```
while (getchar() != '\n')
    ;
```

Such a technique is handy when a program has already read some input from a line and needs to skip to the beginning of the next line. The problem is that the lone semicolon is hard to spot. The code is much more readable if you use `continue`.

```
while (getchar() != '\n')
    continue;
```

Don't use `continue` if it complicates rather than simplifies the code. Consider the following fragment, for instance:

```
while ((ch = getchar() ) != '\n')
{
    if (ch == '\t')
        continue;
    putchar(ch);
}
```

This loop skips over the tabs and quits only when a newline character is encountered. The loop could have been expressed more economically as this:

```
while ((ch = getchar()) != '\n')
    if (ch != '\t')
        putchar(ch);
```

Often, as in this case, reversing an `if` test eliminates the need for a `continue`.

You've seen that the `continue` statement causes the remaining body of a loop to be skipped. Where exactly does the loop resume? For the `while` and `do while` loops, the next action taken after the `continue` statement is to evaluate the loop test expression. Consider the following loop, for example:

```
count = 0;
while (count < 10)
{
    ch = getchar();
    if (ch == '\n')
        continue;
    putchar(ch);
    count++;
}
```

It reads 10 characters (excluding newlines because the `count++;` statement gets skipped when `ch` is a newline) and echoes them, except for newlines. When the `continue` statement is executed, the next expression evaluated is the loop test condition.

For a `for` loop, the next actions are to evaluate the update expression, then the loop test expression. Consider the following loop, for example:

```
for (count = 0; count < 10; count++)
{
    ch = getchar();
    if (ch == '\n')
        continue;
    putchar(ch);
}
```

In this case, when the `continue` statement is executed, first `count` is incremented, and then `count` is compared to `10`. Therefore, this loop behaves slightly differently from the `while` example. As before, only non-newline characters are displayed, but this time newline characters are included in the count, so it reads 10 characters, including newlines.

The break Statement

A `break` statement in a loop causes the program to break free of the loop that encloses it and to proceed to the next stage of the program. In Listing 7.9, replacing `continue` with `break` would cause the loop to quit when, say, 188 is entered instead of just skipping to the next loop cycle. Figure 7.4 compares `break` and `continue`. If the `break` statement is inside nested loops, it affects only the innermost loop containing it.

Figure 7.4 Comparing `break` and `continue`.

Sometimes **break** is used to leave a loop when there are two separate reasons to leave. Listing 7.10 uses a loop that calculates the area of a rectangle. The loop terminates if you respond with non-numeric input for the rectangle's length or width.

Listing 7.10   The `break.c` program.

```
/* break.c -- uses break to exit a loop */
#include <stdio.h>
int main(void)
{
  float length, width;

  printf("Enter the length of the rectangle:\n");
  while (scanf("%f", &length) == 1)
  {
      printf("Length = %0.2f:\n", length);
      printf("Enter its width:\n");
```

continued on next page

continued from previous page

```
                if (scanf("%f", &width) != 1)
                    break;
                printf("Width = %0.2f:\n", width);
                printf("Area = %0.2f:\n", length * width);
                printf("Enter the length of the rectangle:\n");
        }
    return 0;
}
```

You could have controlled the loop this way:

```
while (scanf("%f %f", &length, &width) == 2)
```

However, using `break` makes it simple to echo each input value individually.

As with `continue`, don't use `break` when it complicates code. For instance, consider the following loop:

```
while ((ch = getchar()) != '\n')
{
    if (ch == '\t')
        break;
    putchar(ch);
}
```

The logic is clearer if both tests are in the same place:

```
while ((ch = getchar() ) != '\n' && ch != '\t')
        putchar(ch);
```

The `break` statement is an essential adjunct to the `switch` statement, which you study next.

Multiple Choice: `switch` and `break`

The conditional operator and the `if else` construction make it easy to write programs that choose between *two* alternatives. Sometimes, however, a program needs to choose one of *several* alternatives. You can do this by using `if else if...else`, but in many cases it is more convenient to use the C `switch` statement. Listing 7.11 is an example showing how the `switch` statement works. This program reads in a letter and then responds by printing an animal name that begins with that letter.

Listing 7.11   The `animals.c` program.

```
/* animals.c -- uses a switch statement */
#include <stdio.h>
#include <ctype.h>
int main(void)
```

```
{
  char ch;

  printf("Give me a letter of the alphabet, and I will give ");
  printf("an animal name\nbeginning with that letter.\n");
  printf("Please type in a letter; type # to end my act.\n");
  while ((ch = getchar()) != '#')
  {
    if (islower(ch)) /* lowercase only */
      switch (ch)
      {
        case 'a' :
                printf("argali, a wild sheep of Asia\n");
                break;
        case 'b' :
                printf("babirusa, a wild pig of Malay\n");
                break;
        case 'c' :
                printf("coati, racoonlike mammal\n");
                break;
        case 'd' :
                printf("desman, aquatic, molelike critter\n");
                break;
        case 'e' :
                printf("echidna, the spiny anteater\n");
                break;
        case 'f' :
                printf("fisher, brownish marten\n");
                break;
        default :
                printf("That's a stumper!\n");
      }  /* end of switch */
    else
      printf("I recognize only lowercase letters.\n");
    while (getchar() != '\n')
      continue;                /* skip rest of input line */
    printf("Please type another letter or a #.\n");
  }                            /* while loop end          */
  printf("Bye!\n");
  return 0;
}
```

We got a little lazy and stopped at **f**, but we could have continued in the same manner. Let's look at a sample run before explaining the program further.

```
Give me a letter of the alphabet, and I will give an animal name
beginning with that letter.
Please type in a letter; type # to end my act.
a [enter]
argali, a wild sheep of Asia
Please type another letter or a #.
dab [enter]
desman, aquatic, molelike critter
```

```
Please type another letter or a #.
r [enter]
That's a stumper!
Please type another letter or a #.
Q [enter]
I recognize only lowercase letters.
Please type another letter or a #.
# [enter]
Bye!
```

The program's two main features are its use of the switch statement and its handling of input. We'll look first at how switch works.

Using the switch Statement

The expression in the parentheses following the word switch is evaluated. In this case, it has whatever value you last entered for ch. Then the program scans the list of *labels* (here, case 'a' :, case 'b' :, and so on) until it finds one matching that value. The program then jumps to that line. What if there is no match? If there is a line labeled default :, the program jumps there. Otherwise, the program proceeds to the statement following the switch.

What about the break statement? It causes the program to break out of the switch and skip to the next statement after the switch (see Figure 7.5). Without the break statement, every statement from the matched label to the end of the switch would be processed. For example, if you removed all the break statements from the program and then ran the program using the letter d, you would get this exchange:

```
Give me a letter of the alphabet, and I will give an animal name
beginning with that letter.
Please type in a letter; type # to end my act.
d [enter]
desman, aquatic, molelike critter
echidna, the spiny anteater
fisher, a brownish marten
That's a stumper!
Please type another letter or a #.
# [enter]
Bye!
```

All the statements from case 'd' : to the end of the switch were executed.

Incidentally, a break statement works with loops and with switch, but continue works just with loops. However, continue can be used as part of a switch statement if the statement is in a loop. In that situation, as with other loops, continue causes the program to skip over the rest of the loop, including other parts of the switch.

If you are familiar with Pascal, you will recognize the switch statement as being similar to the Pascal case statement. The most important difference is that the switch statement requires the use of a break if you want only the labeled statement to be processed. Also, you can't use a range as a C case.

```
    switch(number)
    {
    case 1: statement 1;
            break;
 ──► case 2: statement 2;
        ── break;
    case 3: statement 3;
            break
    default: statement 4;
    }
 ──► statement 5;
```

```
    switch(number)
    {
    case 1: statement 1;
 ──► case 2: statement 2;
    case 3: statement 3;
 ── default: statement 4;
    }
 ──► statement 5;
```

Figure 7.5 Program flow in `switch`es, with and without `break`s.

The `switch` test expression in the parentheses should be one with an integer value (includ-ing type `char`). The `case` labels must be integer-type (including `char`) constants or integer constant expressions (expressions containing only integer constants). You can't use a variable for a `case` label. This, then, is the structure of a `switch`:

```
switch (integer expression)
    {
    case constant1:
            statements      <--optional
    case constant2:
            statements      <--optional
    default :      <--optional
            statements      <--optional
    }
```

Reading Only the First Character of a Line

The other new feature incorporated into `animals.c` is how it reads input. As you might have noticed in the sample run, when `dab` was entered, only the first character was processed. Often this behavior is desirable in interactive programs looking for single-character responses. The code responsible for this behavior is the following:

```
while (getchar() != '\n')
    continue;           /* skip rest of input line */
```

This loop reads characters from input up to and including the newline character generated by the Enter key. Note that the function return value is not assigned to ch, so the characters are merely read and discarded. Because the last character discarded is the newline character, the next character to be read is the first character of the next line. It gets read by getchar() and assigned to ch in the outer while loop.

If you omit this loop, the program runs into a bit of trouble. Suppose, for instance, you respond with the letter a. Entering a involves pressing the Enter key, so you actually send the sequence a followed by the newline character. After the program processes the a, it reads the newline character and prints "I recognize only lowercase letters." Therefore, each letter entered causes the program to run through the outer while loop twice, which is disconcerting to the user.

Another approach to the newline problem is to skip only newlines rather than the entire rest of the line. You can do that by using the following code as the first statement in the large while loop:

```
if (ch == '\n')
    continue;
```

Multiple Labels

You can use multiple case labels for a given statement, as shown in Listing 7.12.

Listing 7.12 The vowels.c program.

```
/* vowels.c -- uses multiple labels */
#include <stdio.h>
int main(void)
{
  char ch;
  int a_ct, e_ct, i_ct, o_ct, u_ct;

  a_ct = e_ct = i_ct = o_ct = u_ct = 0;

  printf("Enter some text; enter # to quit.\n");
  while ((ch = getchar()) != '#')
  {
      switch (ch)
      {
        case 'a' :
        case 'A' :  a_ct++;
                    break;
        case 'e' :
        case 'E' :  e_ct++;
                    break;
```

```
        case 'i' :
        case 'I' :   i_ct++;
                     break;
        case 'o' :
        case 'O' :   o_ct++;
                     break;
        case 'u' :
        case 'U' :   u_ct++;
                     break;
        default :    break;
        }                                    /* end of switch */
    }                                        /* while loop end */
    printf("number of vowels:   A    E    I    O    U\n");
    printf("                    %4d %4d %4d %4d %4d\n",
        a_ct, e_ct, i_ct, o_ct, u_ct);
    return 0;
}
```

If ch is, say, the letter i, the switch statement goes to the location labeled case 'i' :.
Because there is no break associated with that label, program flow goes to the next statement, which is i_ct++;. If ch is I, program flow goes directly to that statement. In essence,
both labels refer to the same statement.

Here's a sample run:

```
Enter some text; enter # to quit.
I see under the overseer.#
number of vowels:   A    E    I    O    U
                    0    7    1    1    1
```

In this particular case, you can avoid multiple labels by using the toupper() function
from the ctype.h family (refer to Table 7.2) to convert all letters to uppercase before
testing:

```
while ((ch = getchar()) != '#')
{
    ch = toupper(ch);
    switch (ch)
    {
      case 'A' :   a_ct++;
                   break;
      case 'E' :   e_ct++;
                   break;
      case 'I' :   i_ct++;
                   break;
      case 'O' :   o_ct++;
                   break;
      case 'U' :   u_ct++;
                   break;
      default :    break;
    }                                    /* end of switch */
}                                        /* while loop end */
```

Or, if you want to leave ch unchanged, use the function this way:

```
switch(toupper(ch))
```

Summary: Multiple Choice with `switch`

Keyword:

`switch`

General Comments:

Program control jumps to the `case` label bearing the value of `expression`. Program flow then proceeds through all the remaining statements unless redirected again with a `break` statement. Both `expression` and `case` labels must have integer values (type `char` is included), and the labels must be constants or expressions formed solely from constants. If no `case` label matches the expression value, control goes to the statement labeled `default`, if present. Otherwise, control passes to the next statement following the `switch` statement.

Form:

```
switch (expression)
{
case label1 : statement1 /* use break to skip to end */
    case label2 : statement2
    default     : statement3
}
```

There can be more than two labeled statements, and the `default` case is optional.

Example:

```
switch (choice)
    {
    case 1 :
    case 2 : printf("Darn tootin'!\n");  break;
    case 3 : printf("Quite right!\n");
    case 4 : printf("Good show!\n"); break;
    default  : printf("Have a nice day.\n");
    }
```

If `choice` has the integer value 1 or 2, the first message is printed. If it is 3, the second and third messages are printed. (Flow continues to the following statement because there is no `break` statement after `case` 3.) If it is 4, the third message is printed. Other values print only the last message.

`switch` and `if else`

When should you use a `switch` and when should you use the `if else` construction? Often you don't have a choice. You can't use a `switch` if your choice is based on evaluating a float variable or expression. Nor can you conveniently use a `switch` if a variable must fall into a certain range. It is simple to write the following:

```
if (integer < 1000 && integer > 2)
```

Unhappily, covering this range with a `switch` would involve setting up `case` labels for each integer from 3 to 999. However, if you can use a `switch`, often your program runs a little faster and takes less code.

The `goto` Statement

The `goto` statement, bulwark of the older versions of BASIC and FORTRAN, is available in C. However, C, unlike those two languages, can get along quite well without it. Kernighan and Ritchie refer to the `goto` statement as "infinitely abusable" and suggest that it "be used sparingly, if at all." First, we will show you how to use `goto`. Then, we will show why you usually don't need to.

The `goto` statement has two parts: the `goto` and a label name. The label is named following the same convention used in naming a variable, as in this example:

```
goto part2;
```

For the preceding statement to work, the function must contain another statement bearing the `part2` label. This is done by beginning a statement with the label name followed by a colon:

```
part2: printf("Refined analysis:\n");
```

Avoiding `goto`

In principle, you never need to use the `goto` statement in a C program, but if you have a background in older versions of FORTRAN or BASIC, both of which require its use, you might have developed programming habits that depend on using the `goto`. To help you get over that dependence, we will outline some familiar `goto` situations and then show you a more C-like approach.

1. Handling an `if` situation that requires more than one statement:

   ```
   if (size > 12)
       goto a;
   goto b;
   a: cost = cost * 1.05;
      flag = 2;
   b: bill = cost * flag;
   ```

   In old-style BASIC and FORTRAN, only the single statement immediately following the `if` condition is attached to the `if`. No provision is made for blocks or compound statements. We have translated that pattern into the equivalent C. The standard C approach of using a compound statement or block is much easier to follow:

   ```
   if (size > 12)
   {
       cost = cost * 1.05;
       flag = 2;
   }
   bill = cost * flag;
   ```

2. Choosing from two alternatives:

```
if (ibex > 14)
    goto a;
sheds = 2;
goto b;
a: sheds= 3;
b: help = 2 * sheds;
```

Having the if else structure available allows C to express this choice more cleanly:

```
if (ibex > 14)
        sheds = 3;
else
        sheds = 2;
help = 2 * sheds;
```

Indeed, newer versions of BASIC and FORTRAN have incorporated the else into their syntax.

3. Setting up an indefinite loop:

```
readin: scanf("%d", &score);
if (score < 0)
    goto stage2;
lots of statements;
goto readin;
stage2: more stuff;
```

Use a while loop instead:

```
scanf("%d", &score);
while (score <= 0)
{
        lots of statements;
        scanf("%d", &score);
}
more stuff;
```

4. Skipping to the end of a loop: Use continue instead.

5. Leaving a loop: Use break instead. Actually, break and continue are specialized forms of a goto. The advantages of using them are that their names tell you what they are supposed to do and that, because they don't use labels, there is no danger of putting a label in the wrong place.

6. Leaping madly about to different parts of a program: DON'T!

There is one use of goto tolerated by many C practitioners: getting out of a nested set of loops if trouble shows up. (A single break gets you out of the innermost loop only.)

```
while (funct > 0)
    {
    for (i = 1, i <= 100; i++)
        {
        for (j = 1; j <= 50; j++)
```

```
        {
        statements galore;
        if (bit trouble)
            goto help;
        statements;
        }
    more statements;
    }
yet more statements;
    }
and more statements;
help : bail out;
```

As you can see from the other examples, the alternative forms are clearer than the goto forms. This difference grows even greater when you mix several of these situations. Which gotos are helping ifs, which are simulating if elses, which are controlling loops, which are just there because you have programmed yourself into a corner? By using gotos excessively, you create a labyrinth of program flow. If you aren't familiar with gotos, keep it that way. If you are used to using them, try to train yourself not to. Ironically, C, which doesn't need a goto, has a better goto than most languages because it enables you to use descriptive words for labels instead of numbers.

Summary: Program Jumps

Keywords:

break, continue, goto

General Comments:
These three instructions cause program flow to jump from one location of a program to another location.

The break Command:
The break command can be used with any of the three loop forms and with the switch statement. It causes program control to skip the rest of the loop or the switch containing it and to resume with the next command following the loop or switch.

Example:

```
switch (number)
{
    case 4:  printf("That's a good choice.\n");
             break;
    case 5:  printf("That's a fair choice.\n");
             break;
    default: printf("That's a poor choice.\n");
}
```

The `continue` Command:

The `continue` command can be used with any of the three loop forms but not with a `switch`. It causes program control to skip the remaining statements in a loop. For a `while` or `for` loop, the next loop cycle is started. For a `do while` loop, the exit condition is tested and then, if necessary, the next loop cycle is started.

Example:

```
while ((ch = getchar())   != EOF)
{
    if (ch == ' ')
        continue;
    putchar(ch);
    chcount++;
}
```

This fragment echoes and counts nonspace characters.

The `goto` Command:

A `goto` statement causes program control to jump to a statement bearing the indicated label. A colon is used to separate a labeled statement from its label. Label names follow the rules for variable names. The labeled statement can come either before or after the `goto`.

Form:

```
goto label;
     .
     .
     .
label : statement
```

Example:

```
top : ch = getchar();
      .
      .
      .
if (ch != 'y')
      goto top;
```

Chapter Summary

The `if` statement uses a test condition to control whether a program executes the single simple statement or block following the test condition. Execution occurs if the test expression has a nonzero value and doesn't occur if the value is zero. The `if else` statement enables you to select from two alternatives. If the test condition is nonzero, the statement before the `else` is executed. If the test expression evaluates to zero, the statement following the `else` is executed. By using another `if` statement to immediately follow the `else`, you can set up a structure that chooses between a series of alternatives.

The test condition is often a *relational expression*, that is, an expression formed by using one of the relational operators discussed in Chapter 6, "C Control Statements: Looping." By using C's logical operators, you can combine relational expressions. For example, you can test to see if x is greater than 0 and less than 20.

The *conditional operator* (operand1 ? operand2 : operand3) creates an expression whose value is governed by its first operand and is given by one of the next two operands. If the first operand is nonzero, the whole expression has the value of operand2; otherwise, the value that of operand3.

The ctype.h family of character functions, such as isspace() and isalpha(), offers convenient tools for creating test expressions based on classifying characters.

The switch statement enables you to select from a series of statements labeled with integer values. If the integer value of the test condition following the switch keyword matches a label, execution goes to the statement bearing that label. Execution then proceeds through the statements following the labeled statement unless you use a break statement.

The break, continue, and goto are *jump statements* that cause program flow to jump to another location in a program. A break statement causes the program to jump to the next statement following the end of the loop or switch containing the break. The continue statement causes the program to skip the rest of the containing loop and to start the next cycle.

The control statements presented in these last two chapters will enable you to tackle programs much more powerful and ambitious than those you worked with before. As proof, just compare some of the examples in these chapters to those of the earlier chapters.

Review Questions

1. Determine which expressions are true and which are false.

   a. `100 > 3 && 'a'>'c'`

   b. `100 > 3 || 'a'>'c'`

   c. `!(100>3)`

2. Construct an expression to express the following conditions:

   a. number is equal to or greater than 1 but smaller than 9.

   b. ch is not a q or a k character.

   c. number is between 1 and 9 but is not a 5.

   d. number is not between 1 and 9.

3. The following program has unnecessarily complex relational expressions as well as some outright errors. Simplify and correct it.

```
#include <stdio.h>
int main(void)                                          /* 1   */
{                                                       /* 2   */
   int weight, height;  /* weight in lbs, height in inches */
                                                        /* 4   */
   scanf("%d, weight, height);                          /* 5   */
   if (weight < 100)                                    /* 6   */
      if (height >= 72)                                 /* 7   */
         printf("You are very tall for your weight.\n");
      else if (height < 72 && > 64)                     /* 9   */
         printf("You are tall for your weight.\n");
   else if (weight > 300 && ! (weight <= 300))          /* 11 */
      if (!(height >= 48)                               /* 12 */
         printf(" You are quite short for your weight.\n");
   else                                                 /* 14 */
      printf("Your weight is ideaL.\n");                /* 15 */
                                                        /* 16 */

   return 0;
}
```

4. What is the numerical value of each of the following expressions?

   a. 5 > 2

   b. 3 + 4 > 2 && 3 < 2

   c. x >= y ¦¦ y > x

   d. d = 5 + (6 > 2)

   e. 'X' > 'T' ? 10 : 5

   f. x > y ? y > x : x > y

5. What will the following program print?

```
#include <stdio.h>
int main(void)
{
   int num;
   for (num = 1; num <= 11; num++)
   {
      if (num % 3 == 0)
         putchar('$');
      else
         putchar('*');
         putchar('#');
      putchar('%');
   }
   putchar('\n');
   return 0;
}
```

6. What would the following program print?

```
#include <stdio.h>
int main(void)
{
    int i = 0;
    while ( i < 3) {
        switch(i++) {
            case 0 : printf("Merry");
            case 1 : printf("Merr");
            case 2 : printf("Mer");
            default: printf("Oh no!");
        }
        putchar('\n');
    }
    return 0;
}
```

7. What's wrong with this program?

```
#include <stdio.h>
int main(void)
{
  char ch;
  int lc = 0;    /* lowercase char count */
  int uc = 0;    /* uppercase char count */
  int oc = 0;    /* other char count */

  while ((ch = getchar()) != '#')
  {
      if ('a' <= ch >= 'z')
          lc++;
      else if (!(ch < 'A') || !(ch > 'Z'))
          uc++;
      oc++;
  }
  printf(%d lowercase, %d uppercase, %d other, lc, uc, oc);
  return 0;
}
```

8. What will the following program print?

```
/* retire.c    */
#include <stdio.h>
int main(void)
{
  int age = 20;

  while (age++ <= 65)
  {
    if (( age % 20) == 0) /* is age divisible by 20? */
        printf("You are %d. Here is a raise.\n", age);
    if (age = 65)
        printf("You are %d. Here is your gold watch.\n", age);
  }
  return 0;
}
```

9. What will the following program print when given this input?

```
q
c
g
b
#include <stdio.h>
int main(void)
{
  char ch;

  while ((ch = getchar()) != '#')
  {
      if (ch == '\n')
          continue;
      printf("Step 1\n");
      if (ch == 'c')
          continue;
      else if (ch == 'b')
          break;
      else if (ch == 'g')
          goto laststep;
      printf("Step 2\n");
  laststep:  printf("Step 3\n");
  }
  printf("Done\n");
  return 0;
}
```

10. Rewrite the program in Question 9 so that it exhibits the same behavior but does not use a `continue` or a `goto`.

Programming Exercises

1. Write a program that reads input until encountering the # character and then reports the number of spaces read, the number of newline characters read, and the number of all other characters read.

2. Write a program that reads input until encountering #. Have the program print each input character and its ASCII decimal code. Print eight character-code pairs per line. Suggestion: Use a character count and the modulus operator (%) to print a newline character for every eight cycles of the loop.

3. Write a program that reads integers until 0 is entered. Once input terminates, the program should report the total number of even integers (excluding the 0) entered, the average value of the even integers, the total number of odd integers entered, and the average value of the odd integers.

4. Using if else statements, write a program that reads input up to #, replaces each period with an exclamation mark, replaces each exclamation mark initially present with two exclamation marks, and reports at the end the number of substitutions it has made.

5. Redo Exercise 3, but use a switch.

6. Write a program that reads input up to # and reports the number of times that the sequence ei occurs.

Note

The program will have to "remember" the preceding character as well as the current character. Test it with input like "Receive your eieio award."

7. Write a program that requests the hours worked in a week and then prints the gross pay, the taxes, and the net pay. Assume the following:

   a. Basic pay rate = $10.00/hr

   b. Overtime (in excess of 40 hours) = time and a half

   c. Tax rate   15% of the first $300

                   20% of the next $150

                   25% of the rest

Use #define constants, and don't worry if the example does not conform to current tax law.

8. Modify assumption a. in Exercise 6 so that the program presents a menu of pay rates to choose from. Use a switch to select the pay rate. The beginning of a run should look something like this:

```
******************************************************************
Enter the number corresponding to the desired pay rate or action:
1) $8.75/hr                          2) $9.33/hr
3) $10.00/hr                         4) $11.20/hr
5) quit
******************************************************************
```

If choices 1 through 4 are selected, then the program should request the hours worked. The program should recycle until 5 is entered. If something other than choices 1 through 5 is entered, the program should remind the user what the proper choices are and then recycle. Use #defined constants for the various earning rates and tax rates.

9. Write a program that accepts an integer as input and then displays all the prime numbers smaller than or equal to that number.

10. The 1988 United States Federal Tax Schedule was the simplest in recent times. It had four categories, and each category has two rates. Here is a summary; dollar amounts are taxable income.

Category	Tax
Single	15% of first $17,850 plus 28% of excess
Head of Household	15% of first $23,900 plus 28% of excess
Married, Joint	15% of first $29,750 plus 28% of excess
Married, Separate	15% of first $14,875 plus 28% of excess

For instance, a single wage earner with a taxable income of $20,000 dollars owes $0.15 \times \$17,850 + 0.28 \times (\$20,000 - \$17,850)$. Write a program that lets the user specify the tax category and the taxable income and that then calculates the tax. Use a loop so that the user can enter several tax cases.

## CHAPTER 8

CHARACTER INPUT/OUTPUT AND REDIRECTION

I n this chapter, you learn more about input, output, and the differences between buffered and unbuffered input. You learn how to simulate the end-of-file condition from the keyboard and how to use redirection to connect your programs to files. Finally, you gain some experience in making the user interface friendlier.

In the computing world, we use the words *input* and *output* in several ways. We speak of input and output devices, such as keyboards, disk drives, and laser printers. We talk about the data used for input and output. We discuss the functions that perform input and output. This chapter concentrates on the functions used for input and output (*I/O*, for short).

I/O functions transport information to and from your program; printf(), scanf(), getchar(), and putchar() are examples. You've seen these functions in previous chapters, and now you'll be able to look at their conceptual basis. Along the way, you'll see how to improve the program-user interface.

Originally, input/output functions were not part of the definition of C. Their development was left to C's implementors. In practice, the UNIX implementation of C has served as a model for these functions. The ANSI C library, recognizing past practice, contains a large number of these UNIX I/O functions, including the ones we've used. Because such standard functions must work in a wide variety of computer environments, they seldom take advantage of features peculiar to a particular system. Therefore, many C vendors supply additional I/O functions that do make use of special features, such as the 8086 microprocessor I/O ports or the Macintosh ROM routines. These specialized functions enable you to write programs that use a particular computer more effectively. Unfortunately, they often can't be used on other computer systems. Consequently, we'll concentrate on the standard I/O functions available on all systems, for they enable you to write portable programs that can be moved easily from one system to another.

Single-Character I/O: getchar() and putchar()

As you saw in Chapter 7, "C Control Statements: Branching and Jumps," getchar() and putchar() perform input and output one character at a time. That method might strike you as a rather silly way of doing things. After all, you can easily read groupings larger than a single character, but this method does suit the capability of a computer. Furthermore, this approach is the heart of most programs that deal with text, that is, with ordinary words. To remind yourself of how these functions work, examine Listing 8.1, a very simple example. All it does is fetch characters from keyboard input and send them to the screen. This process is called *echoing the input*. We use a `while` loop that terminates when the # character is encountered.

Listing 8.1 The `echo.c` program.

```
/* echo.c -- repeats input */
#include <stdio.h>
int main(void)
{
  char ch;

  while ((ch = getchar()) != '#')
      putchar(ch);
  return 0;
}
```

On most systems, the definitions of `getchar()` and `putchar()` are in the system file `stdio.h`, which is why we have included that file in the program. (Typically, `getchar()` and `putchar()` are not true functions, but are defined using preprocessor macros, a topic we'll cover in Chapter 16, "The C Preprocessor and the C Library.") Using this program produces exchanges like this:

Hello, there. I would[enter]
Hello, there. I would
like a #3 bag of potatoes.[enter]
like a

After watching this program run, you might wonder why you must type a whole line before the input is echoed. You might also wonder if there is a better way to terminate input. Using a particular character, such as #, to terminate input prevents you from using that character in the text. To answer these questions, you have to look at how C programs handle keyboard input. In particular, you need to examine buffering and the concept of a standard input file.

Buffers

When you run the previous program on some systems, the text you input is echoed immediately. That is, a sample run would look like this:

HHeelllloo,, tthheerree.. II wwoouulldd[enter]

lliikkee aa #

The preceding behavior is the exception. On most systems, nothing happens until you press Enter, as in the first example. The immediate echoing of input characters is an instance of *unbuffered* (or *direct*) input, meaning that the character you type is immediately made available to the waiting program. The delayed echoing, on the other hand, illustrates *buffered* input, in which the characters you type are collected and stored in an area of temporary storage called a *buffer*. Pressing Enter causes the block of characters (or single character, if that is all you typed) to be made available to your program. Figure 8.1 compares these two kinds of input.

Why have buffers? First, it is less time-consuming to transmit several characters as a block than to send them one by one. Second, if you mistype, you can use your keyboard correction features to fix your mistake. When you finally press Enter, you can transmit the corrected version.

Unbuffered input, on the other hand, is desirable for some interactive programs. In a game, for instance, you would like each command to take place as soon as you press a key. Therefore, both buffered and unbuffered input have their uses.

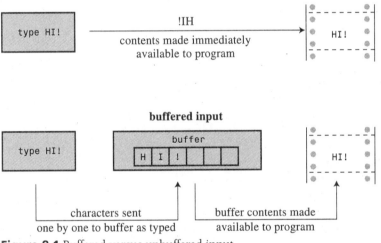

Figure 8.1 Buffered versus unbuffered input.

Buffering comes in two varieties: *fully buffered* I/O and *line-buffered* I/O. For fully buffered input, the buffer is flushed (the contents are sent to their destination) when it is full. This kind of buffering usually occurs with file input. The buffer size depends on the system, but 512 bytes and 4,096 bytes are common values. With line-buffered I/O, the buffer is flushed whenever a newline character shows up. Keyboard input is normally line-buffered, so that pressing Enter flushes the buffer.

Which kind of input do you have: buffered or unbuffered? ANSI C specifies that input should be buffered, but K&R left the choice open to the compiler writer. You can find out by running the `echo.c` program and seeing which behavior results.

The reason ANSI C settled on buffered input as the standard is that some computer designs don't permit unbuffered input. If your particular computer does allow unbuffered input, most likely your C compiler offers unbuffered input as an option. Compilers for IBM PC compatibles, for example, typically supply a special family of functions, supported by the `conio.h` header file, for unbuffered input. These functions include `getche()` for echoed unbuffered input and `getch()` for unechoed unbuffered input. (*Echoed input* means the character you type shows onscreen, and *unechoed input* means the keystrokes don't show.) UNIX systems use a different approach, for there UNIX itself controls buffering. With UNIX, you use the `ioctl()` function to specify the type of input you want, and `getchar()` behaves accordingly. In ANSI C, the `setbuf()` and `setvbuf()` functions (see Chapter 12, "File Input/Output") supply some control over buffering, but the inherent limitations of some systems can restrict the effectiveness of these functions. In short, there is no standard ANSI way of invoking unbuffered input; the means depend on the computer system. In this book, with apologies to our unbuffered friends, we assume you are using buffered input.

Terminating Keyboard Input

The program halts when # is entered, which is convenient as long as you exclude that character from normal input. As you've seen, however, # can show up in normal input. Ideally, you'd like a terminating character that normally does not show up in text. Such a character won't pop up accidentally in the middle of some input, stopping the program before you want it to stop. C has an answer to this need, but, to understand it, you need to know how C handles files.

Files, Streams, and Keyboard Input

A *file* is an area of memory in which information is stored. Normally, a file is kept in some sort of permanent memory, such as a floppy disk, a hard disk, or a tape. You are doubtless aware of the importance of files to computer systems. For instance, your C programs are kept in files, and the programs used to compile your programs are kept in files. This last example points out that some programs need to be able to access particular files. When you compile a program stored in a file called `echo.c`, the compiler opens the `echo.c` file and reads its contents. When the compiler finishes, it closes the file. Other programs, such as word processors, not only open, read, and close files, they also *write* to them.

C, being powerful, flexible, and so on, has many library functions for opening, reading, writing, and closing files. On one level, it can deal with files by using the basic file tools of the host operating system. This is called *low-level I/O*. Because of the many differences among computer systems, it is impossible to create a standard library of universal low-level I/O functions, and ANSI C does not attempt to do so; however, C also deals with files on a second level called the *standard I/O package*. This involves creating a standard model and a standard set of I/O functions for dealing with files. At this higher level, differences between systems are handled by specific C implementations so that you deal with a uniform interface.

What sort of differences are we talking about? Different systems, for example, store files differently. Some store the file contents in one place and information about the file elsewhere. Some build a description of the file into the file itself. In dealing with text, some systems use a single newline character to mark the end of a line. Others might use the combination of the carriage return and linefeed characters to represent the end of a line. Some systems measure file sizes to the nearest byte; some measure in blocks of bytes.

When you use the standard I/O package, you are shielded from these differences. Therefore, to check for a newline, you can use `if (ch == '\n')`. If the system actually uses the carriage-return/linefeed combination, the I/O functions automatically translate back and forth between the two representations.

Conceptually, the C program deals with a stream instead of directly with a file. A *stream* is an idealized flow of data to which the actual input or output is mapped. That means various kinds of input with differing properties are represented by streams with more uniform properties. The process of opening a file then becomes one of associating a stream with the file, and reading and writing take place via the stream.

Chapter 12 discusses files in greater detail. For this chapter, simply note that C treats input and output devices the same as it treats regular files on storage devices. In particular, the keyboard and the display device are treated as files opened automatically by every C program. Keyboard input is represented by a stream called `stdin`, and output to the screen (or teletype, or other output device) is represented by a stream called `stdout`. The `getchar()`, `putchar()`, `printf()`, and `scanf()` functions are all members of the standard I/O package, and they deal with these two streams.

One implication of all this is that you can use the same techniques with keyboard input as you do with files. For example, a program reading a file needs a way to detect the end of the file so that it knows where to stop reading. Therefore, C input functions come equipped with a built-in end-of-file detector. Because keyboard input is treated like a file, you should be able to use that end-of-file detector to terminate keyboard input, too. Let's see how this is done, beginning with files.

The End of File

A computer operating system needs some way to tell where each file begins and ends. One method to detect the end of a file is to place a special character in the file to mark the end. This is the method used, for example, in CP/M, IBM-DOS, and MS-DOS text files. These operating systems use (or once used) the Ctrl+Z character to mark the end of files. (Ctrl+Z is the character generated by holding down the Ctrl key while typing the Z key.) Figure 8.2 illustrates this approach.

prose:

> Ishphat the robot
> slid open the hatch
> and shouted his challenge.

prose in a file:

```
Ishphat the robot\n slid open the hatch\n and shouted his challenge.\n^Z
```

Figure 8.2 A file with an end-of-file marker.

A second approach is for the operating system to store information on the size of the file. If a file has 3,000 bytes and a program has read 3,000 bytes, then the program has reached the end. MS-DOS and its relatives use this approach for binary files because this method allows the files to hold all characters, including Ctrl+Z. Newer versions of DOS also use this approach for text files. UNIX uses this approach for all files.

C handles this variety of methods by having the `getchar()` function return a special value when the end of a file is reached, regardless of how the operating system actually detects the end of file. The name given to this value is EOF (end of file). Therefore, the return value for `getchar()` when it detects an end of file is EOF. The `scanf()` function also returns EOF on detecting the end of a file. Typically, EOF is defined in the `stdio.h` file as follows:

```
#define EOF (-1)
```

Why -1? Normally, `getchar()` returns a value in the range 0 through 127 because those are values corresponding to the standard character set, but it might return values from 0 through 255 if the system recognizes an extended character set. In either case, the value -1 does not correspond to any character, so it can be used to signal the end of a file.

Some systems may define EOF to be a value other than -1, but the definition is always different from a return value produced by a legitimate input character. If you include the `stdio.h` file and use the EOF symbol, you don't have to worry about the numeric definition. The important point is that EOF represents a value that signals the end of a file was detected; it is not a symbol actually found in the file.

Okay, how can you use EOF in a program? Compare the return value of `getchar()` with EOF. If they are different, you have not yet reached the end of a file. In other words, you can use an expression like this:

```
while ((ch = getchar()) != EOF)
```

What if you are reading keyboard input and not a file? Most systems (but not all) have a way to simulate an end-of-file condition from the keyboard. Knowing that, you can rewrite the basic read and echo program, as shown in Listing 8.2.

Listing 8.2   The `echo_eof.c` program.

```
/* echo_eof.c -- repeats input to end of file */
#include <stdio.h>
int main(void)
{
  int ch;

  while ((ch = getchar()) != EOF)
      putchar(ch);
  return 0;
}
```

Note these points:

- You don't have to define EOF because `stdio.h` takes care of that.

- You don't have to worry about the actual value of EOF because the #define statement in `stdio.h` enables you to use the symbolic representation EOF.

- The variable `ch` is changed from type `char` to type `int` because `char` variables may be represented by unsigned integers in the range **0** to **255**, but `EOF` may have the numeric value `-1`. That is an impossible value for an unsigned `char` variable, but not for an `int`. Fortunately, `getchar()` is actually type `int` itself, so it can read the `EOF` character. Implementations that use a signed `char` type may get by with declaring `ch` as type `char`, but it is better to use the more general form.

- The fact that `ch` is an integer doesn't faze `putchar()`. It still prints the character equivalent.

- To use this program on keyboard input, you need a way to type the `EOF` character. No, you can't just type the letters *E-O-F*, and you can't just type `-1`. (Typing `-1` would transmit two characters: a hyphen and the digit *1*.) Instead, you have to find out what your system requires. On most UNIX systems, for example, typing Ctrl+D at the beginning of a line causes the end-of-file signal to be transmitted. Many microcomputing systems recognize a Ctrl+Z typed anywhere on a line as an end-of-file signal.

Here is a buffered example of running `echo_eof.c` on a UNIX system:

```
She walks in beauty, like the night
She walks in beauty, like the night
  Of cloudless climes and starry skies...
  Of cloudless climes and starry skies...
              Lord Byron
              Lord Byron
[Ctrl+D]
```

Each time you press Enter, the characters stored in the buffer are processed, and a copy of the line is printed. This continues until you simulate the end of file, UNIX-style. On a PC, you would type Ctrl+Z instead.

Let's stop for a moment and think about the possibilities for `echo_eof.c`. It copies onto the screen whatever input you feed it. Suppose you could somehow feed a file to it. Then it would print the contents of the file onto the screen, stopping when it reached the end of the file, for it would find an `EOF` signal then. Suppose instead that you could find a way to direct the program's output to a file. Then you could enter data from the keyboard and use `echo_eof.c` to store what you type in a file. Suppose you could do both simultaneously: Direct input from one file into `echo_eof.c` and send the output to another file. Then you could use `echo_eof.c` to copy files. This little program has the potential to look at the contents of files, to create new files, and to make copies of files—pretty good for such a short program! The key is to control the flow of input and output, and that is the next topic.

Simulated EOF and Graphical Interfaces

The concept of simulated `EOF` developed in a command-line environment using a text interface. In such environments, the user interacts with a program through keystrokes, and the operating system generates the `EOF` signal.

Some practices don't translate particularly well to graphical interfaces, such as Windows and the Macintosh, with more complex user interfaces. For them, some behaviors result from the particular implementation rather than from the operating system. For example, a simulated `EOF` is not a basic Macintosh concept. However, Metrowerks CodeWarrior for the Mac provides added support that recognizes Ctrl+Z as the end-of-file simulation, but Symantec C for the Mac chose to implement Ctrl+D as the end-of-file equivalent.

Redirection and Files

Input and output involve functions, data, and devices. Consider, for instance, the `echo_eof.c` program. It uses the input function `getchar()`. The input device (we have assumed) is a keyboard, and the input data stream consists of individual characters. Suppose you want to keep the same input function and the same kind of data, but want to change where the program looks for data. A good question to ask (and to answer) is "How does a program know where to look for its input?"

By default, a C program using the standard I/O package looks to the standard input as its source for input. This is the stream identified earlier as `stdin`. It is whatever has been set up as the usual way for reading data into the computer. It could be magnetic tape, punched cards, a teletype, or (as we will continue to assume) your keyboard. A modern computer is a suggestible tool, however, and you can influence it to look elsewhere for input. In particular, you can tell a program to seek its input from a file instead of from a keyboard.

There are two ways to get a program to work with files. One way is to explicitly use special functions that open files, close files, read files, write in files, and so forth. That method we'll save for Chapter 12. The second way is to use a program designed to work with keyboard and screen, but to *redirect* input and output along different channels, to and from files, for example. In other words, you reassign the `stdin` stream to file. The `getchar()` program continues to get its data from the stream, not really caring from where the stream gets its data. This approach is more limited in some respects than the first, but it is much simpler to use. It is the one you will use now.

One major problem with redirection is that it is associated with the operating system, not C. However, the most popular C environments (UNIX and DOS 2.0 and later) feature redirection, and some C implementations simulate it on systems lacking the feature. We'll look at the UNIX and DOS versions.

UNIX and DOS Redirection

UNIX and current DOS versions enable you to redirect both input and output. Redirecting input enables your program to use a file instead of the keyboard for input, and redirecting output enables it to use a file instead of the screen for output.

Redirecting Input

Suppose you have compiled the `echo_eof.c` program and placed the executable version in a file called `echo_eof` (or `echo_eof.exe` on DOS systems). To run the program, type the executable file's name:

```
echo_eof
```

The program runs as described earlier, taking its input from the keyboard. Now suppose you want to use the program on a text file called **words**. A *text file* is one containing text, that is, data stored as human-readable characters. It could be an essay or a program in C, for example. A file containing machine language instructions, such as the file holding the executable version of a program, is not a text file. Because the program works with characters, it should be used with text files. All you need do is enter this command instead of the previous one:

```
echo_eof < words
```

The < symbol is a UNIX (and DOS) redirection operator. It causes the **words** file to be associated with the **stdin** stream, channeling the file contents into the **echo_eof** program. The **echo_eof** program itself doesn't know (or care) that the input is coming from a file instead of the keyboard. All it knows is that a stream of characters is being fed to it, so it reads them and prints them one character at a time until the end of file shows up. Because C puts files and I/O devices on the same footing, the file is now the I/O *device*. Try it!

Redirection Sidelights

With UNIX and DOS, the spaces on either side of the < are optional. Some systems, such as AmigaDOS, support redirection but don't allow a space between the redirection symbol and the filename.

Here is a sample run for one particular **words** file; the $ is one of the two standard UNIX prompts. On a DOS system, you would see the DOS prompt, perhaps an A> or C>.

```
$ echo_eof < words
The world is too much with us: late and soon,
Getting and spending, we lay waste our powers:
Little we see in Nature that is ours;
We have given our hearts away, a sordid boon!
$
```

Well, that time we got our words' worth.

Redirecting Output

Now suppose you want to have **echo_eof** send your keyboard input to a file called **mywords**. Then you can enter the following and begin typing:

```
echo_eof > mywords
```

The > is a second redirection operator. It causes a new file called `mywords` to be created for your use, and then it redirects the output of `echo_eof` (that is, a copy of the characters you type) to that file. The redirection reassigns `stdout` from the display device (your screen) to the `mywords` file instead. If you already have a file with the name `mywords`, normally it would be erased and then replaced by the new one. (Some UNIX systems, however, give you the option of protecting existing files.) All that appears on your screen are the letters as you type them, and the copies go to the file instead. To end the program, type Ctrl+D (UNIX) or Ctrl+Z (DOS) at the beginning of a line. Try it. If you can't think of anything to type, just imitate the next example. In it, we use the $ UNIX prompt. Remember to end each line by pressing Enter to send the buffer contents to the program.

```
$ echo_eof > mywords
You should have no problem recalling which redirection
operator does what. Just remember that each operator points
in the direction the information flows. Think of it as
a funnel.
[Ctrl+D]
$
```

After the Ctrl+D or Ctrl+Z is processed, the program terminates and your system prompt returns. Did the program work? The UNIX `ls` command or DOS `dir` command, which lists filenames, should show you that the file `mywords` now exists. You can use the UNIX `cat` or DOS `type` command to check the contents, or you can use `echo_eof` again, this time redirecting the file to the program:

```
$ echo_eof < mywords
You should have no problem recalling which redirection
operator does what. Just remember that each operator points
in the direction the information flows. Think of it as a
funnel.
$
```

Combined Redirection

Now suppose you want to make a copy of the file `mywords` and call it `savewords`. Just issue this next command,

```
echo_eof < mywords > savewords
```

and the deed is done. The following command would have served as well because the order of redirection operations doesn't matter:

```
echo_eof > savewords < mywords
```

Beware. Don't use the same file for both input and output to the same command.

```
echo_eof < mywords > mywords....<--WRONG
```

The reason is that > `mywords` causes the original `mywords` to be truncated to zero length before it is ever used as input.

In brief, here are the rules governing the use of the two redirection operators < and > with UNIX or DOS:

- A redirection operator connects an *executable* program (including standard UNIX commands) with a data file. It cannot be used to connect one data file to another, nor can it be used to connect one program to another program.

- Input cannot be taken from more than one file, nor can output be directed to more than one file by using these operators.

- Normally, spaces between the names and operators are optional, except occasionally when some characters with special meaning to the UNIX shell or DOS are used. We could, for example, have used `echo_eof<words`.

You have already seen several proper examples. Here are some wrong examples, with `addup` and `count` as executable programs and `fish` and `beets` as text files:

`fish > beets`	←violates the first rule
`addup < count`	←violates the first rule
`addup < fish < beets`	←violates the second rule
`count > beets fish`	←violates the second rule

UNIX and DOS also feature the `>>` operator, which enables you to add data to the end of an existing file, and the pipe operator (`|`), which enables you to connect the output of one program to the input of a second program. See a UNIX book, such as *UNIX Primer Plus, Second Edition* (Waite, Prata, and Martin; Indianapolis: Sams Publishing), for more information on all these operators.

Comment

Redirection enables you to use keyboard-input programs with files. For this to work, the program has to test for the end of file. For example, Chapter 7 presents a word-counting program that counts words up to the first `|` character. Change `ch` from type `char` to type `int`, and replace `'|'` with `EOF` in the loop test, and you can use the program to count words in text files.

Redirection is a command-line concept because you indicate it by typing special symbols on the command line. If you are not using a command-line environment, you might still be able to try the technique. First, some integrated environments have menu options that let you indicate redirection. Second, the Metrowerks CodeWarrior and the Symantec C/C++ compilers have a mechanism for simulating command-line arguments (see Chapter 11, "Character Strings and String Functions") that also supports redirection. Listing 8.3 shows a Mac-oriented version of Listing 8.2 that enables redirection.

Listing 8.3   The `mac_eof.c` program.

```
/* mac_eof.c -- enables redirection on the Mac */
#include <stdio.h>
#include <console.h>  /* declares ccommand() */
int main(int argc, char *argv[])
```

continued on next page

continued from previous page

```
{
    int ch;

    argc = ccommand(&argv);
    while ((ch = getchar()) != EOF)
        putchar(ch);
    return 0;
}
```

Chapter 11 discusses the altered function heading. The main point is that when the program executes the `ccommand()` function, it displays a dialog box that allows you to specify files be used for input and output.

Summary: How to Redirect Input and Output

With most C systems, you can use redirection, either for all programs through the operating system or else just for C programs, courtesy of the C compiler. In the following, let `prog` be the name of the executable program and let `file1` and `file2` be names of files.

Redirecting Output to a File: >

```
prog >file1
```

Redirecting Input from a File: <

```
prog <file2
```

Combined Redirection:

```
prog <file2 >file1
prog >file1 <file2
```

Both forms use `file2` for input and `file1` for output.

Spacing:

Some systems require a space to the left of the redirection operator and no space to the right. Other systems (UNIX, for example) accept either spaces or no spaces on either side.

A Graphic Example

You can use `getchar()` and `putchar()` to produce geometric patterns using characters. Listing 8.4 shows such a program. It reads a character and then prints it a number of times, the number depending on the character's ASCII value. The program also prints enough spaces to center each line.

Listing 8.4   The `patterns.c` program.

```c
/* patterns.c -- produces a symmetrical pattern of characters */
#include <stdio.h>
int main(void)
{
    int ch;                     /* read character                    */
    int index;
    int chnum;

    while ((ch = getchar()) != '\n')
    {
        chnum = ch % 26;        /* produces a number from 0 to 25 */
        index = 0;
        while (index++ < (30 - chnum))
            putchar(' ');       /* spaces to center pattern          */
        index = 0;
        while (index++ < (2 * chnum + 1))
            putchar(ch);        /* print ch several times            */
        putchar('\n');
    }
    return 0;
}
```

Listing 8.4 uses nested loops. The outer `while` loop gathers input characters. The first inner `while` loop prints leading spaces to center the text, and the second `while` loop prints the character multiple times. The number of characters printed is determined from the numeric value for the character. What you get depends on what you enter. If, for example, you type

What's up?

the response is this:

```
            wwwwwwwwwwwwwwwwwwwwwwwww
                       h
      aaaaaaaaaaaaaaaaaaaaaaaaaaaaaaaaaaaaaaaaaaa
           ttttttttttttttttttttttttttt
                 ! ! ! ! ! ! ! ! ! ! ! ! ! !
            
             sssssssssssssssssssssssss

          uuuuuuuuuuuuuuuuuuuuuuuuuuuuu
               ppppppppppppppppppp
           ?????????????????????????
```

What can you do with this program? You can ignore it, you can tinker with it to change the kinds of patterns it makes, or you can try to find combinations of input characters that produce a pretty pattern. For example, the input

hijklmnopqrstuiii

produces this:

```
               h
              iii
             jjjjj
            kkkkkkk
           lllllllll
          mmmmmmmmmmm
         nnnnnnnnnnnnn
        ooooooooooooooo
       ppppppppppppppppp
      qqqqqqqqqqqqqqqqqqq
     rrrrrrrrrrrrrrrrrrrrr
    sssssssssssssssssssssss
   ttttttttttttttttttttttttt
  uuuuuuuuuuuuuuuuuuuuuuuuuuu
              iii
              iii
              iii
```

Creating a Friendlier User Interface

Most of us have on occasion written programs that are awkward to use. Fortunately, C gives you the tools to make input a smoother, more pleasant process. Unfortunately, learning these tools could, at first, lead to new problems. The goal in this section is to guide you through some of these problems to a friendlier user interface, one that eases data entry and smoothes over the effects of faulty input.

Working with Buffered Input

Buffered input is often a convenience to the user, but it can be bothersome to the programmer when character input is used. The problem, as you've seen in some earlier examples, is that buffered input requires you to press the Enter key to transmit your input. This act also transmits a newline character that the program must handle. Let's examine this and other problems with a guessing program. You pick a number, and the computer tries to guess it. The computer uses a plodding method, but we are concentrating on I/O, not algorithms. See Listing 8.5 for the starting version of the program.

Listing 8.5   The `guess.c` program.

```
/* guess.c -- an inefficient number-guesser */
#include <stdio.h>
int main(void)
{
  int guess = 1;
  char response;
```

```
   printf("Pick an integer from 1 to 100. I will try to guess ");
   printf("it.\nRespond with a y if my guess is right and with");
   printf("\nan n if it is wrong.\n");
   printf("Uh...is your number %d?\n", guess);
   while ((response = getchar()) != 'y')          /* get response */
       printf("Well, then, is it %d?\n", ++guess);
   printf("I knew I could do it!\n");
   return 0;
}
```

Here's a sample run:

```
Pick an integer from 1 to 100. I will try to guess it.
Respond with a y if my guess is right and with
an n if it is wrong.
Uh...is your number 1?
n
Well, then, is it 2?
Well, then, is it 3?
n
Well, then, is it 4?
Well, then, is it 5?
y
I knew I could do it!
```

Out of consideration for the program's pathetic guessing algorithm, we chose a small number. Note that the program makes two guesses every time you enter n. What's happening is that the program reads the n response as a denial that the number is 1 and then reads the newline character as a denial that the number is 2.

One solution is to use a while loop to discard the rest of the input line, including the newline character. This has the additional merit of treating responses such as no or no way the same as a simple n. The version in Listing 8.5 treats no as two responses. Here is a revised loop that fixes the problem:

```
while ((response = getchar()) != 'y')     /* get response */
{
    printf("Well, then, is it %d?\n", ++guess);
    while (getchar() != '\n')
        continue;            /* skip rest of input line     */
}
```

Using this loop produces responses like the following:

```
Pick an integer from 1 to 100. I will try to guess it.
Respond with a y if my guess is right and with
an n if it is wrong.
Uh...is your number 1?
n
Well, then, is it 2?
no
Well, then, is it 3?
no sir
Well, then, is it 4?
forget it
Well, then, is it 5?
y
I knew I could do it!
```

That takes care of the problems with the newline character. However, as a purist, you might not like f being treated as meaning the same as n. To eliminate that defect, you can use an if statement to screen out other responses. Change the loop to this:

```
while ((response = getchar()) != 'y')      /* get response */
{
   if (response == 'n')
      printf("Well, then, is it %d?\n", ++guess);
   else
      printf("Sorry, I understand only y or n.\n");
   while (getchar() != '\n')
      continue;                    /* skip rest of input line */
}
```

Now the program's response looks like this:

```
Pick an integer from 1 to 100. I will try to guess it.
Respond with a y if my guess is right and with
an n if it is wrong.
Uh...is your number 1?
n
Well, then, is it 2?
no
Well, then, is it 3?
no sir
Well, then, is it 4?
forget it
Sorry, I understand only y or n.
n
Well, then, is it 5?
y
I knew I could do it!
```

When you write interactive programs, you should try to anticipate ways in which users might fail to follow instructions. Then you should design your program to handle user failures gracefully. Tell them when they are wrong, and give them another chance.

You should, of course, provide clear instructions to the user, but no matter how clear you make them, someone will always misinterpret them and then blame you for poor instructions.

Mixing Numeric and Character Input

Typically, you use getchar() to read input one character at a time and you use scanf() to read numbers or strings. This mixture can create problems because getchar() reads every character, including spaces, tabs, and newlines. In contrast, scanf(), when reading numbers, skips over spaces, tabs, and newlines. However, when reading characters using the %c specifier, scanf() behaves like getchar().

To illustrate a representative problem, Listing 8.6 presents a program that reads in a character and two numbers as input. It then prints the character using the number of rows and columns specified in the input.

Listing 8.6 The `showchar1.c` program.

```
/* showchar1.c -- program with an I/O problem */
#include <stdio.h>
void display(char c, int lines, int width);
int main(void)
{
    int ch;                /* character to be printed    */
    int rows, cols;        /* number of rows and columns */
    printf("Enter a character and two integers:\n");
    while ((ch = getchar()) != EOF)
    {
      scanf("%d %d", &rows, &cols);
      display(ch, rows, cols);
      printf("Enter another character and two integers;\n");
      printf("Simulate eof to quit.\n");
    }
    return 0;
}

void display(char c, int lines, int width)
{
    int row, col;

    for (row = 1; row <= lines; row++)
    {
        for (col = 1; col <= width; col++)
            putchar(c);
        putchar('\n');    /* end line and start a new one */
    }
}
```

Note: the program reads a character as type `int` to enable the `EOF` test. However, it passes the character as type `char` to the `display()` function. Because `char` is smaller than `int`, some compilers will warn about the conversion. In this case, you can ignore the warning.

The program is set up so that `main()` gets the data, and the `display()` function does the printing. Let's look at a sample run to see what the problem is.

```
Enter a character and two integers:
c 2 3
ccc
ccc
Enter another character and two integers;
Simulate eof to quit.
b 1 2




Enter another character and two integers;
Simulate eof to quit.
```

bb
```
Enter another character and two integers;
Simulate eof to quit.
^Z
```

```
Enter another character and two integers;
Simulate eof to quit.
^Z
```

The program starts off fine. You enter **c 2 3**, and it prints two rows of three c characters, as expected. Then you enter **b 1 2**, and it prints one row with two b characters. In between, it prints eight blank lines! What's wrong? It's that newline character again, this time the one immediately following the **3** on the first input line. Because getchar() doesn't skip over newline characters, this newline character is read by getchar() during the next cycle of the loop, becoming the character to be displayed.

Then scanf() has a turn at exposing our poor programming. Because getchar() reads the newline, the next input is the b character, so the scanf() function attempts to read it as an integer and fails. rows retains its previous value of **2**. (At least, that is how our system behaves on a failed match; ANSI C doesn't require any particular behavior in that instance.) Then scanf() tries to read the cols value. Input is still stuck on the b, so that read fails, too, and cols remains at **3**. The net result is that the program tells display() to print two rows of three newline characters. Each newline character generates a new line, giving a total of eight blank lines. Then the next loop cycle begins, and getchar() finally gets to read the b. This clears the way for scanf() to read the next two numbers. Similarly, the newline following this line forces you to enter Ctrl+Z twice to end the program. (We're assuming the program is run on a DOS system.)

To clear up this problem, the program has to skip over any newlines or spaces between the last number typed for one cycle of input and the character typed at the beginning of the next line. Also, it would be nice if the program could be terminated at the scanf() stage in addition to the getchar() test. The next version, shown in Listing 8.7, accomplishes this.

Listing 8.7 The showr2.c program.

```
/* showchar2.c -- prints characters in rows and columns */
#include <stdio.h>
#include <ctype.h>
void display(char c, int lines, int width);
int main(void)
{
    int ch;          /* character to be printed   */
    int rows, cols;  /* number of rows and columns */

    printf("Enter a character and two integers:\n");
    while ((ch = getchar()) != EOF)
```

```
    {
        if (!isspace(ch))
        {
          if (scanf("%d %d",&rows, &cols) != 2)
            break;
          display(ch, rows, cols);
          printf("Enter another character and two integers;\n");
          printf("Simulate eof to quit.\n");
        }
    }
    return 0;
}

void display(char c, int lines, int width)
{
    int row, col;

    for (row = 1; row <= lines; row++)
    {
        for (col = 1; col <= width; col++)
            putchar(c);
        putchar('\n');    /* end line and start a new one */
    }
}
```

The `if` statement causes the program to skip over the `scanf()` and `display()` statements if ch is whitespace. This means you can enter data fairly freely:

```
Enter a character and two integers:
a 2 3
aaa
aaa
Enter another character and two integers;
Simulate eof to quit.
b 1 2 c 3 5
bb
Enter another character and two integers;
Simulate eof to quit.
ccccc
ccccc
ccccc
Enter another character and two integers;
Simulate eof to quit.
[Ctrl+Z]
```

By using an `if` statement with a `break`, you terminate the program if the return value of `scanf()` is not 2. This occurs if one or both input values are not integers or if end-of-file is encountered.

By using the `if` statement to skip spaces as well as newlines, the program can handle the second input line. If you omit the space skipping, the input line would have to look like this:

```
b 1 2c 3 5
```

Otherwise, a space between the 2 and c would be read into ch, and scanf() would try
to read c as an integer.

Character Sketches

Now let's look at something a little more decorative. The plan is to create a program that
enables you to draw rough, filled-in figures by using characters. Each line of output consists of an unbroken row of characters. You choose the character and the starting and stopping
positions for printing the character in the row. The program, shown in Listing 8.8, keeps
reading your choices until it finds EOF. This program illustrates several programming techniques, which, of course, we'll discuss soon.

Listing 8.8   The sketcher.c program.

```
/* sketcher.c  -- this program makes solid figures */
#include <stdio.h>
#include <ctype.h>
#define TRUE 1
#define FALSE 0
#define MAXLENGTH 80
int badlimits(int begin, int end, int limit);
void display(char c, int first, int last);
int main(void)
{
    int ch;                /* character to be printed    */
    int start, stop;       /* starting and stopping points */
    int badlimits();       /* returns TRUE for bad limits  */

    printf("Enter character and column positions in this ");
    printf("style: D 3 21\n");
    while ((ch = getchar()) != EOF) /* read in character   */
    {
       if (isspace(ch))
          continue;        /* skip newlines, spaces */
       if (scanf("%d %d", &start, &stop) != 2)  /* read limits */
          break;
       if (badlimits(start, stop, MAXLENGTH) == TRUE)
          printf("Inappropriate limits were entered.\n");
       else
          display(ch, start, stop);
    }
    return 0;
}

int badlimits(int begin, int end, int limit)
{
    if (begin > end || begin < 1 || end > limit)
       return TRUE;
    else
       return FALSE;
}
```

```
void display(char c, int first, int last)
{
    int column;

    for (column = 1; column < first; column++)
        putchar(' ');     /* print blanks to starting point */
    for (column = first; column <= last; column++)
        putchar(c);       /* print char to stopping point  */
    putchar('\n');        /* end line and start a new one   */
}
```

The general structure is similar to that of Listing 8.6. The three main differences are these:

- A continue statement is used to skip to the end of the loop if ch is white-space, instead of isolating the relevant code with an if statement.

- The display() function has been rewritten to display the character in a different manner. Here, first represents the first column and last represents the last column for displaying the character.

- A badlimits() function has been added to screen out bad input values.

Suppose you call the executable program sketcher. To run the program, type its name, and then enter a character and two numbers. The program responds, you enter another set of data, and the program responds again until you supply an EOF signal. On a UNIX system using the % prompt, an exchange could look like this:

```
% sketcher
Enter character and column positions in this style: D 3 21
B 10 20
          BBBBBBBBBBB
Y 12 18
            YYYYYYY
[Ctrl+D]
%
```

The program printed the character B in columns 10 to 20, and it printed Y in columns 12 to 18. Unfortunately, when you use the program interactively, your commands are interspersed with the output. A more satisfactory way to use this program is to create a file containing suitable data and then use redirection to feed the file to the program. Suppose, for example, the file fig contains the following data:

```
_ 30 50
| 30 50
| 30 50
| 30 50
| 30 50
| 30 50
= 20 60
: 31 49
: 30 49
: 29 49
: 27 49
: 25 49
```

```
: 30 49
: 30 49
/ 30 49
: 35 48
: 35 48
```

The command `sketcher < fig` produces the output shown in Figure 8.3. (If you use the program with data from a file, you may as well omit the two `printf()` statements providing the original instructions.)

Note

Printers and screens have different values for the vertical-to-horizontal ratio for characters. This difference causes figures of this sort to look more compressed vertically when printed than when displayed on a screen.

Figure 8.3 The output of the character sketch program.

Analyzing the Program

The `sketcher.c` program is short, but it is more involved than the examples we have given before. Let's look at some of its elements.

Line Length

We limited the program to print no farther than the 80th column because 80 characters is the standard width of many video monitors and of regular-width paper. However, you can redefine the value of MAXLENGTH if you want to use the program with a device having a different output width.

Program Structure

We've followed a modular approach, using separate functions (modules) to verify input and to manage the display. The larger a program is, the more vital it is to use modular programming.

The main() function acquires the data:

```
while ((ch = getchar()) != EOF)
{
   if (isspace(ch))
      continue;                         /* skip newlines, spaces */
   if (scanf("%d %d", &start, &stop) != 2)   /* read limits */
      break;
```

With Listing 8.7, we discussed the rationale for skipping whitespace. Next, the program checks to see whether the input makes sense:

```
if (badlimits(start, stop, MAXLENGTH) == TRUE)
   printf("Inappropriate limits were entered.\n");
else
   display(ch, start, stop);
```

The purpose of the **if else** statement is to let the program skirt any values of start and stop that would lead to trouble. We will discuss the details of the badlimits() function later. The important point here is that it returns a value of TRUE if the data fails to pass the testing procedure. In that case, the computer prints a message and skips over the else part, which is the display output.

The display() function uses one for loop to print spaces up to where the character is first to appear. The second for loop then prints the character from the start column to the end column. Finally, it prints a newline to end the line.

```
void display(char c, int first, int last)
{
   int column;

   for (column = 1; column < first; column++)
      putchar(' ');      /* print blanks to starting point */
   for (column = first; column <= last; column++)
      putchar(c);        /* print char to stopping point   */
   putchar('\n');        /* end line and start a new one   */
}
```

Error-Checking

Getting the user to supply data in a form the computer can use properly is a pervasive problem. One technique is to use *error-checking*. In this technique, the computer checks the data to see if it is okay before using it. We have included a beginning effort at error-checking in this program with the `badlimits()` function:

```
int badlimits(int begin, int end, int limit)
{
    if (begin > end ¦¦ begin < 1 ¦¦ end > limit)
        return TRUE;
    else
        return FALSE;
}
```

What is the `badlimits()` function protecting against? First, there's no sense having the starting position come after the final position. Terminals normally print from left to right, not vice versa, so the expression `begin > end` checks for that possible error. Second, the first column on a screen is column 1. You can't write to the left of the left margin, so the `begin < 1` expression guards against making an error there. Finally, the expression `end > limit` checks to see that you don't try to print past the right margin.

Are there any other erroneous values you could give to `begin` and `end`? Well, you could try to make `begin` greater than `limit`. Would that pass the test? No. It's true you don't check for this error directly. However, suppose `begin` is greater than `limit`. Then, either `end` is also greater than `limit`—in which case that error is caught—or else `end` isn't greater than `limit`. If `end` is less than `limit`, it must also be less than `begin`. Therefore, this case gets caught by the first test. Another possible error is that `end` is less than 1. We leave it to you to make sure this error doesn't sneak through, either.

We kept the test pretty simple. If you design a program for serious use, you should put more effort than we did into this part of the program. For instance, you should put in error messages to identify which values are wrong and why, perhaps injecting your personality into the messages. Here are some possibilities:

```
Your value of 897654 for stop exceeds the screen width.
Oh my! Your START is bigger than your STOP. Please try again.
THE START VALUE SHOULD BE BIGGER THAN 0, HONORED USER.
```

The personality you inject, of course, is up to you.

Another input problem occurs if letters show up when `scanf()` expects numbers. As the program is set up, letters cause the program to terminate, which is preferable to it getting stuck or misinterpreting input. It's also possible to have `scanf()` skip over data it can't read; we'll show the technique in Chapter 9, "Functions."

Menu Browsing

Many computer programs use menus as part of the user interface. Menus make programs easier for the user, but they do pose some problems for the programmer. Let's see what's involved.

A menu offers the user a choice of responses. Here's a hypothetical example:

```
Enter the letter of your choice:
a. advice          b. bell
c. count           q. quit
```

Ideally, the user then enters one of these choices, and the program acts on that choice. As a programmer, you want to make this process go smoothly. The first subgoal is for the program to work smoothly when the user follows instructions. The second subgoal is for the program to work smoothly when the user fails to follow instructions. As you might expect, the second goal is the more difficult because it's hard to anticipate all the possible mistreatment that might come your program's way.

Tasks

Let's get more specific and look at the tasks the program needs to perform. It needs to get the user's response, and it needs to select a course of action based on the response. Also, the program should provide a way to return to the menu for further choices. C's switch statement is a natural vehicle for choosing actions because each user choice can be made to correspond to a particular case label. You can use a while statement to provide repeated access to the menu. In pseudocode, you can describe the process this way:

```
get choice
while choice is not 'q'
    switch to desired choice and execute it
    get next choice
```

Toward a Smoother Execution

The goals of program smoothness come into play when you decide how to implement this plan. One thing you can do, for example, is have the "get choice" segment screen out inappropriate responses so that only correct responses are passed on to the switch. That suggests representing the input process with a function that can return only correct responses. Combining that with a while loop and a switch leads to the following program structure:

```c
#include <stdio.h>
int getchoice(void);
void count(void);
int main(void)
{
    int choice;

    while ( (choice = getchoice()) != 'q')
    {
        switch (choice)
        {
            case 'a' :  printf("Buy low, sell high.\n");
                        break;
            case 'b' :  putchar('\a');   /* ANSI */
                        break;
            case 'c' :  count();
                        break;
            default  :  printf("Program error!\n");
                        break;
        }
    }
    return 0;
}
```

The `getchoice()` function is defined so that it can return only the values `'a'`, `'b'`, `'c'`, and `'q'`. You use it much as you use `getchar()`: getting a value and comparing it to a termination value, `'q'`, in this case. We've kept the actual menu choices simple so that you can concentrate on the program structure; we'll get to the `count()` function soon. The `default` case is handy for debugging. If the `getchoice()` function fails to limit its return value to the intended values, the `default` case lets you know something fishy is going on.

The `getchoice()` Function

Here, in pseudocode, is one possible design for this function:

```
show choices
get response
while response is not acceptable
    prompt for more response
    get response
```

And here is a simple, but awkward, implementation:

```
int getchoice(void)
{
    int ch;

    printf("Enter the letter of your choice:\n");
    printf("a. advice          b. bell\n");
    printf("c. count           d. quit\n");
    ch = getchar();
    while ( (ch < 'a' || ch > 'c') && ch != 'q')
    {
        printf("Please respond with a, b, c, or q.\n");
        ch = getchar();
    }
    return ch;
}
```

The problem is that with buffered input, every newline generated by the Return key is treated as an erroneous response. To make the program interface smoother, the function should skip over newlines.

There are several ways to do that. One is to replace `getchar()` with a new function called `getfirst()` that reads the first character on a line and discards the rest. This method also has the advantage of treating an input line consisting of, say, **act**, as being the same as a simple **a** instead of treating it as one good response followed by **c** for **count**. With this goal in mind, you can reprogram the input function as follows:

```
int getchoice(void)
{
    int ch;
    int getfirst(void);

    printf("Enter the letter of your choice:\n");
    printf("a. advice          b. bell\n");
    printf("c. count           q. quit\n");
    ch = getfirst();
    while ( (ch < 'a' || ch > 'c') && ch != 'q')
```

```
    {
        printf("Please respond with a, b, c, or q.\n");
        ch = getfirst();
    }
    return ch;
}

int getfirst(void)
{
    int ch;

    ch = getchar();            /* read next character */
    while (getchar() != '\n')
        continue;              /* skip rest of line */
    return ch;
}
```

Mixing Character and Numeric Input

As you saw in Listing 8.8, mixing character and numeric input poses problems, and that is true with the menu example, too. Suppose, for instance, the count() function (choice c) were to look like this:

```
void count(void)
{
    int n,i;

    printf("Count how far? Enter an integer:\n");
    scanf("%d", &n);
    for (i = 1; i <= n; i++)
        printf("%d\n", i);
}
```

If you then responded by entering 3, scanf() would read the 3 and leave a newline character as the next character in the input queue. The next call to getchoice() would result in getfirst() returning this newline character, leading to undesirable behavior.

One way to fix that problem is to rewrite getfirst() so that it returns the next nonwhitespace character rather than just the next character encountered. We leave that as an exercise for the reader. A second approach is have the count() function tidy up and clear the newline itself. This is the approach to take:

```
void count(void)
{
    int n,i;

    printf("Count how far? Enter an integer:\n");
    if (scanf("%d", &n) != 1)
    {
        printf("Please use digits next time; this time");
        printf(" I'll use the integer 5.\n");
        n = 5;
    }
```

```
        for (i = 1; i <= n; i++)
            printf("%d\n", i);
        while ( getchar() != '\n')
            continue;        /* clear newline, bad input */
}
```

You use the return value of scanf() to detect non-numeric input, too. To simplify matters, have the program substitute a default value for n if the input is bad. Also, in that case, the while loop at the end of the function disposes of the bad input. If you are more ambitious, you can have the function prompt for new input instead of using a default value. We show an example in Chapter 9. Listing 8.9 shows the final menu program. Note that function prototypes can appear either inside or outside function definitions. The main requirement for placement is that the prototype appears before the function is first used.

Listing 8.9   The menuette.c program.

```
/* menuette.c -- menu techniques */
#include <stdio.h>
int getchoice(void);
int getfirst(void);
void count(void);
int main(void)
{
    int choice;
    int getchoice(void);
    void count(void);

    while ( (choice = getchoice()) != 'q')
    {
        switch (choice)
        {
            case 'a' :  printf("Buy low, sell high.\n");
                        break;
            case 'b' :  putchar('\a');  /* ANSI */
                        break;
            case 'c' :  count();
                        break;
            default  :  printf("Program error!\n");
                        break;
        }
    }
    return 0;
}

void count(void)
{
    int n,i;

    printf("Count how far? Enter an integer:\n");
    if (scanf("%d", &n) != 1)
```

```
        {
            printf("Please use digits next time; this time");
            printf(" I'll use the integer 5.\n");
            n = 5;
        }
        for (i = 1; i <= n; i++)
            printf("%d\n", i);
        while ( getchar() != '\n')
            continue;
}

int getchoice(void)
{
    int ch;

    printf("Enter the letter of your choice:\n");
    printf("a. advice          b. bell\n");
    printf("c. count           q. quit\n");
    ch = getfirst();
    while (  (ch < 'a' || ch > 'c') && ch != 'q')
    {
        printf("Please respond with a, b, c, or q.\n");
        ch = getfirst();
    }
    return ch;
}

int getfirst(void)
{
    int ch;

    ch = getchar();
    while (getchar() != '\n')
        continue;
    return ch;
}
```

Here is a sample run:

```
Enter the letter of your choice:
a. advice          b. bell
c. count           q. quit
a
Buy low, sell high.
Enter the letter of your choice:
a. advice          b. bell
c. count           q. quit
count
Count how far? Enter an integer:
two
Please use digits next time; this time I'll use the integer 5.
1
2
3
4
5
```

```
Enter the letter of your choice:
a. advice          b. bell
c. count           q. quit
d
Please respond with a, b, c, or q.
q
```

It can be hard work getting a menu interface to work as smoothly as you might want, but after you develop a viable approach, you can reuse it in a variety of situations.

Chapter Summary

Many programs use `getchar()` to read input character by character. Typically, systems use *line-buffered input,* meaning that input is transmitted to the program when you press Enter. Pressing Enter also transmits a newline character that may require programming attention. ANSI C requires buffered input as the standard.

C features a family of functions, called the *standard I/O package,* that treats different file forms on different systems in a uniform manner. The `getchar()` and `scanf()` functions belong to this family. Both functions return the value `EOF` (defined in the `stdio.h` header) when they detect the end of a file. UNIX systems enable you to simulate the end-of-file condition from the keyboard by typing Ctrl+D at the beginning of a line; DOS systems use Ctrl+Z for the same purpose.

Many operating systems, including UNIX and DOS, feature *redirection,* which enables you to use files instead of the keyboard and screen for input and output. Programs that read input up to `EOF` can then be used either with keyboard input and simulated end-of-file signals or with redirected files.

Interspersing calls to `getchar()` with calls to `scanf()` can cause problems when `scanf()` leaves a newline character in the input just before a call to `getchar()`. By being aware of this problem, however, you can program around it.

When you are writing a program, plan the user interface thoughtfully. Try to anticipate the sort of errors users are likely to make and then design your program to handle them.

Review Questions

1. `putchar(getchar())` is a valid expression; what does it do? Is `getchar(putchar())` also valid?

2. What would each of the following statements accomplish?

    a. `putchar('H');`

    b. `putchar('\007');`

    c. `putchar('\n');`

    d. `putchar('\b');`

3. Suppose you have a program **count** that counts the characters in its input. Devise a command that counts the number of characters in the file **essay** and stores the result in a file named **essayct**.

4. Given the program and files in Question 3, which of the following are valid commands?

    a. `essayct <essay`

    b. `count essay`

    c. `essay >count`

5. What is **EOF**?

6. What is the output of each of the following fragments for the indicated input (assume that **ch** is type **int** and that the input is buffered)?

    a. The input is as follows:

    ```
    If you quit, I will.[enter]
    ```

    The fragment is as follows:

    ```
    while ((ch = getchar()) != 'i')
        putchar(ch);
    ```

    b. The input is as follows:

    ```
    Harhar[enter]
    ```

    The fragment is as follows:

    ```
    while ((ch = getchar()) != '\n')
    {
        putchar(ch++);
        putchar(++ch);
    }
    ```

7. How does C deal with different computer systems having different file and newline conventions?

8. What potential problem do you face when intermixing numeric input with character input on a buffered system?

Programming Exercises

1. Devise a program that counts the number of characters in its input up to the end of file.

2. Write a program that reads input until encountering **EOF**. Have the program print each input character and its ASCII decimal value. Note that

characters preceding the space character in the ASCII sequence are non-printing characters. Treat them specially. If the nonprinting character is a newline or tab, print \n or \t, respectively. Otherwise, use control-character notation. For instance, ASCII 1 is Ctrl+A, which can be displayed as ^A. Note that the ASCII value for A is the value for Ctrl+A plus 64. A similar relation holds for the other nonprinting characters. Print ten pairs per line, but start a fresh line each time a newline character is encountered.

3. Write a program that reads input until encountering EOF. Have it report the number of uppercase letters and the number of lowercase letters in the input. Assume that the numeric values for the lowercase letters are sequential, and assume the same for uppercase.

4. Write a program that reads input until encountering EOF. Have it report the average number of letters per word. Don't count whitespace as being letters in a word. Actually, punctuation shouldn't be counted either, but don't worry about that now. (If you do want to worry about it, consider using the ispunct() function from the ctype.h family.)

5. Modify the guessing program of Listing 8.5 so that it uses a more intelligent guessing strategy. For example, have the program initially guess 50, and have it ask the user whether the guess is high, low, or correct. If, say, the guess is low, have the next guess be halfway between 50 and 100, that is, 75. If that guess is high, let the next guess be halfway between 75 and 50, and so on. Using this *binary search* strategy, the program quickly zeros in on the correct answer, at least if the user does not cheat.

6. Modify the getfirst() function of Listing 8.9 so that it returns the first non-whitespace character encountered. Test it in a simple program.

7. Modify Exercise 7 from Chapter 7 so that the menu choices are labeled by characters instead of by numbers.

CHAPTER 9

FUNCTIONS

You will learn about the following in this chapter:

- Keyword

  return

- Operators

  * (unary) & (unary)

*I*n this chapter, you learn about functions: how to define them, how to use arguments and return values, and how to use pointer variables as function arguments. You find out about function types, ANSI C prototypes, and recursion.

How do you organize a program? C's design philosophy is to use functions as building blocks. You've already relied on the standard C library for functions such as printf(), scanf(), getchar(), putchar(), and strlen(). Now you're ready for a more active role: creating your own functions. You've previewed several aspects of that process in earlier chapters, and this chapter consolidates your earlier information and expands on it.

Review

First, what is a function? A *function* is a self-contained unit of program code designed to accomplish a particular task. A function in C plays the same role that functions, subroutines, and procedures play in other languages, although the details might differ. Some functions cause action to take place. For example, printf() causes data to be printed on your screen. Some functions find a value for a program to use. For instance, strlen() tells a program how long a certain string is. In general, a function can both produce actions and provide values.

Why should you use functions? For one, they save you from repetitious programming. If you have to do a certain task several times in a program, you need to write an appropriate function only once. The program can then use that function wherever needed, or you can use the same function in different programs, just as you have used `putchar()` in many programs. Two, even if you do a task just once in just one program, using a function is worthwhile because functions make a program more modular, hence easier to read and easier to change or fix. Suppose, for example, you want to write a program that does the following:

```
Read in a list of numbers
Sort the numbers
Find their average
Print a bar graph
```

You could use this program:

```c
#include <stdio.h>
#define SIZE 50
int main(void)
{
  float list[SIZE];

  readlist(list, SIZE);
  sort(list, SIZE);
  average(list, SIZE);
  bargraph(list, SIZE);
  return 0;
}
```

Of course, you would also have to write the four functions `readlist()`, `sort()`, `average()`, and `bargraph()`—mere details. Descriptive function names make it quite clear what the program does and how it is organized. You can then work with each function separately until it does its job right, and if you make the functions general enough, you can use them in other programs.

Many programmers like to think of a function as a "black box" defined in terms of the information that goes in (its input) and the value or action it produces (its output). What goes on inside the black box is not your concern, unless you are the one who has to write the function. For example, when you use `printf()`, you know that you have to give it a control string and, perhaps, some arguments. You also know what output `printf()` should produce. You never had to think about the programming that went into creating `printf()`. Thinking of functions in this manner helps you concentrate on the program's overall design rather than the details. Think carefully about what the function should do and how it relates to the program as a whole before worrying about writing the code.

What do you need to know about functions? You need to know how to define them properly, how to call them up for use, and how to set up communication between functions. To refresh your memory on these points, we will begin with a very simple example and then bring in more features until you have the full story.

Creating and Using a Simple Function

Our modest first goal is to create a function that types 65 asterisks in a row. To give the function a context, we will include it in a program that prints a simple letterhead. Listing 9.1 presents the complete program. It consists of the functions `main()` and `starbar()`.

Listing 9.1 The `lethead1.c` program.

```
/* lethead1.c */
#include <stdio.h>
#define NAME "MEGATHINK, INC."
#define ADDRESS "10 Megabuck Plaza"
#define PLACE "Megapolis, CA 94904"
#define LIMIT 65
void starbar(void);  /* prototype the function */

int main(void)
{
    starbar();
    printf("%s\n", NAME);
    printf("%s\n", ADDRESS);
    printf("%s\n", PLACE);
    starbar();                /* use the function */
    return 0;
}

void starbar(void)        /* define the function */
{
    int count;

    for (count = 1; count <= LIMIT; count++)
        putchar('*');
    putchar('\n');
}
```

Here is the output:
```
*****************************************************************
MEGATHINK, INC.
10 Megabuck Plaza
Megapolis, CA 94904
*****************************************************************
```

There are several major points to note about this program:

- It uses the `starbar` identifier in three separate contexts: a *function prototype* that tells the compiler what sort of function `starbar()` is, a *function call* that causes the function to be executed, and a *function definition* that specifies exactly what the function does.

- Like variables, functions have types. Any program that uses a function should declare the type for that function before it is used. Therefore, this ANSI C prototype precedes the `main()` function definition:

```
void starbar(void);
```

The parentheses indicate that `starbar` is a function name. The first `void` is a function type; the `void` type indicates that the function does not return a value. The second `void` (the one in the parentheses) indicates that the function takes no arguments. The semicolon indicates that you are declaring the function, not defining it. That is, this line announces that the program uses a type `void` function called `starbar()` and that the compiler should expect to find the definition for this function elsewhere. For compilers that don't recognize ANSI C prototyping, just declare the type, as follows:

```
void starbar();
```

Note that some very old compilers don't recognize the `void` type. In that case, use type `int` for functions that don't have return values.

- The program places the `starbar()` prototype before `main()`; instead, it can go inside `main()`, at the same location you would place any variable declarations. Either way is fine.

- The program calls (invokes, summons) the function `starbar()` from `main()` by using its name followed by parentheses and a semicolon, creating this statement:

```
starbar();
```

This is one form for calling up a function, but it isn't the only one. Whenever the computer reaches a `starbar();` statement, it looks for the `starbar()` function and follows the instructions there. When finished with the code within `starbar()`, the computer returns to the next line of the *calling function*—`main()`, in this case (see Figure 9.1).

- The program follows the same form in defining `starbar()` as it does in defining `main()`. It starts with the type, name, and parentheses. Then it supplies the opening brace, a declaration of variables used, the defining statements of the function, and then the closing brace (see Figure 9.2). Note that this instance of `starbar()` is not followed by a semicolon. The lack of a semicolon tells the compiler that you are *defining* `starbar()` instead of calling or prototyping it.

- The program includes `starbar()` and `main()` in the same file. You can use two separate files. The single-file form is slightly easier to compile. Two separate files make it simpler to use the same function in different programs. If you do place the function in a separate file, then you would also place the necessary `#define` and `#include` directives in that file. We will discuss using two or more files later. For now, we will keep all the functions together. The closing brace of `main()` tells the compiler where that function ends, and the following `starbar()` header tells the compiler that `starbar()` is a function.

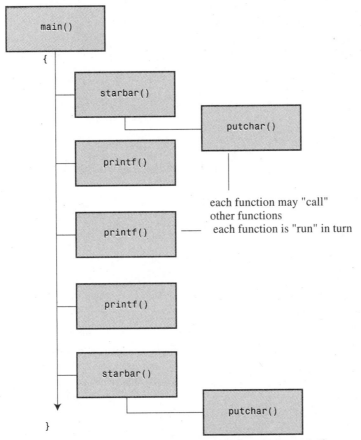

Figure 9.1 Control flow for `lethead1.c` (refer to Listing 9.1).

- The variable `count` in `starbar()` is a *local* variable. This means it is known only to `starbar()`. You can use the name `count` in other functions, including `main()`, and there will be no conflict. You simply wind up with separate, independent variables having the same name.

If you think of `starbar()` as a black box, its action is printing a line of stars. It doesn't have any input because it doesn't need to use any information from the calling function. It doesn't provide (return) any information to `main()`, so `starbar()` doesn't have a return value. In short, `starbar()` doesn't require any communication with the calling function.

Let's create a case where communication is needed.

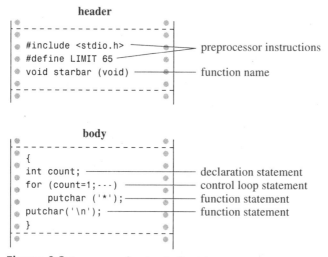

Figure 9.2 Structure of a simple function.

Function Arguments

The letterhead shown earlier would look a little nicer if the text were centered. You can center text by printing the correct number of leading spaces before printing the text. This is similar to the `starbar()` function, which printed a certain number of asterisks, but now you want to print a certain number of spaces. Instead of writing separate functions for each task, we'll follow the C philosophy and write a single, more general function that does both. We'll call the new function `n_char()` (to suggest displaying a character *n* times). Instead of having the display character and number of repetitions built into the function, we will use function arguments to convey those values.

Let's get more specific. The bar of stars is 65 characters wide, and the function call `n_char('*', 65)` should print that. What about spaces? `MEGATHINK, INC.` is 15 spaces wide, so in the first version, there were 50 spaces following the heading. To center it, you should lead off with 25 spaces, which will result in 25 spaces on either side of the phrase. Therefore, you could use the call `n_char(' ', 25)`.

Aside from using arguments, the `n_char()` function will be quite similar to `starbar()`. One difference is that it won't add a newline the way `starbar()` does because you might want to print other text on the same line. Listing 9.2 shows the revised program. To emphasize how arguments work, the program uses a variety of argument forms.

Listing 9.2   The `lethead2.c` program.

```
/* lethead2.c */
#include <stdio.h>
#include <string.h>        /* for strlen() prototype      */
#define NAME "MEGATHINK, INC."
#define ADDRESS "10 Megabuck Plaza"
```

```
#define PLACE "Megapolis, CA 94904"
#define LIMIT 65
#define SPACE ' '
void n_char(char ch, int num);

int main(void)
{
  int spaces;

  n_char('*', LIMIT);        /* using constants as arguments */
  putchar('\n');
  n_char(SPACE, 25);         /* using constants as arguments */
  printf("%s\n", NAME);
  spaces = (65 - strlen(ADDRESS)) / 2;
                             /* Let the program calculate    */
                             /* how many spaces to skip       */
  n_char(SPACE, spaces);     /* use a variable as argument    */
  printf("%s\n", ADDRESS);
  n_char(SPACE, (65 - strlen(PLACE)) / 2);
                             /* an expression as argument     */
  printf("%s\n", PLACE);
  n_char('*', LIMIT);
  putchar('\n');
  return 0;
}

/* here is n_char() */
void n_char(char ch, int num)
{
  int count;

  for (count = 1; count <= num; count++)
  putchar(ch);
}
```

Here is the result of running the program:

```
********************************************************************
                        MEGATHINK, INC.
                       10 Megabuck Plaza
                      Megapolis, CA 94904
********************************************************************
```

Now let's review how to set up a function that takes arguments. After that, you'll look at how the function is used.

Defining a Function with an Argument: Formal Arguments

The function definition begins with this ANSI C declaration:

```
void n_char(char ch, int num)
```

This line informs the compiler that n_char() uses two arguments called ch and num, that ch is type char, and that num is type int. Both the ch and num variables are called *formal arguments*. Like variables defined inside the function, formal arguments are local variables, private to the function. That means you don't have to worry about duplicating variable names used in other functions. These variables will be assigned values each time the function is called.

Note that the ANSI C form requires that each variable be preceded by its type. That is, unlike the case with regular declarations, you can't use a list of variables of the same type:

```
void dibs(int x, y, z)         /* invalid function header */
void dubs(int x, int y, int z)  /* valid function header   */
```

ANSI C also recognizes the pre-ANSI form:

```
void n_char(ch, num)
char ch;
int num;
```

Here, the parentheses contain the list of argument names, but the types are declared afterward. Note that the arguments are declared before the brace that marks the start of the function's body, but ordinary local variables are declared after the brace. This form does enable you to use comma-separated lists of variable names if the variables are of the same type, as shown here:

```
void dibs(x, y, z)
int x, y, z;        /* valid */
```

The intent of the standard is to phase out the pre-ANSI form. You should be aware of it so that you can understand older code, but you should use the modern form for new programs.

Although the n_char() function accepts values from main(), it doesn't return a value. Therefore, n_char() is type void.

Now let's see how this function is used.

Prototyping a Function with Arguments

We used an ANSI prototype to declare the function before it is used:

```
void n_char(char ch, int num);
```

When a function takes arguments, the prototype indicates their number and type by using a comma-separated list of the types. If you like, you can omit variable names in the prototype:

```
void n_char(char, int);
```

Using variable names in a prototype doesn't actually create variables. It merely clarifies the fact that char means a char variable, and so on.

Again, ANSI C also recognizes the older form of declaring a function, which is without an argument list:

```
void n_char();
```

Later, we'll look at the advantages of using the prototype format.

Calling a Function with an Argument: Actual Arguments

You give `ch` and `num` values by using *actual arguments* in the function call. Consider the first use of `n_char()`:

```
n_char(SPACE, 25);
```

The actual arguments are the space character and **25**. These values are assigned to the corresponding formal arguments in `n_char()`—the variables `ch` and `num`. In short, the formal argument is a variable in the called function, and the actual argument is the particular value assigned to the formal variable by the calling function. As we showed in the example, the actual argument can be a constant, a variable, or an even more elaborate expression. Regardless of which it is, the actual argument is evaluated, and its value copied to the corresponding formal argument for the function. For instance, consider the final use of `n_char()`:

```
n_char(SPACE, (65 - strlen(PLACE)) / 2);
```

The long expression forming the second actual argument is evaluated to **23**. Then the value **23** is assigned to the variable `num`. The function neither knows nor cares whether that number came from a constant, a variable, or a more general expression. Again, the actual argument is a specific value that is assigned to the variable known as the formal argument (see Figure 9.3). Because the called function works with data copied from the calling function, the original data in the calling function is protected from whatever manipulations the called function applies to the copies.

The Black Box Viewpoint

Taking a black box viewpoint of `n_char()`, the input is the character to be displayed and the number of spaces to be skipped. The resulting action is printing the character the specified number of times. The input is communicated to the function via arguments. This information is enough to tell you how to use the function in `main()`. Also, it serves as a design specification for writing the function.

The fact that `ch`, `num`, and `count` are local variables private to the `n_char()` function is an essential aspect of the black box approach. If you were to use variables with the same names in `main()`, they would be separate, independent variables. That is, if `main()` had a `count` variable, changing its value wouldn't change the value of `count` in `n_char()`, and vice versa. What goes on inside the black box is hidden from the calling function.

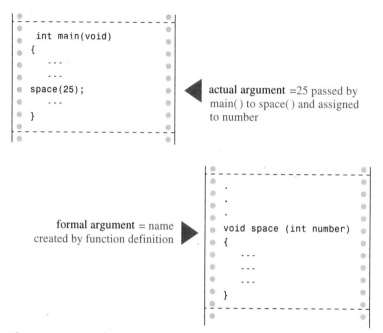

Figure 9.3 Formal arguments and actual arguments.

Returning a Value from a Function with `return`

You have seen how to communicate information from the calling function to the called function. To send information in the other direction, you use the function return value. To refresh your memory on how that works, we'll construct a function that returns the smaller of its two arguments. We'll call the function `imin()` because it's designed to handle `int` values. Also, we will create a simple `main()` whose sole purpose is to check to see whether `imin()` works. A program designed to test functions this way is sometimes called a *driver*. The driver takes a function for a spin. If the function pans out, then it can be installed in a more noteworthy program. Listing 9.3 shows the driver and the minimum value function.

Listing 9.3   The `lesser.c` program.

```
/* lesser.c -- finds the lesser of two evils */
#include <stdio.h>
int imin(int, int);

int main(void)
{
    int evil1, evil2;

    printf("Enter a pair of integers (q to quit):\n");
```

```
    while (scanf("%d %d", &evil1, &evil2) == 2)
    {
        printf("The lesser of %d and %d is %d.\n",
                evil1, evil2, imin(evil1,evil2));
        printf("Enter a pair of integers (q to quit):\n");
    }
    return 0;
}

int imin(int n,int m)
{
    int min;

    if (n < m)
        min = n;
    else
        min = m;
    return min;
}
```

Here is a sample run:

```
Enter a pair of integers (q to quit):
509 333
The lesser of 509 and 333 is 333.
Enter a pair of integers (q to quit):
-9393 6
The lesser of -9393 and 6 is -9393.
Enter a pair of integers (q to quit):
q
```

The keyword **return** causes the value of the following expression to be the return value of the function. In this case, the function returns the value that was assigned to min. Because min is type int, so is the imin() function.

The variable min is private to imin(), but the value of min is communicated back to the calling function with **return**. The effect of a statement such as the next one is to assign the value of min to lesser:

```
lesser = imin(n,m);
```

Could you say the following instead?

```
imin(n,m);
lesser = min;
```

No, because the calling function doesn't even know that min exists. Remember that imin()'s variables are local to imin(). The function call imin(evil1,evil2) copies the values of one set of variables to another set.

Not only can the returned value be assigned to a variable, it can also be used as part of an expression. You can do this, for example:

```
answer = 2 * imin(z, zstar) + 25;
printf("%d\n", imin(-32 + answer, LIMIT));
```

The return value can be supplied by any expression, not just a variable. For example, you can shorten the program to the following:

```
/* minimum value function, second version */
imin(int n,int m)
{
    return (n < m) ? n : m;
}
```

The conditional expression is evaluated to either n or m, whichever is smaller, and that value is returned to the calling function. If you prefer, for clarity or style, to enclose the return value in parentheses, you may, although parentheses are not required.

Using **return** has one other effect. It terminates the function and returns control to the next statement in the calling function. This occurs even if the **return** statement is not the last in the function. Therefore, you can write imin() this way:

```
/* minimum value function, third version */
imin(int n,int m)
{
    if (n < m)
        return n;
    else
        return m;
}
```

Many, but not all, C practitioners deem it better to use **return** just once and at the end of a function to make it easier for someone to follow the control flow through the function. However, it's no great sin to use multiple **returns** in a function as short as this one. Anyway, to the user, all three versions are the same, because all take the same input and produce the same output. Just the innards are different. Even this version works the same:

```
/* minimum value function, fourth version */
imin(int n, int m)
{
    if (n < m)
        return n;
    else
        return m;
    printf("Professor Fleppard is like totally a fopdoodle.\n");
}
```

The **return** statements prevent the **printf()** statement from ever being reached. Professor Fleppard can use the compiled version of this function in his own programs and never learn the true feelings of his student programmer.

You can use a statement like this, too:

```
return;
```

It causes the function to terminate and return control to the calling function. Because no expression follows **return**, no value is returned, and this form should be used only in a type **void** function.

Function Types

Functions should be declared by type. A function with a return value should be declared the same type as the return value. Functions with no return value should be declared as type void. If no type is given for a function, C assumes that the function is type int. This convention stems from the early days of C, when most functions were type int anyway. However, ANSI C recommends providing the type explicitly; eventually, support for the older form of assuming an int type will be dropped.

The type declaration is part of the function definition. Keep in mind that it refers to the return value, not to the function arguments. For instance, the following function heading indicates that you are defining a function that takes two type int arguments but that returns a type double value:

```
double klink(int a, int b)
```

To use a function correctly, a program needs to know the function type before the function is used for the first time. One way to accomplish this is to place the complete function definition ahead of its first use. However, this method could make the program harder to read. Also, the functions might be part of the C library or in some other file. Therefore, you generally inform the compiler about functions by declaring them in advance. For example, the main() function in Listing 9.3 contains these lines:

```
#include <stdio.h>
int imin(int, int);
int main(void)
{
  int evil1, evil2, lesser;
```

The second line establishes that imin is the name of a function that returns a type int value. Now the compiler will know how to treat imin() when it appears later in the program.

We've placed the advance function declarations outside the function using them. They can also be placed inside the function. For example, you can rewrite the beginning of lesser.c as follows:

```
#include <stdio.h>
int main(void)
{
  int imin(int, int);      /* imin() declaration */
  int evil1, evil2, lesser;
```

In either case, your chief concern should be that the function declaration appear before the function is used.

In the ANSI C standard library, functions are grouped into families, each having its own header file. These header files contain, among other things, the declarations for the functions in the family. For instance, the stdio.h header contains function declarations for the standard I/O library functions, such as printf() and scanf(). The math.h header contains function declarations for a variety of mathematical functions. For example, it contains

```
double sqrt(double);
```

(or a pre-ANSI equivalent) to tell the compiler that the `sqrt()` function returns a type `double` value. Don't confuse these declarations with definitions. A function declaration informs the compiler which type the function is, but the function definition supplies the actual code. Including the `math.h` header file tells the compiler that `sqrt()` returns type `double`, but the code for `sqrt()` resides in a separate file of library functions.

ANSI C Function Prototyping

The traditional, pre-ANSI C scheme for declaring functions was deficient in that it declared a function's return type, but not its arguments. Let's look at the kinds of problems that arise when the old form of function declarations is used.

The following pre-ANSI declaration informs the compiler that `imin()` returns a type `int` value:

```
int imin();
```

However, it says nothing about the number or type of `imin()`'s arguments. Therefore, if you use `imin()` with the wrong number or type of arguments, the compiler doesn't catch the error.

The Problem

Let's look at some examples involving `imax()`, a close relation to `imin()`. Listing 9.4 shows a program that declares `imax()` the old-fashioned way and then uses `imax()` incorrectly.

Listing 9.4   The `misuse.c` program.

```
/* misuse.c -- uses a function incorrectly */
#include <stdio.h>
int imax();        /* old-style declaration */
int main(void)
{
  printf("The maximum of %d and %d is %d.\n",
       3, 5, imax(3));
  printf("The maximum of %d and %d is %d.\n",
       3, 5, imax(3.0, 5.0));
  return 0;
}

int imax(n, m)
int n, m;
{
  int max;

  if (n > m)
       max = n;
  else
       max = m;
  return max;
}
```

The first call to `printf()` omits an argument to `imax()`, and the second call uses floating-point arguments instead of integers. Despite these errors, the program compiles and runs.

Here's the output using Microsoft's Visual C++ 5.0:

```
The maximum of 3 and 5 is 6618680.
The maximum of 3 and 5 is 1074266112.
```

With Borland C 3.0 (DOS), we got values of `3` and `0`. The two compilers work fine; they are merely victims of the program's failure to use function prototypes.

What's happening? The mechanics may differ among systems, but here's what goes on with a PC or VAX. The calling function places its arguments in a temporary storage area called the *stack*, and the called function reads those arguments off the stack. These two processes are *not* coordinated with one another. The calling function decides which type to pass based on the actual arguments in the call, and the called function reads values based on the types of its formal arguments. Therefore, the call `imax(3)` places *one* integer on the stack. When the `imax()` function starts up, it reads *two* integers off the stack. Only one was actually placed on the stack, so the second value read is whatever value happened to be sitting in the stack at the time.

The second time the example uses `imax()`, it passes `float` values to `imax()`. This places two `double` values on the stack. (Recall that a `float` is promoted to `double` when passed as an argument.) On our system, that's two 64-bit values, so 128 bits of data are placed on the stack. When `imax()` reads two `ints` from the stack, it reads the first 64 bits on the stack because, on our system, each `int` is 32 bits. These bits happened to correspond to two integer values, the larger of which was 1074266112.

The ANSI Solution

The ANSI standard's solution to the problems of mismatched arguments is to permit the function declaration to declare the variable types, too. The result is a *function prototype*, a declaration that states the return type, the number of arguments, and the types of those arguments. To indicate that `imax()` requires two `int` arguments, you can declare it with either of the following prototypes:

```
int imax(int, int);
int imax(int a, int b);
```

The first form uses a comma-separated list of types. The second adds variable names to the types. Remember that the variable names are dummy names and don't have to match the names used in the function definition.

With this information at hand, the compiler can check to see whether the function call matches the prototype. Are there the right number of arguments? Are they the correct type? If there is a type mismatch and if both types are numbers or pointers, the compiler does a type cast to convert the actual arguments to the same type as the formal arguments. For example, `imax(3.0, 5.0)` becomes `imax ((int) 3.0, (int) 5.0)`. We've modified Listing 9.4 to use a function prototype. The result is shown in Listing 9.5.

Listing 9.5   The proto1.c program.

```
/* proto1.c -- uses a function prototype */
#include <stdio.h>
int imax(int, int);          /* prototype */
int main(void)
{
  printf("The maximum of %d and %d is %d.\n",
      3, 5, imax(3));
  printf("The maximum of %d and %d is %d.\n",
      3, 5, imax(3.0, 5.0));
  return 0;
}

int imax(int n, int m)
{
  int max;

  if (n > m)
      max = n;
  else
      max = m;
  return max;
}
```

When we tried to compile Listing 9.5, our compiler gave an error message stating that the call to `imax()` had too few parameters.

What about the type errors? To investigate those, we replaced `imax(3)` with `imax(3, 5)` and tried compilation again. This time there were no error messages, and we ran the program. Here is the resulting output:

```
The maximum of 3 and 5 is 5.
The maximum of 3 and 5 is 5.
```

As promised, the **3.0** and **5.0** of the second call were converted to **3** and **5** so that the function could handle the input properly.

Although it gave no error message, our compiler did give a warning to the effect that a **double** was converted to **int** and that there was a possible loss of data. The difference between an error and a warning is that an error prevents compilation and a warning permits compilation. One interesting point is that one compiler made this type cast without telling us. Most programmers object to this "silent" correction, but by resetting the warning level on that compiler, we got it to warn us about the type conversion. Many compilers enable you to select which warning you want made. However, the ANSI standard does not require compilers to provide that feature.

No Arguments and Unspecified Arguments

Suppose you give a prototype like this:

```
void print_name();
```

An ANSI C compiler will assume that you have decided to forego function prototyping, and it will not check arguments. To indicate that a function really has no arguments, use the `void` keyword within the parentheses:

```
void print_name(void);
```

ANSI C interprets the preceding expression to mean that `print_name()` takes no arguments. It then checks to see that you, in fact, do not use arguments when calling this function.

A few functions, such as `printf()` and `scanf()`, take a variable number of arguments. In `printf()`, for instance, the first argument is a string, but the remaining arguments are fixed in neither type nor number. ANSI C allows partial prototyping for such cases. You could, for example, use this prototype for `printf()`:

```
int printf(char *, ...);
```

This prototype says that the first argument is a string (Chapter 11, "Character Strings and String Functions," elucidates that point) and that there may be further arguments of an unspecified nature.

Recursion

C permits a function to call itself. This process is termed *recursion*. Recursion is a sometimes tricky, sometimes convenient tool. It's tricky to get recursion to end because a function that calls itself tends to do so indefinitely unless the programming includes a conditional test to terminate recursion.

Recursion Revealed

To see what's involved, let's look at an example. The function `main()` in Listing 9.6 calls the `up_and_down()` function. We'll term this the "first level of recursion." Then `up_and_down()` calls itself; we'll call that the "second level of recursion." The second level calls the third level, and so on. This example is set up to go four levels.

Listing 9.6   The `recur.c` program.

```
/* recur.c -- recursion illustration */
#include <stdio.h>
void up_and_down(int);
int main(void)
{
   up_and_down(1);
   return 0;
}

void up_and_down(int n)
{
   printf("Level %d\n", n);      /* print #1 */
```

continued on next page

continued from previous page

```
    if (n < 4)
        up_and_down(n+1);
    printf("LEVEL %d\n", n);      /* print #2 */
}
```

The output looks like this:

```
Level 1
Level 2
Level 3
Level 4
LEVEL 4
LEVEL 3
LEVEL 2
LEVEL 1
```

Let's trace through the program to see how recursion works. First, main() calls up_and_down() with an argument of 1. As a result, the formal argument n in up_and_down() has the value 1, so print statement #1 prints Level 1. Then, because n is less than 4, up_and_down() (Level 1) calls up_and_down() (Level 2) with an argument of n + 1, or 2. This causes n in the Level 2 call to be assigned the value 2, so print statement #1 prints Level 2. Similarly, the next two calls lead to printing Level 3 and Level 4.

When Level 4 is reached, n is 4, so the if test fails. The up_and_down() function is not called again. Instead, the Level 4 call proceeds to print statement #2, which prints LEVEL 4, because n is 4. Then it reaches the return statement. At this point, the Level 4 call ends, and control passes back to the function that called it, the Level 3 call. The last statement executed in the Level 3 call was the call to Level 4 in the if statement. Therefore, Level 3 resumes with the following statement, which is print statement #2. This causes LEVEL 3 to be printed. Then Level 3 ends, passing control to Level 2, which prints LEVEL 2, and so on.

If you find this a bit confusing, think about when you have a chain of function calls, with fun1() calling fun2(), fun2() calling fun3(), and fun3() calling fun(4). When fun(4) finishes, it passes control back to fun3(). When fun3() finishes, it passes control back to fun(2). And when fun2() finishes, it passes control back to fun1(). The recursive case works the same, except that fun1(), fun2(), fun3(), and fun4()are all the same function.

Recursion Fundamentals

Recursion can be confusing at first, so let's look at a few basic points that will help you understand the process.

First, each level of function call has its own variables. That is, the n of Level 1 is a different variable from the n of Level 2, so the program created four separate variables, each called n, but each having a distinct value. When the program finally returned to the first level call of up_and_down(), the original n still had the value 1 it started with (see Figure 9.4).

variables:	n	n	n	n
after level 1 call	1			
after level 2 call	1	2		
after level 3 call	1	2	3	
after level 4 call	1	2	3	4
after return from level 4	1	2	3	
after return from level 3	1	2		
after return from level 2	1			
after return from level 1				
	(all gone)			

Figure 9.4 Recursion variables.

Second, each function call is balanced with a return. When program flow reaches the `return` at the end of the last recursion level, control passes to the previous recursion level. The program does not jump all the way back to the original call in `main()`. Instead, the program must move back through each recursion level, returning from one level of `up_and_down()` to the level of `up_and_down()` that called it.

Third, statements in a recursive function that come before the recursive call are executed in the same order that the functions are called. For instance, in Listing 9.6 print statement #1 comes before the recursive call. It was executed four times in the order of the recursive calls: Level 1, Level 2, Level 3, and Level 4.

Fourth, statements in a recursive function that come after the recursive call are executed in the opposite order from which the functions are called. For example, print statement #2 comes after the recursive call, and it was executed in this order: Level 4, Level 3, Level 2, Level 1. This feature of recursion is useful for programming problems involving reversals of order. You'll see an example soon.

Finally, although each level of recursion has its own set of variables, the code itself is not duplicated. The code is a sequence of instructions, and a function call is a command to go to the beginning of that set of instructions. A recursive call, then, returns the program to the beginning of that instruction set. Aside from recursive calls creating new variables on each call, they are much like a loop. Indeed, sometimes recursion can be used instead of loops, and vice versa.

Tail Recursion

In the simplest form of recursion, the recursive call is at the end of the function, just before the `return` statement. It is called *tail recursion*, or *end recursion*, because the recursive call comes at the end. Tail recursion is the simplest form because it acts like a loop.

Let's look at both a loop version and a tail recursion version of a function to calculate factorials. The *factorial* of an integer is the product of the integers from 1 through that number. For example, 3 factorial (written `3!`) is `1*2*3`. The `0!` is taken to be 1, and factorials are not defined for negative numbers. Listing 9.7 presents a function that uses a `for` loop to calculate factorials.

Listing 9.7   The factor.c program.

```
/* factor.c -- uses loops to calculate factorials */
#include <stdio.h>
long fact(int n);
int main(void)
{
  int num;

  printf("This program calculates factorials.\n");
  printf("Enter a value in the range 0-16 (q to quit):\n");
  while (scanf("%d", &num) == 1)
  {
    if (num < 0)
      printf("No negative numbers, please.\n");
    else if (num > 15)
      printf("Keep input under 16.\n");
    else
      printf("%d factorial = %ld\n", num, fact(num));
    printf("Enter a value in the range 0-16 (q to quit):\n");
  }
  return 0;
}
long fact(int n)              /* loop finds factorial */
{
  long ans;

  for (ans = 1; n > 1; n--)
    ans *= n;
  return ans;
}
```

The test driver program limits input to the integers 0–15. It turns out that **15!** is slightly over 2 billion, which makes **16!** much larger than **long** on our system. To go beyond **15!**, you would have to use a type **double** function.

The loop initializes **ans** to 1 and then multiplies it by the integers from n down to **2**. Technically, you should multiply by **1**, but that doesn't change the value. Here's a sample run:

```
This program calculates factorials.
Enter a value in the range 0-16 (q to quit):
4
4 factorial = 24
Enter a value in the range 0-16 (q to quit):
11
11 factorial = 39916800
Enter a value in the range 0-16 (q to quit):
q
```

Now let's try a recursive version. The key is that n! = n × (n-1)!. This follows because (n-1)! is the product of all the positive integers through n-1. Therefore, multiplying by n gives the product through n. This suggests a recursive approach. If you call the function rfact(), then rfact(n) is n * rfact(n-1). You can thus evaluate rfact(n) by having it call rfact(n-1), as in Listing 9.8. Of course, you have to end the recursion at some point, and you can do this by setting the return value to 1 when n is 0.

Listing 9.8   rfactor.c.

```
/* rfactor.c -- uses recursion to calculate factorials */
#include <stdio.h>
long rfact(int n);
int main(void)
{
  int num;

printf("This program calculates factorials.\n");
  printf("Enter a value in the range 0-16 (q to quit):\n");
  while (scanf("%d", &num) == 1)
  {
     if (num < 0)
        printf("No negative numbers, please.\n");
     else if (num > 15)
        printf("Keep input under 16.\n");
     else
        printf("%d factorial = %ld\n", num, rfact(num));
     printf("Enter a value in the range 0-16 (q to quit):\n");
  }
  return 0;
}
long rfact(int n)     /* recursive function */
{
  long ans;

  if (n > 0)
     ans= n * rfact(n-1);
  else
     ans = 1;
  return ans;
}
```

The recursive version of Listing 9.8 produces the same output as the previous version. Note that although the recursive call to **rfact()** is not the last line in the function, it is the last statement executed when n > 0, so it is tail recursion.

Given that you can use either a loop or recursion to code a function, which should you use? Normally, the loop is the better choice. First, because each recursive call gets its own set of variables, recursion uses more memory; each recursive call places a new set of variables on the stack. Second, recursion is slower because each function call takes time. So why show this example? Because tail recursion is the simplest form of recursion to understand, and recursion is worth understanding because in some cases, there is no simple loop alternative.

Recursion and Reversal

Now let's look at a problem in which recursion's ability to reverse order is handy. (This is a case for which recursion is simpler than using a loop.) The problem is this: Write a function that prints the binary equivalent of an integer. Binary notation represents numbers in terms of powers of 2. Just as 234 in decimal means $2 \times 10^2 + 3 \times 10^1 + 4 \times 10^0$, so 101 in binary means $1 \times 2^2 + 0 \times 2^1 + 1 \times 2^0$. Binary numbers use only the digits 0 and 1.

You need a method, or *algorithm*. How can you, say, find the binary equivalent of 5? Well, odd numbers must have a binary representation ending in 1. Even numbers end in 0, so you can determine whether the last digit is a 1 or a 0 by evaluating 5 % 2. If the result is 1, then 5 is odd, and the last digit is 1. In general, if n is a number, the final digit is n % 2, so the first digit you find is the last digit you want to print. This suggests using a recursive function in which n % 2 is calculated before the recursive call but in which it is printed after the recursive call. That way, the first value calculated is the last value printed.

To get the next digit, divide the original number by 2. This is the binary equivalent to moving the decimal point one place to the left so that you can examine the next binary digit. If this value is even, the next binary digit is 0. If it is odd, the binary digit is 1. For example, 5/2 is 2 (integer division), so the next digit is 0. This gives 01 so far. Now repeat the process. Divide 2 by 2 to get 1. Evaluate 1 % 2 to get 1, so the next digit is 1. This gives 101. When do you stop? You stop when the result of dividing by 2 is less than 2 because as long as it is 2 or greater, there is one more binary digit. Each division by 2 lops off one more binary digit until you reach the end. (If this seems confusing to you, try working through the decimal analogy. The remainder of 628 divided by 10 is 8, so 8 is the last digit. Integer division by 10 yields 62, and the remainder from dividing 62 by 10 is 2, so that's the next digit, and so on.) Listing 9.9 implements this approach.

Listing 9.9 The binary.c program.

```
/* binary.c -- prints integer in binary form */
#include <stdio.h>
void to_binary(int n);
int main(void)
{
  int number;
  printf("Enter an integer (q to quit):\n");
  while (scanf("%d", &number) == 1)
  {
     printf("Binary equivalent: ");
     to_binary(number);
     putchar('\n');
     printf("Enter an integer (q to quit):\n");
  }
  return 0;
}
void to_binary(int n)    /* recursive function */
{
  int r;
```

```
   r = n % 2;
   if (n >= 2)
      to_binary(n / 2);
   putchar('0' + r);
   return;
}
```

In Listing 9.9, the expression `'0' + r` evaluates to the character `'0'` if r is `0` and to the character `'1'` if r is `1`. This assumes that the numeric code for the `'1'` character is one greater than the code for the `'0'` character. Both the ASCII and the EBCDIC codes satisfy that assumption.

Here's a sample run:

```
Enter an integer (q to quit):
9
Binary equivalent: 1001
Enter an integer (q to quit):
255
Binary equivalent: 11111111
Enter an integer (q to quit):
1024
Binary equivalent: 10000000000
Enter an integer (q to quit):
q
```

Could you use this algorithm for calculating a binary representation without using recursion? Yes, you could. But because the algorithm calculates the final digit first, you'd have to store all the digits somewhere (in an array, for example) before displaying the result. Chapter 15, "Bit Fiddling," shows an example of a non-recursive approach.

Recursion is used in many more advanced algorithms, often involving cases where the recursive function calls itself twice. For example, there are sorting algorithms that divide the items to be sorted into two groups, then recursively divide each of those groups into two groups, and so on.

All C Functions Are Created Equal

Each C function in a program is on equal footing with the others. Each can call any other function or be called by any other function. This makes the C function somewhat different from Pascal and Modula-2 procedures because those procedures can be nested within other procedures. Procedures in one nest are ignorant of procedures in another nest.

Isn't the function `main()` special? Yes, it is a little special in that when a program of several functions is put together, execution starts with the first statement in `main()`, but that is the limit of its preference. Even `main()` can be called by itself recursively or by other functions, although this is rarely done.

Compiling Programs with Two or More Functions

The simplest approach to using several functions is to place them in the same file. Then just compile that file as you would a single-function file. Other approaches are more system dependent, as the next few sections illustrate.

UNIX

This assumes the UNIX system has the standard UNIX C compiler `cc` installed. Suppose that `file1.c` and `file2.c` are two files containing C functions. Then the following command will compile both files and produce an executable file called `a.out`:

```
cc file1.c file2.c
```

In addition, two object files called `file1.o` and `file2.o` are produced. If you later change `file1.c` but not `file2.c`, you can compile the first and combine it with the object code version of the second file by using this command:

```
cc file1.c file2.o
```

Linux

This assumes the Linux system has the GNU C compiler `gcc` installed. Suppose that `file1.c` and `file2.c` are two files containing C functions. Then the following command will compile both files and produce an executable file called `a.out`:

```
gcc file1.c file2.c
```

In addition, two object files called `file1.o` and `file2.o` are produced. If you later change `file1.c` but not `file2.c`, you can compile the first and combine it with the object code version of the second file by using this command:

```
gcc file1.c file2.o
```

DOS Command-Line Compilers

Most DOS command-line compilers work similarly to the UNIX `cc` command. One difference is that object files wind up with an `.obj` extension instead of an `.o` extension. Some compilers produce intermediate files in assembly language or in some other special code instead of object code files.

Windows and Macintosh Compilers

Windows and Macintosh compilers are project-oriented. A *project* describes the resources a particular program uses. The resources include your source code files. If you've been using one of these compilers, you've probably had to create projects to run one-file programs. For multiple file programs, find the menu command that lets you add a source code file to a project. You should make sure all your source code files (the ones with the `.c` extension) are listed as part of the project. Be careful, however, not to place your header files (the ones with the `.h` extension) in a project. The idea is that the project manages which source code files are used, and `#include` directives in the source code files manage which header files get used.

Using Header Files

If you put `main()` in one file and your function definitions in a second file, the first file still needs the function prototypes. Rather than type them in each time you use the function file, you can store the function prototypes in a header file. That is what the standard C library does, placing i/o function prototypes in `stdio.h` and math function prototypes in `math.h`, for example. You can do the same for your function files.

Also, you will often use the C preprocessor to define constants used in a program. Such definitions hold only for the file containing the `#define` directives. If you place the functions of a program into separate files, you also have to make the `#define` directives available to each file. The most direct way is to retype the directives for each file, but this is time-consuming and increases the possibility for error. Also, it poses a maintenance problem: If you revise a `#define` value, you have to remember to do so for each file. A better solution is to place the `#define` directives in a header file and then use the `#include` directive in each source code file.

So it's good programming practice to place function prototypes and defined constants in a header file. Let's examine an example. Suppose you manage a chain of four hotels. Each hotel charges a different room rate, but all the rooms in a given hotel go for the same rate. For people who book multiple nights, the second night goes for 95% of the first night, the third night goes for 95% of the second night, and so on. (Don't worry about the economics of such a policy.) You want a program that enables you to specify the hotel and the number of nights and gives you the total charge. You'd like the program to have a menu that enables you to continue entering data until you choose to quit.

Listings 9.10, 9.11, and 9.12 show what you might come up with. The first listing contains the `main()` function, which provides the overall organization for the program. The second listing contains the supporting functions, which we assume are kept in a separate file. Finally, Listing 9.12 shows a header file that contains the defined constants and function prototypes for all the program's source files. Recall that in UNIX and DOS environments, the double quotes in the directive `#include "hotels.h"` indicate that the `include` file is in the current working directory (typically the directory containing the source code).

Listing 9.10   The `usehotel.c` control module.

```
/* usehotel.c -- room rate program */
/* compile with  Listing 9.11      */
#include <stdio.h>
#include "hotel.h" /* defines constants, declares functions */
int main(void)
```

continued on next page

continued from previous page

```
{
    int nights;
    double hotel;
    int code;

    while ((code = menu()) != QUIT)
    {
        switch(code)
        {
        case 1 : hotel = HOTEL1;
                 break;
        case 2 : hotel = HOTEL2;
                 break;
        case 3 : hotel = HOTEL3;
                 break;
        case 4 : hotel = HOTEL4;
                 break;
        default: hotel = 0.0;
                 printf("Oops!\n");
                 break;
        }
        nights = getnights();
        showprice(hotel, nights);
    }
    return 0;
}
```

Listing 9.11   The `hotel.c` function support module.

```
/* hotel.c -- hotel management functions */
#include <stdio.h>
#include "hotel.h"
int menu(void)
{
    int code, status;

    printf("\n%s%s\n", STARS, STARS);
    printf("Enter the number of the desired hotel:\n");
    printf("1) Fairfield Arms          2) Hotel Olympic\n");
    printf("3) Chertworthy Plaza       4) The Stockton\n");
    printf("5) quit\n");
    printf("%s%s\n", STARS, STARS);
    while ((status = scanf("%d", &code)) != 1  ||
            (code < 1 || code > 5))
    {
        if (status != 1)
            scanf("%*s");
        printf("Enter an integer from 1 to 5, please.\n");
    }
    return code;
}
```

```
int getnights(void)
{
    int nights;

    printf("How many nights are needed? ");
    while (scanf("%d", &nights) != 1)
    {
        scanf("%*s");
        printf("Please enter an integer, such as 2.\n");
    }
    return nights;
}
void showprice(double hotel, int nights)
{
    int n;
    double total = 0.0;
    double factor = 1.0;

    for (n = 1; n <= nights; n++, factor *= DISCOUNT)
        total += hotel * factor;
    printf("The total cost will be $%0.2f.\n", total);
}
```

Listing 9.12 The hotel.h header file.

```
/* hotel.h -- constants and declarations for hotel.c */
#define QUIT       5
#define HOTEL1    50.00
#define HOTEL2    55.00
#define HOTEL3    80.00
#define HOTEL4   100.00
#define DISCOUNT   0.95
#define STARS "********************************"

int menu(void);
int getnights(void);
void showprice(double, int);
```

Here's a sample run:

```
****************************************************************
1) Fairfield Arms        2) Hotel Olympic
3) Chertworthy Plaza     4) The Stockton
5) quit
****************************************************************
3
How many nights are needed? 1
The total cost will be $80.00.

****************************************************************
```

continued on next page

continued from previous page

```
Enter the number of the desired hotel:
1) Fairfield Arms           2) Hotel Olympic
3) Chertworthy Plaza        4) The Stockton
5) quit
*****************************************************************
4
How many nights are needed? 3
The total cost will be $285.25.
*****************************************************************
Enter the number of the desired hotel:
1) Fairfield Arms           2) Hotel Olympic
3) Chertworthy Plaza        4) The Stockton
5) quit
*****************************************************************
5
```

Incidentally, the program itself has some interesting features. In particular, the `menu()` and `getnights()` functions skip over non-numeric data by testing the return value of `scanf()` and by using the `scanf("%*s")` call to skip to the next whitespace. Note how the following excerpt from `menu()` checks for both non-numeric input and out-of-limits numerical input:

```
while ((status = scanf("%d", &code)) != 1 ||
       (code < 1 || code > 5))
```

This code fragment uses C's guarantee that logical expressions are evaluated from left to right and that evaluation ceases the moment the statement is clearly false. In this instance, the values of `code` are checked only after it is determined that `scanf()` succeeded in reading an integer value.

Assigning separate tasks to separate functions encourages this sort of refinement. A first pass at `menu()` or `getnights()` might use a simple `scanf()` without the data verification features that have been added. Then, after the basic version works, you can begin improving each module.

Finding Addresses: The & Operator

One of the most important C concepts (and sometimes one of the most perplexing) is the *pointer*, which is a variable used to store an address. You've already seen that `scanf()` uses addresses for arguments. More generally, any C function that modifies a value in the calling function without using a `return` value uses addresses. We'll cover this topic next, beginning with the unary `&` operator.

The unary `&` operator gives you the address at which a variable is stored. If `pooh` is the name of a variable, then `&pooh` is the address of the variable. You can think of the address as a location in memory. Suppose you have the following statement:

```
pooh = 24;
```

Suppose that the address where pooh is stored is 0B76. (PC addresses often are given as four-digit hexadecimal values.) Then the statement

```
printf("%d %p\n", pooh, &pooh);
```

would produce this (%p is the specifier for addresses):

```
24 0B76
```

In Listing 9.13, let's use this operator to see where variables of the same name—but in different functions—are kept.

Listing 9.13   The loccheck.c program.

```
/* loccheck.c  -- checks to see where variables are stored */
#include <stdio.h>
void mikado(int);                      /* declare function */
int main(void)
{
    int pooh = 2, bah = 5;

    printf("In main(), pooh = %d and &pooh = %p\n",
            pooh, &pooh);
    printf("In main(), bah = %d and &bah = %p\n",
            bah, &bah);
    mikado(pooh);
    return 0;
}
void mikado(int bah)                   /* define function  */
{
    int pooh = 10;

    printf("In mikado(), pooh = %d and &pooh = %p\n",
            pooh, &pooh);
    printf("In mikado(), bah = %d and &bah = %p\n",
            bah, &bah);
}
```

Listing 9.13 used the %p format for printing the addresses. This format specifier is used for displaying addresses but is not available on some pre-ANSI systems. If your system lacks %p, try %u or, perhaps, %lu. On our system, this is the output of this little exercise:

```
In main(), pooh = 2 and &pooh = 0064FDF0
In main(), bah = 5 and &bah = 0064FDF4
In mikado(), pooh = 10 and &pooh = 0064FDE0
In mikado(), bah = 2 and &bah = 0064FDEC
```

The way that %p represents addresses varies between implementations. This one (Microsoft Visual C++ 5.0 on a PC) displays the address in hexadecimal form.

What does this output show? First, the two poohs have different addresses. The same is true for the two bahs. So, as promised, the computer considers them to be four separate variables. Second, the call mikado(pooh) did convey the value (2) of the actual argument (pooh of main()) to the formal argument (bah of mikado()). Note that just the value was transferred. The two variables involved (`pooh` of `main()` and `bah` of `mikado()`) retain their distinct identities.

We raise the second point because it is not true for all languages. In a FORTRAN subroutine, for example, the subroutine affects the original variable in the calling routine. The subroutine's variable might have a different name, but the address is the same. C doesn't do this. Each function uses its own variables. This is preferable because it prevents the original variable from being altered mysteriously by some side effect of the called function. However, it can make for some difficulties, too, as the next section shows.

Altering Variables in the Calling Function

Sometimes you want one function to make changes in the variables of a different function. For example, a common task in sorting problems is interchanging the values of two variables. Suppose you have two variables called x and y and you want to swap their values. The simple sequence

```
x = y;
y = x;
```

does not work because, by the time the second line is reached, the original value of x has already been replaced by the original y value. An additional line is needed to temporarily store the original value of x.

```
temp = x;

x = y;
y = temp;
```

Now that the method works, you can put it into a function and construct a driver to test it. To make clear which variables belong to `main()` and which belong to the `interchange()` function, Listing 9.14 uses x and y for the first, and u and v for the second.

Listing 9.14   The `swap1.c` program.

```c
/* swap1.c -- first attempt at a swapping function */
#include <stdio.h>
void interchange(int u, int v); /* declare function */
int main(void)
{
    int x = 5, y = 10;

    printf("Originally x = %d and y = %d.\n", x , y);
    interchange(x, y);
    printf("Now x = %d and y = %d.\n", x, y);
    return 0;
}
void interchange(int u, int v)  /* define function  */
{
```

```
    int temp;

    temp = u;
    u = v;
    v = temp;
}
```

Running the program gives these results:
```
Originally x = 5 and y = 10.
Now x = 5 and y = 10.
```

Oops! The values didn't get switched! Let's put some print statements into `interchange()` to see what's gone wrong (see Listing 9.15).

Listing 9.15 The `swap2.c` program.

```
/* swap2.c -- researching swap1.c */
#include <stdio.h>
void interchange(int u, int v);
int main(void)
{
    int x = 5, y = 10;

    printf("Originally x = %d and y = %d.\n", x , y);
    interchange(x, y);
    printf("Now x = %d and y = %d.\n", x, y);
    return 0;
}
void interchange(int u, int v)
{
    int temp;

    printf("Originally u = %d and v = %d.\n", u , v);
    temp = u;
    u = v;
    v = temp;
    printf("Now u = %d and v = %d.\n", u, v);
}
```

Here is the new output:
```
Originally x = 5 and y = 10.
Originally u = 5 and v = 10.
Now u = 10 and v = 5.
Now x = 5 and y = 10.
```

Nothing is wrong with `interchange()`; it does swap the values of u and v. The problem is in communicating the results to `main()`. As we pointed out, `interchange()` uses different variables from `main()`, so interchanging the values of u and v has no effect on x and y! Can you somehow use `return`? Well, you could finish `interchange()` with this line:

```
return(u);
```

Then change the call in `main()` to this:

```
x = interchange(x,y);
```

This change gives `x` its new value, but it leaves `y` in the cold. With `return` you can send just one value back to the calling function, but you need to communicate two values. It can be done! All you have to do is use pointers.

Pointers: A First Look

Pointers? What are they? Basically, a *pointer* is a variable (or, more generally, a data object) whose value is an address. Just as a `char` variable has a character as a value and an `int` variable has an integer as a value, the pointer variable has an address as a value. If you give a particular pointer variable the name `ptr`, then you can have statements like the following:

```
ptr = &pooh;  /* assigns pooh's address to ptr */
```

We say that `ptr` "points to" `pooh`. The difference between `ptr` and `&pooh` is that `ptr` is a variable, and `&pooh` is a constant. If you want, you can make `ptr` point elsewhere:

```
ptr = &bah;  /* make ptr point to bah instead of to pooh */
```

Now the value of `ptr` is the address of `bah`.

To create a pointer variable, you need to be able to declare its type. Suppose you want to declare `ptr` so that it can hold the address of an `int`. To make this declaration, you need to use a new operator. Let's examine that operator now.

The Indirection Operator: *

Suppose you know that `ptr` points to `bah`, as shown here:

```
ptr = &bah;
```

Then you can use the *indirection* operator * (also called the *dereferencing* operator) to find the value stored in `bah`. (Don't confuse this unary indirection operator with the binary * operator of multiplication.)

```
val = *ptr;  /* finding the value ptr points to */
```

The statements `ptr = &bah;` and `val = *ptr;` taken together amount to the following statement:

```
val = bah;
```

Using the address and indirection operators is a rather indirect way of accomplishing this result, hence the name "indirection operator."

The Address Operator:

&

General Comments:

When followed by a variable name, & gives the address of that variable.

Example:

&nurse is the address of the variable nurse.

The Indirection Operator:

*

General Comments:

When followed by a pointer name or an address, * gives the value stored at the pointed-to address.

Example:

```
nurse = 22;
ptr = &nurse;   /* pointer to nurse */
val = *ptr;
```

The net effect is to assign the value 22 to val.

Declaring Pointers

You already know how to declare int variables and other fundamental types. How do you declare a pointer variable? You might guess that the form is like this:

```
pointer ptr;     /* not the way to declare a pointer */
```

Why not? Because it is not enough to say that a variable is a pointer. You also have to say what kind of variable the pointer points to. The reason for this is that different variable types take up different amounts of storage, and some pointer operations require knowledge of that storage size. Also, the program has to know what kind of data is stored at the address. A long and a float might use the same amount of storage, but they store numbers quite differently. Here's how pointers are declared:

```
int * pi;        /* pi is a pointer to an integer variable  */
char * pc;       /* pc is a pointer to a character variable */
float * pf, * pg; /* pf, pg are pointers to float variables  */
```

The type specification identifies the type of variable pointed to, and the asterisk (*) identifies the variable itself as a pointer. The declaration int * pi; says that pi is a pointer and that *pi is type int (see Figure 9.5).

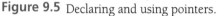

Figure 9.5 Declaring and using pointers.

The space between the * and the pointer name is optional. Often, programmers use the space in a declaration and omit it when dereferencing a variable.

The value (*pc) of what pc points to is of type char. What of pc itself? We describe it as being of type "pointer to char." Its value, being an address, is an unsigned integer on most systems. Therefore, on most systems, you can use the %u format to print the value of pc. As mentioned earlier, that need not hold true universally, so ANSI C provides the %p form specifically for pointers. Also, as the next chapter explains, the allowed operations for a pointer are different from those for an unsigned integer.

Using Pointers to Communicate Between Functions

We have touched only the surface of the rich and fascinating world of pointers, but our concern here is using pointers to solve our communication problem. Listing 9.16 shows a program that uses pointers to make the **interchange()** function work. Let's look at it, run it, and then try to understand how it works.

Listing 9.16   The swap3.c program.

```
/* swap3.c -- using pointers to make swapping work */
#include <stdio.h>
void interchange(int * u, int * v);
int main(void)
{
    int x = 5, y = 10;

    printf("Originally x = %d and y = %d.\n", x, y);
    interchange(&x, &y);  /* send addresses to function  */
    printf("Now x = %d and y = %d.\n", x, y);
```

```
    return 0;
}
void interchange(int * u, int * v)
{
    int temp;

    temp = *u;         /* temp gets value that u points to */
    *u = *v;
    *v = temp;
}
```

After all this trouble, does Listing 9.16 really work?

```
Originally x = 5 and y = 10.
Now x = 10 and y = 5.
```

Yes, it works.

Now, let's see how Listing 9.16 works. First, the function call looks like this:

```
interchange(&x, &y);
```

Instead of transmitting the *values* of x and y, you are transmitting their *addresses*. That means the formal arguments u and v appearing in the prototype and in the definition of interchange() will have addresses as their values. Therefore, they should be declared as pointers. Because x and y are integers, u and v are pointers to integers, so declare them as follows:

```
void interchange (int * u, int * v)
```

Next, in the body of the function, declare

```
int temp;
```

to provide the temporary storage you need. You want to store the value of x in temp, so you say

```
temp = *u;
```

Remember, u has the value &x, so u points to x. This means that *u gives you the value of x, which is what you want. You don't want to write

```
temp = u;    /* NO */
```

because that would assign temp the address of x rather than its value, and you are trying to interchange values, not addresses.

Similarly, to assign the value of y to x, use

```
*u = *v;
```

which translates to

```
x = y;
```

Let's summarize what this example does. You want a function that alters the values x and y. By passing the function the addresses of x and y, you give `interchange()` access to those variables. Using pointers and the * operator, the function can examine the values stored at those locations and change them.

There are a couple of variants you should know about. The pre-ANSI form for the function heading is this:

```
void interchange(u, v)
int * u, * v;
```

You can omit the variable names in the ANSI prototype. Then the prototype declaration looks like this:

```
void interchange(int *, int *);
```

More generally, you can communicate two kinds of information about a variable to a function. If you use a call of the form

```
function1(x);
```

you transmit the value of x. If you use a call of the form

```
function2(&x);
```

you transmit the address of x. The first form requires that the function definition include a formal argument of the same type as x.

```
int function1(int num)
```

The second form requires that the function definition include a formal argument that is a pointer to the right type:

```
int function2(int * ptr)
```

Use the first form if the function needs a value for some calculation or action. Use the second form if the function needs to alter variables in the calling function. You have been doing this all along with the `scanf()` function. When you want to read in a value for a variable num, for example, you use `scanf("%d", &num)`. That function reads a value and then uses the address you give it to store the value.

Pointers enable you to get around the fact that the variables of `interchange()` were local. They let that function reach out into `main()` and alter what was stored there.

Pascal and Modula-2 users might recognize the first form as being the same as Pascal's value parameter and the second form as being similar (but not identical) to Pascal's variable parameter. BASIC users might find the whole setup a bit unsettling. If this section seems strange to you, be assured that a little practice will make at least some uses of pointers seem simple, normal, and convenient (see Figure 9.6).

```
52000 52001 52002 52003 52004 52005 ...    52009  52010 ———— machine address
e|byte|byte|byte|byte|byte|byte|byte|byte|byte| byte |by
```

| G | 7776 | 1942 | 2.015×10^{30} | q | |—— value in memory

```
  ch      feet     date      sunmass    quit ——— variable name
   &ch = 52000              └ float type variable
   &feet = 52001             takes 4 bytes
   &date = 52003
   &sunmass = 52005
   &quit = 52009
   └ address operator
```

Figure 9.6 Names, addresses, and values in a byte-addressable system, such as the IBM PC.

Variables: Names, Addresses, and Values

The preceding discussion of pointers has hinged on the relationships between the names, addresses, and values of variables. Let's discuss these matters further.

When you write a program, you think of a variable as having two attributes: a name and a value. (There are other attributes, including type, but that's another matter.) After the program has been compiled and loaded, the computer also thinks of the same variable as having two attributes: an address and a value. An address is the computer's version of a name.

In many languages, the address is the computer's business, concealed from the programmer. In C, however, you can access the address through the & operator.

&barn is the address of the variable barn.

You can get the value from the name just by using the name.

printf("%d\n", barn) prints the value of barn.

You can get the value from the address by using the * operator.

Given pbarn = &barn;, then *pbarn is the value stored at address &barn.

In short, a regular variable makes the value the primary quantity and the address a derived quantity, via the & operator. A pointer variable makes the address the primary quantity and the value a derived quantity, via the * operator.

Although you can print an address to satisfy your curiosity, that is not the main use for the & operator. More important, using &, *, and pointers enables you to manipulate addresses and their contents symbolically, as in swap3.c (refer to Listing 9.16).

Summary: Functions

Form:

A typical function definition has this form:

```
name(argument list)
argument declarations
function body
```

The presence of the argument list and declarations is optional. Variables other than the arguments are declared within the body, which is bounded by braces.

ANSI C encourages the following form:

```
name(argument declaration list)
function body
```

The argument declaration list is a comma-separated list of variable declarations.

Examples:

```
int diff(x,y)      /* function name and argument list */
int x,y;           /* declare arguments              */
{                  /* begin function body            */
  int z;           /* declare local variable         */

  z = x - y;
  return z;
}                  /* end function body              */

int diff(int x, int y)   /* ANSI version            */
{                        /* begin function body      */
  int z;                 /* declare local variable   */

  z = x - y;
  return z;
}                        /* end function body        */
```

Communicating Values:

Arguments are used to convey values from the calling function to the function. If variables **a** and **b** have the values **5** and **2**, then the call

```
c = diff(a,b);
```

transmits **5** and **2** to the variables **x** and **y**. The values **5** and **2** are called *actual arguments*, and the `diff()` variables x and y are called *formal arguments*. The keyword `return` communicates one value from the function to the calling function. In this example, **c** receives the value of **z**, which is **3**. A function ordinarily has no effect on the variables in a calling function.

To directly affect variables in the calling function, use pointers as arguments. This might be necessary if you want to communicate more than one value back to the calling function.

Function Type:

Functions must have the same type as the value they return. Functions are assumed to be type `int`. If a function is another type, it must be declared as such in the calling function and in the function definition.

Example:

```c
int main(void)
{
  double q, x, duff();  /* declare in calling function   */
  int n;


  ...
   q = duff(x,n);


  ...
}
double duff(u, k)       /* declare in function definition */
double u;
int k;
{
  double tor;
...
   return tor;          /* returns a double value        */
}
```

Chapter Summary

Use functions as building blocks for larger programs. Each function should have a single, well-defined purpose. Use arguments to communicate values to a function, and use the keyword `return` to communicate back a value. If the function returns a value not of type `int`, then you must specify the function type in the function definition and in the declaration section of the calling function. If you want the function to affect variables in the calling function, use addresses and pointers.

ANSI C offers function prototyping, a powerful C enhancement that allows compilers to verify that the proper number and types of arguments are used in a function call.

A C function can call itself; this is called recursion.

Review Questions

1. What is the difference between an actual argument and a formal argument?

2. Write ANSI C function headings for the following functions described. Note we are asking just for the headings, not the body.

   a. `donut()` takes an `int` argument and prints that number of `0`s.

   b. `gear()` takes two `int` arguments and returns type `int`.

   c. `stuff_it()` takes a `double` and the address of a `double` variable and stores the first value in the given location.

3. Write ANSI C function headings for the following functions described. Note that you need write only the headings, not the body.

   a. `n_to_char()` takes an `int` argument and returns a `char`.

   b. `digits()` takes a `double` argument and an `int` argument and returns an `int`.

   c. `random()` takes no argument and returns an `int`.

4. Devise a function that returns the sum of two integers.

5. What changes, if any, would you need to make to have the function of Question 4 add two `double` numbers instead?

6. Devise a function `alter()` that takes two `int` variables x and y and changes their values to their sum and their difference, respectively.

7. Is anything wrong with this function definition?

```
void salami(num)
{
    int num, count;

    for (count = 1; count <= num; num++)
        printf(" O salami mio!\n");
}
```

8. Write a function that returns the largest of three integer arguments.

9. Given the following output:

```
Please choose one of the following:
1) copy files          2) move files
3) remove files        4) quit
Enter the number of your choice:
```

   a. Write a function that displays a menu of four numbered choices and asks you to choose one. (The output should look like the preceding.)

   b. Write a function that has two `int` arguments: a lower limit and an upper limit. The function should read an integer from input. If the integer is outside the limits, the function should print a menu again (using the function from part a. of this question) to reprompt the user, and get a new value. When an integer in the proper limits is entered, the function should return that value to the calling function.

   c. Write a minimal program using the functions from parts a. and b. of this question. By minimal, we mean it need not actually perform the actions promised by the menu; it should just show the choices and get a valid response.

Programming Exercises

1. Devise a function `min(x,y)` that returns the smaller of two `double` values, and test the function with a simple driver.

2. Devise a function `chline(ch,i,j)` that prints the requested character in columns `i` through `j`. Test it in a simple driver.

3. Write a function that takes three arguments: a character and two integers. The character is to be printed. The first integer specifies the number of times that the character is to be printed on a line, and the second integer specifies the number of lines that are to be printed. Write a program that makes use of this function.

4. The harmonic mean of two numbers is obtained by taking the inverses of the two numbers, averaging them, and taking the inverse of the result. Write a function that takes two `double` arguments and returns the harmonic mean of the two numbers.

5. Write a function that replaces the contents of two variables with two new values: the sum and the difference of the original contents.

6. Write a program that reads characters from the standard input to end-of-file. For each character, have the program report whether it is a letter. If it is a letter, also report its numerical location in the alphabet. For example, c and C would each be letter 3. Incorporate a function that takes a character as an argument and returns the numerical location if the character is a letter and that returns –1 otherwise.

7. In Chapter 6, "C Control Statements: Looping," (refer to Listing 6.18) we wrote a `power()` function that returned the result of raising a type `double` number to a positive integer value. Improve the function so that it correctly handles negative powers. Also, build into the function that 0 to any power is 0 and that any number to the 0 power is 1. Use a loop. Test the function in a program.

8. Redo Exercise 7, but this time use a recursive function.

9. Generalize the `to_binary()` function of Listing 9.9 so that it takes a second argument in the range 2–10. It then prints the number that is its first argument to the number base given by the second argument.

CHAPTER 10

ARRAYS AND POINTERS

You will learn about the following in this chapter:

- Keyword
  static

- Operators
  & *(unary)

I n this chapter, you learn how to create and initialize arrays. Along the way, you strengthen your knowledge of pointers and see how they relate to arrays. You also write functions that process arrays and explore two-dimensional arrays. People turn to computers for tasks like tracking monthly expenses or daily rainfall or quarterly sales or weekly weights. As a programmer, you inevitably have to deal with large quantities of related data. Often, arrays offer the best way to handle such data in an efficient, convenient manner. Chapter 6, "C Control Statements: Looping," introduced arrays, and this chapter takes a more thorough look. In particular, it examines how to write array-processing functions. Such functions enable you to extend the advantages of modular programming to arrays. In doing so, you can see the intimate relationship between arrays and pointers.

Arrays

Recall that an *array* is composed of a series of elements of one data type. You use *declarations* to tell the compiler when you want an array. An *array declaration* tells the compiler how many elements the array contains and what the type is for these elements. Armed with this information, the compiler can set up the array properly. Array elements can have the same types as ordinary variables. Consider the following example of array declarations:

```
/* some array declarations */
int main(void)
{
    float candy[365];      /* array of 365 floats */
    char code[12];         /* array of 12 chars    */
    int states[50];        /* array of 50 ints     */
    ...
}
```

The brackets (`[ ]`) identify `candy` and the rest as arrays, and the number enclosed in the brackets indicates the number of elements in the array.

To access elements in an array, you identify an individual element by using its subscript number, also called an *index*. The numbering starts with 0. Hence, `candy[0]` is the first element of the `candy` array, and `candy[364]` is the 365th and last element.

This is rather old hat; let's learn something new.

Initialization and Storage Classes

Arrays are often used to store data needed for a program. For example, a 12-element array can store the number of days in each month. In cases such as these, it's convenient to initialize the array at the beginning of a program, and you can. Let's see how it is done.

You know you can initialize single-valued variables (sometimes called *scalar* variables) in a declaration with expressions like

```
int fix = 1;
float flax = PI * 2;
```

where, you hope, `PI` was defined earlier as a macro. Can you do something similar with arrays? The answer is that old favorite: yes and maybe. It's yes for ANSI C and maybe for K&R C. If the array is an *external* array or a *static* array, it can be initialized. If it is an *automatic* array, it can be initialized under ANSI C but not under the older K&R definition of the language. We'll cover these new terms in Chapter 13, "Storage Classes and Program Development," but we'll preview them now.

The terms *external, static,* and *automatic* describe different *storage classes* that C allows. The storage class determines how widely known a data item is to various functions in a program and for how long it is kept in memory. Until now, we have used only automatic variables. Let's look at these three storage classes.

Automatic Variables and Arrays

An automatic variable or array is one defined *inside* a function (this includes formal arguments). As we've emphasized, a variable defined in a function is private to that function, even if it reuses a name appearing in another function. We haven't mentioned, however, that such a variable exists only for the duration of the function call. When a function finishes and returns to the calling function, the space used to hold its variables is freed.

ANSI C enables you to initialize automatic arrays, as follows:

```
int main(void)
{
  int powers[8] = {1,2,4,6,8,16,32,64}; /* ANSI only */
  ...
}
```

Because the array is defined inside `main()`, it is an automatic array. It is initialized by using a comma-separated list of values enclosed in braces. You can use spaces between the values and the commas, if you want. The first element (`powers[0]`) is assigned the value 1, and so on.

K&R C, however, does not allow this syntax to initialize an array. The only way to give values to an automatic array in K&R is to assign values to the elements individually, perhaps by using a loop.

External Variables and Arrays

An external variable or array is one defined *outside* a function. Here, for example, is how to define an external variable and an external array:

```
int report;
int sows[5] = {12, 10, 8, 9, 6};   /* ok in ANSI and K&R */
int feed(int n);    /* prototype */
int main(void)
{
    ...
}
int feed(int n)
{
    ...
}
```

External variables and arrays differ from their automatic cousins in three respects. First, they are known to all functions following them in a file. Therefore, in this example, both `main()` and `feed()` can use and modify the `int` variable `report` and the array `sows`. Second, external variables and arrays persist as long as the program runs. Because they are not defined in a particular function, they don't expire when a particular function terminates. Third, external variables and arrays are initialized to zeros by default, so `report` is initialized to `0`.

Static Variables and Arrays

You can define a static variable or array inside a function by beginning the definition with the keyword `static`, as shown here:

```
int account(int n, int m)
{
    static int beans[2] = {343, 332}; /* ok in ANSI, K&R */
    ...
}
```

This definition creates an array that, like an automatic array, is local to the function `account()`. However, like an external array, a static array retains its values between function calls and is initialized to zeros by default.

Storage Classes: Comments

C offers multiple storage classes to meet different programming needs. In Chapter 13, we'll investigate the uses of each type. For most cases, automatic variables and arrays are the best choice. However, because K&R doesn't allow automatic arrays to be initialized, many older programs use external or static arrays instead. The ANSI standard has been around several years now, so this book assumes that automatic arrays can be initialized. (If that doesn't work for you, you can modify the examples by adding the `static` keyword.) That said, let's learn a bit more about array initialization.

More Array Initialization

Listing 10.1 presents a short program that prints the number of days per month. (Remember, if your compiler doesn't support initialization of automatic arrays, add the keyword static to the declaration.)

Listing 10.1   The day_mon1.c program.

```
/* day_mon1.c -- prints the days for each month */
#include <stdio.h>
#define MONTHS 12

int main(void)
{
  int days[MONTHS] = {31,28,31,30,31,30,31,31,30,31,30,31};
  int index;

  for (index = 0; index < MONTHS; index++)
    printf("Month %d has %d days.\n", index +1,
           days[index]);
  return 0;
}
```

The output looks like this:

```
Month 1 has 31 days.
Month 2 has 28 days.
Month 3 has 31 days.
Month 4 has 30 days.
Month 5 has 31 days.
Month 6 has 30 days.
Month 7 has 31 days.
Month 8 has 31 days.
Month 9 has 30 days.
Month 10 has 31 days.
Month 11 has 30 days.
Month 12 has 31 days.
```

Not quite a superb program, but it's wrong only one month in every four years. The program intializes days[] with a list of comma-separated values enclosed in braces.

What if you fail to initialize an array? Listing 10.2 shows what happens with the three kinds of arrays (external, static, and automatic) if you fail to initialize them.

Listing 10.2   The no_data.c program.

```
/* no_data.c -- uninitialized arrays */
#include <stdio.h>
#define SIZE 4
int extar[SIZE];            /* uninitialized external array  */
int main(void)
{
  static int statar[SIZE];  /* uninitialized static array */
  int autar[SIZE];          /* uninitialized automatic array */
  int i;
```

```
    printf("%2s%10s%10s%10s\n",
            "i", "extar", "statar", "autar");
    for (i = 0; i < SIZE; i++)
        printf("%2d%10d%10d%10d\n", i, extar[i],
                statar[i], autar[i]);
    return 0;
}
```

Here is the result:

i	extar	statar	autar
0	0	0	3
1	0	0	6618612
2	0	0	4206088
3	0	0	6618628

The rule is that external and static arrays are initialized to 0s by default. The automatic array, on the other hand, is like an ordinary automatic variable—if you don't initialize it, it might have any value. The compiler just uses whatever values were already present at those memory locations.

The number of items in the list should match the size of the array. What if you count wrong? Let's try the last example again, as shown in Listing 10.3, with lists that are two too short.

Listing 10.3 The somedata.c program.

```
/* somedata.c -- partially initialized arrays */
#include <stdio.h>
#define SIZE 4
int extar[SIZE] = {1956, 1966};
int main(void)
{
    static int statar[SIZE]= { -50, -90};
    int autar[SIZE] = {492, 567};
    int i;

    printf("%2s%10s%10s%10s\n",
            "i", "extar", "statar", "autar");
    for (i = 0; i < SIZE; i++)
        printf("%2d%10d%10d%10d\n", i, extar[i],
                statar[i], autar[i]);
    return 0;
}
```

This time the output looks like this:

i	extar	statar	autar
0	1956	-50	492
1	1966	-90	567
2	0	0	0
3	0	0	0

As you can see, the compiler had no problem. When it ran out of values from the list, it initialized the remaining elements to 0. This initializing to 0 holds for automatic arrays as well as for external and static arrays. That is, if you don't initialize an automatic array at all, its elements, like uninitialized ordinary variables, get garbage values, but if you partially initialize an automatic array, the uninitialized elements are set to 0.

The compiler is not so forgiving if you have too many list values. This overgenerosity is considered an error. There is no need, however, to subject yourself to the ridicule of your compiler. Instead, you can let the compiler match the array size to the list by omitting the size from the braces (see Listing 10.4).

Listing 10.4 The day_mon2.c program.

```
/* day_mon2.c -- letting the compiler count elements */
#include <stdio.h>
int main(void)
{
    int days[] = {31,28,31,30,31,30,31,31,30,31};
    int index;

    for (index = 0; index < sizeof days / sizeof (int); index++)
        printf("Month %d has %d days.\n", index +1,
                days[index]);
    return 0;
}
```

There are two main points to note in the program:

- When you use empty brackets to initialize an array, the compiler counts the number of items in the list and makes the array that large.

- Notice what we did in the for loop control statement. Lacking faith (justifiably) in our ability to count correctly, we let the computer give us the size of the array. The sizeof operator gives the size, in bytes, of the object or type following it. On our system, each int element occupies 4 bytes, so we divide the total number of bytes by 4 to get the number of elements. Other systems may have a different size int. Therefore, to be general, we divide by sizeof (int).

Here is the result of running this program:

```
Month 1 has 31 days.
Month 2 has 28 days.
Month 3 has 31 days.
Month 4 has 30 days.
Month 5 has 31 days.
Month 6 has 30 days.
Month 7 has 31 days.
Month 8 has 31 days.
Month 9 has 30 days.
Month 10 has 31 days.
```

Oops! We put in just ten values, but our method of letting the program find the array size kept us from trying to print past the end of the array. This points out a potential disadvantage of automatic counting: Errors in the number of elements could pass unnoticed.

There is one more short method of initializing arrays. Because it works only for character strings, however, we will save it for the next chapter.

Assigning Array Values

You can *assign* values to array members by using an array index, or subscript. For example, the following fragment assigns even numbers to an automatic array:

```
/* array assignment */
#include <stdio.h>
#define SIZE 50
int main(void)
{
  int counter, evens[SIZE];

  for (counter = 0; counter < SIZE; counter++)
        evens[counter] = 2 * counter;
  ...
}
```

Note that this assignment is element by element. C doesn't let you assign one array to another as a unit. Nor can you use the list-in-braces form except when initializing.

```
/* nonvalid array assignment */
#define SIZE 5
int main(void)
{
    int oxen[SIZE] = {5,3,2,8};      /* ok here     */
    int yaks[SIZE];

    yaks = oxen;                     /* not allowed */
    yaks[SIZE] = oxen[SIZE];         /* invalid     */
    yaks[SIZE] = {5,3,2,8};          /* doesn't work */
}
```

Pointers to Arrays

Pointers, as you may recall from Chapter 9, "Functions," provide a symbolic way to use addresses. Because the hardware instructions of computing machines rely heavily on addresses, pointers enable you to express yourself in a way that is close to how the machine expresses itself. This correspondence makes programs with pointers efficient. In particular, pointers offer an efficient way to deal with arrays. Indeed, as you will see, array notation is simply a disguised use of pointers.

An example of this disguised use is that an array name is also the address of the first element of an array. That is, if **flizny** is an array, then the following is true:

```
flizny == &flizny[0]
```

Both `flizny` and `&flizny[0]` represent the memory address of that first element. (Recall that & is the address operator). Both are *constants* because they remain fixed for the duration of the program. However, they can be assigned as values to a pointer *variable*, and you can change the value of a variable, as Listing 10.5 shows. Notice what happens to the value of a pointer when you add a number to it. (Recall that the `%p` specifier for the pointers typically displays hexadecimal values.)

Listing 10.5 The `pnt_add.c` program.

```
/* pnt_add.c -- pointer addition */
#include <stdio.h>
#define SIZE 4
int main(void)
{
  short dates [SIZE], * pti, index;
  double bills[SIZE], * ptf;

  pti = dates;    /* assign address of array to pointer */
  ptf = bills;
  printf("%23s %10s\n", "short", "double");
  for (index = 0; index < SIZE; index ++)
      printf("pointers + %d: %10p %10p\n",
                index, pti + index, ptf + index);
  return 0;
}
```

Here is the output:

```
                short      double
pointers + 0:   0064FDC8   0064FDD8
pointers + 1:   0064FDCA   0064FDE0
pointers + 2:   0064FDCC   0064FDE8
pointers + 3:   0064FDCE   0064FDF0
```

The second line prints the beginning addresses of the two arrays, and the next line gives the result of adding 1 to the address, and so on. Note that A is the hexadecimal digit for 10, C is the digit for 12, and E is the digit for 14. So, for example, 8 + 2 is A. What?

```
0064FDC8 + 1 = 0064FDCA?
0064FDE0 + 1 = 0064FDE8?
```

Pretty crazy? Like a fox! Our system is addressed by individual bytes, but type **short** uses 2 bytes and type **double** uses 4 bytes. What is happening here is that when you say "add 1 to a pointer," C adds one *storage unit*. For arrays, that means the address is increased to the address of the next *element*, not just the next byte (see Figure 10.1). This is one reason you have to declare what sort of object a pointer points to. The address is not enough because the computer needs to know how many bytes are used to store the object. (This is true even for pointers to scalar variables; otherwise, the `*pt` operation to fetch the value wouldn't work correctly.)

int dates[y], *pti;
pti = dates; (or pti = & dates[0];)

pointer variable pti is assigned the
address of the first element of the array dates

Figure 10.1 An array and pointer addition.

Now we can define more clearly what is meant by pointer-to-int or pointer-to-float or pointer to any other data object:

- The value of a pointer is the address of the object to which it points. How the address is represented internally is hardware dependent. Many computers, including PCs and VAXs, are *byte addressable*, meaning that each byte in memory is numbered sequentially. Here, the address of a large object, such as type **double** variable, typically is the address of the first byte of the object.

- Applying the * operator to a pointer yields the value stored in the pointed-to object.

- Adding 1 to the pointer increases its value by the size, in bytes, of the pointed-to object.

As a result of C's cleverness, you have the following equalities:

```
dates +2 == &date[2]        /* same address */
*(dates + 2) == dates[2]     /* same value   */
```

These relationships sum up the close connection between arrays and pointers. They mean you can use a pointer to identify an individual element of an array and to get its value. In essence, you have two different notations for the same thing. Indeed, the C language standard describes array notation in terms of pointers, so the pointer approach is the more basic of the two.

Incidentally, don't confuse *(dates+2) with *dates+2. The indirection operator (*) binds more tightly (has higher precedence) than +, so the latter means (*dates)+2.

```
*(dates +2)      /* value of the 3rd element of dates       */
*dates +2        /* 2 added to the value of the 1st element  */
```

The relationship between arrays and pointers means that you can often use either approach when writing a program. Listing 10.6, for instance, produces the same output as Listing 10.1 when compiled and run.

Listing 10.6   The day_mon3.c program.

```
/* day_mon3.c -- uses pointer notation */
#include <stdio.h>
#define MONTHS 12

int main(void)
{
   int days[MONTHS] = {31,28,31,30,31,30,31,31,30,31,30,31};
   int index;

   for (index = 0; index < MONTHS; index++)
     printf("Month %d has %d days.\n", index +1,
             *(days + index));   // same as days[index]
   return 0;
}
```

Here, days is the address of the first element of the array, days + index is the address of element days[index], and *(days + index) is the value of that element, just as days[index] is. The loop references each element of the array in turn and prints the contents of what it finds.

Is there an advantage to writing the program this way? Not really. The point to Listing 10.6 is that pointer notation and array notation are two equivalent methods. This example shows you can use pointer notation with arrays. The reverse is also true; you can use array notation with pointers. This turns out to be important when you have a function with an array as an argument.

Functions, Arrays, and Pointers

Suppose you want to write a function that operates on an array. For instance, suppose you want a function that returns the sum of the elements of an array. Listing 10.7 shows a program that does this. To point out an interesting fact about array arguments, the program also prints the size of the relevant arrays. (Recall that some pre-ANSI compilers require %ld for printing sizeof quantities.)

Listing 10.7   The sum_arr1.c program.

```
/* sum_arr1.c -- sums the elements of an array */
#include <stdio.h>
#define SIZE 10
long sum(int ar[], int n);
int main(void)
{
    int marbles[SIZE] = {20,10,5,39,4,16,19,26,31,20};
    long answer;
```

```
    answer = sum(marbles, SIZE);
    printf("The total number of marbles is %ld.\n", answer);
    printf("The size of marbles is %d bytes.\n",
        sizeof marbles);
    return 0;
}

long sum(int ar[], int n)        /* how big an array? */
{
    int i;
    long total = 0;

    for( i = 0; i < n; i++)
        total += ar[i];
    printf("The size of ar is %d bytes.\n", sizeof ar);
    return total;

}
```

Recall that the += operator adds the value of the operand on its right to the operand on its left. Therefore, `total` is a running sum of the array elements. The output on our system looks like this:

```
The size of ar is 4 bytes.
The total number of marbles is 190.
The size of marbles is 40 bytes.
```

Array Names as Arguments

Well, the function does successfully sum the number of marbles, but what is `ar`? From the function argument declarations, you might expect that `ar` is a new array into which are copied the values found in `marbles`—the actual argument to the function. After all, the formal argument n is assigned the value of its corresponding actual argument. Yet `ar` is only 4 bytes, so it couldn't be assigned the 40 bytes of data in `marbles`. Therefore, `ar` is not an array of 10 `ints`.

The reason that `ar` is not an array is that C does not allow arrays to be passed as function arguments. Look at this function call:

```
sum(marbles, SIZE);
```

The first argument is `marbles`, the name of an array, and the name of an array, recall, is the *address* of the first element of the array. That is, the identifier `marbles` is not an array; it is the address of an `int`, `marbles[0]`, so the function call `sum(marbles, SIZE)` is the same as `sum(&marbles[0], SIZE)` and passes two numbers: an address and an integer. This means that the formal arguments to `sum()` should be a pointer-to-`int` and an `int`. The function heading should look like this:

```
int sum(int *ar, int n)
```

Indeed, if you replace the heading in Listing 10.7 with this heading, the program works exactly the same as before. When you declare a formal argument (and *only* when you declare a formal argument) in C, the forms

```
int *ar    /* formal argument */
```

and

```
int ar[]   /* formal argument */
```

are exactly equivalent. Both state that `ar` is a pointer-to-int. That is why `sizeof ar` is 4—our system uses 4-byte pointers.

If `ar` is a pointer, why can you use the expression `ar[i]` in `sum()`? In C, remember, `ar[i]` is the same as `*(ar + i)`. Both represent the value stored at address `ar +i`. This is true if `ar` is the name of an array, and it is true if `ar` is the name of a pointer variable. Therefore, you can use pointer notation to process an array, and you can use array notation with a pointer variable. In this instance, `ar` starts out pointing to the first element of the `marbles` array. Increasing `i` then makes `ar + i` point to each element in turn. Because you also pass the size of the array, the `sum()` function knows when the end of the array is reached.

In short, when you use an array name as a function argument, you pass the address of the first element of the array to the function. The function then uses a pointer set to that address to access the original array in the calling program.

Incidentally, we designed the function to use an argument representing the array size, which enables us to use the same function for differently sized arrays. Note that the only way the function can know the array size is if we tell it. As the example shows, applying the `sizeof` operator to an array name yields the size of an array, but applying `sizeof` to a pointer variable yields the size of the pointer, not the size of the object that is pointed to. Another way to indicate the size is to build it into the function. That is, instead of using the `n` argument in `sum()`, we could have made the loop test be `i < 10`. However, such a function would be limited to working with 10-element arrays.

Using Pointer Arguments

The `sum()` function used two items of information to describe an array. First, a pointer identified the beginning of the array and the type of information stored. Then an integer indicated how many elements to process. Another way to describe the array is by passing two pointers, with the first indicating where the array starts (as before) and the second where the array ends. Listing 10.8 illustrates this approach. It also uses the fact that a pointer argument is a variable; that means instead of using an index to indicate which element in an array to access, the function can alter the value of the pointer itself, making it point to each array element in turn. Listing 10.8 also illustrates this technique.

Listing 10.8   The `sum_arr2.c` program.

```
/* sum_arr2.c -- sums the elements of an array */
#include <stdio.h>
#define SIZE 10
```

```
long sump(int * start, int * end);
int main(void)
{
  int marbles[SIZE] = {20,10,5,39,4,16,19,26,31,20};
  long answer;

  answer = sump(marbles, marbles + SIZE);
  printf("The total number of marbles is %ld.\n", answer);
  return 0;
}
/* use pointer arithmetic    */
long sump(int * start, int * end)
{
  long total = 0;

  while (start < end)
  {
    total += *start;   /* add value to total              */
    start++;           /* advance pointer to next element */
  }
  return total;
}
```

The pointer start begins by pointing to the first element of marbles, so the assignment expression total +=*start adds the value of the first element (20) to total. Then the expression start++ increments the pointer variable start so that it points to the next element in the array. Because start points to type int, C increments the value of start by the size of int.

Note that the sump() function uses a different method from sum() to end the summation loop. The sum() function uses the number of elements as a second argument, and the loop uses that value as part of the loop test:

```
for( i = 0; i < n; i++)
```

The sump() function, however, uses a second pointer to end the loop:

```
while (start < end)
```

Because the test is for inequality, the last element processed is the one just before the element pointed to by end. This mean that end actually points to the location after the final element in the array. C guarantees that when it allocates space for an array, a pointer to the first location after the end of the array is a valid pointer. That makes constructions like this one valid, for the final value start gets in the loop is end. Note that using this "past-the-end" pointer makes the function call neat:

```
answer = sump(marbles, marbles + SIZE);
```

Because indexing starts at 0, marbles + SIZE points to the next element after the end. If end pointed to the last element instead of to one past the end, you would have to use this code instead:

```
answer = sump(marbles, marbles + SIZE - 1);
```

Not only is this code less elegant in appearance, it's harder to remember, hence more likely to lead to programming errors. By the way, although C guarantees that the pointer `marbles + SIZE` is a valid pointer, it makes no guarantees about `marbles[SIZE]`, the value stored at that location.

You can also condense the body of the loop to one line:

```
total += *start++;
```

The unary operators `*` and `++` have the same precedence but associate from right to left. This means the `++` applies to ~~start, not to *start. That is, the~~ pointer is incremented, not the value pointed to. The use of the postfix form (`start++` rather than `++start`) means that the pointer is not incremented until after the pointed-to value is added to `total`. If the program used `*++start`, the order would be to increment the pointer, then use the value pointed to. If the program used `(*start)++`, however, it would use the value of `start` and then increment the value, not the pointer. That would leave the pointer pointing to the same element, but the element would contain a new number. Although the `*start++` notation is commonly used, you might prefer to use `*(start++)` for clarity. Listing 10.9 illustrates these niceties of precedence.

Listing 10.9   The `order.c` program.

```
/* order.c -- precedence in pointer operations */
#include <stdio.h>
int data[2] = {100, 300};
int moredata[2] = {200, 400};
int main(void)
{
  int * p1, * p2, * p3;

  p1 = p2 = data;
  p3 = moredata;
  printf("*p1++ = %d, *++p2 = %d, (*p3)++ = %d\n",
            *p1++, *++p2, (*p3)++);
  printf("  *p1 = %d,    *p2 = %d,      *p3 = %d\n",
            *p1, *p2, *p3);
  return 0;
}
```

Here is its output:

```
*p1++ = 100, *++p2 = 300, (*p3)++ = 200
  *p1 = 300,    *p2 = 300,      *p3 = 201
```

The only operation that altered an array value is (`*p3)++`. The other two operations caused `p1` and `p2` to advance to point to the next array element.

Comment: Pointers and Arrays

As you have seen, functions that process arrays actually use pointers as arguments, but you do have a choice between array notation and pointer notation for writing array-processing functions. Using array notation, as in Listing 10.7, makes it more obvious that the function is working with arrays. Also, array notation has a more familiar look to programmers versed in other languages, such as FORTRAN, Pascal, Modula-2, or BASIC. Other programmers may be more accustomed to working with pointers and might find the pointer notation more natural.

As far as C goes, the two notations are equivalent in meaning. Pointer notation, particularly when used with the increment operator, is closer to machine language and, with some compilers, leads to more efficient code. Many programmers, however, believe that the programmer's main concerns should be correctness and clarity and that code optimization should be left to the compiler.

Pointer Operations

Just what can you do with pointers? C offers five basic operations you can perform on pointers, and the next program demonstrates these possibilities. To show the results of each operation, we will print the value of the pointer (which is the address it points to), the value stored in the pointed-to address, and the address of the pointer itself. (If your compiler doesn't support the %p specifier, try %u or perhaps %lu for printing the addresses.)

Listing 10.10 shows the five basic operations that can be performed with or on pointer variables.

Listing 10.10 The pt_ops.c program.

```
/* pt_ops.c -- pointer operations */
#include <stdio.h>
int main(void)
{
  int urn[3] = {100,200,300};
  int * ptr1, * ptr2;

  ptr1 = urn;          /* assign an address to a pointer */
  ptr2 = &urn[2];      /* ditto
                       /* dereference a pointer and take */
                       /* the address of a pointer       */
  printf("ptr1 = %p, *ptr1 =%d, &ptr1 = %p\n",
      ptr1, *ptr1, &ptr1);
  ptr1++;              /* increment a pointer            */
  printf("values after ptr1++\n");
  printf("ptr1 = %p, *ptr1 =%d, &ptr1 = %p\n",
      ptr1, *ptr1, &ptr1);
  printf("ptr2 = %p, *ptr2 =%d, &ptr2 = %p\n",
      ptr2, *ptr2, &ptr2);
  ++ptr2;   /* going past end of the array */
  printf("values after ++ptr1\n");
  printf("ptr2 = %p, *ptr2 = %d, &ptr2 = %p\n",
      ptr2, *ptr2, &ptr2);
  printf("ptr2 - ptr1 = %d\n", ptr2 - ptr1);
                      /* pointer subtraction            */
  return 0;
}
```

Here is the output:

```
ptr1 = 0064FDEC, *ptr1 =100, &ptr1 = 0064FDE8
values after ptr1++
ptr1 = 0064FDF0, *ptr1 =200, &ptr1 = 0064FDE8
ptr2 = 0064FDF4, *ptr2 =300, &ptr2 = 0064FDE4
values after ++ptr2
ptr2 = 0064FDF8, *ptr2 = 6618680, &ptr2 = 0064FDE4
ptr2 - ptr1 = 2
```

The following list describes the five basic operations that can be performed with or on pointer variables:

- *Assignment.* You can assign an address to a pointer. Typically you do this by using an array name or by using the address operator (&). In the example, ptr1 is assigned the address of the beginning of the array urn. This address happens to be memory cell number 0064FDEC. The variable ptr2 gets the address of the third and last element, urn[2].

- *Value-finding (dereferencing).* The * operator gives the value stored in the pointed-to location. Therefore, *ptr1 is initially 100, the value stored at location 0064FDEC.

- *Taking a pointer address.* Like all variables, pointer variables have an address and a value. The & operator tells you where the pointer itself is stored. In this example, ptr1 is stored in memory location 0064FDE8. The content of that memory cell is 0064FDEC, the address of urn.

- *Incrementing a pointer.* You can do this by regular addition or by using the increment operator. Incrementing a pointer to an array element makes it move to the next element of an array. Therefore, ptr1++ increases the numerical value of ptr1 by 4 (4 bytes per int on our system) and makes ptr1 point to urn[1] (see Figure 10.2). Now ptr1 has the value 0064FDF0 (the next array address) and *ptr1 has the value 200, the value of urn[1]. Note that the address of ptr1 itself remains 0064FDE8. After all, a variable doesn't move around just because it changes value!

Of course, you can also decrement a pointer. There are some cautions to remember when incrementing or decrementing a pointer, however. The computer does not keep track of whether a pointer still points to an array element. The operation ++ptr2 in this example caused ptr2 to move up another 4 bytes, and now it points to whatever happened to be stored after the array. Also, you can use the increment or decrement operators for pointer variables, but not for address constants, such as array names, just as you can't use the increment operator on regular constants. However, you can use simple addition, as in urn + 2, for address constants.

Given the following,

```
int urn[3];
int * ptr1, * ptr2;
int x, y;
```

here are some valid and invalid statements:

Valid	Invalid
ptr1++;	urn++;
x++;	3++;
ptr2 = ptr1 + 2;	ptr2 = urn++;
ptr2 = urn + 1;	x = y + 3++;

- *Differencing.* You can find the difference between two pointers. Normally, you do this for two pointers to elements that are in the same array to find out how far apart the elements are. The result is in the same units as the type size. For instance, in the output from Listing 10.10, ptr2 - prt1 has the value 2, meaning these pointers point to objects separated by 2 ints, not by 2 bytes. Subtraction is guaranteed to be a valid operation as long as both pointers point into the same array (or possibly to a position one past the end). Applying the operation to pointers to two different arrays might produce a value or could lead to a runtime error.

Figure 10.2 Incrementing a type int pointer.

These operations open many possibilities. C programmers create arrays of pointers, pointers to functions, arrays of pointers to pointers, arrays of pointers to functions, and so on. Relax, though—we'll stick to the basic uses we have already unveiled. The first basic use for pointers is to communicate information to and from functions. You already know that you must use pointers if you want a function to affect variables in the calling function.

The second use is in functions designed to manipulate arrays. Let's look at a programming example using functions and arrays.

Protecting Array Contents

When you write a function that processes a fundamental type, such as int, you have a choice of passing the int by value or of passing a pointer-to-int. The usual rule is to pass quantities by value unless the program needs to alter the value, in which case you pass a pointer. Arrays don't give you that choice; you *must* pass a pointer. The reason is efficiency. If a function passed an array by value, it would have allocated enough space to hold a copy of the original array, then copied all the data from the original array to the new array. It is much quicker to pass the address of the array and have the function work with the original data.

This technique can raise problems. The reason C ordinarily passes data by value is to preserve the integrity of the data. If a function works with a copy of the original data, it won't accidentally modify the original data. But, because array-processing functions do work with the original data, they *can* modify the array. Sometimes that's desirable. For example, here's a function that adds the same value to each member of an array:

```c
void add_to(double ar[], int n, double val)
{
    int i;
    for( i = 0; i < n; i++)
        ar[i] += val;
}
```

Therefore, the function call

```c
add_to(prices, 100, 2.50);
```

causes each element in the **prices** array to be replaced by a value larger by 2.5; this function modifies the contents of the array. It can do so because, by working with pointers, the function uses the original data.

Other functions, however, do not have the intent of modifying data. The following function, for example, is intended to find the sum of the array's contents; it shouldn't change the array. However, because **ar** is really a pointer, a programming error could lead to the original data being corrupted. Here, for instance, the expression **ar[i]++** results in each element having 1 added to its value:

```c
long sum(int ar[], int n)
{
    int i;
    long total = 0;

    for( i = 0; i < n; i++)
        total += ar[i]++;    /* error increments each element */
    return total;
}
```

Using const with Formal Parameters

With K&R C, the only way to avoid this sort of error was being vigilant. With ANSI C, there is an alternative. If a function's intent is that it not change the contents of the array, use the keyword const when declaring the formal parameter in the prototype and in the function definition. For example, the prototype and definition for sum() should look like this:

```
long sum(const int ar[], int n);  /* prototype */

long sum(const int ar[], int n)   /* definition */
{
    int i;
    long total = 0;

    for( i = 0; i < n; i++)
        total += ar[i];
    return total;
}
```

This tells the compiler that the function should treat the array pointed to by ar as though the array contained constant data. Then, if you accidentally use an expression like ar[i]++, the compiler can catch it and generate an error message, telling you that the function attempts to alter constant data.

It's important to understand that using const this way does not require that the original array *be* constant; it just says that the function has to treat the array *as though* it were constant. Using const this way provides the protection for arrays that passing by value provides for fundamental types; it prevents a function from modifying data in the calling function. In general, if you write a function intended to modify an array, don't use const when declaring the array parameter. If you write a function not intended to modify an array, do use const when declaring the array parameter.

In the program shown in Listing 10.11, one function displays an array and one function multiplies each element of an array by a given value. Because the first function should not alter the array, it uses const. Because the second function has the intent of modifying the array, it doesn't use const.

Listing 10.11   The arf.c program.

```
/* arf.c -- array functions */
#include <stdio.h>
#define SIZE 5
void show_array(const double ar[], int n);
void mult_array(double ar[], int n, double mult);
int main(void)
{
  double dip[SIZE] = {20.0, 17.66, 8.2, 15.3, 22.22};

  printf("The original dip array:\n");
  show_array(dip, SIZE);
  mult_array(dip, SIZE, 2.5);
```

continued on next page

continued from previous page

```
            printf("The dip array after calling mult_array():\n");
            show_array(dip, SIZE);
            return 0;
    }
    void show_array(const double ar[], int n)
    {
      int i;

      for (i = 0; i < n; i++)
            printf("%8.3f ", ar[i]);
      putchar('\n');
    }

    /* multiplies each array member by the same multiplier */
    void mult_array(double ar[], int n, double mult)
    {
      int i;
    Z
      for (i = 0; i < n; i++)
            ar[i] *= mult;
    }
```

Here is the output:

```
The original dip array:
  20.000    17.660     8.200    15.300    22.220
The dip array after calling mult_array():
  50.000    44.150    20.500    38.250    55.550
```

Note that both functions are type `void`. The `mult_array()` function does provide new values to the `dip` array, but not by using the `return` mechanism.

More About const

Earlier, you saw that you can use `const` to create symbolic constants:

```
const double PI = 3.14159;
```

That was something you could do with the `#define` directive also, but `const` lets you create constant arrays, constant pointers, and pointers to constants.

Suppose you use an array to store values that should not be altered. You can use the `const` keyword to protect that array:

```
#define MONTHS 12
const int days[MONTHS] = {31,28,31,30,31,30,31,31,30,31,30,31};
```

If your code subsequently tries to alter the array, you'll get a compile-time error message:

```
days[9] = 44;     /* compile error */
```

Pointers to constants can't be used to change values. Consider the following code:

```
double rates[5] = {88.99, 100.12, 59.45, 183.11, 340.5};
const double * pd = rates;     /* pd points to beginning of the array */
```

The second line of code declares that pd points to a const double. That means you can't use pd to change pointed-to values:

```
*pd = 29.89;      /* not allowed */
pd[2] = 222.22;   /* not allowed */
rates[0] = 99.99; /* allowed because rates is not const */
```

Whether you use pointer notation or array notation, you are not allowed to use pd to change the value of pointed-to data. Note, however, that because rates was not declared as a constant, you can still use rates to change values. Also note that you can make pd point somewhere else:

```
pd++;      /* make pd point to rates[1] -- allowed */
```

A pointer-to-constant is normally used as a function parameter to indicate that the function won't use the pointer to change data. For example, the show_array() function from Listing 10.11 could have been prototyped this way:

```
void show_array(const double *ar, int n);
```

There are some rules you should know. First, it's valid to assign the address of either constant data or non-constant data to a pointer-to-constant:

```
double rates[5] = {88.99, 100.12, 59.45, 183.11, 340.5};
const double locked[4] = {0.08, 0.075, 0.0725, 0.07};
const double * pd = rates;   /* valid */
pd = locked;                 /* valid */
pd = &rates[3];              /* valid */
```

Only the addresses of non-constant data can be assigned to regular pointers, however:

```
double rates[5] = {88.99, 100.12, 59.45, 183.11, 340.5};
const double locked[4] = {0.08, 0.075, 0.0725, 0.07};
double * pd = rates;     /* valid     */
pd = locked;             /* not valid */
pd = &rates[3];          /* valid     */
```

This is a reasonable rule. Otherwise, you could use the pointer to change data that was supposed to be constant.

A practical consequence of these rules is that a function such as show_array() can accept the names of regular arrays and of constant arrays as actual arguments because either can be assigned to a pointer-to-constant:

```
show_array(rates, 5);    /* valid */
show_array(locked, 4);   /* valid */
```

A function like mult_array(), however, can't accept the name of a constant array as an argument:

```
mult_array(rates, 5, 1.2);    /* valid       */
mult_array(locked, 4, 1.2);   /* not allowed */
```

Therefore, using const in a function parameter definition not only protects data, it also allows the function to work with arrays that have been declared const.

There are more possible uses of const. For example, you can declare and initialize a pointer so that it can't be made to point elsewhere. The trick is the placement of the keyword const:

```
double rates[5] = {88.99, 100.12, 59.45, 183.11, 340.5};
double * const pd = rates;    /* pd points to beginning of the array */
pd = &rates[2];               /* not allowed                         */
*pd = 92.99;                  /* ok -- changes rates[0]              */
```

Such a pointer can still be used to change values, but it can point only to the location originally assigned to it.

Finally, you can use const twice to create a pointer that can neither change where it's pointing nor change the value to which it points:

```
double rates[5] = {88.99, 100.12, 59.45, 183.11, 340.5};
const double * const pd = rates;
pd = &rates[2];               /* not allowed */
*pd = 92.99;                  /* not allowed */
```

Multidimensional Arrays

Tempest Cloud, a weather person who takes her subject cirrusly, wants to analyze 5 years of monthly rainfall data. One of her first decisions is how to represent the data. One choice is to use 60 variables, one for each data item. (We mentioned this choice once before, and it is as senseless now as it was then.) Using an array with 60 elements would be an improvement, but it would be nicer still if she could keep each year's data separate. She could use five arrays, each with 12 elements, but that is clumsy and could get really awkward if Tempest decides to study 50 years' worth of rainfall instead of 5. She needs something better.

The better approach is to use an array of arrays. The master array would have five elements, one for each year. Each of those elements, in turn, would be a 12-element array, one for each month. This is how to declare such an array:

```
float rain[5][12];   /* array of 5 arrays of 12 floats */
```

You can also visualize this rain array as a two-dimensional array consisting of five rows, each of 12 columns, as shown in Figure 10.3. By changing the second subscript, you move along a row, month by month. By changing the first subscript, you move vertically along a column, year by year.

The two-dimensional view is merely a convenient way of visualizing an array with two indices. Internally, such an array is stored sequentially, beginning with the first 12-element array, followed by the second 12-element array, and so on.8

Let's use this two-dimensional array in a weather program. The program goal is to find the total rainfall for each year, the average yearly rainfall, and the average rainfall for each month. To find the total rainfall for a year, you have to add all the data in a given row. To find the average rainfall for a given month, you have to add all the data in a given column. The two-dimensional array makes it easy to visualize and execute these activities. Listing 10.12 shows the program.

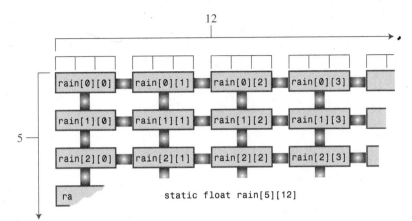

Figure 10.3 Two-dimensional array.

Listing 10.12   The rain.c program.

```
/* rain.c  -- finds yearly totals, yearly average, and monthly
                 average for several years of rainfall data */
#include <stdio.h>
#define MONTHS 12    /* number of months in a year */
#define YRS    5     /* number of years of data    */
int main(void)
{
 /* initializing rainfall data for 1990 - 1994 */
 const float rain[YRS][MONTHS] = {
 {10.2, 8.1, 6.8, 4.2, 2.1, 1.8, 0.2, 0.3, 1.1, 2.3, 6.1, 7.4},
 {9.2, 9.8, 4.4, 3.3, 2.2, 0.8, 0.4, 0.0, 0.6, 1.7, 4.3, 5.2},
 {6.6, 5.5, 3.8, 2.8, 1.6, 0.2, 0.0, 0.0, 0.0, 1.3, 2.6, 4.2},
 {4.3, 4.3, 4.3, 3.0, 2.0, 1.0, 0.2, 0.2, 0.4, 2.4, 3.5, 6.6},
 {8.5, 8.2, 1.2, 1.6, 2.4, 0.0, 5.2, 0.9, 0.3, 0.9, 1.4, 7.2}
 };
 int year, month;
 float subtot, total;

 printf(" YEAR    RAINFALL  (inches)\n");
 for (year = 0, total = 0; year < YRS; year++)
 {             /* for each year, sum rainfall for each month */
    for (month = 0, subtot = 0; month < MONTHS; month++)
      subtot += rain[year][month];
    printf("%5d %15.1f\n", 1990 + year, subtot);
    total += subtot;                    /* total for all years */
 }
 printf("\nThe yearly average is %.1f inches.\n\n", total/YRS);
 printf("MONTHLY AVERAGES:\n\n");
 printf(" Jan  Feb  Mar  Apr  May  Jun  Jul  Aug  Sep  Oct ");
 printf(" Nov  Dec\n");
```

continued on next page

continued from previous page

```
    for (month = 0; month < MONTHS; month++)
    {                 /* for each month, sum rainfall over years */
      for (year = 0, subtot =0; year < YRS; year++)
        subtot += rain[year][month];
      printf("%4.1f ", subtot/YRS);
    }
    printf("\n");
    return 0;
}
```

Here is the output:

```
YEAR      RAINFALL   (inches)
1990             50.6
1991             41.9
1992             28.6
1993             32.2
1994             37.8
```

```
The yearly average is 38.2 inches.
```

```
MONTHLY AVERAGES:
```

```
Jan  Feb  Mar  Apr  May  Jun  Jul  Aug  Sep  Oct  Nov  Dec
7.8  7.2  4.1  3.0  2.1  0.8  1.2  0.3  0.5  1.7  3.6  6.1
```

As you study this program, concentrate on the initialization and on the computation scheme. The initialization is the more involved of the two, so let's look at the computation first.

To find the total for a given year, keep **year** constant and let **month** go over its full range. This is the inner **for** loop of the first part of the program. Then repeat the process for the next value of **year**. This is the outer loop of the first part of the program. A nested loop structure like this one is natural for handling a two-dimensional array. One loop handles the first subscript, and the other loop handles the second subscript.

The second part of the program has the same structure, but now it changes **year** with the inner loop and **month** with the outer. Remember, each time the outer loop cycles once, the inner loop cycles its full allotment. Therefore, this arrangement cycles through all the years before changing months. You get a 5-year average for the first month, and so on.

Initializing a Two-Dimensional Array

For the initialization, we included five embraced lists of numbers, all enclosed by one outer set of braces. The data in the first interior set of braces is assigned to the first row of the array, the data in the second interior set goes to the second row, and so on. The rules we discussed about mismatches between data and array sizes apply to each row. That is, if the first inner set of braces encloses 10 numbers, only the first 10 elements of the first row are affected. The last two elements in that row are then initialized by default to zero. If there are too many numbers, it is an error; the numbers do not get shoved into the next row.

We could have left out the interior braces and just retained the two outermost braces. As long as you have the right number of entries, the effect is the same. If you are short of entries, however, the array is filled sequentially row by row until the data runs out. Then the remaining elements are initialized to 0. Figure 10.4 shows both ways of initializing an array.

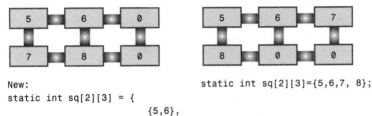

New:
```
static int sq[2][3] = {
                        {5,6},
                        {7,8}
                      };
```

```
static int sq[2][3]={5,6,7, 8};
```

Figure 10.4 Two methods of initializing an array.

Because the `rain` array holds data that should not be modified, the program uses the `const` modifier when declaring the array.

More Dimensions

Everything we have said about two-dimensional arrays can be generalized to three-dimensional arrays and further. You can declare a three-dimensional array this way:

```
int box[10][20][30];
```

You can visualize this array as 10 two-dimensional arrays (each 20 × 30) stacked atop each other, or you can think of it as an array of arrays of arrays. That is, it is a 10-element array, each element of which is a 20-element array. Each 20-element array then has elements that are 30-element arrays. Or you can simply think of arrays in terms of the number of indices needed. We'll stick to two dimensions in our examples.

Pointers and Multidimensional Arrays

How do pointers relate to multidimensional arrays? Let's look at some examples now to find the answer. To simplify the discussion, you'll examine an array that is much smaller than `rain`. Suppose you have this declaration:

```
int zippo[4][2];   /* an array of arrays of ints */
```

Then `zippo`, being the name of an array, is the address of the first element of the array. In this case, the first element of `zippo` is itself an array of two `int`s, so `zippo` is the address of an array of two `int`s. Let's analyze that further in terms of pointer properties:

- Because `zippo` is the address of the array's first element, `zippo` equals `&zippo[0]`. Next, `zippo[0]` is itself an array of two integers, so `zippo[0]` equals `&zippo[0][0]`, the address of its first element, an `int`. In short, `zippo[0]` is the address of an `int`-sized object, and `zippo` is the address of a two-`int`-sized object. Because both the integer and the array of two integers begin at the same location, both `zippo` and `zippo[0]` have the same numeric value.

- Adding 1 to a pointer or address yields a value larger by the size of the referred-to object. In this respect, `zippo` and `zippo[0]` differ, for `zippo` refers to an object two `int`s in size, and `zippo[0]` refers to an object one `int` in size. Therefore, `zippo + 1` and `zippo[0] + 1` do not have the same value.

- Dereferencing a pointer or an address (applying the `*` operator or else the `[ ]` operator with an index) yields the value represented by the referred-to object. Because `zippo[0]` is the address of its first element `zippo[0][0]`, `*(zippo[0])` represents the value stored in `zippo[0][0]`, an `int` value. Similarly, `*zippo` represents the value of its first element, `zippo[0]`, but `zippo[0]` itself is the address of an `int`. It's the address `&zippo[0][0]`, so `*zippo` is `&zippo[0][0]`. Applying the dereferencing operator to both expressions implies that `**zippo` equals `*&zippo[0][0]`, which reduces to `zippo[0][0]`, an `int`. In short, `zippo` is the address of an address and must be dereferenced twice to get an ordinary value. An address of an address or a pointer of a pointer is an example of *double indirection*.

Clearly, increasing the number of array dimensions increases the complexity of the pointer view. At this point, most students of C begin realizing why pointers are considered one of the more difficult aspects of the language. You might want to study the preceding points carefully and see how they are illustrated in the following examples. Listing 10.13 is a program that prints addresses.

Listing 10.13   The `zippo1.c` program.

```
/* zippo1.c -- addresses */
#include <stdio.h>
int main(void)
{
    int zippo[4][2];

    printf("zippo = %p, zippo[0] = %p\n", "zippo, zippo[0]);
    printf("&zippo[0][0] = %p, &zippo = %p\n",
            &zippo[0][0], *zippo);
    return 0;
}
```

Here is the output:

```
zippo = 0064FDD8, zippo[0] = 0064FDD8
&zippo[0][0] = 0064FDD8, &zippo = 0064FDD8
```

The output shows that the address of the two-dimensional array `zippo` and the address of the one-dimensional array `zippo[0]` are the same. Each is the address of the corresponding array's first element, and this is the same numerically as `&zippo[0][0]`. Also, note that `zippo` and `*zippo` have the same value.

Nonetheless, there is a difference. On our system, `int` is 4 bytes. As discussed earlier, `zippo[0]` and `*zippo` point to a 4-byte data object. Adding 1 to either should produce a value larger by 4. The name `zippo` is the address of an array of two `int`s, so it identifies an 8-byte data object. Therefore, adding 1 to `zippo` should produce an address 8 bytes larger. Let's modify the program, as shown in Listing 10.14, to check that.

Listing 10.14 The `zippo2.c` program.

```c
/* zippo2.c -- more zippo info */
#include <stdio.h>
int main(void)
{
    int zippo[4][2];
    printf("zippo = %p, zippo[0] = %p, &zippo[0][0] = %p\n",
    zippo, zippo[0], &zippo[0][0]);
    printf("*zippo = %p\n", *zippo);

    printf("zippo + 1 = %p, zippo[0] + 1 = %p\n",
    zippo + 1, zippo[0] + 1);
    printf("&zippo[0][0] + 1 = %p, *zippo + 1 = %p\n",
            &zippo[0][0] + 1, *zippo + 1);
    printf("*(zippo + 1) = %p\n", *(zippo + 1));
    return 0;
}
```

Here is the new output:

```
zippo = 0064FDD8, zippo[0] = 0064FDD8, &zippo[0][0] = 0064FDD8
*zippo = 0064FDD8
zippo + 1 = 0064FDE0, zippo[0] + 1 = 0064FDDC
&zippo[0][0] + 1 = 0064FDDC, *zippo + 1 = 0064FDDC
*(zippo + 1) = 0064FDE0
```

The results are as we predicted. Adding 1 to `zippo` moves you from one two-`int` array to the next array, and adding 1 to `zippo[0]` moves you from one `int` to the next (see Figure 10.5). Also, note what happens if you add 2 to `zippo[0]` (or, equivalently, to `*zippo`). You would go past the end of the first two-`int` array to the beginning of the next. The last two examples illustrate that `zippo[0]`, `&zippo[0][0]`, and `*zippo` are but three different notations for the same thing. All are addresses of the same `int`.

Note the difference between `*zippo + 1` and `*(zippo +1)`. The former applies the `*` first and then adds, but the latter adds and then dereferences. In the first case, because `*zippo` is the address of an `int`, adding 1 increases the value by 4 bytes on our system. In the second

case, because `zippo` is the address of a two-`int` object, 8 is added. This means that `zippo`
`+ 1` is the address of the second two-`int` array element, and applying the `*` operator yields
the address of the first element of that array. Therefore, `*(zippo + 1)` is the address of an
`int`. In particular, it's the address of the element `zippo[1][0]`. The expression `*zippo + 1`
is also the address of an `int`, but it's the address of `zippo[0][1]`. In short, dereferencing,
then adding, moves the address along a row (changes the second index); adding, then dereferencing, moves the address along a column (changes the first index).

Figure 10.5 An array of arrays.

Another point to note is that *each* element of `zippo` is an array and hence the address
of a first element. Therefore, you have these relationships:

```
zippo[0] == &zippo[0][0] == *zippo
zippo[1] == &zippo[1][0] == *(zippo + 1)
zippo[2] == &zippo[2][0] == *(zippo + 2)
zippo[3] == &zippo[3][0] == *(zippo + 3)
```

Applying the `*` operator to each gives the following results:

```
*zippo[0] == zippo[0][0] == **zippo
*zippo[1] == zippo[1][0] == *(*(zippo + 1))
*zippo[2] == zippo[2][0] == *(*(zippo + 2))
*zippo[3] == zippo[3][0] == *(*(zippo + 3))
```

More generally, you can represent individual elements by using array notation and pointer notation as follows:

```
zippo[m][n] == *(*(zippo + m) + n)
```

The value m, being the index associated with `zippo`, is added to `zippo`. The value n, being
the index associated with the subarray `zippo[m]`, is added to `zippo[m]`, which is `*(zippo`
`+m)` in array notation. This makes `*(zippo + m) + n` the address of element `zippo[m][n]`,
and applying the `*` operator yields the contents at that address.

Now suppose you want to declare a pointer variable `pz` that is compatible with `zippo`.
Such a pointer could be used, for example, in writing a function to deal with `zippo`-like
arrays. Will the type pointer-to-`int` suffice? No. That type is compatible with `zippo[0]`,
which points to a single `int`, but you want `pz` to point to an array of `int`s. Here is what
you can do:

```
int (* pz)[2];
```

This statement says that `pz` is a pointer to an array of two `ints`. Why the parentheses? Well, `[ ]` has a higher precedence than `*`. Therefore, with a declaration like

```
int * pax[2];
```

you apply the brackets first, making `pax` an array of two somethings. Next, you apply the `*`, making `pax` an array of two pointers. Finally, use the `int`, making `pax` an array of two pointers to `int`. This declaration creates *two* pointers, but the original version uses parentheses to apply the `*` first, creating *one* pointer to an array of two `ints`.

Functions and Multidimensional Arrays

You might be wondering if you really have to learn about pointers to pointers. If you want to write functions that process two-dimensional arrays, the answer is yes. Mainly, you need to understand pointers well enough to make the proper declarations for function arguments. In the function body itself, you can usually get by with array notation.

Suppose, then, you want to write a function to deal with two-dimensional arrays. You have several choices. You can use a function written for one-dimensional arrays on each subarray, or you can use the same function on the whole array, but treat the whole array as one-dimensional instead of two-dimensional, or you can write a function that explicitly deals with two-dimensional arrays. To illustrate these three approaches, let's take a small two-dimensional array and apply each of the approaches to double the magnitude of each element.

Applying a One-Dimensional Function to Subarrays

To keep things simple, we'll declare `junk` as a small array of arrays and initialize it. We'll write a function that takes an array address and an array size as arguments and doubles the indicated elements. We'll use a `for` loop to apply this function to each subarray of `junk`, and we'll print the array contents. Listing 10.15 shows the program.

Listing 10.15   The `dubarr1.c` program.

```
/* dubarr1.c -- doubles array elements */
#include <stdio.h>
void dub(int ar[], int size);
int main(void)
{
    int junk[3][4] = {
            {2,4,5,8},
            {3,5,6,9},
            {12,10,8,6}
    };
    int i, j;

    for (i = 0; i < 3 ; i++)
        dub(junk[i], 4);
```

continued on next page

continued from previous page

```
            for (i = 0; i < 3; i++)
            {
                for (j = 0; j < 4; j++)
                    printf("%5d", junk[i][j]);
                putchar('\n');
            }
            return 0;
        }

        void dub(int ar[], int size)     /* or int * ar */
        {
            int i;

            for (i = 0; i < size; i++)
                ar[i] *= 2;
        }
```

The first `for` loop in `main()` uses `dub()` to process the subarrays `junk[0]`, `junk[1]`, and so on. This approach works because `junk[0]`, `junk[1]`, and so forth, *are* each one-dimensional arrays. Note that we pass `dub()` a `size` parameter of 4 because that is the number of elements in each subarray. Here is the output:

```
 4    8   10   16
 6   10   12   18
24   20   16   12
```

Applying a One-Dimensional Function to a Two-Dimensional Array

In the preceding example, you looked at `junk` as being an array of three arrays of four `int`s. For most C implementations, you can also look at `junk` as being an array of 12 `int`s. Suppose, for instance, you pass `dub()` the value `junk[0]` as an argument. This act initializes the pointer `ar` in `dub()` to the address of `junk[0][0]`. As a result, `ar[0]` corresponds to `junk[0][0]`, and `ar[3]` corresponds to `junk[0][3]`. What about `ar[4]`? It represents the element following `junk[0][3]`, which is `junk[1][0]`, the first element of the next subarray. In other words, you've finished one row and gone to the beginning of the next. The program in Listing 10.16 continues in this fashion to cover the whole array, with `ar[11]` representing `junk[2][3]`.

Listing 10.16   The `dubarr2.c` program.

```
/* dubarr2.c -- doubles array elements */
#include <stdio.h>
void dub(int ar[], int size);
int main(void)
{
    static int junk[3][4] = {
        {2,4,5,8},
```

```
             {3,5,6,9},
             {12,10,8,6}
      };
      int i, j;

      dub(junk[0], 3*4);

      for (i = 0; i < 3; i++)
      {
         for (j = 0; j < 4; j++)
            printf("%5d", junk[i][j]);
         putchar('\n');
      }
      return 0;
}

void dub(int ar[], int size)    /* or int * ar */
{
      int i;

      for (i = 0; i < size; i++)
         ar[i] *= 2;
}
```

In Listing 10.15, note that dub() is unchanged from Listing 10.14. We merely changed the limit to 3*4 (or 12) and used one call to dub() instead of three. (We wrote the limit as 3*4 to emphasize that it is the total number of elements calculated by multiplying the number of rows times the number of columns.) Does it work? Here is the output:

```
 4    8   10   16
 6   10   12   18
24   20   16   12
```

Because junk has the same numerical value as junk[0], could you use junk instead of junk[0] as the argument to dub()? K&R implementations let you, but ANSI C implementations point out that junk clashes with the prototype, which says the argument should be a pointer-to-int, not a pointer to a pointer.

Is this a good approach? Not really, because it treats the junk array as though it were one-dimensional, and that's conceptually wrong. However, it does illustrate that a two-dimensional array is implemented internally as one big array.

Applying a Two-Dimensional Function

Both of the approaches described so far lose track of the column-and-row information. In this application (doubling each element), that information is unimportant, but suppose each row represented a year and each column a month. Then you might want a function to, say, total up individual columns. In that case, the function should have the row and column information available. This can be accomplished by declaring the right kind of formal variable so that the function can pass the array properly. In this case, the array junk is an array of three arrays of four ints. As the earlier discussion implied, that means junk is a pointer to an array of four `int`s, and a function parameter of this type can be declared in this way:

```
int (* pj)[4]
```

Alternatively, if `pj` is a formal argument to a function, you can declare it this way:

```
int pj[][4]
```

Note that the first set of brackets is empty. The empty brackets identify `pj` as being a pointer. Such a variable can then be used in the same way as `junk`. That is what we have done in the next example, shown in Listing 10.17.

Listing 10.17   The `dubarr3.c` program.

```
/* dubarr3.c -- doubles array elements */
#include <stdio.h>
void dub2 (int ar[][4], int size);
int main(void)
{
    static int junk[3][4] = {
            {2,4,5,8},
            {3,5,6,9},
            {12,10,8,6}
    };
    int i, j;

    dub2(junk,3);
    for (i = 0; i < 3; i++)
    {
        for (j = 0; j < 4; j++)
            printf("%5d", junk[i][j]);
        putchar('\n');
    }
    return 0;
}

void dub2 (int ar[][4], int size)    /* or int (*ar)[4] */
{
    int i, j;

    for (i = 0; i < size; i++)
        for (j = 0; j < 4; j++)
            ar[i][j] *= 2;
}
```

The program in Listing 10.17 passes as arguments `junk`, which is a pointer to the first array, and **3**, the number of rows. The `dub2()` function then treats `ar` as an array of arrays of four `int`s. The number of columns is built into the function, but the number of rows is left open. The same function will work with, say, a 12-by-4 array if 12 is passed as the number of rows. That's because `size` is the number of elements; however, because each element is an array, or row, `size` becomes the number of rows.

Note that `ar` is used in the same fashion as `junk` is used in `main()`. This is possible because `ar` and `junk` are the same type: pointer to array-of-four-`int`s.

Here is the output:

```
 4    8   10   16
 6   10   12   18
24   20   16   12
```

Be aware that the following declaration will not work properly:

```
int ar[][]; /* faulty declaration */
```

Recall that the compiler converts array notation to pointer notation. This means, for example, that `ar[1]` will become `ar+1`. For the compiler to evaluate this, it needs to know what size of object `ar` points to. The declaration

```
int ar[][4];
```

says that `ar` points to an array of four `int`s, hence to an object 16 bytes long on our system, so `ar+1` means "add 16 bytes to the address." With the empty-bracket version, the compiler would not know what to do.

You can also include a size in the other bracket pair, as shown here, but it is ignored:

```
void dub2(ar, n)
int ar[3][4];     /* the 3 is ignored */
int n;
```

In general, to declare a pointer corresponding to an N-dimensional array, you must supply values for all but the leftmost set of brackets.

Planning a Program

Now that you've seen the mechanics of writing array functions, let's try a more programming-oriented example. Our self-appointed task is to write a program that reads numbers into an array, prints the entered numbers, and reports the average. To make the program more realistic, require that it allow the user to terminate input, if desired, before the array is filled. This will enable the program to process any number of items up to a maximum determined by the array size. Also, you want to avoid calculating the average if no numbers are entered.

General Plan

Conceptually, the program should perform three major tasks: reading in a set of numbers, printing the set of numbers, and calculating the average. Now that you know how to process arrays with functions, let's use functions to modularize the work. As a first pass, you can visualize the program as shown in Listing 10.18.

Listing 10.18 The draft1.c program.

```
/* draft1.c -- first draft of program skeleton */
#include <stdio.h>
#define MAX 25
void read_array(double ar[]);
void show_array(const double ar[]);
double mean(const double ar[]);
int main(void)
{
  double data[MAX];

  read_array(data);
  show_array(data);
  printf("The average is %.2lf.\n", mean(data));
  return 0;
}
```

Now you have a modular program, but this draft doesn't handle data communication well. For instance, the `read_array()` function should know the maximum number of items that it is allowed to read, so it should also take `MAX` as an argument. Incidentally, the fact that `data` is a pointer means that the `read_array()` function will modify the `data` array in `main()` directly, which is exactly what you want for this function.

Similarly, the `show_array()` and `mean()` functions should know how big an array they are using, so they each need an additional argument. In general, this argument should not be `MAX` because the user might enter fewer numbers. You can use a variable `size` to represent the actual number of items entered; it can be the second argument to these two functions. Neither of these functions should modify the array, so the parameter is declared as `const`.

This raises a new problem: How does `main()` know what `size` is? One solution is to have the `read_array()` function return that value. That is, it takes as arguments the array to be filled and the maximum number of values that the array holds. It then reads data into the array and returns the actual number of items read. If this number is zero, you can skip the rest of the program. This line of thought leads to a second draft for the skeleton, which is shown in Listing 10.19.

Listing 10.19 The draft2.c program.

```
/* draft2.c -- second top-level draft for the program */
#include <stdio.h>
#define MAX 25
int read_array(double ar[], int limit);
void show_array(const double ar[], int n);
double mean(const double ar[], int n);
int main(void)
{
  double data[MAX];
  int size;
  double average;

  size = read_array(data, MAX);
  if (size == 0)
```

```
        printf("No data. Bye.\n");
    else
    {
        printf("The following numbers were entered:\n\n");
        show_array(data, size);
        printf("\nThe average of these values is %.2f.\n",
            mean(data, size));
    }
    return 0;
}
```

Note that we changed the prototype for read_array() to reflect that it now has a return value. Now you have the overall design for the program and its data flow, and you can turn to the individual functions.

The read_array() Function

The read_array() function is the most ambitious of the three. It should read in values until the array is filled or until the user wants to stop, whichever occurs first. The main question is how to let the user inform the program that he or she is finished. You can use the properties of scanf() to help here. Recall that scanf() returns the number of values successfully read. Non-numeric input or end of file causes it to return 0 or EOF, respectively. Therefore, you can terminate input if scanf() doesn't return the value 1. Also, you can use a counter to keep track of the number of entries so that you can terminate input if the counter exceeds the size of the array. Here's one approach:

```
int read_array(double ar[], int limit)
{
  int i = 0;

  printf("Enter up to %d numbers. To terminate\n", limit);
  printf("earlier, enter a letter or EOF.\n");
  while (i < limit && scanf("%lf", &ar[i]) == 1)
      i++;
  return i;
}
```

This approach looks simple enough, but there are two subtle points to note. The first is that the test i < limit comes first. Recall that the && operator guarantees that the second operand is not evaluated if the first operand is false. This means that if i equals limit, the expression scanf("%lf", &ar[i]) == 1 is not evaluated. This, in turn, means that the scanf() function is not called, which is good. Suppose you had used the opposite order:

```
while ( scanf("%lf", &ar[i]) == 1 && i < limit)
```

In this case, scanf() reads a value into ar[limit] before finding out that it has gone too far. Remember, because array numbering begins with 0, ar[limit] is one position past the end of the array. You don't want to put data there!

The second subtle point is that the loop increments i after reading a value into ar[i]. This makes i one greater than the index of the last array element filled. Because indexing begins with 0, i at that point equals the number of array items, not the array index. This is convenient because the number of array items is the value you want to return.

If you like, you can use pointers more explicitly. For instance, you could use the following input loop:

```
while (i < limit && scanf("%lf", ar++) == 1)
     i++;
```

Recall that `scanf()` requires the address of the location that is to receive the data. Initially, ar holds the address of the first element of the array, so the first time through the loop, `scanf()` places a number in the first element of the array. Then the increment operator increases ar so that it points to the next element of the array, thus preparing for the next loop cycle.

The show_array() Function

Next, you want a function to display the array values. We already have written one for Listing 10.10. A problem with that function, however, is that it prints everything on one line. Here you have more data, so you would like to insert some newline characters.

One scheme is to use a `for` loop as before and to print a newline after every sixth value. You can do this by using the modulus operator (%):

```
void show_array(const double ar[], int n)
{
    int i;

    for (i = 0; i < n; i++)
    {
        printf("%10.2f ", ar[i]);
        if (i % 6 == 5)
            putchar('\n');
    }
    if (i % 6 != 0)
        putchar('\n');
}
```

Because i starts at 0, i % 6 first becomes 5 after six values have been printed. The expression subsequently becomes 5 after each additional six values have been printed.

The `if (i % 6 != 0)` test causes a newline to be printed after all the values have been printed, unless the last value printed was already at the end of a line—in which case the loop itself prints a newline. If i % 6 is 5 inside the loop, the i++ operation at loop's end causes i % 6 to be 0 after leaving the loop.

The mean() Function

Finding the mean is a simple problem. You can use a `for` loop to sum the numbers and then divide by the total number of items to get the average:

```
double mean(const double ar[], int n)
{
    int i;
    double total = 0;
```

```
    for (i = 0; i < n ; i++)
        total += ar[i];
    return (total / n);
}
```

The only potential trouble spot is if n is 0 because dividing by 0 is a no-no. The `main()` function shields `mean()` from this possibility.

The Result

Putting the parts together results in the program shown in Listing 10.20.

Listing 10.20   The `mean.c` program.

```
/* mean.c -- finds the mean of a set of numbers */
#include <stdio.h>
#define MAX 25
int read_array(double ar[], int limit);
void show_array(const double ar[], int n);
double mean(const double ar[], int n);
int main(void)
{
  double data[MAX];
  int size;

  size = read_array(data, MAX);
  if (size == 0)
        printf("No data. Bye.\n");
  else
    {
        printf("The following numbers were entered:\n\n");
        show_array(data, size);
        printf("\nThe average of these values is %.2f.\n",
            mean(data, size));
    }
  return 0;
}
int read_array(double ar[], int limit)
{
  int i = 0;

  printf("Enter up to %d numbers. To terminate\n", limit);
  printf("earlier, enter a letter or EOF.\n");
  while (i < limit  && scanf("%lf", &ar[i]) == 1)
        i++;
  return i;
}
void show_array(const double ar[], int n)
{
  int i;
```

continued on next page

continued from previous page

```
        for (i = 0; i < n; i++)
        {
            printf("%10.2f ", ar[i]);
            if (i % 6 == 5)
                putchar('\n');
        }
        if (i % 6 != 0)
            putchar('\n');
}
double mean(const double ar[], int n)
{
    int i;
    double total = 0;

    for (i = 0; i < n ; i++)
        total += ar[i];
    return (total/n);
}
```

Here's a sample run:

```
Enter up to 25 numbers. To terminate
earlier, enter a letter or EOF.
1 2 3 4 5 6 7 8 9 10 q
The following numbers were entered:

    1.00        2.00        3.00        4.00        5.00        6.00
    7.00        8.00        9.00       10.00

The average of these values is 5.50.
```

Chapter Summary

An *array* is a set of elements that all have the same data type. Array elements are stored sequentially in memory and are accessed by using an integer index (or offset). In C, the first element of an array has an index of 0, so the final element in an array of n elements has an index of n - 1.

To declare a simple *one-dimensional array*, use this form:

```
type name[size];
```

Here, *type* is the data type for each and every element, *name* is the name of the array, and *size* is the number of elements.

C interprets the name of an array to be the address of the first element of the array. In other terms, the name of an array is equivalent to a pointer to the first element. In general, arrays and pointers are closely connected. If **ar** is an array, then the expressions **ar[i]** and ***(ar + i)** are equivalent.

C does not enable entire arrays to be passed as function arguments, but you can pass the address of an array. The function can then use this address to manipulate the original array. If the intent of the function is not to modify the original array, you should use the const keyword when declaring the formal parameter representing the array. You can use either array notation or pointer notation in the called function. In either case, you're actually using a pointer variable.

Adding an integer to a pointer or incrementing a pointer changes the value of the pointer by the number of bytes of the object being pointed to. That is, if **pd** points to an 8-byte **double** value in an array, adding 1 to **pd** increases its value by 8 so that it will point to the next element of the array.

Two-dimensional arrays represent an array of arrays. For instance, the declaration

```
double sales[5][12];
```

creates an array **sales** having five elements, each of which is an array of 12 **doubles**. The first of these one-dimensional arrays can be referred to as **sales[0]**, the second as **sales[1]**, and so on, with each being an array of 12 **ints**. Use a second index to access a particular element in these arrays. For instance, **sales[2][5]** is the sixth element of **sales[2]**, and **sales[2]** is the third element of **sales**.

We've used **int** arrays and **double** arrays in this discussion, but the same concepts apply to other types. Character strings, however, have many special rules. This stems from the fact that the terminal null character in a string provides a way for functions to detect the end of a string without being passed a size. We will look at character strings in detail in Chapter 11, "Character Strings and String Functions."

Review Questions

1. What will this program print?

```
#include <stdio.h>
char ref[] = { 'D', 'O', 'L', 'T'};
int main(void)
{
   char *ptr;
   int index;

   for (index = 0, ptr = ref; index < 4; index++, ptr++)
      printf("%c %c\n", ref[index], *ptr);
   return 0;
}
```

2. In Question 1, what storage class is **ref**?

3. In Question 1, **ref** is the address of what? What about **ref + 1**? What does ++**ref** point to?

4. What is the value of ***ptr** and of *(**ptr** + 2) in each case?

   a.

   ```
   int *ptr;
   int torf[2][2] = {12, 14, 16};
   ptr = torf[0];
   ```

b.
```
int * ptr;
int fort[2][2] = { {12}, {14,16} };
ptr = fort[0];
```

5. What is the value of `**ptr` and of `**(ptr + 1)` in each case?

   a.
   ```
   int (*ptr)[2];
   int torf[2][2] = {12, 14, 16};
   ptr = torf;
   ```

   b.
   ```
   int (*ptr)[2];
   int fort[2][2] = { {12}, {14,16} };
   ptr = fort;
   ```

6. Suppose you have the following declaration:

   `int grid[30][100];`.

   a. Express the address of `grid[22][56]` one way.

   b. Express the address of `grid[22][0]` two ways.

   c. Express the address of `grid[0][0]` three ways.

7. Create an appropriate declaration for each of the following variables:

   a. `digits` is an array of ten `int`s.

   b. `rates` is an array of six `float`s.

   c. `mat` is an array of three arrays of five integers.

   d. `pstr` is a pointer to an array of 20 `char`s.

   e. `psa` is an array of 20 pointers to `char`.

8.

   a. Declare an array of six `int`s and initialize it to the values 1, 2, 4, 8, 16, and 32.

   b. Use array notation to represent the third element (the one with the value 4) of the array in part a.

9. What is the index range for a ten-element array?

10. Suppose you have these declarations:

    ```
    float rootbeer[10], things[10][5], *pf, value = 2.2;
    int i = 3;
    ```

    Identify each of the following statements as valid or invalid:

    a. `rootbeer[2] = value;`

    b. `scanf("%f", &rootbeer );`

```
c. rootbeer = value;

d. printf("%f", rootbeer);

e. things[4][4] = rootbeer[3];

f. things[5] = rootbeer;

g. pf = value;

h. pf = rootbeer;
```

Programming Exercises

1. Modify the rain program in Listing 10.12 so that it does the calculations using pointers instead of subscripts. (You still have to declare and initialize the array.)

2. Write a program that initializes an array and then copies the contents of the array into two other arrays. (All three arrays should be declared in the main program.) To make the first copy, use a function with array notation. To make the second copy, use a function with pointer notation and pointer incrementing. Have each function take as arguments the name of the source array, the name of the target array, and the number of elements to be copied.

3. Write a function that returns the largest value stored in an array. Test the function in a simple program.

4. Write a function that returns the index of the largest value stored in an array. Test the function in a simple program.

5. Write a function that returns the difference between the largest and smallest elements of an array. Test the function in a simple program.

6. Write a program that initializes a two-dimensional array and uses one of the copy functions from Exercise 2 to copy it to a second two-dimensional array. (Because a two-dimensional array is an array of arrays, a one-dimensional copy function can be used with each subarray.)

7. Use a copy function from Exercise 2 to copy the third through fifth elements of a seven-element array into a three-element array. The function itself need not be altered; just choose the right actual arguments. (The actual arguments need not be an array name and array size. They only have to be the address of an array element and a number of elements to be processed.)

8. Write a function that sets each element in an array to the sum of the corresponding elements in two other arrays. That is, if array 1 has the values

2, 4, 5, and 8 and array 2 has the values 1, 0, 4, and 6, the function assigns array 3 the values 3, 4, 9, and 14. The function should take three array names and an array size as arguments. Test the function in a simple program.

9. Write a program that declares a 3-by-5 array and initializes it to some values of your choice. Have the program print the values, double all the values, and then display the new values. Write a function to do the displaying and a second function to do the doubling. Have the functions take the array name and the number of rows as arguments.

10. Rewrite the rain program in Listing 10.12 so that the main tasks are performed by functions instead of in `main()`.

11. Write a program that prompts the user to enter three sets of five `double` numbers each. The program should accomplish all of the following:

   a. Store the information in a 3-by-5 array.

   b. Compute the average of each set of five values.

   c. Compute the average of the values.

   d. Determine the largest value of the 15 values.

   e. Report the results.

   Each major task should be handled by a separate function.

CHAPTER 11

CHARACTER STRINGS AND STRING FUNCTIONS

You will learn about the following in this chapter:

- Functions
  gets(), puts(), strcat(), strncat(), strcmp(), strncmp()
  strcpy(), strncpy(), sprint(), strchr(), isalnum()
  isalpha(), iscntrl(), isdigit(), isgraph()
  islower(), isprint(), ispunct(), isspace()
  isupper(), isxdigit()

*I*n this chapter, you learn more about creating and using strings. You use several string and character functions from the C library and practice creating your own string functions. Also, you learn how to use command-line arguments.

Character strings are one of the most useful and important data types in C. You have been using character strings all along, but there still is much to learn about them. Of course, you already know the most basic fact: A *character string* is a char array terminated with a null character (\0). This chapter discusses the nature of strings, how to declare and initialize strings, how to get them into and out of programs, and how to manipulate strings.

Listing 11.1 presents a busy program that illustrates several ways to set up strings, read them, and print them. It uses two new functions: gets(), which reads a string, and puts(), which prints a string. (You probably notice a family resemblance to getchar() and putchar().) The rest of the program should look fairly familiar.

Listing 11.1 The strings.c program.

```
/* strings.c -- stringing the user along */
#include <stdio.h>
#define MSG "You must have many talents. Tell me some."
                            /* a symbolic string constant */
#define LIM  5
#define LINELEN 81          /* maximum string length + 1  */
char m1[] = "Just limit yourself to one line's worth.";
                            /* initializing an external   */
                            /* character array            */
```

continued on next page

continued from previous page

```
char * m2 = "If you can't think of anything, fake it.";
                            /* initializing an external   */
                            /* character pointer          */
int main(void)
{
  char name[LINELEN];
  char talents[LINELEN];
  int i;
  char *m3 = "\nEnough about me -- what's your name?";
                            /* initializing a pointer      */
  char *mytal[LIM] = {  "Adding numbers swiftly",
          "Multiplying accurately", "Stashing data",
          "Following instructions to the letter",
          "Understanding the C language"};
                            /* initializing an array of    */
                            /* string pointers             */

  printf("Hi! I'm Clyde the Computer. I have many talents.\n");

  printf("Let me tell you some of them.\n");
  puts("What were they? Ah, yes, here's a partial list.");
  for (i = 0; i < LIM; i++)
      puts(mytal[i]);  /* print list of computer talents */
  puts(m3);
  gets(name);
  printf("Well, %s, %s\n", name, MSG);
  printf("%s\n%s\n", m1, m2);
  gets(talents);
  puts("Let's see if I've got that list:");
  puts(talents);
  printf("Thanks for the information, %s.\n", name);
  return 0;
}
```

To show you what this program does, here is a sample run:

```
Hi! I'm Clyde the Computer. I have many talents.
Let me tell you some of them.
What were they? Ah, yes, here's a partial list.
Adding numbers swiftly
Multiplying accurately
Stashing data
Following instructions to the letter
Understanding the C language

Enough about me -- what's your name?
Nigel Barntwit
Well, Nigel Barntwit, You must have many talents. Tell me some.
Just limit yourself to one line's worth.
If you can't think of anything, fake it.
Fencing, yodeling, malingering, cheese tasting, and sighing.
Let's see if I've got that list:
Fencing, yodeling, malingering, cheese tasting, and sighing.
Thanks for the information, Nigel Barntwit.
```

Let's see how Listing 11.1 works. However, rather than go through it line by line, let's take a more encompassing approach. First, you will look at ways of defining a string within a program. Then you will see what is involved in reading a string into a program. Finally, you will study ways to output a string.

Defining Strings Within a Program

As you probably noticed when you read Listing 11.1, there are many ways to define a string. Here are the principal ways: using string constants, using char arrays, using char pointers, and using arrays of character strings. A program should make sure there is a place to store a string, and we will cover that topic, too.

Character String Constants

A *string constant* is anything enclosed in double quotation marks. The enclosed characters, plus a terminating \0 character automatically provided by the compiler, are stored in memory as a character string. The program uses several such character string constants, most often as arguments for the printf() and puts() functions. Note, too, that you can #define character string constants.

If you want to use a double quotation mark within a string, precede the quotation mark with a backslash, as follows:

```
printf("\"Run, Spot, run!\" exclaimed Dick.\n");
```

This produces the following output:

```
"Run, Spot, run!" exclaimed Dick.
```

Character string constants are placed in the *static storage* class. Static storage means that if you use a string constant in a function, the string is stored just once and lasts for the duration of the program, even if the function is called several times. The entire quoted phrase acts as a pointer to where the string is stored. This action is analogous to the name of an array acting as a pointer to the array's location. If this is true, what kind of output should the program in Listing 11.2 produce?

Listing 11.2 The quotes.c program.

```
/* quotes.c -- strings as pointers */
#include <stdio.h>
int main(void)
{
    printf("%s, %p, %c\n", "We", "are", *"space farers");
    return 0;
}
```

The %s format should print the string We. The %p format produces an address. So if the phrase "are" is an address, then %p should print the address of the first character in the string. (Pre-ANSI implementations might have to use %u or %lu instead of %p.) Finally, *"space farers" should produce the value of the address pointed to, which should be the first character of the string "space farers". Does this really happen? Well, here is the output:

```
We, 00410A40, s
```

Character String Arrays and Initialization

When you define a character string array, you must let the compiler know how much space is needed. One way to do this is to initialize the array with a string constant. With older C implementations, you must use static or external arrays for this purpose, but we'll assume you're using ANSI C and can initialize arrays of any storage class. The following declaration initializes the external array m1 to the characters of the indicated string:

```
char m1[] = "Just limit yourself to one line's worth.";
```

This form of initialization is short for the standard array initialization form:

```
char m1[] = { 'J', 'u', 's', 't', ' ', 'l', 'i', 'm', 'i',
't', ' ', 'y', 'o', 'u', 'r', 's', 'e', 'l',
'f', ' ', 't', 'o', ' ', 'o', 'n', 'e', ' ',
'l', 'i', 'n', 'e', '\", 's', ' ', 'w', 'o', 'r',
't', 'h', '.', '\0'
};
```

Note the closing null character. Without it, you have a character array, but not a string. For either form (and we do recommend the first), the compiler counts the characters and sizes the array accordingly. Initializing character arrays is one case when it really does make sense to let the compiler determine the array size.

The array name m1, like any array name, yields the address of the first element of the array:

```
m1 == &m1[0] , *m1 == 'J', and *(m1+1) == m1[1] == 'u'
```

Indeed, you can use pointer notation to set up a string. For example, Listing 11.1 uses this declaration:

```
char *m3 = "\nEnough about me -- what's your name?";
```

This declaration is very nearly the same as this one:

```
char m3[] = "\nEnough about me -- what's your name?"
```

Both declarations amount to saying that m3 is a pointer to the indicated string. In both cases, the string itself determines the amount of storage set aside for the string. Nonetheless, the forms are not identical.

Array Versus Pointer

What is the difference, then, between an array and a pointer form? The array form (m3[ ]) causes an array of 38 elements (one for each character plus one for the terminating ' \0 ') to be created in static storage. (The storage is static because the declaration is external.) Each element is initialized to the corresponding character. Hereafter, the compiler will recognize the name m3 as a synonym for the address of the first array element, &m3[0]. One important point here is that in the array form, m3 is an address *constant*. You can't change m3 because that would mean changing the location (address) where the array is stored. You can use operations like m3+1 to identify the next element in an array, but ++m3 is not allowed. The increment operator can be used only with the names of variables, not with constants.

The pointer form (*m3) also causes 38 elements in static storage to be set aside for the string. In addition, it sets aside one more storage location for the pointer *variable* m3. This variable initially points to the first character of the string, but the value can be changed. Therefore, you can use the increment operator. For instance, ++m3 would point to the second character (E). Note that *m3 does not have to be declared as static, even for K&R C. The reason is that you are not initializing an array of 38 elements; rather, you are initializing a single pointer variable. There are no storage class restrictions for initializing ordinary, non-array variables, either in K&R C or in ANSI C.

Are these differences important? Often they are not, but it depends on what you try to do. See the following discussion for some examples.

Array and Pointer Differences

Let's examine the differences between initializing a character array to hold a string and initializing a pointer to point to a string. (By "pointing to a string," we really mean pointing to the first character of a string.) For example, consider these two declarations:

```c
char heart[] = "I love Tillie!";
char *head = "I love Millie!";
```

The chief difference is that the array name heart is a constant, but the pointer head is a variable. What practical difference does this make?

First, both can use array notation:

```c
for (i = 0; i < 6; i++)
    putchar(heart[i]);
putchar('\n');
for (i = 0; i < 6; i++)
    putchar(head[i]));
putchar('\n');
```

This is the output:

```
I love
I love
```

Next, both can use pointer addition:

```c
for (i = 0; i < 6; i++)
    putchar(*(heart + i));
```

```
putchar('\n');
for (i = 0; i < 6; i++)
    putchar(*(head + i));
putchar('\n');
```

Again, the output is this:

```
I love
I love
```

Only the pointer version, however, can use the increment operator:

```
while (*(head) != '\0')   /* stop at end of string            */
    putchar(*(head++));   /* print character, advance pointer */
```

This produces the following output:

```
I love Millie!
```

Suppose you want **head** to agree with **heart**. You can say this:

```
head = heart;  /* head now points to the array heart */
```

This makes the **head** pointer point to the first element of the **heart** array. However, you cannot say this:

```
heart = head;   /* illegal construction */
```

The situation is analogous to x = 3; versus 3 = x;. The left side of the assignment statement must be a variable or, more generally, an lvalue, such as *p_int. Incidentally, head = heart; does not make the Millie string vanish; it just changes the address stored in head. Unless you've saved the address of "I love Millie!" elsewhere, however, you won't be able to access that string when head points to another location.

There is a way to alter the **heart** message—go to the individual array elements:

```
heart[7]= 'M';
```

or

```
*(heart + 7) = 'M';
```

The *elements* of an array are variables (unless the array was declared as **const**), but the *name* is not a variable.

Specifying Array Size Explicitly

Another way to set up storage is to be explicit. In the external declaration, you could have said

```
char m1[44] = "Just limit yourself to one line's worth.";
```

instead of

```
char m1[] = "Just limit yourself to one line's worth.";
```

Just be sure that the number of elements is at least one more (that null character again) than the string length. As with other static or external arrays, any unused elements are automatically initialized to **0** (which in **char** form is the null character, not the zero digit character). See Figure 11.1.

```
static char pets[12] = "nice cat.";
```
Figure 11.1 Initializing an array.

Note that in the program you had to assign a size for the array **name**:

```
#define LINELEN 81          /* maximum string length + 1  */
char name[LINELEN];
```

Because the contents for **name** are to be read when the program runs, the compiler has no way of knowing in advance how much space to set aside unless you tell it. There is no string constant present whose characters the compiler can count, so we gambled that 80 characters would be enough to hold the user's name. When you declare an array, the array size must evaluate to an integer constant. You can't use a variable that gets set at runtime. The array size is locked into the program at compile time.

```
int n = 8;
char cakes[2 + 5];   /* valid, size is a constant expression */
char crumbs[n];      /* invalid, size is a variable          */
```

Arrays of Character Strings

Often it is convenient to have an array of character strings. Then you can use a subscript to access several different strings. Listing 11.1 used this example:

```
static char *mytal[LIM] = {"Adding numbers swiftly",
        "Multiplying accurately", "Stashing data",
        "Following instructions to the letter",
        "Understanding the C language"};
```

Let's study this declaration. Because **LIM** is **5**, you can say that **mytal** is an array of 5 pointers-to-**char**. That is, **mytal** is a one-dimensional array, and each element in the array holds the address of a **char**. The first pointer is **mytal[0]**, and it points to the first character of the first string. The second pointer is **mytal[1]**, and it points to the beginning of the second string. In general, each pointer points to the first character of the corresponding string.

```
*mytal[0] == 'A', *mytal[1] == 'M', *mytal[2] == 'S'
```

And so on. The **mytal** array doesn't actually hold the strings; it just holds the addresses of the strings. You can think of **mytal[0]** as representing the first string and ***mytal[0]** as the first character of the first string. Because of the relationship between array notation and pointers, you can also use `mytal[0][0]` to represent the first character of the first string, even though `mytal` is not defined as a two-dimensional array.

The initialization follows the rules for arrays. The braced portion is equivalent to this:

```
{{...}, {...},...,{...} };
```

The ellipses indicate the stuff we were too lazy to type in. The main point is that the first set of double quotation marks corresponds to a brace-pair and so is used to initialize the first character string pointer. The next set of double quotation marks initializes the second pointer, and so on. A comma separates adjacent strings.

Another approach is to create a two-dimensional array:

```
char mytal_2[LIM][LINLIM];
```

Here, `mytal_2` is an array of five elements, and each of these elements is itself an array of 81 `char` values. In this case, the strings themselves are stored in the array. One difference is that this second choice sets up a *rectangular* array with all the rows of the same length. That is, 81 elements are used to hold each string. The array of pointers, however, sets up a *ragged* array, with each row's length determined by the string it was initialized to:

```
char *mytal[LIM];
```

This ragged array doesn't waste any storage space. Figure 11.2 shows the two kinds of arrays. (Actually, the strings pointed to by the `mytal` array elements don't necessarily have to be stored consecutively in memory, but the figure does illustrate the difference in storage requirements.)

Another difference is that `mytal` and `mytal_2` have different types; `mytal` is an array of pointers-to-char, but `mytal_2` is an array of arrays of `char`. In short, `mytal` holds five addresses, but `mytal_2` holds five complete character arrays.

Pointers and Strings

Perhaps you noticed an occasional reference to pointers in this discussion of strings. Most C operations for strings actually work with pointers. Consider, for example, the instructive program shown in Listing 11.3.

Listing 11.3   The `p_and_s.c` program.

```
/* p_and_s.c -- pointers and strings */
#include <stdio.h>
int main(void)
{
  char * mesg = "Don't be a fool!";
  char * copy;

  copy = mesg;
  printf("%s\n", copy);
  printf("mesg = %s; &mesg = %p; value = %p\n",
      mesg, &mesg, mesg);
  printf("copy = %s; &copy = %p; value = %p\n",
      copy, &copy, copy);
  return 0;
}
```

Figure 11.2 Rectangular versus ragged array.

Note

Use `%u` or `%lu` instead of `%p` if your compiler doesn't support `%p`.

Looking at this program, you might think that it makes a copy of the string `"Don't be a fool!"`, and your first glance at the output might seem to confirm this guess.

```
Don't be a fool!
mesg = Don't be a fool!; &mesg = 0064FDF0; value = 00410A30
copy = Don't be a fool!; &copy = 0064FDF4; value = 00410A30
```

Study the `printf()` output. First, `mesg` and `copy` are printed as strings (`%s`). No surprises here; all the strings are `"Don't be a fool!"`.

The next item on each line is the address of the specified pointer. The two pointers `mesg` and `copy` are stored in locations `0064FDF0` and `0064FDF4`, respectively.

Now notice the final item, the one we called `value`. It is the value of the specified pointer. The value of the pointer is the address it contains. You can see that `mesg` points to location

`00410A30`, and so does `copy`. Therefore, the string itself was never copied. All that `copy = mesg;` does is produce a second pointer pointing to the very same string.

Why all this pussyfooting around? Why not just copy the whole string? Well, ask yourself which is more efficient: copying one address or copying, say, 50 separate elements? Often, the address is all that is needed to get the job done. If you truly require a copy that is a duplicate, you can use the `strcpy()` or `strncpy()` functions discussed later in this chapter.

Now that we have discussed defining strings within a program, let's turn to strings that are read in.

String Input

If you want to read a string into a program, you must first set aside space to store the string and then use an input function to fetch the string.

Creating Space

The first order of business is setting up a place to put the string after it is read. As mentioned earlier, this means you need to allot enough storage to hold whatever strings you expect to read. Don't expect the computer to count the string length as it is read and then allot space for it. The computer won't (unless you write a function to do so). For example, suppose you try something like this:

```
char *name;

scanf("%s", name);
```

It will probably get by the compiler, but when the name is read, the name will be written over data or code in your program. That's because `scanf()` copies information to the address given by the argument, and in this case, the argument is an uninitialized pointer; `name` might point anywhere. Most programmers regard this as highly humorous, but only in other people's programs.

The simplest course is to include an explicit array size in the declaration:

```
char name[81];
```

Now `name` is the address of an allocated block of 81 bytes. Another possibility is to use the C library functions that allocate memory, and we'll touch on those in Chapter 16, "The C Preprocessor and the C Library." In this program, we used an automatic array for `name`. You can do that even under K&R C because you don't have to initialize the array.

After you have set aside space for the string, you can read the string. The C library supplies a trio of functions that can read strings: `scanf()`, `gets()`, and `fgets()`. The most commonly used one is `gets()`, which we discuss first.

The `gets()` Function

The `gets()` (*get string*) function is very handy for interactive programs. It gets a string from your system's standard input device, normally your keyboard. Because a string has no predetermined length, gets() needs a way to know when to stop. Its method is to read characters until it reaches a newline (\n) character, which you generate by pressing the Enter key. It takes all the characters up to (but not including) the newline, tacks on a null character (\0), and gives the string to the calling program. The newline character itself is read and discarded so that the next read begins at the start of the next line. Listing 11.4 shows a simple means of using gets().

Listing 11.4 The name1.c program.

```
/* name1.c -- reads a name */
#include <stdio.h>
#define MAX 81
int main(void)
{
  char name[MAX];         /* allot space                */

  printf("Hi, what's your name?\n");
  gets(name);                /* place string into name array */
  printf("Nice name, %s.\n", name);
  return 0;
}
```

Here is a sample run:

```
Hi, what's your name?
Davina Sprocket
Nice name, Davina Sprocket.
```

Listing 11.4 accepts and stores any name (including spaces) up to 80 characters. (Remember to reserve one space for the \0 in the array.) Note that you want gets() to affect something (name) in the calling function. This means you should use an address as an argument, and, of course, the name of an array is an address.

The gets() function is more sophisticated than this preceding example suggests. Look at Listing 11.5.

Listing 11.5 The name2.c program.

```
/* name2.c -- reads a name */
#include <stdio.h>
#define MAX 81
int main(void)
{
    char name[MAX];
    char * ptr;

    printf("Hi, what's your name?\n");
    ptr = gets(name);
    printf("%s? Ah! %s!\n", name, ptr);
    return 0;
}
```

Here is a sample exchange:

```
Hi, what's your name?
Tony de Tuna
Tony de Tuna? Ah! Tony de Tuna!
```

The `gets()` function gets input in two ways:

- It uses an address to feed the string into `name`.

- The code for `gets()` uses the `return` keyword to return the address of the string, and the program assigns that address to `ptr`. Notice that `ptr` is a pointer to `char`. This means that `gets()` must return a value that is a pointer to `char`.

ANSI C mandates that the **stdio.h** header file include a function prototype for `gets()`. With newer implementations, then, you need not declare the function yourself as long as you remember to include that header file. However, some older versions of C require that you provide your own function declaration for `gets()`.

The design of a `gets()` function could look something like this:

```
char *gets(char * s)
{
    ...
    return(s);
}
```

The function header indicates that `gets()` returns a pointer to a `char`. Note that `gets()` returns the same pointer that was passed to it. There is but one copy of the input string; the one placed at the address passed as a function argument, so `ptr` in Listing 11.5 winds up pointing to the name `array`. The actual design is slightly more complicated because `gets()` has two possible returns. If everything goes well, then it returns the address of the read string, as we have said. If something goes wrong or if `gets()` encounters end of file, it returns a null, or zero, address. This null address is called the *null pointer* and is represented in **stdio.h** by the defined constant **NULL**. Therefore, `gets()` incorporates a bit of error-checking, making it convenient to use constructions like this:

```
while (gets(name) != NULL)
```

Such a construction enables you to both check for **end of file** and read a value. If **end of file** is encountered, nothing is read into `name`. This two-pronged approach is more compact than that of `getchar()`, which has a return value but no argument:

```
while ((ch = getchar()) != EOF)
```

By the way, don't confuse the null pointer with the null character. The null pointer is an address, and the null character is a type `char` data object with the value zero. Numerically, both can be represented by **0**, but they differ conceptually from each other.

The `fgets()` Function

One weakness of `gets()` is that it doesn't check to see whether the input actually fits into the reserved storage area. Extra characters simply overflow into the adjoining memory.

The `fgets()` function improves on this questionable behavior by enabling you to specify an upper limit for the number of characters to be read. Because `fgets()` is designed for file I/O, it's slightly more awkward than `gets()` for keyboard input. It differs from `gets()` in three respects:

- It takes a second argument indicating the maximum number of characters to read. If this argument has the value n, `fgets()` reads up to n-1 characters or through the newline character, whichever comes first.

- If `fgets()` reads the newline, it stores it in the string, unlike `gets()`, which discards it.

- It takes a third argument indicating which file to read. To read from the keyboard, use `stdin` (for *standard input*) as the argument; this identifier is defined in `stdio.h`.

Listing 11.6 modifies Listing 11.5 to use `fgets()` instead of `gets()`.

Listing 11.6   The `name3.c` program.

```
/* name3.c -- reads a name using fgets() */
#include <stdio.h>
#define MAX 81
int main(void)
{
    char name[MAX];
    char * ptr;

    printf("Hi, what's your name?\n");
    ptr = fgets(name, MAX, stdin);
    printf("%s? Ah! %s!\n", name, ptr);
    return 0;
}
```

Here is some sample output, which reveals one of the awkward aspects of `fgets()`:

```
Hi, what's your name?
Jon Dough
Jon Dough
? Ah! Jon Dough
!
```

The problem is that `fgets()` stores the newline in the string, so that a newline gets displayed every time you display the string. Later in this chapter, you'll learn a way to remove the newline.

Because `gets()` doesn't check whether the input will fit in the destination array, it is considered unsafe. Indeed, a few years ago someone exploited the fact that some UNIX operating system code used `gets()` to overwrite code, creating a "worm" that propagated through the UNIX network. That system code has since been replaced by `gets()`-free code. So in serious programming, you should use `fgets()` rather than `gets()`, but this book takes a more relaxed approach.

The `scanf()` Function

You've used `scanf()` with the `%s` format before to read a string. The chief difference between `scanf()` and `gets()` lies in how they decide when they have reached the end of the string: `scanf()` is more of a "get word" than a "get string" function. The `gets()` function, as you've seen, takes in all the characters up to the first newline. The `scanf()` function has two choices for terminating input. For either choice, the string starts at the first non-whitespace character encountered. If you use the `%s` format, the string runs up to (but not including) the next whitespace character (blank, tab, or newline). If you specify a field width, as in `%10s`, the `scanf()` collects up to 10 characters or up to the first whitespace character, whichever comes first (see Figure 11.3).

Input Statement	Original Input Queue*	Name Contents	Remaining Queue
`scanf('%s', name);`	Fleebert☐Hup	Fleebert	☐Hup
`scanf('%5s', name);`	Fleebert☐Hup	Fleeb	ert☐Hup
`scanf('%5s', name);`	Ann☐Ular	Ann	☐Ular

*the ☐ represents the space character

Figure 11.3 Field widths and `scanf()`.

Recall that the `scanf()` function returns an integer value that equals the number of items successfully read or returns `EOF` if it encounters the end of file.

Listing 11.7 illustrates how `scanf()` works when you specify a field width.

Listing 11.7   The `scan_str.c` program.

```
/* scan_str.c -- using scanf() */
#include <stdio.h>
int main(void)
{
    char name1[11], name2[11];
    int count;

    printf("Please enter 2 names.\n");
    count = scanf("%5s %10s",name1, name2);
    printf("I read the %d names %s and %s.\n",
            count, name1, name2);
    return 0;
}
```

Here are three runs:

```
Please enter 2 names.
Jesse Jukes
I read the 2 names Jesse and Jukes.
```

```
Please enter 2 names.
Liza Applebottham
I read the 2 names Liza and Applebotth.

Please enter 2 names.
Portensia Callowit
I read the 2 names Porte and nsia.
```

In the first example, both names fell within the allowed size limits. In the second example, only the first 10 characters of **Applebottham** were read because we used a **%10s** format. In the third example, the last four letters of **Portensia** went into **name2** because the second call to **scanf()** resumed reading input where the first ended; in this case, that was still inside the word **Portensia**.

You are better off using **gets()** to read text from the keyboard. It is easier to use, faster, and more compact. The typical use for **scanf()** is reading and converting a mixture of data types in some standard form. For example, if each input line contained the name of a tool, the number in stock, and the cost of the item, you might use **scanf()**, or you might throw together a function of your own that did some entry error-checking.

Now let's discuss how to print strings.

String Output

Again, we will use library functions. C has three standard library functions for printing strings. They are **puts()**, **fputs()**, and **printf()**.

The **puts()** Function

The **puts()** function is very easy to use. Just give it the address of a string for an argument. Listing 11.8 illustrates some of the many ways to do this.

Listing 11.8   The put_out.c program.

```c
/* put_out.c -- using puts() */
#include <stdio.h>
#define DEF "I am a #defined string."
int main(void)
{
   char str1[80] = "An array was initialized to me.";
   char * str2 = "A pointer was initialized to me.";

   puts("I'm an argument to puts().");
   puts(DEF);
   puts(str1);
   puts(str2);
   puts(&str1[4]);
   puts(str2+4);
   return 0;
}
```

The output is this:

```
I'm an argument to puts().
I am a #defined string.
An array was initialized to me.
A pointer was initialized to me.
rray was initialized to me.
inter was initialized to me.
```

Note that each string appears on its own line. Unlike `printf()`, `puts()` automatically appends a newline when it displays a string.

This example reminds you that phrases in double quotation marks are string constants and are treated as addresses. Also, the names of character array strings are treated as addresses. The expression `&str1[4]` is the address of the fifth element of the array `str1`. That element contains the character `'r'`, and that is what `puts()` uses for its starting point. Similarly, `str2+4` points to the memory cell containing the `'i'` of `"pointer"`, and the printing starts there.

How does `puts()` know when to stop? It stops when it encounters the null character, so there had better be one. Don't emulate the program in Listing 11.9!

Listing 11.9   The nono.c program.

```
/* nono.c -- no! */
#include <stdio.h>
int main(void)
{
    char c1 = 'A';
    char dont[] = {'W', 'O', 'W', '!' };
    char c2 = 'B';

    puts(dont);    /* dont is not a string */
    return 0;
}
```

Because **dont** lacks a closing null character, it is not a string, so `puts()` won't know where to stop. It will just keep printing from memory following **dont** until it finds a null somewhere. Here's a sample run:

WOW!B$@

You may get different results, depending upon what is in your computer's memory when you run the program. There are usually lots of nulls in memory, and if you're lucky, `puts()` might find one soon, but don't count on it.

The `fputs()` Function

The `fputs()` function is the file-oriented version of `gets()`. The main differences are these:

- The `fputs()` takes a second argument indicating the file to write to. You can use `stdout` (for *standard output*), which is defined in `stdio.h`, as an argument to output to your display.

- Unlike `puts()`, `fputs()` does not automatically append a newline to the output.

Note that `gets()` discards a newline on input, but `puts()` adds a newline on output. On the other hand, `fgets()` stores the newline on input, and `fputs()` doesn't add a newline on output. Suppose you want to write a loop that reads a line and echoes it on the next line. You can do this:

```
char line[81];
while (gets(line))
    puts(line);
```

Recall that `gets()` returns the null pointer if it encounters end-of-file. The null pointer evaluates as zero, or false, so that terminates the loop. Or you can do this:

```
char line[81];
while (fgets(line, 81, stdin))
    fputs(line, stdout);
```

With the first loop, the string in the `line` array is displayed on a line of its own because `puts()` adds a newline. With the second loop, the string in the `line` array is displayed on a line of its own because `fgets()` stores a newline. Note that if you mixed `fgets()` input with `puts()` output, you'd get two newlines displayed for each string. The point is that `puts()` is designed to work with `gets()`, and `fputs()` is designed to work with `fgets()`.

The `printf()` Function

We discussed `printf()` pretty thoroughly in Chapter 4, "Character Strings and Formatted Input/Output." Like `puts()`, it takes a string address as an argument. The `printf()` function is less convenient to use than `puts()`, but it is more versatile because it formats various data types.

One difference is that `printf()` does not automatically print each string on a new line. Instead, you must indicate where you want new lines. Therefore,

```
printf("%s\n", string);
```

has the same effect as

```
puts(string);
```

As you can see, the first form takes more typing. It also takes longer for the computer to execute. On the other hand, `printf()` makes it simple to combine strings for one line of printing. For example, the following statement combines `Well,` with the user's name and a `#define`d character string, all on one line:

```
printf("Well, %s, %s\n", name, MSG);
```

The Do-It-Yourself Option

You aren't limited to the standard C library options for input and output. If you don't have these options or don't like them, you can prepare your own versions, building on getchar() and putchar(). Suppose you want a function like puts() that doesn't automatically add a newline. Listing 11.10 shows one way to do it.

Listing 11.10   The put1.c program.

```
/* put1.c -- prints a string  without adding \n */
#include <stdio.h>
void put1(const char * string) /* string not altered */
{
    while (*string != '\0')
        putchar(*string++);
}
```

The char pointer string initially points to the first element of the called argument. Because this function doesn't change the string, use the const modifier. After the contents of that element are printed, the pointer increments and points to the next element. This goes on until the pointer points to an element containing the null character. Remember, the higher precedence of ++ compared to * means that putchar(*string++) prints the value pointed to by string but increments string itself, not the character it points to.

You can regard put1.c as a model for writing string-processing functions. Because each string has a null character marking its end, you don't have to pass a size to the function. Instead, the function processes each character in turn until it encounters the null character.

A somewhat longer way of writing the function is to use array notation:

```
int i = 0;
while (string[i]!= '\0')
        putchar(string[i++]);
```

This involves an additional variable for the index.

Many C programmers would use the following test for the while loop:

```
while (*string)
```

When string points to the null character, *string has the value 0, which terminates the loop. This approach certainly takes less typing than the previous version. If you are not familiar with C practice, it is less obvious. It could result in more efficient code, depending on the compiler. Regardless of its merits, this idiom is widespread.

Note

Why does Listing 11.10 use const char * string rather than const char string[] as the formal argument? Technically, the two are equivalent, so either form will work. One reason to use bracket notation is to remind the user that the function processes an array. With strings, however, the actual argument can be the name of an array, a quoted string, or a variable that has been declared as type char *. Using const char * string reminds you that the actual argument isn't necessarily an array.

Suppose you want a function like puts() that also tells you how many characters are printed. As Listing 11.11 demonstrates, it's easy to add that feature.

Listing 11.11   The put2.c program.

```
/* put2.c -- prints a string and counts characters */
#include <stdio.h>
int put2(const char * string)
{
    int count = 0;
    while (*string != '\0')
    {
        putchar(*string++);
        count++;
    }
    putchar('\n');              /* newline not counted */
    return(count);
}
```

The following call prints the string pizza:

```
put1("pizza");
```

The next call also returns a character count that is assigned to num, in this case, the value 5.

```
num = put2("pizza");
```

Listing 11.12 presents a driver using put1() and put2() and showing nested function calls.

Listing 11.12   The put_put.c program.

```
#include <stdio.h>
void put1(const char *);
int put2(const char *);
int main(void)
{
    put1("If I'd as much money");
    put1(" as I could spend,\n");
    printf("I count %d characters.\n",
        put2("I never would cry old chairs to mend."));
    return 0;
}
```

We assume you'll place the put1() and put2() functions in the same file. Note that we used #include stdio.h because on our system, putchar() is defined there, and our new functions use putchar().

Hmmm, we are using printf() to print the value of put2(), but in the act of finding the value of put2(), the computer first must execute that function, causing the string to be printed. Here's the output:

```
If I'd as much money as I could spend,
I never would cry old chairs to mend.
I count 37 characters.
```

String Functions

The C library supplies several string-handling functions; ANSI C uses the `string.h` header file to provide the prototypes. We'll look at some of the most useful and common ones: `strlen()`, `strcat()`, `strncat()`, `strcmp()`, `strncmp()`, `strcpy()`, and `strncpy()`. We'll also examine `sprintf()`, supported by the `stdio.h` header file. For a complete list of the `string.h` family of functions, see Appendix F, "The Standard ANSI C Library."

The `strlen()` Function

The `strlen()` function, as you already know, finds the length of a string. It's used in the next example, a function that shortens lengthy strings:

```
/* fit.c -- procrustean function */
void fit(char * string, unsigned int size)
{
    if (strlen(string) > size)
        *(string + size) = '\0';
}
```

This function does change the string, so the function header doesn't use **const** in declaring the formal parameter `string`.

Try the `fit()` function in the test program of Listing 11.13.

Listing 11.13   The `test.c` program.

```
/* test.c -- try the string-shrinking function */
#include <stdio.h>
#include <string.h> /* contains string function prototypes */
void fit(char *, unsigned int);
int main(void)
{
    char mesg[] = "Hold on to your hats, hackers.";

    puts(mesg);
    fit(mesg,7);
    puts(mesg);
    return 0;
}
void fit(char *string, unsigned int size)
{
    if (strlen(string) > size)
        *(string + size) = '\0';
}
```

The output is this:

```
Hold on to your hats, hackers.
Hold on
```

The `fit()` function placed a '\0' character in the eighth element of the array, replacing a blank. The rest of the array is still there, but `puts()` stops at the first null character and ignores the rest of the array.

The ANSI `string.h` file contains function prototypes for the C family of string functions, so we will include it in our examples.

Note

Some pre-ANSI systems use `strings.h` instead, and others might lack a string header file entirely.

The `strcat()` and `strncat()` Functions

Listing 11.14 illustrates what `strcat()` can do.

Listing 11.14   The `str_cat.c` program.

```
/* str_cat.c -- joins two strings */
#include <stdio.h>
#include <string.h>   /* declares the strcat() function */
#define SIZE 80
int main(void)
{
    char flower[SIZE];
    char addon[] = "s smell like old shoes.";

    puts("What is your favorite flower?");
    gets(flower);
    strcat(flower, addon);
    puts(flower);
    puts(addon);
    return 0;
}
```

This is the output:

```
What is your favorite flower?
Rose
Roses smell like old shoes.
s smell like old shoes.
```

As you can see, `strcat()` (for *string* con*cat*enation) takes two strings for arguments. A copy of the second string is tacked onto the end of the first, and this combined version becomes the new first string. The second string is not altered. Function `strcat()` is type `char *`, that is, a pointer to `char`. It returns the value of its first argument—the address of the first character of the string to which the second string is appended.

The `strcat()` function does not check to see whether the second string will fit in the first array. If you fail to allot enough space for the first array, you will run into problems as excess characters overflow into adjacent memory locations. Of course, you can use `strlen()` to look before you leap, as shown in Listing 11.15. Note that we add 1 to the combined lengths to allow space for the null character. Or you can use `strncat()`, which takes a second argument indicating the maximum number of characters to add. For example, `strncat(bugs, addon, 13)` will add the contents of the `addon` string to `bugs`, stopping when it reaches 13 additional characters or the null character, whichever comes first. Therefore, counting the null character (which is appended in either case), the `bugs` array should be large enough to hold the original string (not counting the null character), a maximum of 13 additional characters, and the terminal null character. Listing 11.15 uses this information to calculate a value for the `available` variable, which is used as the maximum number of additional characters allowed.

Listing 11.15   The `join_chk.c` program.

```
/* join_chk.c -- joins two strings, check size first */
#include <stdio.h>
#include <string.h>
#define SIZE 30
#define BUGSIZE 13
int main(void)
{
    char flower[SIZE];
    char addon[] = "s smell like old shoes.";
    char bug[BUGSIZE];
    int available;

    puts("What is your favorite flower?");
    gets(flower);
    if ((strlen(addon) + strlen(flower) + 1) <= SIZE)
        strcat(flower, addon);
    puts(flower);
    puts("What is your favorite bug?");
    gets(bug);
    available = BUGSIZE - strlen(bug) - 1;
    strncat(bug, addon, available);
    puts(bug);
    return 0;
}
```

Here is a sample run:

```
What is your favorite flower?
Rose
Roses smell like old shoes.
What is your favorite bug?
Aphid
Aphids smell
```

The `strcmp()` and `strncmp()` Functions

Suppose you want to compare someone's response to a stored string, as shown in Listing 11.16.

Listing 11.16   The nogo.c program.

```
/* nogo.c -- will this work? */
#include <stdio.h>
#define ANSWER "Grant"
int main(void)
{
    char try[40];

    puts("Who is buried in Grant's tomb?");
    gets(try);
    while (try != ANSWER)
    {
        puts("No, that's wrong. Try again.");
        gets(try);
    }
    puts("That's right!");
    return 0;
}
```

As nice as this program might look, it will not work correctly. ANSWER and try really are pointers, so the comparison try != ANSWER doesn't check to see whether the two strings are the same. Rather, it checks to see whether the two strings have the same address. Because ANSWER and try are stored in different locations, the two addresses are never the same, and the user is forever told that he or she is wrong. Such programs tend to discourage people.

What you need is a function that compares string *contents*, not string *addresses*. You could devise one, but the job has been done for you with strcmp() (for *string comparison*). This function does for strings what relational operators do for numbers. In particular, it returns 0 if its two string arguments are the same. The revised program is shown in Listing 11.17.

Listing 11.17   The compare.c program.

```
/* compare.c -- this will work */
#include <stdio.h>
#include <string.h>    /* declares strcmp() */
#define ANSWER "Grant"
#define MAX 40
int main(void)
{
    char try[MAX];

    puts("Who is buried in Grant's tomb?");
    gets(try);
    while (strcmp(try,ANSWER) != 0)
    {
        puts("No, that's wrong. Try again.");
        gets(try);
    }
    puts("That's right!");
    return 0;
}
```

Note

Because any nonzero value is "true," some programmers would abbreviate the while statement to while (strcmp(try,ANSWER)).

One of the nice features of strcmp() is that it compares strings, not arrays. Although the array try occupies 40 memory cells and "Grant" only 6 (one for the null character), the comparison looks only at the part of try up to its first null character. Therefore, strcmp() can be used to compare strings stored in arrays of different sizes.

What if the user answers "GRANT" or "grant" or "Ulysses S. Grant"? The user is told that he or she is wrong. To make a friendlier program, you have to anticipate all possible correct answers. There are some tricks. You can #define the answer as "GRANT" and write a function that converts all input to uppercase. That eliminates the problem of capitalization, but you still have the other forms to worry about. We leave that as an exercise for you.

The strcmp() Return Value

What value does strcmp() return if the strings are not the same? Listing 11.18 shows a sample.

Listing 11.18   The compback.c program.

```
/* compback.c -- strcmp returns */
#include <stdio.h>
#include <string.h>
int main(void)
{

  printf("%d\n", strcmp("A", "A"));
  printf("%d\n", strcmp("A", "B"));
  printf("%d\n", strcmp("B", "A"));
  printf("%d\n", strcmp("C", "A"));
  printf("%d\n", strcmp("Z", "a"));
  printf("%d\n", strcmp("apples", "apple"));
  return 0;
}
```

Here is the output on one system:

```
0
-1
1
1
-1
1
```

Comparing "A" to itself returns a 0. Comparing "A" to "B" gives a -1, and reversing the comparison gives a 1. These results suggest that strcmp() returns a negative number if the first string precedes the second alphabetically and that it returns a positive number if the order is the other way. Therefore, comparing "C" to "A" gives a 1. Other systems might return 2—the difference in ASCII code values. The ANSI standard says that strcmp() returns a negative number if the first string comes before the second alphabetically, returns a 0 if they are the same, and returns a positive number if the first string follows the second alphabetically. The exact numerical values, however, are left open to the implementation.

What if the initial characters are identical? In general, strcmp() moves along until it finds the first pair of disagreeing characters. It then returns the corresponding code. For instance, in the very last example, "apples" and "apple" agree until the final s of the first string. This matches up with the sixth character in "apple", which is the null character, ASCII 0. Because the null character is the very first character in the ASCII sequence, s comes after it, and the function returns a positive value.

The last comparison points out that strcmp() compares all characters, not just letters, so instead of saying the comparison is alphabetic, we should say that strcmp() goes by the machine *collating sequence*. That means characters are compared according to their numeric representation, typically the ASCII values. In ASCII, the codes for uppercase letters precede those for lowercase letters. Therefore, strcmp("Z", "a") is negative.

Most often, you won't care about the exact value returned. You just want to know if it is zero or nonzero—that is, whether there is a match or not—or you might be trying to sort the strings alphabetically, in which case you want to know if the comparison is positive, negative, or zero.

Note

The strcmp() function is for comparing *strings*, not *characters*. So you can use arguments like "apples" and "A", but you cannot use character arguments, such as 'A'. However, recall that the char type is an integer type, so you can use the relational operators for character comparisons. Suppose word is a string stored in an array of char and that ch is a char variable. Then the following statements are valid:

```
if (strcmp(word, "quit") == 0)
    puts("Bye!");
if (ch == 'q')
    puts("Bye!");
```

However, don't use ch or 'q' as arguments for strcmp().

Listing 11.19 uses the strcmp() function for checking to see whether a program should stop reading input.

Listing 11.19   The input.c program.

```
/* input.c -- beginning of some program */
#include <stdio.h>
#include <string.h>
#define SIZE 81
#define LIM 100
```

continued on next page

continued from previous page

```
#define STOP "quit"
int main(void)
{
  char input[LIM][SIZE];
  int ct = 0;

  printf("Enter up to %d lines (type quit to quit):\n");
  while (ct < LIM && gets(input[ct]) != NULL &&
          strcmp(input[ct],STOP) != 0)
  {
      ct++;
  }
  printf("%d strings entered\n", ct);
  return 0;
}
```

This program quits reading input when it encounters an EOF character (gets() returns null in that case), or when you enter the word *quit,* or when you reach the limit LIM.

Incidentally, sometimes it is more convenient to terminate input by entering an empty line, that is, by pressing the Enter key or Return key without entering anything else. To do so, you can modify the while loop control statement so that it looks like this:

```
while (ct < LIM && gets(input[ct]) != NULL
                        && input[ct][0] != '\0')
```

Here, input[ct] is the string just entered and input[ct][0] is the first character of that string. If the user enters an empty line, gets() places the null character in the first element, so the expression

```
input[ct][0] != '\0')
```

tests for an empty input line.

The strncmp() Variation

The strcmp() function compares strings until it finds corresponding characters that differ, and that could take the search to the end of one of the strings. The strncmp() function compares the strings until they differ or until it has compared a number of characters specified by a third argument. For example, if you wanted to search for strings that begin with "astro", you could limit the search to the first five characters. Listing 11.20 shows how.

Listing 11.20   The starsrch.c program.

```
/* starsrch.c -- use strncmp() */
#include <stdio.h>
#include <string.h>
#define LISTSIZE 5
int main()
```

```
{
    char * list[LISTSIZE] = {
            "astronomy", "astounding",
            "astrophysics", "ostracize",
            "asterism"      };
    int count = 0;
    int i;

    for (i = 0; i < LISTSIZE; i++)
        if (strncmp(list[i],"astro", 5) == 0)
            count++;
    printf("The list contained %d words beginning"
            " with astro.\n", count);
    return 0;
}
```

Here is the output:

```
The list contained 2 words beginning with astro.
```

The `strcpy()` and `strncpy()` Functions

We've said that if **pts1** and **pts2** are both pointers to strings, then the expression

```
pts2 = pts1;
```

copies only the address of a string, not the string itself. Suppose, though, that you do want to copy a string. Then you can use the **strcpy()** function. Listing 11.21 asks the user to enter words beginning with *q*. The program copies the input into a temporary array, and if the first letter is a *q*, the program uses **strcpy()** to copy the string from the temporary array to a permanent destination. The **strcpy()** function is the string equivalent of the assignment operator.

Listing 11.21   The copy1.c program.

```
/* copy1.c -- strcpy() demo */
#include <stdio.h>
#include <string.h>   /* declares strcpy() */
#define SIZE 40
#define LIM 5
int main(void)
{
    char qwords[LIM][SIZE];
    char temp[SIZE];
    int i = 0;
    printf("Enter %d words beginning with q:\n", LIM);
    while (i < LIM && gets(temp))
    {
        if (temp[0] != 'q')
            printf("%s doesn't begin with q!\n", temp);
        else
```

continued on next page

continued from previous page

```
        {
            strcpy(qwords[i], temp);
            i++;
        }
      }
    puts("Here are the words accepted:");
    for (i = 0; i < LIM; i++)
        puts(qwords[i]);
    return 0;
}
```

Here is a sample run:

```
Enter 5 words beginning with q:
quackery
quasar
quilt
quotient
no more
no more doesn't begin with q!
quiz
Here are the words accepted:
quackery
quasar
quilt
quotient
quiz
```

Note that the counter `i` is incremented only when the word entered passes the *q* test. Also note that the program uses a character-based test:

```
if (temp[0] != 'q')
```

That is, is the first character in the `temp` array not a *q*? Another possibility is using a string-based test:

```
if (strncmp(temp, "q", 1) != 0)
```

That is, are the strings `temp` and `"q"` different from each other in the first element?

Note that the string pointed to by the second argument (`temp`) is copied into the array pointed to by the first argument (`qword[i]`). The copy is called the *target*, and the original string is called the *source*. You can remember the order of the arguments by noting that it is the same as the order in an assignment statement: The target string is on the left.

```
char target[20];
int x;
x = 50;                      /* assignment for numbers */
strcpy(target, "Hi ho!");    /* assignment for strings */
target = "So long";          /* syntax error           */
```

It is your responsibility to make sure the destination array has enough room to copy the source. The following is asking for trouble:

```
char * str;
strcpy(str, "The C of Tranquility"); /* a problem */
```

The function will copy the string `"The C of Tranquility"` to the address specified by `str`, but `str` is uninitialized, so the copy might wind up anywhere.

In short, `strcpy()` takes two string pointers as arguments. The second pointer, which points to the original string, can be a declared pointer, an array name, or a string constant, but the first pointer, which points to the copy, should point to a data object, such as an array, roomy enough to hold the string.

Further `strcpy()` Properties

The `strcpy()` function has two more properties that you might find useful. First, it is type `char *`. It returns the value of its first argument—the address of a character. Second, the first argument need not point to the beginning of an array; this lets you copy just part of an array. Listing 11.22 illustrates both these points.

Listing 11.22   The `copy2.c` program.

```
/* copy2.c -- strcpy() demo */
#include <stdio.h>
#include <string.h>              /* declares strcpy() */
#define WORDS  "beast"
#define SIZE 40
int main(void)
{
    char *orig = WORDS;
    char copy[SIZE] = "Be the best that you can be.";
    char * ps;

    puts(orig);
    puts(copy);
    ps = strcpy(copy + 7, orig);
    puts(copy);
    puts(ps);
    return 0;
}
```

Here is the output:

```
beast
Be the best that you can be.
Be the beast
beast
```

Note that `strcpy()` copies the null character from the source string. In this example, the null character overwrites the **t** in **that** in `copy` so that the new string ends with **beast** (see Figure 11.4). Also note that **ps** points to the eighth element (index of 7) of `copy` because the first argument is `copy + 7`. Therefore, `puts(ps)` prints the string starting at that point.

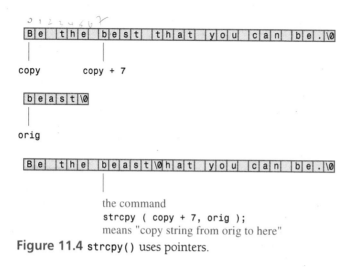

Figure 11.4 `strcpy()` uses pointers.

The Careful Choice: `strncpy()`

The `strcpy()` function shares a problem with `gets()`—neither check to see whether the source string actually fits in the target string. The safer way to copy strings is to use `strncpy()`. It takes a third argument, which is the maximum number of characters to copy. Listing 11.23 is a rewrite of Listing 11.21, using `strncpy()` instead of `strcpy()`. To illustrate what happens if the source string is too large, it uses a rather small size (seven elements, six characters) for the target strings.

Listing 11.23 The `copy3.c` program.

```
/* copy1.c -- strncpy() demo */
#include <stdio.h>
#include <string.h>   /* declares strncpy() */
#define SIZE 40
#define TARGSIZE 7
#define LIM 5
int main(void)
{
    char qwords[LIM][TARGSIZE];
    char temp[SIZE];
    int i = 0;
    printf("Enter %d words beginning with q:\n", LIM);
    while (i < LIM && gets(temp))
    {
        if (temp[0] != 'q')
            printf("%s doesn't begin with q!\n", temp);
        else
        {
            strncpy(qwords[i], temp, TARGSIZE - 1);
            qwords[i][TARGSIZE - 1] = '\0';
            i++;
        }
    }
```

```
    puts("Here are the words accepted:");
    for (i = 0; i < LIM; i++)
        puts(qwords[i]);
    return 0;
}
```

Here is a sample run:

```
Enter 5 words beginning with q:
quack
quadratic
quisling
quota
quagga
Here are the words accepted:
quack
quadra
quisli
quota
quagga
```

The function call `strncpy(target, source, n)` copies up to n characters or up through the null character (whichever comes first) from `source` to `target`. Therefore, if the number of characters in source is less than n, the entire string is copied, including the null character. The function never copies more than n characters, so if it reaches the limit before reaching the end of the source string, no null character is added. As a result, the final string may or may not have a null character. For this reason, the program sets n to one less than the size of the target array and then sets the final element in the array to the null character:

```
strncpy(qwords[i], temp, TARGSIZE - 1);
qwords[i][TARGSIZE - 1] = '\0';
```

This ensures that you've stored a string. If the source string actually fits, the null character copied with it marks the true end of the string. If the source string doesn't fit, this final null character marks the end of the string.

The `sprintf()` Function

The `sprintf()` function is declared in `stdio.h` instead of `string.h`. It works like `printf()`, but it writes to a string instead of writing to a display. Therefore, it provides a way to combine several elements into a single string. The first argument to `sprintf()` is the address of the target string. The remaining arguments are the same as for `printf()`— a conversion specification string followed by a list of items to be written.

Listing 11.24 uses `sprintf()` to combine three items (two strings and a number) into a single string. Note that it uses `sprintf()` the same way you would use `printf()`, except that the resulting string is stored in the array `formal` instead of being displayed on the screen.

Listing 11.24   The `format.c` program.

```
/* format.c -- format a string */
#include <stdio.h>
#define MAX 20
int main(void)
{
    char first[MAX];
    char last[MAX];
    char formal[2 * MAX + 10];
    double prize;

    puts("Enter your first name:");
    gets(first);
    puts("Enter your last name:");
    gets(last);
    puts("Enter your prize money:");
    scanf("%lf", &prize);
    sprintf(formal, "%s, %-19s: $%6.2f\n", last, first, prize);
    puts(formal);
    return 0;
}
```

Here's a sample run:

```
Enter your first name:
Teddy
Enter your last name:
Behr
Enter your prize money:
450
Behr, Teddy              : $450.00
```

The `sprintf()` command took the input and formatted it into a standard form, which it then stored in the string `formal`.

Other String Functions

The ANSI C library has more than 20 string-handling functions, and the following list summarizes some of the more commonly used ones:

- `char *strcpy(char * s1, const char * s2);`

   This function copies the string (including the null character) pointed to by s2 to the location pointed to by s1. The return value is s1.

- `char *strncpy(char * s1, const char * s2, size_t n);`

   This function copies to the location pointed to by s1 no more than n characters from the string pointed to by s2. The return value is s1. No characters after a null character are copied, and if the source string is shorter than n characters, the target string is padded with null characters. If the source string has n or more characters, no null character is copied. The return value is s1.

- `char *strcat(char * s1, const char * s2);`

  The string pointed to by s2 is copied to the end of the string pointed to by s1. The first character of the s2 string is copied over the null character of the s1 string. The return value is s1.

- `char *strncat(char * s1, const char * s2, size_t n);`

  No more than the first n characters of the s2 string are appended to the s1 string, with the first character of the s2 string being copied over the null character of the s1 string. The null character and any characters following it in the s1 string are not copied, and a null character is appended to the result. The return value is s1.

- `int strcmp(const char * s1, const char * s2);`

  The function returns a positive value if the s1 string follows the s2 string in the machine collating sequence, the value 0 if the two strings are identical, and a negative value if the first string precedes the second string in the machine collating sequence.

- `int strncmp(const char * s1, const char * s2, size_t n);`

  This function works like strcmp() except that the comparison stops after n characters or when the first null character is encountered, whichever comes first.

- `char *strchr(const char * s, int c);`

  This function returns a pointer to the first location in the string s that holds the character c. (The terminating null character is part of the string, so it can be searched for.) The function returns the null pointer if the character is not found.

- `char *strpbrk(const char * s1, const char * s2);`

  This function returns a pointer to the first location in the string s1 that holds any character found in the s2 string. The function returns the null pointer if no character is found.

- `char *strrchr(const char * s, int c);`

  This function returns a pointer to the last occurrence of the character c in the string s. (The terminating null character is part of the string, so it can be searched for.) The function returns the null pointer if the character is not found.

- `char *strstr(const char * s1, const char * s2);`

  This function returns a pointer to the first occurrence of string s2 in string s1. The function returns the null pointer if the string is not found.

- `size_t strlen(const char * s);`

    This function returns the number of characters, not including the terminating null character, found in the string s.

Note that these prototypes use the keyword **const** to indicate which strings are not altered by a function. For example, consider the following:

```
char *strcpy(char * s1, const char * s2);
```

It means **s2** points to a string that can't be changed, at least not by the **strcpy()** function, but **s1** points to a string that can be changed. This makes sense, for **s1** is the target string, which gets altered, and **s2** is the source string, which should be left unchanged.

The **size_t** type is whatever type the **sizeof** operator returns. C states that the **sizeof** operator returns an integer type, but it doesn't specify which integer type, so **size_t** can be **unsigned int** on one system and **unsigned long** on another. Your **string.h** file defines **size_t** for your particular system or else refers to another header file having the definition.

As mentioned earlier, Appendix F lists all the functions in the **string.h** family. Many implementations provide additional functions beyond those required by the ANSI standard. You should check the documentation for your implementation to see what is available.

Now that we have outlined some string functions, let's look at a full program that handles strings.

A String Example: Sorting Strings

Let's tackle the practical problem of sorting strings alphabetically. This task can show up in preparing name lists, in making up an index, and in many other situations. One of the main tools in such a program is **strcmp()**, because it can be used to determine the order of two strings. The general plan will be to read an array of strings, sort them, and print them. A little while ago, we presented a scheme for reading strings, and we will start the program that way. Printing the strings is no problem. We'll use a standard sorting algorithm that we'll explain later. We will do one slightly tricky thing; see whether you can spot it. Listing 11.25 presents the program.

Listing 11.25   The sort_str.c program.

```
/* sort_str.c -- reads in strings and sorts them */
#include <stdio.h>
#include <string.h>
#define SIZE 81        /* string length limit, including \0  */
#define LIM 20         /* maximum number of lines to be read */
#define HALT ""        /* null string to stop input          */
void stsrt(char *strings[], int num);/* string-sort function */
int main(void)
```

```
{
   char input[LIM][SIZE];       /* array to store input      */
   char *ptstr[LIM];            /* array of pointer variables */
   int ct = 0;                  /* input count               */
   int k;                       /* output count              */

   printf("Input up to %d lines, and I will sort them.\n",LIM);
   printf("To stop, press the Enter key at a line's start.\n");
   while (ct < LIM && gets(input[ct]) != NULL
                             && input[ct][0] != '\0')
   {
      ptstr[ct] = input[ct];    /* set ptrs to strings       */
      ct++;
   }
   stsrt(ptstr, ct);            /* string sorter             */
   puts("\nHere's the sorted list:\n");
   for (k = 0; k < ct; k++)
      puts(ptstr[k]) ;          /* sorted pointers           */
   return 0;
}
/* string-pointer-sorting function */
void stsrt(char *strings[], int num)
{
   char *temp;
   int top, seek;

   for (top = 0; top < num-1; top++)
      for (seek = top + 1; seek < num; seek++)
         if (strcmp(strings[top],strings[seek]) > 0)
         {
            temp = strings[top];
            strings[top] = strings[seek];
            strings[seek] = temp;
         }
}
```

We fed Listing 11.22 an obscure nursery rhyme to test it:

```
Input up to 20 lines, and I will sort them.
To stop, press the Enter key at a line's start.
O that I was where I would be,
Then would I be where I am not;
But where I am I must be,
And where I would be I can not.

Here's the sorted list:

And where I would be I can not.
But where I am I must be,
O that I was where I would be,
Then would I be where I am not;
```

Hmm, the nursery rhyme doesn't seem to suffer much from being alphabetized.

The tricky part of the program is that instead of rearranging the strings themselves, we just rearranged *pointers* to the strings. Let us explain. Originally, `ptrst[0]` is set to `input[0]`, and so on. That means the pointer `ptrst[i]` points to the first character in the array `input[i]`. Each `input[i]` is an array of 81 elements, and each `ptrst[]` is a single variable. The sorting procedure rearranges `ptrst`, leaving `input` untouched. If, for example, `input[1]` comes before `input[0]` alphabetically, the program switches `ptrsts`, causing `ptrst[0]` to point to the beginning of `input[1]` and causing `ptrst[1]` to point to the beginning of `input[0]`. This is much easier than using, say, `strcpy()` to interchange the contents of the two `input` strings. See Figure 11.5 for another view of this process.

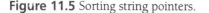

Figure 11.5 Sorting string pointers.

Sorting

To sort the pointers, we use the *selection sort* algorithm. The idea is to use a **for** loop to compare each element in turn with the first element. If the compared element precedes the current first element, the program swaps the two. By the time the program reaches the end of the loop, the first element contains a pointer to whichever string is first in the machine collating sequence. Then the outer **for** loop repeats the process, this time starting with the second element of **input**. When the inner loop completes, the pointer to the second-ranking string ends up in the second element of **ptrst**. The process continues until all the elements have been sorted. We'll take a more detailed look at this algorithm in Chapter 13, "Storage Classes and Program Development."

The `ctype.h` Character Functions and Strings

Chapter 7, "C Control Statements: Branching and Jumps," introduced the `ctype.h` family of character-related functions. These functions can't be applied to a string as a whole, but they can be applied to the individual characters in a string. Listing 11.26, for example, defines a function that applies the `toupper()` function to each character in a string, thus converting the whole string to uppercase. It also defines a function that uses `ispunct()` to count the number of punctuation characters in a string.

Listing 11.26   The `convert.c` program.

```
/* convert.c -- modifies a string */
#include <stdio.h>
#include <string.h>
#include <ctype.h>
#define LIMIT 80
void ToUpper(char *);
int PunctCt(const char *);
int main(void)
{
  char line[LIMIT];

  puts("Please enter a line:");
  gets(line);
  ToUpper(line);
  puts(line);
  printf("That line has %d punctuation characters.\n",
         PunctCt(line));
  return 0;
}

void ToUpper(char * str)
{
  while (*str != '\0')
  {
      *str = toupper(*str);
      str++;
  }
}

int PunctCt(const char * str)
{
  int ct = 0;
  while (*str != '\0')
  {
      if (ispunct(*str))
         ct++;
      str++;
  }
  return ct;
}
```

The `while (*str != '\0')` loop processes each character in the string pointed to by `str` until the null character is reached. Here is a sample run:

```
Please enter a line:
Me? You talkin' to me? Get outta here!
ME? YOU TALKIN' TO ME? GET OUTTA HERE!
That line has 4 punctuation characters.
```

The `ToUpper()` function applies `toupper()` to each character in a string. (The fact that C distinguishes between uppercase and lowercase makes these two function names different from one another.) As defined by ANSI C, the `toupper()` function alters only characters that are lowercase. However, very old implementations of C don't do that check automatically, so old code normally does something like this:

```
if (islower(*str))          /* pre-ANSI C -- check before converting */
    *str = toupper(*str);
```

Incidentally, the `ctype.h` functions are usually implemented as *macros*. These are C pre-processor constructions that act much like functions, but have some important differences. We'll cover macros in Chapter 16.

Next, let's try to fill an old emptiness in our lives, namely, the void between the parentheses in `main()`.

Command-Line Arguments

Before the modern graphical interface, there was the command-line interface. DOS and UNIX are examples. The *command line* is the line you type to run your program in a command-line environment. Suppose you have a program in a file named **fuss**. Then the command line to run it might look like this in UNIX:

```
$ fuss
```

Or it might look like this in DOS:

```
C> fuss
```

Command-line arguments are additional items on the same line.

```
% fuss -r Ginger
```

A C program can read those additional items for its own use (see Figure 11.6).

A C program reads these items by using arguments to `main()`. Listing 11.27 shows a typical example.

Listing 11.27   The `echo.c` program.

```
/* echo.c -- main() with arguments */
#include <stdio.h>
int main(int argc, char *argv[])
{
    int count;
```

```
    printf("The command line has %d arguments:\n", argc - 1);
    for (count = 1; count < argc; count++)
        printf("%d: %s\n", count, argv[count]);
    printf("\n");
    return 0;
}
```

Figure 11.6 Command-line arguments.

Compile this program into an executable file called echo; this is what happens when you run it:

```
C>echo Resistance is futile
The command line has 3 arguments:
1: Resistance
2: is
3: futile
```

You can see why it is called echo, but you might wonder how it works. We'll explain now.

C compilers allow main() to have no arguments or else to have two arguments. The first argument is the number of strings in the command line. By tradition (but not by necessity), this int argument is called argc for *argument count*. The system uses spaces to tell when one string ends and the next begins. Therefore, the echo example has four strings, including the command name, and the fuss example has three. The second argument is an array of pointers to strings. Each string on the command line is stored in memory and has a pointer assigned to point to it. By convention, this array of pointers is called argv, for *argument values*. When possible (some operating systems don't allow this), argv[0] is assigned the name of the program itself. Then `argv[1]` is assigned the first following string, and so on. For our example, we have the following relationships:

`argv[0]`	points to	echo (for most systems)
`argv[1]`	points to	Resistance
`argv[2]`	points to	is
`argv[3]`	points to	futile

The program in Listing 11.27 uses a `for` loop to print each string in turn. Recall that the `printf()` `%s` specifier expects the address of a string to be provided as an argument. Each element, `argv[0]`, `argv[1]`, and so on, is just such an address.

With pre-ANSI C, use this form to declare `argc` and `argv`:

```
main(argc, argv)
int argc;
char *argv[];
```

The form is the same as for any other function having formal arguments. Many programmers use a different declaration for `argv`:

```
int main(int argc, char **argv)
```

This alternative declaration for `argv` really is equivalent to `char *argv[]`. It says that `argv` is a pointer to a pointer to `char`. The example comes down to the same thing. It had an array with seven elements. The name of the array is a pointer to the first element, so `argv` points to `argv[0]`, and `argv[0]` is a pointer to `char`. Hence, even with the original definition, `argv` is a pointer to a pointer to `char`. You can use either form, but we think that the first more clearly suggests that `argv` represents a set of strings.

Incidentally, many environments, including UNIX and DOS, allow the use of quotation marks to lump several words into a single argument. For example, the command

```
echo "I am hungry" now
```

would assign the string `"I am hungry"` to `argv[1]` and the string `"now"` to `argv[2]`.

Command-Line Arguments in Integrated Environments

Integrated Windows environments like Metrowerks CodeWarrior, Microsoft Visual C++, and Borland C/C++ don't use command lines to run programs. However, some have menu selections that enable you to specify a command-line argument. In other cases, you may be able to compile the program in the IDE, and then open an MS-DOS window to run the program in command-line mode.

Command-Line Arguments with the Macintosh

The Macintosh operating system doesn't use command lines, but Metrowerks CodeWarrior and Symantec C++ enable you to simulate a command-line environment with the `ccommand()` function. Use the `console.h` header file and start your programs like this:

```
#include <stdio.h>
#include <console.h>
int main(int argc, char *argv[])
{
    ...        /* variable declarations */
    argc = ccommand(&argv);
    ...
}
```

When the program reaches the `ccommand()` function call, it puts a dialog box onscreen and provides a box in which you can type a command line. The command then places the command-line words in the `argv` strings and returns the number of words. The current project name will appear as the first word in the command-line box, so you should type the command-line arguments after that name. The `ccommand()` function also enables you to simulate redirection.

String to Number Conversions

Numbers can be stored either as strings or in numeric form. Storing a number as a string means storing the digit characters. For instance, the number 213 can be stored in a character string array as the digits `'2'`, `'1'`, `'3'`, `'\0'`. Storing 213 in numeric form means storing it as, say, an `int`.

C requires numeric forms for numeric operations, such as addition and comparison, but displaying numbers on your screen requires a string form because a screen displays characters. The `printf()` and `sprintf()` functions, through their `%d` and other specifiers, convert numeric forms to string forms and vice versa. C also has functions whose sole purpose is to convert string forms to numeric forms.

Suppose, for example, you want a program to use a numeric command-line argument. Unfortunately, command-line arguments are read as strings. Therefore, to use the numeric value, you must first convert the string to a number. If the number is an integer, you can use the `atoi()` function (for *alphanumeric to* integer). It takes a string as an argument and returns the corresponding integer value. Listing 11.28 shows a sample use.

Listing 11.28   The `hello.c` program.

```
/* hello.c -- converts command-line argument to number */
#include <stdio.h>
#include <stdlib.h>
int main(int argc, char *argv[])
```

continued on next page

continued from previous page

```
{
   int i, times;
   if (argc < 2 || (times = atoi(argv[1])) < 1)
       printf("Usage: %s positive-number\n", argv[0]);
   else
       for (i = 0; i < times; i++)
           puts("Hello, good looking!");
   return 0;
}
```

Here's a sample run:

```
% hello 3
Hello, good looking!
Hello, good looking!
Hello, good looking!
```

The % is a UNIX prompt. The command-line argument of 3 was stored as the string "3\0". The atoi() function converted this string to the integer value 3, which was assigned to times. This then determined the number of for loop cycles executed.

If you run the program without a command-line argument, the argc < 2 test aborts the program and prints a usage message. The same thing happens if times is 0 or negative. C's order-of-evaluation rule for logical operators guarantees that if argc < 2, then atoi(argv[1]) is not evaluated.

The atoi() function still works if the string only begins with an integer. In that case, it converts characters until it encounters something that is not part of an integer. For example, atoi("42regular") returns the integer 42. What if the command line is something like hello what? On the implementations we've used, the atoi() function returns a value of 0 if its argument is not recognizable as a number. However, the ANSI standard does not require that behavior.

We include the stdlib.h header because, under ANSI C, it contains the function declaration for atoi(). That header file also includes declarations for atof() and atol(). The atof() function converts a string to a type double value, and the atol() function converts a string to a type long value. They work analogously to atoi(), so they are type double and long, respectively.

ANSI C has supplied more sophisticated versions of these functions: strtol() converts a string to a long, stsroul() converts a string to an unsigned long, and strtod() converts a string to double. The more sophisticated aspect is that the functions identify and report the first character in the string that is not part of a number. Also, strtol() and strtoul() allow you to specify a number base.

Let's look at an example involving strtol(). Its prototype is this:

```
long strtol(const char *nptr, char **endptr, int base);
```

Here, nptr is a pointer to the string you want to convert, endptr is the address of a pointer that gets set to the address of the character terminating the input number, and base is the number base the number is written in. An example, given in Listing 11.29, makes this clearer.

Listing 11.29   The strcnvt.c program.

```
/* strcnvt.c -- try strtol()  */
#include <stdio.h>
#include <stdlib.h>
int main()
{
    char number[30];
    char * end;
    long value;

    puts("Enter a number (empty line to quit):");
    while(gets(number) && number[0] != '\0')
    {
        value = strtol(number, &end, 10);
        printf("value: %ld, stopped at %s (%d)\n",
                    value, end, *end);
        value = strtol(number, &end, 16);
        printf("value: %ld, stopped at %s (%d)\n",
                    value, end, *end);
        puts("Next number:");
    }
    puts("Bye!\n");
    return 0;
}
```

Here is some sample output:

```
Enter a number (empty line to quit):
10
value: 10, stopped at  (0)
value: 16, stopped at  (0)
Next number:
10atom
value: 10, stopped at atom (97)
value: 266, stopped at tom (116)
Next number:

Bye!
```

First, note that the string "10" is converted to the number 10 when base is 10 and to 16 when base is 16. Also note that if end points to a character, then *end is a character. Therefore, the first conversion ended when the null character was reached, so end pointed to the null character. Printing end displays an empty string, and printing *end with the %d format displays the ASCII code for the null character.

For the second input string (base 10 interpretation), end is given the address of the 'a' character. So printing end displays the string "atom", and printing *end displays the ASCII code for the 'a' character. When the base is changed to 16, however, the 'a' character is recognized as a valid hexadecimal digit, and the function converts the hexadecimal number 10a to 266, base 10.

The strtol() function goes up to base 36, using the letters through 'z' as digits. The strtoul() function does the same, but converts unsigned values. The strtod() function does only base 10, so it uses just two arguments.

Many implementations have `itoa()` and `ftoa()` functions for converting integers and floating-point values to strings. However, they are not part of the ANSI C library; use `sprintf()`, instead, for greater compatibility.

Chapter Summary

A C *string* is a series of `chars` terminated by the null character, `'\0'`. A string can be stored in a character array. A string can also be represented with a *string constant*, in which the characters, aside from the null character, are enclosed in double quotation marks. The compiler supplies the null character. Therefore, `"joy"` is stored as the four characters `j`, `o`, `y`, and `\0`. The length of a string, as measured by `strlen()`, doesn't count the null character.

String constants can be used to initialize character arrays. In pre-ANSI C, only external and static arrays can be initialized, but ANSI C permits automatic arrays to be initialized, too. The array size should be at least one greater than the string length to accommodate the terminating null character. String constants can also be used to initialize pointers of type pointer-to-`char`.

Functions use pointers to the first character of a string to identify which string to act on. Typically, the corresponding actual argument is an array name, a pointer variable, or a quoted string. In each case, the address of the first character is passed. In general, it is not necessary to pass the length of the string because the function can use the terminating null character to locate the end of a string.

The `gets()` and `puts()` functions fetch a line of input and print a line of output, respectively. They are part of the `stdio.h` family of functions.

The C library includes several *string-handling* functions. Under ANSI C, these functions are declared in the `string.h` file. The library also has several *character-processing* functions; they are declared in the `ctype.h` file.

You can give a program access to *command-line arguments* by providing the proper two formal variables to the `main()` function. The first argument, traditionally called `argc`, is an `int` and is assigned the count of command-line words. The second argument, traditionally called `argv`, is a pointer to an array of pointers of `char`. Each pointer-to-`char` points to one of the command-line argument strings, with `argv[0]` pointing to the command name, `argv[1]` pointing to the first command-line argument, and so on.

The `atoi()`, `atol()`, and `atof()` functions convert string representations of numbers to type `int`, `long`, and `double` forms, respectively. The `strtol()`, `strtoul()`, and `strtod()` functions convert string representations of numbers to type `long`, `unsigned long`, and `double` forms, respectively.

Review Questions

1. What's wrong with this attempted declaration of a character string?

```
int main(void)
{
    char name[] = {'F', 'e', 's', 's' };
    ...
}
```

2. What will this program print?

```
#include <stdio.h>
int main(void)
{
    char note[] = "See you at the snack bar.";
    char *ptr;

    ptr = note;
    puts(ptr);
    puts(++ptr);
    note[7] = '\0';
    puts(note);
    puts(++ptr);
    return 0;
}
```

3. What will this program print?

```
#include <stdio.h>
#include <string.h>
int main(void)
{
    char food[] = "Yummy";
    char *ptr;

    ptr = food + strlen(food);
    while (--ptr >= food)
        puts(ptr);
    return 0;
}
```

4. What will the following program print?

```
#include <stdio.h>
#include <string.h>
int main(void)
{
    char goldwyn[40] = "art of it all ";
    char samuel[40] = "I read p";
    char *quote = "the way through.";

    strcat(goldwyn, quote);
    strcat( samuel, goldwyn);
    puts(samuel);
    return 0;
}
```

5. Here is an exercise providing practice with strings, loops, pointers, and pointer incrementing. First, suppose you have this function definition:

```
#include <stdio.h>
char *pr (char *str)
{
    char *pc;
```

```
        pc = str;
        while (*pc)
            putchar(*pc++);
        do {
            putchar(*—pc);
            } while (pc - str);
        return (pc);
    }
```

Consider the following function call:

```
x = pr("Ho Ho Ho!");
```

a. What is printed?

b. What type should x be?

c. What value does x get?

d. What does the expression *--pc mean, and how is it different from --*pc?

e. What would be printed if *--pc were replaced with *pc--?

f. What do the two while expressions test for?

g. What happens if pr() is supplied with a null string as an argument?

h. What must be done in the calling function so that pr() can be used as shown?

6. How many bytes does '$' use? What about "$"?

7. What does the following program print?

```
#include <stdio.h>
#include <string.h>
#define M1    "How are ya, sweetie? "
char M2[40] = "Beat the clock.";
char * M3  = "chat";
int main(void)
{
    char words[80];
    printf(M1);
    puts(M1);
    puts(M2);
    puts(M2 + 1);
    strcpy(words,M2);
    strcat(words, " Win a toy.");
    puts(words);
    words[4] = '\0';
    puts(words);
    while (*M3)
        puts(M3++);
    puts(—M3);
    puts(—M3);
```

```
        M3 = M1;
        puts(M3);
        return 0;
    }
```

8. What does the following program print?

```
#include <stdio.h>
int main(void)
{
    static char str1[] = "gawsie";
    static char str2[] = "bletonism";
    char *ps;
    int i = 0;

    for (ps = str1; *ps != '\0'; ps++) {
        if ( *ps == 'a' || *ps == 'e' )
                putchar(*ps);
        else
                (*ps)--;
        putchar(*ps);
        }
    putchar('\n');
    while (str2[i] != '\0' ) {
        printf("%c", i % 3 ? str2[i] : '*');
        ++i;
        }
    return 0;
}
```

9. The strlen() function takes a pointer to a string as an argument and returns the length of the string. Write your own version of this function.

10. Design a function that takes a string pointer as argument and returns a pointer to the first space character in the string on or after the pointed-to position. Have it return a null pointer if it finds no spaces.

11. Rewrite Listing 11.17 using ctype.h functions so that the program recognizes a correct answer regardless of the user's choice of uppercase and lowercase.

Programming Exercises

1. Design a function that fetches the next n characters from input, including blanks, tabs, and newlines.

2. Modify the function in Exercise 1 so that it stops after n characters or after the first blank, tab, or newline, whichever comes first. (Don't just use scanf().)

3. Design a function that fetches the first word from a line of input and discards the rest of the line. Define a word as a sequence of characters with no blanks, tabs, or newlines in it.

4. Design a function that searches the specified string for the first occurrence of a specified character. Have the function return a pointer to the character if successful, and a null if the character is not found in the string. (This duplicates the way that the library `strchr()` function works.)

5. Write a function `is_within()` that takes a character and a string pointer as arguments. Have the function return a nonzero value (true) if the character is in the string and zero (false) otherwise.

6. The `strncpy(s1,s2,n)` function copies exactly n characters from `s2` to `s1`, truncating `s2` or padding it with extra null characters as necessary. The target string may not be null-terminated if the length of `s2` is n or more. The function returns `s1`. Write your own version of this function.

7. Write a function `string_in()` that takes two string pointers as arguments. If the second string is contained in the first string, have the function return the address at which the contained string begins. For instance, `string_in("hats", "at")` would return the address of the a in `hats`. Otherwise, have the function return the null pointer.

8. Write a function that replaces the contents of a string with the string reversed.

9. Write a function that takes a string as an argument and which removes the spaces from the string. Test in a program that uses a loop to read lines until you enter an empty line. The program should apply the function to each input string and display the result.

10. Write a program that reads in up to 10 strings or to `EOF`, whichever comes first. Have it offer the user a menu with five choices: print the original list of strings, print the strings in ASCII collating sequence, print the strings in order of increasing length, print the strings in order of the length of the first word in the string, and quit. Have the menu recycle until the user enters the quit request. The program, of course, should actually perform the promised tasks.

11. Write a program that reads input up to `EOF` and reports the number of words, the number of uppercase letters, the number of lowercase letters, the number of punctuation characters, and the number of digits. Use the `ctype.h` family of functions.

12. Write a program that echoes the command-line arguments in reverse word order. That is, if the command-line arguments are `see you later`, the program should print `later you see`.

13. Write a power-law program that works on a command-line basis. The first command-line argument should be the type **double** number to be raised to a power, and the second argument should be the integer power.

14. Use the character classification functions to prepare an implementation of **atoi()**.

15. Write a program that reads input until end of file and echoes it to the display. Have the program recognize and implement the following command-line arguments:

    -p   Print input as is

    -u   Map input to all uppercase

    -1   Map input to all lowercase

CHAPTER 12

FILE INPUT/OUTPUT

You will learn about the following in this chapter:

- Functions
  fopen(), getc(), putc(),
  exit(), fclose()
  fprintf(), fscanf(), fgets(),
  fputs()

rewind(), fseek(), ftell(),
fflush()
fgetpos(), fsetpos(), feof(),
ferror()
ungetc(), setvbuf(), fread(),

*I*n this chapter, you learn how to process files using C's standard I/O family of functions. You learn about text modes and binary modes, text and binary formats, and buffered and nonbuffered I/O. You practice using functions that can access files both sequentially and randomly.

Files are essential to today's computer systems. They are used to store programs, documents, data, correspondence, forms, graphics, and myriad other kinds of information. As a programmer, you will have to write programs that create files, write into files, and read from files. In this chapter, we show you how.

Communicating with Files

Often you need programs that can read information from files or can write results into a file. One such form of program-file communication is file redirection, as you saw in Chapter 8, "Character Input/Output and Redirection." This method is simple but limited. For instance, suppose you want to write an interactive program that asks you for book titles and then saves the complete listing in a file. If you use redirection, as in

```
books > bklist
```

your interactive prompts are redirected into `bklist`. Not only does this put unwanted text into `bklist`, it prevents you from seeing the questions you are supposed to answer.

Fortunately, C offers more powerful methods of communicating with files. It enables you to open a file from within a program and then use special I/O functions to read from or write to that file. Before investigating these methods, however, let's briefly review the nature of a file.

What Is a File?

A *file* is a named section of storage, usually on a disk. You think of `stdio.h`, for instance, as the name of a file containing some useful information. To the operating system, however, a file is a bit more complicated. A large file, for example, could wind up stored in several scattered fragments, or it might contain additional data that allows the operating system to determine what kind of file it is, but these are the operating system's concerns, not yours (unless you are writing operating systems). Your concern is how files appear to a C program.

C views a file as a continuous sequence of bytes, each of which can be read individually. This corresponds to the file structure in the UNIX environment, where C grew up. Because other environments may not correspond exactly to this model, ANSI C provides two ways to view files.

The Text View and the Binary View

The two ANSI-mandated views of a file are *binary* and *text*. In the binary view, each and every byte of the file is accessible to a program. In the text view, what the program sees can differ from what is in the file. With the text view, the local environment's representation of such things as the end of a line are mapped to the C view when a file is read. Similarly, the C view is mapped to the local representation of output. For example, MS-DOS text files represent the end of a line with the carriage-return, linefeed combination: \r\n. Macintosh text files represent the end of a line with just a carriage-return \r. C programs represent the end of a line with just \n. Therefore, when a C program takes the text view of an MS-DOS text file, it converts \r\n to \n when reading from a file, and it converts \n to \r\n when writing to a file. When a C program takes the text view of a Macintosh text file, it converts the \r to \n when reading from a file, and it converts \n to \r when writing to a file.

You aren't restricted to using only the text view for an MS-DOS text file. You can also use the binary view of the same file. If you do, your program sees both the \r and the \n characters in the file; no mapping takes place (see Figure 12.1). MS-DOS distinguishes between text and binary *files*, but C provides for text and binary *views*. Normally, you use the text view for text files and the binary view for binary files. However, you can use either view of either type of file, although a text view of a binary file works poorly.

Although ANSI C provides for both a binary and a text view, these views can be implemented identically. For instance, because UNIX uses just one file structure, both views are the same for UNIX implementations.

Figure 12.1 Binary view and text view.

Levels of I/O

In addition to selecting the view of a file, you can, in most cases, choose between two levels of I/O, that is, between two levels of handling access to files. *Low-level I/O* uses the fundamental I/O services provided by the operating system. *Standard high-level I/O* uses a standard package of C library functions and `stdio.h` header file definitions. ANSI C supports only the standard I/O package because there is no way to guarantee that all operating systems can be represented by the same low-level I/O model. Because ANSI C establishes the portability of the standard I/O model, we will concentrate on it.

Standard Files

C programs automatically open three files on your behalf. They are termed the *standard input*, the *standard output*, and the *standard error output*. The standard input, by default, is the normal input device for your system, usually your keyboard. Both the standard output and the standard error output, by default, are the normal output device for your system, usually your display screen.

The standard input, naturally, provides input to your program. It's the file that is read by `getchar()`, `gets()`, and `scanf()`. The standard output is where normal program output goes. It is used by `putchar()`, `puts()`, and `printf()`. Redirection, as you learned in Chapter 8, causes other files to be recognized as the standard input or standard output. The purpose of the standard error output file is to provide a logically distinct place to send error messages. If, for example, you use redirection to send output to a file instead of to the screen, output sent to the standard error output still goes to the screen. This is good because if the error messages were routed to the file, you would not see them until you viewed the file.

Standard I/O

The standard I/O package has two advantages, besides portability, over low-level I/O. First, it has many specialized functions that simplify handling different I/O problems. For instance, printf() converts various forms of data to string output suitable for terminals. Second, input and output are *buffered*. That is, information is transferred in large chunks (typically 512 bytes at a time or more) instead of a byte at a time. When a program reads a file, for example, a chunk of data is copied to a buffer—an intermediate storage area. This buffering greatly increases the data transfer rate. The program can then examine individual bytes in the buffer. The buffering is handled behind the scenes, so you have the illusion of character-by-character access. (You can also buffer low-level I/O, but you have to do much of the work yourself.) Listing 12.1 shows how to use standard I/O to read a file and count the number of characters in the file. We'll discuss the features of Listing 12.1 in the next several sections. (Windows users might have to run the program in an MS-DOS window after compiling. Macintosh users should use console.h and the ccommand() function as described in Chapter 11, "Characters Strings and String Functions," and in the Think C documentation.)

Listing 12.1   The count.c program.

```
/* count.c -- using standard I/O */
#include <stdio.h>
#include <stdlib.h> /* ANSI C exit() prototype           */
int main(int argc, char *argv[])
{
    int ch;         /* place to store each character as read */
    FILE *fp;       /* "file pointer"                        */
    long count = 0;

    if (argc != 2)
    {
        printf("Usage: %s filename\n", argv[0]);
        exit(1);
    }
    if ((fp = fopen(argv[1], "r")) == NULL)
    {
        printf("Can't open %s\n", argv[1]);
        exit(1);
    }
    while ((ch = getc(fp)) != EOF)
    {
        putc(ch,stdout);
        count++;
    }
    fclose(fp);
```

```
    printf("File %s has %ld characters\n", argv[1], count);
    return 0;
}
```

Checking for Command-Line Arguments

First, the program in Listing 12.1 checks the value of `argc` to see if there is a command-line argument. If there isn't, the program prints a usage message and exits. The string `argv[0]` is the name of the program. Using `argv[0]` instead of the program name explicitly causes the error message to change automatically if you change the name of the executable file. This feature is also handy in environments like UNIX that permit multiple names for a single file. But beware—some operating systems, such as pre–MS-DOS 3.0, don't recognize `argv[0]`, so this usage is not completely portable.

The `exit()` function causes the program to terminate, closing any open files. The argument to `exit()` is passed on to some operating systems, including UNIX and PC DOS, where it can be used by other programs. The usual convention is to pass a value of `0` for programs that terminate normally and to pass nonzero values for abnormal termination. Different exit values can be used to distinguish between different causes of failure, and this is the usual practice in UNIX and DOS programming. However, not all operating systems recognize the same range of possible return values. Therefore, the ANSI C standard mandates a rather restricted minimum range. In particular, the standard requires that the value `0` or the macro `EXIT_SUCCESS` be used to indicate successful termination, and the macro `EXIT_FAILURE` be used to indicate unsuccessful termination. These macros, along with the `exit()` prototype, are found in the `stdlib.h` header file. This book will follow the common practice of using integer exit values, but for maximum portability, use `EXIT_SUCCESS` and `EXIT_FAILURE`.

Under ANSI C, using `return` in the initial call to `main()` has the same effect as calling `exit()`. Therefore, the following statement

```
return 0;
```

which you've been using all along, is equivalent in effect to this statement:

```
exit(0);
```

Note, however, the qualifying phrase "the initial call." If you make `main()` into a recursive program, `exit()` still terminates the program, but `return` passes control to the previous level of recursion until the original level is reached. Then `return` terminates the program. Another difference between `return` and `exit()` is that `exit()` terminates the program even if called in a function other than `main()`.

The `fopen()` Function

Next, the program uses `fopen()` to open the file. This function is declared in `stdio.h`. Its first argument is the name of the file to be opened; more exactly, it is the address of a string containing that name. The second argument is a string identifying the mode in which the file is to be opened. The C library provides for several possibilities, as shown in Table 12.1.

Table 12.1 Mode strings for `fopen()`.

Mode String	Meaning
`"r"`	Open a text file for reading
`"w"`	Open a text file for writing, truncating an existing file to zero length, or creating the file if it does not exist
`"a"`	Open a text file for writing, appending to the end of an existing file, or creating the file if it does not exist
`"r+"`	Open a text file for update, that is, for both reading and writing
`"w+"`	Open a text file for update (reading and writing), first truncating the file to zero length if it exists or creating the file if it does not exist
`"a+"`	Open a text file for update (reading and writing), appending to the end of an existing file, or creating the file if it does not yet exist; the whole file can be read, but writing can only be appended
`"rb"`, `"wb"`, `"ab"`, `"ab+"`, `"a+b"`, `"wb+"`, `"w+b"`, `"ab+"`, `"a+b"`	Like the preceding modes, except using binary mode instead of text mode mode

For systems like UNIX, which have just one file type, the modes with the **b** are equivalent to the corresponding modes lacking the **b**.

Caution

If you use any of the `"w"` modes for an existing file, the file contents are truncated so that your program can start with a clean slate.

After your program successfully opens a file, `fopen()` returns a *file pointer*, which the other I/O functions can then use to specify the file. The file pointer, `fp` in this example, is of type pointer-to-**FILE**; FILE is a derived type defined in `stdio.h`. The pointer `fp` doesn't point to the actual file. Instead, it points to a data package containing information about the file, including information about the buffer used for the file's I/O. Because the I/O functions in the standard library use a buffer, they need to know where the buffer is. They also need to know how full the buffer is and which file is being used. This enables the functions to refill or empty the buffer when necessary. The data package pointed to by `fp` has all that information. (This data package is an example of a C structure, a topic we discuss in Chapter 14, "Structures and Other Data Forms.")

The `fopen()` function returns the null pointer (also defined in `stdio.h`) if it cannot open the file. The program exits if `fp` is **NULL**. The `fopen()` function can fail because the disk is full, because the name is illegal, because access is restricted, or because of a hardware problem, to name just a few reasons, so check for trouble; a little error-trapping can go a long way.

The `getc()` and `putc()` Functions

The two functions `getc()` and `putc()` work very much like `getchar()` and `putchar()`. The difference is that you must tell these newcomers which file to use. So the following old standby means get a character from the standard input:

```
ch = getchar();
```

However, this statement means get a character from the file identified by `fp`:

```
ch = getc(fp);
```

Similarly, this statements means put the character `ch` into the file identified by the `FILE` pointer `fpout`:

```
putc(ch, fpout);
```

In the `putc()` argument list, the character comes first, then the file pointer.

Listing 12.1 uses `stdout` for the second argument of `putc()`. It is defined in `stdio.h` as being the file pointer associated with the standard output, so `putc(ch,stdout)` is the same as `putchar(ch)`. Indeed, the latter function is normally defined as being the former. Similarly, `getchar()` is defined as being `getc()` using the standard input.

The `fclose()` Function

The `fclose(fp)` closes the file identified by `fp`, flushing buffers as needed. For a program less casual than this one, you would check to see whether the file had been closed successfully. The function `fclose()` returns a value of `0` if successful, and `EOF` if not.

```
if (fclose(fp) != 0)
  printf("Error in closing file %s\n", argv[1]);
```

The `fclose()` function can fail if, for example, the disk is full, the diskette has been removed, or there has been an I/O error.

Standard Files

The `stdio.h` file associates three file pointers with the three standard files automatically opened by C programs.

Standard File	File Pointer	Normally
Standard input	`stdin`	Your keyboard
Standard output	`stdout`	Your screen
Standard error	`stderr`	Your screen

These pointers are all type pointer-to-`FILE`, so they can be used as arguments to the standard I/O functions, just as `fp` was in the example. Let's move on to an example that creates a new file and writes to it.

A Simple-Minded File-Condensing Program

This next program copies selected data from one file to another. It opens two files simultaneously, using the "r" mode for one and the "w" mode for the other. The program (see Listing 12.2) condenses the contents of the first file by the brutal expedient of retaining only every third character. Finally, it places the condensed text into the second file. The name for the second file is the old name with .red (for reduced) appended. Command-line arguments, opening more than one file simultaneously, and filename appending are generally quite useful techniques. This particular form of condensing is of more limited appeal, but it can have its uses, as you will see.

Listing 12.2   The reducto.c program.

```
/* reducto.c -- reduces your files by two-thirds ! */
#include <stdio.h>
#include <stdlib.h>
#include <string.h>       /* for strcpy(), strcat() */
int main(int argc, char *argv[])
{
    FILE  *in, *out;   /* declare two FILE pointers    */
    int ch;
    char name[40];      /* storage for output filename   */
    int count = 0;

    if (argc < 2)       /* check for an input file       */
    {
        fprintf(stderr, "Usage: %s filename\n", argv[0]);
        exit(1);
    }
    if ((in = fopen(argv[1], "r")) == NULL)
    {
        fprintf(stderr, "I couldn't open the file \"%s\"\n",
                argv[1]);
        exit(2);
    }
    strcpy(name,argv[1]);    /* copy filename into array   */
    strcat(name,".red");     /* append .red to name        */
    if ((out = fopen(name, "w")) == NULL)
    {                        /* open file for writing      */
        fprintf(stderr,"Can't create output file.\n");
        exit(3);
    }
    while ((ch = getc(in)) != EOF)
        if (count++ % 3 == 0)
            putc(ch, out); /* print every 3rd char        */
    if (fclose(in) != 0 || fclose(out) != 0)
        fprintf(stderr,"Error in closing files\n");
    return 0;
}
```

The executable file is called `reducto`. We applied it to a file called `eddy`, which contained this single line:

```
So even Eddy came oven ready.
```

The command was as follows:

```
reducto eddy
```

The output was written to a file called `eddy.red`. The program doesn't produce any onscreen output, but displaying the `eddy.red` file revealed the following:

```
Send money
```

This example illustrates several programming techniques. Let's examine some of them now.

The `fprintf()` function is like `printf()` except that it requires a file pointer as its first argument. We've used the `stderr` pointer to send error messages to the standard error; this is a standard C practice.

To construct the new name for the output file, the program uses `strcpy()` to copy the name `eddy` into the array `name`. Then it uses the `strcat()` function to combine that name with `.red`, producing `eddy.red`. We also checked to see whether the program succeeded in opening a file by that name. This is particularly important in the DOS environment because a filename like, say, `strange.c.red` is invalid; you can't add extensions to extensions under DOS. (The proper MS-DOS approach is to replace any existing extension with `.red`, so that the reduced version of `strange.c` would be `strange.red`. You could use the `strchr()` function, for example, to locate the period, if any, in a name and copy only the part of the string before the period.)

This program had two files open simultaneously, so we declared two **FILE** pointers. Note that each file is opened and closed independently of the other. There are limits to how many files you can have open at one time. The limit depends on your system and implementation; the range is often 10 to 20. You can use the same file pointer for different files, providing those files are not open at the same time.

File I/O: `fprintf()`, `fscanf()`, `fgets()`, and `fputs()`

For each of the I/O functions in the preceding chapters, there is a similar file I/O function. The main distinction is that you need to use a **FILE** pointer to tell the new functions which file to work with. Like `getc()` and `putc()`, these functions require that you identify a file by using a pointer-to-**FILE** such as `stdout` or that you use the return value of `fopen()`.

The `fprintf()` and `fscanf()` Functions

The file I/O functions `fprintf()` and `fscanf()` work just like `printf()` and `scanf()`, except that they require an additional first argument to identify the proper file. You've already used `fprintf()`. Listing 12.3 illustrates both of these file I/O functions along with the `rewind()` function.

Listing 12.3   The addaword.c program.

```c
/* addaword.c -- uses fprintf(), fscanf(), and rewind() */
#include <stdio.h>
#include <stdlib.h>
#define MAX 40
int main(void)
{
    FILE *fp;
    char words[MAX];

    if ((fp = fopen("wordy", "a+")) == NULL)
    {
        fprintf(stdin,"Can't open \"words\" file.\n");
        exit(1);
    }
    puts("Enter words to add to the file; press the Enter");
    puts("key at the beginning of a line to terminate.");
    while (gets(words) != NULL  && words[0] != '\0')
        fprintf(fp, "%s ", words);
    puts("File contents:");
    rewind(fp);               /* go back to beginning of file */
    while (fscanf(fp,"%s",words) == 1)
        puts(words);
    if (fclose(fp) != 0)
        fprintf(stderr,"Error closing file\n");
    return 0;
}
```

This program enables you to add words to a file. By using the "a+" mode, the program can both read and write in the file. The first time the program is used, it creates the words file and enables you to place words in it. When you use the program subsequently, it enables you to add (append) words to the previous contents. The append mode only enables you to add material to the end of the file, but the "a+" mode does enable you to read the whole file. The rewind() command takes the program to the file beginning so that the final while loop can print the file contents. Note that rewind() takes a file pointer argument.

If you enter an empty line, gets() places a null character in the first element of the array. Use that fact to terminate the loop.

Here's a sample run from a DOS environment:

```
C>addaword
Enter words to add to the file; press the Enter
key at the beginning of a line to terminate.
The fabulous programmer[enter]
[enter]
File contents:
The
fabulous
programmer
C>addaword
Enter words to add to the file; press the Enter
key at the beginning of a line to terminate.
```

```
enchanted the[enter]
large[enter]
[enter]
File contents:
The
fabulous
programmer
enchanted
the
large
```

As you can see, `fprintf()` and `fscanf()` work like `printf()` and `scanf()`. Unlike `putc()`, the `fprintf()` and `fscanf()` functions take the `FILE` pointer as the first argument instead of as the last argument.

The `fgets()` and `fputs()` Functions

You met `fgets()` in Chapter 11. The `fgets()` function takes three arguments to the `gets()` function's one. The first argument, as with `gets()`, is the address (type `char *`) where input should be stored. The second argument is an integer representing the maximum size of the input string. The final argument is the file pointer identifying the file to be read. A function call, then, looks like this:

```
fgets(buf, MAX, fp);
```

Here, `buf` is the name of a `char` array, `MAX` is the maximum size of the string, and `fp` is the pointer-to-`FILE`.

The `fgets()` function reads input through the first newline character or until one fewer than the upper limit of characters is read or until the end of file is found; `fgets()` then adds a terminating null character to form a string. Therefore, the upper limit represents the maximum number of characters plus the null character. If `fgets()` reads in a whole line before running into the character limit, it adds the newline character marking the end of the line into the string, just before the null character. Here it differs from `gets()`, which reads the newline but discards it.

Like `gets()`, `fgets()` returns the value `NULL` when it encounters `EOF`. You can use this to check for the end of a file. Otherwise, it returns the address passed to it.

The `fputs()` function takes two arguments: first, an address of a string, and then a file pointer. It writes the string found at the pointed-to location into the indicated file. Unlike `puts()`, `fputs()` does not append a newline when it prints. A function call looks like this:

```
fputs(buf, fp);
```

Here, `buf` is the string address, and `fp` identifies the target file.

Because `fgets()` keeps the newline and `fputs()` doesn't add one, they work well in tandem. Listing 12.4 shows an echo program using these two functions.

Listing 12.4   The echo.c program.

```
/* echo.c -- using fgets() and fputs() */
#include <stdio.h>
#define MAXLINE 20
int main(void)
{
    char line[MAXLINE];

    while (fgets(line, MAXLINE, stdin) != NULL &&
            line[0] != '\n')
        fputs(line, stdout);
    return 0;
}
```

When you press the Enter key at the beginning of a line, `fgets()` reads the newline and places it into the first element of the array `line`. Use that fact to terminate the input loop. Encountering end of file also terminates it. (Listing 12.3 tested for `'\0'` instead of `'\n'` because `gets()` discards the newline.)

Here is a sample run. Do you notice anything odd?

```
The silent knight
The silent knight
strode solemnly down the dank and dark hall.
strode solemnly down the dank and dark hall.
[enter]
```

The program works fine. This should seem surprising because the second line you entered contains 44 characters, and the `line` array holds only 20, including the newline character! What happened? When `fgets()` read the second line, it read just the first 19 characters, through the w in `down`. They were copied into `line`, which `fputs()` printed. Because `fgets()` hadn't reached the end of a line, `line` did not contain a newline character, so `fputs()` didn't print a newline. The third call to `fgets()` resumed where the second call left off. Therefore, it read the next 19 characters into `line`, beginning with the n after the w in `down`. This next block replaced the previous contents of `line` and, in turn, was printed on the same line as the output. Remember, the last output didn't have a newline. In short, `fgets()` read the second line in chunks of 19 characters, and `fputs()` printed it in the same-size chunks.

This program also terminates input if a line has exactly 19 characters. In that case, `fgets()` stops reading input after the 19 characters, so the next call to `fgets()` starts with the newline at the end of the line. This newline becomes the first character read, thus terminating the loop. So although the program worked with the sample input, it doesn't work correctly in all cases. You really should use a storage array big enough to hold entire lines.

You might be wondering why the program didn't print the first 19 characters of the second line as soon as you typed them. That is where screen buffering comes in. The second line wasn't sent to the screen until the newline character had been reached.

Commentary: `gets()` and `fgets()`

Because `fgets()` can be used to prevent storage overflow, it is a better function than `gets()` for serious programming. Because it does read a newline into a string and because `puts()` appends a newline to output, `fgets()` should be used with `fputs()`, not `puts()`. Otherwise, one newline in input can become two on output.

The six I/O functions we have just discussed should give you tools aplenty for reading and writing text files. So far, we have used them only for sequential access, that is, processing the file contents in order. Next, we look at random access—in other words, accessing the contents in any order you want.

Adventures in Random Access: `fseek()` and `ftell()`

The `fseek()` function enables you to treat a file like an array and move directly to any particular byte in a file opened by `fopen()`. To see how it works, let's create a program (see Listing 12.5) that displays a file in reverse order. Borrowing from the earlier examples, it uses a command-line argument to get the name of the file it will read. Note that `fseek()` has three arguments and returns an `int` value. The `ftell()` function returns the current position in a file as a `long` value.

Listing 12.5   The `reverse.c` program.

```
/* reverse.c -- displays a file in reverse order */
#include <stdio.h>
#include <stdlib.h>
#define CNTL_Z '\032'   /* eof marker in DOS text files */
#define SLEN 50
int main(void)
{
    char file[SLEN];
    char ch;
    FILE *fp;
    long count, last;

    puts("Enter the name of the file to be processed:");
    gets(file);
    if ((fp = fopen(file,"rb")) == NULL)
    {                       /* read-only and binary modes */
        printf("reverse can't open %s\n", file);
        exit(1);
    }
    fseek(fp, 0L, SEEK_END);        /* go to end of file */
    last = ftell(fp);
    for (count = 1L; count <= last; count++)
    {
        fseek(fp, -count, SEEK_END);  /* go backward      */
```

continued on next page

continued from previous page

```
      ch = getc(fp);
  /* for DOS, works with UNIX */
    if (ch != CNTL_Z && ch != '\r')
      putchar(ch);
  /* for Macintosh            */
  /*  if (ch == '\r')
      putchar('\n');
    else
      putchar(ch);            */
  }
  putchar('\n');
  fclose(fp);
  return 0;
}
```

Here is the output for a sample file:

```
Enter the name of the file to be processed:
cluv

.C ni eno naht ylevol erom margorp a
ees reven llahs I taht kniht I
```

Note

If you run the program from a command-line environment, this program expects the filename to be in the same directory (or folder) as the executable program. If you run the program from an IDE, the program looks depend on the implementation. For example, Microsoft Visual C++ 5.0 looks in the directory containing the source code, but Metrowerks CodeWarrior looks in the directory containing the executable file.

We need to discuss three topics: how `fseek()` and `ftell()` work, how to use a binary stream, and how to make the program portable.

How `fseek()` and `ftell()` Work

The first of the three arguments to `fseek()` is a `FILE` pointer to the file being searched. The file should have been opened by using `fopen()`.

The second argument to `fseek()` is called the *offset*. This argument tells how far to move from the starting point (see the following list of mode starting points). The argument must be a `long` value. It can be positive (move forward), negative (move backward), or zero (stay put).

The third argument is the mode, and it identifies the starting point. Under ANSI, the `stdio.h` header file specifies the following manifest constants for the mode:

Mode	Measure Offset From
SEEK_SET	Beginning of file
SEEK_CUR	Current position
SEEK_END	End of file

Older implementations may lack these definitions and, instead, use the numeric values 0L, 1L, and 2L, respectively, for these modes. Recall that the L suffix identifies type long values, or the implementation might have the constants defined in a different header file. When in doubt, consult your usage manual or the online manual.

The value returned by fseek() is 0 if everything is okay, and -1 if there is an error, such as attempting to move past the bounds of the file.

The ftell() function is type long, and it returns the current file location. Under ANSI, it is declared in stdio.h. As originally implemented in UNIX, ftell() specifies the file position by returning the number of bytes from the beginning, with the first byte being byte 0, and so on. Under ANSI C, this definition applies to files opened in the binary mode, but not necessarily to files opened in the text mode. That is one reason we used the binary mode for Listing 12.5.

Now we can explain the basic elements of Listing 12.5. First, the statement

```
fseek(fp, 0L, SEEK_END);
```

takes you to an offset of 0 bytes from the file end. That is, it takes you to the end of the file. Next, the statement

```
last = ftell(fp);
```

assigns to last the number of bytes from the beginning to the end of the file.

Then, you have this loop:

```
for (count = 1L; count <= last; count++)
{
  fseek(fp, -count, SEEK_END);     /* go backward */
    ch = getc(fp);
 }
```

The first cycle positions the program at the first character before the end of the file, that is, at the file's final character. Then the program prints that character. The next loop positions the program at the preceding character and prints it. This process continues until the first character is reached and printed.

Binary Versus Text Mode

We designed Listing 12.5 to work in both the UNIX and the MS-DOS environments. UNIX has only one file format, so no special adjustments are needed. MS-DOS, however, does require extra attention. Many MS-DOS editors mark the end of a text file with the character Ctrl+Z. When such a file is opened in the text mode, C recognizes this character as marking the end of the file. When the same file is opened in the binary mode, however, the Ctrl+Z character is just another character in the file, and the actual end-of-file comes later. It might come immediately after the Ctrl+Z, or the file could be padded with null characters to make the size a multiple of, say, 256. Null characters don't print under DOS, and we included code to prevent the program from trying to print the Ctrl+Z character.

Another difference is one we've mentioned before: MS-DOS represents a text file newline with the \r\n combination. A C program opening the same file in a text mode "sees" \r\n as a simple \n, but, when using the binary mode, the program sees both characters. Therefore, we included coding to suppress printing \r. (Different coding is needed for Macintosh text files because they use the \r as the end-of-line marker. Listing 12.5 shows the Macintosh version as a comment.)

Because a UNIX text file normally contains neither Ctrl+Z nor \r, this extra coding does not affect most UNIX text files.

The ftell() function may work differently in the text mode than in the binary mode. Many systems have text file formats that are different enough from the UNIX model that a byte count from the beginning of the file is not a meaningful quantity. ANSI C states that, for the text mode, ftell() returns a value that can be used as the second argument to fseek(). For MS-DOS, for example, ftell() can return a count that sees \r\n as a single byte.

Portability

Ideally, fseek() and ftell() should conform to the UNIX model. However, differences in real systems sometimes make this impossible. Therefore, ANSI provides lowered expectations for these functions. Here are some limitations:

- In the binary mode, implementations need not support the SEEK_END mode. (Listing 12.5, then, is not guaranteed to be portable.)

- In the text mode, the only calls to fseek() that are guaranteed to work are these:

fseek(file, 0L, SEEK_SET)	Go to beginning of file
fseek(file, 0L, SEEK_CUR)	Stay at current position
fseek(file, 0L, SEEK_END)	Go to file end
fseek(file,ftell-pos, SEEK_SET)	Go to position ftell-pos from the beginning; ftell-pos is a value returned by ftell()

Fortunately, many common environments allow stronger implementations of these functions.

The fgetpos() and fsetpos() Functions

One potential problem with fseek() and ftell() is that they limit file sizes to values that can be represented by type long. Perhaps two billion bytes seems more than adequate, but the ever-increasing capacities of storage devices makes larger files possible. ANSI C introduced two new positioning functions designed to work with larger file sizes. Instead of using a `long` value to represent a position, it uses a new type, called `fpos_t` (for file position type) for that purpose. The `fpos_t` type is not a fundamental type; rather, it is defined in terms of other types. A variable or data object of `fpos_t` type can specify a location within a file, and it can be used with `fseek()` and `ftell()`, but its nature is not specified beyond that. Implementors can then design a type to meet the needs of a particular platform; the type could, for example, be implemented as a structure.

ANSI C does define how the `fpos_t` is used. The `fgetpos()` has this prototype:

```
int fgetpos(FILE *stream, fpos_t *pos);
```

When called, it places an `fpos_t` value in the location pointed to by `pos`; the value describes a location in the file. The function returns zero if successful, and a non-zero value for failure.

The `fsetpos()` function has this prototype:

```
int fsetpos(FILE *stream, const fpos_t *pos);
```

When called, it uses the `fpos_t` value in the location pointed to by `pos` to set the file pointer to the location indicated by that value. The function returns zero if successful, and a non-zero value for failure. The `fpos_t` value should have been obtained by a previous call to `fgetpos()`.

Behind the Scenes with Standard I/O

Now that you've seen some of the features of the standard I/O package, let's examine a representative conceptual model to see how standard I/O works.

Normally, the first step in using standard I/O is to use `fopen()` to open a file. (Recall, however, that the `stdin`, `stdout`, and `stderr` files are opened automatically.) The `fopen()` function not only opens a file but sets up a buffer (two buffers for read-write modes), and it sets up a data structure containing data about the file and about the buffer. Also, `fopen()` returns a pointer to this structure so that other functions know where to find it. Assume that this value is assigned to a pointer variable named `fp`. The `fopen()` function is said to open a stream. If the file is opened in the text mode, you get a text stream, and if the file is opened in the binary mode, you get a binary stream.

The data structure typically includes a file position indicator to specify the current position in the stream. It also has indicators for errors and end-of-file, a pointer to the beginning of the buffer, a file identifier, and a count for the number of bytes actually copied into the buffer.

Let's concentrate on file input. Usually, the next step is to call on one of the input functions declared in `stdio.h`, such as `fscanf()`, `getc()`, or `fgets()`. Calling any one of these functions causes a chunk of data to be copied from the file to the buffer. The buffer size is implementation dependent, but it typically is 512 bytes or some multiple thereof.

In addition to filling the buffer, the initial function call sets values in the structure pointed to by **fp**. In particular, the current position in the stream, and the number of bytes copied into the buffer are set. Usually the current position starts at byte 0.

After the data structure and buffer are initialized, the input function reads the requested data from the buffer. As it does so, the file position indicator is set to point to the character following the last character read. Because all the input functions from the **stdio.h** family use the same buffer, a call to any one function resumes where the previous call to any of the functions stopped.

When an input function finds that it has read all the characters in the buffer, it requests that the next buffer-sized chunk of data be copied from the file into the buffer. In this manner, the input functions can read all the file contents up to the end of the file. After a function reads the last character of the final buffer's worth of data, it sets the end-of-file indicator to true. The next call to an input function then returns **EOF**.

In a similar manner, output functions write to a buffer. When the buffer is filled, the data is copied to the file.

Other Standard I/O Functions

The ANSI standard library contains over three dozen functions in the standard I/O family. Although we don't cover them all here, we will briefly describe a few more to give you a better idea of what is available. We'll list each function by its ANSI C prototype to indicate its arguments and return values. Of those functions we discuss here, all but **setvbuf()** are also available in pre-ANSI implementations. Appendix F, "The Standard ANSI C Library," lists the full ANSI C standard I/O package.

The `int ungetc(int c, FILE *fp)` Function

The **int ungetc(int c, FILE *fp)** function pushes the character specified by **c** back onto the input stream. If you push a character onto the input stream, the next call to a standard input function reads that character (see Figure 12.2). Suppose, for example, you want a function to read characters up to, but not including, the next colon. You can use **getchar()** or **getc()** to read characters until a colon is read and then use **ungetc()** to place the colon back in the input stream. The ANSI C standard guarantees only one pushback at a time. If an implementation permits you to push back several characters in a row, the input functions read them in the reversed order of pushing.

The `int fflush(FILE *fp)` Function

Calling the **int fflush(FILE *fp)** function causes any unwritten data in the buffer to be sent to the output file identified by **fp**. This process is called *flushing a buffer*. If **fp** is the null pointer, all output buffers are flushed.

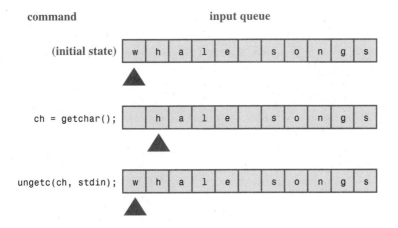

Figure 12.2 The ungetc() function.

The int setvbuf(FILE *fp, char *buf, int mode, size_t size) Function

The int setvbuf(FILE *fp, char *buf, int mode, size_t size) function sets up an alternative buffer to be used by the standard I/O functions. It is called after the file has been opened and before any other operations have been performed on the stream. The pointer **fp** identifies the stream, and **buf** points to the storage to be used. If the value of **buf** is not **NULL**, you must create the buffer. For instance, you could declare an array of 1,024 **chars** and pass the address of that array. However, if you use **NULL** for the value of **buf**, the function allocates a buffer itself. The **size** variable tells **setvbuf()** how big the array is. (The **size_t** type is a derived integer type; see Chapters 11 and 16, "The C Preprocessor and the C Library.") The **mode** is selected from the following choices: **_IOFBF** means fully buffered, **_IOLBF** means line-buffered, and **_IONBF** means nonbuffered. The function returns zero if successful, nonzero otherwise.

Suppose you had a program that worked with stored data objects having, say, a size of 3,000 bytes each. You could use **setvbuf()** to create a buffer whose size matched that of the data object. Many pre-ANSI implementations use **setbuf()** instead. It takes two arguments. The first is a pointer-to-**FILE** to identify the file to be buffered. The second is the desired buffer size in bytes. The **setbuf()** function does not select among different buffering modes, nor does it have a return value.

Binary I/O: fread() and fwrite()

The **fread()** and **fwrite()** functions are next on the list, but first some background. The standard I/O functions you've used to this point are text oriented, dealing with characters and strings. What if you want to save numeric data in a file? True, you can use **fprintf()** and the **%f** format to save a floating-point value, but then you are saving it as a string. For instance, the sequence

```
double num = 1./3.;
fprintf(fp,"%f", num);
```

saves num as a string of eight characters: 0.333333. Using a %.2f specifier saves it as four characters: 0.33. Using a %.12f specifier saves it as 14 characters: 0.333333333333. Changing the specifier alters the amount of space needed to store the value; it can also result in different values being stored. After the value of num is stored as 0.33, there is no way to get back the full precision when reading the file. In general, fprintf() converts numeric values to strings, possibly altering the value.

The most accurate and consistent way to store a number is to use the same pattern of bits that the program does. Therefore, a **double** value should be stored in a size **double** container. When data is stored in a file using the same representation that the program uses, we say that the data is stored in *binary form*. There is no conversion from numeric forms to strings. For standard I/O, the **fread()** and **fwrite()** functions provide this binary service (see Figure 12.3).

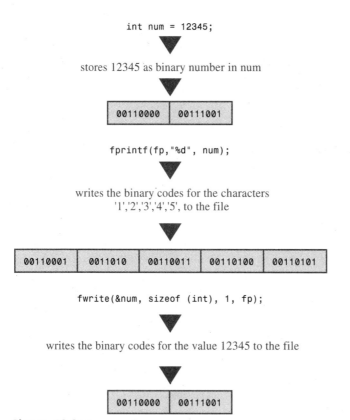

Figure 12.3 Binary and text output.

Actually, all data is stored in binary form. Even characters are stored using the binary representation of the character code. However, if all data in the file is interpreted as character codes, we say that the file contains text data. If some or all of the data is interpreted as numeric data in binary form, we say that the file contains binary data. (Also, files in which the data represents machine language instructions are binary files.)

The uses of the terms *binary* and *text* can get confusing. ANSI C recognizes two modes for opening files: binary and text. Many operating systems recognize two file formats: binary and text. Information can be stored or read as binary data or as text data. These are all related, but not identical. You can open a text format file in the binary mode. You can store text in a binary format file. You can use `getc()` to copy files containing binary data. In general, however, you use the binary mode to store binary data in a binary format file. Similarly, you most often use text data in text files opened in the text format.

The `size_t fwrite(void *ptr, size_t size, size_t nmemb, FILE *fp)` Function

The `size_t fwrite(void *ptr, size_t size, size_t nmemb, FILE *fp)` function writes binary data to a file. The `size_t` type is defined in terms of the standard C types. It is the type returned by the `sizeof` operator. Typically it is `unsigned int`, but an implementation can choose another type. The pointer `ptr` is the address of the chunk of data to be written. The `size` represents the size, in bytes, of the chunks to be written, and the `nmemb` represents the number of chunks to be written. As usual, `fp` identifies the file to be written to. For instance, to save a data object (such as an array) that is 256 bytes in size, you can do this:

```
char buffer[256];
fwrite(buffer, 256, 1, fp);
```

This call writes one chunk of 256 bytes from `buffer` to the file, or to save an array of 10 `double` values, you can do this:

```
double earnings[10];
fwrite(earnings, sizeof (double), 10, fp);
```

This call writes data from the `earnings` array to the file in 10 chunks, each of size `double`.

You probably noticed the odd declaration of `void *ptr` in the `fwrite()` prototype. One problem with `fwrite()` is that its first argument is not a fixed type. For instance, the first example used `buffer`, which is type pointer-to-`char`, and the second example used `earnings`, which is type pointer-to-`double`. Under ANSI C function prototyping, these actual arguments are converted to the pointer-to-`void` type, which acts as a sort of catchall type for pointers. (Pre-ANSI C uses type `char *` for this argument, requiring you to typecast actual arguments to that type.)

The `fwrite()` function returns the number of items successfully written. Normally, this equals `nmemb`, but it can be less if there is a write error.

The `size_t fread(void *ptr, size_t size, size_t nmemb, FILE *fp)` Function

The `size_t fread(void *ptr, size_t size, size_t nmemb, FILE *fp)` function takes the same set of arguments that `fwrite()` does. This time `ptr` is the address of the memory storage into which file data is read, and `fp` identifies the file to be read. Use this function to read data that was written to a file using `fwrite()`. For example, to recover the array of 10 `double`s saved in the previous example, use this call:

```
double earnings[10];
fread(earnings, sizeof (double), 10, fp);
```

This call copies 10 size `double` values into the `earnings` array.

The `fread()` function returns the number of items successfully read. Normally, this equals `nmemb`, but it can be less if there is a read error or if the end of file is reached.

The `int feof(FILE *fp)` and `int ferror(FILE *fp)` Functions

When the standard input functions return `EOF`, it usually means they have reached the end of a file. However, it can also indicate that a read error has occurred. The `feof()` and `ferror()` functions enable you to distinguish between the two possibilities. The `feof()` function returns a non-zero value if the last input call detected the end of file and returns zero otherwise. The `ferror()` function returns a non-zero value if a read or write error has occurred and zero otherwise.

An Example

Let's use some of these functions in a program that appends the contents from a list of files to the end of another file. One problem is passing the file information to the program. This can be done interactively or by using command-line arguments. We'll take the first approach, which suggests a plan along the following lines:

* Request a name for the destination file and open it.
* Use a loop to request source files.
* Open each source file in turn in the read mode and add it to the append file.

To illustrate `setvbuf()`, we'll use it to specify a different buffer size. The next stage of refinement examines opening the append file. We will use the following steps:

* Open the final command-line file in the append mode.
* If this cannot be done, quit.
* Establish a 1,024-byte buffer for this file.
* If this cannot be done, quit.

Similarly, we can refine the copying portion by doing the following for each file:

- If it is the same as the append file, skip to the next file.

- If it cannot be opened in the read mode, skip to the next file.

- Add the contents of the file to the append file.

For practice, we'll use `fread()` and `fwrite()` for the copying. Listing 12.6 shows the result.

Listing 12.6   The `append.c` program.

```
/* append.c -- appends files to a file */
#include <stdio.h>
#include <stdlib.h>
#include <string.h>
#define BUFSIZE 1024
#define SLEN 50
char temp[BUFSIZE];
void append(FILE *source, FILE *dest);

int main(void)
{
    FILE *fa, *fs;
    int files = 0;
    char file_app[SLEN];
    char file_src[SLEN];
    puts("Enter name of destination file:");
    gets(file_app);
    if ((fa = fopen(file_app, "a")) == NULL)
    {
        fprintf(stderr, "Can't open %s\n", file_app);
        exit(2);
    }
    if (setvbuf(fa, NULL, _IOFBF, BUFSIZE) != 0)
    {
        fputs("Can't create output buffer\n", stderr);
        exit(3);
    }
    puts("Enter name of first source file (empty line to quit):");
    while (gets(file_src) && file_src[0] != '\0')
    {
        if (strcmp(file_src, file_app) == 0)
            fputs("Can't append file to itself\n",stderr);
        else if ((fs = fopen(file_src, "r")) == NULL)
            fprintf(stderr, "Can't open %s\n", file_src);
        else
        {
            if (setvbuf(fs, NULL, _IOFBF, BUFSIZE) != 0)
            {
                fputs("Can't create output buffer\n",stderr);
                continue;
            }
```

continued on next page

continued from previous page

```
            append(fs, fa);
            if (ferror(fs) != 0)
                fprintf(stderr,"Error in reading file %s.\n",
                        file_src);
            if (ferror(fa) != 0)
                fprintf(stderr,"Error in writing file %s.\n",
                        file_app);
            fclose(fs);
            files++;
            printf("File %s appended.\n", file_src);
            puts("Next file (empty line to quit):");
        }
    }
    printf("Done. %d files appended.\n", files);
    fclose(fa);
    return 0;
}

void append(FILE *source, FILE *dest)
{
    size_t bytes;
    extern char temp[]; /* use the external temp array */

    while ((bytes = fread(temp,sizeof(char),BUFSIZE,source)) > 0)
        fwrite(temp, sizeof (char), bytes, dest);
}
```

The following code creates a buffer 1024 bytes in size to be used with the append file:

```
if (setvbuf(fa, NULL, _IOFBF, BUFSIZE) != 0)
{
    fputs("Can't create output buffer\n", stderr);
    exit(3);
}
```

If setvbuf() is unable to create the buffer, it returns a non-zero value, and the code then terminates the program. Similar coding establishes a 1,024-byte buffer for the file currently being copied. By using NULL as the second argument to setvbuf(), we let that function allocate storage for the buffer.

This code prevents the program from trying to append a file to itself:

```
if (strcmp(file_src, file_app) == 0)
    fputs("Can't append file to itself\n",stderr);
```

The argument file_app represents the name of the destination file, and file_src represents the name of the file currently being processed.

The append() function does the copying. Instead of copying a byte at a time, it uses fread() and fwrite() to copy 1024 bytes at a time:

```
void append(source, dest)
FILE *source, *dest;
{
    size_t bytes;
    extern char temp[];
```

```
    while ((bytes = fread(temp,sizeof(char),BUFSIZE,source)) > 0)
        fwrite(temp, sizeof (char), bytes, dest);
}
```

Because the file specified by **dest** is opened in the append mode, each source file is added to the end of the destination file, one after the other.

The example uses text-mode files; by using the "**ab**" and "**rb**" modes, it could handle binary files.

Random Access with Binary I/O

Random access is most often used with binary files written using binary I/O, so let's look at a short example. The program in Listing 12.7 creates a file of **double** numbers, and then lets you access the contents.

Listing 12.7   The randbin.c program.

```
/* randbin.c -- random access, binary i/o */
#include <stdio.h>
#include <stdlib.h>
#define ARSIZE 1000
int main()
{
    double numbers[ARSIZE];
    double value;
    const char * file = "numbers.dat";
    int i;
    long pos;
    FILE *iofile;

    /* create a set of double values */
    for(i = 0; i < ARSIZE; i++)
        numbers[i] = 100.0 * i + 1.0 / (i + 1);
    if ((iofile = fopen(file, "wb")) == NULL)
    {
        fprintf(stderr, "Could not open %s for output.\n", file);
        exit(1);
    }
    /* write array in binary format to file */
    fwrite(numbers, sizeof (double), ARSIZE, iofile);
    fclose(iofile);
    if ((iofile = fopen(file, "rb")) == NULL)
    {
        fprintf(stderr,
            "Could not open %s for random access.\n", file);
        exit(1);
    }
    /* read selected items from file */
    printf("Enter an index in the range 0-%d.\n", ARSIZE - 1);
    scanf("%d", &i);
    while (i >= 0 && i < ARSIZE)
    {
```

continued on next page

continued from previous page

```
            pos = (long) i * sizeof(double); /* find offset */
            fseek(iofile, pos, SEEK_SET);     /* go there    */
            fread(&value, sizeof (double), 1, iofile);
            printf("The value there is %f.\n", value);
            printf("Next index (out of range to quit):\n");
            scanf("%d", &i);
        }
        fclose(iofile);
        puts("Bye!");
        return 0;
    }
```

First, the program creates an array and places some values into it. Then it creates a file called numbers.dat in binary mode and uses fwrite() to copy the array contents to the file. The 64-bit pattern for each double value is copied from memory to the file. You can't read the resulting binary file with a text editor because the values are not translated to strings. However, each value is stored in the file precisely as it was stored in memory, so there is no loss of precision. Furthermore, each value occupies exactly 64 bits of storage in the file, so it is a simple matter to calculate the location of each value.

The second part of the program opens the file for reading and asks the user to enter the index for a value. Multiplying the index by the number of bytes per double yields the location in the file. The program then uses fseek() to go to that location and fread() to read the value there. Note that there are no format specifiers. Instead, fread() copies the 8 bytes starting at that location into the memory location indicated by &value. Then it can use printf() to display value. Here is a sample run:

```
Enter an index in the range 0-999.
500
The value there is 50000.001996.
Next index (out of range to quit):
900
The value there is 90000.001110.
Next index (out of range to quit):
0
The value there is 1.000000.
Next index (out of range to quit):
-1
Bye!
```

Chapter Summary

Writing to and reading from files is essential for most C programs. Most C implementations offer both low-level I/O services and standard high-level I/O services for these purposes. Because the ANSI C library includes the standard I/O services but not the low-level services, the standard package is more portable.

The standard I/O package automatically creates input and output buffers to speed up data transfer. The fopen() function opens a file for standard I/O and creates a data structure designed to hold information about the file and the buffer. The fopen() function returns a pointer to that data structure, and this pointer is used by other functions to identify the file to be processed. The `feof()` and `ferror()` functions report the reason an I/O operation failed.

ANSI C provides two file-opening modes: binary and text. When a file is opened in binary mode, it can be read byte-for-byte. When a file is opened in text mode, its contents may be mapped from the system representation of text to the C representation. For UNIX systems, the two modes are identical because the C model for text files is derived from the UNIX file model.

The input functions `getc()`, `fgets()`, `fscanf()`, and `fread()` normally read a file sequentially, starting at the beginning of the file. However, the `fseek()` and `ftell()` functions let a program move to an arbitrary position in a file, enabling random access. The `fgetpos()` and `fsetpos()` extend similar capabilities to larger files. Random access works better in the binary than in the text mode.

Review Questions

1. What's wrong with this program?

```
int main(void)
{
    int * fp;
    int k;

    fp = fopen("gelatin");
    for (k = 0; k < 30; k++)
        fputs(fp, "Nanette eats gelatin.");
    fclose("gelatin");
    return 0;
}
```

2. What would the following program do? (Mac users can assume the program correctly uses `console.h` and the `ccommand()` function.)

```
#include <stdio.h>
#include <stdlib.h>
#include <ctype.h>
int main(int argc, char *argv[])
{
    int ch;
    FILE *fp;

    if ( (fp = fopen(argv[1], "r")) == NULL)
        exit(1);
    while ( (ch= getc(fp)) != EOF )
        if( isdigit(ch) )
            putchar(ch);
    fclose (fp);
    return 0;
}
```

3. Suppose you have these statements in a program:

```
#include <stdio.h>
FILE * fp1,* fp2;
char ch;

fp1 = fopen("terky", "r");
fp2 = fopen("jerky", "w");
```

Also, suppose that both files were opened successfully. Supply the missing arguments in the following function calls:

a. `ch = getc();`

b. `fprintf( ,"%c\n", );`

c. `putc( , );`

d. `fclose(); /* close the terky file */`

4. Write a program that takes zero command-line arguments or one command-line argument. If there is one argument, it is interpreted as the name of a file. If there is no argument, the standard input (**stdin**) is to be used for input. Assume that the input consists entirely of floating-point numbers. Have the program calculate and report the arithmetic mean (the average) of the input numbers.

5. Write a program that takes two command-line arguments. The first is a character, and the second is a filename. The program should print only those lines in the file containing the given character.

Note

Lines in a file are identified by a terminating '\n'. Assume that no line is more than 256 characters long. You might want to use `fgets()`.

6. What's the difference between binary files and text files on the one hand versus binary streams and text streams on the other?

7. What is the difference between

a. Saving **8238201** by using **fprintf()** and saving it by using **fwrite()**?

b. Saving the character *S* by using **putc()** and saving it by using **fwrite()**?

8. What's the difference among the following?

```
printf("Hello, %s\n", name);
```

```
fprintf(stdout, "Hello, %s, name);
fprintf(stderr, "Hello, %s, name);
```

9. The "a+", "r+", and "w+" modes all open files for both reading and writing. Which one is best suited for altering material already present in a
   file?

Programming Exercises

1. Write a file copy program that takes the original filename and the copy
   file from the command line. Use standard I/O and the binary mode, if
   possible.

2. Write a program that sequentially displays onscreen all the files listed in
   the command line. Use **argc** to control a loop.

3. Modify the program in Listing 12.6 so that it uses a command-line interface instead of an interactive interface.

4. Programs using command-line arguments rely on the user's memory of
   how to use them correctly. Rewrite the program in Listing 12.2 so that,
   instead of using command-line arguments, it prompts the user for the
   required information.

5. Write a program that opens two files whose names are provided by
   command-line arguments.

   a. Have the program print line 1 of the first file, line 1 of the second
      file, line 2 of the first file, line 2 of the second file, and so on, until
      the last line of the longer file (in terms of lines) is printed.

   b. Modify the program so that lines with the same line number are
      printed on the same line.

6. Write a program that takes as command-line arguments a character and
   zero or more filenames. If no arguments follow the character, have the
   program read the standard input. Otherwise, have it open each file in
   turn and report how many times the character appears in each file. The
   filename and the character itself should be reported along with the count.
   Include error-checking to see whether the number of arguments is correct
   and whether the files can be opened. If a file can't be opened, have the
   program report that fact and go on to the next file.

7. Modify the program in Listing 12.3 so that each word is numbered
   according to the order in which it was added to the list, starting with 1.
   Make sure that, when the program is run a second time, new word numbering resumes where the previous numbering left off.

8. Write a program that opens a text file whose name is obtained interactively. Set up a loop that asks the user to enter a file position. The program then prints the part of the file starting at that position and proceeding to the next newline character. Let non-numeric input terminate the user-input loop.

9. Write a program that takes two command-line arguments. The first is a string; the second is the name of a file. The program should then search the file, printing all lines containing the string. Because this task is line-oriented rather than character-oriented, use `fgets()` instead of `getc()`. Use the standard C library function `strstr()` (briefly described in Exercise 7, Chapter 11) to search each line for the string.

10. Write a function that reads one word from a file, leaving the boundary character (a tab, space, or newline) in the input buffer. Don't use `scanf()` or `fscanf()`.

11. Create a text file consisting of 20 rows of 30 integers. The integers should be in the range 0–9 and be separated by spaces. The file is a digital representation of a picture, with the values **0** through **9** representing increasing levels of darkness. Write a program that reads the contents of the file into a 20-by-30 array of `int`. In a crude approach toward converting this digital representation to a picture, have the program use the values in this array to initialize a 20-by-31 array of `char`, with a **0** value corresponding to a space character, a **1** value to the period character, and so on, which each larger number represented by a character that occupies more space. For example, you might use # to represent 9. The last character (the 31st) in each row should be a null character, making it an array of 20 strings. Have the program display the resulting picture (that is, print the strings) and also store the result in a text file. For example, suppose you start with this data:

```
0 0 9 0 0 0 0 0 0 0 0 5 8 9 9 8 5 2 0 0 0 0 0 0 0 0 0 0 0 0
0 0 0 0 9 0 0 0 0 0 0 5 8 9 9 8 5 5 2 0 0 0 0 0 0 0 0 0 0 0
0 0 0 0 0 0 0 0 0 0 0 5 8 1 9 8 5 4 5 2 0 0 0 0 0 0 0 0 0 0
0 0 0 0 9 0 0 0 0 0 0 5 8 9 9 8 5 0 4 5 2 0 0 0 0 0 0 0 0 0
0 0 9 0 0 0 0 0 0 0 0 5 8 9 9 8 5 0 0 4 5 2 0 0 0 0 0 0 0 0
0 0 0 0 0 0 0 0 0 0 0 5 8 9 1 8 5 0 0 0 4 5 2 0 0 0 0 0 0 0
0 0 0 0 0 0 0 0 0 0 0 5 8 9 9 8 5 0 0 0 0 4 5 2 0 0 0 0 0 0
5 5 5 5 5 5 5 5 5 5 5 5 8 9 9 8 5 5 5 5 5 5 5 5 5 5 5 5 5 5
8 8 8 8 8 8 8 8 8 8 8 5 8 9 9 8 5 8 8 8 8 8 8 8 8 8 8 8 8 8
9 9 9 9 0 9 9 9 9 9 9 9 9 9 9 9 9 9 9 9 9 3 9 9 9 9 9 9 9 9
8 8 8 8 8 8 8 8 8 8 8 5 8 9 9 8 5 8 8 8 8 8 8 8 8 8 8 8 8 8
5 5 5 5 5 5 5 5 5 5 5 5 8 9 9 8 5 5 5 5 5 5 5 5 5 5 5 5 5 5
0 0 0 0 0 0 0 0 0 0 0 5 8 9 9 8 5 0 0 0 0 0 0 0 0 0 0 0 0 0
0 0 0 0 0 0 0 0 0 0 0 5 8 9 9 8 5 0 0 0 6 6 0 0 0 0 0 0 0 0
0 0 0 0 2 2 0 0 0 0 0 5 8 9 9 8 5 0 0 5 6 0 0 6 5 0 0 0 0 0
0 0 0 0 3 3 0 0 0 0 0 5 8 9 9 8 5 0 5 6 1 1 1 1 6 5 0 0 0 0
0 0 0 0 4 4 0 0 0 0 0 5 8 9 9 8 5 0 0 5 6 0 0 6 5 0 0 0 0 0
0 0 0 0 5 5 0 0 0 0 0 5 8 9 9 8 5 0 0 0 6 6 0 0 0 0 0 0 0 0
```

```
0 0 0 0 0 0 0 0 0 0 0 5 8 9 9 8 5 0 0 0 0 0 0 0 0 0 0 0
0 0 0 0 0 0 0 0 0 0 0 5 8 9 9 8 5 0 0 0 0 0 0 0 0 0 0 0
```

The output could look like this:
```
    #              *%##%*'
      #            *%##%**'
                   *%.#%*~*'
      #            *%##%*  ~*'
    #              *%##%*   ~*'
                   *%#.%*    ~*'
                   *%##%*      ~*'
    ***************%##%**************
    %%%%%%%%%%%%*%##%*%%%%%%%%%%%%%%
    #### ################:#######
    %%%%%%%%%%%%*%##%*%%%%%%%%%%%%%%
    ***************%##%**************
                   *%##%*
                   *%##%*        ==
         ' '       *%##%*    *=   =*
         : :       *%##%*    *=....=*
         ~~        *%##%*    *=   =*
         * *       *%##%*        ==
                   *%##%*
                   *%##%*
```

12. Digital images, particularly those radioed back from spacecraft, may have glitches. Add a deglitching function to Programming Exercise 11. It should compare each value to its immediate neighbors to the left and right, above and below. If the value differs by more than 1 from each of its neighbors, replace the value with the average of the neighboring values. You should round the average to the nearest integer value. Note that the points along the boundaries have fewer than four neighbors, so they require special handling.

CHAPTER 13

STORAGE CLASSES AND PROGRAM DEVELOPMENT

You will learn about the following in this chapter:

- Keywords

  auto, extern, static
  register, const, volatile

- Function

  rand()

*I*n this chapter, you learn how C allows you to determine the scope of a variable (how widely known it is) and the lifetime of a variable (how long it remains in existence). Also, you gain experience in designing more complex programs.

One of C's strengths is that it enables you to control a program's fine points. C's storage classes exemplify that control by letting you determine which functions know which variables and for how long a variable persists in a program. Using storage classes is one more element of program design. There is more to programming than just knowing the rules of the language, just as there is more to writing a novel (or even a memo) than knowing the rules of English. In this chapter, we reinforce some of the general principles and concepts of program design introduced earlier. We also develop several useful functions. As we do so, we try to demonstrate some of the general considerations that go into designing a function. In particular, we emphasize the value of a modular approach—the division of a job into smaller, more manageable tasks.

Storage Classes and Scope

We gave storage classes a passing mention in Chapter 10, "Arrays and Pointers," but let's take a more in-depth look now. As mentioned in Chapter 10, *local variables* are known only to the functions containing them. However, C also offers the possibility of *global variables*, those known to several functions. Suppose you want both main() and critic() to have access to the variable Units. You can do this by declaring Units so that it belongs to the external storage class, as shown in Listing 13.1. (Here we follow a common, but not universal, convention of uppercasing the first character of a global variable name.)

Listing 13.1   The global.c program.

```
/* global.c  -- uses an external variable */
#include <stdio.h>
int Units;                    /* an external variable    */
void critic(void);
int main(void)
{
    extern int Units;         /* an optional redeclaration */

    printf("How many pounds to a firkin of butter?\n");
    scanf("%d", &Units);
    while ( Units != 56)
        critic();
    printf("You must have looked it up!\n");
    return 0;
}
void critic(void)
{
    /* optional redeclaration omitted */
    printf("No luck, chummy. Try again.\n");
    scanf("%d", &Units);
}
```

Here is a sample output:

```
How many pounds to a firkin of butter?
14
No luck, chummy. Try again.
56
You must have looked it up!
```

(We did.)

Note how the second value for Units was read by the critic() function, yet main() also knew the new value when it finished the while loop. We made Units an external variable by defining it outside of (external to) any function definition. That's all you need to do to make Units available to all the subsequent functions in the file.

There are three ways to treat Units within a function. The simplest is to have no further declarations. In that case, the function uses the externally defined Units by default; critic() does this.

The second way, and the one main() took, is to place the following declaration in the function:

```
extern int Units;
```

In the example, inserting this declaration is mainly a matter of documentation. It tells the compiler that any mention of Units in this particular function refers to a variable defined outside the function, perhaps even outside the file. Again, both functions use the externally defined Units.

The third way, and one quite different in meaning, is to use this declaration in the functions:

```
int Units;
```

Suppose you do this for `main()` but not for `critic()`. Omitting the keyword `extern` causes the compiler to create a *separate* variable private to `main()`, but also named `Units`. The new `Units` would be visible while `main()` is running, but when control passes to `critic()`, the program would interpret `Units` as the externally defined one, and the value assigned to `Units` in `main()` would not affect the value of `Units` in `critic()`.

Each variable, as you know, has a type. In addition, each variable has a storage class. There are four keywords used to describe storage classes: `extern` (for external), `auto` (for automatic), `static`, and `register`. Variables declared within a function are considered to be class `auto` unless declared otherwise. The formal arguments to functions normally are class `auto`, but they can be made class `register`.

A variable's storage class is determined by where it is defined and by what keyword, if any, is used. The storage class determines three things. First, it controls which functions in a file have access to a variable. If a section of code can use a particular variable, we say the variable is visible in that section. A variable's visibility to the parts of a program is its *scope*. Second, the storage class determines in how many places the same variable can be declared; this property is described by a variable's *linkage*. Finally, the storage class specifies how long the variable persists in memory—its storage *duration*. Let's look at each of these terms briefly, then see how they relate to the different storage types.

Scope, Linkage, and Storage Duration

A C variable has one of the following three scopes: *file scope*, *block scope*, or *function prototype scope*. A variable with file scope is visible from the point it is defined to the end of the file containing the definition. For instance, the variable `Units` in Listing 13.1 has file scope, and it's visible to all the functions following its definition.

A variable with block scope is visible from the point it is defined until the end of the block containing the definition. (A block, recall, is marked by braces.) The local variables we've used to date, including formal function arguments, have block scope. Indeed, block scope is what makes them local, confining them to the functions in which they are defined. The function body is considered to be the block containing the formal function arguments. Therefore, the variables `cleo` and `patrick` in the following code both have block scope extending to the closing brace:

```
double blocky(double cleo)
{
    double patrick = 0.0;
    ...
    return patrick;
}
```

Function prototype scope applies to variable names used in function prototypes, as in the following:

```
int mighty(int mouse, double large);
```

Function prototype scope runs from the point the variable is defined to the end of the prototype declaration. What this means is that all the compiler cares about when handling a function prototype arguments are the types; the names you use, if any, don't matter.

A C variable has one of the following linkages: *external linkage, internal linkage,* or *no linkage.* A variable with external linkage can be used anywhere in a multifile program. A variable with internal linkage can be used anywhere in a single file, and a variable with no linkage can be used only in the block where it is defined. Variables with internal or external linkage can appear in more than one declaration, but variables with no linkage can be declared only once.

As you may have noticed, the concepts of linkage and scope are related. Variables with block scope or function prototype scope have no linkage, which is why the descriptions of no linkage and block scope are similar. As you'll see later, you can use the concepts of internal and external linkage to divide variables with file scope into two groups.

A C variable has one of the following two storage durations: *static storage duration* or *automatic storage duration.* If a variable has static storage duration, it exists throughout program execution. External variables, such as `Units` from Listing 13.1, have static storage duration. A variable with automatic storage duration is guaranteed to exist only while the program is executing the block where the variable is defined. The local variables we've used so far fall into this category. For instance, in the following code, the variables `number` and `index` come into being each time the `bore()` function is called and pass away each time the function completes:

```
void bore(int number)
{
    int index;
    for (index = 0; index < number; index++)
        puts("They don't make them the way they used to.\n");
    return 0;
}
```

Now let's discuss C's storage classes in more detail.

Automatic Variables

By default, variables declared in a function are automatic. You can, however, make your intentions perfectly clear by explicitly using the keyword `auto`, as shown here:

```
int main(void)
{
  auto int plox;
```

You might do this, for example, to document that you are intentionally overriding an external function definition or that it is important not to change the variable to another storage class.

An automatic variable has block scope. Only the function in which the variable is defined can access that variable by name. (Of course, arguments can be used to communicate the variable's value and address to another function, but that is indirect knowledge.) Another function can use a variable with the same name, but it will be an independent variable stored in a different memory location.

An automatic variable has no linkage. You can't declare it twice in the same block. You can declare variables having the same name but existing in different blocks, but they would be separate, independent variables with no links between them.

An automatic variable has automatic storage duration. It comes into existence when the function that contains it is called. When the function finishes its task and returns control to its caller, the automatic variable disappears. Its memory location can now be used for something else.

One more point about the scope of an automatic variable: Its scope is confined to the block (paired braces) where the variable is declared. We have always declared variables at the beginning of the function block, so the scope is the whole function, but in principle you could declare a variable within a sub-block. Then that variable would be known only to that subsection of the function. Here's an example:

```c
int loop(int n)
{
    int m;
    scanf("%d", &m);
    {
        int i;    /* local to this sub-block */
        for (i = m; i < n; i++)
            puts("i is local to a sub-block\n");
    }
    return m;
}
```

In this code, i is visible only within the inner braces. You'd get a compiler error if you tried to use it before or after the inner block. Normally, you wouldn't use this feature when designing a program. Sometimes, however, it is useful to define a variable in a sub-block if it is not used elsewhere. In that way, you can document the meaning of a variable close to where it is used. Also, the variable doesn't sit unused, occupying memory when it is no longer needed.

What if you reuse a name? Then the name defined inside the block is the variable used inside the block. We say it *hides* the outer definition, but when execution exits the inner block, the outer variable comes back into scope. Listing 13.2 illustrates these points and more.

Listing 13.2   The hiding.c program.

```c
/* hiding.c -- variables in blocks */
#include <stdio.h>
int main()
{
    int x = 30;
    printf("x in outer block: %d\n", x);
    {
        int x = 77;   /* new x, hides first x */
        printf("x in inner block: %d\n", x);
    }
    printf("x in outer block: %d\n", x);
    while (x++ < 33)
    {
        int x = 100;  /* new x, hides first x */
        x++;
        printf("x in while loop: %d\n", x);
    }
    return 0;
}
```

Here's the output:

```
x in outer block: 30
x in inner block: 77
x in outer block: 30
x in while loop: 101
x in while loop: 101
x in while loop: 101
```

First, the program creates an x with the value 30, as the first printf() statement shows. Then it defines a new x with the value of 77, as the second printf() statement shows. That it is a new variable hiding the first x is shown by the third printf() statement. It is located after the first inner block, and it displays the original x value, showing that the original x variable never went away and never got changed.

Perhaps the most intriguing part of the program is the while loop. The while loop test uses the original x:

```
while(x++ < 33)
```

Inside the loop, however, the program sees a third x variable, one defined just inside the while loop block. So when the code uses x++ in the body of the loop, it is the new x that is incremented to 101, and then displayed. When each loop cycle is completed, that new x disappears. Then the loop test condition uses and increments the original x, the loop block is entered again, and the new x is created again. In this example, that x is created and destroyed three times. Note that, to terminate, this loop had to increment x in the test condition because incrementing x in the body increments a different x than the one used for the test.

The intent of this example is not to encourage you to write code like this. Rather, it is to illustrate what happens when you define variables inside a block.

Initialization of Automatic Variables

Automatic variables are not initialized unless you do so explicitly. Consider the following declarations:

```
int main(void)
{
  int repid;
  int tents = 5;
```

The tents variable is initialized to 5; but the repid variable winds up with whatever value happened to previously occupy the space assigned to repid. You cannot rely on this value being 0.

External Variables

A variable defined outside a function is external. As a matter of documentation, an external variable can also be declared inside a function that uses it by using the extern keyword. If the variable is defined in *another* file, declaring the variable with extern is mandatory. Declarations look like this:

```
int Errupt;           /* externally defined variable  */
double Up[100];       /* externally defined array      */
extern char Coal;     /* mandatory declaration         */
                      /* Coal defined in another file  */
void next(void);
int main(void)
{
  extern int Errupt;  /* optional declaration          */

  extern double Up[]; /* optional declaration          */
  ...
}
void next(void)
{
  ...
}
```

The two declarations of `Errupt` are examples of linkage, for they both refer to the same variable. External variables have external linkage, a point we'll return to later.

Note that you don't have to give the array size in the optional declaration of `double Up`. That's because the original declaration already supplied that information. The group of `extern` declarations inside `main()` can be omitted entirely because external variables have file scope, so they are known from the point of declaration to the end of the file.

If only the `extern` is omitted from the declaration inside a function, then a separate automatic variable is set up. That is, replacing

```
extern int Errupt;
```

with

```
int Errupt;
```

in `main()` causes the compiler to create an automatic variable named `Errupt`. It would be a separate, local variable, distinct from the original `Errupt`. The local variable would be in scope while the program executes `main()`, but the external `Errupt` would be in scope for other functions, such as `next()`, in the same file. In short, a variable in block scope "hides" a variable of the same name in file scope while the program executes statements in the block.

External variables have static storage duration. Therefore, the array `double_Up` maintains its existence and values regardless of whether the program is executing `main()`, `next()`, or some other function.

The following three examples show four possible combinations of external and automatic variables. In Example 1, there is one external variable: `Hocus`. It is known to both `main()` and `magic()`.

```
/* Example 1 */
int Hocus;
int magic();
int main(void)
{
    extern int Hocus;  /* Hocus declared external */
    ...
}
```

```
int magic()
{
   extern int Hocus;
   ...
}
```

Example 2 has one external variable, `Hocus`, known to both functions. This time, `magic()` knows it by default.

```
/* Example 2 */
int Hocus;
int magic();
int main(void)
{
   extern int Hocus;   /* Hocus declared external */
   ...
}
int magic()
{
                      /* Hocus not declared at all */
   ...
}
```

In Example 3, four separate variables are created. The `Hocus` in `main()` is automatic by default and is local to `main`. The `Hocus` in `magic()` is automatic explicitly and is known only to `magic()`. The external `Hocus` is not known to `main()` or `magic()` but would be known to any other function in the file that did not have its own local `Hocus`. Finally, `Pocus` is an external variable known to `magic()` but not to `main()` because `Pocus` follows `main()`.

```
/* Example 3 */
int Hocus;
int magic();
int main(void)
{
   int Hocus;        /* Hocus declared, is auto by default */
   ...
}
int Pocus;
int magic()
{
   auto int Hocus;   /* Hocus declared automatic          */
   ...
}
```

These examples illustrate the scope of external variables. They also illustrate the lifetimes of variables. The external `Hocus` and `Pocus` variables persist as long as the program runs, and, because they aren't confined to any one function, they don't fade away when a particular function returns.

Note

If you use the keyword `extern` without a type, the compiler interprets it as being `extern int`.

Initializing External Variables

Like automatic variables, external variables can be initialized explicitly. Unlike automatic variables, external variables are automatically initialized to zero if you don't initialize them. This rule applies to elements of an externally defined array, too.

External Names

The rules for names of external variables are more restrictive than for local variables. The reason is that external names need to comply with the rules of the local environment, which may be more limiting. For local names, the ANSI C standard requires that a compiler distinguish between uppercase and lowercase and that it recognize the first 31 characters in a name. For external variables, the compiler does not need to distinguish between uppercase and lowercase, and it need recognize only the first 6 characters in a name. These rules apply to function names, too. The preceding limitations stem from the desire to make C programs compatible with some of the older, more limited operating systems and languages.

The C9X committee feels that it is now time to break the shackles of the past; it proposes that compilers recognize the first 63 characters for local identifiers and the first 31 characters for external identifiers.

Definitions and Declarations

There is a difference between defining a variable and declaring it. Consider this example:

```
int tern;              /* tern defined              */
main()
{
     external int tern;  /* use a tern defined elsewhere */
```

Here `tern` is declared twice. The first declaration causes storage to be set aside for the variable. It constitutes a definition of the variable. The second declaration merely tells the compiler to use the `tern` variable that has been created previously, so it is not a definition. The first declaration is called a *defining declaration,* and the second is called a *referencing declaration.* The keyword `extern` *always* indicates that a declaration is not a definition because it instructs the compiler to look elsewhere.

Suppose you do this:

```
extern int tern;
int main(void)
{
```

Then the compiler assumes that the actual definition of `tern` is somewhere else in your program, perhaps in another file. This declaration does not cause space to be allocated. Therefore, don't use the keyword `extern` to create an external definition; use it only to *refer* to an existing external definition.

An external variable can be initialized only once, and that must occur when the variable is defined. A statement like

```
extern char permis = 'Y';   /* error */
```

is in error because the presence of the keyword `extern` signifies a referencing declaration, not a defining declaration.

Static Variables

The name *static variable* sounds like a contradiction, like a variable that can't vary. Actually, "static" means that the variable stays put. These variables have the same scope as automatic variables, but they don't vanish when the containing function ends its job. That is, static storage class variables have block scope, but static storage duration. The computer remembers their values from one function call to the next. The example in Listing 13.3 illustrates this point and shows how to declare a static variable.

Listing 13.3   The static.c program.

```
/* static.c -- using a static variable */
#include <stdio.h>
void trystat(void);
int main(void)
{
    int count;

    for (count = 1; count <= 3; count++)
    {
        printf("Here comes iteration %d:\n", count);
        trystat();
    }
    return 0;
}
void trystat(void)
{
    int fade = 1;
    static int stay = 1;

    printf("fade = %d and stay = %d\n", fade++, stay++);
}
```

Note that trystat() increments each variable after printing its value. Running the program gives this output:

```
Here comes iteration 1:
fade = 1 and stay = 1
Here comes iteration 2:
fade = 1 and stay = 2
Here comes iteration 3:
fade = 1 and stay = 3
```

The static variable stay remembers that its value was increased by 1, but the fade variable starts anew each time. This points out a difference in initialization: fade is initialized each time trystat() is called, but stay is initialized just once, when trystat() is compiled. Like external variables, static variables are initialized to zero if you don't explicitly initialize them to some other value.

The two declarations look similar:

```
int fade = 1;
static int stay = 1;
```

However, the first statement is really part of the `trystat()` function and is executed each time the function is called. It is a runtime action. The second statement isn't actually part of the `trystat()` function. If you use a debugger to execute the program step-by-step, you'll see that the program seems to skip that step. That's because static variables and external variables are already in place after a program is loaded into memory. Placing the statement in the `trystat()` function tells the compiler that only the `trystat()` function is allowed to see the variable; it's not a statement that's executed during runtime.

External Static Variables

You can also declare a `static` variable outside all functions. This creates an *external static variable*. The difference between an ordinary external variable and an external static variable lies in its linkage (see Figure 13.1). The ordinary external variable can be used by functions in any file, but the external static variable can be used only by functions in the same file. In other words, an ordinary external variable has external linkage, but a static external variable has internal linkage. You set up an external static variable by placing the definition outside all functions and by using the keyword `static` in that definition:

```
static int randx = 1;
int rand()
{
```

Later on, Listing 13.4 shows an example with a static variable.

file 1

```
int twit;

static int turn;

int main(void)

  {

  - - -

  - - -

  }

int figaro(void)

  {

  - - -

  - - -

  }
```

file 2

```
extern int twit:

int hedge(void)

  {

  - - -

  - - -

  }

void mostly(char*)

  {

  - - -

  - - -

  }
```

Figure 13.1 External variable versus external static variable.

Multiple Files

Complex C programs often use several separate files of code. Sometimes these files might need to share an external variable. The ANSI C way to do this is to have a defining declaration in one file and referencing declarations in the other files. That is, all but one declaration (the defining declaration) should use the `extern` keyword, and only the defining declaration can be used to initialize the variable.

Note that an external variable defined in one file is not available to a second file unless it is also declared (by using `extern`) in the second file. An external declaration by itself only makes a variable potentially available to other files.

Historically, however, many compilers have followed different rules in this regard. Many UNIX systems, for example, enable you to declare a variable in several files without using the `extern` keyword, provided that no more than one declaration includes an initialization. If there is a declaration with an initialization, it is taken to be the definition.

Scope and Functions

Functions, too, have storage classes. A function can be either external (the default) or static. An external function can be accessed by functions in other files, but a static function can be used only within the defining file. Consider, for example, a file containing these function declarations:

```
double gamma();          /* external by default */
static double beta();
extern double delta();
```

The functions `gamma()` and `delta()` can be used by functions in other files that are part of the program, but `beta()` cannot. Because this `beta()` is restricted to one file, you can use a different function having the same name in the other files. One reason to use the `static` storage class is to create functions that are private to a particular module, thereby avoiding the possibility of name conflicts.

We recommend that you use the `extern` keyword when declaring functions defined in other files. This practice is mostly a matter of clarity because a function declaration is assumed to be `extern` unless the keyword `static` is used.

Register Variables

Variables are normally stored in computer memory. With luck, register variables are stored in the CPU registers or, more generally, in the fastest memory available, where they can be accessed and manipulated more rapidly than regular variables. In other respects, register variables are the same as automatic variables. They are declared this way:

```
int main(void)
{
    register int quick;
```

We say "with luck" because declaring a variable as register class is more a request than a direct order. The compiler has to weigh your demands against the number of registers or amount of fast memory available, so you might not get your wish. In that case, the variable becomes an ordinary automatic variable.

You can request that formal parameters be register variables. Just use the keyword in the function heading:

```
void macho(register int n)
```

The types that can be declared `register` may be restricted. For example, the registers in a processor might not be large enough to hold type `double`. Also, the `&` operator does not work with `register` variables.

Summary: Scopes

Automatic variables have block scope, no linking, and automatic storage duration. They are local and private to the block (typically a function) where they are defined. When a variable is declared external to any function in a file, it's an external variable and has file scope, external linking, and static storage duration. An external variable will be known to all functions following it in that file, whether or not those functions explicitly declare the variable as `extern`. If you want a function in a second file to access an external variable in the first file, you must declare the variable in the second file by using the keyword `extern`.

A static variable is defined inside a function by using the keyword `static`. It is local to that function. It has block scope, no linkage, and static storage duration. A static external variable is defined outside a function by using the keyword `static`. It has file scope, internal linking, and static storage duration. A static external variable is local to its file.

Which Storage Class?

The answer to the question "Which storage class?" is most often "automatic." After all, why else was automatic selected as the default? Yes, we know that at first glance external storage is quite alluring. Just make all your variables external, and you never have to worry about using arguments and pointers to communicate between functions. There is a subtle pitfall, however. You will have to worry about function `A()` sneakily altering the variables used in function `B()`, despite your intentions to the contrary. The unquestionable evidence of untold years of collective computer experience is that this one subtle danger far outweighs the superficial attraction of using external storage indiscriminately.

One of the golden rules of protective programming is the "need to know" principle. Keep the inner workings of each function as private to that function as possible, sharing only those variables that need to be shared. The other classes are useful, and they are available. Before using one, though, ask yourself if it is necessary.

General Comments:

The storage class of a variable determines its scope, its linkage, and its storage duration. Storage class is determined both by where the variable is defined and by its associated keyword. Variables defined outside all functions are external, have file scope, external linkage, and static storage duration. Variables declared inside a function are automatic unless one of the other keywords is used. They have block scope, no linkage, and automatic storage duration. Variables defined with the keyword static inside a function have block scope, no linkage, and static storage duration. Variables defined with the keyword static outside a function have file scope, internal linkage, and static storage duration.

Properties:

In the following list, those variables in storage classes above the dotted line are declared inside a function; those below the line are defined outside a function.

Storage Class	Keyword	Duration	Scope and Linkage
automatic	auto	temporary	local
register	register	temporary	local
static	static	persistent	local
external	extern*	persistent	global (all files)
external	static	persistent	global (one file)
static			

The keyword extern is used only to redeclare variables that have been defined externally elsewhere. The act of defining the variable outside a function makes it external.

A Random Number Function

Now let's look at a function that makes use of an external static variable: a random number function. The ANSI C library provides the rand() function to generate random numbers. There are a variety of algorithms for generating random numbers, and ANSI C enables implementors to choose the best algorithm for a particular machine. However, the ANSI C standard also supplies a standard, portable algorithm that produces the same random numbers on different systems. Actually, rand() is a "pseudorandom number generator," meaning that the actual sequence of numbers is predictable (computers are not known for their spontaneity), but the numbers are spread pretty uniformly over the possible range of values.

Instead of using your compiler's built-in `rand()` function, we'll use the portable ANSI version so that you can see what goes on inside. The scheme starts with a number called the "seed." The function uses the seed to produce a new number, which becomes the new seed. Then the new seed can be used to produce a newer seed, and so on. For this scheme to work, the random number function must remember the seed it used the last time it was called. Aha! This calls for a static variable. Listing 13.4 is version 0. (Yes, version 1 comes soon.)

Listing 13.4 The `and0.c` function file.

```
/* rand0.c -- produces random numbers        */
/*               uses ANSI C portable algorithm  */
static unsigned long int next = 1;  /* the seed   */
int rand0(void)
{
/* magic formula to generate pseudorandom number */
    next = next * 1103515245 + 12345;
    return (unsigned int) (next/65536) % 32768;
}
```

In Listing 13.4 the static variable **next** starts with the value 1 and is altered by the magic formula each time the function is called. The result is a return value somewhere in the range of 0 to 32767. Note that **next** is external static, rather than merely static. That's because the example will be expanded later so that **next** is shared between two functions in the same file.

Let's try the `rand0()` function with the simple driver shown in Listing 13.5.

Listing 13.5 The `r_drive1.c` driver.

```
/* r_drive1.c -- test the rand0() function */
/* compile with rand0.c               */
#include <stdio.h>
extern int rand0(void);
int main(void)
{
    int count;

    for (count = 0; count < 5; count++)
        printf("%hd\n", rand0());
    return 0;
}
```

Here's a good chance to practice using multiple files. Use one file for Listing 13.4 and one for Listing 13.5. (See Chapter 9, "Functions," or your compiler manual for guidance.) The **extern** keyword reminds you that `rand0()` is defined in a separate file.

The output is this:

```
16838
5758
10113
17515
31051
```

The output looks random, but let's run it again. This time the result is as follows:

```
16838
5758
10113
17515
31051
```

Hmmm, that looks familiar; this is the "pseudo" aspect. Each time the main program is run, you start with the same seed of 1. You can get around this problem by introducing a second function srand1() that enables you to reset the seed. The trick is to make **next** an external static variable known only to **rand1()** and **srand1()**. (The C library equivalent to **srand1()** is called **srand()**.) Keep **rand1()** and **srand1()** in their own file and compile that file separately. Listing 13.6 is the modification.

Listing 13.6 The s_and_r.c program.

```
/* s_and_r.c -- file for rand1() and srand1()   */
/*               uses ANSI C portable algorithm */
static unsigned long int next = 1;  /* the seed  */
int rand1(void)
{
/* magic formula to generate pseudorandom number */
    next = next * 1103515245 + 12345;
    return (unsigned int) (next/65536) % 32768;
}

void srand1(unsigned int seed)
{
    next = seed;
}
```

Notice that **next** is an external static variable. That means it can be used by both **rand1()** and **srand1()**, but not by functions in other files. To test these functions, use the driver in Listing 13.7.

Listing 13.7 The r_drive2.c program.

```
/* r_drive2.c -- test rand1() and srand1() */
/* compile with s_and_r.c                  */
#include <stdio.h>
extern void srand1(unsigned int x);
extern int rand1(void);
int main(void)
{
    int count;
    unsigned seed;
```

```
    printf("Please enter your choice for seed.\n");
    scanf("%u", &seed);
    srand1(seed);    /* reset seed */
    for (count = 0; count < 5; count++)
        printf("%hd\n", rand1());
    return 0;
}
```

Again, use two files. Run the program once.

```
Please enter your choice for seed.
1
16838
5758
10113
17515
31051
```

Using a value of 1 for **seed** yields the same values as before. Now let's try a value of 3:

```
Please enter your choice for seed.
3
17747
7107
10365
8312
20622
```

Very good! You get a different set of numbers.

Automated Reseeding

If your C implementation gives you access to some changing quantity, such as the system clock, you can use that value (possibly truncated) to initialize the seed value. For instance, ANSI C has a `time()` function that returns the system time. The time units are system dependent, but what matters here is that the return value is an arithmetic type and that its value changes with time. The exact type is system dependent and is given the label `time_t`, but you can use a type cast. Here's the basic setup:

```
#include <time.h>    /* ANSI prototype for clock() */
            srand1((unsigned int) time(0));    /* initialize seed */
```

In general, `time()` takes an argument that is the address of a type `time_t` object. In that case, the time value is also stored at that address. However, you can pass the null pointer (0) as an argument, in which case the value is supplied only through the return value mechanism.

You can use the same technique with the standard ANSI C functions `srand()` and `rand()`. If you do use these functions, include the `stdlib.h` header file. In fact, now that you've seen how `srand1()` and `rand1()` use an external static variable, you might as well use the versions your compiler supplies. We'll do that for the next example.

Roll 'Em

We are going to simulate that very popular random activity, dice-rolling. The most popular form of dice-rolling uses two six-sided dice, but there are other possibilities. Many adventure-fantasy games use all of the five geometrically possible dice: 4, 6, 8, 12, and 20 sides. Those clever ancient Greeks proved that there are but five regular solids having all faces the same shape and size, and these solids are the basis for the dice varieties. You could make dice with other numbers of sides, but the faces would not all be the same, so they wouldn't all have equal odds of turning up.

Computer calculations aren't limited by these geometric considerations, so we can devise an electronic die that has any number of sides. Let's start with six sides and then generalize.

We want a random number from 1 to 6. However, `rand()` produces an integer in the range 0 to `RAND_MAX`; `RAND_MAX` is defined in `stdlib.h`. It is typically `INT_MAX`. Therefore, we have some adjustments to make. Here's one approach:

1. Take the random number modulus 6. It produces an integer in the range 0 through 5.

2. Add 1. The new number is in the range 1 through 6.

3. To generalize, just replace the number 6 in step 1 by the number of sides.

Listing 13.8 shows a function that does these steps for a general number of sides. The listing includes some explicit type casts to emphasize where type conversions take place.

Listing 13.8   The `diceroll.c` file.

```
/* diceroll.c -- dice role simulation*/
#include <stdlib.h>   /* for rand() */
int rollem(int sides)
{
    int roll;

    roll = rand() % sides + 1;
    return roll;
}
```

Listing 13.9 shows a program that uses the `rand()`, `srand()`, and `rollem()` functions.

Listing 13.9   The `manydice.c` program.

```
/* manydice.c -- multiple dice roll */
/* compile with diceroll.c        */
#include <stdio.h>
#include <stdlib.h>   /* for srand() */
#include <time.h>     /* for time() */
extern int rollem(int);

int main(void)
{
  int dice, count, roll;
  int sides;
```

```
    srand((unsigned int) time(0));   /* randomize rand() */
    printf("Enter the number of sides per die, 0 to stop.\n");
    while (scanf("%d", &sides) == 1 && sides > 0)
    {
        printf("How many dice?\n");
        scanf("%d", &dice);
        for (roll = 0, count = 0; count < dice; count++)
            roll += rollem(sides);
            /* running total of dice pips */
        printf("You have rolled a %d using %d %d-sided dice.\n",
                roll, dice, sides);
        printf("How many sides? Enter 0 to stop.\n");
    }
    printf("GOOD FORTUNE TO YOU!\n");
    return 0;
}
```

Compile Listing 13.9 with the file containing Listing 13.8, and then use the resulting program. The output should look like this:

```
Enter the number of sides per die, 0 to stop.
6
How many dice?
2
You have rolled a 10 using 2 6-sided dice.
How many sides? Enter 0 to stop.
6
How many dice?
2
You have rolled a 11 using 2 6-sided dice.
How many sides? Enter 0 to stop.
0
GOOD FORTUNE TO YOU!
```

You can use **rollem()** in many ways. With **sides** equal to 2, the program simulates a coin toss with "heads" being 2 and "tails" being 1 (or vice versa, if you really prefer it). You can easily modify the program to show the individual results as well as the total, or you can construct a craps simulator. If you require a large number of rolls, as in some role-playing games, you can easily modify the program to produce output like this:

```
Enter the number of sets; enter q to stop.
18
How many sides and how many dice?
6 3
Here are 18 sets of 3 6-sided throws.
  12  10   6   9   8  14   8  15   9  14  12  17  11   7  10
  13   8  14
How many sets? Enter q to stop.
q
```

Another use for **rand1()** or **rand()** (but not of **rollem()**) is creating a number-guessing program so that the computer chooses and you guess. You can try that yourself.

Now let's develop some more functions. The first project is designing a program that reads in a list of integers and sorts them.

Sorting Numbers

One of the most common tasks for a computer is sorting, so we'll develop a program to sort integers. We'll take a black box approach and think in terms of input and output. The overall plan, shown in Figure 13.2, is pretty simple.

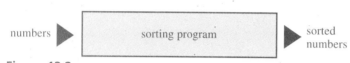

Figure 13.2 Sorting program: a black box view.

At this point, the program is still too vaguely defined for us to begin writing code. The next step is to identify the main tasks that the program must do to accomplish our goals. We can break the example down to three such tasks:

1. Read the numbers.

2. Sort them.

3. Print the sorted numbers.

Figure 13.3 shows this breakdown as we descend from the top level of organization to a more detailed level.

Figure 13.3 Sorting program: peeking inside.

Global Decisions

Before designing the individual modules, we need to make some global decisions. We need to choose a data form and decide what information will be passed to the individual modules.

Data Form

How do we represent a collection of numbers? We could use a collection of variables, one for each number, but that is just too much trouble to even think about. Using an array is an immensely superior approach.

What kind of an array? Type `int`? Type `double`? We need to know how the program is going to be used. Assuming it is to be used with modestly sized integers, we will use an array of `ints` to store the numbers we read.

Information Flow

The first module gathers input. It should know where to place the values it reads. It should also know the maximum number of values it can accept and report the actual number of items read. The sorting module should know which array to sort and how many elements are present. The printing module should know which array to use and how many elements to print. These considerations suggest the `main()` function shown in Listing 13.10.

Listing 13.10   The `sort_int.c` program.

```
/* sort_int.c -- sorts integers */
#include <stdio.h>
#define MAXSIZE  100     /* limit to number of integers to sort */
extern int getarray(int ar[], int n);
extern void sort(int ar[], int n);
extern void print(const int ar[], int n);
int main(void)
{
    int numbers[MAXSIZE];              /* array to hold input    */
    int size;                          /* number of input items  */

    size = getarray(numbers, MAXSIZE); /* put input into array    */
    printf("\nOriginal data (%d values):\n", size);
    print(numbers, size);              /* print original array   */
    sort(numbers, size);               /* sort the array         */
    puts("Sorted data: ");
    print(numbers, size);              /* print the sorted array */
    return 0;
}
```

Here we have the skeleton of the program. The function `getarray()` places the values read into the array `numbers` and reports how many values were read. That value is assigned to `size`. The program reports the number of elements entered and displays the original array. Then `sort()` sorts the array, and `print()` prints the sorted results.

Now that we have refined our picture of the information flow, we should modify the black box sketch. As Figure 13.4 shows, we now have three black boxes, each with its own input and output. Because we are emphasizing modularity, we have broken the original problem into three smaller, more manageable pieces. We can assign each part to a different programming team, provided that the numbers output by "read 'em" are in the same form that "sort 'em" uses for input.

We will apply our efforts to each of the three boxes separately, breaking them down to simpler units until we reach a point where the code is obvious. As we do this, we must pay attention to these important points: data-form choice, error-trapping, and information flow. Let's continue with the example, tackling the reading portion first (see Figure 13.5).

sorting program

Figure 13.4 Sorting program: adding details.

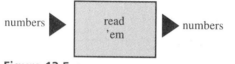

Figure 13.5 Sorting program: the first task.

Reading Numeric Data

Many programs read numbers, so the ideas we develop here will be useful elsewhere. The general form for this part of the program is clear: Use a loop to read in numbers until all the numbers are read. However, there is more to reading numbers than you might think!

Ending Input

How will the function know when to quit reading numbers? We faced a similar problem in Chapter 10. There, we had a `read_array()` function that quit reading numbers when the user either simulated EOF or entered a non-numeric value. This time we'll take a different tack. The main change is how we handle non-numeric input. We'll design the function so that it alerts the user when the input is non-numeric and then gives the user the option of trying again.

Why this change? Suppose you are entering data at the keyboard and accidentally enter 1o instead of 10. Would you rather have the program terminate, forcing you to reenter all the data or have it just reject that one entry and let you continue? It is simpler to rely on the "perfect user theory," which states that the user makes no entry errors. However, we recognize that this theory might not apply to users other than ourselves. Therefore, we opt for the second choice. This checking input for suitability is termed *data validation*.

Here is one approach:

1. Read a word.

2. While not EOF.

3. If the word is an integer, assign it to an array.

4. Else skip that word and provide the option of entering a number again.

5. Terminate if input is non-numeric.

6. Otherwise, read the next word if the array isn't full.

Note that there are three separate conditions that bring this portion of the program to a close: an EOF signal, filling the array, or entering non-numeric data twice in succession.

The getarray() Function

Now let's look at getarray(), shown in Listing 13.11.

Listing 13.11   The getarray.c file.

```
/* getarray.c -- reads in an array */
#include <stdio.h>
#define NONUM 0
#define YESNUM 1
int getarray(int array[], int limit)
{
  int num, status;
  int index = 0;        /* array index */

  printf("This program stops reading numbers after %d ",
         limit);
  printf("values\nor if EOF is encountered. First value: ");
  status = scanf("%d", &num);
  while (index < limit && status != EOF)
  {
    if (status == YESNUM)
    {
      array[index++] = num;
      printf("%d accepted. ", num);
      if (index < limit)                /* if there's room, */
      {                                 /* get next value   */
        printf("Next value: ");
        status = scanf("%d", &num);
      }
    }
    else if (status == NONUM)
    {
      scanf("%*s"); /* dispose of bad input    */
      printf("That was no integer! Enter an integer to \n");
      printf("continue or non-numeric input to quit: ");
      if ((status = scanf("%d", &num)) == NONUM)
        break;        /* quit loop if nonnumeric */
    }
    else
    {
      printf("Oops! Program should never reach here!\n");
      break;
    }
  }
  if (index == limit )    /* report if array gets filled */
    printf("All %d elements of the array were filled.\n",
         limit);
  return(index);
}
```

This is not a simple function, so we have quite a few points to note.

Explanation

We set up `getarray()` to handle each of the possible return values for `scanf()`. Recall that `scanf()` returns the number of items successfully read. If it finds an `int`, it returns `1`, or `YESNUM`. If it finds a non-integer, it returns `0`, or `NONUM`, and if it finds the end of file, it returns `EOF`.

An `EOF` return causes the `while` loop to end. A `YESNUM` return results in a valid entry being stored in the awaiting array and the index being incremented. Also, that number is echoed back to the user showing that it was accepted.

A `NONUM` return initiates a more complex chain of events. The program first disposes of the invalid input with this line:

```
scanf("%*s"); /* dispose of bad input    */
```

Recall that the `%*s` specifier causes `scanf()` to skip over the next word. If `status` is `NONUM`, then the word is not an integer, so we want to skip it. Otherwise, `scanf()` will remain stuck on that word forever. Next, the program sends the user back for another try. If the user responds with another non-integer, the program uses `break` to exit the loop, terminating input. If the user responds with an integer or with end-of-file, the program continues to the loop test. The loop test will catch an `EOF` return; otherwise, the value is added to the array.

There is one more `else` statement. Logically, the only way this final `else` statement can be reached is if `scanf()` returns a value other than `YESNUM`, `NONUM`, or `EOF`, but those are the only values that can be returned, so it seems to be a useless statement. We included it as an example of defensive programming, the art of protecting a program from future fiddling. Someday, we, or someone else, might decide to rewrite `getarray()` so that, say, it reads two values at a time, making `2` a possible return value. Most likely, we will have forgotten by then—and they might never have known—that `getarray()` assumes there are just three possible responses. Therefore, to help future debugging, we include this final `else` to trap any new responses that show up.

We use the keyword `return` to communicate the number of items read, so the function call

```
size = getarray(numbers, MAXSIZE);
```

assigns a value to `size` and puts values into the `numbers` array.

In functions such as this one that involve counters and limits, the most likely place to find an error is at the boundary conditions, where counts reach their limits. Are you going to read a maximum of `MAXSIZE` numbers, or are you going to be off by 1? You need to pay attention to details such as `++index` versus `index++` and `<` versus `<=`. You also have to keep in mind that arrays start their subscripting with `0`, not `1`. Take a moment to check our code and see whether it works as it should. The easiest way to do that is to imagine that `limit` is `1` and then walk through the procedure step by step.

Finally, the function informs the user when the array is full so that he or she is not taken by surprise.

Getting a program to interact in a convenient, dependable manner with the user is often the most difficult part of writing code. That is the case with this part of the program. You'll find `sort()` and `print()` easier. Let's move on to `sort()` now.

Sorting the Data

Let's look at `main()` again from Listing 13.10:

```c
/* sort_int.c -- sorts integers */
#include <stdio.h>
#define MAXSIZE  100     /* limit to number of integers to sort */
extern int getarray(int ar[], int n);
extern void sort(int ar[], int n);
extern void print(const int ar[], int n);
int main(void)
{
  int numbers[MAXSIZE];                /* array to hold input    */
  int size;                            /* number of input items  */

  size = getarray(numbers, MAXSIZE); /* put input into array    */
  printf("\nOriginal data (%d values):\n", size);
  print(numbers, size);                /* print original array   */
  sort(numbers, size);                 /* sort the array         */
  puts("Sorted data: ");
  print(numbers, size);                /* print the sorted array */
  return 0;
}
```

You can see that the two arguments to `sort()` are an array of integers to be sorted and a count of the number of elements to be sorted. The function sorts the numbers but has no return value. We still haven't decided how to do the sorting, so we need to refine this description further.

One obvious decision is the direction of the sort. Are we going to sort from largest to smallest or vice versa? Again, we'll be arbitrary and say that we'll sort from largest to smallest (see Figure 13.6). (We could design a function to do either, but then we would have to develop a way to tell the function which choice we want.)

Figure 13.6 Sorting function: the second task.

Now let's consider the method we will use to sort. Many sorting algorithms have been developed for computers, but we'll use one of the simplest—the selection sort.

Here is our plan in pseudocode:

```
for n = first to n = next-to-last element,
    find largest remaining number and place it in the nth element
```

The plan works like this. First, start with n = 1. Scan the entire array, find the largest number, and swap it with the first element. Next, set n = 2, and scan all but the first element of the array. Find the largest remaining number, and swap it with the second element. Continue this process until reaching the next-to-last element. Now only two elements are left. Compare them and place the larger in the next-to-last position. This leaves the smallest element of all in the final position.

It looks like a `for` loop task, but we still have to describe the "find and place" process in more detail. Here is one way to select the largest remaining value. Compare the first and second elements of the remaining array. If the second is larger, swap the two values. Now compare the first element with the third. If the third is larger, swap those two. Each swap moves a larger element to the top. Continue this way until you have compared the first with the last element. When you finish, the largest number is now in the first element of the remaining array. You have sorted the array for the first element, but the rest of the array is in a jumble. Here is the procedure in pseudocode:

```
for n - second element to last element,
    compare nth element with first element; if nth is greater, swap values
```

This process looks like another `for` loop. It will be nested in the first `for` loop. The outer loop indicates which array element is to be filled, and the inner loop finds the value to put there. Putting the two parts of the pseudocode together and translating them into C, we get the function in Listing 13.12.

Listing 13.12   The `sort.c` file.

```c
/* sort.c -- sorts an integer array in decreasing order */
void sort(int array[], int limit)
{
    int top, search, temp;

    for (top = 0; top < limit -1; top++)
        for (search = top + 1; search < limit; search++)
            if (array[search] > array[top])
            {
                temp = array[search];
                array[search] = array[top];
                array[top] = temp;
            }
}
```

In Listing 13.12, we were clever enough to remember that the first element has **0** for a subscript. Also, we used the swapping technique discussed in Chapter 9. We used `top` as the subscript for the array element that is to be filled because it is at the top of the unsorted part of the array. The `search` index roams over the array below the current `top` element. Now we just have `print()` left to write.

Printing the Data

The last task is to write the function that will print the sorted numbers (see Figure 13.7). This function, as shown in Listing 13.13, is pretty simple. Because the function does not modify the array, it declares `array` as `const`.

Figure 13.7 Printing results: the third task.

Listing 13.13   The print.c file.

```
/* print.c -- prints an array */
#include <stdio.h>
void print(const int array[], int limit)
{
    int index;

    for (index = 0; index < limit; index++)
    {
        printf("%d ", array[index]);
        if (index % 10 == 9)
            putchar('\n');
    }
    if (index % 10 != 0)
        putchar('\n');
}
```

Listing 13.13 uses the modulus operator to control printing newlines:

```
if (index % 10 == 9)
    putchar('\n');
```

The condition is true when index is 9, 19, 29, and so on. Because array indexing begins with 0, this results in displaying a newline after every tenth element. The function also displays a new line at the end unless the very last thing printed inside the loop was a new line:

```
if (index % 10 != 0)
        putchar('\n');
```

Suppose a newline is the last thing printed in the loop before it terminates; then the value of the modulus is **9**. However, the **for** loop update condition increments **index**, so the value of the modulus is **10** after the loop terminates.

If you want something a little different, such as printing in one column or using fixed-width fields, you can always change this function, leaving the other functions untouched. Similarly, if you found a sorting algorithm that you liked better, you could replace the **sort()** module. That is one of the advantages of a modular program.

Results

Let's compile and test this package. That is, compile Listings 13.10, 13.11, 13.12, and 13.13 together as a single program or project. To make checking the boundary conditions simpler, we'll temporarily change MAXSIZE to 5. For the first test, we will feed numbers to the program until it refuses to take more:

```
This program stops reading numbers after 5 values
or if EOF is encountered. First value: 78
78 accepted. Next value: 85
85 accepted. Next value: ninety
That was no integer! Enter an integer to
continue or non-numeric input to quit: 90
90 accepted. Next value: 88
88 accepted. Next value: 95
95 accepted. All 5 elements of the array were filled.

Original data (5 values):
78 85 90 88 95
Sorted data:
95 90 88 85 78
```

Good, it stopped when five numbers were read, and it sorted the results. Now we'll restore the limit to 100 values, recompile, and test to see whether it stops when the end of file is encountered.

```
This program stops reading numbers after 100 values
or if EOF is encountered. First value: 87
87 accepted. Next value: 88
88 accepted. Next value: 67
67 accepted. Next value: 93
93 accepted. Next value: <Control-Z>
Original data (4 values):
87 88 67 93
Sorted data:
93 88 87 67
```

Faster than you can say "oikology is the science of housekeeping," the whole enormous array is sorted. Recall that Ctrl+D transmits EOF on UNIX systems.

Finally, let's see if consecutive non-numeric responses halt input:

```
This program stops reading numbers after 100 values
or if EOF is encountered. First value: 56
56 accepted. Next value: 68
68 accepted. Next value: 74
74 accepted. Next value: 54
54 accepted. Next value: no
That was no integer! Enter an integer to
continue or non-numeric input to quit: q

Original data (4 values):
56 68 74 54
Sorted data:
74 68 56 54
```

Success wasn't easy, but it was possible. By breaking the problem into smaller parts and by thinking about what information should flow into and out of each part, we reduced the problem to manageable proportions. Furthermore, the individual modules we produced could be used as parts of similar programs.

Comments

One major advantage of the modular design is that it makes it simpler to tinker with the program. For instance, consider the sorting module. After thinking about it, you might decide that you can improve the efficiency by changing the algorithm slightly. As the program moves through the inner loop, instead of immediately promoting each new claimant to the top ranking to the top, just keep track of the index of the claimant. Then, when the inner loop finishes, just swap the current top claimant with the current top position. Or you might want to modify the printing module to print six numbers to a line. With a modular approach, you can fix just that module and leave the rest of the program unchanged. If each function has its own file, you need only recompile the altered one, and then link it to the compiled versions of the other files. Integrated environments do this automatically when you have a project file. That is, they keep track of which files need to be recompiled and which have been unaltered.

ANSI C Type Qualifiers

You've seen that a variable is characterized by both its type and its storage class. ANSI C adds two more properties: constancy and volatility. These properties are declared with the keywords `const` and `volatile`, which create *qualified types*. The C9X committee proposes adding a third qualifier, `restrict`, designed to facilitate compiler optimizations; Appendix H, "The C9X Committee," discusses it briefly.

The `const` Type Qualifier

Chapter 4, "Character Strings and Formatted Input/Output," and Chapter 10 have already introduced `const`. To review, the `const` keyword in a declaration establishes a variable whose value cannot be modified by assignment or by incrementing or decrementing. On an ANSI-compliant compiler, the code

```
const int nochange;   /* qualifies m as being constant */
nochange = 12;        /* not allowed                    */
```

should produce an error message. You can, however, initialize a `const` variable. Therefore, the following code is fine:

```
const int nochange = 12;  /* ok */
```

The preceding declaration makes `nochange` a read-only variable. Once initialized, it cannot be changed.

You can use the `const` keyword to, for example, create an array of data that the program can't alter:

```
const int days1[12] = {31,28,31,30,31,30,31,31,30,31,30,31};
```

Using const with Pointers and Parameter Declarations

Using the const keyword when declaring a simple variable and an array is pretty easy. Pointers are more complicated because you have to distinguish between making the pointer itself const and making the value that is pointed to const. The declaration

```
const float * pf;   /* pf points to a constant float value */
```

establishes that pf points to a value that must remain constant. The value of pf itself can be changed. For example, it can be set to point at another const value. In contrast, the declaration

```
float * const pt;     /* pt is a const pointer */
```

says that the pointer pt itself cannot have its value changed. It must always point to the same address, but the pointed-to value can change. Finally, the declaration

```
const float * const ptr;
```

means both that ptr must always point to the same location and that the value stored at the location must not change.

One common use for this new keyword is declaring pointers that serve as formal function parameters. For example, consider the function print() from Listing 13.13. If you pass it a pointer to the beginning of the string, the function returns the length of the string. In general, passing a pointer to a function enables that function to alter data in the calling function, but the following prototype prevents that from happening:

```
void print(const int array[], int limit);
```

In a prototype and a function header, the parameter declaration const int array[] is the same as const int * array, so the declaration says that the data to which array points cannot be changed.

The ANSI C library follows this practice. If a pointer is used only to give a function access to values, the pointer is declared as a pointer to a const-qualified type. If the pointer is used to alter data in the calling function, then the const keyword isn't used. For instance, the ANSI C declaration for strcat() is this:

```
char *strcat(char *, const char *);
```

Recall that strcat() adds a copy of the second string to the end of the first string. This modifies the first string, but leaves the second string unchanged. The declaration reflects this.

Using const with Global Data

Recall that using global variables is considered a risky approach because it exposes data to being mistakenly altered by any part of a program. That risk disappears if the data is const, so it is perfectly reasonable to use global variables with the const qualifier. You can have const variables, const arrays, and const structures. (Structures are a compound data type discussed in the next chapter.)

One area that requires care, however, is sharing `const` data across files. There are two strategies you can use. The first is to follow the usual rules for external variables—use defining declarations in one file and reference declarations (using the keyword `extern`) in the other files:

```
/* file1.c -- defines some global constants */
const double PI = 3.14159;
const char * MONTHS[12] =
    {"January", "February", "March", "April", "May", "June", "July",
     "August", "September", "October", "November", "December"};

/* file2.c -- use global constants defined elsewhere */
extern const double PI;
extern const * MONTHS[];
```

The second approach is to place the constants in an include file. Here you must take the additional step of using the static external storage class:

```
/* constant.h -- defines some global constants */
static const double PI = 3.14159;
static const char * MONTHS[12] =
    {"January", "February", "March", "April", "May", "June", "July",
     "August", "September", "October", "November", "December"};

/* file1.c -- use global constants defined elsewhere */
#include "constant.h"

/* file2.c -- use global constants defined elsewhere */
#include "constant.h"
```

If you don't use the keyword `static`, then including `constant.h` in `file1.c` and in `file2.c` would result in each file having a defining declaration of the same identifier, which is not supported by the ANSI standard. (Some compilers, however, do allow it.) By making each identifier static external, you actually give each file a separate copy of the data. That wouldn't work if the files were supposed to use the data to communicate with one another because each file would see only its own copy. Because the data is constant (by using the `const` keyword) and identical (by having both files include the same header file), however, that's not a problem.

The advantage of the header file approach is that you don't have to remember to use defining declarations in one file and reference declarations in the next; all files simply include the same header file. The disadvantage is that the data is duplicated. For the preceding examples, that's not a real problem, but it might be one if your constant data includes enormous arrays.

The `volatile` Type Qualifier

The `volatile` qualifier tells the compiler that a variable can have its value altered by agencies other than the program. It is typically used for hardware addresses and for data shared with other programs running simultaneously. For instance, an address might hold the current clock time. The value at that address changes as time changes, regardless of what your program is doing. Or an address could be used to receive information transmitted from, say, another computer.

The syntax is the same as for `const`:

```
volatile int loc1;    /* loc1 is a volatile location      */
volatile int * ploc; /* ploc points to a volatile location */
```

These statements declare `loc1` to be a `volatile` value and `ploc` to point to a `volatile` value.

You may think that `volatile` is an interesting concept, but you might be wondering why the ANSI committee felt it necessary to make `volatile` a keyword. The reason is that it facilitates compiler optimization. Suppose, for example, you have code like this:

```
val1 = x;
 /* some code not using x */
val2 = x;
```

A smart (optimizing) compiler might notice that you use x twice without changing its value. It would temporarily store the x value in a register. Then, when x is needed for `val2`, it can save time by reading the value from a register instead of from the original memory location. This procedure is called *caching*. Ordinarily, caching is a good optimization, but not if x is changed between the two statements by some other agency. If there were no `volatile` keyword, a compiler would have no way of knowing whether this might happen. Therefore, to be safe, the compiler couldn't cache. That was the pre-ANSI situation. Now, however, if the `volatile` keyword is not used in the declaration, the compiler can assume that a value hasn't changed between uses, and it can then attempt to optimize the code.

A value can be both `const` and `volatile`. For instance, the hardware clock setting normally should not be changed by the program, making it `const`, and it is changed by an agency other than the program, making it `volatile`. Just use both qualifiers in the declaration, as shown here; the order doesn't matter:

```
volatile const int loc;
const volatile int * ploc;
```

Chapter Summary

What have you accomplished? On the practical side, you have seen how to develop a random-number generator and an integer-sorting program. In the process, you met `getint()` and `sort()` functions that you can use in other programs. On the educational side, you have learned some general principles and concepts useful in designing complex programs.

Programs should be designed rather than allowed to evolve through some random process of growth, trial, and error. You should think carefully about the form and content of input and output for a program. You should break the program into well-defined tasks and then write the code for these tasks separately, keeping in mind how they interface with one another. The idea is to achieve modularity. When necessary, break a module into smaller modules, and use functions to enhance the program's modularity and clarity.

When designing a program, try to anticipate what might go wrong and then write the program accordingly. Use error-trapping to circumvent potential problems or, at least, to alert the user if a problem shows up. It's much better to give the user a second chance to enter data than to let the program crash in ignominy.

When designing a function, first decide how it will interact with the calling function. Decide what information flows in and what information flows out. What will the arguments be? Will you use pointers, or `return`, or both? After you have these design parameters in mind, you can turn your attention to the mechanics of the function.

As you put these ideas to use, you'll produce programs with greater reliability, and you might acquire a body of functions that you can use in other programs. If so, your programming will take less time.

Don't forget about storage classes. Variables can be defined outside functions, in which case they are external (or global) and are available to more than one function. Variables defined within a function are local to that function and are not known to other functions. When possible, use local variables. This keeps variables in one function from being contaminated by the actions of other functions.

Review Questions

1. Which storage classes create variables local to the function containing them?

2. Which storage classes create variables that persist for the duration of the containing program?

3. Which storage class creates variables that can be used across several files? Restricted to just one file?

4. What might make the sorting algorithm inefficient?

5. How would you change the sorting routine to make it sort in increasing order instead of decreasing order?

6. How would you change `getarray()` to handle strings that represent octal numbers?

7. Which functions know each variable in the following? Are there any errors?

```
/* file 1 */
int daisy;
int main(void)
{
    int lily;
    ...;
}
int petal()
```

```
{
  extern int daisy, lily;
  ...;
}
/* file 2 */
extern int daisy;
static int lily;
int rose;
int stem()
{
  int rose;
  ...;
}
void root()
{
  ...;
}
```

8. What will the following program print?

```
#include <stdio.h>
char color= 'B';
void first(void);
void second(void);

int main(void)
{
  extern char color;

  printf("color in main() is %c\n", color);
  first();
  printf("color in main() is %c\n", color);
  second();
  printf("color in main() is %c\n", color);
  return 0;
}

void first(void)
{
  char color;

  color = 'R';
  printf("color in first() is %c\n", color);
}

void second(void)
{
  color = 'G';
  printf("color in second() is %c\n", color);
}
```

9. A file begins with the following declarations:

```
static int plink;
int value_ct(const int arr[], int value, int n);
```

    a. What do these declarations tell you about the programmer's intent?

    b. Will replacing `int value` and `int n` with `const int value` and `const int n` enhance the protection of values in the calling program?

Programming Exercises

1. Some users might be daunted by being asked to enter an EOF character. Modify `getarray()` so that a # character terminates input the first time it is entered.

2. Create a program that sorts `float` numbers in increasing order.

3. Modify the `sort()` function in Listing 13.12 so that it uses the suggestion given in the "Comments" section following the sample output; namely, that the function keep track of the index of the largest value and swap values only after the inner loop terminates.

4. Write and test in a loop a function that returns the number of times it has been called.

5. Write a program that generates a list of 100 random numbers in the range 1–10 in sorted decreasing order.

6. Write a program that generates 1,000 random numbers in the range 1–10. Don't save or print the numbers, but do print how many times each number was produced. Have the program do this for ten different seed values. Do the numbers appear in equal amounts? You can use the functions from this chapter or ANSI C `rand()` and `srand()` functions, which follow the same format that our functions do. This is one way to test the randomness of a particular random-number generator.

7. Write a program that behaves like the modification of Listing 13.9, which we discussed after showing the output of Listing 13.9. That is, have the program produce output like the following:

```
Enter the number of sets; enter q to stop.
18
How many sides and how many dice?
6 3
Here are 18 sets of 3 6-sided throws.
   12  10   6   9   8  14   8  15   9  14  12  17  11   7  10
   13   8  14
How many sets? Enter q to stop.
q
```

8. Write an interactive program that lets the user enter as many as 20 words. Have the program display the words in sorted order (recall the string

sorting example from Chapter 11, "Character Strings and String Functions") and then ask the user if the words should be saved in a file. If the user responds with a yes, have the program request a name for the file and then write the words into a file by that name.

9. Write a function that skips over input until encountering a digit. It then stores that digit and subsequent digits in a string until encountering a nondigit. The nondigit is placed back in the input, and the function converts the digit string to a numeric value. The function should use a pointer argument to supply the numeric value to the calling program. Use the function return value to return EOF if the function encounters end of file; have it return 1 otherwise. Use getc() and ungetc(). In short, this function finds the next integer in output, whether it is isolated or embedded in text, as in be22again.

10. Modify Exercise 8 so that the function recognizes an optional minus sign. That is, confronted with an input of be-22now, it extracts the value -22.

11. Construct a text file containing ten lines, each composed of a name, a colon, and three integers. Write a program that reads the file and prints the lines in order of increasing average value of the integers in the line. That is, the line

```
Shalla Woogie: 80 70 84
```

would precede the line

```
Hagar Joe Plinty: 70 90 80
```

because the average of its three values is less than the second average. Also, have the program append the average to each line when it is printed. Note that the name part of the input need not consist of exactly two names.

CHAPTER 14

STRUCTURES AND OTHER DATA FORMS

You will learn about the following in this chapter:

- Keywords

  `struct, union, typedef`

- Operators

  `. ->`

In this chapter, you learn what C structures are and how to create structure templates and variables. Then you learn how to access the members of a structure and how to write functions to handle structures. A short look at C's `typedef` facility and at unions and pointers to functions concludes the chapter.

One of the most important steps in designing a program is choosing a good way to represent the data. In many cases, a simple variable or even an array is not enough. C takes your ability to represent data a step further with the C *structure variables*. The C structure is flexible enough in its basic form to represent a diversity of data, and it enables you to invent new forms. If you are familiar with the "records" of Pascal, you should be comfortable with structures. If not, this chapter will introduce you to C structures. Let's study a concrete example to see why a C structure might be needed and how to create and use one.

Sample Problem: Creating an Inventory of Books

Gwen Glenn wants to print an inventory of her books. She would like to print a variety of information for each book: title, author, publisher, copyright date, the number of pages, the number of copies, and the dollar value. Some of these items, such as the titles, can be stored in an array of strings. Other items require an array of `int` or an array of `float`. With seven different arrays, keeping track of everything can get complicated, especially if Gwen wants to generate several complete lists, one sorted by title, one sorted by author, one sorted by value, and so on. A better solution is to use one array, in which each member contained all the information about one book.

Gwen needs a data form, then, that can contain both strings and numbers and somehow keep the information separate. The C structure meets this need. To see how a structure is set up and how it works, we'll start with a limited example. To simplify the problem, we will impose two restrictions. First, we'll include only title, author, and current market value. Second, we'll limit the inventory to one book. If you have more books than that, don't worry; we'll extend the program soon.

Look at the program in Listing 14.1 and its output. Then read our explanation of the main points.

Listing 14.1   The `book.c` program.

```
/* book.c -- one-book inventory */
#include <stdio.h>
#define MAXTITL  41    /* maximum length of title + 1       */
#define MAXAUTL  31    /* maximum length of author's name + 1 */
struct book {          /* structure template: tag is book   */
    char title[MAXTITL];
    char author[MAXAUTL];
    float value;
};                     /* end of structure template         */
int main(void)
{
    struct book libry; /* declare libry as book-type variable */
    printf("Please enter the book title.\n");
    gets(libry.title);         /* access to the title portion */
    printf("Now enter the author.\n");
    gets(libry.author);
    printf("Now enter the value.\n");
    scanf("%f", &libry.value);
    printf("%s by %s: $%.2f\n",libry.title,
           libry.author, libry.value);
    printf("%s: \"%s\" ($%.2f)\n", libry.author,
           libry.title, libry.value);
    return 0;
}
```

Here is a sample run:

```
Please enter the book title.
Chicken of the Alps
Now enter the author.
Bismo Lapoult
Now enter the value.
14.95
Chicken of the Alps by Bismo Lapoult: $14.95
Bismo Lapoult: "Chicken of the Alps" ($14.95)
```

The structure created in Listing 14.1 has three parts (called *members* or *fields*): one to store the title, one to store the author, and one to store the value. These are the three main skills you must acquire:

- Setting up a format or layout for a structure

- Declaring a variable to fit that layout
- Gaining access to the individual components of a structure variable

Setting Up the Structure Declaration

A *structure declaration* is the master plan that describes how a structure is put together. The declaration looks like this:

```
struct book {
    char title[MAXTITL];
    char author[MAXAUTL];
    float value;
};
```

This declaration describes a structure made up of two character arrays and one `float` variable. It does not create an actual data object, but it describes what constitutes such an object. (Occasionally, we'll refer to a structure declaration as a *template* because it outlines how data will be stored. If you've heard of templates in C++, that's a different use of the word.) Let's look at the details. First comes the keyword `struct`. It identifies what comes next as a structure. Next comes an optional tag—the word `book`—which is a shorthand label you can use to refer to this structure. Therefore, later on we have this declaration:

```
struct book libry;
```

It declares `libry` to be a structure variable using the `book` structure design.

Next in the structure declaration, the list of structure members are enclosed in a pair of braces. Each member is described by its own declaration, complete with a terminating semicolon. For instance, the `title` portion is a `char` array with `MAXTITL` elements. A member can be any C data type—and that includes other structures!

A semicolon after the closing brace ends the definition of the structure design. You can place this declaration outside any function (externally), as we have done, or inside a function definition. If the declaration is placed inside a function, then its tag can be used only inside that function. If the declaration is external, it is available to all the functions following the declaration in the file. For example, in a second function, you could define

```
struct book dickens;
```

and that function would have a variable `dickens` that followed the form of the `book` design.

The tag name is optional, but you must use one when you set up structures as we did, with the structure design defined one place and the actual variables defined elsewhere. We will return to this point soon, after we look at defining structure variables.

Defining a Structure Variable

The word *structure* is used in two senses. One is the sense "structure plan," which is what we just discussed. The structure plan tells the compiler *how* to represent the data, but it doesn't make the computer *allocate* space for the data. The next step is to create a "structure variable," the second sense of the word. The line in the program that causes a structure variable to be created is this:

```
struct book libry;
```

Seeing this instruction, the compiler creates the variable `libry`. Using the `book` template, the compiler allots space for a `char` array of `MAXTITL` elements, for a `char` array of `MAXAUTL` elements, and for a `float` variable. This storage is lumped together under the single name `libry` (see Figure 14.1). (The next section explains how to unlump it as needed.)

In declaring a structure variable, `struct book` plays the same role that `int` or `float` does in simpler declarations. For example, you could declare two variables of the `struct book` type or even a pointer to that kind of structure:

```
struct book doyle, panshin, * ptbook;
```

The structure variables `doyle` and `panshin` would each have the parts `title`, `author`, and `value`. The pointer `ptbook` could point to `doyle`, `panshin`, or any other `book` structure. In essence, the `book` structure declaration creates a new type called `struct book`.

```
struct stuff {
            int number;
            char code[4];
            float cost;
            };
```

Figure 14.1 Memory allocation for a structure.

As far as the computer is concerned, the following declaration

```
struct book libry;
```

is short for

```
struct book {
   char title[MAXTITL];
   char author[AXAUTL];
   float value;
} libry;    /* follow declaration with variable name */
```

In other words, the process of declaring a structure and the process of defining a structure variable can be combined into one step. Combining the declaration and the variable definitions, as shown here, is the one circumstance in which a tag need not be used:

```
struct {            /* no tag */
    char title[MAXTITL];
    char author[MAXAUTL];
    float value;
} libry;
```

Use the tag form, however, if you plan to use a structure template more than once.

There is one aspect of defining a structure variable that did not come up in this example: initialization. We'll look at that now.

Initializing a Structure

You've seen how to initialize variables and arrays:

```
int count = 0;
int fibo[7] = {0,1,1,2,3,5,8};
```

Can a structure variable be initialized, too? Yes, although many pre-ANSI implementations limit initialization to external or static structure variables. Whether a structure variable is external depends on where the *variable* is defined, not on the location of the declaration describing the structure layout. In the example, the declaration for the book structure is external, but the variable libry is not because it is defined inside the function and is, by default, placed in the automatic storage class.

Similarly, the declaration

```
static struct book libry;
```

would create a structure with the static storage class.

To initialize a structure (any storage class for ANSI C, but excluding automatic variables for pre-ANSI C), you use a syntax similar to that used for arrays:

```
struct book libry = {
    "The Pirate and the Damsel",
    "Renee Vivotte",
    1.95
};
```

In short, you use a comma-separated list of initializers enclosed in braces. Each initializer should match the type of structure member being initialized. Therefore, you can initialize the title member to a string and the value member to a number. To make the associations more obvious, we gave each member its own line of initialization, but all the compiler needs are commas to separate one member's initialization from the next.

Now, let's continue with structure properties.

Gaining Access to Structure Members

A structure is like a "superarray," in which one element can be `char`, the next element `float`, and the next an `int` array. You can access the individual elements of an array by using a subscript. How do you access individual members of a structure? Use a dot (`.`), the structure member operator. For example, `libry.value` is the `value` portion of `libry`. You can use `libry.value` exactly as you would use any other `float` variable. Similarly, you can use `libry.title` exactly as you would use a `char` array. Therefore, the program uses expressions like

```
gets(libry.title);
```

and

```
scanf("%f", &libry.value);
```

In essence, `.title`, `.author`, and `.value` play the role of subscripts for a **book** structure.

Note that although `libry` is a structure, `libry.value` is a `float` type and is used like any other `float` type. For example, `scanf("%f",...)` requires the address of a `float` location, and that is what `&libry.float` is. The dot has higher precedence than the `&` here, so the expression is the same as `&(libry.float)`.

If you had a second structure variable of the same type, you would use the same method:

```
struct book bill, newt;

gets(bill.title);
gets(newt.title);
```

The `.title` refers to the first member of the **book** structure. Notice how in the initial program we printed the contents of the structure `libry` in two different formats. This illustrates the freedom you have in using the members of a structure.

Now that you have these basics in hand, you're ready to expand your horizons and look at several ramifications of structures. You'll see arrays of structures, structures of structures, pointers to structures, and functions that process structures.

Arrays of Structures

Let's extend our book program to handle more books. Clearly, each book can be described by one structure variable of the **book** type. To describe two books, you need to use two such variables, and so on. To handle several books, you can use an array of such structures, and that is what we have created in the next program, shown in Listing 14.2. (If you're using Borland C/C++, read the box "Borland C and Floating Point.")

Structures and Memory

The `manybook.c` program uses an array of 100 structures. Because the array is an automatic storage class object, the information is typically placed on the stack. Such a large array requires a good-sized chunk of memory, which can cause problems. If you get a runtime error, perhaps complaining about the stack size or stack overflow, your compiler probably uses a default size for the stack that is too small for this example. To fix things, you can use the compiler options to set the stack size to 10,000 to accommodate the array of structures, or you can make the array static or external (so that it isn't placed in the stack), or you can reduce the array size to 16. Why didn't we just make the stack small to begin with? Because you should know about the potential stack size problem so that you can cope with it if you run into it on your own.

Borland C and Floating Point

Older Borland C compilers attempt to make programs more compact by using a small version of `scanf()` if the program doesn't use floating-point values. However, the compilers (through Borland C/C++ 3.1 for DOS, but not Borland C/C++ 4.0) are fooled if the only floating-point values are in an array of structures, as in the case for Listing 14.2. As a result, you get a message like this:

```
scanf : floating point formats not linked
Abnormal program termination
```

One workaround is adding this code to your program:

```
#include <math.h>
double dummy = sin(0.0);
```

This code forces the compiler to load the floating-point version of `scanf()`.

Listing 14.2 The `manybook.c` program.

```
/* manybook.c -- multiple book inventory */
#include <stdio.h>
#define MAXTITL    40
#define MAXAUTL    40
#define MAXBKS    100          /* maximum number of books  */
struct book {                  /* set up book template     */
    char title[MAXTITL];
    char author[MAXAUTL];
    float value;
};
```

continued on next page

continued from previous page

```
int main(void)
{
    struct book libry[MAXBKS]; /* array of book structures */
    int count = 0;
    int index;

    printf("Please enter the book title.\n");
    printf("Press [enter] at the start of a line to stop.\n");
    while (count < MAXBKS && gets(libry[count].title) != NULL
                    && libry[count].title[0] != '\0')
    {
        printf("Now enter the author.\n");
        gets(libry[count].author);
        printf("Now enter the value.\n");
        scanf("%f", &libry[count++].value);
        while (getchar() != '\n')
            continue;                    /* clear input line */
        if (count < MAXBKS)
        printf("Enter the next title.\n");
    }
    printf("Here is the list of your books:\n");
    for (index = 0; index < count; index++)
    printf("%s by %s: $%.2f\n", libry[index].title,
        libry[index].author, libry[index].value);
    return 0;
}
```

Here is a sample program run:

```
Please enter the book title.
Press [enter] at the start of a line to stop.
My Life as a Budgie
Now enter the author.
Mack Zackles
Now enter the value.
12.95
Enter the next title.
    ...more entries...
Here is the list of your books:
My Life as a Budgie by Mack Zackles: $12.95
Thought and Unthought Rethought by Kindra Schlagmeyer: $43.50
The Business of a Bee by Salome Deschamps: $14.99
The CEO Power Diet by Buster Downsize: $19.25
C++ Primer Plus by Stephen Prata: $32.95
Coping with Coping by Dr. Rubin Thonkwacker: $0.00
Delicate Frivolity by Neda McFey: $29.99
Murder Wore a Bikini by Mickey Splats: $18.95
A History of Buvania, Volume 2, by Prince Nikoli Buvan: $50.00
Mastering Your Digital Watch, 2nd Edition, by Miklos Mysz: $18.95
A Foregone Confusion by Phalty Reasoner: $5.99
```

First, we'll describe how to declare arrays of structures and how to access individual members. Then we will highlight two aspects of the program.

Declaring an Array of Structures

Declaring an array of structures is like declaring any other kind of array.

```
struct book libry[MAXBKS];
```

This declares `libry` to be an array with **MAXBKS** elements. Each element of this array is a structure of **book** type. Thus, `libry[0]` is one **book** structure, `libry[1]` is a second **book** structure, and so on. Figure 14.2 may help you visualize this. The name `libry` itself is not a structure name; it is the name of the array whose elements are type **struct book** structures.

Identifying Members of an Array of Structures

To identify members of an array of structures, you apply the same rule used for individual structures: Follow the structure name with the dot operator and then with the member name.

```
libry[0].value    /* the value associated with the first array element */
libry[4].title    /* the title associated with the fifth array element */
```

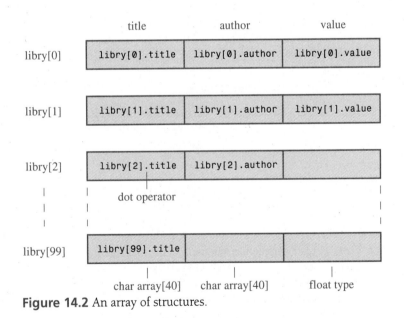

Figure 14.2 An array of structures.

Note that the array subscript is attached to `libry`, not to the end of the name:

```
libry.value[2]    /* WRONG */
libry[2].value    /* RIGHT */
```

The reason `libry[2].value` is used is that `libry[2]` is the structure variable name, just as `libry[1]` is another structure variable name.

By the way, what do you suppose the following represents?

`libry[2].title[4]`

It's the fifth character in the title (the `title[4]` part) of the book described by the third structure (the `libry[2]` part). In the example, it would be the character **A**. This example points out that subscripts found to the right of the dot operator apply to individual members, but subscripts to the left of the dot operator apply to arrays of structures.

Let's finish the program now.

Program Details

The main change from the first program is that we inserted a loop to read multiple entries. The loop begins with this `while` condition:

```
while (count < MAXBKS && gets(libry[count].title) != NULL
              && libry[count].title[0] != '\0')
```

The expression `gets(libry[count].title)` reads a string for the title of a book; the expression evaluates to `NULL` if `gets()` attempts to read past the end-of-file. The expression `libry[count].title[0] != '\0'` tests whether the first character in the string is the null character, that is, if the string is empty. If the user presses the Enter key at the beginning of a line, the empty string is transmitted, and the loop ends. We also have a check to keep the number of books entered from exceeding the array's size limit.

Then the program has these lines:

```
while (getchar() != '\n')
  continue;                /* clear input line */
```

As you might recall from earlier chapters, this code overcomes the `scanf()` function ignoring spaces and newlines. When you respond to the request for the book's value, you type something like this:

`12.50[enter]`

This statement transmits the following sequence of characters:

`12.50\n`

The `scanf()` function collects the **1**, the **2**, the **.**, the **5**, and the **0**, but it leaves the `\n` sitting there, awaiting whatever read statement comes next. If the precautionary code were missing, the next read statement, `gets(libry[count].title)`, would read the leftover newline character as an empty line, and the program would think you had sent a stop signal. The code we inserted will eat up characters until it finds and disposes of the newline. It doesn't do anything with the characters except remove them from the input queue. This gives `gets()` a fresh start.

Now let's return to exploring structures.

Nested Structures

Sometimes it is convenient for one structure to contain, or nest, another. For example, Shalala Pirosky is building structure of information about her friends. One member of the structure, naturally enough, is the friend's name. The name, however, can be represented by a structure itself, with separate entries for first and last name members. Listing 14.3 is a condensed example of Shalala's work.

Listing 14.3   The `friend.c` program.

```
/* friend.c -- example of a nested structure */
#include <stdio.h>
#define LEN 20
const char * msgs[5] =
{
    "     Thank you for the wonderful evening, ",
    "You certainly prove that a ",
    "is a special kind of guy. We must get together",
    "over a delicious ",
    " and have a few laughs"
};
struct names {                     /* first template    */
    char first[LEN];
    char last[LEN];
};
struct guy {                       /* second template   */
    struct names handle;           /* nested structure  */
    char favfood[LEN];
    char job[LEN];
    float income;
};
int main(void)
{
    struct guy fellow = {    /* initialize a variable */
        { "Chip", "Vejer" },
        "nachos plate",
        "memory broker",
        36827.00
    };

    printf("Dear %s, \n\n", fellow.handle.first);
    printf("%s%s.\n", msgs[0], fellow.handle.first);
    printf("%s%s\n", msgs[1], fellow.job);
    printf("%s\n", msgs[2]);
    printf("%s%s%s", msgs[3], fellow.favfood, msgs[4]);
    if (fellow.income > 150000.0)
        puts("!!");
    else if (fellow.income > 75000.0)
        puts("!");
```

continued on next page

continued from previous page

```
      else
          puts(".");
      printf("\n%40s%s\n", " ", "See you soon,");
      printf("%40s%s\n", " ", "Shalala");
      return 0;
}
```

Here is the output:

```
Dear Chip,

    Thank you for the wonderful evening, Chip.
You certainly prove that a memory broker
is a special kind of guy. We must get together
over a delicious nachos plate and have a few laughs.

                              See you soon,
                              Shalala
```

First, note how the nested structure is set up in the template. It is simply declared, just as an **int** variable would be:

```
struct names handle;
```

This declaration says that **handle** is a variable of the **struct names** type. Of course, the file should also include the declaration for the **names** structure.

Second, note how you gain access to a member of a nested structure; you merely use the dot operator twice:

```
fellow.handle.first == "Chip"
```

The construction is interpreted this way, going from left to right:

```
(fellow.handle).first
```

That is, find **fellow**, then find the **handle** member of **fellow**, and then find the **first** member of that.

Pointers to Structures

Pointer lovers will be glad to know that you can have pointers to structures. There are at least three reasons why having pointers to structures is a good idea. First, just as pointers to arrays are easier to manipulate (in a sorting problem, say) than the arrays themselves, so pointers to structures are often easier to manipulate than structures themselves. Second, in some older implementations, a structure can't be passed as an argument to a function, but a pointer to a structure can. Third, many wondrous data representations use structures containing pointers to other structures.

The next short example (see Listing 14.4) shows how to define a pointer to a structure and how to use it to access the members of a structure.

Listing 14.4   The `friends.c` program.

```
/* friends.c -- uses pointer to a structure */
#include <stdio.h>
#define LEN 20
struct names {
    char first[LEN];
    char last[LEN];
};
struct guy {
    struct names handle;
    char favfood[LEN];
    char job[LEN];
    float income;
};
int main(void)
{
    struct guy fellow[2] = {
        {{ "Chip", "Vejer"},
         "nachos plate",
         "memory broker",
         36827.00
         },
        {{"Rodney", "Swillbelly"},
         "salmon mousse",
         "tabloid editor",
         148500.00
         }
    };
    struct guy * him;     /* here is a pointer to a structure */
    printf("address #1: %p #2: %p\n", &fellow[0], &fellow[1]);
    him = &fellow[0];      /* tell the pointer where to point */
    printf("pointer #1: %p #2: %p\n", him, him + 1);
    printf("him->income is $%.2f: (*him).income is $%.2f\n",
        him->income, (*him).income);
    him++;                     /* point to the next structure     */
    printf("him->favfood is %s:  him->handle.last is %s\n",
        him->favfood, him->handle.last);
    return 0;
}
```

The output, please:

```
address #1: 0064FD50 #2: 0064FDA4
pointer #1: 0064FD50 #2: 0064FDA4
him->income is $36827.00: (*him).income is $36827.00
him->favfood is salmon mousse:  him->handle.last is Swillbelly
```

Let's look first at how we created a pointer to a **guy** structure. Then we'll explain how to specify individual structure members by using the pointer.

Declaring and Initializing a Structure Pointer

Declaration is as easy as can be:

```
struct guy * him;
```

First is the keyword struct, then the structure tag guy, and then an * followed by the pointer name. The syntax is the same as for the other pointer declarations you have seen.

This declaration does not create a new structure, but the pointer him can now be made to point to any existing structure of the guy type. The example initializes him by making it point to fellow[0]. Note that you use the address operator:

```
him = &fellow[0];
```

The first two output lines show the success of this assignment. Comparing the two lines, you see that him points to fellow[0], and him + 1 points to fellow[1]. Note that adding 1 to him adds 84 to the address. In hexadecimal, A4 – 50 = 54 (hex) = 84 (base 10) because each guy structure occupies 84 bytes of memory: names.first is 20, names.last is 20, favfood is 20, job is 20, and income is 4, the size of float on our system. Incidentally, on some systems the size of a structure may be greater than the sum of its parts. That's because those systems can align individual numbers on, for example, only even addresses or on addresses that are multiples of four. Such structures might wind up with unused "holes" in them.

Member Access by Pointer

The pointer him is pointing to the structure fellow[0]. How can you use him to get a value of a member of fellow[0]? The third output line shows two methods.

The first method, and the most common, uses a new operator, ->. This operator is formed by typing a hyphen (-) followed by the greater-than symbol (>). The example helps make the meaning clear:

```
him->income  is  fellow[0].income  if  him == &fellow[0]
```

In other words, a structure pointer followed by the -> operator works the same way as a structure name followed by the . (dot) operator. (You can't properly say him.income because him is not a structure name.)

It is important to note that him is a pointer, but him->income is a member of the pointed-to structure. So in this case, him->income is a float variable.

The second method for specifying the value of a structure member follows from this sequence: If him == &fellow[0], then *him == fellow[0] because & and * are reciprocal operators. Hence, by substitution

```
fellow[0].income == (*him).income
```

The parentheses are required because the . operator has higher precedence than *.

In summary, if him is a pointer to the structure fellow[0], the following are all equivalent:

```
fellow[0].income == (*him).income == him->income
```

Now let's look at the interaction between structures and functions.

Telling Functions About Structures

Recall that function arguments pass values to the function. Each value is a number, perhaps `int`, perhaps `float`, perhaps ASCII character code, or perhaps an address. A structure is a bit more complicated than a single value, so it is not surprising that older implementations do not allow a structure to be used as an argument for a function. This limitation has been removed in newer implementations, and ANSI C allows structures to be used as arguments. Therefore, modern implementations give you a choice between passing structures as arguments or passing pointers to structures as arguments, or if you are concerned with just part of a structure, you can pass structure members as arguments. We'll examine all three methods, beginning with passing structure members as arguments.

Passing Structure Members

As long as a structure member is a data type with a single value (that is, an `int` or one of its relatives, a `char`, a `float`, a `double`, or a pointer), it can be passed as a function argument. The fledgling financial analysis program in Listing 14.5, which adds the client's bank account to his or her savings and loan account, illustrates this point.

Listing 14.5   The funds1.c program.

```
/* funds1.c -- passing structure members as arguments */
#include <stdio.h>
#define FUNDLEN 50
struct funds {
    char    bank[FUNDLEN];
    double  bankfund;
    char    save[FUNDLEN];
    double  savefund;
};
double sum(double, double);
int main(void)
{
    struct funds stan = {
        "Garlic-Melon Bank",
        2024.72,
        "Lucky's Savings and Loan",
        8237.11
    };

    printf("Stan has a total of $%.2f.\n",
            sum(stan.bankfund, stan.savefund) );
    return 0;
}
/* adds two double numbers */
double sum(double x, double y)
{
    return(x + y);
}
```

Here is the result of running this program:

```
Stan has a total of $10261.83.
```

Ah, it works. Notice that the function `sum()` neither knows nor cares whether the actual arguments are members of a structure; it requires only that they be type `double`.

Of course, if you want a called function to affect the value of a member in the calling function, you can transmit the address of the member:

```
modify(&stan.bankfund);
```

This would be a function that altered Stan's bank account.

The next approach to telling a function about a structure involves letting the called function know that it is dealing with a structure.

Using the Structure Address

We will solve the same problem as before, but this time we will use the address of the structure as an argument. Because the function has to work with the `funds` structure, it, too, has to make use of the `funds` template. See Listing 14.6 for the program.

Listing 14.6   The `funds2.c` program.

```
/* funds2.c -- passing a pointer to a structure */
#include <stdio.h>
#define FUNDLEN 50
struct funds {
    char    bank[FUNDLEN];
    double bankfund;
    char    save[FUNDLEN];
    double savefund;
};
double sum(const struct funds *);   /* argument is a pointer */
int main(void)
{
    struct funds stan = {
        "Garlic-Melon Bank",
        2024.72,
        "Lucky's Savings and Loan",
        8237.11
    };
    printf("Stan has a total of $%.2f.\n", sum(&stan));
    return 0;
}
double sum(const struct funds * money)
{
    return(money->bankfund + money->savefund);
}
```

This, too, produces the following output:

```
Stan has a total of $10261.83.
```

The sum() function uses a pointer (money) to a fund structure for its single argument. Passing the address &stan to the function causes the pointer money to point to the structure stan. Then the -> operator is used to gain the values of stan.bankfund and stan.savefund. Because the function does not alter the contents of the pointed-to value, it declares money as a pointer-to-const.

This function also has access to the institution names, although it doesn't use them. Note that you must use the & operator to get the structure's address. Unlike the array name, the structure name alone is not a synonym for its address.

Passing a Structure as an Argument

For compilers that permit passing structures as arguments, the last example can be rewritten as shown in Listing 14.7.

Listing 14.7   The funds3.c program.

```
/* funds3.c -- passing a pointer to a structure */
#include <stdio.h>
#define FUNDLEN 50
struct funds {
    char    bank[FUNDLEN];
    double bankfund;
    char    save[FUNDLEN];
    double savefund;
};
double sum(struct funds moolah);   /* argument is a structure */
int main(void)
{
    struct funds stan = {
        "Garlic-Melon Bank",
        2024.72,
        "Lucky's Savings and Loan",
        8237.11
    };
    printf("Stan has a total of $%.2f.\n", sum(stan));
    return 0;
}
double sum(struct funds moolah)
{
    return(moolah.bankfund + moolah.savefund);
}
```

Again, the output is this:

```
Stan has a total of $10261.83.
```

We replaced money, which was a pointer to struct funds, with moolah, which is a struct funds variable. When sum() is called, an automatic variable moolah is created according to the funds template. The members of this structure are then initialized to be copies of the values held in the corresponding members of the structure stan. Therefore, the computations are done by using a copy of the original structure, whereas the preceding program used the original structure itself. Because `moolah` is a structure, the program uses `moolah.bankfund`, not `moolah->bankfund`. Listing 14.6 used `money->bankfund` because `money` is a pointer, not a structure.

More on the New, Improved Structure Status

Under modern C, including ANSI C, not only can structures be passed as function arguments, they can also be returned as function return values. To make this return mechanism workable, the values in one structure can be assigned to another. That is, if `n_data` and `o_data` are both structures of the same type, you can do the following:

```
o_data = n_data;    /* assigning one structure to another */
```

This causes each member of `o_data` to be assigned the value of the corresponding member of `n_data`. Also, you can initialize one structure to another of the same type:

```
struct names right_field = {"Ruthie", "George"};
struct names captain = right_field;  /* initialize a structure */
```

Using structures as function arguments enables you to convey structure information to a function, and using functions to return structures enables you to convey structure information from a called function to the calling function. Structure pointers also allow two-way communication, so you can often use either approach to solve programming problems. Let's look at another set of examples illustrating these two approaches.

To contrast the two approaches, we'll write a simple program that handles structures by using pointers; then we'll rewrite it by using structure passing and structure returns. The program itself asks for your first and last names and reports the total number of letters in them. This project hardly requires structures, but it offers a simple framework for seeing how they work. Listing 14.8 presents the pointer form.

Listing 14.8　The `nameln1.c` program.

```
/* nameln1.c -- uses pointers to a structure */
#include <stdio.h>
#include <string.h>
struct namect {
    char fname[20];
    char lname[20];
    int letters;
};
void getinfo(struct namect *);
void makeinfo(struct namect *);
void showinfo(const struct namect *);
int main(void)
{
    struct namect person;

    getinfo(&person);
    makeinfo(&person);
    showinfo(&person);
    return 0;
}
```

```
void getinfo (struct namect * pst)
{
    printf("Please enter your first name.\n");
    gets(pst->fname);
    printf("Please enter your last name.\n");
    gets(pst->lname);
}

void makeinfo (struct namect * pst)
{
    pst->letters = strlen(pst->fname) +
                    strlen(pst->lname);
}

void showinfo (const struct namect * pst)
{
    printf("%s %s, your name contains %d letters.\n",
        pst->fname, pst->lname, pst->letters);
}
```

Compiling and running the program produces results like the following:

```
Please enter your first name.
Viola
Please enter your last name.
Plunderfest
Viola Plunderfest, your name contains 16 letters.
```

The work of the program is allocated to three functions called from main(). In each case, the address of the person structure is passed to the function.

The getinfo() function transfers information from itself to main(). In particular, it gets names from the user and places them in the person structure, using the pst pointer to locate it. Recall that pst->lname means the lname member of the structure pointed to by pst. This makes pst->lname equivalent to the name of a char array, hence a suitable argument for gets(). Note that although getinfo() feeds information to the main program, it does not use the return mechanism, so it is type void.

The makeinfo() function performs a two-way transfer of information. By using a pointer to person, it locates the two names stored in the structure. It uses the C library function strlen() to calculate the total number of letters in each name and then uses the address of person to stow away the sum. Again, the type is void. Finally, the showinfo() function uses a pointer to locate the information to be printed. Because this function does not alter the contents of an array, it declares the pointer as const.

In all these operations, there has been but one structure variable, person, and each of the functions used the structure address to access it. One function transferred information from itself to the calling program, one transferred information from the calling program to itself, and one did both.

Now let's see how you can program the same task using structure arguments and return values. First, to pass the structure itself, use the argument person rather than &person. The corresponding formal argument, then, is declared type struct namect instead of being a pointer to that type. Second, to provide structure values to main(), you can return a structure. Listing 14.9 presents the nonpointer version.

Listing 14.9 The nameln2.c program.

```
/* nameln2.c -- passes and returns structures */
#include <stdio.h>
#include <string.h>
struct namect {
    char fname[20];
    char lname[20];
    int letters;
};
struct namect getinfo(void);
struct namect makeinfo(struct namect);
void showinfo(struct namect);
int main(void)
{
    struct namect person;

    person = getinfo();
    person = makeinfo(person);
    showinfo(person);
    return 0;
}

struct namect getinfo(void)
{
    struct namect temp;
    printf("Please enter your first name.\n");
    gets(temp.fname);
    printf("Please enter your last name.\n");
    gets(temp.lname);
    return temp;
}

struct namect makeinfo(struct namect info)
{
    info.letters = strlen(info.fname) + strlen(info.lname);
    return info;
}

void showinfo(struct namect info)
{
    printf("%s %s, your name contains %d letters.\n",
        info.fname, info.lname, info.letters);
}
```

This version produces the same final result as the preceding one, but it proceeds in a different manner. Each of the three functions creates its own copy of **person**, so this program uses four distinct structures instead of just one.

Consider the makeinfo() function, for example. In the first program, the address of **person** was passed, and the function fiddled with the actual **person** values. In this second version, a new structure called **info** is created. The values stored in **person** are copied to **info**, and the function works with the copy, so when the number of letters is calculated, it is stored in `info`, but not in `person`. The return mechanism, however, fixes that. The `make-info()` line

```
return info;
```

combines with the `main()` line

```
person = makeinfo(person);
```

to copy the values stored in `info` into `person`. Note that the `makeinfo()` function had to be declared type `struct namect` because it returns a structure.

Structures or Pointer to Structures?

Suppose you have to write a structure-related function. Should you use structure pointers as arguments, or should you use structure arguments and return values? Each approach has its strengths and weaknesses.

The two advantages of the pointer argument method are that it works on older as well as newer C implementations and that it is quick; you just pass a single address. The disadvantage is that you have less protection for your data. Some operations in the called function could inadvertently affect data in the original structure. However, the ANSI C addition of the `const` qualifier solves that problem. For example, if you put code into the `showinfo()` function that changes any member of the structure, the compiler will catch it as an error.

One advantage of passing structures as arguments is that the function works with copies of the original data, which is safer than working with the original data. Also, the programming style tends to be clearer. Suppose you define the following structure type:

```
struct vector = {double x; double y;};
```

You want to set the vector **ans** to the sum of the vectors **a** and **b**. You could write a structure-passing and returning function that would make the program like this:

```
struct vector ans, a, b, sum_vect();
...
ans = sum_vect(a,b);
```

The preceding version is more natural-looking to an engineer than a pointer version, which might look like this:

```
struct vector ans, a, b;
void sum_vect();
...
sum_vect(&a, &b, &ans);
```

Also, in the pointer version, the user has to remember whether the address for the sum should be the first or the last argument.

The two main disadvantages to passing structures are that older implementations might not handle the code and that it wastes time and space. It's especially wasteful to pass large structures to a function that uses only one or two members of the structure. In that case, passing a pointer or passing just the required members as individual arguments makes more sense.

Typically, programmers use structure pointers as function arguments for reasons of efficiency, using `const` when needed to protect data from unintended changes. Passing structures by value is most often done for structures that are small to begin with.

Character Arrays or Character Pointers in a Structure

The examples so far have used character arrays to store strings in a structure. You might have wondered if you can use pointers-to-`char` instead. For example, Listing 14.3 had this declaration:

```
#define LEN 20
struct names {
    char first[LEN];
    char last[LEN];
};
```

Can you do this instead?

```
struct pnames {
    char * first;
    char * last;
};
```

The answer is that you can, but you might get into trouble unless you understand the implications. Consider the following code:

```
struct names veep = {"Talia", "Summers"};
struct pnames treas = {"Brad", "Fallingjaw"};
printf("%s and %s\n", veep.first, treas.first);
```

This is valid code, and it works, but consider where the strings are stored. For the `struct names` variable `veep`, the strings are stored inside the structure; the structure has allocated a total of 40 bytes to hold the two named. For the `struct pnames` variable `treas`, however, the strings are stored wherever the compiler stores string constants. All the structure holds are the two addresses, which, on our system, take a total of 8 bytes. In particular, the `struct pnames` structure allocates no space to store strings. It can be used only with strings that have had space allocated for them elsewhere, such as string constants or strings in arrays. In short, the pointers in a `pnames` structure should be used only to manage strings that were created and allocated elsewhere in the program.

Let's see where this restriction is a problem. Consider the following code:

```
struct names accountant;
struct pnames attorney;
puts("Enter the last name of your accountant:");
scanf("%s", accountant.last);
puts("Enter the last name of your attorney:");
scanf("%s", attorney.last);   /* here lies the danger */
```

As far as syntax goes, this code is fine. But where does the input get stored? For the accountant, the name is stored in the last member of the `accountant` variable; this structure has an array to hold the string. For the attorney, `scanf()` is told to place the string at the address given by `attorney.last`. Because this is an uninitialized variable, the address could have any value, and the program could try to put the name anywhere. If you were lucky, the program might work, at least some of the time. Or the attempt could bring your program to a crashing halt. Actually, if the program works, you're unlucky, for the program will have a dangerous programming error of which you are unaware.

So if you want a structure to store the strings, use character array members. Storing pointers-to-`char` has its uses, but has the potential for serious misuse.

Functions Using an Array of Structures

Suppose you have an array of structures that you want to process with a function. The name of an array is a synonym for its address, so it can be passed to a function. Again, the function needs access to the structure template. To show how this works, Listing 14.10 expands our monetary program to two people so that it has an array of two **funds** structures.

Listing 14.10   The `funds4.c` program.

```c
/* funds4.c -- passing an array of structures to a function */
#include <stdio.h>
#define FUNDLEN 50
#define N 2
struct funds {
    char    bank[FUNDLEN];
    double bankfund;
    char    save[FUNDLEN];
    double savefund;
};
double sum(const struct funds *money, int n);
int main(void)
{
    struct funds jones[N] = {
        {
            "Garlic-Melon Bank",
            2024.72,
            "Lucky's Savings and Loan",
            8237.11
        },
        {
            "Honest Jack's Bank",
            1834.28,
            "Party Time Savings",
            2903.89
        }
    };

    printf("The Joneses have a total of $%.2f.\n",
            sum(jones,N));
    return 0;
}
```

continued on next page

continued from previous page

```
double sum(const struct funds *money, int n)
{
    double total;
    int i;

    for (i = 0, total = 0; i < n; i++, money++)
        total += money->bankfund + money->savefund;
    return(total);
}
```

The output is this:

```
The Joneses have a total of $15000.00.
```

(What an even sum! One would almost think the figures were invented.)

The array name `jones` is the address of the array. In particular, it is the address of the first element of the array, which is the structure `jones[0]`. Therefore, initially the pointer `money` is given by this expression:

```
money = &jones[0];
```

Then the `->` operator enables you to add the two funds for the first Jones. This is very much like Listing 14.6. Next, the `for` loop increments the pointer `money` by 1. Now it points to the next structure, `jones[1]`, and the rest of the funds can be added to `total`.

These are the main points:

- You can use the array name to pass the address of the first structure in the array to a function.

- You can then use pointer arithmetic to move the pointer to successive structures in the array. Note that the function call

  ```
  sum(&jones[0],N)
  ```

  would have the same effect as using the array name because both refer to the same address. Using the array name is just an indirect way of passing the structure address.

- Because the `sum()` function isn't supposed to alter the original data, we used the ANSI C `const` qualifier.

Saving the Structure Contents in a File

Because structures can hold a wide variety of information, they are an important tool for constructing databases. For example, you could use a structure to hold all the pertinent information about an employee or an auto part. Ultimately, you would want to be able to save this information in, and retrieve it from, a file. A database file could contain an arbitrary number of such data objects. The entire set of information held in a structure is termed a *record*, and the individual items are *fields*. Let's investigate these topics.

What is perhaps the most obvious way to save a record is the least efficient way, and that is to use `fprintf()`. For example, recall the `book` structure introduced in Listing 14.1:

```
#define MAXTITL    40
#define MAXAUTL    40
struct book {
    char title[MAXTITL];
    char author[MAXAUTL];
    float value;
};
```

If `pbooks` identified a file stream, you could save the information in a `struct book` variable called `primer` with the following statement:

```
fprintf(pbooks, "%s %s %.2f\n", primer.title,
        primer.author,primer.value);
```

This setup becomes unwieldy for structures with, say, 30 members. Also, it poses a retrieval problem because the program would need some way of telling where one field ends and another begins. This problem can be fixed by using a format with fixed-size fields, for example, `"%39s%39s%8.2f"`, but the awkwardness remains.

A better solution is to use `fread()` and `fwrite()` to read and write structure-sized units. Recall that these functions read and write using the same binary representation that the program uses. For example,

```
fwrite(&primer, sizeof (struct book), 1, pbooks);
```

goes to the beginning address of the `primer` structure and copies all the bytes of the structure to the file associated with `pbooks`. The `sizeof (struct book)` term tells the function how large a block to copy, and the `1` indicates that it should copy just one block. The `fread()` function with the same arguments copies a structure-sized chunk of data from the file to the location pointed to by `&primer`. In short, these functions read and write one whole record at a time instead of a field at a time.

To show how these functions can be used in a program, we've modified the program in Listing 14.2 so that the book titles are saved in a file called `book.dat`. If the file already exists, the program shows you its current contents and then enables you to add to the file. Listing 14.11 presents the new version. (If you're using an older Borland compiler, review the "Borland C and Floating Point" discussion in the box near Listing 14.2.)

Listing 14.11   The `booksave.c` program.

```
/* booksave.c -- saves structure contents in a file */
#include <stdio.h>
#include <stdlib.h>
#define MAXTITL    40
#define MAXAUTL    40
#define MAXBKS     10                  /* maximum number of books */
```

continued on next page

continued from previous page

```
struct book {                    /* set up book template   */
    char title[MAXTITL];
    char author[MAXAUTL];
    float value;
};
int main(void)
{
    struct book libry[MAXBKS]; /* array of structures     */
    int count = 0;
    int index, filecount;
    FILE * pbooks;
    int size = sizeof (struct book);

    if ((pbooks = fopen("book.dat", "a+b")) == NULL)
    {
        fputs("Can't open book.dat file\n",stderr);
        exit(1);
    }
    rewind(pbooks);              /* go to start of file    */
    while (count < MAXBKS &&  fread(&libry[count], size,
              1, pbooks) == 1)
    {
        if (count == 0)
            puts("Current contents of book.dat:");
        printf("%s by %s: $%.2f\n",libry[count].title,
            libry[count].author, libry[count].value);
        count++;
    }
    filecount = count;
    if (count == MAXBKS)
    {
        fputs("The book.dat file is full.", stderr);
        exit(2);
    }
    puts("Please add new book titles.");
    puts("Press [enter] at the start of a line to stop.");
    while (count < MAXBKS && gets(libry[count].title) != NULL
                    && libry[count].title[0] != '\0')
    {
        puts("Now enter the author.");
        gets(libry[count].author);
        puts("Now enter the value.");
        scanf("%f", &libry[count++].value);
        while (getchar() != '\n')
            continue;                /* clear input line  */
        if (count < MAXBKS)
            puts("Enter the next title.");
    }
    puts("Here is the list of your books:");
    for (index = 0; index < count; index++)
        printf("%s by %s: $%.2f\n",libry[index].title,
            libry[index].author, libry[index].value);
```

```
        fwrite(&libry[filecount], size, count - filecount,
                pbooks);
        fclose(pbooks);
        return 0;
}
```

We'll look at a couple of sample runs and then discuss the main programming points.

```
% booksave
Please add new book titles.
Press [enter] at the start of a line to stop.
Metric Merriment
Now enter the author.
Polly Poetica
Now enter the value.
18.99
Enter the next title.
Deadly Farce
Now enter the author.
Dudley Forse
Now enter the value.
15.99
Enter the next title.
[enter]
Here is the list of your books:
Metric Merriment by Polly Poetica: $18.99
Deadly Farce by Dudley Forse: $15.99
% booksave
Current contents of book.dat:
Metric Merriment by Polly Poetica: $18.99
Deadly Farce by Dudley Forse: $15.99
Please add new book titles.
The Third Jar
Now enter the author.
Nellie Nostrum
Now enter the value.
22.99
Enter the next title.
[enter]
Here is the list of your books:
Metric Merriment by Polly Poetica: $18.99
Deadly Farce by Dudley Forse: $15.99
The Third Jar by Nellie Nostrum: $22.99
%
```

Running the `booksave` program again would show all three books as current file records.

Program Points

First, the `"a+b"` mode is used for opening the file. The `a+` part lets the program read the whole file and append data to the end of the file. The `b` is the ANSI way of signifying that the program will use the binary file format. For UNIX systems that don't accept the `b`, you can omit it because UNIX has only one file form, anyway. For other pre-ANSI implementations, you might need to find the local equivalent to using b.

We chose the binary mode because fread() and fwrite() are intended for binary files. True, some of the structure contents are text, but the .value member is not. If you use a text editor to look at book.dat, the text part will show up okay, but the numeric part will be unreadable and could even cause your text editor to barf.

The rewind() command ensures that the file position pointer is situated at the start of the file, ready for the first read.

The initial while loop reads one structure at a time into the array of structures, stopping when the array is full or when the file is exhausted. The variable filecount keeps track of how many structures were read.

The next while loop prompts for, and takes, user input. As in Listing 14.2, this loop quits when the array is full or when the user presses the Enter key at the beginning of a line. Notice that the count variable starts with the value it had after the preceding loop. This causes the new entries to be added to the end of the array.

The for loop then prints the data both from the file and from the user. Because the file was opened in the append mode, new writes to the file are appended to the existing contents.

We could have used a loop to add one structure at a time to the end of the file. However, we decided to use the ability of fwrite() to write more than one block at a time. The expression count - filecount yields the number of new book titles to be added, and the call to fwrite() writes that number of structure-sized blocks to the file. The expression &libry[filecount] is the address of the first new structure in the array, so copying begins from that point.

This example is, perhaps, the simplest way to write structures to a file and to retrieve them, but it can waste space because the unused parts of a structure are saved, too. The size of this structure is 2 x 40 x sizeof (char) + sizeof (float), which totals 84 bytes on our system. None of the entries actually needed all that space. However, each data chunk being the same size makes retrieving the data easy.

Another approach is to use variably sized records. To facilitate reading such records from a file, each record can begin with a numerical field specifying the record size. This is a bit more complex than what we have done. Normally, this method involves "linked structures," which we describe next, and dynamic memory allocation, which we discuss in Chapter 16, "The C Preprocessor and the C Library."

Structures: What Next?

Before we end our explanation of structures, we would like to mention one of the more important uses of structures: creating new data forms. Computer users have developed data forms much more efficient for certain problems than the arrays and simple structures we have presented. These forms have names such as queues, binary trees, heaps, hash tables, and graphs. Many such forms are built from linked structures. Typically, each structure contains one or two items of data plus one or two pointers to other structures of the same type. Those pointers link one structure to another and furnish a path to enable you to search through the overall tree of structures. For example, Figure 14.3 shows a binary tree structure, with each individual structure (or node) connected to the two below it.

Figure 14.3 A binary tree structure.

Is the hierarchical, or tree, structure shown in Figure 14.3 more efficient than an array? Consider the case of a tree with ten levels of nodes. It has $2^{10}-1$, or 1,023, nodes in which you could store up to 1,023 words. If the words were arranged according to some sensible plan, you could start at the top level and find any word in—at most—nine moves as your search moved down one level to the next. If you had the words in an array, you might have to search all 1,023 elements before finding the word you sought.

If you are interested in more advanced concepts such as this, you can consult any number of computer science texts on data structures. With the C structures, you can create and use virtually every form presented in these texts. Also, Chapter 17, "Advanced Data Representation," investigates some of these advanced forms.

That's our final word on structures for this chapter, but we will present examples of linked structures in Chapter 17. Next, we'll look at two other C features for dealing with data: the union and `typedef`.

Unions: A Quick Look

A *union* is a type that enables you to store different data types in the same memory space (but not simultaneously). A typical use is a table designed to hold a mixture of types in some order that is neither regular nor known in advance. With a union, you can create an array of equal-sized units, each of which can hold a variety of data types.

Unions are set up in much the same way as structures. There is a union template and a union variable. They can be defined in one step or, by using a union tag, in two. Here is an example of a union template with a tag:

```
union hold {
    int digit;
    double bigfl;
    char letter;
};
```

Here is an example of defining three union variables of the `hold` type:

```
union hold fit;       /* union variable of hold type      */
union hold save[10]; /* array of 10 union variables       */
union hold * pu;      /* pointer to a variable of hold type */
```

The first declaration creates a single variable `fit`. The compiler allots enough space so that it can hold the largest of the described possibilities. In this case, the biggest possibility listed is `double`, which requires 64 bits, or 8 bytes, on our system. The second declaration creates an array `save` with ten elements, each 8 bytes in size. The third declaration creates a pointer that can hold the address of a `hold` union.

You can initialize a union. Because the union holds only one value, the rules are different from those in a structure. In particular, you have two choices: You can initialize a union to another union of the same type, or you can initialize the first element of a union:

```
union hold valA;
valA.letter = 'R';
union hold valB = valA;  /* initialize one union to another  */
union hold valC = {88};  /* initialize digit member of union */
```

You can use the `->` operator with pointers to unions in the same fashion that you use the operator with pointers to structures:

```
pu = &fit;
x = pu->digit;  /* same as x = fit.digit */
```

Here is how a union is used:

```
fit.digit = 23;    /* 23 is stored in fit; 2 bytes used    */
fit.bigfl = 2.0;   /* 23 cleared, 2.0 stored; 8 bytes used */
fit.letter = 'h';  /* 2.0 cleared, h stored; 1 byte used   */
```

The dot operator shows which data type is being used. Only one value is stored at a time. You can't store a `char` and an `int` at the same time, even though there is enough space to do so. It is your responsibility to keep track of the data type currently being stored in a union.

You can use the `->` operator with pointers to unions in the same fashion that you use the operator with pointers to structures:

```
pu = &fit;
x = pu->digit;  /* same as x = fit.digit */
```

The next sequence shows what not to do:

```
fit.letter = 'A';
flnum = 3.02*fit.bigfl;   /* ERROR ERROR ERROR */
```

This sequence is wrong because a `char` type is stored, but the next line assumes that the content of `fit` is a `double` type.

However, sometimes it can be useful to use one member to place values into a union and to then use a different member for viewing the contents. Listing 15.4 in the next chapter "Bit Fiddling," shows an example.

Another place you might use a union is in a structure for which the stored information depends on one of the members. For instance, suppose you have a structure representing an automobile. If the automobile is owned by the user, you want a structure member describing the owner. If the automobile is leased, you want the member to describe the leasing company. Then you can do something along the following lines:

```
struct owner {
    char socsecurity[12];
    ...
};
struct leasecompany  {
    char name[40];
    char headquarters[40];
    ...
}
union data {
    struct owner owncar;
    struct leasecompany leasecar;
};
struct car_data {
    char make[15];
    int status; /* 0 = owned, 1 = leased */
    union data ownerinfo;
    ...
};
```

Suppose `flits` is a `car_data` structure. Then if `flits.status` were 0, the program would use `flits.status.ownerinfo.owncar`, and if `flits.status` were 1, the program would use `flits.status.ownerinfo.leasecar`.

Summary: Structure and Union Operators

The Membership Operator:

.

General Comments:

The . operator is used with a structure or union name to specify a member of that structure or union. If `name` is the name of a structure and `member` is a member specified by the structure template, then the following identifies that member of the structure:

`name.member`

The type of `name.member` is the type specified for `member`. The membership operator can also be used in the same fashion with unions.

Example:

```
struct {
        int code;
        float cost;
} item;

item.code = 1265;
```

The last statement assigns a value to the `code` member of the structure `item`.

The Indirect Membership Operator:

->

General Comments:

This operator is used with a pointer to a structure or union to identify a member of that structure or union. Suppose that `ptrstr` is a pointer to a structure and that `member` is a member specified by the structure template. Then the statement

```
ptrstr->member
```

identifies that member of the pointed-to structure. The indirect membership operator can be used in the same fashion with unions.

Example:

```
struct {
        int code;
        float cost;
} item, * ptrst;
ptrst = &item;
ptrst->code = 3451;
```

The last statement assigns an `int` value to the `code` member of `item`. The following three expressions are equivalent:

```
ptrst->code    item.code    (*ptrst).code
```

typedef: A Quick Look

The `typedef` function is an advanced data feature that enables you to create your own name for a type. It is similar to `#define` in that respect, but with three differences:

- Unlike `#define`, `typedef` is limited to giving symbolic names to types only and not to values.

- The `typedef` function is performed by the compiler, not the preprocessor.

- Within its limits, `typedef` is more flexible than `#define`.

Let's see how `typedef` works. Suppose you want to use the term **BYTE** for one-byte numbers. You simply define **BYTE** as if it were a `char` variable and precede the definition by the keyword `typedef`.

```
typedef unsigned char BYTE;
```

From then on, you can use **BYTE** to define variables:

```
BYTE x, y[10], * z;
```

The scope of this definition depends on the location of the `typedef` statement. If the definition is inside a function, then the scope is local, confined to that function. If the definition is outside a function, then the scope is global.

Often, uppercase letters are used for these definitions to remind the user that the type name is really a symbolic abbreviation, but you could have used lowercase instead:

```
typedef unsigned char byte;
```

The same rules that govern the valid names of variables govern the name used for a `typedef`.

Creating a name for an existing type might seem a bit frivolous, but it can be useful. With the preceding example, using `BYTE` instead of `unsigned char` helps document that you plan to use `BYTE` variables to represent numbers rather than character codes. Using `typedef` also helps increase portability. For example, we've mentioned the `size_t` type that represents the type returned by the `sizeof` operator and the `time_t` type that represents the type of value returned by the `time()` function. The C standard says `sizeof` and `time()` return integer types, but it leaves it up to the implementation to determine which type. The reason for this lack of specificity is that the ANSI C committee feels that no one choice is likely to be the best choice for every computer platform. So they make up a new type name, such as `time_t`, and let the implementation use a `typedef` to set that name to some specific type. That way they can provide a general prototype such as the following:

```
time_t time(time_t *);
```

On one system, `time_t` can be `unsigned int`; on another, it can be `unsigned long`. As long as you include the `time.h` header file, your program can access the appropriate definition, and you can declare `time_t` variables in your code.

Some features of `typedef` can be duplicated with a `#define`. For example,

```
#define BYTE unsigned char
```

cause the preprocessor to replace `BYTE` with unsigned `char`. Here is one that can't be duplicated with a `#define`:

```
typedef char * STRING;
```

Without the keyword `typedef`, this example would identify `STRING` itself as a pointer to `char`. With the keyword, it makes `STRING` an identifier for pointers to `char`. Therefore,

```
STRING name, sign;
```

means

```
char * name, * sign;
```

Suppose, instead, you did this:

```
#define STRING char *
```

Then

```
STRING name, sign;
```

would translate to the following:

```
char * name, sign;
```

In this case, only `name` would be a pointer.

You can use `typedef` with structures, too:

```
typedef struct complex {
        float real;
        float imag;
} COMPLEX;
```

You can then use the type `COMPLEX` instead of the `struct complex` to represent complex numbers. One reason to use `typedef` is to create convenient, recognizable names for types that turn up often. For instance, many people prefer to use `STRING` or its equivalent, as in the earlier example.

A second reason for using `typedef` is that `typedef` names are often used for complicated types. For example, the declaration

```
typedef char (* FRPTC ()) [5];
```

makes `FRPTC` announce a type that is a function that returns a pointer to a five-element array of `char`. (See the upcoming discussion on fancy declarations.)

When using `typedef`, bear in mind that it does not create new types; it just creates convenient labels. This means, for example, that variables using the `STRING` type we created can be used as arguments for functions expecting type pointer-to-`char`.

With structures, unions, and `typedef`, C gives you the tools for efficient and portable data handling.

Fancy Declarations

C enables you to create elaborate data forms. Although we are sticking to simpler forms, we feel it is our duty to point out the potentialities. When you make a declaration, the name (or identifier) you use can be modified by tacking on a modifier.

Modifier	Significance
*	Indicates a pointer
()	Indicates a function
[]	Indicates an array

C enables you to use more than one modifier at a time, and that enables you to create a variety of types.

```
int board[8][8];     /* an array of arrays of int          */
int ** ptr;          /* a pointer to a pointer to int       */
int * risks[10];     /* a 10-element array of pointers to int */
int (* rusks)[10];   /* a pointer to an array of 10 ints     */
int * oof[3][4];     /* a 3 x 4 array of pointers to int     */
int (* uuf)[3][4];   /* a pointer to a 3 x 4 array of ints   */
int (* uof[3])[4];   /* a 3-element array of pointers to
                        4-element arrays of int              */
```

The trick to unraveling these declarations is figuring out the order in which to apply the modifiers. These rules should get you through:

1. The [], which indicates an array, and the (), which indicates a function, have the same precedence. This precedence is higher than that of the * indirection operator, which means that the following declaration makes risks an array of pointers rather than a pointer to an array:

```
int * risks[10];
```

2. The [] and () associate from left to right. This next declaration makes goods an array of 12 arrays of 50 ints, not an array of 50 arrays of 12 ints:

```
int goods[12][50];
```

3. The [] and () have the same precedence, but because they associate from left to right, the following declaration groups the * and rusks together before applying the brackets. This means that the following declaration makes rusks a pointer to an array of 10 ints:

```
int (* rusks)[10];
```

Let's apply these rules to this declaration:

```
int * oof[3][4];
```

The [3] has higher precedence than the *, and, because of the left-to-right rule, it has higher precedence than the [4]. Hence, oof is an array with three elements. Next in order is [4], so the elements of oof are arrays of four elements. The * tells us that these elements are pointers. The int completes the picture: oof is a three-element array of four-element arrays of pointers to int, or, for short, a 3 x 4 array of pointers to int. Storage is set aside for 12 pointers.

Now look at this declaration:

```
int (* uuf)[3][4];
```

The parentheses cause the * modifier to have first priority, making uuf a pointer to a 3 x 4 array of ints. Storage is set aside for a single pointer.

These rules also yield the following types:

```
char * fump();       /* function returning pointer to char   */
char (* frump)();    /* pointer to a function that returns[sr]
                        type char                            */
char (* flump[3])();/* array of 3 pointers to functions that
                        return type char                     */
```

When you bring structures into the picture, the possibilities for declarations truly grow baroque. And the applications—well, we'll leave that for more advanced texts.

Functions and Pointers

As the discussion on declarations illustrated, it's possible to declare pointers to functions. You might wonder if such a beast has any usefulness. Typically, a function pointer is used as an argument to another function, telling the second function which function to use. For instance, the `qsort()` function from the C library takes a pointer to a function as one of its arguments. We've used one sorting function for integers and another for strings. The algorithm was the same, but we used > for comparing integers and `strcmp()` for strings. The `qsort()` function takes a more general approach. You pass it a pointer to a comparison function appropriate to the type you want to sort, and `qsort()` then uses that function to sort the type, whether it be integer, string, or structure.

Let's take a closer look at function pointers. First, what does it mean? A pointer to, say, an `int` holds the address of a location in memory at which an `int` can be stored. Functions, too, have addresses, for the machine-language implementation of a function consists of code loaded into memory. A pointer to a function can hold the address marking the start of the function code.

Next, when you declare a data pointer, you have to declare the type of data pointed to. When declaring a function pointer, you have to declare the type of function pointed to. To specify the function type, you indicate the return type for the function and the parameter types for a function. For example, consider this prototype:

```
void ToUpper(char *);    /* convert string to uppercase  */
```

The type for the `ToUpper()` function is "function with `char *` parameter and return type `void`." To declare a pointer `pf` to this function type, do this:

```
void (*pf)(char *);      /* pf a pointer-to-function     */
```

Reading this declaration, you see the first parentheses pair associates the * operator with `pf`, meaning that `pf` is a pointer to a function. This makes `(*pf)` a function, which makes `(char *)` the parameter list for the function and `void` the return type. Probably the simplest way to create this declaration is to note that it replaces the function name `ToUpper` with the expression `(*pf)`. So if you want to declare a pointer to a specific type of function, you can declare a function of that type, then replace the function name with an expression of the form `(*pf)` to create a function pointer declaration. As mentioned earlier, the first parentheses are needed because of operator precedence rules. Omitting them leads to something quite different:

```
void *pf(char *);        /* pf a function that returns a pointer   */
```

Tip

To declare a pointer to a particular type of function, first declare a function of the desired type, and then replace the function name with an expression of the form `(*pf)`; `pf` then becomes a pointer to a function of that type.

After you have a function pointer, you can assign to it the addresses of functions of proper type. In this context, the *name* of a function can be used to represent the address of the function:

```
void ToUpper(char *);
void ToLower(char *);
int round(double);
void (*pf)(char *);
pf = ToUpper;        /* valid, ToUpper is address of the function   */
pf = ToLower;        /* valid, ToLower is address of the function   */
pf = round;          /* invalid, round is the wrong type of function */
pf = ToLower();      /* invalid, ToLower() is not an address         */
```

The last assignment is also invalid because you can't use a void function in an assignment statement. Note that the pointer pf can point to any function that takes a char * argument and has a return type of void, but not to functions with other characteristics.

Just as you can use a data pointer to access data, you can use a function pointer to access a function. Strangely, there are two logically inconsistent syntaxes for doing so, as the following illustrates:

```
void ToUpper(char *);
void ToLower(char *);
void (*pf)(char *);
char mis[] = "Nina Metier";
pf = ToUpper;
(*pf)(mis);        /* apply ToUpper to mis (syntax 1) */
pf = ToLower;
pf(mis);           /* apply ToLower to mis (syntax 2) */
```

Each approach sounds sensible. Here is the first approach: Because pf points to the ToUpper function, *pf is the ToUpper function, so the expression (*pf)(mis) is the same as ToUpper(mis). Just look at the declarations of ToUpper and of pf to see that ToUpper and (*pf) are equivalent. Here is the second approach: Because the name of a function is a pointer, you can use a pointer and a function name interchangeably, hence pf(mis) is the same as ToLower(mis). Just look at the assignment statement for pf to see that pf and ToLower are equivalent. Historically, the developers of C and UNIX at Bell Labs took the first view and the extenders of UNIX at Berkeley took the second view. K&R C did not allow the second form, but to maintain compatibility with existing code, ANSI C accepts both forms as equivalent.

Just as one of the most common uses of a data pointer is an argument to a function, one of the most common uses of a function pointer is an argument to a function. For instance, consider this function prototype:

```
void show(void (* fp)(char *), char * str);
```

It looks messy, but it declares two parameters, fp and str. The fp parameter is a function pointer, and the str is a data pointer. More specifically, fp points to a function that takes a char * parameter and has a void return type, and str points to a char. So, given the declarations we had earlier, you can make function calls such as the following:

```
show(ToLower, mis);  /* show() uses ToLower() function: fp = ToLower   */
show(pf, mis);       /* show() uses function pointed to by pf: fp = pf */
```

And how does `show()` use the function pointer passed to it? It uses either the `fp()` or the `(*fp)()` syntax to invoke the function:

```
void show(void (* fp)(char *), char * str)
{
    (*fp)(str); /* apply chosen function to str */
    puts(str);  /* display result             */
}
```

Here, for example, `show()` first transforms the string `str` by applying to it the function pointed to by `fp`, and then it displays the transformed string.

By the way, functions with return values can be used two different ways as arguments to other functions. For example, consider the following:

```
function1(sqrt);      /* passes address of sqrt function    */
function2(sqrt(4.0)); /* passes return value of sqrt function */
```

The first passes the address of the `sqrt()` function and, presumably, `function1()` will use that function in its code. The second statement initially calls the `sqrt()` function, evaluates it, and then passes the return value (2.0, in this case) to `function2()`.

To show the essential ideas, the program in Listing 14.12 uses `show()` with a variety of transforming functions as arguments. The listing also shows some useful techniques for handling a menu.

Listing 14.12   The `func_ptr.c` program.

```
/* func_ptr.c -- uses function pointers */
#include <stdio.h>
#include <string.h>
#include <ctype.h>
char showmenu(void);
void eatline(void);      /* read through end of line    */
void show(void (* fp)(char *), char * str);
void ToUpper(char *);    /* convert string to uppercase */
void ToLower(char *);    /* convert string to uppercase */
void Transpose(char *);  /* transpose cases             */
void Dummy(char *);      /* leave string unaltered      */

int main(void)
{
    char line[81];
    char copy[81];
    char choice;
    void (*pfun)(char *); /* points a function having a */
                          /* char * argument and no     */
                          /* return value               */
    puts("Enter a string (empty line to quit):");
    while (gets(line) != NULL && line[0] != '\0')
    {
        while ((choice = showmenu()) != 'n')
        {
            switch (choice   )  /* switch sets pointer */
```

```
                {
                    case 'u' : pfun = ToUpper;   break;
                    case 'l' : pfun = ToLower;   break;
                    case 't' : pfun = Transpose; break;
                    case 'o' : pfun = Dummy;     break;
                }
                strcpy(copy, line);/* make copy for show()  */
                show(pfun, copy);  /* use selected function */
            }
            puts("Enter a string (empty line to quit):");
        }
        puts("Bye!");
        return 0;
    }

char showmenu(void)
{
    char ans;
    puts("Enter menu choice:");
    puts("u) uppercase        l) lowercase");
    puts("t) transposed case o) original case");
    puts("n) next string");
    ans = getchar();    /* get response          */
    ans = tolower(ans); /* convert to lowercase  */
    eatline();          /* dispose of rest of line */
    while (strchr("ulton", ans) == NULL)
    {
        puts("Please enter a u, l, t, o, or n:");
        ans = tolower(getchar());
        eatline();
    }
    return ans;
}

void eatline(void)
{
    while (getchar() != '\n')
        continue;
}

void ToUpper(char * str)
{
    while (*str != '\0')
    {
        *str = toupper(*str);
        str++;
    }
}

void ToLower(char * str)
{
    while (*str != '\0')
```

continued on next page

continued from previous page

```
        {
            *str = tolower(*str);
            str++;
        }
    }
    void Transpose(char * str)
    {
        while (*str != '\0')
        {
            if (islower(*str))
                *str = toupper(*str);
            else if (isupper(*str))
                *str = tolower(*str);
            str++;
        }
    }
    void Dummy(char * str)
    {
        /* leaves string unchanged */
    }

    void show(void (* fp)(char *), char * str)
    {
        (*fp)(str); /* apply chosen function to str */
        puts(str);  /* display result                */''''
    }
```

Here is a sample run:

```
Enter a string (empty line to quit):
Does C make you feel loopy?
Enter menu choice:
u) uppercase        l) lowercase
t) transposed case o) original case
n) next string
t
dOES c MAKE YOU FEEL LOOPY?
Enter menu choice:
u) uppercase        l) lowercase
t) transposed case o) original case
n) next string
l
does c make you feel loopy?
Enter menu choice:
u) uppercase        l) lowercase
t) transposed case o) original case
n) next string
n
Enter a string (empty line to quit):

Bye!
```

Note that the `ToUpper()`, `ToLower()`, `Transpose()`, and `Dummy()` functions all have the same type, so all four can be assigned to the `pfun` pointer. This program uses `pfun` as the argument to `show()`, but you can also use any of the four function names directly as arguments, as in `show(Transpose, line)`.

You can use `typedef` in situations like these. For example, the program could have done this:

```
typedef void (*V_FP_CHARP)(char *);
void show (V_FP_CHARP fp, char *);
V_FP_CHARP pfun;
```

If you're feeling adventurous, you can declare and initialize an array of such pointers:

```
V_FP_CHARP arpf[4] = {ToUpper, ToLower, Transpose, Dummy};
```

If you then modify the `showmenu()` function so that is type `int` and returns `0` if the user enters u, 1 if the user enters 1, 2 if the user enters t, and so on, you could replace the loop holding the `switch` statement with the following:

```
index = showmenu();
while (index >= 0 && index <= 3)
{
    strcpy(copy, line);          /* make copy for show() */
    show(arpf[index], copy);  /* use selected function */
    index = showmenu();
}
```

You can't have an array of functions, but you can have an array of function pointers.

```
function name used in a prototype declaration:  int comp(int x, int y);
              function name used in a function call:  status = comp(q,r);
   function name used in a function definition:  int comp(intx, inty)

                                                 { ...
function name used as a pointer in assignment:  pfunct = comp;
     function name used as pointer argument:  slowsort(arr,n,comp);
```

Figure 14.4 Uses for a function name.

You've now seen all four ways in which a function name can be used: in defining a function, in declaring a function, in calling a function, and as a pointer. Figure 14.4 sums up the uses.

As far as menu handling goes, the `showmenu()` function shows several techniques. First, the code

```
ans = getchar();     /* get response        */
ans = tolower(ans); /* convert to lowercase    */
```

and

```
ans = tolower(getchar());
```

show two ways to convert user input to one case so that you don't have to test for both `'u'` and `'U'`, and so on.

The `eatline()` function disposes of the rest of the entry line. This is useful on two accounts. First, to enter a choice, the user types a letter, then presses the Enter key, which generates a newline character. That newline character will be read as the next response unless you get rid of it first. Second, suppose the user responds by typing the entire word **uppercase** instead of **u**. Without the `eatline()` function, the program would treat each character in the word **uppercase** as a separate response. With `eatline()`, the program processes the u and discards the rest of the line.

Next, the `showmenu()` function is designed to return only valid choices to the program. To help with that task, the program uses the standard library function `strchr()` from the `string.h` header file:

```
while (strchr("ulton", ans) == NULL)
```

This function looks for the location of the first occurrence of the character `ans` in the string `"ulton"` and returns a pointer to it. If it doesn't find the character, it returns the null pointer. Therefore, this `while` loop test is a more convenient replacement for the following:

```
while (ans != 'u' && ans != 'l' && ans != 't' && ans != 'o' && ans != 'n')
```

The more choices you have to check, the more convenient using `strchr()` becomes.

Chapter Summary

A C structure provides the means to store several data items, usually of different types, in the same data object. You can use a tag to identify a specific structure template and to declare variables of that type. The membership dot operator (.) enables you to access the individual members of a structure by using labels from the structure template.

If you have a pointer to a structure, you can use the pointer and the indirect membership operator (->) instead of a name and the dot operator to access individual members. To find the address of a structure, use the & operator. Unlike arrays, the name of a structure does not serve as the address of the structure.

Traditionally, structure-related functions have used pointers to structures as arguments. Modern C, including ANSI C, permits structures to be passed as arguments, used as return values, and assigned to structures of the same type.

Unions use the same syntax as structures. However, with unions, the members share a common storage space. Instead of storing several data types simultaneously in the manner of a structure, the union stores a single data item type from a list of choices. That is, a structure can hold, say, an `int` and a `double` and a `char`, and the corresponding union can hold an `int` or a `double` or a `char`.

The `typedef` facility enables you to establish aliases or shorthand representations of standard C types.

The name of a function yields the address of that function. Such addresses can be passed as arguments to functions, which then use the pointed-to function.

Review Questions

1. What's wrong with this template?

   ```
   structure {
          char itable;
          int  num[20];
          char * togs
   }
   ```

2. Here is a portion of a program. What will it print?

   ```
   #include <stdio.h>
   struct house {
       float sqft;
       int rooms;
       int stories;
       char address[40];
   };
   int main(void)
   {
     struct house fruzt = {1560.0, 6, 1, "22 Spiffo Road"};
     struct house *sign;

     sign = &fruzt;
     printf("%d %d\n", fruzt.rooms, sign->stories);
     printf("%s \n", fruzt.address);
     printf("%c %c\n", sign->address[3], fruzt.address[4]);
     return 0;
   }
   ```

3. Devise a structure template that will hold the name of a month, a three-letter abbreviation for the month, the number of days in the month, and the month number.

4. Define an array of 12 structures of the sort in Question 3 and initialize it for a non-leap year.

5. Write a function that, when given the month number, returns the total days in the year up to and including that month. Assume that the structure template of Question 2 and an appropriate array of such structures are declared externally.

6. Given the following **typedef**, declare a ten-element array of the indicated structure. Then, using individual member assignment (or the string equivalent), let the third element describe a Remarkatar lens of focal length 500 mm and aperture f/2.0.

   ```
   typedef struct lens {     /* lens descriptor */
       float foclen;         /* focal length,mm */
       float fstop;          /* aperture        */
       char brand[30];       /* brand name      */
   } LENS;
   ```

7. Consider the following programming fragment:

```
struct name {
        char first[20];
        char last[20];
};
struct bem {
        int limbs;
        struct name title;
        char type[30];
};
struct bem * pb;
struct bem deb = {
        6,
        {"Berbnazel", "Gwolkapwolk"},
        "Arcturan"

};

pb = &deb;
```

   a. What would each of the following statements print?

```
printf("%d\n", deb.limbs);
printf("%s\n", pb->type);
printf("%s\n", pb->type + 2);
```

   b. How could you represent "Gwolkapwolk" in structure notation (two ways)?

   c. Write a function that takes the address of a bem structure as its argument and prints the contents of that structure in the form shown below. Assume that the structure template is in a file called starfolk.h.

   Berbnazel Gwolkapwolk is a 6-limbed Arcturan.

8. Consider the following declarations:

```
struct fullname {
                char fname[20];
                char lname[20];
                };
struct bard      {
                struct fullname name;
                int born;
                int died;
                };
struct bard willie;
struct bard *pt = &willie;
```

   a. Identify the born member of the willie structure using the willie identifier.

     b. Identify the **born** member of the **willie** structure using the **pt** identifier.

     c. Use a **scanf()** call to read in a value for the **born** member using the **willie** identifier.

     d. Use a **scanf()** call to read in a value for the **born** member using the **pt** identifier.

     e. Construct an identifier for the third letter of the first name of someone described by the **willie** variable.

     f. Construct an expression representing the total number of letters in the first and last names of someone described by the **willie** variable.

9. Define a structure template suitable for holding the following items: the name of an automobile, its horsepower, its EPA city-driving mpg rating, its wheelbase, and its year. Use **car** as the template tag.

10. Suppose you have this structure:

```
struct gas {
    float distance;
    float gals;
    float mpg;
};
```

Devise a function that takes a **struct gas** argument. Assume that the passed structure contains the **distance** and **gals** information. Have the function calculate the correct value for the **mpg** member and return the now completed structure.

11. Declare a pointer to a function that returns a pointer to **char** and that takes a pointer to **char** and a **char** as arguments.

12. Declare four functions and initialize an array of pointers to point to them. Each function should take two **double** arguments and return a **double**.

Programming Exercises

1. Redo Review Question 3, but make the argument the spelled-out name of the month instead of the month number. (Don't forget about **strcmp()**.)

2. Write a program that prompts the user to enter the day, month, and year. The month can be a month number, a month name, or a month abbreviation. The program then returns the total number of days in the year up through the given day.

3. Revise the book-listing program in Listing 14.2 so that it prints both the book descriptions alphabetized by title and the total value of the books.

4. Write a program that creates a structure template with two members according to the following criteria:

   a. The first member is a Social Security number. The second member is a structure with three members. Its first member contains a first name, its second member contains a middle name, and its final member contains a last name. Create and initialize an array of five such structures. Have the program print the data in this form:

   ```
   Dribble, Flossie M. -- 302039823
   ```

   Only the initial of the middle name is printed, and a period is added. Neither the initial (of course) nor the period should be printed if the middle name member is empty. Write a function to do the printing; pass the structure array to the function.

   b. Modify part a. by passing the structure value instead of the address.

5. Write a program that fits the following recipe:

   a. Externally define a name structure template with two members: a string to hold the first name and a string to hold the second name.

   b. Externally define a student structure template with three members: a name structure, a grade array to hold floating-point scores, and a variable to hold the average of those three scores.

   c. Have the main() function declare an array of CSIZE (with CSIZE = 4) student structures and initialize the name portions to names of your choice. Use functions to perform the tasks described in parts d, e, f, and g.

   d. Interactively acquire scores for each student by prompting the user with a student name and a request for scores. Place the scores in the grade array portion of the appropriate structure. The required looping can be done in main() or in the function, as you prefer.

   e. Calculate the average score value for each structure and assign it to the proper member.

   f. Print the information in each structure.

   g. Print the class average for each of the numeric structure members.

6. A text file holds information about a softball team. Each line has data arranged as follows:

   ```
   4 Jessie Joybat 5 2 1 1
   ```

The first item is the player's number, conveniently in the range 0–18. The second is the player's first name, and the third is the player's last name. Each name is a single word. The next item is the player's official times at bat, followed by the number of hits, walks, and runs batted in (RBIs). The file may contain data for more than one game, so the same player may have more than one line of data, and there may be data for other players between those lines. Write a program that stores the data into an array of structures. The structure should have members to represent the first and last names, the runs, hits, walks, and RBIs, and the batting average (to be calculated later). You can use the player number as an array index. The program should read to end-of-file, and it should keep cumulative totals for each player.

The simplest way to do this is to initialize the structure contents to zeros, read the file data into temporary variables, and then add them to the contents of the corresponding structure. After the program has finished reading the file, it should then calculate the batting average for each player and store it in the corresponding structure member. The batting average is calculated by dividing the cumulative number of hits for a player by the cumulative number of at-bats; it should be a floating-point calculation. The program should then display the cumulative data for each player along with a line showing the combined statistics for the entire time.

7. Modify Listing 14.11 so that as each record is read from the file and shown to you, you are given the chance to delete the record or to modify its contents. If you delete the record, use the vacated array position for the next record to be read. To allow changing the existing contents, you'll need to use the "r+b" mode instead of the "a+b" mode, and you'll have to pay more attention to positioning the file pointer so that appended records don't overwrite existing records. It's simplest to make all changes in the data stored in program memory, and then write the final set of information to the file.

8. The Colossus Airlines fleet consists of one plane with a seating capacity of 12. It makes one flight daily. Write a seating reservation program with the following features:

   a. The program uses an array of 12 structures. Each structure should hold a seat identification number, a marker that indicates whether the seat is assigned, the last name of the seat holder, and the first name of the seat holder.

   b. The program displays the following menu:

```
To choose a function, enter its letter label:
a) Show number of empty seats
b) Show list of empty seats
c) Show alphabetical list of seats
```

```
d) Assign a customer to a seat assignment
e) Delete a seat assignment
f) Quit
```

c. The program successfully executes the promises of its menu. Choices d) and e) require additional input, and each should enable the user to abort entry.

d. After executing a particular function, the program shows the menu again, except for choice f).

e. Data is saved in a file between runs. When the program is restarted, it first loads in the data, if any, from the file.

9. Colossus Airlines (Exercise 7) acquires a second plane (same capacity) and expands its service to four flights daily (Flights 102, 311, 444, and 519). Expand the program to handle four flights. Have a top-level menu that offers a choice of flights and quitting. Selecting a particular flight should then bring up a menu similar to that of Exercise 7. However, one new item should be added: confirming a seat assignment. Also, the quit choice should be replaced with the choice of exiting to the top-level menu. Each display should indicate which flight is currently being handled. Also, the seat assignment display should indicate the confirmation status.

10. Write a program that implements a menu by using an array of pointers to functions. For instance, choosing a from the menu would activate the function pointed to by the first element of the array.

## CHAPTER 15

BIT FIDDLING

You will learn about the following in this chapter:

- Operators
  ~ & | ^
  >> <<
  &= |= ^= >>= <<=

I n this chapter, you review binary, octal, and hexadecimal number notations. Then you learn about two C facilities for handling the individual bits in a value: bitwise operators and bit fields.

With C, you can manipulate the individual bits in a variable. Perhaps you are wondering why anyone would want to. Be assured that sometimes this ability is necessary, or at least useful. For example, a hardware device is often controlled by sending it a byte in which each bit has a particular meaning. Also, operating system information about files is often stored by using particular bits to indicate particular items.

We'll investigate C's bit powers in this chapter after we supply you with some background about bits, bytes, binary notation, and other number bases.

Binary Numbers, Bits, and Bytes

The usual way to write numbers is based on the number 10. For instance, 2,157 has a 2 in the thousands place, a 1 in the hundreds place, a 5 in the tens place, and a 7 in the ones place. This means you can think of 2,157 as being the following:

```
2 x 1000 + 1 x 100 + 5 x 10 + 7 x 1
```

However, 1,000 is 10 cubed, 100 is 10 squared, 10 is 10 to the first power, and, by convention, 1 is 10 (or any positive number) to the zero power. Therefore, you can also write 2,157 as this:

$$2 \times 10^3 + 1 \times 10^2 + 5 \times 10^1 + 7 \times 10^0$$

Because our system of writing numbers is based on powers of ten, we say that 2,157 is written in *base 10*.

Presumably, the decimal system evolved because we have ten fingers. A computer bit, in a sense, has only two fingers because it can be set only to 0 or 1, off or on. Therefore, a *base 2* system is natural for a computer. It uses powers of two instead of powers of ten. Numbers expressed in base 2 are termed *binary numbers*. The number 2 plays the same role for binary numbers that the number 10 does for base 10 numbers. For example, a binary number such as 1,101 mean this:

$$1 \times 2^3 + 1 \times 2^2 + 0 \times 2^1 + 1 \times 2^0$$

In decimal numbers, it becomes this:

$$1 \times 8 + 1 \times 4 + 0 \times 2 + 1 \times 1 = 13$$

You can use the binary system to express any number (if you have enough bits) as a combination of 1s and 0s. This system is very convenient for digital computers, which express information in combinations of on and off states that can be interpreted as 1s and 0s. Let's see how the binary system works for a 1-byte integer.

Binary Integers

Usually, a byte contains 8 bits. C, remember, uses the term *byte* to denote the size used to hold a system's character set, so a C byte could be 8 bits, 9 bits, 16 bits, or some other value. However, the 8-bit byte is the byte used to describe memory chips and the byte used to describe data transfer rates. To keep matters simple, this chapter assumes an 8-bit byte. You can think of these 8 bits as being numbered from 7 to 0, left to right. Bit 7 is called the *high-order bit,* and bit 0 is the *low-order bit* in the byte. Each bit number corresponds to a particular exponent of 2. Imagine the byte as looking like Figure 15.1.

Here, 128 is 2 to the 7th power, and so on. The largest number this byte can hold is 1, with all bits set to 1: 11111111. The value of this binary number is as follows:

$$128 + 64 + 32 + 16 + 8 + 4 + 2 + 1 = 255$$

The smallest binary number would be 00000000, or a simple 0. A byte can store numbers from 0 to 255, for a total of 256 possible values. By changing the interpretation, a byte can store numbers from −128 to +127, again a total of 256 values.

This example shows bits 6, 3, and 0 set to 1.
The value of this byte is 64 + 8 + 1 or 73.

Figure 15.1 Bit numbers and bit values.

Signed Integers

The representation of signed numbers is determined by the hardware, not by C. Probably the simplest way to represent signed numbers is to reserve 1 bit, such as the high-order bit, to represent the sign. In a 1-byte value, this leaves 7 bits for the number itself. In such a *sign-magnitude* representation, 10000001 is –1 and 00000001 is 1. The total range, then, is –127 to +127.

One disadvantage of this approach is that it has two zeros: +0 and –0. This is confusing, and it also uses up two bit patterns for just one value.

The *two's-complement* method avoids that problem and is the most common system used today. We'll discuss this method as it applies to a 1-byte value. In that context, the values 0 through 127 are represented by the last 7 bits, with the high-order bit set to 0. So far, that's the same as the sign-magnitude method. Also, if the high-order bit is 1, the value is negative. The difference comes in determining the value of that negative number. Subtract the bit-pattern for a negative number from the 9-bit pattern 100000000 (256 expressed in binary), and the result is the magnitude of value. For example, suppose the pattern is 10000000. As an unsigned byte, it would be 128. As a signed value, it is negative (bit 7 is 1) and has a value of 100000000 – 10000000, or 10000000 (128). Therefore, the number is –128. (It would have been -0 in the sign-magnitude system.) Similarly, 10000001 is –127, and 11111111 is –1. The method represents numbers in the range –128 to +127.

The simplest method for reversing the sign of a two's-complement binary number is to invert each bit (convert 0s to 1s and 1s to 0s) and then add 1. Because 1 is 00000001, –1 is 11111110 + 1, or 11111111, just as you saw earlier.

The *one's-complement* method forms the negative of a number by inverting each bit in the pattern. For instance, 00000001 is 1 and 11111110 is –1. This method also has a –0: 11111111. Its range (for a 1-byte value) is –127 to +127.

Binary Floating Point

Floating-point numbers are stored in two parts: a binary fraction and a binary exponent. Let's see how this is done.

Binary Fractions

The ordinary fraction 0.527 represents

```
5/10 + 2/100 + 7/1000
```

with the denominators representing increasing powers of ten. In a binary fraction, you use powers of two for denominators, so the binary fraction .101 represents

```
1/2 + 0/4 + 1/8
```

which in decimal notation is

```
0.50 + 0.00 + 0.125
```

or 0.625.

Many fractions, such as 1/3, cannot be represented exactly in decimal notation. Similarly, many fractions cannot be represented exactly in binary notation. Indeed, the only fractions that can be represented exactly are combinations of multiples of powers of 1/2. Therefore, 3/4 and 7/8 can be represented exactly as binary fractions, but 1/3 and 2/5 cannot be.

Floating-Point Representation

To represent a floating-point number in a computer, a certain number of bits (depending on the system) are set aside to hold a binary fraction. Additional bits hold an exponent. In general terms, the actual value of the number consists of the binary fraction times 2 to the indicated exponent. Multiplying a floating-point number by, say, 4, increases the exponent by 2 and leaves the binary fraction unchanged. Multiplying by a number that is not a power of 2 changes the binary fraction and, if necessary, the exponent.

Other Bases

Computer workers often use number systems based on 8 and on 16. Because 8 and 16 are powers of 2, these systems are more closely related to a computer's binary system than the decimal system is.

Octal

Octal refers to a base 8 system. In this system, the different places in a number represent powers of 8. You use the digits 0 to 7. For example, the octal number 451 (written 0451 in C) represents this:

```
4 x 8² + 5 x 8¹ + 1 x 8⁰ = 297 (base 10)
```

A handy thing to know about octal is that each octal digit corresponds to three binary digits. Table 15.1 shows the correspondence. This correspondence makes it simple to translate between the two systems. For example, the octal number 0377 is 11111111 in binary. We replaced the 3 with 011, dropped the leading 0, and then replaced each 7 with 111. The only awkward part is that a 3-digit octal number might take up to 9 bits in binary form, so an octal value larger than 0377 requires more than a byte. Note that internal 0s are not dropped: 0173 is 01 111 011, not 01 111 11.

Table 15.1   Binary equivalents for octal digits.

Octal Digit	Binary Equivalent
0	000
1	001
2	010

Octal Digit	Binary Equivalent
3	011
4	100
5	101
6	110
7	111

Hexadecimal

Hexadecimal (or "hex") refers to a base 16 system. Here you use powers of 16 and the digits 0 to 15, but because you don't have single digits to represent the values 10 to 15, use the letters A to F for that purpose. For instance, the hex number A3F (written 0xA3F in C) represents

```
10 x 16² + 3 x 16¹ + 15 x 16⁰ = 2623 (base 10)
```

because A represents 10 and F represents 15. In C, you can use either lowercase or uppercase letters for the additional hex digits. Therefore, you can also write 2623 as `0xa3f`.

Each hexadecimal digit corresponds to a 4-digit binary number, so two hexadecimal digits correspond exactly to an 8-bit byte. The first digit represents the upper 4 bits, and the second digit the last 4 bits. This makes hexadecimal a natural choice for representing byte values. Table 15.2 shows the correspondence. For example, the hex value 0xC2 translates to 11000010.

Table 15.2 Decimal, hexadecimal, and binary equivalents.

Decimal Digit	Hexadecimal Digit	Binary Equivalent	Decimal Digit	Hexadecimal Digit	Binary Equivalent
0	0	0000	8	8	1000
1	1	0001	9	9	1001
2	2	0010	10	A	1010
3	3	0011	11	B	1011
4	4	0100	12	C	1100
5	5	0101	13	D	1101
6	6	0110	14	E	1110
7	7	0111	15	F	1111

Now that you've seen what bits and bytes are, let's examine what C can do with them. C has two facilities to help you manipulate bits. The first is a set of six bitwise operators that act on bits. The second is the `field` data form, which gives you access to bits within an `int`. The following discussion outlines these C features.

C's Bitwise Operators

C offers bitwise logical operators and shift operators. In the following examples, we will write out values in binary notation so that you can see what happens to the bits. In an actual program, you would use integer variables or constants written in the usual forms. For instance, instead of `00011001`, you would use `25` or `031` or `0x19`. For our examples, we will use 8-bit numbers, with the bits numbered 7 to 0, left to right.

Bitwise Logical Operators

The four bitwise logical operators work on integer-type data, including `char`. They are called *bitwise* because they operate on each bit independently of the bit to the left or right. Don't confuse them with the regular logical operators (`&&`, `¦¦`, and `!`), which operate on values as a whole.

One's Complement, or Bitwise Negation: ~

The unary operator ~ changes each 1 to a 0 and each 0 to a 1, as in the following example:

`~(10011010) == (01100101)`

Suppose that `val` is an `unsigned char` assigned the value 2. In binary, 2 is `00000010`. Then ~`val` has the value `11111101`, or `253`. Note that the operator does not change the value of `val`, just as `3 * val` does not change the value of `val`; `val` is still `2`, but it does create a new value that can be used or assigned elsewhere.

```
newval = ~val;
printf("%d", ~val);
```

If you want to change the value of `val` to ~`val`, use simple assignment:

```
val = ~val;
```

Bitwise AND: &

The binary operator & produces a new value by making a bit-by-bit comparison between two operands. For each bit position, the resulting bit is 1 only if both corresponding bits in the operands are 1. (In terms of true-false, the result is true only if each of the two bit operands is true.) Therefore,

`(10010011) & (00111101) == (00010001)`

because only bits 4 and 0 are 1 in both operands.

C also has a combined bitwise AND-assignment operator: `&=`. The statement

```
val &= 0377;
```

produces the same final result as the following:

```
val = val & 0377;
```

Bitwise OR: ¦

The binary operator ¦ produces a new value by making a bit-by-bit comparison between two operands. For each bit position, the resulting bit is 1 if either of the corresponding bits in the operands is 1. (In terms of true-false, the result is true if one or the other bit operands are true or if both are true.) Therefore,

```
(10010011) ¦ (00111101) == (101111111)
```

because all bit positions but bit 6 have the value 1 in one or the other operands.

C also has a combined bitwise OR-assignment operator: `¦=`. The statement

```
val ¦= 0377;
```

produces the same final result as this:

```
val = val ¦ 0377;
```

Bitwise EXCLUSIVE OR: ^

The binary operator ^ makes a bit-by-bit comparison between two operands. For each bit position, the resulting bit is 1 if one or the other (but not both) of the corresponding bits in the operands is 1. (In terms of true-false, the result is true if one or the other bit operands— but not both— are true.) Therefore,

```
(10010011) ^ (00111101) == (10101110)
```

Note that because bit position 0 has the value 1 in both operands, the resulting 0 bit has value 0.

C also has a combined bitwise OR-assignment operator: `^=`. The statement

```
val ^= 0377;
```

produces the same final result as this:

```
val = val ^ 0377;
```

Usage: Masks

The bitwise AND operator is often used with a mask. A *mask* is a bit pattern with some bits set to ON (1) and some bits to OFF (0). To see why a mask is called a mask, let's see what happens when a quantity is combined with a mask by using `&`. For example, suppose you define the symbolic constant MASK as 2, that is, binary 00000010, with only bit number 1 being nonzero. Then the statement

```
flags = flags & MASK;
```

would cause all the bits of **flags** (except bit 1) to be set to 0 because any bit combined with 0 by using the **&** operator yields 0. Bit number 1 will be left unchanged. (If the bit is 1, then **1 & 1** is 1; if the bit is 0, then **0 & 1** is 0.) This process is called "using a mask" because the zeros in the mask hide the corresponding bits in **flags**.

Extending the analogy, you can think of the 0s in the mask as being opaque and the 1s as being transparent. The expression **flags & MASK** is like covering the **flags** bit pattern with the mask; only the bits under **MASK**'s 1s are visible (see Figure 15.2).

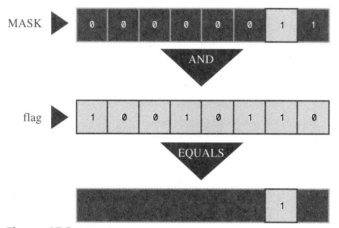

Figure 15.2 A mask.

You can shorten the code by using the AND-assignment operator, as shown here:

```
flags &= MASK;
```

One common C usage is this statement:

```
ch &= 0377;   /* or ch &= 0xff; */
```

The value **0377**, recall, is 11111111 in binary, as is the value **0xff**. This mask leaves the final 8 bits of **ch** alone and sets the rest to 0. Regardless of whether the original **ch** is 8 bits, 16 bits, or more, the final value is trimmed to something that fits into a single byte.

Usage: Turning Bits On

Sometimes you might need to turn on particular bits in a value while leaving the remaining bits unchanged. For instance, an IBM PC controls hardware through values sent to ports. To turn on, say, the speaker, you might have to turn on 1 bit while leaving the others unchanged. You can do this with the bitwise **OR** operator.

For example, consider the **MASK**, which has bit 1 set to 1. The statement

```
flags = flags | MASK;
```

sets bit number 1 in **flags** to 1 and leaves all the other bits unchanged. This follows because any bit combined with 0 by using the ¦ operator is itself, and any bit combined with 1 by using the ¦ operator is 1.

For short, you can use the bitwise OR-assignment operator:

```
flags |= MASK;
```

This, too, sets to 1 those bits in `flags` that are also on in `MASK`, leaving the other bits unchanged.

Usage: Turning Bits Off

Just as it's useful to be able to turn on particular bits without disturbing the other bits, it's useful to be able to turn them off. Suppose you want to turn off bit 1 in the variable `flags`. Once again, `MASK` has only the 1 bit turned on. You can do this:

```
flags = flags & ~MASK;
```

Because `MASK` is all 0s except for bit 1, `~MASK` is all 1s except for bit 1. A 1 combined with any bit by using & is that bit, so the statement leaves all the bits other than bit 1 unchanged. Also, a 0 combined with any bit by using & is 0, so bit 1 is set to 0 regardless of its original value.

You can use this short form instead:

```
flags &= ~MASK;
```

Usage: Toggling Bits

Toggling a bit means turning it off if it is on, and turning it on if it is off. You can use the bitwise **EXCLUSIVE OR** operator to toggle a bit. The idea is that if `b` is a bit setting (1 or 0), then `1 ^ b` is `0` if `b` is `1` and is `1` if `b` is `0`. Also `0 ^ b` is `b`, regardless of its value. Therefore, if you combine a value with a mask by using ^, values corresponding to 1s in the mask are toggled, and values corresponding to 0s in the mask are unaltered. To toggle bit 1 in `flag`, you can do either of the following:

```
flag = flag ^ MASK;
flag ^= MASK;
```

Usage: Checking the Value of a Bit

You've seen how to change the values of bits. Suppose, instead, that you want to check the value of a bit. For example, does `flag` have bit 1 set to 1? You shouldn't simply compare `flag` to `MASK`.

```
if (flag == MASK)
  puts("Wow!");    /* doesn't work right */
```

Even if bit 1 in `flag` is set to 1, the other bit setting in `flag` can make the comparison untrue. Instead, you must first mask the other bits in `flag` so that you compare only bit 1 of `flag` with `MASK`:

```
if ((flag & MASK) == MASK)
  puts("Wow!");
```

The bitwise operators have lower precedence than ==, so the parentheses around `flag & MASK` are needed.

Bitwise Shift Operators

Now let's look at C's shift operators. The bitwise shift operators shift bits to the left or right. Again, we will write binary numbers explicitly to show the mechanics.

Left Shift: <<

The << left shift operator shifts the bits of the value of the left operand to the left by the number of places given by the right operand. The vacated positions are filled with 0s, and bits moved past the end of the left operand are lost. In this statement, then,

```
(10001010) << 2 == (00101000)
```

each bit is moved two places to the left.

This operation produces a new bit value, but it doesn't change its operands. For example, suppose `stonk` is 1. Then `stonk<<2` is 4, but `stonk` is still 1. You can use the left-shift assignment operator (<<=) to actually change a variable's value. This operator shifts the bit in the variable to its left by the number of places given by the right-hand value.

```
int stonk = 1;
int onkoo;
onkoo = stonk << 2;    /* assigns 4 to onkoo */
stonk <<= 2;           /* changes stonk to 4 */
```

Right Shift: >>

The >> right shift operator shifts the bits of the value of the left operand to the right by the number of places given by the right operand. Bits moved past the right end of the left operand are lost. For **unsigned** types, the places vacated at the left end are replaced by 0s. For signed types, the result is machine dependent. The vacated places may be filled with 0s, or they may be filled with copies of the sign (leftmost) bit:

```
(10001010) >> 2 == (00100010)  /* signed value, some systems  */
(10001010) >> 2 == (11100010)  /* signed value, other systems */
```

For an unsigned value, you have the following:

```
(10001010) >> 2 == (00100010)  /* unsigned value, all system  */
```

Each bit is moved two places to the right, and the vacated places are filled with 0s.

The right-shift assignment operator (>>=) shifts the bits in the lefthand variable to the right by the indicated number of places, as shown here:

```
int sweet = 16;
int ooosw;

ooosw = sweet >> 3;  /* ooosw = 2, sweet still 16 */
sweet >>=3;          /* sweet changed to 2        */
```

Usage: Bitwise Shift Operators

The bitwise shift operators can provide swift, efficient (depending on the hardware) multiplication and division by powers of 2.

number << n	Multiplies number by 2 to the nth power.
number >> n	Divides number by 2 to the nth power if number is not negative.

These shift operations are analogous to the decimal system procedure of shifting the decimal point to multiply or divide by 10.

The shift operators can also be used to extract groups of bits from larger units. Suppose, for example, you use an unsigned long value to represent color values, with the low-order byte holding the red intensity, the next byte holding the green intensity, and the third byte holding the blue intensity. Suppose you then wanted to store the intensity of each color in its own unsigned char variable. Then you could do something like this:

```
#define BYTE_MASK 0xff
unsigned long color = 0x002a162f;
unsigned char blue, green, red;
red = color & BYTE_MASK;
green = (color >> 8) & BYTE_MASK;
blue = (color >> 16) & BYTE_MASK;
```

The code uses the right-shift operator to move the 8-bit color value to the low-order byte, and then uses the mask technique to assign the low-order byte to the desired variable.

Programming Example

In Chapter 9, "Functions," we used recursion to write a program to convert numbers to a binary representation. Now we'll solve the same problem by using the bitwise operators. The program in Listing 15.1 reads an integer from the keyboard and passes it and a string address to a function called itobs() (for integer *to* binary string, of course). This function then uses the bitwise operators to figure out the correct pattern of 1s and 0s to put into the string.

Listing 15.1   The binary.c program.

```
/* binary.c -- using bit operations to display binary */
#include <stdio.h>
char * itobs(int, char *);
int main(void)
{
    char bin_str[8 * sizeof(int) + 1];
    int number;

    puts("Enter integers and see them in binary.");
    puts("Non-numeric input terminates program.");
```

continued on next page

continued from previous page

```
        while (scanf("%d", &number) == 1)
            printf("%d is %s\n", number, itobs(number,bin_str));
        return 0;
    }

char * itobs(int n, char * ps)
{
    int i;
    static int size = 8 * sizeof(int);

    for (i = size - 1; i >= 0; i--, n >>= 1)
        ps[i] = (01 & n) + '0';
    ps[size] = '\0';
    return ps;
}
```

Listing 15.1 assumes that the system uses 8 bits to a byte. Therefore, the expression
8 * sizeof(int) is the number of bits in an int. The bin_str array has that many elements plus 1 to allow for the terminating null character.

The itobs() function returns the same address passed to it, so you can use the function as, say, an argument to printf(). The first time through the for loop, the function
evaluates the quantity 01 & n. The term 01 is the octal representation of a mask with all
but the zero bit set to 0. Therefore, 01 & n is just the value of the final bit in n. This value
is a 0 or a 1, but for the array, you need the *character* '0' or the *character* '1'. Adding the
ASCII code for '0' accomplishes that conversion. The result is placed in the next-to-last
element of the array. (The last element is reserved for the null character.)

By the way, you can just as well use 1 & n as 01 & n. Using octal 1 instead of decimal
1 just makes the mood a bit more computerish.

Then the loop executes the statements i-- and n >>= 1. The first statement moves you
one element earlier in the array, and the second shifts the bits in n over one position to the
right. The next time through the loop, then, you find the value of the new rightmost bit.
The corresponding digit character is then placed in the element preceding the final digit.
In this fashion, the function fills the array from right to left.

Here is a sample run:

```
Enter integers and see them in binary.
Non-numeric input terminates program.
7
7 is 00000000000000000000000000000111
1999
1999 is 00000000000000000000011111001111
-1
-1 is 11111111111111111111111111111111
32123
32123 is 00000000000000000111110101111011
q
```

Another Example

Let's work through one more example. The goal this time is to write a function that inverts the last n bits in a value, with both n and the value being function arguments.

The ~ operator inverts bits, but it inverts all the bits in a byte, not just a select few. However, the ^ operator (exclusive or), as you have seen, can be used to toggle individual bits. Suppose you create a mask with the last n bits set to 1 and the remaining bits set to 0. Then applying ^ to that mask and a value toggles, or inverts, the last n bits, leaving the other bits unchanged. That's the approach used here:

```
int invert_end(int num, int bits)
{
    int mask = 0;
    int bitval = 1;

    while (bits-- > 0)
    {
        mask |= bitval;
        bitval <<= 1;
    }
    return num ^ mask;
}
```

The while loop creates the mask. Initially, mask has all its bits set to 0. The first pass through the loop sets bit 0 to 1 and then increases the value of bitval to 2; that is, it sets bit 0 to 0 and bit 1 to 1. The next pass through then sets bit 1 of mask to 1, and so on. Finally, the num ^ mask operation produces the desired result.

To test the function, you can slip it into the preceding program, as shown in Listing 15.2.

Listing 15.2 The invert4.c program.

```
/*  invert4.c -- inverts last 4 bits of integers */
#include <stdio.h>
char * itobs(int n, char * ps);
int invert_end(int num, int bits);
int main(void)
{
    char bin_str[8 * sizeof(int) + 1];

    int number;

    puts("Enter integers and see them in binary.");
    puts("Non-numeric input terminates program.");
    while (scanf("%d", &number) == 1)
    {
        printf("%d is %s\n", number, itobs(number,bin_str));
        printf("Inverting the last 4 bits gives\n%s\n",
                itobs(invert_end(number,4),bin_str));
    }
    return 0;
}
```

continued on next page

continued from previous page

```
char * itobs(int n, char * ps)
{
    int i;
    static int size = 8 * sizeof(int);

    for (i = size - 1; i >= 0; i--, n >>= 1)
        ps[i] = (01 & n) + '0';
    ps[size] = '\0';
    return ps;
}
int invert_end(int num, int bits)
{
    int mask = 0;
    int bitval = 1;

    while (bits-- > 0)
    {
        mask |= bitval;
        bitval <<= 1;
    }
    return num ^ mask;
}
```

Here's a sample run:

```
Enter integers and see them in binary.
Non-numeric input terminates program.
7
7 is 00000000000000000000000000000111
Inverting the last 4 bits gives
00000000000000000000000000001000
255
255 is 00000000000000000000000011111111
Inverting the last 4 bits gives
00000000000000000000000011110000
q
```

Bit Fields

The second method of manipulating bits is to use a *bit field*, which is just a set of neighboring bits within an `unsigned int`. A bit field is set up with a structure declaration that labels each field and determines its width. For instance, the following declaration sets up four 1-bit fields:

```
struct   {
         unsigned int autfd  : 1;
         unsigned int bldfc  : 1;
         unsigned int undln  : 1;
         unsigned int itals  : 1;
} prnt;
```

This definition causes `prnt` to contain four 1-bit fields. Now you can use the usual structure membership operator to assign values to individual fields:

```
prnt.itals = 0;
prnt.undln = 1;
```

Because each of these particular fields is just 1 bit, `1` and `0` are the only values you can use for assignment. The variable `prnt` is stored in an `int`-sized memory cell, but only 4 bits are used in this example.

Fields aren't limited to 1-bit sizes. You can also do this:

```
struct {
        unsigned int code1 : 2;
        unsigned int code2 : 2;
        unsigned int code3 : 8;
} prcode;
```

This code creates two 2-bit fields and one 8-bit field. You can now make assignments such as the following:

```
prcode.code1 = 0;
prcode.code2 = 3;
prcode.code3 = 102;
```

Just make sure the value doesn't exceed the capacity of the field.

What if the total number of bits you declare exceeds the size of an `int`? Then the next `int` storage location is used. A single field is not allowed to overlap the boundary between two `int`s. The compiler automatically shifts an overlapping field definition so that the field is aligned with the `int` boundary. When this occurs, it leaves an unnamed hole in the first `int`.

You can "pad" a field structure with unnamed holes by using unnamed field widths. Using an unnamed field width of 0 forces the next field to align with the next integer:

```
struct {
    unsigned int field1 : 1;
    unsigned int        : 2;
    unsigned int field1 : 1;
    unsigned int        : 0;
    unsigned int field1 : 1;
} stuff;
```

Here, there is a 2-bit gap between `stuff.field1` and `stuff.field2`, and `stuff.field3` is stored in the next `int`.

One important machine dependency is the order in which fields are placed into an `int`. On some machines the order is left to right, and on others it is right to left. Also, machines differ in the location of boundaries between fields. For these reasons, bit fields tend not to be very portable. Typically, however, they are used for nonportable purposes, such as putting data in the exact form used by a particular hardware device.

Bit-Field Example

Often bit fields are used as a more compact way of storing data. Suppose, for example, you decided to represent the properties of an onscreen box. Let's keep the graphics simple and suppose the box has the following properties:

- The box is opaque or transparent.

- The fill color is selected from the following palette of colors: black, red, green, yellow, blue, magenta, cyan, or white.

- The border can be shown or hidden.

- The border color is selected from the same palette used for the fill color.

- The border can use one of three line styles: solid, dotted, or dashed.

You could use a separate variable or a full-sized structure member for each property, but that is a bit wasteful of bits. For example, you need only a single bit to indicate whether the box is opaque or transparent, and you need only a single bit to indicate if the border is shown or hidden. The eight possible color values can be represented by the eight possible values of a 3-bit unit, and a 2-bit unit is more than enough to represent the three possible border styles. A total of 10 bits, then, is enough to represent the possible settings for all five properties.

Here's one possible representation of the information; the `struct box_props` declaration uses padding to place the fill-related information in one byte and the border-related information in a second byte.

```
struct box_props {
    unsigned int opaque        : 1;
    unsigned int fill_color    : 3;
    unsigned int               : 4;
    unsigned int show_border   : 1;
    unsigned int border_color  : 3;
    unsigned int border_style  : 2;
    unsigned int               : 2;
};
```

The padding brings the structure size up to 16 bits. Without padding, the structure would be 10 bits. However, because memory allocation is usually aligned with the beginning of bytes or words, creating a 10-bit structure most likely would not save any memory compared to a 16-bit structure.

You can use a value of 1 for the `opaque` member to indicate that the box is opaque and a 0 value to indicate transparency. You can do the same for the `show_border` member. For colors, you can use a simple RGB (red-green-blue) representation. These are the primary colors for mixing light. A monitor blends red, green, and blue pixels to reproduce different colors. In the early days of computer color, each pixel could be either on or off, so you could use one bit to represent the intensity of each of the three binary colors. The usual order is for the left bit to represent blue intensity, the middle bit green intensity, and the right bit red intensity. Table 15.3 shows the eight possible combinations. They can be used as values for the `fill_color` and `border_color` members. Finally, you can choose to let 0, 1, and 2 represent the solid, dotted, and dashed styles; they can be used as values for the `border_style` member.

Table 15.3 Simple color representation.

Bit Pattern	Decimal	Color
000	0	Black
001	1	Red
010	2	Green
011	3	Yellow
100	4	Blue
101	5	Magenta
110	6	Cyan
111	7	White

Listing 15.3 uses the `box_props` structure in a simple example. It uses `#define` to create symbolic constants for the possible member values. Note that the primary colors are represented by a single bit being on. The other colors can be represented by combinations of the primary colors. For example, magenta consists of the blue bit and the red bit being on, so it can be represented by the combination `BLUE ¦ RED`.

Listing 15.3 The `fields.c` program.

```
/* fields.c -- define and use fields */
#include <stdio.h>
/* opaque and show */
#define YES     1
#define NO      0
/* line styles     */
#define SOLID   0
#define DOTTED  1
#define DASHED  2
/* primary colors  */
#define BLUE    4
#define GREEN   2
#define RED     1
/* mixed colors    */
#define BLACK   0
#define YELLOW  (RED ¦ GREEN)
#define MAGENTA (RED ¦ BLUE)
#define CYAN    (GREEN ¦ BLUE)
#define WHITE   (RED ¦ GREEN ¦ BLUE)
```

continued on next page

continued from previous page

```
struct box_props {
    unsigned int opaque          : 1;
    unsigned int fill_color      : 3;
    unsigned int                 : 4;
    unsigned int show_border     : 1;
    unsigned int border_color    : 3;
    unsigned int border_style    : 2;
    unsigned int                 : 2;
};
const char * colors[8] = {"black", "red", "green", "yellow",
            "blue", "magenta", "cyan", "white"};
int main(void)
{
    /* create and initialize box_props stucture */
    struct box_props box = {YES, YELLOW , YES, GREEN, DASHED};

    printf("Box is %s.\n",
        box.opaque == YES? "opaque": "transparent");
    printf ("The border style is ");
    switch(box.border_style)
    {
        case SOLID  : printf("solid.\n"); break;
        case DOTTED : printf("dotted.\n"); break;
        case DASHED : printf("dashed.\n"); break;
        default     : printf("unknown type.\n");
    }
    printf("The fill color is %s.\n", colors[box.fill_color]);
    printf("The border color is %s.\n", colors[box.border_color]);
    box.opaque = NO;
    box.fill_color = WHITE;
    box.border_color = MAGENTA;
    box.border_style = SOLID;
    printf("After changes, box is %s.\n",
        box.opaque == YES? "opaque": "transparent");
    printf ("The border style is ");
    switch(box.border_style)
    {
        case SOLID  : printf("solid.\n"); break;
        case DOTTED : printf("dotted.\n"); break;
        case DASHED : printf("dashed.\n"); break;
        default     : printf("unknown type.\n");
    }
    printf("The fill color is %s.\n", colors[box.fill_color]);
    printf("The border color is %s.\n", colors[box.border_color]);
    return 0;
}
```

Here is the output:

```
Box is opaque.
The border style is dashed.
The fill color is yellow.
The border color is green.
```

```
After changes, box is transparent.
The border style is solid.
The fill color is white.
The border color is magenta.
```

There are some points to note. First, you can initialize a bit-field structure by using the same syntax regular structures use:

```
struct box_props box = {YES, YELLOW , YES, GREEN, DASHED};
```

Similarly, you can assign to bit-field members:

```
box.fill_color = WHITE;
```

Also, you can use a bit-field member as the value expression for a `switch` statement. You can even use a bit-field member as an array index:

```
printf("The fill color is %s.\n", colors[box.fill_color]);
```

Notice that the `colors` array was defined so that each index value corresponds to a string representing the name of the color having the index value as its numeric color value. For example, an index of 1 corresponds to the string `"red"`, and red has the color value of 1.

Bit Fields and Bitwise Operators

Bit fields and bitwise operators are two alternative approaches to the same type of programming problem. That is, often you could use either approach. For instance, the previous example used a 2-byte structure to hold information about a graphics box, or you could use a 2-byte integer value, such as the typical `unsigned short`, to hold the same information. Then, instead of using structure member notation to access different parts, you could use the bitwise operators for that purpose. Typically, this is a bit more awkward to do. Let's look at an example that takes both approaches. (The reason for taking both approaches is to illustrate the differences, not to suggest that taking both approaches simultaneously is a good idea!)

You can use a union as a means of combining the structure approach with the bitwise approach. Given the existing declaration of the `struct box_props` type, you can declare the following union:

```
union Views      /* look at data as struct or as unsigned short */
{
    struct box_props st_view;
    unsigned short   sh_view;
};
```

On many systems, including ours, an `unsigned short` and a `box_props` structure both occupy 16 bits of memory. With this union, you can use the `st_view` member to look at that memory as a structure or use the `sh_view` member to look at the same block of memory as an `unsigned short`. Which bit fields of the structure correspond to which bits in the `unsigned short`? That depends on the implementation and the hardware. On an IBM PC using Microsoft Visual C/C++ 5.0, structures are loaded into memory from the low-bit end to the high-bit end of a byte. That is, the first bit field in the structure goes into bit 0 of the word (see Figure 15.3).

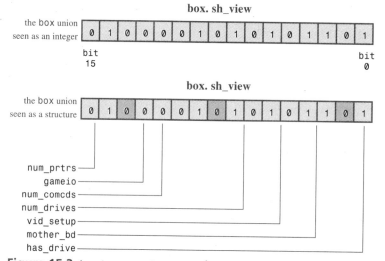

Figure 15.3 A union as an integer and as a structure.

Listing 15.4 uses the Views union to let you compare the bit field and bitwise approaches. In it, box is a Views union, so box.st_view is a box_prop structure using bit fields, and box.sh_view is the same data viewed as an unsigned short. The program also uses a shtobs() function, based on the itobs() function defined earlier in this chapter, to display the data as a binary string so that you can see which bits are on and which are off.

Listing 15.4   The dual.c program.

```
/* dual.c -- bit fields and bitwise operators */
#include <stdio.h>
/* BIT-FIELD CONSTANTS */
/* opaque and show */
#define YES      1
#define NO       0
/* line styles      */
#define SOLID    0
#define DOTTED   1
#define DASHED   2
/* primary colors   */
#define BLUE     4
#define GREEN    2
#define RED      1
/* mixed colors     */
#define BLACK    0
#define YELLOW   (RED ¦ GREEN)
#define MAGENTA  (RED ¦ BLUE)
#define CYAN     (GREEN ¦ BLUE)
#define WHITE    (RED ¦ GREEN ¦ BLUE)
```

```c
/* BITWISE CONSTANTS     */
#define OPAQUE          1
#define FILL_BLUE       8
#define FILL_GREEN      4
#define FILL_RED        2
#define FILL_MASK       14
#define BORDER          256
#define BORDER_BLUE     2048
#define BORDER_GREEN    1024
#define BORDER_RED      512
#define BORDER_MASK     3584
#define B_DOTTED        4096
#define B_DASHED        9192
#define STYLE_MASK      13288

struct box_props {
    unsigned int opaque        : 1;
    unsigned int fill_color    : 3;
    unsigned int               : 4;
    unsigned int show_border   : 1;
    unsigned int border_color  : 3;
    unsigned int border_style  : 2;
    unsigned int               : 2;
};
const char * colors[8] = {"black", "red", "green", "yellow",
        "blue", "magenta", "cyan", "white"};
char * shtobs(int n, char * ps); /* display short as binary string */
int main(void)
{
    union Views      /* look at data as struct or as unsigned short */
    {
        struct box_props st_view;
        unsigned short   sh_view;
    };
    /* create Views object, initialize struct box view */
    union Views box = {{YES, YELLOW , YES, GREEN, DASHED}};
    char bin_str[8 * sizeof(int) + 1];

    printf("Box is %s.\n",
        box.st_view.opaque == YES? "opaque": "transparent");
    printf ("The border style is ");
    switch(box.st_view.border_style)
    {
        case SOLID  : printf("solid.\n"); break;
        case DOTTED : printf("dotted.\n"); break;
        case DASHED : printf("dashed.\n"); break;
        default     : printf("unknown type.\n");
    }
    printf("The fill color is %s.\n",
        colors[box.st_view.fill_color]);
    printf("The border color is %s.\n",
        colors[box.st_view.border_color]);
```

continued on next page

continued from previous page

```
            printf("bits are %s\n",
                shtobs(box.sh_view,bin_str));
            box.sh_view &= ~FILL_MASK;             /* clear fill bits */
            box.sh_view |= (FILL_BLUE | FILL_GREEN); /* reset fill */
            box.sh_view ^= OPAQUE;                 /* toggle opacity */
            printf("After changes, box is %s.\n",
                box.st_view.opaque == YES? "opaque": "transparent");
            printf("The fill color is %s.\n",
                colors[box.st_view.fill_color]);
            printf("The border color is %s.\n",
                colors[(box.sh_view >> 9) & 07]);
            printf("bits are %s\n",
                shtobs(box.sh_view,bin_str));
            return 0;
}

/* convert short to binary string */
char * shtobs(int n, char * ps)
{
    int i;
    static int size = 8 * sizeof(short);

    for (i = size - 1; i >= 0; i--, n >>= 1)
        ps[i] = (01 & n) + '0';
    ps[size] = '\0';
    return ps;
}
```

Here is the output:

```
Box is opaque.
The border style is dashed.
The fill color is yellow.
The border color is green.
bits are 0010010100000111
After changes, box is transparent.
The fill color is cyan.
The border color is green.
bits are 0010010100001100
```

There are several points to discuss. One difference between the bit-field and bitwise views is that the bitwise view needs positional information. For example, we've used **BLUE** to represent the color blue. This constant has the numerical value of 4. But, because of the way the data is arranged in the structure, the actual bit holding the blue setting for the fill color is bit 3 (remember, numbering starts at 0), and the bit holding the blue setting for the border color is bit 11. Therefore, the program defines some new constants:

```
#define FILL_BLUE        8
#define BORDER_BLUE   2048
```

Here, **8** is the value if just bit 3 is set to 1, and **2048** is the value if just bit 11 is set to 1. You can use the first constant to set the blue bit for the fill color and the second constant to set the blue bit for the border color.

Note that using bitwise operators to change settings is more complicated. For example, consider setting the fill color to cyan. It is not enough just to turn the blue bit and the green bit on:

```
box.sh_view |= (FILL_BLUE | FILL_GREEN); /* reset fill */
```

The problem is that the color also depends on the red bit setting. If that bit is already set (as it is for the color yellow), then this code leaves the red bit set and sets the blue and green bits, resulting in the color white. The simplest way around this problem is to turn all the color bits off first, before setting the new values. That is why the program used the following code:

```
box.sh_view &= ~FILL_MASK;              /* clear fill bits */
box.sh_view |= (FILL_BLUE | FILL_GREEN); /* reset fill */
```

In a case like this, the bit-field equivalent is simpler:

```
box.st_view.fill_color = CYAN;  /*bit-field equivalent */
```

You don't need to clear the bits first. Also, with the bit-field members, you can use the same color values for the border as for the fill, but you need to use different values (values reflecting the actual bit positions) for the bitwise operator approach.

Next, compare the following two print statements:

```
printf("The border color is %s.\n",
       colors[box.st_view.border_color]);
printf("The border color is %s.\n",
       colors[(box.sh_view >> 9) & 07]);
```

In the first statement, the expression `box.st_view.border_color` has a value in the range 0–7, so it can be used as an index for the `colors` array. Getting the same information with bitwise operators is more complex. One approach is to use `box.sh_view >> 9` to right-shift the border-color bits to the rightmost position in the value (bits 0–2). Then combine this value with a mask of `07` so that all bits but the rightmost 3 are turned off. Then what is left is in the range 0–7 and can be used as an index for the `colors` array.

Caution

The correspondence between bit fields and bit positions is implementation dependent. For example, running Listing 15.4 on a Macintosh produces the following output:

```
Box is opaque.
The border style is dashed.
The fill color is yellow.
The border color is green.
bits are 1011000010101000
After changes, box is opaque.
The fill color is yellow.
The border color is black.
bits are 1011000010101101
```

The code changed the same bits as before, but the Macintosh loads the structure into memory differently. In particular, it loads the first bit field into the highest-order bit instead of the lowest-order bit. Therefore, the assumptions that Listing 15.4 makes about the location of bits is incorrect for the Macintosh, and using bitwise operators to change the opacity and fill color settings alters the wrong bits.

Chapter Summary

Computing hardware is closely tied to the binary number system because the 1s and 0s of binary numbers can be used to represent the on and off states of bits in computer memory and registers. Although C does not allow you to write numbers in binary form, it does recognize the related octal and hexadecimal notations. Just as each binary digit represents 1 bit, each octal digit represents 3 bits, and each hexadecimal digit represents 4 bits. This relationship makes it relatively simple to convert binary numbers to octal or hexadecimal form.

C features several bitwise operators, so called because they operate independently on each bit within a value. The bitwise negation operator (~) inverts each bit in its operand, converting 1s to 0s and vice versa. The bitwise AND operator (&) forms a value from two operands. Each bit in the value is set to 1 if both corresponding bits in the operands are 1. Otherwise, the bit is set to 0. The bitwise OR operator (¦) also forms a value from two operands. Each bit in the value is set to 1 if either or both corresponding bits in the operands are 1; otherwise, the bit is set to 0. The bitwise EXCLUSIVE OR operator (^) acts similarly, except that the resulting bit is set to 1 only if one or the other, but not both, of the corresponding bits in the operands is 1.

C also has left-shift (<<) and right-shift (>>) operators. Each produces a value formed by shifting the bits in a pattern the indicated number of bits to the left or right. For the left-shift operator, the vacated bits are set to 0. For the right-shift operator, the vacated bits are set to 0 if the value is unsigned. The behavior of the right-shift operator is implementation dependent for signed values.

You can use bit fields in a structure to address individual bits or groups of bits in a value. The details are implementation independent.

These bit tools help C programs deal with hardware matters, so they most often appear in implementation-dependent contexts.

Review Questions

1. Convert the following decimal values to binary:

   a. 3

   b. 13

    c. 59

    d. 119

2. Convert the following binary values to decimal, octal, and hexadecimal:

    a. 00010101

    b. 01010101

    c. 01001100

    d. 10011101

3. Evaluate the following expressions; assume each value is 8 bits:

    a. `~3`

    b. `3 & 6`

    c. `3 | 6`

    d. `1 | 6`

    e. `3 ^ 6`

    f. `7 >> 1`

    g. `7 << 2`

4. Evaluate the following expressions; assume each value is 8 bits:

    a. `~0`

    b. `!0`

    c. `2 & 4`

    d. `2 && 4`

    e. `2 | 4`

    f. `2 || 4`

    g. `5 << 3`

5. Because the ASCII code uses only the final 7 bits, sometimes it is desirable to mask off the other bits. What's the appropriate mask in binary? In decimal? In octal? In hexadecimal?

6. In Listing 15.2, you can replace

```
while (bits-- > 0)
    {
        mask |= bitval;
        bitval <<= 1;
    }
```

with

```
while (bits-- > 0)
    {
        mask += bitval;
        bitval *= 2;
    }
```

and the program still works. Does this mean the operation `*= 2` is equivalent to `<<= 1`? What about `|=` and `+=`?

8.

a. The Tinkerbell computer has a hardware byte that can be read into a program. This byte contains the following information:

Bit(s)	Meaning
0–1	Number of 1.4MB floppy drives
2	Not used
3–4	Number of CD-ROM drives
5	Not used
6–7	Number of hard drives

Like the IBM PC, the Tinkerbell fills in structure bit fields from right to left. Create a bit-field template suitable for holding the information.

b. The Klinkerbell, a near Tinkerbell clone, fills in structures from left to right. Create the corresponding bit-field template for the Klinkerbell.

Programming Exercises

1. Write a function that converts a binary string to a numeric value. That is, if you have

```
char * pbin = "01001001";
```

then you can pass `pbin` as an argument to the function and have the function return an `int` value of **25**.

2. Write a program that reads two binary strings as command-line arguments and prints the results of applying the `~` operator to each number and the results of applying the `&`, `|`, and `^` operators to the pair. Show the results as binary strings.

3. Write a function that takes an `int` argument and returns the number of ON bits in the argument.

4. Write a function that takes two int arguments: a value and a bit position. Have the function return 1 if that particular bit position is 1, and have it return 0 otherwise.

5. Write a function that rotates the bits of an unsigned int by a specified number of bits to the left. For instance, rotate_l(x,4) would move the bits in x four places to the left, and the bits lost from the left end would reappear at the right end. That is, the bit moved out of the high-order position is placed in the low-order position.

6. Write a program with the same functionality as Listing 15.3. However, instead of using a structure with bit fields, it should use an unsigned int and the bitwise operators.

CHAPTER 16

THE C PREPROCESSOR AND THE C LIBRARY

You will learn about the following in this chapter:

- Keywords

  #define, #include, #ifdef
  #else, #endif, #ifndef
  #if, #elif, enum

- Functions

  sqrt(), atan(), atan2()
  exit(), atexit(), malloc()

I n this chapter, you investigate further the capabilities of the C preprocessor, learning about macro "functions" and conditional compilation. Also, you are introduced to the **enum** facility and learn more about the C library and dynamic memory allocation.

The ANSI C standard encompasses more than just the C language. It also describes how the C preprocessor should perform, establishes which functions form the standard C library, and details how these functions work. We'll explore the C preprocessor and the C library in this chapter, beginning with the preprocessor.

The preprocessor looks at your program before it is compiled (hence the term *preprocessor*). Following your preprocessor directives, the preprocessor replaces the symbolic abbreviations in your program with the directions they represent. The preprocessor can include other files at your request, and it can select which code the compiler sees. This description does not do justice to its true utility and value, so let's turn to examples. With **#define** and **#include**, we have provided examples all along. Now we can gather what you have learned in one place and add to it.

Manifest Constants: #define

The **#define** preprocessor directive, like all preprocessor directives, begins with a # symbol. The ANSI standard permits the # symbol to be preceded by spaces or tabs, and it allows for space between the # and the remainder of the directive. Older versions of C, however, typically require that the directive begin in the leftmost column and that there be no spaces between the # and the remainder of the directive. A directive can appear anywhere in the source file, and the definition holds from its place of appearance to the end of the file. We have used directives heavily to define symbolic, or manifest, constants in our programs, but they have more range than that, as we will show. Listing 16.1 illustrates some of the possibilities and properties of the `#define` directive.

Preprocessor directives run until the first newline following the #. That is, a directive is limited to one line in length. However, the combination backslash-newline is treated as a space, not an end-of-line marker, so you can spread the directive over several physical lines. These lines, however, constitute a single *logical* line.

Listing 16.1 The `preproc.c` program.

```
/* preproc.c -- simple preprocessor examples */
#include <stdio.h>
#define TWO 2          /* you can use comments if you like    */
#define OW "Consistency is the last refuge of the unimagina\
tive. - Oscar Wilde" /* a backslash continues a definition */
                        /* to the next line                   */
#define FOUR  TWO*TWO
#define PX printf("X is %d.\n", x)
#define FMT   "X is %d.\n"
int main(void)
{
    int x = TWO;

    PX;
    x = FOUR;
    printf(FMT, x);
    printf("%s\n", OW);
    printf("TWO: OW\n");
    return 0;
}
```

Each `#define` line (logical line, that is) has three parts. The first part is the `#define` directive itself. The second part is your chosen abbreviation, known as a *macro* or *alias* in the computer world. (Some programmers reserve the term *macro* for the macro functions we discuss later and use the term *alias* for the symbolic constants we are discussing now.) The macro name must have no spaces in it, and its name must conform to the same rules that C variables follow: Only letters, digits, and the underscore (_) character can be used, and the first character cannot be a digit. The third part (the remainder of the line) is termed the *body* (see Figure 16.1). When the preprocessor finds an example of one of your aliases within your program, it almost always replaces it with the body. (There is one exception, as we will show you in just a moment.) This process of going from a macro to a final replacement is called *macro expansion*. Note that you can use standard C comments on a `#define` line; they are ignored by the preprocessor. Also, in most systems (and the ANSI C standard), you can use the backslash (\) to extend a definition over more than one line, as shown in Listing 16.1.

Figure 16.1 Parts of a macro definition.

Let's run the example and see how it works:

```
X is 2.
X is 4.
Consistency is the last refuge of the unimaginative. - Oscar Wilde
TWO: OW
```

Here's what happened. The statement

```
int x = TWO;
```

becomes

```
int x = 2;
```

as 2 is substituted for TWO. Then the statement

```
PX;
```

becomes

```
printf("X is %d.\n", x);
```

as that wholesale substitution is made. This is a new wrinkle because up to now we've used macros only to represent constants. Here you see that a macro can express any string, even a whole C expression. Note, though, that this is a constant string; PX will print only a variable named x.

The next line also represents something new. You might think that FOUR is replaced by 4, but the actual process is this:

```
x = FOUR;
```

becomes

```
x = TWO*TWO;
```

which then becomes

```
x = 2*2;
```

The macro expansion process ends there. The actual multiplication takes place not while the preprocessor works, but during compilation because the C compiler evaluates all constant expressions (expressions with just constants) at compile time. The preprocessor does no calculation; it just makes the suggested substitutions very literally.

Note that a macro definition can include other macros. (Some compilers do not support this nesting feature.)

In the next line

```
printf (FMT, x);
```

becomes

```
printf("X is %d.\n",x);
```

as **FMT** is replaced by the corresponding string. This approach could be handy if you had a lengthy control string that you had to use several times. Alternatively, you can do the following:

```
char * fmt = "X is %d.\n";
```

Then you can use **fmt** as the **printf()** control string.

In the next line, **OW** is replaced by the corresponding string. The double quotation marks make the replacement string a character string constant. The compiler will store it in an array terminated with a null character. Therefore,

```
#define HAL 'Z'
```

defines a character constant, but

```
#define HAP "Z"
```

defines a character string: Z\0.

In the example, we used a backslash immediately before the end of the line to extend the string to the next line:

```
#define OW "Consistency is the last refuge of the unimagina\
tive. - Oscar Wilde"
```

Note that the second line is flush left. Suppose, instead, we did this:

```
#define OW "Consistency is the last refuge of the unimagina\
     tive. - Oscar Wilde"
```

Then the output would be this:

```
Consistency is the last refuge of the unimagina     tive. - Oscar Wilde
```

The space between the beginning of the line and **tive** counts as part of the string.

In general, wherever the preprocessor finds one of your macros in your program, it literally replaces it with the equivalent replacement text. If that string also contains macros, they, too, are replaced. The one exception to replacement is a macro found within double quotation marks. Therefore,

```
printf("TWO: OW");
```

prints **TWO: OW** literally instead of printing

```
2: Consistency is the last refuge of the unimaginative. - Oscar Wilde
```

To print this last line, you would use this:

```
printf("%d: %s\n", TWO, OW);
```

Here, the macros are outside the double quotation marks.

When should you use symbolic constants? You should use them for most numbers. If the number is some constant used in a calculation, a symbolic name makes its meaning clearer. If the number is an array size, a symbolic name makes it simpler to change the array size and loop limits later. If the number is a system code for, say, EOF, a symbolic representation makes your program much more portable; just change one EOF definition. Mnemonic value, easy alterability, portability—these features all make symbolic constants worthwhile.

Tokens

Technically, the body of a macro is considered to be a string of *tokens* rather than a string of characters. C preprocessor tokens are the separate "words" in the body of a macro definition. They are separated from one another by whitespace. For example, the definition

```
#define FOUR 2*2
```

has one token—the sequence 2*2—but the definition

```
#define SIX 2 * 3
```

has three tokens in it: 2, *, and 3.

Character strings and token strings differ in how multiple spaces in a body are treated. Consider this definition:

```
#define EIGHT 4    *    8
```

A preprocessor that interpreted the body as a character string would replace EIGHT with 4   *   8. That is, the extra spaces would be part of the replacement, but a preprocessor that interprets the body as tokens will replace EIGHT with three tokens separated by single spaces: 4 * 8. In other words, the character string interpretation views the spaces as part of the body, but the token interpretation views the spaces as separators between the tokens of the body. In practice, some C compilers have viewed macro bodies as strings rather than tokens. The difference is of practical importance only for more intricate usages than what we're attempting here.

Incidentally, the C compiler takes a more complex view of tokens than the preprocessor does. The compiler understands the rules of C and doesn't necessarily require spaces to separate tokens. For instance, the C compiler would view 2*2 as three tokens because it recognizes that each 2 is a constant and the * is an operator.

Redefining Constants

Suppose you define LIMIT to be 20, and then later in the same file you define it again as 25. This process is called *redefining a constant*. Implementations differ on redefinition policy. Some consider it an error unless the new definition is the same as the old. Others allow redefinition, perhaps issuing a warning. The ANSI standard takes the first view, allowing redefinition only if the new definition duplicates the old.

Having the same definition means the bodies must have the same tokens in the same order. Therefore, these two definitions agree:

```
#define SIX 2 * 3
#define SIX 2      *    3
```

Both have the same three tokens, and the extra spaces are not part of the body. The next definition is considered different.

```
#define SIX 2*3
```

It has just one token, not three, so it doesn't match. If you want to redefine a macro, use the #undef directive, which we discuss later.

If you do have constants that you need to redefine, it might be easier to use the const keyword and scope rules to accomplish that end.

Using Arguments with #define

By using arguments, you can create macros that look and act much like functions. A macro with arguments looks very similar to a function because the arguments are enclosed within parentheses. Listing 16.2 provides some examples that illustrate how such a *macro function* is defined and used. Some of the examples also point out possible pitfalls, so read them carefully.

Listing 16.2   The mac_arg.c program.

```
/* mac_arg.c -- macros with arguments */
#include <stdio.h>
#define SQUARE(X) X*X
#define PR(X)    printf("The result is %d.\n", X)
int main(void)
{
    int x = 4;
    int z;

    z = SQUARE(x);
    PR(z);
    z = SQUARE(2);
    PR(z);
    PR(SQUARE(x+2));
    PR(100/SQUARE(2));
    printf("x is %d\n.", x);
    PR(SQUARE(++x));
    printf("After incrementing, x is %x.\n", x);
    return 0;
}
```

Wherever SQUARE(x) appears in Listing 16.2, it is replaced by x*x. This differs from the earlier examples in that you are free to use symbols other than x when you use this macro. The x in the macro definition is replaced by the symbol used in the macro call in the program. Therefore, SQUARE(2) is replaced by 2*2, so the x really does act as an argument.

However, as you will soon see, a macro argument does not work exactly like a function argument. Here are the results of running the program. Note that some of the answers are different from what you might expect. Indeed, your compiler might not even give the same answer as what's shown here for the next to last line:

```
The result is 16.
The result is 4.
The result is 14.
The result is 100.
x is 4.
The result is 30.
After incrementing, x is 6.
```

The first two lines are predictable, but then you come to some peculiar results. Recall that x has the value 4. This might lead you to expect that SQUARE(x+2) would be 6*6, or 36, but the printout says it is 14, which sure doesn't look like a square to us! The simple reason for this misleading output is the one we have already stated—the preprocessor doesn't make calculations; it just substitutes strings. Wherever the definition shows an x, the preprocessor substitutes the string x+2. Therefore,

```
x*x
```

becomes

```
x+2*x+2
```

The only multiplication is 2*x. If x is 4, then this is the value of this expression:

```
4+2*4+2 = 4 + 8 + 2 = 14
```

This example pinpoints an important difference between a function call and a macro call. A function call passes the value of the argument to the function while the program is running. A macro call passes the argument token to the program before compilation; it's a different process at a different time. Can the definition be fixed to make SQUARE(x+2) yield 36? Sure. You simply need more parentheses.

```
#define SQUARE(x)  (x)*(x)
```

Then SQUARE(x+2) becomes (x+2)*(x+2), and you get the desired multiplication as the parentheses carry over in the replacement string.

This doesn't solve all the problems, however. Consider the events leading to the next output line:

```
100/SQUARE(2)
```

becomes

```
100/2*2
```

By the laws of precedence, the expression is evaluated from left to right:

```
(100/2)*2    or    50*2    or    100
```

This mix-up can be cured by defining SQUARE(x) as

```
#define SQUARE(x)  (x*x)
```

This produces `100/(2*2)`, which eventually evaluates to `100/4`, or `25`.

To handle both of the previous two examples, you need this definition:

```
#define SQUARE(x)  ((x)*(x))
```

The lesson here is to use as many parentheses as necessary to ensure that operations and associations are done in the right order.

Even these precautions fail to save the final example from grief.

```
SQUARE(++x)
```

becomes

```
++x*++x
```

and x gets incremented twice, once before the multiplication and once afterward.

```
++x*++x = 5*6 = 30
```

Because the order of operations is left open, some compilers render the product `6*5`. Yet other compilers might increment both terms before multiplication, yielding `6*6`. In all these cases, however, x starts with the value `4` and ends up with the value `6` even though the code looks as though x were incremented just once.

The simplest remedy for this problem is to avoid using `++x` as a macro argument. In general, don't use increment or decrement operators with macros. Note that `++x` would work as a function argument because it would be evaluated to `6`, and then the value `6` would be sent to the function.

Including the Macro Argument in a String

Under K&R C, you could define macros like the following:

```
#define PSQR(X)  printf("The square of X is %d.\n", ((X)*(X)));
```

Suppose you used the preceding macro like this:

```
PSQR(8);
PSQR(2 + 3);
```

Then the output would be this:

```
The square of 8 is 64.
The square of 2 + 3 is 25.
```

That is, the macro argument inside the double quotes would be replaced by the actual argument, contrary to the normal rule that tokens inside double quotes are left unaltered. ANSI C does not allow this substitution within quotes. Running the same code under ANSI C produces the following output:

```
The square of X is 64.
The square of X is 25.
```

The X in the quoted string is treated as ordinary text, not as a token that can be replaced.

Suppose you do want to include the macro argument in a string. A new feature of ANSI C enables you to do that. If, say, x is a macro parameter, then `#x` is that parameter converted to a string. Listing 16.3 illustrates how this process works.

Listing 16.3   The subst.c program.

```
/* subst.c -- substitute in string */
#include <stdio.h>
#define PSQR(x) printf("The square of " #x " is %d.\n",((x)*(x)))
int main(void)
{
    int y = 5;

    PSQR(y);
    PSQR(2 + 4);
    return 0;
}
```

Here's the output:

```
The square of y is 25.
The square of 2 + 4 is 36.
```

In the first call to the macro, #x was replaced by "y", and in the second call it was replaced by "2 + 4". ANSI C string concatenation then combined these strings with the other strings in the printf() statement to produce the final strings that were used.

Macro or Function?

Many tasks can be done by using a macro with arguments or by using a function. Which one should you use? There is no hard and fast rule, but here are some considerations.

Macros are somewhat trickier to use than regular functions because they can have odd side effects if you are unwary. Some compilers limit the macro definition to one line, and it is probably best to observe that limit even if your compiler does not.

The macro-versus-function choice represents a trade-off between time and space. A macro produces in-line code; that is, you get a statement in your program. If you use the macro 20 times, then you get 20 lines of code inserted into your program. If you use a function 20 times, you have just one copy of the function statements in your program, so less space is used. On the other hand, program control must shift to where the function is and then return to the calling program, and this takes longer than in-line code.

Macros have an advantage in that they don't worry about variable types. (This is because they deal with character strings, not with actual values.) Therefore, the SQUARE(x) macro can be used equally well with int or float.

Programmers typically use macros for simple functions such as the following:

```
#define MAX(X,Y)   ((X) > (Y) ? (X) : (Y))
#define ABS(X)     ((X) < 0 ? -(X) : (X))
#define ISSIGN(X)  ((X) == '+' || (X) == '-' ? 1 : 0)
```

(The last macro has the value 1—true—if x is an algebraic sign character.)

Here are some points to note:

- Remember that there are no spaces in the macro name, but spaces can appear in the replacement string. With K&R C, there can be no spaces in the argument list. The preprocessor thinks the macro ends at the first space, so anything after that space is lumped into the replacement string, as shown in Figure 16.2. ANSI C, however, does permit spaces in the argument list.

- Use parentheses around each argument and around the definition as a whole. This ensures that the enclosed terms are grouped properly in an expression such as `forks = 2 * MAX(guests + 3, last);`.

- Use capital letters for macro function names. This convention is not as widespread as that of using capitals for macro constants. However, one good reason for using capitals is to remind yourself to be alert to possible macro side effects.

- If you intend to use a macro instead of a function primarily to speed up a program, first try to determine if it is likely to make a significant difference. A macro that is used once in a program probably won't make any noticeable improvement in running time. A macro inside a nested loop is a much better candidate for speed improvements. Many systems offer program profilers to help you pin down where a program spends the most time.

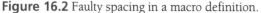

Figure 16.2 Faulty spacing in a macro definition.

Suppose you have developed some macro functions you like. Do you have to retype them each time you write a new program? Not if you remember the `#include` directive, reviewed in the following section.

File Inclusion: `#include`

When the preprocessor spots an `#include` directive, it looks for the following filename and includes the contents of that file within the current file. The `#include` directive in your source code file is replaced with the text from the included file. It's as though you sat down and typed in the entire contents of the included file at that particular location in your source file. The `#include` directive comes in two varieties.

```
#include <stdio.h>          ←Filename in angle brackets
#include "mystuff.h"        ←Filename in double quotation marks
```

On a UNIX system, the angle brackets tell the preprocessor to look for the file in one or more standard system directories. The double quotation marks tell it to first look in your current directory (or some other directory that you have specified in the filename) and then look in the standard places.

```
#include <stdio.h>          ←Searches system directories
#include "hot.h"            ←Searches your current working directory
#include "/usr/biff/p.h"    ←Searches the /usr/biff directory
```

Integrated development environments (IDEs) also have a standard location or locations for the system header files. Many provide menu choices for specifying additional locations to be searched when angle brackets are used. As with UNIX, using double quotes means to search a local directory first, but the exact directory searched depends on the compiler. Some search the same directory as that holding the source code; some search the current working directory; and some search the same directory as that holding the project file.

ANSI C doesn't demand adherence to the directory model for files because not all computer systems are organized similarly. In general, the method used to name files is system dependent, but the use of the angle brackets and double quotation marks is not.

Why include files? Because they have information the compiler needs. The stdio.h file, for example, typically includes definitions of EOF, NULL, getchar(), and putchar(). The last two are defined as macro functions.

The .h suffix is conventionally used for *header files*—files with information that are placed at the head of your program. Header files usually consist of preprocessor statements. Some, like stdio.h, come with the system, but you are free to create your own.

Including a large header file doesn't necessarily add much to the size of your program. The content of header files, for the most part, is information used by the compiler to generate the final code, not material to be added to the final code.

Header Files: An Example

Suppose you like using Boolean values. That is, instead of having 1 be true and 0 be false, you prefer using the words TRUE and FALSE. You could create a file called, say, bool.h that contains these definitions:

```
/* bool.h file */
#define BOOLEAN int  /* or typedef int BOOLEAN; */
#define TRUE 1
#define FALSE 0
```

Listing 16.4 is an example of a program using this header.

Listing 16.4   The cnt_en.c program.

```
/* cnt_en.c -- counts even numbers */
#include <stdio.h>
#include <stdlib.h>
#include "bool.h"
```

continued on next page

continued from previous page

```
BOOLEAN even_gt(int val, int lim);
#define ASIZE 100
int main(void)
{
    int data[ASIZE];
    int i;
    int count = 0;
    int num;
    int num2;

    printf("Enter a positive integer: ");
    scanf("%d", &num);
    num2 = num / 2;
    for (i = 0; i < ASIZE; i++)
        data[i] = rand() % num;
    for (i = 0; i < ASIZE; i++)
        if ( even_gt(data[i], num2))
            count++;

    printf("The sample of %d numbers contains ", ASIZE);
    printf("%d even values greater than %d.\n", count, num2);
    return 0;
}

/* returns true if val > lim and if val is even */
BOOLEAN even_gt(int val, int lim)
{
    if (val > lim && val %2 == 0)
        return(TRUE);
    else
        return(FALSE);
}
```

Here is a sample run:

```
Enter a positive integer: 500
The sample of 100 numbers contains 31 even values greater than 250.
```

Note the following points about this program:

- If the two functions in this program, main() and even_gt(), were compiled separately, you would use the #include "bool.h" directive with each.

- We have not created a new type BOOLEAN because BOOLEAN is just int. The purpose of labeling the function BOOLEAN is to remind the programmer that the function is being used for a logical (as opposed to arithmetic) calculation.

- Using a function for involved logical comparisons can make a program clearer. It also can save effort if the comparison is made in more than one place in a program.

Uses for Header Files

A look through any of the standard header files can give you a good idea of the sort of information found in them. Typical header contents include the following:

- *Manifest constants.* A typical `stdio.h` file, for instance, defines `EOF`, `NULL`, and `BUFSIZE` (the size of the standard I/O buffer).

- *Macro functions.* For example, `getchar()` is usually defined as `getc(stdin)`, `getc()` is usually defined as a rather complex macro, and the `ctype.h` header typically contains macro definitions for the `ctype` functions.

- *Function declarations.* The `string.h` header (`strings.h` on some older systems), for instance, contains function declarations for the family of string functions. Under ANSI C, the declarations are in function prototype form.

- *Structure template definitions.* The standard I/O functions make use of a structure containing information about a file and its associated buffer. The `stdio.h` file holds the template for this structure.

- *Type definitions.* You might recall that the standard I/O functions use a pointer-to-`FILE` argument. Typically, `stdio.h` uses a `#define` or a `typedef` to make `FILE` represent a pointer to a structure. Similarly, the `size_t` and `time_t` types are defined in header files.

Many programmers develop their own standard header files to use with their programs. Some files might be for special purposes; others might be used with almost every program. Because included files can incorporate `#include` directives, you can create concise, well-organized header files, if you like.

Consider this example:

```
/* header file mystuff.h */
#include <stdio.h>
#include "bool.h"
#include "funct.h"
#define YES 1
#define NO 0
```

First, it's a good idea to use a comment to identify the name of the header file. Second, we have included three files. Presumably the third one contains some macro functions or function prototypes that we use often. Third, we have defined `YES` as `1`, although in `bool.h` we defined `TRUE` as `1`. There is no conflict here. We can use `YES` and `TRUE` in the same program. Each will be replaced by a `1`.

Also, you can use header files to declare external variables to be shared by several files. Some programmers think it's okay to do so. Others think it is poor style because you have to check another file to see whether a variable is declared. However, external data that is both `static` and `const` works well in header files. The `const` part protects against accidental changes, and the `static` part means that each file including the header gets its own copy of the constants so that there isn't the problem of needing one file with a defining declaration and the rest with reference declarations.

The `#include` and `#define` directives are the most heavily used C preprocessor features. We'll look at the other directives in less detail.

Other Directives

The `#undef` directive cancels an earlier `#define` definition. The `#if`, `#ifdef`, `#ifndef`, `#else`, `#elif`, and `#endif` directives are typically used to produce files that can be compiled in more than one way.

The #undef Directive

The `#undef` directive undefines a given `#define`. That is, suppose you have this definition:

```
#define LIMIT 400
```

Then the directive

```
#undef LIMIT
```

removes that definition. Now, if you like, you can redefine `LIMIT` so that it has a new value. Even if `LIMIT` is not defined in the first place, it is still valid to undefine it. If you want to use a particular name and you are unsure whether it has been used previously, you can undefine it to be on the safe side.

With some compilers, you can redefine a defined name and nest `#define` and `#undef` directives so that undefining a name causes it to revert to its original value. This is not, however, the standard practice, and it is not part of the ANSI standard. More typically, you'll get a warning or error message if you redefine a name, so use `#undef` first if you want to redefine. Remember, however, that you can nest **const** constants as long as each new definition is in its own subblock, as Listing 16.5 shows.

Listing 16.5   The `nestcnst.c` program.

```
/* nestcnst.c -- use const for nested constants */
#include <stdio.h>
const int BIG = 20;
void big(void);
int main(void)
{
    const int BIG = 3;        /* hides global BIG             */
    {
        const int BIG = 100;  /* hides the BIG that equals 3 */
        printf("%d\n", BIG);  /* displays 100                */
    }
    printf("%d\n", BIG);      /* displays 3                  */
    big();
    return 0;
}
void big(void)
{
    printf("%d\n", BIG);      /* displays 20                 */
}
```

Conditional Compilation

You can use the other directives mentioned to set up conditional compilations. That is, you can use them to tell the compiler to accept or ignore blocks of information or code according to conditions at the time of compilation.

The #ifdef, #else, and #endif Directives

A short example will clarify what conditional compilation does. Consider the following:

```
#ifdef MAVIS
    #include "horse.h"  /* gets done if MAVIS is #defined    */
    #define  STABLES    5
#else
    #include "cow.h"    /* gets done if MAVIS isn't #defined */
    #define  STABLES  15
#endif
```

Here we've used the indentation allowed by newer implementations and by the ANSI standard. If you have an older implementation, you might have to move all the directives, or at least the # symbols (see the next example), to flush left:

```
#ifdef MAVIS
#    include "horse.h"  /* gets done if MAVIS is #defined    */
#    define  STABLES    5
#else
#    include "cow.h"    /* gets done if MAVIS isn't #defined */
#    define  STABLES  15
#endif
```

The #ifdef directive says that if the following identifier (MAVIS) has been defined by the preprocessor, then follow all the directives and compile all the C code up to the next #else or #endif, whichever comes first. If there is an #else, then everything from the #else to the #endif is done if the identifier isn't defined.

Incidentally, an "empty" definition like

```
#define MAVIS
```

is sufficient to define MAVIS for the purposes of #ifdef.

The form #ifdef #else is much like that of the C if else. The main difference is that the preprocessor doesn't recognize the braces ({}) method of marking a block, so it uses the #else (if any) and the #endif (which must be present) to mark blocks of directives. These conditional structures can be nested. You can use these directives to mark blocks of C statements, too, as Listing 16.6 illustrates.

Listing 16.6 The ifdef.c program.

```
/* ifdef.c -- uses conditional compilation */
#include <stdio.h>
#define JUST_CHECKING
#define LIMIT 4
int main(void)
```

continued on next page

continued from previous page

```
    {
        int i;
        int total = 0;

        for (i = 1; i <= LIMIT; i++)
        {
            total += 2*i*i + 1;
#ifdef JUST_CHECKING
            printf("i=%d, running total = %d\n", i, total);
#endif
        }
        printf("Grand total = %d\n", total);
        return 0;
}
```

Compiling and running the program as shown produces this output:

```
i=1, running total = 3
i=2, running total = 12
i=3, running total = 31
i=4, running total = 64
Grand total = 64
```

If you omit the **JUST_CHECKING** definition (or enclose it inside a C comment) and recompile the program, only the final line is displayed. You can use this approach, for instance, to help in program debugging. Define **JUST_CHECKING** and use a judicious selection of **#ifdefs**, and the compiler will include program code for printing intermediate values for debugging. After everything is working, you can remove the definition and recompile. If, later, you find that you need the information again, you can reinsert the definition and avoid having to retype all the extra print statements. Another possibility is using **#ifdef** to select among alternative chunks of codes suited for different C implementations.

The #ifndef Directive

The **#ifndef** directive can be used with **#else** and **#endif** in the same way that **#ifdef** is. The **#ifndef** asks if the following identifier is not defined; **#ifndef** is the negative of **#ifdef**. This directive is often used to define a constant if it is not already defined.

```
#ifndef SIZE
    #define SIZE 100
#endif
```

Again, older implementations might not permit indenting the **#define** directive. Suppose this directive were in an **include** file called **arrays.h**. Placing the line

```
#include "arrays.h"
```

at the head of a file would result in **SIZE** being defined as 100, but placing

```
#define SIZE 10
#include "arrays.h"
```

at the head would set SIZE to 10. Here, SIZE is defined by the time the lines in arrays.h are processed, so the #define SIZE 100 line is skipped. You might do this, for example, to test a program using a smaller array size. When it works to your satisfaction, you can remove the #define SIZE 10 statement and recompile. That way, you never have to worry about modifying the header array itself.

The #ifndef directive is commonly used to prevent multiple inclusions of a file. That is, a header file can be set up along the following lines:

```
/* things.h */
#ifndef _THINGS__H_
    #define _THINGS_H_
    /* rest of include file */
#endif
```

Suppose this file somehow got included several times. The first time the preprocessor encounters this include file, _THINGS_H_ is undefined, so the program proceeds to define _THINGS_H_ and to process the rest of the file. The next time the preprocessor encounters this file, _THINGS_H_ is defined, so the preprocessor skips the rest of the file.

Why would you include a file more than once? The most common reason is that many include files include other files, so you may include a file explicitly that another include file has already included. Why is this a problem? Some items that appear in include files, such as declarations of structure types, can appear only once in a file. The standard C header files use the #ifndef technique to avoid multiple inclusions. One problem is to make sure the identifier you are testing hasn't been defined elsewhere. The usual solution is to use the filename as the identifier, using uppercase, replacing periods with an underscore, and using an underscore (or, perhaps, two underscores) as a prefix and a suffix. Listing 16.7 shows an example

Listing 16.7 The names.h header file.

```
/* names.h -- define names structure */
#ifndef _NAMES_H_
#define _NAMES_H_

#define SLEN 32
struct names
{
    char first[SLEN];
    char last[SLEN];
};

#endif
```

You can test this header file with the program shown in Listing 16.8. This program should work correctly when using the header file shown in Listing 16.7, and it should fail to compile if you remove the #ifndef protection from Listing 16.7.

Listing 16.8 The `doubincl.c` program.

```
/* doubincl.c -- include header twice */
#include <stdio.h>
#include "names.h"
#include "names.h"    /* accidental second inclusion */
int main()
{
    struct names winner = {"Less", "Ismoor"};
    printf("The winner is %s %s.\n", winner.first,
            winner.last);
    return 0;
}
```

The #if and #elif Directives

The `#if` directive is more like the regular C `if`. It is followed by a constant integer expression that is considered true if non-zero, and you can use C's relational and logical operators with it.

```
#if SYS == 1
#include "ibm.h"
#endif
```

You can use the `#elif` (not available in some older implementations) directive to extend an `if-else` sequence. For example, you could do this:

```
#if SYS == 1
    #include "ibmpc.h"
#elif SYS == 2
    #include "vax.h"
#elif SYS == 3
    #include "mac.h"
#else
    #include "general.h"
#endif
```

Many newer implementations offer a second way to test whether a name is defined. Instead of using

```
#ifdef VAX
```

you can use this form:

```
#if defined (VAX)
```

Here, `defined` is a preprocessor operator that returns 1 if its argument is `#defined` and 0 otherwise. The advantage of this newer form is that it can be used with `#elif`. Using it, you can rewrite the previous example this way:

```
#if defined (IBMPC)
    #include "ibmpc.h"
#elif defined (VAX)
    #include "vax.h"
```

```
#elif defined (MAC)
    #include "mac.h"
#else
    #include "general.h"
#endif
```

If you were using these lines on, say, a VAX, you would have defined VAX somewhere earlier in the file with this line:

```
#define VAX
```

One use for these conditional compilation features is to make a program more portable. By changing a few key definitions at the beginning of a file, you can set up different values and include different files for different systems.

The ANSI C standard stipulates that implementations conforming to the standard predefine the name __STDC__. Therefore, you can use the test

```
#if defined (__STDC__)
```

to check whether the compiler is ANSI C compliant.

Enumerated Types

You can use the *enumerated type* to declare symbolic names to represent integer constants. It is a common C extension that has been incorporated into the ANSI C standard. By using the enum keyword, you can create a new "type" and specify the values it may have. (Actually, enum constants are type int, so they can be used wherever you would use an int.) The purpose of enumerated types is to enhance the readability of a program. The syntax is similar to that used for structures. For example, you can make these declarations:

```
enum spectrum {red, orange, yellow, green, blue, violet};
enum spectrum color;
```

The first declaration establishes spectrum as a type name, and the second declaration makes color a variable of that type. The identifiers within the braces enumerate the possible values that a spectrum variable can have. Therefore, the possible values for color are red, orange, yellow, and so on. Then, you can use statements like the following:

```
color = blue;
if (color == yellow)
   ...;
for (color = red; color <= violet; color++)
   ...;
```

Although enumerated constants are type int, enumerated variables are more loosely constrained to be an integral type as long as the type can hold the enumerated constants. For example, the enumerated constants for spectrum have the range 0–7, so a compiler could choose to use unsigned char to represent the color variable.

enum Constants

Just what are `blue` and `red`? Technically, they are integer type constants. For instance, given the preceding enumeration declaration, you can try this:

```
printf("red = %d, orange = %d\n", red, orange);
```

Here is the output:

```
red = 0, orange = 1
```

What has happened is that `red` has become a named constant representing the integer 0. Similarly, the other identifiers are named constants representing the integers 1 through 5. The process is similar to using defined constants, except that these definitions are set up by the compiler rather than the preprocessor.

Default Values

By default, the constants in the enumeration list are assigned the integer values 0, 1, 2, and so on. Therefore, the declaration

```
enum kids {nippy, slats, skippy, nina, liz};
```

results in `nina` having the value `3`.

Assigned Values

You can choose the integer values that you want the constants to have. Just include the desired values in the declaration:

```
enum levels {low = 100, medium = 500, high = 2000};
```

If you assign a value to one constant but not to the following constants, the following constants will be numbered sequentially. For example, suppose you have this declaration:

```
enum feline {cat, lynx = 10, puma, tiger};
```

Then `cat` is `0`, by default, and `lynx`, `puma`, and `tiger` are `10`, `11`, and `12`, respectively.

Usage

Recall that the purpose of enumerated types is to enhance a program's readability. If you are dealing with colors, using `red` and `blue` is much more obvious than using `0` and `1`. Note that the enumerated types are for internal use. If you want to enter a value of `orange` for `color`, you have to enter a `1`, not the word `orange`, or you can read in the string `"orange"` and have the program convert it to the value `orange`.

Because the enumerated type is an integer type, `enum` variables can be used in expressions in the same manner as integer variables. They make convenient labels for a `case` statement.

Listing 16.9 shows a short example using `enum`. The example relies on the default value-assignment scheme. This gives `red` the value `0`, which makes it the index for the pointer to the string `"red"`.

Listing 16.9 The enum.c program.

```
/* enum.c -- uses enumerated values */
#include <stdio.h>
#include <string.h>
enum BOOL {FALSE, TRUE};
typedef enum BOOL BOOLEAN;
enum spectrum {red, orange, yellow, green, blue, violet};
const char * colors[] = {"red", "orange", "yellow",
                         "green", "blue", "violet"};

#define LEN 30
int main(void)
{
    char choice[LEN];
    enum spectrum color;
    BOOLEAN found = FALSE;

    puts("Enter a color (empty line to quit):");
    while (gets(choice) != NULL && choice[0] != '\0')
    {
        for (color = red; color <= violet; color++)
        {
            if (strcmp(choice, colors[color]) == 0)
            {
                found = TRUE;
                break;
            }
        }
        if (found == TRUE)
            switch(color)
            {
                case red    : puts("Roses are red.");
                              break;
                case orange : puts("Poppies are orange.");
                              break;
                case yellow : puts("Sunflowers are yellow.");
                              break;
                case green  : puts("Grass is green.");
                              break;
                case blue   : puts("Bluebells are blue.");
                              break;
                case violet : puts("Violets are violet.");
                              break;
            }
        else
            printf("I don't know about the color %s.\n", choice);
        found = FALSE;
        puts("Next color, please (empty line to quit:");
    }
    return 0;
}
```

Note

Some compilers predefine **FALSE** and **TRUE**, so you would have to use, say, **False** and **True** instead in this **enum** definition.

Many programs use a single **enum** statement instead of several **#define** directives to create named constants.

The C Library

Originally, there was no official C library. Later, a de facto standard emerged based on the UNIX implementation of C. The ANSI C committee, in turn, developed an official standard library, largely based on the de facto standard. Recognizing the expanded C universe, the committee then sought to redefine the library so that it could be implemented on a wide variety of systems.

We've already discussed some I/O functions, character functions, and string functions from the library. In this chapter, we'll browse through several more. First, however, let's talk about how to use a library.

Gaining Access to the C Library

How you gain access to the C library depends on your implementation, so you need to see how the more general statements apply to your system. First, there are often several different places to find library functions. For example, **getchar()** is usually defined as a macro in the file **stdio.h**, but **strlen()** is usually kept in a library file. Second, different systems have different ways to reach these functions. The following sections outline three possibilities.

Automatic Access

On many systems, you just compile the program and the more common library functions are made available automatically.

Keep in mind that you should declare the function type for functions you use. Usually you can do that by including the appropriate header file. User manuals describing library functions tell you which files to include. On some older systems, however, you might have to enter the function declarations yourself. Again, the user manual indicates the function type.

In the past, header filenames have not been consistent among different implementations. The ANSI C standard groups the library functions into families, with each family having a specific header file for its function prototypes.

File Inclusion

If a function is defined as a macro, you can include the file containing its definition by using the **#include** directive. Often, similar macros are collected in an appropriately named header file. For example, many systems, including all ANSI C systems, have a `ctype.h` file containing several macros that determine the nature of a character: uppercase, digit, and so forth.

Library Inclusion

At some stage in compiling or linking a program, you might have to specify a library option. Even a system that automatically checks its standard library can have other libraries of functions less frequently used. These libraries have to be requested explicitly by using a compile-time option. Note that this process is distinct from including a header file. A header file provides a function declaration or prototype. The library option tells the system where to find the function code. Clearly, we can't go through all the specifics for all systems, but these discussions should alert you to what you should look for.

Using the Library Descriptions

We haven't the space to discuss the complete library, but we will look at some representative examples. First, though, let's take a look at documentation.

You can find function documentation in several places. Your system might have an online manual, and integrated environments often have online help. C vendors may supply printed user's guides describing library functions, or they might place equivalent material on a reference CD-ROM. Several publishers have issued reference manuals for C library functions. Some are generic in nature, and some are targeted toward specific implementations.

The key skill you need in reading the documentation is interpreting function headings. The idiom has changed with time. Here, for instance, is how `fread()` is listed in older UNIX documentation:

```
#include <stdio.h>

fread(ptr, sizeof(*ptr), nitems, stream)
FILE *stream;
```

First, the proper `include` file is given. No type is given for `fread()`, `ptr`, `sizeof(*ptr)`, or `nitems`. By default, then, they are taken to be type `int`, but the context makes it clear that `ptr` is a pointer. (In C's early days, pointers were handled as integers.) The `stream` argument is declared as a pointer to `FILE`. The declaration makes it look as though you are supposed to use the `sizeof` operator as the second argument. Actually, it's saying that the value of this argument should be the size of the object pointed to by `ptr`. Often, you would use `sizeof` as illustrated, but any type `int` value satisfies the syntax.

Later, the form changed to this:

```
#include <stdio.h>

int fread(ptr, size, nitems, stream;)
char *ptr;
int size, nitems;
FILE *stream;
```

Now all types are given explicitly, and `ptr` is treated as a pointer to `char`.

The ANSI C standard provides the following description:

```
#include <stdio.h>
size_t fread(void *ptr, size_t size, size_t nmemb, FILE *stream);
```

First, it uses the new prototype format. Second, it changes some types. The `size_t` type is defined as the unsigned integer type that the `sizeof` operator returns. Usually, it is either `unsigned int` or `unsigned long`. The `stddef.h` file contains a `typedef` or a `#define` for `size_t`, as do several other files, including `stdio.h`, typically by including `stddef.h`. Many functions, including `fread()`, often incorporate the `sizeof` operator as part of an actual argument. The `size_t` type makes that formal argument match this common usage.

Also, ANSI C uses pointer-to-`void` as a kind of generic pointer for situations in which pointers to different types may be used. For instance, the actual first argument to `fread()` may be a pointer to an array of `double` or to a structure of some sort. If the actual argument is, say, a pointer-to-array-of-20-`double` and the formal argument is pointer-to-`void`, the compiler makes the appropriate type version without complaining about type clashes.

Now let's turn to some specific functions.

The Math Library

The math library contains many useful mathematical functions. The `math.h` header file provides the function declarations or prototypes for these functions. Table 16.1 lists several functions declared in `math.h`. Note that all angles are measured in radians. (One radian = $180/\pi$ = 57.296 degrees.) (Appendix F, "The Standard ANSI C Library," supplies a complete list of the functions specified by the C90 standard.)

Table 16.1   ANSI C standard math functions.

Prototype	Description
`double acos(double x)`	Returns the angle (0 to π radians) whose cosine is x
`double asin(double x)`	Returns the angle ($-\pi/2$ to $\pi/2$ radians) whose sine is x
`double atan(double x)`	Returns the angle ($-\pi/2$ to $\pi/2$ radians) whose tangent is x
`double atan2(double y, double x)`	Returns the angle ($-\pi$ to π radians) whose tangent is y / x
`double cos(double x)`	Returns the cosine of x (x in radians)
`double sin(double x)`	Returns the sine of x (x in radians)
`double tan(double x)`	Returns the tangent of x (x in radians)
`double exp(double x)`	Returns the exponential function of x (e^x)
`double log(double x)`	Returns the natural logarithm of x
`double log10(double x)`	Returns the base 10 logarithm of x

Prototype	Description
`double pow(double x, double y)`	Returns the x to the y power
`double sqrt(double x)`	Returns the square root of x
`double ceil(double x)`	Returns the smallest integral value not less than x
`double fabs(double x)`	Returns the absolute value of x
`double floor(double x)`	Returns the largest integral value not greater than x

Let's use the math library to solve a common problem: converting from x-y coordinates to magnitudes and angles. For example, suppose you draw, on a gridwork, a line that transverses four units horizontally (the x value), and three units vertically (the y value). What is the length (magnitude) of the line and what is its direction? Trigonometry tells us the following:

```
magnitude = square root (x² + y²)
```

and

```
angle = arctangent (y/x)
```

The math library provides a square root function and a couple of arctangent functions, so you can express this solution in a C program. The square root function, called `sqrt()`, takes a `double` argument and returns the argument's square root, also as a type `double` value.

The `atan()` function takes a double argument—the tangent—and returns the angle having that value as its tangent. Unfortunately, the `atan()` function is confused by, say, a line with x and y values of –5 and –5. Because (–5)/(–5) is 1, `atan()` would report 45°, the same as it does for a line with x and y of 5 and 5. In other words, `atan()` doesn't distinguish between a line of a given angle and one 180° in the opposite direction. (Actually, `atan()` reports in radians, not degrees; we'll discuss that conversion soon.)

Fortunately, the C library also provides the `atan2()` function. It takes two arguments: the x value and the y value. That way, it can examine the signs of x and y and figure out the correct angle. Like `atan()`, `atan2()` returns the angle in radians. To convert to degrees, multiply the resulting angle by 180 and divide by pi. Listing 16.10 illustrates these steps. It also gives you a chance to use structures and the `typedef` facility.

Listing 16.10 The `convert.c` program.

```c
/* convert.c -- converts rectangular coordinates to polar */
#include <stdio.h>
#include <math.h>
#define RAD_TO_DEG (180/3.141592654)
typedef struct polar_v {
    double magnitude;
    double angle;
} POLAR_V;
typedef struct rect_v {
    double x;
    double y;
```

continued on next page

continued from previous page

```
    } RECT_V;
    POLAR_V rect_to_polar(RECT_V);
    int main(void)
    {
        RECT_V input;
        POLAR_V result;

        puts("Enter x,y coordinates; enter q to quit:");
        while (scanf("%lf %lf", &input.x, &input.y) == 2)
        {
            result = rect_to_polar(input);
            printf("magnitude = %0.2f, angle = %0.2f\n",
                    result.magnitude, result.angle);
        }
        return 0;
    }
    POLAR_V rect_to_polar(RECT_V rv)
    {
        POLAR_V pv;

        pv.magnitude = sqrt(rv.x * rv.x + rv.y * rv.y);
        if (pv.magnitude == 0)
            pv.angle = 0.0;
        else
            pv.angle = RAD_TO_DEG * atan2(rv.y, rv.x);
        return pv;
    }
```

Here's a sample run:

```
Enter x,y coordinates; enter q to quit:
10 10
magnitude = 14.14, angle = 45.00
-12 -5
magnitude = 13.00, angle = -157.38
q
```

If, when you compile, you get a message like

```
Undefined:      _sqrt
```

or

```
'sqrt': unresolved external
```

or something similar, then your compiler-linker is not finding the math library. UNIX systems require that you instruct the linker to search the math library by using the -lm flag.

```
cc spring.c -lm
```

The General Utilities Library

The general utilities library contains a grab bag of functions, including a random number generator, searching and sorting functions, conversion functions, and memory management functions. Under ANSI C, prototypes for these functions exist in the stdlib.h header file. Appendix F lists all the functions in this family; we'll take a closer look at a few of them now.

The exit() and atexit() Functions

We've already used exit() explicitly in several examples. In addition, the exit() function is invoked automatically upon return from main(). The ANSI standard has added a couple of nice features that we haven't used yet. The most important addition is that you can specify particular functions to be called when exit() executes. The atexit() function provides this feature by registering the functions to be called on exit; the atexit() function takes a function pointer as its argument. Listing 16.11 shows how this works.

Listing 16.11   The byebye.c program.

```
/* byebye.c -- atexit() example */
#include <stdio.h>
#include <stdlib.h>
void sign_off(void);
void too_bad(void);
int main(void)
{
    int n;

    atexit(sign_off);    /* register the sign_off() function */
    puts("Enter an integer:");
    if (scanf("%d",&n) != 1)
    {
        puts("That's no integer!");
        atexit(too_bad); /* register the too_bad()  function */
        exit(EXIT_FAILURE);
    }
    printf("%d is %s.\n", n,  (n % 2 == 0)? "even" : "odd");
    return 0;
}

void sign_off(void)
{
    puts("Thus terminates another magnificent program from");
    puts("SeeSaw Software!");
}

void too_bad(void)
{
    puts("SeeSaw Software extends its heartfelt condolences");
    puts("to you upon the failure of your program.");
}
```

Here's one sample run:

```
Enter an integer:
212
212 is even.
Thus terminates another magnificent program from
SeeSaw Software!
```

Here's a second run:

```
Enter an integer:
what?
That's no integer!
SeeSaw Software extends its heartfelt condolences
to you upon the failure of your program.
Thus terminates another magnificent program from
SeeSaw Software!
```

Let's look at two main areas: the use of the `atexit()` and `exit()` arguments.

Using `atexit()`

Here's a function that uses function pointers! To use the `atexit()` function, simply pass it the address of the function you want called on exit. Because the name of a function acts as an address when used as a function argument, you use `sign_off` or `too_bad` as the argument. Then `atexit()` registers that function in a list of functions to be executed when `exit()` is called. ANSI guarantees that you can place at least 32 functions on the list. Each function is added with a separate call to `atexit()`. When the `exit()` function is finally called, it executes these functions, with the last function added being executed first.

Notice that both `sign_off()` and `too_bad()` were called when input failed, but only `sign_off()` was called when input worked. That's because the `if` statement registers `too_bad()` only if input fails. Also note that the last function registered was the first called.

The functions registered by `atexit()` should, like `sign_off()` and `too_bad()`, be type `void` functions taking no arguments. Typically, they would perform housekeeping tasks, such as updating a program-monitoring file or resetting environmental variables.

Note that `sign_off()` is called even when `exit()` is not called explicitly; that's because `exit()` is called implicitly when `main()` terminates.

Using `exit()`

After `exit()` executes the functions specified by `atexit()`, it does some tidying of its own. It flushes all output streams, closes all open streams, and closes temporary files created by calls to the standard I/O function `tmpfile()`. Then `exit()` returns control to the host environment and, if possible, reports a termination status to the environment. Traditionally, UNIX programs have used 0 to indicate successful termination and non-zero to report failure. UNIX return codes don't necessarily work with all systems, so ANSI C defined a macro called `EXIT_FAILURE` that can be used portably to indicate failure. Similarly, it defined `EXIT_SUCCESS` to indicate success, but `exit()` also accepts 0 for that purpose. Under ANSI C, using the `exit()` function in a nonrecursive `main()` function is equivalent to using the keyword `return`. However, `exit()` also terminates programs when used in functions other than `main()`.

Memory Allocation: `malloc()` and `free()`

All programs have to set aside enough memory to store the data they use. Some of this memory allocation is done automatically. For example, you can declare

```
char place[] = "Pork Liver Creek";
```

and enough memory to store that string is set aside, or you can be more explicit and ask for a certain amount of memory:

```
int plates[100];
```

This declaration sets aside 100 memory locations, each fit to store an `int` value.

C goes beyond this. You can allot more memory as a program runs. The main tool is the `malloc()` function, which takes one argument: the number of bytes of memory you want. Then `malloc()` finds a suitable block of free memory and returns the address of the first byte of that block. Because `char` represents a byte, `malloc()` has traditionally been defined as type pointer-to-`char`. The ANSI C standard, however, uses a new type: pointer-to-`void`. This type is intended to be a "generic pointer." The `malloc()` function can be used to return pointers to arrays, structures, and so forth, so normally the return value is typecast to the proper value. Under ANSI C, you should still typecast for clarity, but assigning a pointer-to-`void` value to a pointer of another type is not considered a type clash. If `malloc()` fails to find the required space, it returns the null pointer.

Let's apply `malloc()` to the task of creating an array. You can use `malloc()` to request a block of storage. You also need a pointer to keep track of where the block is in memory. For example, consider this code:

```
double * ptd;
ptd = (double *) malloc(30 * sizeof(double));
```

This code requests space for 30 type `double` values and sets `ptd` to point to the location. Note that `ptd` is declared as a pointer to a single `double` and not to a block of 30 `double` values. Remember that the name of an array is the address of its first element. Therefore, if you make `ptd` point to the first element of the block, you can use it just like an array name. That is, you can use the expression `ptd[0]` to access the first element of the block, `ptd[1]` to access the second element, and so on. As you've learned earlier, you can use pointer notation with array names, and you can use array notation with pointers.

You now have two ways to create an array:

- Declare an array and use the array name to access elements.

- Declare a pointer, call `malloc()`, and use the pointer to access elements.

You can use the second method to do something you can't do with a declared array—create a *dynamic array*, one that's allocated while the program runs and that you can choose a size for while the program runs. Suppose, for example, that n is an integer variable. You can't do the following:

```
double item[n];    /* not allowed if n is a variable */
```

However, you can do the following:

```
ptd = (double *) malloc(n * sizeof(double)); /* okay */
```

By using malloc(), then, a program can decide what size array is needed and create it while the program runs. Listing 16.12 illustrates this possibility. It assigns the address of block of memory to the pointer ptd, then it uses ptd in the same fashion you would use an array name.

Listing 16.12   The dyn_arr.c program.

```
/* dyn_arr.c -- dynamically allocated array */
#include <stdio.h>
#include <stdlib.h>
int main(void)
{
    double * ptd;
    int max;
    int number;
    int i = 0;

    puts("What is the maximum number of type double entries?");
    scanf("%d", &max);
    ptd = (double *) malloc(max * sizeof (double));
    if (ptd == NULL)
    {
        puts("Memory allocation failed. Goodbye.");
        exit(EXIT_FAILURE);
    }
    /* ptd now points to an array of max elements */
    puts("Enter the values (q to quit):");
    while (i < max && scanf("%lf", &ptd[i]) == 1)
        ++i;
    printf("Here are your %d entries:\n", number = i);
    for (i = 0; i < number; i++)
    {
        printf("%7.2f ", ptd[i]);
        if (i % 7 == 6)
            putchar('\n');
    }
    if (i % 7 != 0)
        putchar('\n');
    puts("Done.");
    free(ptd);
    return 0;
}
```

Here's a sample run. In it, we entered six numbers, but the program processes just five of them because we limited the array size to 5.

```
What is the maximum number of entries?
5
Enter the values (q to quit):
20 30 35 25 40 80
Here are your 5 entries:
  20.00   30.00   35.00   25.00   40.00
Done.
```

Let's look at the code. The program finds the desired array size with the following lines:

```
puts("What is the maximum number of type double entries?");""
scanf("%d", &max);
```

Next, the following line allocates enough space to hold the requested number of entries and then assigns the address of the block to the pointer `ptd`:

```
ptd = (double *) malloc(max * sizeof (double));
```

It's possible that `malloc()` can fail to procure the desired amount of memory. In that case, the function returns the null pointer, and the program terminates.

```
if (ptd == NULL)
{
    puts("Memory allocation failed. Goodbye.");
    exit(EXIT_FAILURE);
}
```

If the program clears this hurdle, then it can treat `ptd` as though it were the name of an array of `max` elements, and so it does.

Note the `free()` function near the end of the program. It frees memory allocated by `malloc()`. Think of `malloc()` and `free()` as managing a pool of memory. Each call to `malloc()` allocates memory for program use, and each call to `free()` restores memory to the pool so it can be reused. The `free()` function frees only the block of memory that its argument points to. The argument to `free()` should be a pointer to a block of memory allocated by `malloc()`; you can't use `free()` to free memory allocated by other means, such as declaring a structure or array. In this particular example, using `free()` isn't really necessary, for any allocated memory automatically is freed when the program terminates. In a more complex program, however, the ability to free and reuse memory can be important.

What have you gained by using a dynamic array? Primarily, you've gained program flexibility. Suppose you know that most of the time the program will need no more than 100 elements, but that sometimes it would need 10,000 elements. If you declared an array, you would have to allow for the worst case and declare an array with 10,000 elements. Most of the time, that program would be wasting memory. Then, the one time you need 10,001 elements, the program will fail. You can use a dynamic array to adjust the program to fit the circumstances.

The `calloc()` Function

Another option for memory allotment is to use `calloc()`. A typical use looks like this:

```
long * newmem;

newmem = (long *)calloc(100, sizeof (long));
```

Like `malloc()`, `calloc()` returns a pointer-to-`char` in its pre-ANSI version and a pointer-to-`void` under ANSI. You should use the cast operator if you want to store a different type. This new function takes two arguments, both of which should be unsigned integers (type `size_t` under ANSI). The first argument is the number of memory cells you want.

The second argument is the size of each cell in bytes. In our case, `long` uses 4 bytes, so this instruction sets up 100 4-byte units, using 400 bytes in all for storage.

Using `sizeof (long)` instead of `4` makes this coding more portable. It will work on those rare systems where `long` is some size other than 4.

The `calloc()` function throws in one more feature: It sets all the bits in the block to zero. (Note, however, that on some hardware systems, a floating-point value of `0` is not represented by all bits set to 0.)

The `free()` function can also be used to free memory allocated by `calloc()`.

Dynamic memory allocation is the key to many advanced programming techniques. We'll examine some in Chapter 17, "Advanced Data Representation." Your own C library probably offers several other memory-management functions, some portable, some not. You might want to take a moment to look them over.

Storage Classes and Dynamic Memory Allocation

You might be wondering about the connection between storage classes and dynamic memory allocation. Let's look at an idealized model. You can think of a program as dividing its available memory into three separate sections: one for external, static, and static external variables; one for automatic variables; and one for dynamically allocated memory.

The amount of memory needed for the external, static, and external static storage classes is known at compile time, and the data stored in this section is available as long as the program runs. Each variable of these classes comes into being when the program starts and expires when the program ends.

An automatic variable, however, comes into existence when a program enters the block of code containing the variable's definition and expires when its block of code is exited. Therefore, as a program calls functions and as functions terminate, the amount of memory used by automatic variables grows and shrinks. This section of memory is typically handled as a stack. That means new variables are added sequentially in memory as they are created and then are removed in the opposite order as they pass away.

Dynamically allocated memory comes into existence when `malloc()` or a related function is called, and is freed when `free()` is called. Memory persistence is controlled by the programmer, not by a set of rigid rules, so a memory block can be created in one function and disposed of in another function. Because of this, the section of memory used for dynamic memory allocation can wind up fragmented, that is, having unused chunks interspersed among active blocks of memory. Using dynamic memory tends to be a slower process than using stack memory, however.

The `qsort()` Function

The "quick sort" method is one of the most effective sorting algorithms, particularly for larger arrays. Developed by C. A. R. Hoare in 1962, it uses a recursive approach to partition arrays into ever smaller sizes until the element level is reached. First, the array is divided into two parts, with every value in one partition being less than every value in the other partition.

This process continues until the array is fully sorted. The quick sort algorithm is an example of the divide-and-conquer form of recursion mentioned in Chapter 9, "Functions."

The name for the C implementation of the quick sort algorithm is `qsort()`. The `qsort()` function sorts an array of data objects. It has the following ANSI prototype:

```
void qsort (void *base, size_t nmemb, size_t size,
            int (*compar)(const void *, const void *));
```

The first argument is a pointer to the beginning of the array to be sorted. ANSI C permits any data pointer type to be typecast to a pointer-to-**void**, thus permitting the first actual argument to `qsort()` to refer to any kind of array.

The second argument is the number of items to be sorted. The prototype converts this value to type **size_t**. As you might recall from the discussion of **fread()** and **fwrite()** in Chapter 12, "File Input/Output," **size_t** is the integer type returned by the **sizeof** operator and is defined in the standard header files.

Because `qsort()` converts its first argument to a **void** pointer, `qsort()` loses track of how big each array element is. To compensate, you must tell `qsort()` explicitly the size of the data object. That's what the third argument is for. For instance, if you are sorting an array of type **double**, you would use **sizeof(double)** for this argument.

Finally, `qsort()` requires a pointer to the function to be used to determine the sorting order. The comparison function should take two arguments: pointers to the two items being compared. It should return a positive integer if the first item should follow the second value, zero if the two items are the same, and a negative integer if the second item should follow the first. The `qsort()` will use this function, passing it pointer values that it calculates from the other information given to it.

The form the comparison function must take is set forth in the `qsort()` prototype for the final argument:

```
int (*compar)(const void *, const void *)
```

This states that the final argument is a pointer to a function that returns an **int** and that takes two arguments, each of which is a pointer to type **const void**. These two pointers point to the items being compared.

Listing 16.13 and the discussion following it illustrate how to define a comparison function and how to use `qsort()`. The program creates an array of random floating-point values and sorts the array.

Listing 16.13   The `qsorter.c` program.

```
/* qsorter.c -- using qsort to sort groups of numbers */
#include <stdio.h>
#include <stdlib.h>

#define NUM 40
void fillarray(double ar[], int n);
void showarray(const double ar[], int n);
int mycomp(const void * p1, const void * p2);
```

continued on next page

continued from previous page

```
int main(void)
{
    double vals[NUM];
    fillarray(vals, NUM);
    puts("Random list:");
    showarray(vals, NUM);
    qsort(vals, NUM, sizeof(double), mycomp);
    puts("\nSorted list:");
    showarray(vals, NUM);
    return 0;
}

void fillarray(double ar[], int n)
{
    int index;

    for( index = 0; index < n; index++)
        ar[index] = (double)rand()/((double) rand() + 0.1);
}

void showarray(const double ar[], int n)
{
    int index;

    for( index = 0; index < n; index++)
    {
        printf("%9.4f ", ar[index]);
        if (index % 6 == 5)
            putchar('\n');
    }
    if (index % 6 != 0)
        putchar('\n');
}

/* sort values by increasing */
int mycomp(const void * p1, const void * p2)
{
    /* need to use pointers to double to access values   */
    const double * a1 = p1; /* a1 is proper pointer type */
    const double * a2 = p2;

    if (*a1 < *a2)
        return -1;
    else if (*a1 == *a2)
        return 0;
    else
        return 1;
}
```

Here is a sample run:

```
Random list:
    0.0022      0.2390      1.2191      0.3910      1.1021      0.2027
    1.3836     20.2872      0.2508      0.8880      2.2180     25.5033
    0.0236      0.9308      0.9911      0.2507      1.2802      0.0939
    0.9760      1.7218      1.2055      1.0326      3.7892      1.9636
    4.1137      0.9241      0.9971      1.5582      0.8955     35.3843
    4.0580     12.0467      0.0096      1.0110      0.8506      1.1530
    2.3614      1.5876      0.4825      6.8751

Sorted list:
    0.0022      0.0096      0.0236      0.0939      0.2027      0.2390
    0.2507      0.2508      0.3910      0.4825      0.8506      0.8880
    0.8955      0.9241      0.9308      0.9760      0.9911      0.9971
    1.0110      1.0326      1.1021      1.1530      1.2055      1.2191
    1.2802      1.3836      1.5582      1.5876      1.7218      1.9636
    2.2180      2.3614      3.7892      4.0580      4.1137      6.8751
   12.0467     20.2872     25.5033     35.3843
```

Let's look at two main areas: the use of `qsort()` and the definition of `mycomp()`.

Using qsort()

The `qsort()` function sorts an array of data objects. It has the following ANSI prototype:

```
void qsort (void *base, size_t nmemb, size_t size,
        int (*compar)(const void *, const void *));
```

The first argument is a pointer to the beginning of the array to be sorted. In this program, the actual argument is `vals`, the name of an array of `double`, hence a pointer to the first element of the array. The ANSI prototype causes the `vals` argument to be typecast to type pointer-to-`void`. That's because ANSI C permits any data pointer type to be typecast to a pointer-to-`void`, thus permitting the first actual argument to `qsort()` to refer to any kind of array.

The second argument is the number of items to be sorted. In Listing 16.13, it is N, the number of array elements. The prototype converts this value to type `size_t`.

The third argument is the size of each element—`sizeof(double)`, in this case.

The final argument is `mycomp`, the address of the function to be used for comparing elements.

Defining mycomp()

As mentioned before, the `qsort()` prototype mandates the form of the comparison function:

```
int (*compar)(const void *, const void *)
```

This states that the final argument is a pointer to a function that returns an `int` and that takes two arguments, each of which is a pointer to type `const void`. We made the prototype for the `mycomp()` function agree with this prototype:

```
int mycomp(const void * p1, const void * p2);
```

Remember that the name of the function is a pointer to the function when used as an argument, so `mycomp` matches the `compar` prototype.

The `qsort()` function passes the addresses of the two elements to be compared to the comparison function. In this program, then, `p1` and `p2` are assigned the addresses of two type `double` values to be compared. Note that the first argument to `qsort()` refers to the whole array, and the two arguments in the comparison function refer to two elements in the array. There is a problem. To compare the pointed-to values, you need to dereference a pointer. Because the values are type `double`, you need to dereference a pointer to type `double`. However, `qsort()` requires pointers to type `void`. The way to get around this problem is to declare pointers of the proper type inside the function and initialize them to the values passed as arguments:

```
int mycomp(const void * p1, const void * p2)
{
    /* need to use pointers to double to access values   */
    const double * a1 = p1; /* a1 is proper pointer type */
    const double * a2 = p2;

    if (*a1 < *a2)
        return -1;
    else if (*a1 == *a2)
        return 0;
    else
        return 1;
}
```

In short, `qsort()` and the comparison function use `void` pointers for generality. As a consequence, you have to tell `qsort()` explicitly how large each element of the array is, and within the definition of the comparison function, you have to convert its pointer arguments to pointers of the proper type for your application.

Let's look at one more example of a comparison function. Suppose you have these declarations:

```
struct names {
    char first[40];
    char last[40];
};
struct names staff[100];
```

What should a call to `qsort()` look like? Following the model in Listing 16.13, a call could look like this:

```
qsort(staff, 100, sizeof(struct names), comp);
```

Here, `comp` is the name of the comparison function. What should this function look like? Suppose you want to sort by last name, and then by first name. You could write the function this way:

```
#include <string.h>
int comp(const void * p1, const void * p2)    /* mandatory form */
{
    const struct names *ps1 = p1; /* get right type of pointer */
    const struct names *ps2 = p2;
    int res;
```

```
        res = strcmp(ps1->last, ps2->last);   /* compare last names */
        if (res != 0)
            return res;
        else                                  /* last names identical    */
            return strcmp(ps1->first, ps2->first);
    }
```

This function uses the strcmp() function to do the comparison; its possible return values match the requirements for the comparison function. Note that you need a pointer to a structure to use the -> operator.

The Assert Library

The assert library, supported by the assert.h header file, is a small one designed to help with debugging programs. It consists of a macro named assert(). It takes as its argument an integer expression. If the expression evaluates as false (non-zero), the assert() macro writes an error message to the standard error stream (stderr) and calls the abort() function, which terminates the program. (The abort() function is prototyped in the stdlib.h header file.) The idea is to identify critical locations in a program where certain conditions should be true and to use the assert() statement to terminate the program if the condition is not true. Typically, the argument is a relational or logical expression. If assert() does abort the program, it first displays the test that failed, the name of the file containing the test, and a line number. Listing 16.14 shows a short example. It asserts that z is greater than or equal to 0 before attempting to take its square root. It also mistakenly subtracts a value instead of adding it, making it possible for z to obtain forbidden values.

Listing 16.14   The checking.c program.

```
/* checking.c -- use assert() */
#include <stdio.h>
#include <math.h>
#include <assert.h>
int main()
{
    double x, y, z;
    puts("Enter a pair of numbers (0 0 to quit): ");
    while (scanf("%lf%lf", &x, &y) == 2
                && (x != 0 || y != 0))
    {
        z = x * x - y * y;   /* should be + */
        assert(z >= 0);
        printf("answer is %f\n", sqrt(z));
        puts("Next pair of numbers: ");
    }
    return 0;
}
```

Here is a sample run:

```
Enter a pair of numbers (0 0 to quit):
4 3
answer is 2.645751
Next pair of numbers:
5 3
answer is 4.000000
Next pair of numbers:
3 5
Assertion failed: z >= 0, file C:\checking.c, line 13
```

One potentially confusing point to note is that the message is not saying that `z >= 0`; instead, it's saying that the claim `z >= 0` failed.

You could accomplish something similar with an `if` statement:

```
if (z < 0)
{
    puts("z less than 0");
    abort();
}
```

The `assert()` approach has several advantages, however. It identifies the file automatically. It identifies the line number where the problem occurs automatically. Finally, there's a mechanism for turning the `assert()` macro on and off without changing code. If you think you've eliminated the program bugs, place the macro definition

```
#define NDEBUG
```

before the location where `assert.h` is included and then recompile the program, and the compiler will deactivate all `assert()` statements in the file. If problems pop up again, you can remove the `#define` directive, and recompile, thus reactivating all the `assert()` statements.

Chapter Summary

The C preprocessor and the C library are two important adjuncts to the C language. The C preprocessor, following preprocessor directives, adjusts your source code before it is compiled. The C library provides many functions designed to help with tasks such as input, output, file handling, memory management, sorting and searching, mathematical calculations, and string processing, to name a few. Appendix F lists the complete ANSI C library.

Review Questions

1. Here are groups of one or more macros followed by a source code line that uses them. What code results in each case? Is it valid code?

   a.   `#define FPM  5280     /* feet per mile */`
        `dist = FPM * miles;`

b. #define FEET 4
```
#define POD FEET + FEET
plort = FEET * POD;
```

c. #define SIX = 6;
```
nex = SIX;
```

d. #define NEW(X) X + 5
```
y = NEW(y);
berg = NEW(berg) * lob;
est = NEW(berg) / NEW(y);
nilp = lob * NEW(-berg);
```

2. Fix the definition in 1.d. to make it more reliable.

3. Define a macro function that returns the minimum of two values.

4. Replace the even_gt() macro in Listing 16.4 with a macro of your own devising.

5. Define a macro function that prints the representations and the values of two integer expressions. For example, it might print

   3+4 is 7 and 4*12 is 48

   if its arguments are 3+4 and 4*12.

6. Create #define statements to accomplish the following goals:

   a. Create a named constant of value 25.

   b. Have SPACE represent the space character.

   c. Have PS() represent printing the space character.

   d. Have BIG(X) represent adding 3 to X.

   e. Have SUMSQ(X,Y) represent the sums of the squares of X and Y.

7. Define a macro that prints the name, value, and address of an int variable in the following format:

   name: fop; value: 23; address: ff464016

8. Suppose you have a block of code you want to skip over temporarily while testing a program. How can you do so without actually removing the code from the file?

9. a. How would you create an enumerated type days that makes the abbreviations sun, mon, tue, wed, thu, fri, and sat stand for the integers 0–6? For the integers 1–7?

   b. How would you create a variable visit of that type?

10. What's wrong with this program?

```
#include <stdio.h>
int main(int argc, char argv[])
{
    printf("The square root of %f is %f\n", argv[1],
            sqrt(argv[1]) );
}
```

11. Suppose **scores** is an array of 1000 **int** values that you want to sort into descending order. You will use **qsort()** and a comparison function called **comp()**.

    a. What is a suitable call to **qsort()**?

    b. What is a suitable definition for **comp()**?

12. How could you dynamically allot space to hold an array of structures?

Programming Exercises

1. Start developing a header file of preprocessor definitions that you want to use.

2. The harmonic mean of two numbers is obtained by taking the inverses of the two numbers, averaging them, and taking the inverse of the result. Use a **#define** directive to define a macro "function" that performs this operation. Write a simple program that tests the macro.

3. Polar coordinates describe a vector in terms of magnitude and the counterclockwise angle from the x-axis to the vector. Rectangular coordinates describe the same vector in terms of x and y components (see Figure 16.3). Write a program that reads the magnitude and angle (in degrees) of a vector and then displays the x and y components. The relevant equations are these:

```
x = r cos A     y = r sin A
```

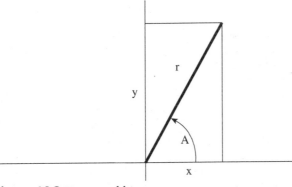

Figure 16.3 Unary and binary operators.

To do the conversion, use a function that takes a structure containing the polar coordinates and returns a structure containing the rectangular coordinates (or use pointers to such structures, if you prefer).

4. Modify the program in Listing 16.12 so that it processes TV show names instead of numbers and saves the strings in a file. If the file already exists when the program is run, have it first load the contents into memory and then display them. Use a fixed-size record for storing each string, and use `fread()` and `fwrite()`.

5. This exercise is the same as Exercise 4 except that you should use variable-sized records to store the strings. Each string should be preceded in storage by a byte holding the length of the string. On input, the program will first read the number byte and then use that information to determine the number of bytes to read for the string.

6. The ANSI library features a `clock()` function with this description:

```
#include <time.h>
clock_t clock (void);
```

Here, `clock_t` is a type defined in `time.h`. The function returns the processor time, which is given in some implementation-dependent units. (If the processor time is unavailable or cannot be represented, the function returns a value of `-1`.) However, `CLOCKS_PER_SEC`, also defined in `time.h`, is the number of processor time units per second. Therefore, dividing the difference between two return values of `clock()` by `CLOCKS_PER_SEC` gives you the number of seconds elapsed between the two calls. Typecasting the values to `double` before division enables you to get fractions of a second. Write a function that takes a `double` argument representing a desired time delay and then runs a loop until that amount of time has passed. Write a simple program that tests the function.

7. Write a function that takes as arguments the name of an array of type `int` elements, the size of an array, and a value representing the number of picks. The function then selects the indicated number of items at random from the array and prints them. No array element is to be picked more than once. (This simulates picking lottery numbers or jury members.) Also, if your implementation has `time()` (discussed in Chapter 13, "Storage Classes and Program Development") or a similar function available, use its output with `srand()` to initialize the `rand()` random number generator. Write a simple program that tests the function.

8. Modify Listing 16.13 so that it uses an array of `struct names` elements (as defined after the listing) instead of an array of `double`. Use fewer elements, and initialize the array explicitly to a suitable selection of names.

CHAPTER 17

ADVANCED DATA REPRESENTATION

You will learn about the following in this chapter:

- Functions

  more malloc()

*I*n this chapter, you learn more about using C to represent a variety of data types. You'll encounter new algorithms and increase your ability to develop programs conceptually. Also, you'll learn about abstract data types (ADTs).

Learning a computer language is like learning music, carpentry, or engineering. At first, you work with the tools of the trade, playing scales, learning which end of the hammer to hold and which end to avoid, solving countless problems involving falling, sliding, and balanced objects. Acquiring and practicing skills is what you've been doing so far in this book, learning to create variables, structures, functions, and the like. Eventually, however, you move to a higher level in which using the tools is second nature and the real challenge is designing and creating a project. You develop an ability to see the project as a coherent whole. This chapter concentrates on that higher level. You may find the material covered here a little more challenging than the preceding chapters, but you may also find it more rewarding as it helps you move from the role of apprentice to the role of craftsperson.

We'll start by examining a vital aspect of program design: the way a program represents data. Often the most important aspect of program development is finding a good representation of the data manipulated by that program. Getting data representation right can make writing the rest of the program simple. By now you've seen C's built-in data types: simple variables, arrays, pointers, structures, and unions.

Finding the right data representation, however, often goes beyond simply selecting a type. You should also think about what operations will be necessary. That is, you should decide how to store the data, and you should define what operations are valid for the data type. For instance, C implementations typically store both the C `int` type and the C pointer type as integers, but the two types have different sets of valid operations. You can multiply one integer by another, for example, but you can't multiply a pointer by a pointer. You can use the `*` operator to dereference a pointer, but that operation is meaningless for an integer. The C language defines the valid operations for its fundamental types. However, when you design a scheme to represent data, you might need to define the valid operations yourself. In C, you can do so by designing C functions to represent the desired operations. In short, then, designing a data type consists of deciding on how to store the data and of designing a set of functions to manage the data.

You will also look at some *algorithms*, recipes for manipulating data. As a programmer, you will acquire a repertoire of such recipes that you apply over and over again to similar problems.

This chapter looks into the process of designing data types, a process that matches algorithms to data representations. In it, you'll meet some common data forms, such as the queue, the list, and the binary search tree.

You'll also be introduced to the concept of the abstract data type (ADT). An ADT packages methods and data representations in a way that is problem-oriented rather than language-oriented. After you've designed an ADT, you can easily reuse it in different circumstances. Understanding ADTs prepares you conceptually for entering the world of object-oriented programming (OOP) and the C++ language.

Exploring Data Representation

Let's begin by thinking about data. Suppose you had to create an address book program. What data form would you use to store information? Because there's a variety of information associated with each entry, it makes sense to represent each entry with a structure. How do you represent several entries? With a standard array of structures? With a dynamic array? With some other form? Should the entries be alphabetized? Should you be able to search through the entries by zip code? by area code? The actions you want to perform might affect how you decide to store the information. In short, you have a lot of design decisions to make before plunging into coding.

How would you represent a bitmapped graphics image that you want to store in memory? A bitmapped image is one in which each pixel on the screen is set individually. In the days of black-and-white screens, you could use one computer bit (1 or 0) to represent one pixel (on or off), hence the name *bitmapped*. With color monitors, it takes more than one bit to describe a single pixel. For instance, you can get 256 colors if you dedicate 8 bits to each pixel. Now the industry has moved to 65,536 colors (16 bits per pixel), 16,777,216 colors (24 bits per pixel), and even 2,147,483,648 colors (32 bits per pixel). If you have 16 million colors and if your monitor has a resolution of 1024 × 768, you'll need 18.9 million bits (2.25 MB) to represent a single screen of bitmapped graphics. Is this the way to go, or can you develop a way of compressing the information? Should this compression be *lossless* (no data lost) or *lossy* (relatively unimportant data lost)? Again, you have a lot of design decisions to make before diving into coding.

Let's tackle a particular case of representing data. Suppose you want to write a program that enables you to enter a list of all the movies (including videotapes) you've seen in a year. For each movie, you'd like to record a variety of information, such as the title, the year it was released, the director, the lead actors, the length, the kind of film (comedy, science fiction, romance, drivel, and so forth), your evaluation, and so on. That suggests using a structure for each film and an array of structures for the list. To simplify matters, let's limit the structure to two members: the film title and your evaluation, a ranking on a 0 to 10 scale. Listing 17.1 shows a bare-bones implementation using this approach.

Listing 17.1 The `films1.c` program.

```
/* films1.c -- using an array of structures */
#include <stdio.h>
#define TSIZE        45      /* size of array to hold title    */
#define FMAX          5      /* maximum number of film titles */
struct film {
    char title[TSIZE];
    int rating;
};
int main(void)
{
    struct film movies[FMAX];
    int i = 0;
    int j;

    puts("Enter first movie title:");
    while (i < FMAX && gets(movies[i].title) != NULL &&
           movies[i].title[0] != '\0')
    {
        puts("Enter your rating <0-10>:");
        scanf("%d", &movies[i++].rating);
        while(getchar() != '\n')
            continue;
        puts("Enter next movie title (empty line to stop):");
    }
    if (i == 0)
        printf("No data entered. ");
    else
        printf ("Here is the movie list:\n");

    for (j = 0; j < i; j++)
        printf("Movie: %s  Rating: %d\n", movies[j].title,
            movies[j].rating);
    printf("Bye!\n");
    return 0;
}
```

The program creates an array of structures and then fills the array with data entered by the user. Entry continues until the array is full (the **FMAX** test), until end of file (the **NULL** test) is reached, or until the user presses the Enter key at the beginning of a line (the '\0' test).

This formulation has some problems. First, the program will most likely waste a lot of space because most movies don't have titles 40 characters long, but some movies do have long titles, such as *The Discreet Charm of the Bourgeoisie* and *Won Ton Ton, The Dog Who Saved Hollywood*. Second, many people will find the limit of five movies a year too restrictive. Of course, you can increase that limit, but what would be a good value? Some people see

500 movies a year, so you could increase FMAX to 500, but that still might be too small for some, yet it might waste enormous amounts of memory for others. Also, some compilers set a default limit for the amount of memory available for automatic storage class variables such as movies, and such a large array could exceed that value. You can fix that by making the array a static or external array or by instructing the compiler to use a larger stack, but that's not fixing the real problem.

The real problem here is that the data representation is too inflexible. You have to make decisions at compile time that are better made at runtime. This suggests switching to a data representation that uses dynamic memory allocation. You could try something like this:

```
#define TSIZE   45            /* size of array to hold title   */
struct film {
   char title[TSIZE];
   int rating;
};
...
int n, i;
struct film * movies;         /* pointer to a structure        */
...
printf("Enter the maximum number of movies you'll enter:\n");
scanf("%d", &n);
movies = (struct film *) malloc(n * sizeof(struct film));
```

Here, as in the preceding chapter, you can use the pointer movies just as though it were an array name:

```
while (i < FMAX && gets(movies[i].title) != NULL &&
        movies[i].title[0] != '\0')
```

By using malloc(), you can postpone determining the number of elements until the program runs, so the program need not allocate 500 elements if only 20 are needed. However, it puts the burden on the user to supply a correct value for the number of entries.

Beyond the Array to the Linked List

Ideally, you'd like to be able to add data indefinitely (or until the program runs out of memory) without specifying in advance how many entries you'll make and without committing the program to allocating huge chunks of memory unnecessarily. You can do this by calling malloc() after each entry and allocating just enough space to hold the new entry. If the user enters three films, the program calls malloc() three times. If the user enters 300 films, the program calls malloc() 300 times.

This fine idea raises a new problem. To see what it is, compare calling malloc() once, asking for enough space for 300 film structures, and calling malloc() 300 times, each time asking for enough space for one film structure. The first case allocates the memory as one contiguous memory block and all you need to keep track of the contents is a single pointer-to-struct film variable that points to the first structure in the block. Simple array notation lets the pointer access each structure in the block, as shown in the preceding code segment. The problem with the second approach is that there is no guarantee that consecutive calls to `malloc()` yield adjacent blocks of memory. This means the structures won't necessarily be stored contiguously (see Figure 17.1). Therefore, instead of storing one pointer to a block of 300 structures, you need to store 300 pointers, one for each independently allocated structure!

```
struct film * movie;

movie = (struct film *) malloc(5*sizeof(struct film);
```

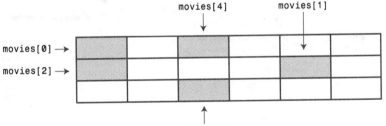

```
int i;
struct film * movies[s];

for (i = 0; i<< 5; i++)
movies[i] = (struct films *) malloc(sizeof(struct films));
```

Figure 17.1 Allocating structures in a block versus allocating them individually.

One solution, which we won't use, is to create a large array of pointers and assign values to the pointers one by one as new structures are allocated:

```
#define TSIZE  45        /* size of array to hold titles   */
#define FMAX   500        /* maximum number of film titles   */
struct film {
   char title[TSIZE];
   int rating;
};
...
struct film * movies[FMAX];    /* array of pointers to structures */
int i;
...
movies[i] = (struct film *) malloc (sizeof (struct film));
```

This approach saves a lot of memory if you don't use the full allotment of pointers, because an array of 500 pointers takes much less memory than an array of 500 structures. It still wastes the space occupied by unused pointers, however, and it still imposes a 500-structure limit.

There's a better way. Each time you use `malloc()` to allocate space for a new structure, you can also allocate space for a new pointer. "But," you say, "then I need another pointer to keep track of the newly allocated pointer, and that needs a pointer to keep track of it, and so on." The trick to avoiding this potential problem is to redefine the structure so that each structure includes a pointer to the *next* structure. Then, each time you create a new structure, you can store its address in the preceding structure. In short, you need to redefine the `film` structure this way:

```
#define TSIZE  45       /* size of array to hold titles  */
struct film {
   char title[TSIZE];
   int rating;
   struct film * next;
};
```

True, a structure can't contain in itself a structure of the same type, but it can contain a pointer to a structure of the same type. Such a definition is the basis for defining a *linked list*—a list in which each item contains information describing where to find the next item.

Before looking at C code for a linked list, let's take a conceptual walk through such a list. Suppose a user enters `Modern Times` as a title and `10` as a rating. The program would allocate space for a `film` structure, copy the string `Modern Times` into the `title` member, and set the `rating` member to `10`. To indicate that no structure follows this one, the program would set the `next` member pointer to `NULL`. (`NULL`, recall, is a symbolic constant defined in the `stdio.h` file and representing the null pointer.) Of course, you need to keep track of where the first structure is stored. You can do this by assigning its address to a separate pointer that we'll refer to as the *head pointer*. The head pointer points to the first item in a linked list of items. Figure 17.2 represents how this structure looks. (The empty space in the `title` member is suppressed to save space in the figure.)

```
#define TSIZE 45
struct film {
   char title[TSIZE]
   int rating;
   struct film * next;
};
struct film * head;
```

Figure 17.2 First item in a linked list.

Now suppose the user enters a second movie and rating, for example, `Titanic` and `8`. The program allocates space for a second `film` structure, storing the address of the new structure in the `next` member of the first structure (overwriting the `NULL` previously stored there) so that the `next` pointer of one structure points to the following structure in the linked list. Then the program copies `Titanic` and `8` to the new structure and sets its `next` member to `NULL`, indicating that it is now the last structure in the list. Figure 17.3 shows this list of two items.

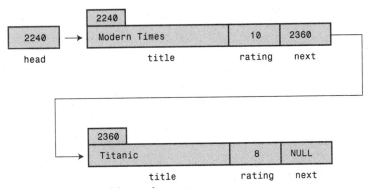

Figure 17.3 Linked list with two items.

Each new movie will be handled the same way. Its address will be stored in the preceding structure, the new information goes into the new structure, and its `next` member is set to `NULL`, setting up a linked list like that shown in Figure 17.4.

Suppose you want to display the list. Each time you display an item, you can use the address stored in the corresponding structure to locate the next item to be displayed. For this scheme to work, however, you need a pointer to keep track of the very first item in the list because no structure in the list stores the address of the first item. Fortunately, you've already accomplished this with the head pointer.

Using a Linked List

Now that you have a picture of how a linked list works, let's implement it. Listing 17.2 modifies Listing 17.1 so that it uses a linked list instead of an array to hold the movie information.

Listing 17.2   The `films2.c` program.

```
/* films2.c -- using a linked list of structures */
#include <stdio.h>
#include <stdlib.h>      /* has the malloc prototype    */
#include <string.h>      /* has the strcpy prototype    */
#define TSIZE    45      /* size of array to hold title */
```

continued on next page

continued from previous page

```
struct film {
   char title[TSIZE];
   int rating;
   struct film * next;    /* points to next struct in list */
};

int main(void)
{
   struct film * head = NULL;
   struct film * prev, * current;
   char input[TSIZE];

   puts("Enter first movie title:");
   while (gets(input) != NULL && input[0] != '\0')
   {
      current = (struct film *) malloc(sizeof(struct film));
      if (head == NULL)            /* first structure       */
         head = current;
      else                         /* subsequent structures */
         prev->next = current;
      current->next = NULL;
      strcpy(current->title, input);
      puts("Enter your rating <0-10>:");
      scanf("%d", &current->rating);
      while(getchar() != '\n')
         continue;
      puts("Enter next movie title (empty line to stop):");
      prev = current;
   }
   if (head == NULL)
      printf("No data entered. ");
   else
      printf ("Here is the movie list:\n");
   current = head;
   while (current != NULL)
   {
      printf("Movie: %s  Rating: %d\n", current->title, current->rating);
      current = current->next;
   }
   printf("Bye!\n");
   return 0;
}
```

The program performs two tasks using the linked list. First, it constructs the list and fills it with the incoming data. Second, it displays the list. Displaying is the simpler task, so let's look at it first.

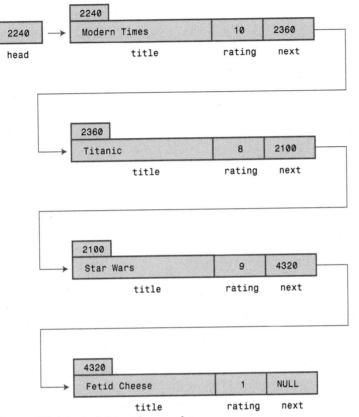

Figure 17.4 Linked list with several items.

Displaying a List

The idea is to begin by setting a pointer (call it **current**) to point to the first structure. Because the head pointer (call it **head**) already points there, this code suffices:

```
current = head;
```

Then you can use pointer notation to access the members of that structure:

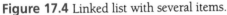

```
printf("Movie: %s   Rating: %d\n", current->title, current->rating);
```

The next step is to reset the **current** pointer to point to the next structure in the list. That information is stored in the **next** member of the structure, so this code accomplishes the task:

```
current = current->next;
```

After this is accomplished, repeat the whole process. When the last item in the list is displayed, **current** will be set to **NULL**, for that's the value of the **next** member of the final structure. You can use that fact to terminate the printing. Here's all the code `films2.c` uses to display the list:

```
while (current != NULL)
{
    printf("Movie: %s  Rating: %d\n", current->title, current->rating);
    current = current->next;
}
```

Why not just use **head** instead of creating a new pointer **current** to march through the list? Because using **head** would change the value of **head**, and the program would no longer have a way to find the beginning of the list.

Creating the List

Creating the list involves three steps:

1. Use `malloc()` to allocate enough space for a structure.

2. Store the address of the structure.

3. Copy the correct information into the structure.

There's no point in creating a structure if none is needed, so the program uses temporary storage (the **input** array) to get the user's choice for a movie name. If the user simulates **EOF** from the keyboard or enters an empty line, the input loop quits:

```
while (gets(input) != NULL && input[0] != '\0')
```

If there is input, the program requests space for a structure and assigns its address to the pointer variable **current**:

```
current = (struct film *) malloc(sizeof(struct film));
```

The address of the very first structure should be stored in the pointer variable **head**. The address of each subsequent structure should be stored in the **next** member of the structure that precedes it. Therefore, the program needs a way to know whether it's dealing with the first structure or not. A simple way is to initialize the **head** pointer to NULL when the program starts. Then the program can use the value of **head** to decide what to do.

```
if (head == NULL)          /* first structure       */
    head = current;
else                       /* subsequent structures */
    prev->next = current;
```

In this code, **prev** is a pointer that points to the structure allocated the previous time.

Next, you have to set the structure members to the proper values. In particular, you should set the **next** member to NULL to indicate that the current structure is the last one in the list. You should copy the film title from the **input** array to the **title** member, and you should get a value for the **rating** member. The following code does these things:

```
current->next = NULL;
strcpy(current->title, input);
puts("Enter your rating <0-10>:");
scanf("%d", &current->rating);
```

Finally, you should prepare the program for the next cycle of the input loop. In particular, you need to set `prev` to point to the current structure, for it will become the previous structure after the next movie name is entered and the next structure is allocated. The program sets this pointer at the end of the loop:

```
prev = current;
```

Does it work? Here is a sample run:

```
Enter first movie title:
The Full Monty
Enter your rating <0-10>:
7
Enter next movie title (empty line to stop):
The Duelists
Enter your rating <0-10>:
8
Enter next movie title (empty line to stop):
Devil Dog: The Hound of Hell
Enter your rating <0-10>:
1
Enter next movie title (empty line to stop):

Here is the movie list:
Movie: The Full Monty  Rating: 7
Movie: The Duelists  Rating: 8
Movie: Devil Dog: The Hound of Hell  Rating: 1
Bye!
```

Afterthoughts

The `films2.c` program is a bit skimpy. For example, it fails to check whether `malloc()` finds the requested memory, and it doesn't have any provisions for deleting items from the list. These failings can be fixed, however. For instance, you can add code that checks whether `malloc()`'s return value is `NULL` (the sign it failed to obtain the memory you wanted). If the program needs to delete entries, you can write some more code to do that. This approach to solving problems and adding features as the need arises isn't the best programming method. In particular, it tends to intermingle coding details and the conceptual model. For instance, in the sample program, the conceptual model is that you add items to a list. The program obscures that interface by pushing details such as `malloc()` and the `current->next` pointer into the foreground. It would be nice if you could write a program in a way that made it obvious you're adding something to a list and in which bookkeeping details, such as calling memory-management functions and setting pointers, were hidden. By making a fresh start, you can meet these goals. Let's see how.

Abstract Data Types (ADTs)

In programming, you try to match the data type to the needs of a programming problem. For instance, you would use the `int` type to represent the number of shoes you own and the `float` or `double` type to represent your average cost per pair of shoes. In the movie examples, the data formed a list of items, each of which consisted of a movie name (a C string) and rating (an `int`). No basic C type matches that description, so we defined a structure to represent individual items, and then we devised a couple of methods for tying together a series of structures to form a list. In essence, we used C's capabilities to design a new data type that matched our needs, but we did so unsystematically. Now we'll take a more systematic approach to defining types.

What constitutes a type? A *type* specifies two kinds of information: a set of properties and a set of operations. For instance, the `int` type's property is that it represents an integer value and, therefore, shares the properties of integers. The allowed arithmetic operations are changing the sign, adding two `int`s, subtracting two `int`s, multiplying two `int`s, dividing one `int` by another, and taking the modulus of one `int` with respect to another. When you declare a variable to be an `int`, you're saying that these and only these operations can affect it.

Integer Properties

Behind the C `int` type is a more abstract concept, that of the *integer*. Mathematicians can, and do, define the properties of integers in a formal abstract manner. For instance, if N and M are integers, then N + M = M + N, or for every two integers N and M, there is an integer S, such that N + M = S. If N + M = S and if N + Q = S, M = Q. You can think of mathematics as supplying the abstract concept of the integer and of C as supplying an implementation of that concept. For example, C provides a means of storing an integer and of performing integer operations such as addition and multiplication. Note that providing support for arithmetic operations is an essential part of representing integers. The `int` type would be much less useful if all you could do was store a value but not use it in arithmetic expressions. Note also that the implementation doesn't do a perfect job of representing integers. For instance, there are an infinity of integers, but a 2-byte `int` can represent only 65,536 of them; don't confuse the abstract idea with a particular implementation.

Suppose you want to define a new data type. First, you have to provide a way to store the data, perhaps by designing a structure. Second, you have to provide ways of manipulating the data. For instance, consider the `films2.c` program (refer to Listing 17.2). It has a linked set of structures to hold the information and supplies code for adding information and displaying information. This program, however, doesn't do these things in a way that makes it clear we were creating a new type. What should we have done?

Computer science has developed a very successful way to define new data types. It's a three-step process that moves from the abstract to the concrete:

1. Provide an abstract description of the type's properties and of the operations you can perform on the type. This description shouldn't be tied to any particular implementation. It shouldn't even be tied to a particular programming language. Such a formal abstract description is called an *abstract data type* (ADT).

2. Develop a programming interface that implements the ADT. That is, indicate how to store the data and describe a set of functions that perform the desired operations. In C, for instance, you might supply a structure definition along with prototypes for functions to manipulate the structures. These functions play the same role for the user-defined type that C's built-in operators play for the fundamental C types. Someone who wants to use the new type will use this interface for her or his programming.

3. Write code to implement the interface. This step is essential, of course, but the programmer using the new type need not be aware of the details of the implementation.

Let's work through an example to see how this process works. Because you've already invested some effort into the movie listing example, let's redo it using the new approach.

Getting Abstract

Basically, all you need for the movie project is a list of items. Each item contains a movie name and a rating. You need to be able to add new items to the end of the list, and you need to be able to display the contents of the list. Let's call the abstract type that will handle these needs a *list*. What properties should a list have? Clearly, a list should be able to hold a sequence of items. That is, a list can hold several items, and these items are arranged in some kind of order, so you can speak of the first item in a list or of the second item or of the last item. Next, the list type should support operations such as adding an item to the list. Here are some useful operations:

- Initializing a list to empty.

- Adding an item to the end of a list.

- Determining whether the list is empty.

- Determining whether the list is full.

- Determining how many items are in the list.

- Visiting each item in a list to perform some action, such as displaying the item.

You don't need any further operations for this project, but a more general list of operations for lists might include the following:

- Inserting an item anywhere in the list.

- Removing an item from the list.

- Retrieving an item from the list (list left unaltered).

- Replacing one item in the list with another.

- Searching for an item in the list.

The informal, but abstract, definition of a list, then, is that it is a data object capable of holding a sequence of items and to which you can apply any of the preceding operations. This definition doesn't state what kind of items can be stored in the list. It doesn't specify whether an array or a linked set of structures or some other data form should be used to hold the items. It doesn't dictate what method to use, for example, to find the number of elements in a list. These matters are all details left to the implementation.

To keep the example simple, adopt a simplified list as the abstract data type, one that embodies only the features needed for the movie project. Here's a summary of the type:

Type Name: Simple List

Type Properties: Can hold a sequence of items.

Type Operations: Initialize list to empty.

Determine whether list is empty.

Determine whether list is full.

Determine number of items in the list.

Add item to end of list.

Traverse list, processing each item in list.

The next step is to develop a C-language interface for the simple list ADT.

Building an Interface

The interface for the simple list has two parts. The first part describes how the data will be represented, and the second part describes functions that implement the ADT operations. For instance, there will be functions for adding an item to a list and for reporting the number of items in the list. The interface design should parallel the ADT description as closely as possible. Therefore, it should be expressed in terms of some general `Item` type instead of in terms of some specific type, such as `int` or `struct film`. One way to do this is to use C's `typedef` facility to define `Item` as the needed type:

```
#define TSIZE 45      /* size of array to hold title   */
struct film
{
   char title[TSIZE];
   int rating;
};

typedef struct film Item;
```

Then you can use the `Item` type for the rest of the definitions. If you later want a list of some other form of data, you can redefine the `Item` type and leave the rest of the interface definition unchanged.

Having defined `Item`, you now have to decide how to store items of that type. This step really belongs to the implementation stage, but making a decision now makes the example easier to follow. The linked structure approach worked pretty well in the `films2.c` program, so let's adapt it as shown here:

```
typedef struct node
{
    Item item;
    struct node * next;
} Node;
typedef Node * List;
```

In a linked list implementation, each link is called a *node*. Each node contains information that forms the contents of the list along with a pointer to the next node. To emphasize this terminology, we've used the tag name `node` for a node structure, and we've used `typedef` to make `Node` the type name for a `struct node` structure. Finally, to manage a linked list, we need a pointer to its beginning, and we've used `typedef` to make `List` the name for a pointer of this type. Therefore, the declaration

```
List movies;
```

establishes `movies` as a pointer suitable for referring to a linked list.

Is this the only way to define the `List` type? No. For instance, you could incorporate a variable to keep track of the number of entries:

```
typedef struct list
{
    Node * head;    /* pointer to head of list          */
    int size;       /* number of entries in list        */
} List;             /* alternative definition of list */
```

You could add a second pointer to keep track of the end of the list. Later, you'll see an example that does that. For now, let's stick to the first definition of a `List` type. The important point is that you should think of the declaration

```
List movies;
```

as establishing a list, not as establishing a pointer to a node or as establishing a structure. The exact data representation of `movies` is an implementation detail that should be invisible at the interface level.

For example, a program should initialize the head pointer to `NULL` when starting out, but you should not use code like this:

```
movies = NULL;
```

Why not? Because later you might find you like the structure implementation of a `List` type better, and that would require the following initializations:

```
movies.next = NULL;
movies.size = 0;
```

Anyone using the `List` type shouldn't have to worry about such details. Instead, they should be able do something along the following lines:

```
InitializeList(movies);
```

Programmers need to know only that they should use the `InitializeList()` function to initialize a list. They don't have to know the exact data implementation of a `List` variable. This is an example of *data hiding*, the art of concealing details of data representation from the higher levels of programming.

To guide the user, you can supply a function prototype along these lines:

```
/* operation:        initialize a list                   */
/* preconditions:    plist points to a list              */
/* postconditions:   the list is initialized to empty    */
void InitializeList(List * plist);
```

There are three points you should notice. First, the comments outline *preconditions*, that is, conditions that should hold before the function is called. Here, for instance, you need a list to initialize. Second, the comments outline *postconditions*, that is, conditions that should hold after the function executes. Finally, the function uses a pointer to a list instead of a list as its argument, so this would be the function call:

```
InitializeList(&movies);
```

The reason is that C passes arguments by value, so the only way a C function can alter a variable in the calling program is by using a pointer to that variable. Here the restrictions of the language make the interface deviate slightly from the abstract description.

The C way to tie all the type and function information into a single package is to place the type definitions and function prototypes (including precondition and postcondition comments) in a header file. This file should supply all the information a programmer needs to use the type. Listing 17.3 shows a header file for the simple list type. It defines a particular structure as the `Item` type, and then defines `Node` in terms of `Item` and `List` in terms of `Node`. The functions representing list operations then use `Item` types and `List` types as arguments. If the function needs to modify an argument, it uses a pointer to the corresponding type instead of using the type directly. The file capitalizes each function name as a way of marking it as part of an interface package. Also, the file uses the `#ifndef` technique discussed in Chapter 16, "The C Preprocessor and the C Library," to protect against multiple inclusions of a file.

Listing 17.3   The `list.h` interface header file.

```
/* list.h -- header file for a simple list type */
#ifndef _LIST_H_
#define _LIST_H_

/* program-specific declarations */

#define TSIZE     45    /* size of array to hold title */
struct film
{
   char title[TSIZE];
   int rating;
};

/* general type definitions */
```

```
typedef struct film Item;
typedef enum boolean {False, True} BOOLEAN;
typedef struct node
{
    Item item;
    struct node * next;
} Node;
typedef Node * List;

/* function prototypes */

/* operation:        initialize a list                        */
/* preconditions:    plist points to a list                   */
/* postconditions:   the list is initialized to empty         */
void InitializeList(List * plist);

/* operation:        determine if list is empty               */
/* preconditions:    l is an initialized list                 */
/* postconditions:   function returns True if list is empty   */
/*                   and returns False otherwise              */
BOOLEAN EmptyList(List l);

/* operation:        determine if list is full                */
/* preconditions:    l is an initialized list                 */
/* postconditions:   function returns True if list is full    */
/*                   and returns False otherwise              */
BOOLEAN FullList(List l);

/* operation:        determine number of items in list        */
/* preconditions:    l is an initialized list                 */
/* postconditions:   function returns number of items in list */
unsigned int ListItems(List l);

/* operation:        add item to end of list                 */
/* preconditions:    item is an item to be added to list      */
/*                   plist points to an initialized list      */
/* postconditions:   if possible, function adds item to end   */
/*                   of list and returns True; otherwise the  */
/*                   function returns False                   */
BOOLEAN AddItem(Item item, List * plist);

/* operation:        apply a function to each item in list    */
/* preconditions:    l is an initialized list                 */
/*                   pfun points to a function that takes an  */
/*                   Item argument and has no return value    */
/* postcondition:    the function pointed to by pfun is       */
/*                   executed once for each item in the list  */
void Traverse (List l, void (* pfun)(Item item) );

#endif
```

One of the prototypes in the header file is a bit more complex than the others.

```
/* operation:        apply a function to each item in list    */
/* preconditions:    l is an initialized list                 */
/*                   pfun points to a function that takes an   */
/*                   Item argument and has no return value     */
/* postcondition:    the function pointed to by pfun is        */
/*                   executed once for each item in the list   */
void Traverse (List l, void (* pfun)(Item item) );
```

The argument **pfun** is a pointer to a function. In particular, it is a pointer to a function that takes an item as an argument and that has no return value. As you might recall from Chapter 14, "Structures and Other Data Forms," you can pass a pointer to a function as an argument to a second function, and the second function can then use the pointed-to function. Here, for instance, you can let **pfun** point to a function that displays an item. The **Traverse()** function would then apply this function to each item in the list, thus displaying the whole list.

Using the Interface

Our claim is that you should be able to use this interface to write a program without knowing any further details, for example, without knowing how the functions are written. Let's write a new version of the movie program right now before we write the supporting functions. Because the interface is in terms of **List** and **Item** types, the program should be phrased in those terms. Here's a pseudocode representation of one possible plan:

```
Create a List variable.
Create an Item variable.
Initialize the list to empty.
While the list isn't full and while there's more input:
    Read the input into the Item variable.
    Add the item to the end of the list.
Visit each item in the list and display it.
```

The program shown in Listing 17.4 follows this basic plan, with some error-checking. Note how it makes use of the interface described in the **list.h** file (refer to Listing 17.3). Also note that the listing has code for a **showmovies()** function that conforms to the prototype required by **Traverse()**. Therefore, the program can pass the pointer **showmovies** to **Traverse()** so that **Traverse()** can apply the **showmovies()** function to each item in the list. (Recall that the name of a function is a pointer to the function.)

Listing 17.4 The `films3.c` program.

```
/* films3.c -- using an ADT-style linked list */
#include <stdio.h>
#include <stdlib.h>    /* prototype for exit() */
#include "list.h"      /* defines List, Item   */
void showmovies(Item item);
```

```
int main(void)
{
    List movies;
    Item temp;

    InitializeList(&movies);
    if (FullList(movies))
    {
        fprintf(stderr,"No memory available! Bye!\n");
        exit(1);
    }
    puts("Enter first movie title:");
    while (gets(temp.title) != NULL && temp.title[0] != '\0')
    {
        puts("Enter your rating <0-10>:");
        scanf("%d", &temp.rating);
        while(getchar() != '\n')
            continue;
        if (AddItem(temp, &movies)== False)
        {
            fprintf(stderr,"Problem allocating memory\n");
            break;
        }
        if (FullList(movies))
        {
            puts("The list is now full.");
            break;
        }
        puts("Enter next movie title (empty line to stop):");
    }
    if (EmptyList(movies))
        printf("No data entered. ");
    else
    {
        printf ("Here is the movie list:\n");
        Traverse(movies, showmovies);
    }
    printf("Bye!\n");
    return 0;
}

void showmovies(Item item)
{
        printf("Movie: %s  Rating: %d\n", item.title,
            item.rating);
}
```

Implementing the Interface

Of course, you still have to implement the List interface. The C approach is to collect
the function definitions in a file called list.c. The complete program, then, consists of
three files: list.h, which defines the data structures and provides prototypes for the user

interface, list.c, which provides the function code to implement the interface, and films3.c, which is a source code file that applies the list interface to a particular programming problem. Listing 17.5 shows one possible implementation of list.c. To run the program, you must compile both films3.c and list.c and link them. (You might want to review the discussion in Chapter 9, "Functions," on compiling multiple-file programs.) Together, the files list.h, list.c, and films3.c constitute a complete program (see Figure 17.5).

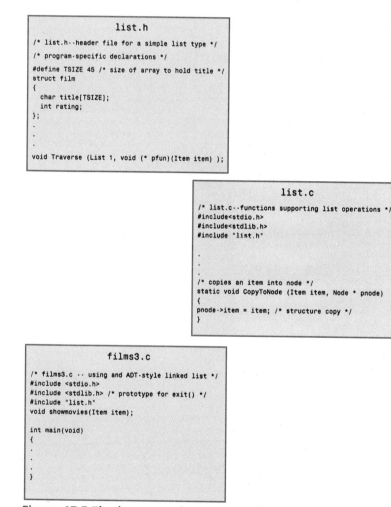

Figure 17.5 The three parts of a program package.

Listing 17.5   The list.c implementation file.

```
/* list.c -- functions supporting list operations */
#include <stdio.h>
#include <stdlib.h>
#include "list.h"
```

```
/* local functions */
static void CopyToNode(Item item, Node * pnode);

/* interface functions */
/* set the list to empty   */
void InitializeList(List * plist)
{
    * plist = NULL;
}

/* returns true if list is empty */
BOOLEAN EmptyList(List l)
{
    if (l == NULL)
        return True;
    else
        return False;
}

/* returns true if list is full */
BOOLEAN FullList(List l)
{
    Node * pt;
    BOOLEAN full;

    pt = (Node *) malloc(sizeof(Node));
    if (pt == NULL)
        full = True;
    else
        full = False;
    free(pt);
    return full;
}

/* returns number of nodes */
unsigned int ListItems(List l)
{
    unsigned int count = 0;

    while (l != NULL)
    {
        ++count;
        l = l->next;    /* set l to next node */
    }
    return count;
}

/* creates node to hold item and adds it to the end of */
/* the list pointed to by plist (slow implementation)  */
BOOLEAN AddItem(Item item, List * plist)
{
    Node * pnew;
    Node * scan = *plist;
```

continued on next page

continued from previous page

```
            pnew = (Node *) malloc(sizeof(Node));
            if (pnew == NULL)
               return False;  /* quit function on failure  */

            CopyToNode(item, pnew);
            pnew->next = NULL;
            if (scan == NULL)        /* empty list, so place */
               * plist = pnew;       /* pnew at head of list */
            else
            {
               while (scan->next != NULL)
                   scan = scan->next;  /* find end of list  */
               scan->next = pnew;      /* add pnew to end   */
            }
            return True;
        }

        /* visit each node and execute function pointed to by pfun */
        void Traverse (List l, void (* pfun)(Item item) )
        {
           while (l != NULL)
           {
              (*pfun)(l->item);    /* apply function to item in list */
              l = l->next;
           }
        }

        /* copies an item into a node */
        static void CopyToNode(Item item, Node * pnode)
        {
           pnode->item = item;  /* structure copy */
        }
```

Program Notes

The list.c file has many interesting points. For one, it illustrates when you might use static storage class functions. As described in Chapter 13, "Storage Classes and Program Development," static functions are known only in the file where they are defined. When implementing an interface, you might find it convenient sometimes to write auxiliary functions that aren't part of the official interface. For instance, the example uses a function CopyToNode() to copy a type Item value to a type Item variable. Because this function is part of the implementation but not part of the interface, we hid it in the list.c file by making it static. Now, examine the other functions.

The InitializeList() function initializes a list to empty. In our implementation, that means setting a type List variable to NULL. As mentioned earlier, this requires passing a pointer to the List variable to the function.

The EmptyList() function is quite simple, but it does depend on the list variable being set to NULL when the list is empty. Therefore, it's important to initialize a list before first using the EmptyList() function. Also, if you were to extend the interface to include deleting items, you should make sure the deletion function resets the list to empty when the last item is deleted. Because this function doesn't alter the list, you don't need to pass a pointer as an argument, so the argument is a `List` instead of a pointer to a `List`.

With a linked list, the size of the list is limited by the amount of memory available. The `FullList()` function tries to allocate enough space for a new item. If it fails, the list is full. If it succeeds, it has to free the memory it just allocated so that it is available for a real item.

The `ListItems()` function uses the usual linked-list algorithm to traverse the list, counting items as it goes:

```
unsigned int ListItems(List l)
{
    unsigned int count = 0;

    while (l != NULL)
    {
        ++count;
        l = l->next;    /* set l to next node */
    }
     return count;
}
```

The `AddItem()` function is the most elaborate of the group:

```
BOOLEAN AddItem(Item item, List * plist)
{
    Node * pnew;
    Node * scan = *plist;

    pnew = (Node *) malloc(sizeof(Node));
    if (pnew == NULL)
        return False;           /* quit function on failure */

    CopyToNode(item, pnew);
    pnew->next = NULL;
    if (scan == NULL)           /* empty list, so place     */
        * plist = pnew;         /* pnew at head of list      */
    else
    {
        while (scan->next != NULL)
            scan = scan->next;   /* find end of list         */
        scan->next = pnew;       /* add pnew to end          */
    }
    return True;
}
```

The first thing the `AddItem()` function does is allocate space for a new node. If this succeeds, the function uses `CopyToNode()` to copy the item to the node. Then it sets the `next` member of the node to `NULL`. This, recall, indicates that the node is the last node in the linked list. Finally, after creating the node and assigning the correct values to its members, the function attaches the node to the end of the list. If the item is the first item added to the list, the program sets the head pointer to the first item. (Remember, `AddItem()` is called with the address of the head pointer as its second argument, so `* plist` is the value of the head pointer.) Otherwise, the code marches through the linked list until it finds the item having its **next** member set to **NULL**. That node is currently the last node, so the function resets its **next** member to point to the new node.

Good programming practice dictates that you call **FullList()** before trying to add an item to the list. However, a user might fail to observe this dictate, so **AddItem()** checks for itself whether **malloc()** has succeeded. Also, it's possible a user might do something else to allocate memory between calling **FullList()** and calling **AddItem()**, so it's best to check whether **malloc()** worked.

Finally, the **Traverse()** function is similar to the **ListItems()** function with the addition of applying a function to each item in the list:

```c
void Traverse (List l, void (* pfun)(Item item) )
{
    while (l != NULL)
    {
        (*pfun)(l->item);        /* apply function to item in list */
        l = l->next;
    }
}
```

Recall that **l->item** represents the data stored in a node, and the **l->next** identifies the next node in the linked list. For example, the function call

```c
Traverse(movies, showmovies);
```

applies the **showmovies()** function to each item in the list.

Contemplating Your Work

Take a little time now to evaluate what the ADT approach has done for you. First, compare Listing 17.2 with Listing 17.4. Both programs use the same fundamental method (dynamic allocation of linked structures) to solve the movie listing problem, but Listing 17.2 exposes all the programming plumbing, putting **malloc()** and **prev->next** in public view. Listing 17.4, on the other hand, hides these details and expresses the program in a language that relates directly to the tasks. That is, it talks about creating a list and adding items to the list, not about calling memory functions or resetting pointers. In short, Listing 17.4 expresses the program in terms of the problem to be solved, not in terms of the low-level tools needed to solve the problem. The ADT version is oriented to the end user's concerns and is much easier to read.

Next, the **list.h** and **list.c** files together constitute a reusable resource. If you need another simple list, just haul out these files. Suppose you need to store an inventory of your relatives: names, relationships, addresses, and phone numbers. First, you would go to the **list.h** file and redefine the **Item** type:

```c
typedef struct itemtag
{
    char fname[14];
    char lname [24];
    char relationship[36];
    char address [60];
    char phonenum[20];
}   Item;
```

Next. . .well, that's all you have to do in this case because all the simple list functions are defined in terms of the `Item` type. In some cases, you would also have to redefine the `CopyToNode()` function. For example, if an item were an array, you couldn't copy it by assignment.

Another important point is that the user interface is defined in terms of abstract list operations, not in terms of some particular set of data representation and algorithms. This leaves you free to fiddle with the implementation without having to redo the final program. For instance, the current `AddItem()` function is a bit inefficient because it always starts at the beginning of the list, and then searches for the end. You can fix this problem by keeping track of the end of the list. For instance, you can redefine the `List` type this way:

```
typedef struct list
{
    Node * head;      /* points to head of list */
    Node * end;       /* points to end of list  */
} List;
```

Of course, you would then have to rewrite the list-processing functions using this new definition, but you wouldn't have to change a thing in Listing 17.4. This sort of isolating implementation from the final interface is particularly useful for large programming projects. It's called *data hiding* because the detailed data representation is hidden from the final user.

Note that this particular ADT doesn't even force you to implement the simple list as a linked list. Here's another possibility:

```
#define MAXSIZE 100
typedef struct list
{
    Item entries[MAXSIZE];   /* array of items          */
    int items;               /* number of items in list */
} List;
```

Again, this would require rewriting the `list.c` file, but the program using the list doesn't need to be changed.

Getting Queued with an ADT

The abstract data type approach to programming in C, as you've seen, involves the following three steps:

1. Describing a type, including its operations, in an abstract, general fashion.

2. Devising a function interface to represent the new type.

3. Writing detailed code to implement the interface.

You've seen this approach applied to a simple list. Now, apply it to something slightly more complex: the queue.

Defining the Queue Abstract Data Type

A *queue* is a list with two special properties. First, new items can be added only to the end of the list. In this respect, the queue is like the simple list. Second, items can be removed from the list only at the beginning. You can visualize a queue as a line of people buying tickets to a theater. You join the line at the end, and you leave the line at the front, after purchasing your tickets. A queue is a *first in, first out* (FIFO) data form, just the way a movie line is (if no one cuts into the line). Once again, let's frame an informal, abstract definition, as shown here:

Type Name:	Queue
Type Properties:	Can hold an ordered sequence of items.
Type Operations:	Initialize queue to empty.
	Determine whether queue is empty.
	Determine whether queue if full.
	Determine number of items in the queue.
	Add item to rear of queue.
	Remove and recover item from front of queue.

Defining an Interface

The interface definition will go into a file called `queue.h`. We'll use C's `typedef` facility to create names for two types: `Item` and `Queue`. The exact implementation for the corresponding structures should be part of the `queue.h` file, but conceptually, designing the structures is part of the detailed implementation stage. For the moment, just assume that the types have been defined and concentrate on the function prototypes.

First, consider initialization. It involves altering a `Queue` type, so the function should take the address of a `Queue` as an argument:

```
void InitializeQueue (Queue * pq);
```

Next, determining whether the queue is empty or full involves a function that should return a true or false value. Because the function doesn't alter the queue, it can take a `Queue` argument. On the other hand, it can be faster and less memory intensive to just pass the address of a `Queue`, depending on how large a `Queue`-type object is. Let's try that approach this time. To indicate that these functions don't change a queue, you can, and should, use the `const` qualifier:

```
BOOLEAN FullQueue(const Queue * pq);
BOOLEAN EmptyQueue(const Queue * pq);
```

Paraphrasing, the pointer `pq` points to a `Queue` data object that cannot be altered through the agency of `pq`. You can define a similar prototype for a function that returns the number of items in a queue.

```
int QueueItems(const Queue * pq);
```

Adding an item to the end of the queue involves identifying the item and the queue. This time the queue is altered, so using a pointer is necessary, not optional. The function could be type `void`, or you can use the return value to indicate whether the operation of adding an item succeeded. Let's take the second approach:

```
BOOLEAN EnQueue(Item item, Queue * pq);
```

Finally, removing an item can be done several ways. If the item is defined as a structure or as one of the fundamental types, it could be returned by the function. The function argument could be either a `Queue` or a pointer to a `Queue`. Therefore, one possible prototype is this:

```
Item DeQueue(Queue q);
```

However, the following prototype is a bit more general:

```
BOOLEAN DeQueue(Item * pitem, Queue * pq);
```

The item removed from the queue goes to the location pointed to by the `pitem` pointer, and the return value indicates whether the operation succeeded.

Implementing the Interface Data Representation

The first step is deciding what C data form to use for a queue. One possibility is an array. The advantages to arrays are that they're easy to use and that adding an item to the end of an array's filled portion is easy. The problem comes with removing an item from the front of the queue. In the analogy of people in a ticket line, removing an item from the front of the queue consists of copying the value of the first element of the array (simple), and then moving each item left in the array one element toward the front. That is easy to program, but it wastes a lot of computer time (see Figure 17.6).

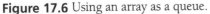

Figure 17.6 Using an array as a queue.

A second way to handle the removal problem in an array implementation is to leave the remaining elements where they are and, instead, change which element you call the front (see Figure 17.7). This method's problem is that the vacated elements become dead space, so the available space in the queue keeps decreasing.

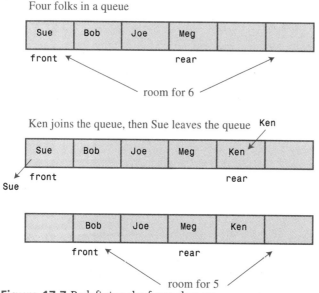

Figure 17.7 Redefining the front element.

A clever solution to the dead space problem is to make the queue *circular*. This means wrapping around from the end of the array to the beginning. That is, consider the first element of the array as immediately following the last element so that when you reach the end of the array, you can start adding items to the beginning elements if they have been vacated (see Figure 17.8). You can imagine drawing the array on a strip of paper, and then pasting one end of the array to the other to form a band. Of course, you now have to do some fancy bookkeeping to make sure the end of the queue doesn't pass the front.

Yet another solution is to use a linked list. This has the advantage that removing the front item doesn't require moving all the other items. Instead, you just reset the front pointer to point to the new first element. Because we've already been working with linked lists, we'll take this tack. To test our ideas, we'll start with a queue of integers:

```
typedef int Item;
```

A linked list is built from nodes, so let's define a node next:

```
typedef struct node
{
    Item item;
    struct node * next;
} Node;
```

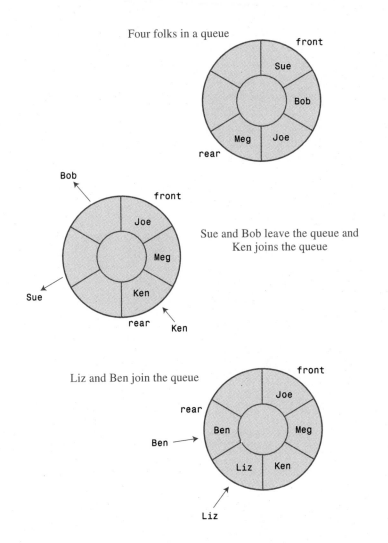

Four folks in a queue

Sue and Bob leave the queue and
Ken joins the queue

Liz and Ben join the queue

Circular queue wraps around to front of array

Figure 17.8 A circular queue.

For the queue, you need to keep track of the front and rear items. You can use pointers to do this. Also, you can use a counter to keep track of the number of items in a queue.

```
typedef struct queue
{
    Node * front;    /* pointer to front of queue */
    Node * rear;     /* pointer to rear of queue  */
    int items;       /* number of items in queue  */
} Queue;
```

Note that a `Queue` is a structure with three members, so the earlier decision to use pointers to queues instead of entire queues as arguments is a time and space saver.

Next, think about the size of a queue. With a linked list, the amount of available memory sets the limit, but often a much smaller size is more appropriate. For example, you might use a queue to simulate airplanes waiting to land at an airport. If the number of waiting planes gets too large, new arrivals might be rerouted to other airports. We'll set a maximum queue size of 10. Listing 17.6 contains the definitions and prototypes for the queue interface. It leaves open the exact definition of the `Item` type. When using the interface, you would insert the appropriate definition for your particular program.

Listing 17.6   The `queue.h` interface header file.

```
/* queue.h -- interface for a queue */
#ifndef _QUEUE_H_
#define _QUEUE_H_

/* INSERT ITEM TYPE HERE */
/* INSERT ITEM TYPE HERE */
/* FOR EXAMPLE, */
typedef int Item;
/* OR typedef struct item {int gumption; int charisma;} Item; */

#define MAXQUEUE 10

typedef enum boolean {False, True} BOOLEAN;

typedef struct node
{
   Item item;
   struct node * next;
} Node;

typedef struct queue
{
   Node * front;  /* pointer to front of queue  */
   Node * rear;   /* pointer to rear of queue   */
   int items;     /* number of items in queue   */
} Queue;

/* operation:      initialize the queue                     */
/* precondition:   pq points to a queue                     */
/* postcondition:  queue is initialized to being empty      */
void InitializeQueue(Queue * pq);

/* operation:      check if queue is full                   */
/* precondition:   pq points to previously initialized queue */
/* postcondition:  returns True if queue is full, else False */
BOOLEAN FullQueue(const Queue * pq);

/* operation:      check if queue is empty                  */
/* precondition:   pq points to previously initialized queue */
/* postcondition:  returns True if queue is empty, else False */
BOOLEAN EmptyQueue(const Queue *pq);
```

```
/* operation:        determine number of items in queue      */
/* precondition:     pq points to previously initialized queue  */
/* postcondition:    returns number of items in queue        */
int QueueItems(const Queue * pq);

/* operation:        add item to rear of queue               */
/* precondition:     pq points to previously initialized queue */
/*                   item is to be placed at rear of queue    */
/* postcondition:    if queue is not empty, item is placed at */
/*                   rear of queue and function returns       */
/*                   True; otherwise, queue is unchanged and  */
/*                   function returns False                   */
BOOLEAN EnQueue(Item item, Queue * pq);

/* operation:        remove item from front of queue         */
/* precondition:     pq points to previously initialized queue */
/* postcondition:    if queue is not empty, item at head of   */
/*                   queue is copied to *pitem and deleted from */
/*                   queue, and function returns True; if the  */
/*                   operation empties the queue, the queue is */
/*                   reset to empty. If the queue is empty to  */
/*                   begin with, queue is unchanged and the    */
/*                   function returns False                    */
BOOLEAN DeQueue(Item *pitem, Queue * pq);

#endif
```

Implementing the Interface Functions

Now we can get down to writing the interface code. First, initializing a queue to empty means setting the front and rear pointers to NULL and setting the item count (the **items** member) to **0**:

```
void InitializeQueue(Queue * pq)
{
    pq->front = pq->rear = NULL;
    pq->items = 0;
}
```

Next, the **items** member makes it easy to check for a full queue or empty queue and to return the number of items in a queue:

```
BOOLEAN FullQueue(const Queue * pq)
{
    return pq->items == MAXQUEUE;
}

BOOLEAN EmptyQueue(const Queue * pq)
{
    return pq->items == 0;
}
```

```
int QueueItems(const Queue * pq)
{
    return pq->items;
}
```

Adding an item to the queue involves the following steps:

1. Creating a new node.

2. Copying the item to the node.

3. Setting the node's **next** pointer to NULL, identifying the node as the last in the list.

4. Setting the current rear node's **next** pointer to point to the new node, linking the new node to the queue.

5. Setting the **rear** pointer to the new node, making it easy to find the last node.

6. Adding 1 to the item count.

Also, the function has to handle two special cases. First, if the queue is empty, the **front** pointer should be set to point to the new node. That's because when there is just one node, that node is both the front and the rear of the queue. Second, if the function is unable to obtain memory for the node, it should do something. Because we envision using small queues, such failure should be rare, so we'll simply have the function terminate the program if the program runs out of memory.

```
BOOLEAN EnQueue(Item item, Queue * pq)
{
    Node * pnew;

    if (FullQueue(pq))
        return False;
    pnew = (Node *) malloc( sizeof(Node));
    if (pnew == NULL)
    {
        fprintf(stderr,"Unable to allocate memory!\n");
        exit(1);
    }
    CopyToNode(item, pnew);
    pnew->next = NULL;
    if (EmptyQueue(pq))
        pq->front = pnew;           /* item goes to front     */
    else
        pq->rear->next = pnew;      /* link at end of queue   */
    pq->rear = pnew;                /* record location of end */
    pq->items++;                    /* one more item in queue */
    return True;
}
```

The CopyToNode() function is a static function to handle copying the item to a node:

```
static void CopyToNode(Item item, Node * pn)
{
    pn->item = item;
}
```

Removing an item from the front of the queue involves the following steps:

1. Copying the item to a waiting variable.

2. Freeing the memory used by the vacated node.

3. Resetting the front pointer to the next item in the queue.

4. Resetting the front and rear pointers to NULL if the last item is removed.

5. Decrementing the item count.

Here's code that does all these things:

```
BOOLEAN DeQueue(Item * pitem, Queue * pq)
{
    Node * pt;

    if (EmptyQueue(pq))
        return False;
    CopyToItem(pq->front, pitem);
    pt = pq->front;
    pq->front = pq->front->next;
    free(pt);
    pq->items--;
    if (pq->items == 0)
        pq->rear = NULL;
    return True;
}
```

There are a couple of pointer facts you should note. First, the code doesn't explicitly set the front pointer to NULL when the last item is deleted. That's because it already sets the front pointer to the next pointer of the node being deleted. If that node is the last node, its next pointer is NULL, so the front pointer gets set to NULL. Second, the code uses a temporary pointer pt to keep track of the deleted node's location. That's because the official pointer to the first node (pq->front) gets reset to point to the next node, so without the temporary pointer, the program would lose track of which block of memory to free.

Keeping Your ADT Pure

After you've defined an ADT interface, you should use only the functions of the interface to handle the data type. Note, for instance, that Dequeue() depends on the EnQueue() function doing its job of setting pointers correctly and setting the next pointer of the rear node to NULL. If, in a program using the ADT, you decided to manipulate parts of the queue directly, you might mess up the coordination between the functions in the interface package.

Listing 17.7 shows all the functions of the interface, including the `CopyToItem()` function used in `EnQueue()`.

Listing 17.7   The `queue.c` implementation file.

```
/* queue.c -- the Queue type implementation*/
#include <stdio.h>
#include <stdlib.h>
#include "queue.h"

/* local functions */
static void CopyToNode(Item item, Node * pn);
static void CopyToItem(Node * pn, Item * pi);

void InitializeQueue(Queue * pq)
{
    pq->front = pq->rear = NULL;
    pq->items = 0;
}

BOOLEAN FullQueue(const Queue * pq)
{
    return pq->items == MAXQUEUE;
}

BOOLEAN EmptyQueue(const Queue * pq)
{
    return pq->items == 0;
}

int QueueItems(const Queue * pq)
{
    return pq->items;
}

BOOLEAN EnQueue(Item item, Queue * pq)
{
    Node * pnew;

    if (FullQueue(pq))
        return False;
    pnew = (Node *) malloc( sizeof(Node));
    if (pnew == NULL)
    {
        fprintf(stderr,"Unable to allocate memory!\n");
        exit(1);
    }
    CopyToNode(item, pnew);
    pnew->next = NULL;
    if (EmptyQueue(pq))
        pq->front = pnew;
    else
        pq->rear->next = pnew;
```

```
        pq->rear = pnew;
        pq->items++;
        return True;
    }

    BOOLEAN DeQueue(Item * pitem, Queue * pq)
    {
        Node * pt;

        if (EmptyQueue(pq))
            return False;
        CopyToItem(pq->front, pitem);
        pt = pq->front;
        pq->front = pq->front->next;
        free(pt);
        pq->items--;
        if (pq->items == 0)
            pq->rear = NULL;
        return True;
    }

    static void CopyToNode(Item item, Node * pn)
    {
        pn->item = item;
    }

    static void CopyToItem(Node * pn, Item * pi)
    {
        *pi = pn->item;
    }
```

Testing the Queue

It's a good idea to test a new design, like the queue package, before inserting it into a critical program. One approach to testing is writing a short program, sometimes called a *driver*, whose sole purpose is to test the package. For instance, Listing 17.8 uses a queue that enables you to add and delete integers. Before using the program, make sure the following line is present in queue.h:

```
typedef int item;
```

Remember, too, that you have to link queue.c and use_q.c.

Listing 17.8   The use.qc program.

```
/* use_q.c -- driver testing the Queue interface */
/* compile with queue.c                          */
#include <stdio.h>
#include "queue.h"  /* defines Queue, Item       */
```

continued on next page

continued from previous page

```
int main(void)
{
    Queue line;
    Item temp;
    char ch;

    InitializeQueue(&line);
    puts("Testing the Queue interface. Type a to add a value,");
    puts("type d to delete a value, and type q to quit.");
    while ((ch = getchar()) != 'q')
    {
        if (ch != 'a' && ch != 'd')    /* ignore other input */
            continue;
        if ( ch == 'a')
        {
            printf("Integer to add: ");
            scanf("%d", &temp);
            if (!FullQueue(&line))
            {
                printf("Putting %d into queue\n", temp);
                EnQueue(temp,&line);
            }
            else
                puts("Queue is full!");
        }
        else
        {
            if (EmptyQueue(&line))
                puts("Nothing to delete!");
            else
            {
                DeQueue(&temp,&line);
                printf("Removing %d from queue\n", temp);
            }
        }
        printf("%d items in queue\n", QueueItems(&line));
        puts("Type a to add, d to delete, q to quit:");
    }
    puts("Bye!");

    return 0;
}
```

Here is a sample run. You should also test to see that the implementation behaves correctly when the queue is full.

```
Testing the Queue interface. Type a to add a value,
type d to delete a value, and type q to quit.
a
Integer to add: 40
Putting 40 into queue
1 items in queue
Type a to add, d to delete, q to quit:
```

```
a
Integer to add: 20
Putting 20 into queue
2 items in queue
Type a to add, d to delete, q to quit:
a
Integer to add: 55
Putting 55 into queue
3 items in queue
Type a to add, d to delete, q to quit:
d
Removing 40 from queue
2 items in queue
Type a to add, d to delete, q to quit:
d
Removing 20 from queue
1 items in queue
Type a to add, d to delete, q to quit:
d
Removing 55 from queue
0 items in queue
Type a to add, d to delete, q to quit:
d
Nothing to delete!
0 items in queue
Type a to add, d to delete, q to quit:
q
Bye!
```

Simulating with a Queue

Well, the queue works! Now let's do something more interesting with it. Many real-life situations involve queues. For instance, customers queue in banks and in supermarkets, airplanes queue at airports, and tasks queue in multitasking computer systems. You can use the queue package to simulate such situations.

Suppose, for example, that Sigmund Landers has set up an advice booth in a mall. Customers can purchase one, two, or three minutes of advice. To ensure a free flow of foot traffic, mall regulations limit the number of customers waiting in line to ten (conveniently equal to the program's maximum queue size.) Suppose people show up randomly and that the time they want to spend in consultation is spread randomly over the three choices (one, two, or three minutes). How many customers, on average, will Sigmund handle an hour? How long, on average, will customers have to wait? How long, on average, will the line be? These are the sort of questions a queue simulation can answer.

First, let's decide what to put in the queue. You can describe each customer in terms of the time when he or she joins the queue and in terms of how many minutes of consultation he or she wants. This suggests the following definition for the `Item` type:

```
typedef struct item
{
    long arrive;      /* the time when a customer joins the queue    */
    int processtime;  /* the number of consultation minutes desired */
} Item;
```

To convert the queue package to handle this structure, instead of the `int` type the last example used, all you have to do is replace the former `typedef` for `Item` with the one shown here. After that's done, you don't have to worry about the detailed mechanics of a queue. Instead, you can proceed to the real problem—simulating Sigmund's waiting line.

Here's one approach. Let time move in one-minute increments. Each minute, check to see whether a new customer has arrived. If a customer arrives and the queue isn't full, add the customer to the queue. This involves recording in an `Item` structure the customer's arrival time and the amount of consultation time the customer wants, and then adding the item to the queue. If the queue is full, however, turn the customer away. For bookkeeping, keep track of the total number of customers and the total number of turnaways (people who can't get in line because it is full).

Next, process the front of the queue. That is, if the queue isn't empty and if Sigmund isn't occupied with a previous customer, remove the item at the front of the queue. The item, recall, contains the time when the customer joined the queue. By comparing this time with the current time, you get the number of minutes the customer has been in the queue. The item also contains the number of consultation minutes the customer wants, which determines how long Sigmund will be occupied with the new customer. Use a variable to keep track of this waiting time. If Sigmund is busy, no one is "dequeued." However, the variable keeping track of the waiting time should be decremented.

The core code can look like this, with each cycle corresponding to one minute of activity:

```
for (cycle = 0; cycle < cyclelimit; cycle++)
{
    if (newcustomer(min_per_cust))
    {
        if (FullQueue(&line))
            turnaways++;
        else
        {
            customers++;
            temp = customertime(cycle);
            EnQueue(temp, &line);
        }
    }
    if (wait_time <= 0 && !EmptyQueue(&line))
    {
        DeQueue (&temp, &line);
        wait_time = temp.processtime;
        line_wait += cycle - temp.arrive;
        served++;
    }
    if (wait_time > 0)
        wait_time--;
    sum_line += QueueItems(&line);
}
```

Here are the meanings of some of the variables and functions:

- `min_per_customer` is the average number of minutes between customer arrivals.

- newcustomer() uses the C rand() function to determine whether a customer shows up during this particular minute.

- turnaways is the number of arrivals turned away.

- customers is the number of arrivals who join the queue.

- temp is an Item variable describing the new customer.

- customertime() sets the arrive and processtime members of the temp structure.

- wait_time is the number of minutes remaining until Sigmund finishes with the current client.

- line_wait is the cumulative time spent in line by all customers to date.

- served is the number of clients actually served.

- sum_line is the cumulative length of the line to date.

Think of how much messier and more obscure this code would look if it were sprinkled with malloc() and free() functions and pointers to nodes. Having the queue package enables you to concentrate on the simulation problem, not on programming details.

Listing 17.9 shows the complete code for the mall advice booth simulation. It uses the standard rand(), srand(), and time() functions to generate random values, following the method suggested in Chapter 13, "Storage Classes and Program Development." To use the program, remember to update the Item definition in queue.h with the following:

```
typedef struct item
{
    long arrive;        /* the time when a customer joins the queue   */
    int processtime;  /* the number of consultation minutes desired */
} Item;
```

Also remember to link the code for mall.c with queue.c.

Listing 17.9   The mall.c program.

```
/* mall.c -- use the Queue interface */
/* compile with queue.c              */
#include <stdio.h>
#include <stdlib.h>     /* for rand() and srand() */
#include <time.h>       /* for time()             */
#include "queue.h"
#define MIN_PER_HR 60.0

BOOLEAN newcustomer(double x);    /* is there a new customer? */
Item customertime(long when);     /* set customer parameters  */
```

continued on next page

continued from previous page

```
int main(void)
{
    Queue line;
    Item temp;                   /* new customer data          */
    int hours;                   /* hours of simulation        */
    int perhour;                 /* average # of arrivals per hour */
    long cycle, cyclelimit;      /* loop counter, limit        */
    long turnaways = 0;          /* turned away by full queue  */
    long customers = 0;          /* joined the queue           */
    long served = 0;             /* served during the simulation */
    long sum_line = 0;           /* cumulative line length     */
    int wait_time = 0;           /* time until Sigmund is free */
    double min_per_cust;         /* average time between arrivals */
    long line_wait = 0;          /* cumulative time in line    */

    InitializeQueue(&line);
    srand(time(0));              /* random initializing of rand() */
    puts("Case Study: Sigmund Lander's Advice Booth");
    puts("Enter the number of simulation hours:");
    scanf("%d", &hours);
    cyclelimit = MIN_PER_HR * hours;
    puts("Enter the average number of customers per hour:");
    scanf("%d", &perhour);
    min_per_cust = MIN_PER_HR / perhour;

    for (cycle = 0; cycle < cyclelimit; cycle++)
    {
        if (newcustomer(min_per_cust))
        {
            if (FullQueue(&line))
                turnaways++;
            else
            {
                customers++;
                temp = customertime(cycle);
                EnQueue(temp, &line);
            }
        }
        if (wait_time <= 0 && !EmptyQueue(&line))
        {
            DeQueue (&temp, &line);
            wait_time = temp.processtime;
            line_wait += cycle - temp.arrive;
            served++;
        }
        if (wait_time > 0)
            wait_time--;
        sum_line += QueueItems(&line);
    }
```

```
    if (customers > 0)
    {
        printf("customers accepted: %ld\n", customers);
        printf("   customers served: %ld\n", served);
        printf("         turnaways: %ld\n", turnaways);
        printf("average queue size: %.2f\n",
            (double) sum_line / cyclelimit);
        printf(" average wait time: %.2f minutes\n",
            (double) line_wait / served);
    }
    else
        puts("No customers!");

    return 0;
}

/* x = average time, in minutes, between customers      */
/* return value is true if customer shows up this minute */
BOOLEAN newcustomer(double x)
{
    if (rand() * x / RAND_MAX < 1)
        return True;
    else
        return False;
}

/* when is the time at which the customer arrives         */
/* function returns an Item structure with the arrival time  */
/* set to when and the processing time set to a random value */
/* in the range 1 - 3                                     */
Item customertime(long when)
{
    Item cust;

    cust.processtime = rand() % 3 + 1;
    cust.arrive = when;
    return cust;
}
```

The program enables you to specify the number of hours to simulate and the average number of customers per hour. Choosing a large number of hours gives you good average values, and choosing a small number of hours shows the sort of random variation you can get from hour to hour. The following runs illustrate these points. Note that the average queue sizes and wait times for 80 hours are about the same as for 800 hours, but that the two one-hour samples differ quite a bit from each other and from the long-term averages. That's because smaller statistical samples tend to have larger relative variations.

```
Case Study: Sigmund Lander's Advice Booth
Enter the number of simulation hours:
80
```

```
Enter the average number of customers per hour:
20
customers accepted: 1633
  customers served: 1633
        turnaways: 0
average queue size: 0.46
average wait time: 1.35 minutes
Case Study: Sigmund Lander's Advice Booth
Enter the number of simulation hours:
800
Enter the average number of customers per hour:
20
customers accepted: 16020
  customers served: 16019
        turnaways: 0
average queue size: 0.44
average wait time: 1.32 minutes
Case Study: Sigmund Lander's Advice Booth
Enter the number of simulation hours:
1
Enter the average number of customers per hour:
20
customers accepted: 20
  customers served: 20
        turnaways: 0
average queue size: 0.23
average wait time: 0.70 minutes
Case Study: Sigmund Lander's Advice Booth
Enter the number of simulation hours:
1
Enter the average number of customers per hour:
20
customers accepted: 22
  customers served: 22
        turnaways: 0
average queue size: 0.75
 average wait time: 2.05 minutes
```

Another way to use the program is to keep the numbers of hours constant, but try different average numbers of customers per hour. Here are a few sample runs exploring this variation:

```
Case Study: Sigmund Lander's Advice Booth
Enter the number of simulation hours:
80
Enter the average number of customers per hour:
25
customers accepted: 1960
  customers served: 1959
        turnaways: 3
average queue size: 1.43
average wait time: 3.50 minutes
Case Study: Sigmund Lander's Advice Booth
Enter the number of simulation hours:
80
```

```
Enter the average number of customers per hour:
30
customers accepted: 2376
  customers served: 2373
        turnaways: 94
average queue size: 5.85
average wait time: 11.83 minutes
```

Note how the average wait time takes a sharp upturn as the frequency of customers increases. The average wait for 20 customers per hour (80-hour simulation) was 1.35 minutes. It climbs to 3.50 minutes at 25 customers per hour and soars to 11.83 minutes at 30 customers an hour. Also, the number of turnaways climbs from 0 to 3 to 94. Sigmund could use this sort of analysis to decide whether he needs a second booth.

The Linked List Versus the Array

Many programming problems, such as creating a list or a queue, can be handled with a linked list—by which we mean a linked sequence of dynamically allocated structures—or with an array. Each form has its strengths and weaknesses, so the choice of which to use depends on the particular requirements of a problem. Table 17.1 summarizes the qualities of linked lists and arrays.

Table 17.1 Comparing arrays to linked lists.

Data Form	Pros	Cons
Array	Directly supported by C Provides random access	Size determined at compile time
		Inserting and deleting elements is time-consuming
Linked List	Size determined during runtime	No random access
	Inserting and deleting elements is quick	User must provide programming support

Take a closer look at the process of inserting and deleting elements. To insert an element in an array, you have to move elements to make way for the new element, as shown in Figure 17.9. The closer to the front the new element goes, the more elements have to be moved. To insert a node in a linked list, however, you just have to assign values to two pointers, as shown in Figure 17.10. Similarly, removing an element from an array involves a wholesale relocation of elements, but removing a node from a linked list involves resetting a pointer and freeing the memory used by the deleted node.

make room by shifting items

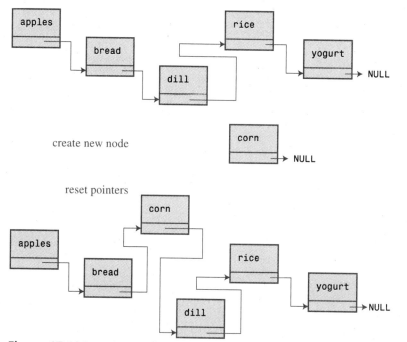

Figure 17.9 Inserting an element into an array.

Figure 17.10 Inserting an element into a linked list.

Next, consider how to access the members of a list. With an array, you can use the array index to access any element immediately. This is called *random access*. With a linked list, you have to start at the top of the list, and then move from node to node until you get to the node you want, which is termed *sequential access*. You can have sequential access with an array, too. Just increment the array index by one step each to move through the array in order. For some situations, sequential access is sufficient. For instance, if you want to display every item in a list, sequential access is fine. Other situations greatly favor random access, as you will see next.

Suppose you want to search a list for a particular item. One algorithm is to start at the beginning of the list and search through it in sequence, called a *sequential search*. If the items aren't arranged in some sort of order, a sequential search is about all you can do. If the sought-for item isn't in the list, you'll have to look at every item in the list before concluding the item isn't there.

You can improve the sequential search by sorting the list first. That way, you can terminate a search if you haven't found an item by the time you reach an item that would come later. For instance, suppose you're seeking *Susan* in an alphabetical list. Starting from the top of the list, you look at each item and eventually encounter *Sylvia* without finding *Susan*. At that point you can quit searching because *Susan*, if in the list, would precede *Sylvia*. On average, this method would cut search times in half for attempting to find items not in the list.

With an ordered list, you can do much better than a sequential search by using the *binary search* method. Here's how it works. First, call the list item you want to find the *goal* and assume the list is in alphabetical order. Next, pick the item halfway down the list and compare it to the goal. If the two are the same, the search is over. If the list item comes before the goal alphabetically, the goal, if it's in the list, must be in the second half. If the list item follows the goal alphabetically, the goal must be in the first half. Either way, the comparison rules out half the list as a place to search. Next, apply the method again. That is, choose an item midway in the half of the list that remains. Again, this method either finds the item or rules out half the remaining list. Proceed in this fashion until you find the item or until you've eliminated the whole list (see Figure 17.11). This method is quite efficient. Suppose, for example, that the list is 127 items long. A sequential search, on the average, would take 64 comparisons before finding an item or ruling out its presence. The binary search method, on the other hand, will take at most 7 comparisons. The first comparison prunes the possible matches to 63, the second comparison cuts the possible matches to 31, and so on, until the sixth comparison cuts down the possibilities to 1. The seventh comparison then determines if the one remaining choice is the goal or not. In general, n comparisons let you process an array with $2n - 1$ members, so the advantage of a binary search over a sequential search gets greater the longer the list is.

It's simple to implement a binary search with an array, for you can use the array index to determine the midpoint of any list or subdivision of a list. Add the subscripts of the initial and final elements of the subdivision and divide by 2. For instance, in a list of 100 elements, the first index is 0, the final index is 99, and the initial guess would be $(0 + 99) / 2$, or 49 (integer division). If the element having index 49 were too far down the alphabet, the correct choice must be in the range 0–48, so the next guess would be $(0 + 48) / 2$, or 24. If element 24 were too early in the alphabet, the next guess would be $(25 + 48) / 2$, or 36. This is where the random access feature of the array comes into play. It enables you to jump from one location to another without visiting every location in between. Linked lists, which support only sequential access, don't provide a means to jump to the midpoint of a list, so you can't use the binary search technique with linked lists.

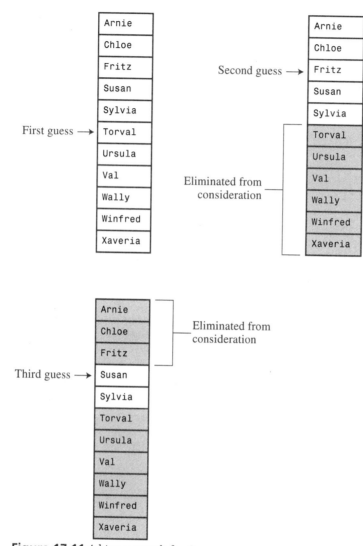

Figure 17.11 A binary search for Susan.

You can see, then, that the choice of data type depends on the problem. If the situation calls for a list that is continuously resized with frequent insertions and deletions but that isn't searched often, the linked list is the better choice. If the situation calls for a stable list with only occasional insertions and deletions but that has to be searched often, an array is the better choice.

What if you need a data form that supports frequent insertions and deletions and frequent searches? Neither a linked list nor an array is ideal for that set of purposes. Another form, the binary search tree, may be just what you need.

Binary Search Trees

The *binary search tree* is a linked structure that incorporates the binary search strategy. Each node in the tree contains an item and two pointers to other nodes, called *child nodes*. Figure 17.12 shows how the nodes in a binary search tree are linked. The idea is that each node has two child nodes, a left node and a right node. The ordering comes from the fact that the item in a left node precedes the item in the parent node, and the item in the right node follows the item in the parent node. This relationship holds for every node with children. Furthermore, all items that can trace their ancestry back to a left node of a parent contain items that precede the parent item in order, and every item descended from the right node contains items that follow the parent item in order. The tree in Figure 17.12 stores words in this fashion. The top of the tree, in an interesting inversion of botany, is called the root. A tree is a *hierarchical* organization, meaning that the data are organized in ranks, or levels, with each rank, in general, having ranks above and below it. If a binary search tree is fully populated, each level has twice as many nodes as the level above it.

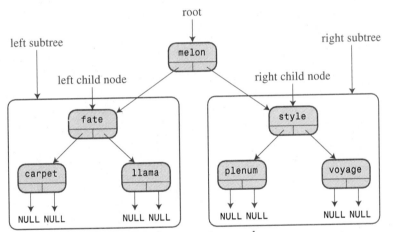

Figure 17.12 A binary search tree storing words.

Each node in the binary search tree is itself the root of the nodes descending from it, making the node and its descendants a *subtree*. In Figure 17.12, for example, the nodes containing the words *fate*, *carpet*, and *llama* form the left subtree of the whole tree, and the word *voyage* is the right subtree of the *style-plenum-voyage* subtree.

Suppose you want to find an item—call it the *goal*—in such a tree. If the item precedes the root item, you need search only the left half of the tree, and if the goal follows the root item, you need search only the right subtree of the root node. Therefore, one comparison eliminates half the tree. Suppose you search the left half. That means comparing the goal with the item in the left child. If the goal precedes the left-child item, you need search only the left half of its descendants, and so on. As with the binary search, each comparison cuts the number of potential matches in half.

Let's apply this method to see if the word *puppy* is in the tree shown in Figure 17.12. Comparing *puppy* to *melon* (the root node item), you see that *puppy*, if present, must be in the right half of the tree. Therefore, you go to the right child and compare *puppy* to *style*. In this case, *puppy* precedes the node item, so you must follow the link to the left node. There you find *plenum*, which precedes *puppy*. You now have to follow the right branch, but it is empty, so three comparisons show you that *puppy* is not in the tree.

A binary search tree, then, combines a linked structure with binary search efficiency. The programming price is that putting a tree together is more involved than creating a linked list. Let's make a binary tree the next, and final, ADT project.

A Binary Tree ADT

As usual, we'll start by defining a binary tree in general terms. This particular definition assumes the tree contains no duplicate items. Many of the operations are the same as list operations. The difference is in the hierarchical arrangement of data. Here is an informal summary of this ADT:

Type Name: Binary Search Tree

Type Properties: A binary tree is either an empty set of nodes (an empty tree) or a set of nodes with one node designated as the root.

Each node has exactly two trees, called the *left subtree* and the *right subtree*, descending from it.

Each subtree is itself a binary tree, which includes the possibility of being an empty tree.

A binary search tree is an ordered binary tree in which each node contains an item, in which all items in the left subtree precede the root item, and in which the root item precedes all items in the right subtree.

Type Operations: Initializing tree to empty.

Determining whether tree is empty.

Determining whether tree if full.

Determining the number of items in the tree.

Adding an item to the tree.

Removing an item from the tree.

Searching the tree for an item.

Visiting each item in the tree.

The Binary Search Tree Interface

In principle, you can implement a binary search tree in a variety of ways. You can even implement one as an array by manipulating array indices. But the most direct way to implement a binary search tree is by using dynamically allocated nodes linked together by using pointers, so we'll start with definitions like these:

```
typedef SOMETHING Item;
typedef struct node
{
    Item item;
    struct node * left;
    struct node * right;
} Node;
typedef struct tree
{
    Node * root;
    int size;
} Tree;
```

Each node contains an item, a pointer to the left child node, and a pointer to the right child node. You could define a `Tree` to be type pointer-to-`Node`, for you only need know the location of the root node to access the entire tree. Using a structure with a size member, however, makes it simpler to keep track of the size of the tree.

The example we'll be developing is maintaining the roster of the Nerfville Pet Club, with each item consisting of a pet name and a pet kind. With that in mind, we can set up the interface shown in Listing 17.10. We've limited the tree size to 10. The small size makes it easier to test whether the program behaves correctly when the tree fills. You can always set `MAXITEMS` to a larger value, if necessary.

Listing 17.10 The `tree.h` interface header file.

```
/* tree.h -- binary search tree                          */
/*           no duplicate items are allowed in this tree */
#ifndef _TREE_H_
#define _TREE_H_

/* redefine Item as appropriate */
typedef struct item
{
    char petname[20];
    char petkind[20];
} Item;

#define MAXITEMS 10

typedef enum boolean {False, True} BOOLEAN;
```

continued on next page

continued from previous page

```
typedef struct node
{
    Item item;
    struct node * left;     /* pointer to right branch  */
    struct node * right;    /* pointer to left branch   */
} Node;

typedef struct tree
{
    Node * root;            /* pointer to root of tree  */
    int size;               /* number of items in tree  */
} Tree;

/* function prototypes */

/* operation:     initialize a tree to empty       */
/* preconditions: ptree points to a tree           */
/* postconditions: the tree is initialized to empty */
void InitializeTree(Tree * ptree);

/* operation:     determine if tree is empty        */
/* preconditions: ptree points to a tree            */
/* postconditions: function returns True if tree is  */
/*                 empty and returns False otherwise */
BOOLEAN EmptyTree(const Tree * ptree);

/* operation:     determine if tree is full         */
/* preconditions: ptree points to a tree            */
/* postconditions: function returns True if tree is  */
/*                 full and returns False otherwise  */
BOOLEAN FullTree(const Tree * ptree);

/* operation:     determine number of items in tree */
/* preconditions: ptree points to a tree            */
/* postconditions: function returns number of items in */
/*                 tree                              */
int TreeItems(const Tree * ptree);

/* operation:     add an item to a tree             */
/* preconditions: pi is address of item to be added */
/*                ptree points to an initialized tree */
/* postconditions: if possible, function adds item to */
/*                 tree and returns True; otherwise,  */
/*                 the function returns False         */
BOOLEAN AddItem(const Item * pi, Tree * ptree);

/* operation:     find an item in a tree            */
/* preconditions: pi points to an item              */
/*                ptree points to an initialized tree */
/* postconditions: function returns True if item is in */
/*                 tree and returns False otherwise  */
BOOLEAN InTree(const Item * pi, const Tree * ptree);
```

```
/* operation:      delete an item from a tree        */
/* preconditions:  pi is address of item to be deleted */
/*                 ptree points to an initialized tree */
/* postconditions: if possible, function deletes item  */
/*                 from tree and returns True;        */
/*                 otherwise, the function returns False*/
BOOLEAN DeleteItem(const Item * pi, Tree * ptree);

/* operation:      apply a function to each item in   */
/*                 the tree                           */
/* preconditions:  ptree points to a tree            */
/*                 pfun points to a function that takes*/
/*                 an Item argument and has no return */
/*                 value                              */
/* postcondition:  the function pointed to by pfun is */
/*                 executed once for each item in tree */
void Traverse (const Tree * ptree, void (* pfun)(Item item));

#endif
```

The Binary Tree Implementation

Next, proceed to the task of implementing the splendid functions outlined in `tree.h`. The `InitializeTree()`, `EmptyTree()`, `FullTree()`, and `TreeItems()` functions are pretty simple, working like their counterparts for the list and queue ADTs, so we'll concentrate on the remaining ones.

Adding an Item

When adding an item to the tree, you should first check whether the tree has room for a new node. Then, because the binary search tree is defined so that it has no duplicate items, you should check that the item is not already in the tree. If the new item clears these first two hurdles, you create a new node, copy the item to the node, and set the node's left and right pointers to NULL. This indicates that the node has no children. Then you should update the size member of the Tree structure to mark the adding of a new item. Next, you have to find where the node should be located in the tree. If the tree is empty, you should set the root pointer to point to the new node. Otherwise, look through the tree for a place to add the node. The AddItem() function follows this recipe, offloading some of the work to functions not yet defined: SeekItem(), MakeNode(), and AddNode().

```
BOOLEAN AddItem(const Item * pi, Tree * ptree)
{
    Node * new;

    if (FullTree(ptree))
    {
        fprintf(stderr,"Tree is full\n");
        return False;              /* early return        */
    }
```

```
        if (SeekItem(pi, ptree).child != NULL)
        {
            fprintf(stderr, "Attempted to add duplicate item\n");
            return False;               /* early return            */
        }
        new = MakeNode(pi);             /* new points to new node */
        if (new == NULL)
        {
            fprintf(stderr, "Couldn't create node\n");
            return False;               /* early return            */
        }
        /* succeeded in creating a new node */
        ptree->size++;

        if (ptree->root == NULL)        /* case 1: tree is empty   */
            ptree->root = new;          /* new node is tree root   */
        else                            /* case 2: not empty       */
            AddNode(new,ptree->root); /* add new node to tree    */
        return True;
    }
```

The SeekItem(), MakeNode(), and AddNode() functions are not part of the public interface for the Tree type. Instead, they are static functions hidden in the **tree.c** file. They
deal with implementation details, such as nodes, pointers, and structures, that don't
belong in the public interface.

The MakeNode() function is pretty simple. It handles the dynamic memory allocation
and the initialization of the node. The function argument is a pointer to the new item, and
the function's return value is a pointer to the new node. Recall that **malloc()** returns the
null pointer if it can't make the requested allocation. The MakeNode() function initializes
the new node only if memory allocation succeeds.

```
static Node * MakeNode(const Item * pi)
{
    Node * new;

    new = (Node *) malloc(sizeof(Node));
    if (new != NULL)
    {
        new->item = *pi;
        new->left = NULL;
        new->right = NULL;
    }
    return new;
}
```

The AddNode() function is the second most difficult function in the binary search tree
package. It has to determine where the new node goes, and then it has to add it. In particular, it needs to compare the new item with the root item to see whether the new item
goes into the left subtree or the right subtree. If the item were a number, you could use <
and > to make comparisons. If the item were a string, you could use **strcmp()** to make
comparisons. But the item is a structure containing two strings, so you'll have to define your
own functions for making comparisons. The ToLeft() function, to be defined later,

returns `True` if the new item should be in the left subtree, and the `ToRight()` function returns `True` if the new item should be in the right subtree. These two functions are analogous to < and >, respectively. Suppose the new item goes to the left subtree. It could be that the left subtree is empty. In that case, the function just makes the left child pointer point to the new node. What if the left subtree isn't empty? Then the function should compare the new item to the item in the left child node, deciding whether the new item should go in the left subtree or right subtree of the child node. This process should continue until the function arrives at an empty subtree, at which point the new node can be added. One way to implement this search is to use recursion, that is, apply the `AddNode()` function to a child node instead of to the root node. The recursive series of function calls ends when a left or right subtree is empty, that is, when `root->left` or `root->right` is `NULL`. Keep in mind that `root` is a pointer to the top of the current subtree, so it points to a new, and lower-level, subtree each recursive call. (You might want to review the discussion of recursion in Chapter 9.)

```
static void AddNode (Node * new, Node * root)
{
    if (ToLeft(&new->item, &root->item))
    {
        if (root->left == NULL)        /* empty subtree      */
            root->left = new;          /* so add node here   */
        else
            AddNode(new, root->left);/* else process subtree*/
    }
    else if (ToRight(&new->item, &root->item))
    {
        if (root->right == NULL)
            root->right = new;
        else
            AddNode(new, root->right);
    }
    else                                /* should be no duplicates */
    {
        fprintf(stderr,"location error in AddNode()\n");
        exit(1);
    }
}
```

The `ToLeft()` and `ToRight()` functions depend on the nature of the `Item` type. The members of the Nerfville Pet Club will be ordered alphabetically by name. If two pets have the same name, order them by kind. If they are also the same kind, then the two items are duplicates, which aren't allowed in the basic search tree. Recall that the standard C library function `strcmp()` returns a negative number if the string represented by the first argument precedes the second string, returns zero if the two strings are the same, and returns a positive number if the first string follows the second. The `ToRight()` function has similar code. Using these two functions instead of making comparisons directly in `AddNode()` makes the code easier to adapt to new requirements. Instead of rewriting `AddNode()` when a different form of comparison is needed, you rewrite `ToLeft()` and `ToRight()`.

```
static BOOLEAN ToLeft(const Item * i1, const Item * i2)
{
    int comp1;

    if ((comp1 = strcmp(i1->petname, i2->petname)) < 0)
        return True;
    else if (comp1 == 0 &&
                strcmp(i1->petkind, i2->petkind) < 0 )
        return True;
    else
        return False;
}
```

Finding an Item

Three of the interface functions involve searching the tree for a particular item: AddItem(), InTree(), and DeleteItem(). This implementation uses a SeekItem() function to provide that service. The DeleteItem() function has an additional requirement: It needs to know the parent node of the deleted item so that the parent's child pointer can be updated when the child is deleted. Therefore, we designed SeekItem() to return a structure containing two pointers: one pointing to the node containing the item (NULL if the item isn't found) and one pointing to the parent node (NULL if the node is the root and has no parent). The structure type is defined as follows:

```
typedef struct pair {
    Node * parent;
    Node * child;
} Pair;
```

The SeekItem() function can be implemented recursively. However, to expose you to a variety of programming techniques, we'll use a while loop to handle descending through the tree. Like AddNode(), SeekItem() uses ToLeft() and ToRight() to navigate through the tree. SeekItem() initially sets the look.child pointer to point to the root of the tree, and then resets look.child to successive subtrees as it traces the path to where the item should be found. Meanwhile, look.parent is set to point to successive parent nodes. If no matching item is found, look.child will be NULL. If the matching item is in the root node, then look.parent is NULL, for the root node has no parent.

```
static Pair SeekItem(const Item * pi, const Tree * ptree)
{
    Pair look;
    look.parent = NULL;
    look.child = ptree->root;

    if (look.child == NULL)
        return look;                    /* early return        */
    while (look.child != NULL)
    {
        if (ToLeft(pi, &(look.child->item)))
        {
            look.parent = look.child;
            look.child = look.child->left;
        }
```

```
        else if (ToRight(pi, &(look.child->item)))
        {
            look.parent = look.child;
            look.child = look.child->right;
        }
        else        /* must be same if not to left or right   */
            break;/* look.child is address of node with item*/
    }
    return look;
}
```

Note that because the `SeekItem()` function returns a structure, it can be used with the structure membership operator. For example, the `AddItem()` function used the following code:

```
    if (SeekItem(pi, ptree).child != NULL)
```

After you have `SeekItem()`, it's simple to code the `InTree()` public interface function:

```
BOOLEAN InTree(const Item * pi, const Tree * ptree)
{
    return (SeekItem(pi, ptree).child == NULL) ? False : True;
}
```

Deleting an Item

Removing an item is the most difficult of the tasks because you have to reconnect the remaining subtrees to form a valid tree. Before attempting to program this task, it's a good idea to develop a visual picture of what has to be done.

Figure 17.13 illustrates the simplest case. Here the node to be deleted has no children. Such a node is called a *leaf*. All that has to be done in this case is to reset a pointer in the parent node to `NULL` and to use the `free()` function to reclaim the memory used by the deleted node.

Next in complexity is deleting a node with one child. Deleting the node leaves the child subtree separate from the rest of the tree. To fix this, the address of the child subtree needs to be stored in the parent node at the location formerly occupied by the address of the deleted node (see Figure 17.14).

Finally, you have deleting a node with two subtrees. One subtree, say the left, can be attached to where the deleted node was formerly attached. But where should the remaining subtree go? Keep in mind the basic design of a tree. Every item in a left subtree precedes the item in the parent node, and every item in a right subtree follows the item in the parent node. This means that every item in the right subtree comes after every item in the left subtree. Also, because the right subtree once was part of the subtree headed by the deleted node, every item in the right subtree comes before the parent node of the deleted node. Imagine coming down the tree looking for where to place the head of the right subtree. It comes before the parent node, so you have to go down the left subtree from there. However, it comes after every item in the left subtree, so you have to take the right branch of the left subtree and see whether it has an opening for a new node. If not, you must go down the right side of the left subtree until you do find an opening. Figure 17.15 illustrates the approach.

node to be deleted

revised tree segment

Figure 17.13 Deleting a leaf.

Deleting a Node

Now you can begin to plan the necessary functions, separating the job into two tasks. One is associating a particular item with the node to be deleted, and the second is actually deleting the node. One point to note is that all the cases involve modifying a pointer in the parent node, which has two important consequences:

- The program has to identify the parent node of the node to be deleted.

- To modify the pointer, the code must pass the *address* of that pointer to the deleting function.

We'll come back to the first point later. Meanwhile, the pointer to be modified is itself of type **Node ***, or pointer-to-**Node**. Because the function argument is the address of that pointer, the argument will be of type **Node ****, or pointer-to-pointer-to-**Node**. Assuming you have the proper address available, you can write the deletion function as the following:

```
static void DeleteNode(Node **ptr)
/* ptr is address of parent member pointing to target node  */
{
    Node * temp;

    if ( (*ptr)->left == NULL)
    {
        temp = *ptr;
        *ptr = (*ptr)->right;
        free(temp);
    }
```

```
    else if ( (*ptr)->right == NULL)
    {
        temp = *ptr;
        *ptr = (*ptr)->left;
        free(temp);
    }
    else    /* deleted node has two children */
    {
        /* find where to reattach right subtree */
        for (temp = (*ptr)->left; temp->right != NULL;
                temp = temp->right)
            continue;
        temp->right = (*ptr)->right;
        temp = *ptr;
        *ptr =(*ptr)->left;
        free(temp);
    }
}
```

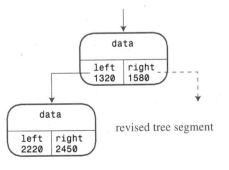

Figure 17.14 Deleting a one-child node.

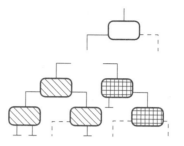

original tree

deleting the node leaves two
unconnected subtrees

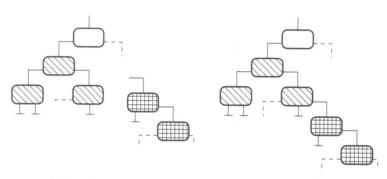

attach left subtree to original
parent node

attach right subtree to first open
location along the rightmost
branches of first subtree

Figure 17.15 Deleting a two-child node.

This function explicitly handles three cases: a node with no left child, a node with no right child, and a node with two children. A node with no children can be considered a special case of a node with no left child. If the node has no left child, the code assigns the address of the right child to the parent pointer. But if the node also has no right child, that pointer is NULL, which is the proper value for the no-child case.

Notice that the code uses a temporary pointer to keep track of the address of the deleted node. After the parent pointer (*ptr) is reset, the program would lose track of where the deleted node is, but you need that information for the free() function. So the program stores the original value of *ptr in temp, and then uses temp to free the memory used for the deleted node.

The code for the two-child case first uses the temp pointer in a for loop to search down the right side of the left subtree for an empty spot. When it finds an empty spot, it attaches the right subtree there. Then it reuses temp to keep track of where the deleted node is. Next, it attaches the left subtree to the parent, and then frees the node pointed to by temp.

Note that because ptr is type Node **, *ptr is of type Node *, making it the same type as temp.

Deleting an Item

The remaining part of the problem is associating a node with a particular item. You can use the SeekNode() function to do so. Recall that it returns a structure containing a pointer to the parent node and a pointer to the node containing the item. Then you can use the parent node pointer to get the proper address to pass to the DeleteNode() function. The DeleteItem() function, shown here, follows this plan:

```
BOOLEAN DeleteItem(const Item * pi, Tree * ptree)
{
    Pair look;
    look = SeekItem(pi, ptree);
    if (look.child == NULL)
        return False;
    if (look.parent == NULL)        /* delete root item      */
        DeleteNode(&ptree->root);
    else if (look.parent->left == look.child)
        DeleteNode(&look.parent->left);
    else
        DeleteNode(&look.parent->right);
    ptree->size--;
    return True;
}
```

First, the return value of the SeekItem() function is assigned to the look structure variable. If look.child is NULL, the search failed to find the time, and the DeleteItem() function quits, returning False. If the Item is found, the function handles three cases. First, a NULL value for look.parent means the item was found in the root node. In this case, there is no parent node to update. Instead, the program has to update the root pointer in the Tree structure. Therefore, the function passes the address of that pointer to the DeleteNode() function. Otherwise, the program determines whether the node to be deleted is the left child or the right child of the parent, and then it passes the address of the appropriate pointer.

Note that the public interface function (DeleteItem()) speaks in terms of end-user concerns (items and trees), and the hidden DeleteNode() function handles the nitty-gritty of pointer shuffling.

Traversing the Tree

Traversing a tree is more involved than traversing a linked list because each node has two branches to follow. This branching nature makes divide-and-conquer recursion (Chapter 9) a natural choice for handling the problem. At each node, the function should do the following:

- Process the item in the node.
- Process the left subtree (a recursive call).
- Process the right subtree (a recursive call).

You can break this process down into two functions: Traverse() and InOrder(). Note that the InOrder() function processes the left subtree, then processes the item, and then processes the right subtree. This order results in traversing the tree in alphabetical order.

If you have the time, you might want to see what happens if you use different orders, such as item-left-right and left-right-item.

```c
void Traverse (const Tree * ptree, void (* pfun)(Item item))
{

    if (ptree != NULL)
        InOrder(ptree->root, pfun);
}

static void InOrder(const Node * root, void (* pfun)(Item item))
{
    if (root != NULL)
    {
        InOrder(root->left, pfun);
        (*pfun)(root->item);
        InOrder(root->right, pfun);
    }
}
```

Listing 17.11 shows the entire **tree.c** code. Together, **tree.h** and **tree.c** constitute a tree programming package.

Listing 17.11 The **tree.c** implementation file.

```c
/* tree.c -- tree support functions */
#include <string.h>
#include <stdio.h>
#include <stdlib.h>
#include "tree.h"

/* local data type */
typedef struct pair {
    Node * parent;
    Node * child;
} Pair;

/* protototypes for local functions */
static Node * MakeNode(const Item * pi);
static BOOLEAN ToLeft(const Item * i1, const Item * i2);
static BOOLEAN ToRight(const Item * i1, const Item * i2);
static void AddNode (Node * new, Node * root);
static void InOrder(const Node * root, void (* pfun)(Item item));
static Pair SeekItem(const Item * pi, const Tree * ptree);
static void DeleteNode(Node **ptr);

/* function definitions */

void InitializeTree(Tree * ptree)
{
    ptree->root = NULL;
    ptree->size = 0;
}
```

```
BOOLEAN EmptyTree(const Tree * ptree)
{
    if (ptree->root == NULL)
        return True;
    else
        return False;
}

BOOLEAN FullTree(const Tree * ptree)
{
    if (ptree->size == MAXITEMS)
        return True;
    else
        return False;
}

int TreeItems(const Tree * ptree)
{
    return ptree->size;
}

BOOLEAN AddItem(const Item * pi, Tree * ptree)
{
    Node * new;

    if (FullTree(ptree))
    {
        fprintf(stderr,"Tree is full\n");
        return False;               /* early return          */
    }
    if (SeekItem(pi, ptree).child != NULL)
    {
        fprintf(stderr, "Attempted to add duplicate item\n");
        return False;               /* early return          */
    }
    new = MakeNode(pi);             /* new points to new node */
    if (new == NULL)
    {
        fprintf(stderr, "Couldn't create node\n");
        return False;               /* early return          */
    }
    /* succeeded in creating a new node */
    ptree->size++;

    if (ptree->root == NULL)      /* case 1: tree is empty  */
        ptree->root = new;        /* new node is tree root  */
    else                          /* case 2: not empty      */
        AddNode(new,ptree->root); /* add new node to tree   */
    return True;
}
```

continued on next page

continued from previous page

```
BOOLEAN InTree(const Item * pi, const Tree * ptree)
{
    return (SeekItem(pi, ptree).child == NULL) ? False : True;
}

BOOLEAN DeleteItem(const Item * pi, Tree * ptree)
{
    Pair look;
    look = SeekItem(pi, ptree);
    if (look.child == NULL)
        return False;
    if (look.parent == NULL)        /* delete root item       */
        DeleteNode(&ptree->root);
    else if (look.parent->left == look.child)
        DeleteNode(&look.parent->left);
    else
        DeleteNode(&look.parent->right);
    ptree->size--;
    return True;
}

void Traverse (const Tree * ptree, void (* pfun)(Item item))
{

    if (ptree != NULL)
        InOrder(ptree->root, pfun);
}

/* local functions */
static void InOrder(const Node * root, void (* pfun)(Item item))
{
    if (root != NULL)
    {
        InOrder(root->left, pfun);
        (*pfun)(root->item);
        InOrder(root->right, pfun);
    }
}

static void AddNode (Node * new, Node * root)
{
    if (ToLeft(&new->item, &root->item))
    {
        if (root->left == NULL)         /* empty subtree       */
            root->left = new;           /* so add node here    */
        else
            AddNode(new, root->left);/* else process subtree*/
    }
    else if (ToRight(&new->item, &root->item))
    {
        if (root->right == NULL)
            root->right = new;
```

```
        else
            AddNode(new, root->right);
    }
    else                           /* should be no duplicates */
    {
        fprintf(stderr,"location error in AddNode()\n");
        exit(1);
    }
}

static BOOLEAN ToLeft(const Item * i1, const Item * i2)
{
    int comp1;

    if ((comp1 = strcmp(i1->petname, i2->petname)) < 0)
        return True;
    else if (comp1 == 0 &&
                strcmp(i1->petkind, i2->petkind) < 0 )
        return True;
    else
        return False;
}

static BOOLEAN ToRight(const Item * i1, const Item * i2)
{
    int comp1;

    if ((comp1 = strcmp(i1->petname, i2->petname)) > 0)
        return True;
    else if (comp1 == 0 &&
                strcmp(i1->petkind, i2->petkind) > 0 )
        return True;
    else
        return False;
}

static Node * MakeNode(const Item * pi)
{
    Node * new;

    new = (Node *) malloc(sizeof(Node));
    if (new != NULL)
    {
        new->item = *pi;
        new->left = NULL;
        new->right = NULL;
    }
    return new;
}
```

continued on next page

continued from previous page

```
static Pair SeekItem(const Item * pi, const Tree * ptree)
{
    Pair look;
    look.parent = NULL;
    look.child = ptree->root;

    if (look.child == NULL)
        return look;                    /* early return         */
    while (look.child != NULL)
    {
        if (ToLeft(pi, &(look.child->item)))
        {
            look.parent = look.child;
            look.child = look.child->left;
        }
        else if (ToRight(pi, &(look.child->item)))
        {
            look.parent = look.child;
            look.child = look.child->right;
        }
        else      /* must be same if not to left or right   */
            break;/* look.child is address of node with item*/
    }
    return look;
}

static void DeleteNode(Node **ptr)
/* ptr is address of parent member pointing to target node   */
{
    Node * temp;

    if ( (*ptr)->left == NULL)
    {
        temp = *ptr;
        *ptr = (*ptr)->right;
        free(temp);
    }
    else if ( (*ptr)->right == NULL)
    {
        temp = *ptr;
        *ptr = (*ptr)->left;
        free(temp);
    }
    else    /* deleted node has two children */
    {
        /* find where to reattach right subtree */
        for (temp = (*ptr)->left; temp->right != NULL;
                temp = temp->right)
            continue;
        temp->right = (*ptr)->right;
        temp = *ptr;
        *ptr =(*ptr)->left;
        free(temp);
    }
}
```

Trying the Tree

Now that you have the interface and the function implementations, let's use them. The program in Listing 17.12 uses a menu to offer a choice of adding pets to the club membership roster, listing members, reporting the number of members, checking for membership, and quitting. The brief `main()` function concentrates on the essential program outline. Supporting functions do most of the work.

Listing 17.12   The `petclub.c` program.

```
/* petclub.c -- use a binary search tree */
#include <stdio.h>
#include <string.h>
#include <ctype.h>
#include "tree.h"

char menu(void);
void addpet(Tree * pt);
void droppet(Tree * pt);
void showpets(const Tree * pt);
void findpet(const Tree * pt);
void printitem(Item item);
void uppercase(char * str);

int main(void)
{
    Tree pets;
    char choice;

    InitializeTree(&pets);
    while ((choice = menu()) != 'q')
    {
        switch (choice)
        {
            case 'a' :  addpet(&pets);
                        break;
            case 'l' :  showpets(&pets);
                        break;
            case 'f' :  findpet(&pets);
                        break;
            case 'n' :  printf("%d pets in club\n",
                               TreeItems(&pets));
                        break;
            case 'd' :  droppet(&pets);
                        break;
            default  :  puts("Switching error");
        }
    }
    puts("Bye.");
    return 0;
}
```

continued on next page

continued from previous page

```c
char menu(void)
{
    int ch;

    puts("Nerfville Pet Club Membership Program");
    puts("Enter the letter corresponding to your choice:");
    puts("a) add a pet          l) show list of pets");
    puts("n) number of pets     f) find pets");
    puts("d) delete a pet       q) quit");
    while ((ch = getchar()) != EOF)
    {
        while (getchar() != '\n')  /* discard rest of line */
            continue;
        ch = tolower(ch);
        if (strchr("alrfndq",ch) == NULL)
            puts("Please enter an a, l, f, n, d, or q:");
        else
            break;
    }
    if (ch == EOF)          /* make EOF cause program to quit */
        ch = 'q';

    return ch;
}

void addpet(Tree * pt)
{
    Item temp;

    if (FullTree(pt))
        puts("No room in the club!");
    else
    {
        puts("Please enter name of pet:");
        gets(temp.petname);
        puts("Please enter pet kind:");
        gets(temp.petkind);
        uppercase(temp.petname);
        uppercase(temp.petkind);
        AddItem(&temp, pt);
    }
}

void showpets(const Tree * pt)
{
    if (EmptyTree(pt))
        puts("No entries!");
    else
        Traverse(pt, printitem);
}
```

```
void printitem(Item item)
{
    printf("Pet: %-19s  Kind: %-19s\n", item.petname,
            item.petkind);
}

void findpet(const Tree * pt)
{
    Item temp;

    if (EmptyTree(pt))
    {
        puts("No entries!");
        return;     /* quit function if tree is empty */
    }

    puts("Please enter name of pet you wish to find:");
    gets(temp.petname);
    puts("Please enter pet kind:");
    gets(temp.petkind);
    uppercase(temp.petname);
    uppercase(temp.petkind);
    printf("%s the %s ", temp.petname, temp.petkind);
    if (InTree(&temp, pt))
        printf("is a member.\n");
    else
        printf("is not a member.\n");
}

void droppet(Tree * pt)
{
    Item temp;

    if (EmptyTree(pt))
    {
        puts("No entries!");
        return;     /* quit function if tree is empty */
    }

    puts("Please enter name of pet you wish to delete:");
    gets(temp.petname);
    puts("Please enter pet kind:");
    gets(temp.petkind);
    uppercase(temp.petname);
    uppercase(temp.petkind);
    printf("%s the %s ", temp.petname, temp.petkind);
    if (DeleteItem(&temp, pt))
        printf("is dropped from the club.\n");
    else
        printf("is not a member.\n");
}
```

continued on next page

continued from previous page

```
void uppercase(char * str)
{
    while (*str != '\0')
    {
        *str = toupper(*str);
        str++;
    }
}
```

The program converts all letters to uppercase so that *SNUFFY*, *Snuffy*, and *snuffy* are not considered distinct names. Here is a sample run:

```
Nerfville Pet Club Membership Program
Enter the letter corresponding to your choice:
a) add a pet        l) show list of pets
n) number of pets   f) find pets
q) quit
a
Please enter name of pet:
Quincy
Please enter pet kind:
pig
Nerfville Pet Club Membership Program
Enter the letter corresponding to your choice:
a) add a pet        l) show list of pets
n) number of pets   f) find pets
q) quit
a
Please enter name of pet:
Betty
Please enter pet kind:
Boa
Nerfville Pet Club Membership Program
Enter the letter corresponding to your choice:
a) add a pet        l) show list of pets
n) number of pets   f) find pets
q) quit
a
Please enter name of pet:
Hiram Jinx
Please enter pet kind:
domestic cat
Nerfville Pet Club Membership Program
Enter the letter corresponding to your choice:
a) add a pet        l) show list of pets
n) number of pets   f) find pets
q) quit
n
3 pets in club
Nerfville Pet Club Membership Program
Enter the letter corresponding to your choice:
a) add a pet        l) show list of pets
n) number of pets   f) find pets
q) quit
```

```
1
Pet: BETTY              Kind: BOA
Pet: HIRAM JINX         Kind: DOMESTIC CAT
Pet: QUINCY             Kind: PIG
Nerfville Pet Club Membership Program
Enter the letter corresponding to your choice:
a) add a pet          l) show list of pets
n) number of pets     f) find pets
q) quit
q
Bye.
```

Tree Thoughts

The binary search tree has some drawbacks. For instance, the binary search tree is efficient only if it is fully populated, or *balanced*. Suppose you're storing words that are entered randomly. Chances are the tree will have a fairly bushy look, as in Figure 17.12. Now suppose you enter data in alphabetical order. Then each new node would be added to the right, and the tree might look like Figure 17.16. The Figure 17.12 tree is said to be *balanced*, and the Figure 17.16 tree is *unbalanced*. Searching this tree is no more effective than sequentially searching a linked list.

One way to avoid stringy trees is use more care when building a tree. If a tree or subtree begins to get too unbalanced on one side or the other, rearrange the nodes to restore a better balance. Similarly, you might need to rearrange the tree after a deletion. The Russian mathematicians Adel'son-Vel'skii and Landis developed an algorithm to do this. Trees built with their method are called AVL trees. It takes longer to build a balanced tree because of the extra restructuring, but you ensure maximum, or nearly maximum, search efficiency.

You might want a binary search tree that does allow duplicate items. Suppose, for example, you wanted to analyze some text by tracking how many times each word in the text appears. One approach is to define `Item` as a structure that holds one word and a number. The first time a word is encountered, it's added to the tree, and the number is set to 1. The next time the same word is encountered, the program finds the node containing the word and increments the number. It doesn't take much work to modify the basic binary search tree to behave in this fashion.

For another possible variation, consider the Nerfville Pet Club. The example ordered the tree by both name and kind, so it could hold Sam the cat in one node, Sam the dog in another node, and Sam the goat in a third node. You couldn't have two cats called Sam, however. Another approach is to order the tree just by name. Making that change alone would allow for only one Sam, regardless of kind, but you could then define `Item` to be a list of structures instead of being a single structure. The first time a Sally shows up, the program would create a new node, then create a new list, and then add Sally and her kind to the list. The next Sally that shows up would be directed to the same node and added to the list.

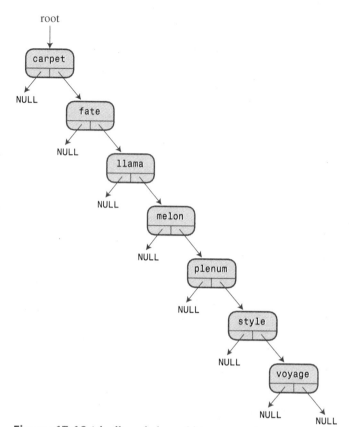

Figure 17.16 A badly unbalanced binary search tree.

Other Directions

In this book, we've covered the essential features of C, but we've only touched upon the library. The ANSI C library contains scores of useful functions. Most implementations also offer extensive libraries of functions specific to particular systems. DOS compilers offer functions to facilitate hardware control, keyboard input, and the generation of graphics for IBM PCs and clones. Windows-based compilers support the Windows graphic interface. Macintosh C compilers provide functions to access the Macintosh toolbox to facilitate producing programs with the standard Macintosh interface. Take the time to explore what your system has to offer. If it doesn't have what you want, make your own functions. That's part of C. If you think you can do a better job on, say, an input function, do it! And as you refine and polish your programming technique, you will go from C to shining C.

If you've found the concepts of lists, queues, and trees exciting and useful, you might want to read a book or take a course on advanced programming techniques. Computer scientists have invested a lot of energy and talent into developing and analyzing algorithms and ways of representing data. You may find that someone has already developed exactly the tool you need.

After you are comfortable with C, you might want to investigate C++, Objective C, or Java. These *object-oriented* languages have their roots in C. C already has data objects ranging in complexity from a simple `char` variable to large and intricate structures. Object-oriented languages carry the idea of the object even further. For instance, the properties of an object include not only what kinds of information it can hold, but also what kinds of operations can be performed on it. The ADTs in this chapter follow that pattern. Also, objects can inherit properties from other objects. OOP carries modularizing to a higher level of abstraction than does C, and it facilitates writing large programs.

You might want to check out the bibliography in Appendix A, "Additional Reading," for books that might further your interests.

Chapter Summary

A data type is characterized by how the data is structured and stored and also by what operations are possible. An abstract data type (ADT) specifies in an abstract manner the properties and operations characterizing a type. Conceptually, you can translate an ADT to a particular programming language in two steps. The first step is defining the programming interface. In C, you can do this by using a header file to define type names and to provide function prototypes that correspond to the allowed operations. The second step is implementing the interface. In C, you can do this with a source code file that supplies the function definitions corresponding to the prototypes.

The list, the queue, and the binary tree are examples of ADTs commonly used in computer programming. Often they are implemented using dynamic memory allocation and linked structures, but sometimes implementing them with an array is a better choice.

When you program using a particular type, say a queue or a tree, you should write the program in terms of the type interface. That way, you can modify and improve the implementation without having to alter programs by using the interface.

Review Questions

1. What's involved in defining a data type?

2. Why can the linked list in Listing 17.2 can be traversed in only one direction? How could you modify the `struct film` definition so that the list could be traversed in both directions?

3. What's an ADT?

4. The `EmptyList()` function took a list as an argument, but the `EmptyQueue()` function took a pointer to a queue as an argument. What are the advantages and disadvantages of each approach?

5. The *stack* is another data form from the list family. In a stack, additions and deletions can be made from only one end of the list. Items are said to be "pushed onto" the top of the stack and to be "popped off" the stack.

Therefore, the stack is a LIFO structure, that is, *Last In, First Out*.

   a. Devise an ADT for a stack.

   b. Devise a C programming interface for a stack.

6. What is the maximum number of comparisons a sequential search and a binary search would need to determine that a particular item is not in a sorted list of 3 items? 1,023 items? 65,535 items?

7. Suppose a program constructs a binary search tree of words, using the algorithm developed in this chapter. Draw the tree, assuming words are entered in the following orders:

   a. nice food roam dodge gate office wave

   b. wave roam office nice gate food dodge

   c. food dodge roam wave office gate nice

   d. nice roam office food wave gate dodge

8. Consider the binary trees constructed in Review Question 7. What would each one look like after the word *food* was removed from each tree using the algorithm from this chapter?

Programming Exercises

1. Modify Listing 17.2 so that it displays the movie list both in the original order and in reverse order. One approach is to modify the linked-list definition so that the list can be traversed in both directions. Another approach is to use recursion.

2. Suppose `list.h` (refer to Listing 17.3) uses the following definition of a list:

```
typedef struct list
{
    Node * head;    /* points to head of list */
    Node * end;     /* points to end of list  */
} List;
```

Rewrite the `list.c` (refer to Listing 17.5) functions to fit this definition and test the resulting code with the `films3.c` (refer to Listing 17.4) program.

3. Suppose `list.h` (refer to Listing 17.3) uses the following definition of a list:

```
#define MAXSIZE 100
typedef struct list
{
    Item entries[MAXSIZE];    /* array of items           */
    int items;                /* number of items in list */
} List;
```

Rewrite the `list.c` (refer to Listing 17.5) functions to fit this definition and test the resulting code with the `films3.c` (refer to Listing 17.4) program.

4. Rewrite `mall.c` (refer to Listing 17.7) so that it simulates a double booth having two queues.

5. Write a program that lets you input a string. The program then pushes the characters of the string onto a stack one by one (see Review Question 5), and then pops the characters from the stack and displays them. This results in displaying the string in reverse order.

6. Write a function that takes three arguments: the name of an array of sorted integers, the number of elements of the array, and an integer to seek. The function returns the value 1 if the integer is in the array, and 0 if it isn't. Have the function use the binary search technique.

7. Write a program that opens and reads a text file and records how many times each word occurs in the file. Use a binary search tree modified to store both a word and the number of times it occurs. After the program has read the file, it offers a menu with three choices. The first is to list all the words along with the number of occurrences. The second is to let you enter a word, and the program reports how many times the word occurred in the file. The third choice is to quit.

8. Modify the Pet Club program so that all pets with the same name are stored in a list in the same node. When the user chooses to find a pet, the program requests the pet name and then lists all pets (along with their kinds) having that name.

APPENDIX A

ADDITIONAL READING

If you want to learn more about C and programming, you will find the following references useful.

C Language

C/C++ Users Journal.
   This monthly magazine (subtitled *Advanced Solutions for C/C++ Programmers*) is a useful resource for C and C++ programmers.

Feuer, Alan R. *The C Puzzle Book*, Second Edition. Englewood Cliffs, NJ: Prentice Hall, 1989.
   This book contains many programs whose output you are supposed to predict. Predicting the output gives you a good opportunity to test and expand your understanding of C. The book includes answers and explanations.

Kernighan, Brian W., and Dennis M. Ritchie. *The C Programming Language.* Englewood Cliffs, NJ: Prentice Hall, 1978.
   This is the first book on C. (Note that the creator of C, Dennis Ritchie, is one of the authors.) It constitutes the definition of "K&R" C, the unofficial standard for many years. The book includes many interesting examples. It does, however, assume that the reader is familiar with systems programming.

Kernighan, Brian W., and Dennis M. Ritchie. *The C Programming Language*, Second Edition. Englewood Cliffs, NJ: Prentice Hall, 1988.
   This edition incorporates ANSI changes based on the ANSI draft that was standard at the time the book was written.

Koenig, Andrew. *C Traps and Pitfalls*. Reading, MA: Addison-Wesley, 1988.
   The title says it all.

Prata, Stephen. *C++ Primer Plus*, Third Edition. Corte Madera, CA: Waite Group Press, 1998.
   This book introduces you to the C++ language and to the philosophy of object-oriented programming.

Ritchie, Dennis M., S.C. Johnson, M.E. Lesk, and Brian W. Kernighan. "The C Programming Language," *The Bell System Technical Journal* 57, no. 6 (July/August 1978).

This article discusses the history of C and offers an overview of its design features.

Stroustrup, Bjarne. *The C++ Programming Language*, Third Edition. Reading, MA: Addison-Wesley, 1997.

This book, by the creator of C++, presents the C++ language and includes the Reference Manual for C++.

Summit, Steve. *C Programming FAQs*. Reading, MA: Addison-Wesley, 1995.

This book is an extended version of the FAQ (Frequently Asked Questions) file that Summit provides for the Usenet `comp.lang.c` newsgroup. It lists over 400 questions about C along with answers. A briefer version can be found online at `http://www.eskimo.com/~scs/C-faq/top.html`.

Programming

Kernighan, Brian W., and P.J. Plauger. *The Elements of Programming Style*, Second Edition. New York: McGraw-Hill, 1978.

This slim classic draws on examples from other texts to illustrate the do's and don'ts of clear, effective programming.

Knuth, Donald E. *The Art of Computer Programming*, Volume 1 (Fundamental Algorithms), Second Edition. Reading, MA: Addison-Wesley, 1973.

This standard reference examines data representation and algorithm analysis in great detail. Volume 2 (Seminumerical Algorithms, 1980) includes an extensive discussion of pseudo-random numbers. Volume 3 (Sorting and Searching, 1973), as the name suggests, examines sorting and searching. Examples are given in pseudocode and assembly language.

Kruse, Robert L., Leung, Bruce P., and Tondo, Clovis L. *Data Structures and Program Design in C*, Second Edition. Englewood Cliffs, NJ: Prentice Hall, 1997.

This textbook covers advanced topics such as software engineering, linked lists, searching, sorting, trees, and graphs. The examples, although in C, show their Pascal heritage.

Reference

Harbison, Samuel P. and Steele, Guy L. *C: A Reference Manual*, Fourth Edition. Englewood Cliffs, NJ: Prentice Hall, 1994.

This reference manual presents the rules of the C language and describes most of the standard library functions. It points out differences between K&R C and ANSI C, and provides many examples.

Plauger, P.J. *The Standard C Library*. Englewood Cliffs, NJ: Prentice Hall, 1991.

This large reference manual describes the standard library functions, with more explanation than you would find in a typical compiler manual.

APPENDIX B

C OPERATORS

C is rich in operators. Table B.1 lists the C operators in order of decreasing precedence and indicates how they associate. All operators are binary (two operands) unless otherwise indicated. Note that some binary and unary operators, such as * (multiplication) and * (indirection), share the same symbol but have different precedence. Following the table are summaries of each operator.

Table B.1 The C operators.

Operators (from high to low precedence)	Associativity
++ (postfix) -- (postfix) ( ) [ ] . ->	L–R
++ (prefix) -- (prefix) - + ~ !	
sizeof * (dereference) & (address)	
(type) (all unary)	R–L
* / %	L–R
+ - (both binary)	L–R
<< >>	L–R
< > <= >=	L–R
== !=	L–R
&	L–R
^	L–R
|	L–R
&&	L–R
||	L–R
? : (conditional expression)	R–L
= *= /= %= += -= <<= >>= &= |= ^=	R–L
, (comma operator)	L–R

Arithmetic Operators

+ adds the value at its right to the value at its left.

– subtracts the value at its right from the value at its left.

–, as a unary operator, changes the sign of the value at its right.

* multiplies the value at its right by the value at its left.

/ divides the value at its left by the value at its right. Answer is truncated if both operands are integers.

% yields the remainder when the value at its left is divided by the value to its right (integers only).

++ adds 1 to the value of the variable to its right (prefix mode) or adds 1 to the value of the variable to its left (postfix mode).

– is like ++, but subtracts 1.

Relational Operators

Each operator compares the value at its left to the value at its right.

<	Less than
<=	Less than or equal to
==	Equal to
>=	Greater than or equal to
>	Greater than
!=	Unequal to

Relational Expressions

A simple relational expression consists of a relational operator with an operand on each side. If the relation is true, the relational expression has the value 1. If the relation is false, the relational expression has the value 0.

5 > 2 is true and has the value 1.

(2 + a) == a is false and has the value 0.

Assignment Operators

= assigns the value at its right to the lvalue on its left.

Each of the following assignment operators updates the lvalue at its left by the value at its right, using the indicated operation. We use R–H for right-hand and L–H for left-hand.

+= adds the R–H quantity to the L–H variable and places the result in the L–H variable.

-= subtracts the R–H quantity from the L–H variable and places the result in the L-H variable.

*= multiplies the L–H variable by the R–H quantity and places the result in the L-H variable.

/= divides the L–H variable by the R–H quantity and places the result in the L–H variable.

%= gives the remainder from dividing the L-H quantity by the R-H quantity and places the result in the L-H variable.

&= assigns L–H & R–H to the L–H quantity and places the result in the L–H variable.

¦= assigns L–H ¦ R–H to the L–H quantity and places the result in the L–H variable.

^= assigns L–H ^ R–H to the L–H quantity and places the result in the L–H variable.

>>= assigns L–H >> R–H to the L–H quantity and places the result in the L–H variable.

<<= assigns L–H << R–H to the L–H quantity and places the result in the L–H variable.

Example

`rabbits *= 1.6;` is the same as `rabbits = rabbits * 1.6;`

Logical Operators

Logical operators normally take relational expressions as operands. The ! operator takes one operand. The rest take two: one to the left, and one to the right.

&&	AND
¦¦	OR
!	NOT

Logical Expressions

expression1 && expression2 is true if, and only if, both expressions are true.

expression1 ¦¦ expression2 is true if either one or both expressions are true.

!expression is true if the expression is false, and vice versa.

Order of Evaluation for Logical Expressions

Logical expressions are evaluated from left to right. Evaluation stops as soon as something is discovered that renders the expression false.

Examples

6 > 2 && 3 == 3 is true.

! (6 > 2 && 3 == 3) is false.

x != 0 && 20/x < 5 The second expression is evaluated only if x is nonzero.

The Conditional Operator

? : takes three operands, each of which is an expression. They are arranged this way: expression1 ? expression2 : expression3. The value of the whole expression equals the value of expression2 if expression1 is true, and equals the value of expression3 otherwise.

Examples

(5 > 3) ? 1 : 2 has the value 1.

(3 > 5) ? 1 : 2 has the value 2.

(a > b) ? a : b has the value of the larger of a or b.

Pointer-Related Operators

& is the address operator. When followed by a variable name, & gives the address of that variable.

* is the indirection or dereferencing operator. When followed by a pointer, * gives the value stored at the pointed-to address.

Example

&nurse is the address of the variable nurse.

```
nurse = 22;
ptr = &nurse; /* pointer to nurse */
val = *ptr;
```

The net effect is to assign the value 22 to val.

Sign Operators

– is the minus sign, which reverses the sign of the operand.

+ is the plus sign, which leaves the sign unchanged.

Structure and Union Operators

Structures and unions use operators to identify individual members. The membership operator is used with structures and unions, and the indirect membership operator is used with pointers to structures or unions.

The Membership Operator

. is used with a structure or union name to specify a member of that structure or union. If name is the name of a structure and member is a member specified by the structure template, then name.member identifies that member of the structure. The type of name.member is the type specified for member. The membership operator can also be used in the same fashion with unions.

Example

```
struct {
        int code;
        float cost;
} item;

item.code = 1265;
```

This statement assigns a value to the code member of the structure item.

The Indirect Membership Operator (or Structure Pointer Operator)

-> is used with a pointer to a structure or union to identify a member of that structure or union. Suppose that `ptrstr` is a pointer to a structure and that `member` is a member specified by the structure template. Then `ptrstr->member` identifies that member of the pointed-to structure. The indirect membership operator can be used in the same fashion with unions.

Example

```
struct {
        int code;
        float cost;
} item, * ptrst;
ptrst = &item;
ptrst->code = 3451;
```

This program fragment assigns a value to the `code` member of `item`. The following three expressions are equivalent:

```
ptrst->code    item.code    (*ptrst).code
```

Bitwise Operators

All of the following bitwise operators, except ~, are binary operators:

~ is the unary operator and produces a value with each bit of the operand inverted.

& is AND and produces a value in which each bit is set to 1 only if both corresponding bits in the two operands are 1.

¦ is OR and produces a value in which each bit is set to 1 if either, or both, corresponding bits of the two operands are 1.

^ is EXCLUSIVE OR and produces a value in which each bit is set to 1 only if one or the other (but not both) of the corresponding bits of the two operands is 1.

<< is left-shift and produces a value obtained by shifting the bits of the left-hand operand to the left by the number of places given by the right-hand operand. Vacated slots are filled with zeros.

>> is right-shift and produces a value obtained by shifting the bits of the left-hand operand to the right by the number of places given by the right-hand operand. For unsigned integers, the vacated slots are filled with zeros. The behavior for signed values is implementation dependent.

Examples

Suppose you have the following:

```
int x = 2;
int y = 3;
```

Then x & y has the value 2 because only bit 1 is ON for both x and y. Also, y<<x has the value 12 because that is the value obtained when the bit pattern for 3 is shifted two bits to the left.

Miscellaneous Operators

sizeof yields the size, in units the size of a char value, of the operand to its right. Typically, a char value is one byte in size. The operand can be a type-specifier in parentheses, as in sizeof (float), or it can be the name of a particular variable, array, or so on, as in size-of foo. A sizeof expression is of type size_t.

(type) is the cast operator and converts the following value to the type specified by the enclosed keyword(s). For example, (float) 9 converts the integer 9 to the floating-point number 9.0.

, is the comma operator; it links two expressions into one and guarantees that the left-most expression is evaluated first. The value of the whole expression is the value of the right-hand expression. This operator is typically used to include more information in a for loop control expression.

Example

```
for (step = 2, fargo = 0; fargo < 1000; step *= 2)
        fargo += step;
```

APPENDIX C

BASIC TYPES AND STORAGE CLASSES

Summary: The Basic Data Types

C's basic types fall into two categories: integers and floating-point numbers. The different varieties give you choices for range and precision.

Keywords

The basic data types are set up using the following eight keywords: `int`, `long`, `short`, `unsigned`, `char`, `float`, `double`, and `signed` (ANSI C).

Signed Integers

Signed integers can have positive or negative values.

`int` is the basic integer type for a given system.

`long` or `long int` can hold an integer at least as large as the largest `int` and possibly larger; `long` is at least 32 bits.

The largest `short` or `short int` integer is no larger than the largest `int`, and may be smaller. A `short` is at least 16 bits. Typically, `long` is bigger than `short`, and `int` is the same as one of the two. For example, C DOS compilers for the PC provide 16-bit `short` and `int` and 32-bit `long`. It all depends on the system.

The `long long` type provided by the C9X committee is at least as big as `long` and is at least 64 bits.

Unsigned Integers

Unsigned integers have zero or positive values only, which extends the range of the largest possible positive number. Use the keyword `unsigned` before the desired type: `unsigned int`, `unsigned long`, `unsigned short`, or `unsigned long long`. A lone `unsigned` is the same as `unsigned int`.

Characters

Characters are typographic symbols such as A, &, and +. By definition, one byte of memory is used for a `char` variable. In the past, 8 bits has been the most typical size for `char`. However, the internationalization of C might lead to 16-bit bytes.

`char` is the keyword for this type.

Some implementations use a signed `char`, but others use an unsigned `char`. ANSI C allows you to use the keywords `signed` and `unsigned` to specify which form you want. Technically, `char`, `unsigned char`, and `signed char` are three distinct types, with the `char` type having the same representation as one of the other two.

Floating Point

Floating-point numbers can have positive or negative values.

`float` is the basic floating-point type for the system. It can represent at least six significant digits accurately. Typically, `float` uses 32 bits.

`double` is a (possibly) larger unit for holding floating-point numbers. It may allow more significant figures and perhaps larger exponents than `float`. It can represent at least ten significant digits accurately. Typically, `double` uses 64 bits.

`long double` is a (possibly) even larger unit for holding floating-point numbers. It may allow more significant figures and perhaps larger exponents than `double`.

Summary: How to Declare a Simple Variable

1. Choose the type you need.

2. Choose a name for the variable.

3. Use this format for a declaration statement: `type-specifier variable-name;`. The `type-specifier` is formed from one or more of the type keywords. Here are some examples:

```
int erest;
unsigned short cash;
```

4. To declare more than one variable of the same type, separate the variable names with commas:

```
char ch, init, ans;
```

5. You can initialize a variable in a declaration statement:

```
float mass = 6.0E24;
```

Summary: Storage Classes

Keywords:

```
auto, extern, static, register
```

General Comments:

The storage class of a variable determines its scope, its linkage, and its storage duration. Storage class is determined both by where the variable is defined and by its associated keyword. Variables defined outside all functions are external, have file scope, external linkage, and static storage duration. Variables declared inside a function are automatic unless one of the other keywords is used. They have block scope, no linkage, and automatic storage duration. Variables defined with the keyword **static** inside a function have block scope, no linkage, and static storage duration. Variables defined with the keyword **static** outside a function have file scope, internal linkage, and static storage duration.

Properties:

In the following list, those variables in storage classes above the dotted line are declared inside a function; those below the line are defined outside a function.

Storage Class	Keyword	Duration	Scope and Linkage
automatic	auto	temporary	local
register	register	temporary	local
static	static	persistent	local
external	extern*	persistent	global (all files)
external	static	persistent	global (one file)
static			

*The keyword **extern** is used only to redeclare variables that have been defined externally elsewhere. The act of defining the variable outside a function makes it external.*

Summary: Qualifiers

Keywords

Use the following keywords to qualify variables:

```
const, volatile
```

General Comments

A qualifier constrains a variable's ability to be modified. A `const` variable, after it's initialized, can't be altered. The compiler can't assume that a volatile variable hasn't been changed by some outside agency, such as a hardware update.

Properties

Note

The declaration

```
const int joy = 101;
```

establishes that the value of `joy` is fixed at `101`.

The declaration

```
volatile unsigned int incoming;
```

establishes that the value of `incoming` might change between one occurrence of `incoming` in a program and its next occurrence.

The declaration

```
const int * ptr = &joy;
```

establishes that the pointer `ptr` can't be used to alter the value of the variable `joy`. The pointer can, however, be made to point to another location.

The declaration

```
int * const ptr = &joy;
```

establishes that the pointer `ptr` can't have its value changed; that is, it can point only to `joy`. However, it can be used to alter `joy`.

The prototype

```
void simple (const char * s);
```

establishes that after the formal argument `s` is initialized to whatever value is passed to `simple()` in a function call, `sample()` may not alter the value to which `s` points.

EXPRESSIONS, STATEMENTS, AND PROGRAM FLOW

Summary: Expressions and Statements

In C, expressions represent values, and statements represent instructions to the computer.

Expressions

An *expression* is a combination of operators and operands. The simplest expression is just a constant or a variable with no operator, such as **22** or **beebop**. More complex examples are **55 + 22** and **vap = 2 * (vip + (vup = 4))**.

Statements

A *statement* is a command to the computer. Any expression followed by a semicolon forms a statement, although not necessarily a meaningful one. Statements can be simple or compound. *Simple statements* terminate in a semicolon, as shown in these examples:

Declaration statement	`int toes;`
Assignment statement	`toes = 12;`
Function call statement	`printf("%d\n", toes);`
Control statement	`while (toes < 20) toes = toes + 2;`
Null statement	`; /* does nothing */`

Compound statements, or *blocks*, consist of one or more statements (which themselves can be compound) enclosed in braces. The following `while` statement is an example:

```c
while (years < 100)
{
    wisdom = wisdom + 1;
    printf("%d %d\n", years, wisdom);
    years = years + 1;
}
```

Summary: The `while` Statement

Keyword

The keyword for the `while` statement is `while`.

General Comments

The `while` statement creates a loop that repeats until the test **expression** becomes false, or zero. The `while` statement is an *entry-condition* loop; the decision to go through one more pass of the loop is made *before* the loop has been traversed. Therefore, it is possible that the loop is never traversed. The **statement** part of the form can be a simple statement or a compound statement.

Form

```
while (expression)
        statement
```

The *statement* portion is repeated until the *expression* becomes false or zero.

Examples

```
while (n++ < 100)
        printf(" %d %d\n",n, 2*n+1);

while (fargo < 1000)
{
        fargo = fargo + step;
        step = 2 * step;
}
```

Summary: The `for` Statement

Keyword

The `for` statement keyword is `for`.

General Comments

The `for` statement uses three control expressions, separated by semicolons, to control a looping process. The **initialize** expression is executed once, before any of the loop statements are executed. If the **test** expression is true (or nonzero), the loop is cycled through once. Then the **update** expression is evaluated, and it is time to check the **test** expression again. The `for` statement is an *entry-condition* loop; the decision to go through one more pass of the loop is made *before* the loop has been traversed. Therefore, it is possible that the loop is never traversed. The `statement` part of the form can be a simple statement or a compound statement.

Form

```
for (initialize ; test ; update)
        statement
```

The loop is repeated until `test` becomes false or zero.

Example

```
for (n = 0;  n < 10 ; n++)
        printf("%d %d\n", n, 2 * n+1);
```

Summary: The `do while` Statement

Keywords

The keywords for the `do while` statement are `do` and `while`.

General Comments

The `do while` statement creates a loop that repeats until the test `expression` becomes false or zero. The `do while` statement is an *exit-condition* loop; the decision to go through one more pass of the loop is made *after* the loop has been traversed. Therefore, the loop must be executed at least once. The `statement` part of the form can be a simple statement or a compound statement.

Form

```
do
    statement
while (expression);
```

The `statement` portion is repeated until the `expression` becomes false or zero.

Example

```
do
    scanf("%d", &number)
while(number != 20);
```

Summary: Using `if` Statements for Making Choices

Keywords

The keywords for `if` statements are `if` and `else`.

General Comments

In each of the following forms, the `statement` can be either a simple statement or a compound statement. A "true" expression, more generally, means one with a nonzero value.

Form 1

```
if (expression)
    statement
```

The `statement` is executed if the `expression` is true.

Form 2

```
if (expression)
    statement1
  else
      statement2
```

If the `expression` is true, `statement1` is executed. Otherwise, `statement2` is executed.

Form 3

```
if (expression1)
    statement1
  else if (expression2)
    statement2
  else
      statement3
```

If `expression1` is true, `statement1` is executed. If `expression1` is false but `expression2` is true, `statement2` is executed. Otherwise, if both expressions are false, `statement3` is executed.

Example

```
if (legs == 4)
    printf("It might be a horse.\n");
else if (legs > 4)
    printf("It is not a horse.\n");
else    /* case of legs < 4 */
```

```
{
    legs++;
    printf("Now it has one more leg.\n")
}
```

Summary: Multiple Choice with `switch`

Keyword

The keyword for the `switch` statement is `switch`.

General Comments

Program control jumps to the statement bearing the value of **expression** as a label. Program flow then proceeds through the remaining statements unless redirected again. Both **expression** and labels must have integer values (type **char** is included), and the labels must be constants or expressions formed solely from constants. If no label matches the expression value, control goes to the statement labeled **default**, if present. Otherwise, control passes to the next statement following the **switch** statement. After control goes to a particular label, all the subsequent statements in the **switch** are executed until the end of the **switch**, or a **break** statement, is encountered, whichever comes first.

Form

```
switch (expression)
{
    case label1 : statement1
    case label2 : statement2
    default     : statement3
}
```

There can be more than two labeled statements, and the **default** case is optional.

Examples

```
switch (value)
    case 1  : find_sum(ar, n);
              break;
    case 2  : show_array(ar, n);
              break;
    case 3  : puts("Goodbye!");
              break;
    default : puts("Invalid choice, try again.");
              break;
}
```

```
switch (letter)
{
    case 'a' :
    case 'e' : printf("%d is a vowel\n", letter);
    case 'c' :
    case 'n' : printf("%d is in \"cane\"\n", letter);
    default  : printf("Have a nice day.\n");
}
```

If `letter` has the value `'a'` or `'e'`, all three messages are printed; `'c'` and `'n'` cause the last two to be printed. Other values print only the last message.

Summary: Program Jumps

Keywords

The keywords for program jumps are `break`, `continue`, and `goto`.

General Comments

The three instructions `break`, `continue`, and `goto` cause program flow to jump from one location of a program to another location.

The `break` Command

The `break` command can be used with any of the three loop forms and with the `switch` statement. It causes program control to skip the rest of the loop or `switch` containing it and to resume with the next command following the loop or `switch`.

Example

```
switch (number)
{
    case  4:  printf("That's a good choice.\n");
              break;
    case  5:  printf("That's a fair choice.\n");
              break;
    default:  printf("That's a poor choice.\n");
}
```

The `continue` Command

The `continue` command can be used with any of the three loop forms, but not with a `switch`. It causes program control to skip the remaining statements in a loop. For a `while` or `for` loop, the next loop cycle is started. For a `do while` loop, the exit condition is tested and then, if necessary, the next loop cycle is started.

Example

```
while ((ch = getchar())  != EOF)
{
    if (ch == ' ')
        continue;
    putchar(ch);
    chcount++;
}
```

This fragment echoes and counts nonspace characters.

The `goto` Command

A `goto` statement causes program control to jump to a statement bearing the indicated label.
A colon is used to separate a labeled statement from its label. Label names follow the rules
for variable names. The labeled statement can come either before or after the `goto`.

Form

```
goto label;
    label : statement
```

Example

```
top : ch = getchar();
      if (ch != 'y')
        goto top;
```

APPENDIX E

THE ASCII CHARACTER SET

Computers store characters by using a numeric code. The ASCII code (American Standard Code for Information Interchange) is the most commonly used code in the United States. C lets you represent most single characters directly, by including the character in single quotation marks, as in `'A'` for the A character. You can also represent a single character by using the octal or hex code preceded by a backslash; for example, `'\012'` and `'\0xa'` both represent the linefeed (LF) character. Such escape sequences can also be part of a string, as in `"Hello,\012my dear"`.

When used as a prefix in the following table, the ^ character denotes using the Ctrl key.

Decimal	Octal	Hex	Binary	Character	ASCII Name
0	0	0	00000000	^@	NUL
1	01	0x1	00000001	^A	SOH
2	02	0x2	00000010	^B	STX
3	03	0x3	00000011	^C	ETX
4	04	0x4	00000100	^D	EOT
5	05	0x5	00000101	^E	ENQ
6	06	0x6	00000110	^F	ACK
7	07	0x7	00000111	^G	BEL
8	010	0x8	00001000	^H	BS
9	011	0x9	00001001	^I, tab	HT
10	012	0xa	00001010	^J	LF
11	013	0xb	00001011	^K	VT
12	014	0xc	00001100	^L	FF
13	015	0xd	00001101	^M	CR
14	016	0xe	00001110	^N	SO

continued on next page

continued from previous page

Decimal	Octal	Hex	Binary	Character	ASCII Name
15	017	0xf	00001111	^O	SI
16	020	0x10	00010000	^P	DLE
17	021	0x11	00010001	^Q	DC1
18	022	0x12	00010010	^R	DC2
19	023	0x13	00010011	^S	DC3
20	024	0x14	00010100	^T	DC4
21	025	0x15	00010101	^U	NAK
22	026	0x16	00010110	^V	SYN
23	027	0x17	00010111	^W	ETB
24	030	0x18	00011000	^X	CAN
25	031	0x19	00011001	^Y	EM
26	032	0x1a	00011010	^Z	SUB
27	033	0x1b	00011011	^[, esc	ESC
28	034	0x1c	00011100	^\	FS
29	035	0x1d	00011101	^]	GS
30	036	0x1e	00011110	^^	RS
31	037	0x1f	00011111	^_	US
32	040	0x20	00100000	space	SP
33	041	0x21	00100001	!	
34	042	0x22	00100010	"	
35	043	0x23	00100011	#	
36	044	0x24	00100100	$	
37	045	0x25	00100101	%	
38	046	0x26	00100110	&	
39	047	0x27	00100111	'	
40	050	0x28	00101000	(	
41	051	0x29	00101001	)	
42	052	0x2a	00101010	*	

Decimal	Octal	Hex	Binary	Character	ASCII Name
43	053	0x2b	00101011	+	
44	054	0x2c	00101100	'	
45	055	0x2d	00101101	-	
46	056	0x2e	00101110	.	
47	057	0x2f	00101111	/	
48	060	0x30	00110000	0	
49	061	0x31	00110001	1	
50	062	0x32	00110010	2	
51	063	0x33	00110011	3	
52	064	0x34	00110100	4	
53	065	0x35	00110101	5	
54	066	0x36	00110110	6	
55	067	0x37	00110111	7	
56	070	0x38	00111000	8	
57	071	0x39	00111001	9	
58	072	0x3a	00111010	:	
59	073	0x3b	00111011	;	
60	074	0x3c	00111100	<	
61	075	0x3d	00111101	=	
62	076	0x3e	00111110	>	
63	077	0x3f	00111111	?	
64	0100	0x40	01000000	@	
65	0101	0x41	01000001	A	
66	0102	0x42	01000010	B	
67	0103	0x43	01000011	C	
68	0104	0x44	01000100	D	
69	0105	0x45	01000101	E	
70	0106	0x46	01000110	F	

continued on next page

continued from previous page

Decimal	Octal	Hex	Binary	Character	ASCII Name
71	0107	0x47	01000111	G	
72	0110	0x48	01001000	H	
73	0111	0x49	01001001	I	
74	0112	0x4a	01001010	J	
75	0113	0x4b	01001011	K	
76	0114	0x4c	01001100	L	
77	0115	0x4d	01001101	M	
78	0116	0x4e	01001110	N	
79	0117	0x4f	01001111	O	
80	0120	0x50	01010000	P	
81	0121	0x51	01010001	Q	
82	0122	0x52	01010010	R	
83	0123	0x53	01010011	S	
84	0124	0x54	01010100	T	
85	0125	0x55	01010101	U	
86	0126	0x56	01010110	V	
87	0127	0x57	01010111	W	
88	0130	0x58	01011000	X	
89	0131	0x59	01011001	Y	
90	0132	0x5a	01011010	Z	
91	0133	0x5b	01011011	[	
92	0134	0x5c	01011100	\	
93	0135	0x5d	01011101	]	
94	0136	0x5e	01011110	^	
95	0137	0x5f	01011111	_	
96	0140	0x60	01100000	'	
97	0141	0x61	01100001	a	
98	0142	0x62	01100010	b	

Decimal	Octal	Hex	Binary	Character	ASCII Name
99	0143	0x63	01100011	c	
100	0144	0x64	01100100	d	
101	0145	0x65	01100101	e	
102	0146	0x66	01100110	f	
103	0147	0x67	01100111	g	
104	0150	0x68	01101000	h	
105	0151	0x69	01101001	i	
106	0152	0x6a	01101010	j	
107	0153	0x6b	01101011	k	
108	0154	0x6c	01101100	l	
109	0155	0x6d	01101101	m	
110	0156	0x6e	01101110	n	
111	0157	0x6f	01101111	o	
112	0160	0x70	01110000	p	
113	0161	0x71	01110001	q	
114	0162	0x72	01110010	r	
115	0163	0x73	01110011	s	
116	0164	0x74	01110100	t	
117	0165	0x75	01110101	u	
118	0166	0x76	01110110	v	
119	0167	0x77	01110111	w	
120	0170	0x78	01111000	x	
121	0171	0x79	01111001	y	
122	0172	0x7a	01111010	z	
123	0173	0x7b	01111011	{	
124	0174	0x7c	01111100	l	
125	0175	0x7d	01111101	}	
126	0176	0x7e	01111110	~	
127	0177	0x7f	01111111	del, rubout	

APPENDIX F

THE STANDARD ANSI C LIBRARY

The ANSI C library classifies functions into several groups, with each group having an associated header file. This appendix gives you an overview of the library, listing the header files and briefly describing the associated function. Some of these functions (for example, several I/O functions) are discussed in much greater detail in the text. More generally, for complete descriptions, consult the documentation for your implementation or a reference manual.

Diagnostics: `assert.h`

This header file defines `assert()` as a macro. Defining the macro identifier NDEBUG before including the `assert.h` header file deactivates the `assert()` macro. The expression used as an argument is typically a relational or logical expression that should be true at that point in the program if the program is functioning properly.

Table F.1   Diagnostic macro.

Prototype	Description
`void assert(int exprs);`	If `exprs` evaluates to non-zero (or true), the macro does nothing. If it evaluates to zero (false), `assert()` displays expression, the line number for the `assert()` statement, and the name of the file containing the statement. Then it calls `abort()`.

Character Handling: `ctype.h`

These functions take `int` arguments, which should be able to be represented as either unsigned char values or as EOF; the effect of supplying other values is undefined. In Table F.2, "true" is used as shorthand for "a non-zero value." Interpretation of some definitions depends on the current locale setting, which is controlled by the functions of `locale.h`.

Table F.2   Character-handling functions.

Prototype	Description
`int isalnum(int c);`	Returns true if c is alphanumeric (alphabetic or numeric).
`int isalpha(int c);`	Returns true if c is alphabetic.
`int iscntrl(int c);`	Returns true if c is a control character, such as Ctrl+B.
`int isdigit(int c);`	Returns true if c is a digit.
`int isgraph(int c);`	Returns true if c is any printing character other than a space.
`int islower(int c);`	Returns true if c is a lowercase character.
`int isprint(int c);`	Returns true if c is a printing character.
`int ispunct(int c);`	Returns true if c is a punctuation character (any printing character other than a space or an alphanumeric character).
`int isspace(int c);`	Returns true if c is a whitespace character: space, newline, formfeed, carriage return, vertical tab, horizontal tab, or, possibly, other implementation-defined characters.
`int isupper(int c);`	Returns true if c is an uppercase character.
`int isxdigit(int c);`	Returns true if c is a hexadecimal-digit character.
`int tolower(int c);`	If the argument is an uppercase character, returns the lowercase version; otherwise, just returns the original argument.
`int toupper(int c);`	If the argument is a lowercase character, returns the uppercase version; otherwise, just returns the original argument.

Localization: `locale.h`

A *locale* is a group of settings controlling things such as the symbol used as a decimal point. Locale values are stored in a structure of type `struct lconv`, defined in the `locale.h` header file. A locale can be specified by a string, which acts to specify a particular set of values for the structure members. The default locale is designated by the string `"C"`. Table F.3 lists the localization functions, and a brief discussion follows.

Table F.3   Localization functions.

Prototype	Description
`char * setlocale(int category, const char * locale);`	The function sets certain locale values to the values specified by the locale and indicated by `locale`. The `category` value controls which locale values get set (see Table F.4). The function returns the null

Prototype	Description
	pointer if it cannot honor the request. Otherwise, it returns a pointer associated with the specified category in the new locale.
`struct lconv * localeconv(void);`	Returns a pointer to a `struct lconv` structure filled in with the values of the current locale.

The required possible values for the `locale` parameter to `setlocale()` are `"C"`, which is the default, and `""`, which represents the implementation-defined native environment. An implementation can define additional locales. The possible values for the `category` parameter to `setlocale()` are represented by the macros listed in Table F.4.

Table F.4   Category macros.

Macro	Description
NULL	Leave the locale unchanged and return a pointer to the current locale.
LC_ALL	Change all locale values.
LC_COLLATE	Change locale values for the collating sequence used by `strcoll()` and `strxfrm()`.
LC_CTYPE	Change locale values for the character-handling functions and to the multibyte functions.
LC_MONETARY	Change locale values for monetary formatting information.
LC_NUMERIC	Change locale values for the decimal point symbol and non-monetary formatting used by formatted I/O and by string conversion functions.
LC_TIME	Change locale values for the time formatting used by `strftime()`.

Table F.5 lists the required members of a `struct lconv` structure.

Table F.5   Required `struct lconv` members.

Macro	Description
`char *decimal_point`	Decimal-point character for non-monetary values.
`char *thousands_sep`	Character used to separate groups of digits before the decimal point for non-monetary quantities.
`char *grouping`	A string whose elements indicate the size of each group of digits for non-monetary quantities.

continued on next page

continued from previous page

Macro	Description
char *int_curr_symbol	The international currency symbol.
char *currency_symbol	The local currency symbol.
char *mon_decimal_point	Decimal-point character for monetary values.
char *mon_thousands_sep	Character used to separate groups of digits before the decimal point for non-monetary quantities.
char *mon_grouping	A string whose elements indicate the size of each group of digits for monetary quantities.
char *positive_sign	String used to indicate a non-negative formatted monetary value.
char *negative_sign	String used to indicate a negative formatted monetary value.
char int_frac_digits	Number of digits displayed after the decimal point for an internationally formatted monetary quantity.
char frac_digits	Number of digits displayed after the decimal point for a locally formatted monetary quantity.
char p_cs_precedes	Set to 1 or 0 depending on whether currency_symbol precedes or follows the value of a non-negative formatted monetary quantity.
char p_sep_by_space	Set to 1 or 0 depending on whether currency_symbol is separated by a space from the value of a non-negative formatted monetary quantity.
char n_cs_precedes	Set to 1 or 0 depending on whether currency_symbol precedes or follows the value of a negative formatted monetary quantity.
char n_sep_by_space	Set to 1 or 0 depending on whether currency_symbol is separated by a space from the value of a negative formatted monetary quantity.
char p_sign_posn	Set to a value indicating the positioning of positive_sign string; 0 means parentheses surround the quantity and currency symbol, 1 means the string precedes the quantity and currency symbol, 2 means the string follows the quantity and currency symbol, 3 means the string immediately precedes the currency symbol, and 4 means the string immediately follows the currency symbol.
char n_sign_posn	Set to a value indicating the positioning of negative_sign string; the meaning is the same as for char p_sign_posn.

Math Library: `math.h`

Table F.6 lists the functions of the math library. The header file defines a macro **HUGE_VAL** that is used as the return value for functions when the magnitude of the result exceeds the largest representable value.

Table F.6   ANSI C standard math functions.

Prototype	Description
`double acos(double x);`	Returns the angle (0 to π radians) whose cosine is x.
`double asin(double x);`	Returns the angle ($-\pi/2$ to $\pi/2$ radians) whose sine is x.
`double atan(double x);`	Returns the angle ($-\pi/2$ to $\pi/2$ radians) whose tangent is x.
`double atan2(double y, double x);`	Returns the angle ($-\pi$ to π radians) whose tangent is y / x.
`double cos(double x);`	Returns the cosine of x (x in radians).
`double sin(double x);`	Returns the sine of x (x in radians).
`double tan(double x);`	Returns the tangent of x (x in radians).
`double cosh(double x);`	Returns the hyperbolic cosine of x.
`double sinh(double x);`	Returns the hyperbolic sine of x.
`double tanh(double x);`	Returns the hyperbolic tangent of x.
`double exp(double x);`	Returns the exponential function of x (e^x).
`double frexp(double v, int *pt_e);`	Breaks a value v into a normalized fraction, which is returned, and a power of 2, which is placed in the location pointed to by `pt_e`.
`double ldexp(double x, int p);`	Returns 2 to the p power times x.
`double log(double x);`	Returns the natural logarithm of x.
`double log10(double x);`	Returns the base 10 logarithm of x
`double modf(double x, double *p);`	Breaks x into an integral part and a fraction part, both of the same sign, returns the fractional part and stores the integral part in the location pointed to by p.
`double pow(double x, double y);`	Returns the x to the y power.
`double sqrt(double x);`	Returns the square root of x.
`double ceil(double x);`	Returns the smallest integral value not less than x.
`double fabs(double x);`	Returns the absolute value of x.
`double floor(double x);`	Returns the largest integral value not greater than x.
`int fmod(double x, double y);`	Returns the fractional part of x / y.

Non-Local Jumps: `setjmp.h`

The `setjmp.h` header file enables you to bypass the usual function call, function return sequence. The `setjmp()` function stores information about the current execution environment, for example, a pointer to the current instruction, in a type `jmp_buf` variable (an array type defined in this header file), and the `longjmp()` function transfers execution to such an environment. The functions are intended to help handle error conditions, not to be used as part of normal program flow control. Table F.7 lists the functions.

Table F.7   Localization functions.

Prototype	Description
`int setjump(jmp_buf env);`	Saves the calling environment in the array `env` and returns `0` if called directly, non-zero if the return is from a call to `longjmp()`.
`void longjmp(jmp_buf env, int val);`	Restores the environment saved by the most recent evocation of `setjmp()` that set the `env` array; after completing this change, the program continues as though that evocation of `setjmp()` had returned `val`, except that a return value of `0` is not allowed and is converted to `1`.

Signal Handling: `signal.h`

A *signal* is a condition that can be reported during program execution. It is represented by a positive integer. The `raise()` function sends, or *raises*, a signal, and the `signal()` function sets the response to a particular signal.

The standard provides the macros listed in Table F.8 to represent possible signals; an implementation can add further values. They can be used as arguments to `raise()` and `signal()`.

Table F.8   Signal macros.

Macro	Description
SIGABRT	Abnormal termination, such as initiated by a call to `abort()`.
SIGFPE	Erroneous arithmetic operation.
SIGILL	Invalid function image (such as illegal instruction) detected.
SIGINT	Interactive attention signal received (such as a DOS interrupt).

Macro	Description
SIGSEGV	Invalid access to storage.
SIGTERM	Termination request sent to program.

The `signal()` function takes as its second argument a pointer to a `void` function that takes an `int` argument. It also returns a pointer of the same type. A function invoked in response to a signal is termed a *signal handler*. The standard defines three macros fitting this prototype:

```
void   (*funct)(int);
```

Table F.9 lists these macros.

Table F.9   Type `void (*f)(int)` macros.

Macro	Description
SIG_DFL	When used as an argument to `signal()`, along with a signal value, indicates that the default handling for that signal will occur.
SIG_ERR	Used as a return value for `signal()` if it cannot return its second argument.
SIG_IGN	When used as an argument to `signal()`, along with a signal value, indicates that the signal will be ignored.

If a signal `sig` is raised and `func` points to a function (see `signal()` prototype in Table F.10), first, under most circumstances, `signal(sig, SIG_DFL)` is called to reset signal handling to the default, and then `(*func)(sig)` is called. The signal-handling function pointed to by `func` can terminate by executing a return statement or by calling `abort()`, `exit()`, or `longjmp()`.

Table F.10 lists the signal functions.

Table F.10   Signal functions.

Prototype	Description
`void (*signal(int sig, void (*func)(int)))(int);`	Causes the function pointed to by `func` to be executed if signal `sig` is raised. If possible, returns `func`; otherwise, returns `SIG_ERR`.
`int raise(int sig);`	Sends the signal `sig` to the executing program; returns zero if successful, and non-zero otherwise.

Variable Arguments: `stdarg.h`

The `stdarg.h` header file provides a means for defining a function having a variable number of arguments. The prototype for such a function should have a parameter list with at least one parameter followed by ellipses:

```
void f1(int n, ...);              /* valid   */
int f2(int n, const char * s, ...);  /* valid   */
double  f3(…);                     /* invalid */
```

In the following, the term *lastparm* is the identifier used for the last parameter preceding the ellipses. In the preceding examples, *lastparm* would be n for the first case and s for the second case.

The header file declares a `va_list` type to represent a data object used to hold the parameters corresponding to the ellipses part of the parameter list. Table F.11 lists three macros to be used in the function with the variable parameter list. An object of type `va_list` should be declared before using these macros.

Table F.11   Variable argument list macros.

Prototype	Description
`void va_start(va_list ap, `*lastparm*`);`	This macro initializes ap before use by `va_arg ()` and `va_end()`; *lastparm* is the identifier for the last named parameter in the argument list.
type `va_arg(va_list ap, `*type*`);`	This macro expands to an expression having the same value and type as the next item in the argument list represented by ap; *type* is the type for that item. Each call advances to the next item in ap.
`void va_end(va_list ap);`	This macro closes out the process and may render ap unusable without another call to `va_start()`.

Here is a short example of how the facilities can be used to create a function that sums a variable number of arguments; here, the first argument to `sum()` is the number of items to be summed.

```
#include <stdio.h>
#include <stdarg.h>
double sum(int, ...);
int main(void)
{
  double s,t;
  s = sum(3, 1.1 ,2.2,3.3);
  t = sum(6, 1.1,2.1,3.1,4.1,5.1,6.1);
  printf("%f %f\n", s, t);
  return 0;
}
```

```
double sum(int lim,...)
{
  va_list ap;                        /* declare object to hold arguments  */
  double tot = 0;
  int i;
  va_start(ap, lim);                 /* initialize ap to argument list    */
  for (i = 0; i < lim; i++)
      tot += va_arg(ap, double);     /* access each item in argument list */
  va_end(ap);                        /* clean up                          */
  return tot;
}
```

Standard I/O Library: `stdio.h`

The ANSI C standard library includes several standard I/O functions associated with streams and the `stdio.h` file. Table F.12 presents the ANSI prototypes for these functions along with a brief explanation of what they do. The header file also defines the `FILE` type, the values `EOF` and `NULL`, and the standard I/O streams `stdin`, `stdout`, and `stderr`, along with several constants used by the functions in this library.

Table F.12   ANSI C standard I/O functions.

Prototype	Description
`void clearerr(FILE *);`	Clears end-of-file and error indicators
`int fclose(FILE *);`	Closes the indicated file
`int feof(FILE *);`	Tests for end of file
`int ferror(FILE *);`	Tests error indicator
`int fflush(FILE *);`	Flushes the indicated file
`int fgetc(FILE *);`	Gets the next character from the indicated input stream
`int fgetpos(FILE *,`	Stores the current value `fpos_t *);` of the file position indicator
`char * fgets(char *,`	Gets the next line (or `int, FILE *);` indicated number of characters) from the indicated stream
`FILE * fopen(const char *, const char *);`	Opens the indicated file
`int fprintf(FILE *, const char *, ...);`	Writes the formatted output to the indicated stream
`int fputc(int, FILE *);`	Writes the indicated character to the indicated stream

continued on next page

continued from previous page

Prototype	Description
`int fputs(const char *, FILE *);`	Writes the character string pointed to by the first argument to indicated stream
`size_t fread(void *, size_t, size_t, FILE *);`	Reads binary data from the indicated stream
`FILE * freopen(const char *, const char *, FILE *);`	Opens the indicated file and associates it with the indicated stream
`int fscanf(FILE *, const char *, ...);`	Reads formatted input from the indicated stream
`int fsetpos(FILE *, const fpos_t *);`	Sets the file-position pointer to the indicated value
`int fseek(FILE *, long, int);`	Sets the file-position pointer to the indicated value
`long ftell(FILE *);`	Gets the current file position
`size_t fwrite(const void *, size_t, size_t, FILE *);`	Writes binary data to the indicated stream
`int getc(FILE *);`	Reads the next character from the indicated input
`int getchar();`	Reads the next character from the standard input
`char * gets(char *);`	Gets the next line from the standard input
`void perror(const char *);`	Writes system error messages to the standard error
`int printf(const char *, ...);`	Writes formatted output to the standard output
`int putc(int, FILE *);`	Writes the indicated character to the indicated output
`int putchar(int);`	Writes the indicated character to the standard output
`int puts(const char *);`	Writes the string to the standard output
`int remove(const char *);`	Removes the named file
`int rename(const char *, constchar *);`	Renames the named file
`void rewind(FILE *);`	Sets the file-position pointer to the start of the file
`int scanf(const char *, ...);`	Reads formatted input from the standard input
`void setbuf(FILE *, char *);`	Sets the buffer size and location
`int setvbuf(FILE *, char *, int, size_t);`	Sets the buffer size, location, and mode

Prototype	Description
`int sprintf(char *,` `const char *, ...);`	Writes formatted output to the indicated string
`int sscanf(const char *,` `const char *, ...);`	Reads formatted input from the indicated string
`FILE * tmpfile(void);`	Creates a temporary file
`char * tmpnam(char *);`	Generates a unique name for a temporary file
`int ungetc(int, FILE *);`	Pushes the indicated character back onto the input stream
`int vfprintf(FILE *,` `const char *, va_list);`	Like `fprintf();`, except uses a single list-argument of type `va_list` initialized by `va_start` instead of a variable argument list
`int vprintf(const char *,` `va_list);`	Like `printf();`, except uses a single list-argument of type `va_list` initialized by `va_start` instead of a variable argument list
`int vsprintf(char *,` `const char *, va_list);`	Like `sprintf();`, except uses a single list-argument of type `va_list` initialized by `va_start` instead of a variable argument list

General Utilities: `stdlib.h`

The ANSI C standard library includes a variety of utility functions defined in `stdlib.h`. The header file defines the types shown in Table F.13.

Table F.13   Types defined in `stdlib.h`.

Type	Description
`size_t`	The integer type returned by the `sizeof` operator.
`wchar_t`	The integer type used to represent wide characters.
`div_t`	The structure type returned by `div()`; it has a `quot` and a `rem` member, both of type `int`.
`ldiv_t`	The structure type returned by `ldiv()`; it has a `quot` and a `rem` member, both of type `long`.

The header file defines the constants listed in Table F.14.

Table F.14   Constants defined in `stdlib.h`.

Type	Description
NULL	The null pointer (equivalent to 0).
EXIT_FAILURE	Can be used as an argument to `exit()` to indicate unsuccessful execution of a program.
EXIT_SUCCESS	Can be used as an argument to `exit()` to indicate successful execution of a program.
RAND_MAX	The maximum value (an integer) returned by `rand()`.
MB_CUR_MAX	The maximum number of bytes for a multibyte character for the extended character set corresponding to the current locale.

Table F.15 lists the functions whose prototypes are found in `stdlib.h`.

Table F.15   General utilities.

Prototype	Description
`double atof(const char * nptr);`	Returns the initial portion of the string `nptr` converted to a type `double` value; conversion ends upon reaching the first character that is not part of the number; initial whitespace is skipped; zero is returned if no number is found.
`int atoi(const char * nptr);`	Returns the initial portion of the string `nptr` converted to a type `int` value; conversion ends upon reaching the first character that is not part of the number; initial whitespace is skipped; zero is returned if no number is found.
`int atol(const char * nptr);`	Returns the initial portion of the string `nptr` converted to a type `long` value; conversion ends upon reaching the first character that is not part of the number; initial whitespace is skipped; zero is returned if no number is found.
`double strtod(const char * npt, char **ept);`	Returns the initial portion of the string `nptr` converted to a type `double` value; conversion ends upon reaching the first character that is not part of the number; initial whitespace is skipped; zero is returned if no number is found; if conversion is successful, the address of the first character after the number is assigned to the location pointed to by `ept`; if conversion fails, `npt` is assigned to the location pointed to by `ept`.
`long strtol(const char * npt, char **ept, int base);`	Returns the initial portion of the string `nptr` converted to a type `long` value; conversion ends upon reaching the first character that is not part of the number; initial whitespace

Prototype	Description
	is skipped; zero is returned if no number is found; if conversion is successful, the address of the first character after the number is assigned to the location pointed to by ept; if conversion fails, npt is assigned to the location pointed to by ept; the number in the string is assumed to be written in a base specified by base.
unsigned long strtoul(const char * npt, char **ept, int base);	Returns the initial portion of the string nptr converted to a type unsigned long value; conversion ends upon reaching the first character that is not part of the number; initial whitespace is skipped; zero is returned if no number is found; if conversion is successful, the address of the first character after the number is assigned to the location pointed to by ept; if conversion fails, npt is assigned to the location pointed to by ept; the number in the string is assumed to be written in a base specified by base.
int rand(void);	Returns a pseudorandom integer in the range 0 to RAND_MAX.
void srand(unsigned int seed);	Sets the random-number generator seed to seed; if rand() is called before a call to srand(), the seed is 1.
void *calloc(size_t nmem, size_t size);	Allocates space for an array of nmem members, each element of which is size bytes in size; all bits in the space are initialized to 0; the function returns the address of the array if successful, and NULL otherwise.
void free(void *ptr);	Deallocates the space pointed to by ptr; ptr should be a value previously returned by a call to calloc(), malloc(), or realloc(), or ptr can be the null pointer, in which case no action is taken; the behavior is undefined for other pointer values.
void *malloc(size_t size);	Allocates an uninitialized block of memory of size bytes; the function returns the address of the array if successful, and NULL otherwise.
void *realloc(void *ptr, size_t size);	Changes the size of the block of memory pointed to by ptr to size bytes; the contents of the block up to the lesser of the old and new sizes are unaltered; the function returns the location of block, which may have been moved; if space cannot be reallocated, the function returns NULL and leaves the original block unchanged; if ptr is NULL, the behavior is the same as calling malloc() with an argument of size; if size is zero and ptr is not NULL, the behavior is the same as calling free() with ptr as an argument.

continued on next page

continued from previous page

Prototype	Description
`void abort(void);`	Causes abnormal program termination unless the signal `SIGABRT` is caught and the corresponding signal handler does not return; closing of I/O streams and temporary files is implementation-dependent; the function executes `raise(SIGABRT)`.
`int atexit(void (*func)(void));`	Registers the function pointed to by `func` to be called upon normal program termination; the implementation should support registration of at least 32 functions, which will be called opposite the order in which they are registered; the function returns zero if registration succeeds, and non-zero otherwise.
`void exit(int status);`	Causes normal program termination to occur, first invoking the functions registered by `atexit()`, then flushing all open output streams, then closing all I/O streams, then closing all files created by `tmpfile()`, and then returning control to the host environment; if `status` is `0` or `EXIT_SUCCESS`, an implementation-defined value indicating successful termination is returned to the host environment; if `status` is `EXIT_FAILURE`, an implementation-defined value indicating unsuccessful termination is returned to the host environment; the effect of other values of `status` is implementation-defined.
`char *getenv(const char * name);`	Returns a pointer to a string representing the value of the environmental variable pointed to by `name`; returns `NULL` if it cannot match the specified `name`.
`int system(const char *str);`	Passes the string pointed to by `str` to the host environment to be executed by a command processor, such as `DOS` or `UNIX`; if `str` is the `NULL` pointer, the function returns non-zero if a command processor is available, and zero otherwise; if `str` is not `NULL`, the return value is implementation-dependent.
`void *bsearch(const void *key, const void *base, size_t nmem, size_t size, int (*comp)(const void *, const void *));`	Searches an array pointed to by `base` having `nmem` members of size `size` for an element matching the object pointed to by `key`; items are compared by the function pointed to by `comp`; the comparison function shall return a value less than zero if the key object is less than an array element, zero if they are equivalent, and more if the key object is greater; the function returns a pointer to a matching element, or `NULL` if no element matches; if two or more elements match the key, it is unspecified which of the matching elements will be selected.

Prototype	Description
`void qsort(void *base, size_t nmem, size_t size, int (*comp) (const void *, const void *));`	Sorts the array pointed to by `base` in the order provided by the function pointed to by `comp`; the array has `nmem` elements each of `size` bytes; the comparison function shall return a value less than zero if the object pointed to by the first argument is less than the object pointed to by the second argument, zero if the objects are equivalent, and more if the first object is greater.
`int abs(int n);`	Returns the absolute value of `n`; the return value may be undefined if `n` is a negative value with no positive counterpart, which can happen if `n` is `INT_MIN` in two's complement representation.
`div_t div(int numer, int denom);`	Computes the quotient and remainder from dividing `numer` by `denom`, placing the quotient in the `quot` member of a `div_t` structure and the remainder in the `rem` member; for inexact division, the quotient is the integer of lesser magnitude that is nearest the algebraic quotient (that is, truncate toward zero).
`long labs(int n);`	Returns the absolute value of `n`; the return value may be undefined if `n` is a negative value with no positive counterpart, which can happen if `n` is `LONG_MIN` in two's complement representation.
`ldiv_t ldiv(long numer, long denom);`	Computes the quotient and remainder from dividing `numer` by `denom`, placing the quotient in the `quot` member of a `ldiv_t` structure and the remainder in the `rem` member; for inexact division, the quotient is the integer of lesser magnitude that is nearest the algebraic quotient (that is, truncate toward zero).
`int mblen(const char *s, size_t n);`	Returns the number of bytes (up to `n`) constituting the multibyte character pointed to by `s`, returns `0` if `s` points to the null character, returns `-1` if `s` does not point to a multibyte character; if `s` is `NULL`, returns non-zero if multibyte characters have state-dependent encoding, and zero otherwise.
`int mbtowc(wchar_t *pw, const char *s, size_t n);`	If `s` is not `NULL`, determines the number of bytes (up to `n`) constituting the multibyte character pointed to by `s` and determines the type `wchar_t` code for that character; if `pw` is not `NULL`, assigns the code to the location pointed to be `pw`; returns the same value as `mblen(s, n)`.
`int wctomb(char *s, wchar_t wc);`	Converts the character code in `wc` to the corresponding multibyte character representation and stores it in the array pointed to by `s`, unless `s` is `NULL`; if `s` is not `NULL`, returns `-1` if `wc` does not correspond to a valid multibyte chararacter or, if `wc` is valid, the

continued on next page

continued from previous page

Prototype	Description
	number of bytes constituting the multibyte character; if **s** is NULL, returns non-zero if multibyte characters have state-dependent encoding, and zero otherwise.
`size_t mbstowcs(wchar_t *pwcs, const char *s, size_t n);`	Converts the array of multibyte characters pointed to by s to an array of wide character codes stored at the location beginning at **pwcs**; conversion proceeds up to n elements in the **pwcs** array or a null byte in the s array, whichever occurs first; if an invalid multibyte character is encountered, returns `(size_t)(-1)`; otherwise, returns the number of array elements filled (excluding a null character, if any).
`size_t wcstombs(char *s, const wchart_t *pwcs, size_t n);`	Converts the sequence of wide-character codes stored in the array pointed to by **pwcs** into a multibyte character sequence copied to the location pointed to by **s**, stopping after storing n bytes or a null character, whichever comes first; if an invalid wide character code is encountered, returns `(size_t)(-1)`; otherwise, returns the number of array bytes filled (excluding a null character, if any).

String Handling: `string.h`

The `string.h` library defines the `size_t` type and the NULL macro for the null pointer. It provides several functions for analyzing and manipulating character strings and a few that deal with memory more generally. Table F.16 lists the functions.

Table F.16   Localization functions.

Prototype	Description
`void *memchr(const void *s, int c, size_t n);`	Searches for the first occurrence of c (converted to unsigned char) in the initial n characters of the object pointed to by s; returns a pointer to the first occurrence, NULL if none is found.
`int memcmp(const void *s1, const void *s2, size_t n);`	Compares the first n characters of the object pointed to by s1 to the first n characters of the object pointed to by s2, interpreting each value as unsigned char; the two objects are identical if all n pairs match; otherwise, the objects compare as the first unmatching

Prototype	Description
	pair; returns zero if the objects are the same, less than zero if the first object is numerically less than the second, and greater than zero if the first object is greater.
`void *memcpy(void *s1, const void *s2, size_t n);`	Copies n bytes from the location pointed to by s2 to the location pointed to by s1; behavior is undefined if the two locations overlap; returns the value of s1.
`void *memmove(void *s1, const void *s2, size_t n);`	Copies n bytes from the location pointed to by s2 to the location pointed to by s1; behaves as if copying; first uses a temporary location so that copying to an overlapping location works; returns the value of s1.
`void *memset(void *s, int v, size_t n);`	Copies the value v (converted to type `unsigned char`) to the first n bytes pointed to by s; returns s.
`char *strcat(char *s1, const char *s2);`	Appends a copy of the string pointed to by s2 (including the null character) to the location pointed to by s1; the first character of the s2 string overwrites the null character of the s1 string; returns s1.
`char *strncat(char *s1, const char *s2, size_t n);`	Appends a copy up to n characters or up to the null character from the string pointed to by s2 to the location pointed to by s1, with the first character of s2 overwriting the null character of s1; a null character is always appended; the function returns s1.
`char *strcpy(char *s1, const char *s2);`	Copies the string pointed to by s2 (including the null character) to the location pointed to by s1; returns s1.
`char *strncpy(char *s1, const char *s2, size_t n);`	Copies up to n characters or up to the null character from the string pointed to by s2 to the location pointed to by s1; if the null character in s2 occurs before n characters are copied, null characters are appended to bring the total to n; if n characters are copied before reaching a null character, no null character is appended; the function returns s1.
`int strcmp(const char *s1, const char *s2);`	Compares the strings pointed to by s1 and s2; two strings are identical if all pairs match; otherwise, the strings compare as the first unmatching pair; characters are compared using the character code values; the function returns zero if the strings are the same, less than zero if the first string is less than the second, and greater than zero if the string array is greater.

continued on next page

continued from previous page

Prototype	Description
`int strcoll(const char *s1, const char *s2);`	Works like `strcmp()` except that it uses the collating sequence specified by the `LC_COLLATE` category of the current locale as set by the `setlocale()` function.
`int strncmp(const char *s1, const char *s2, size_t n);`	Compares up to the first n characters or up to the first null character of the arrays pointed to by s1 and s2; two arrays are identical if all tested pairs match; otherwise, the arrays compare as the first unmatching pair; characters are compared using the character code values; the function returns zero if the arrays are the same, less than zero if the first array is less than the second, and greater than zero if the first array is greater.
`size_t strxfrm(char *s1, const char *s2, size_t n);`	Transforms the string in s2 and copies up to n characters, including a terminating null character, to the array pointed to by s1; the criterion for the transformation is that two transformed strings will be placed in the same order by `strcmp()` as `strcoll()` would place the untransformed strings; the function returns the length of the transformed string (not including the terminal null character).
`char *strchr(const char *s, int c);`	Searches for the first occurrence of c (converted to char) in the string pointed to by s; the null character is part of the string; returns a pointer to the first occurrence, or NULL if none is found.
`size_t strcspn(const char *s1, const char *s2);`	Returns the length of the maximum initial segment of s1 that does not contain any of the characters found in s2.
`char *strpbrk(const char *s1, const char *s2);`	Returns a pointer to th elocation of the first character in s1 to match any of the characters in s2; returns NULL if no match is found.
`char *strrchr(const char *s, int c);`	Searches for the last occurrence of c (converted to char) in the string pointed to by s; the null character is part of the string; returns a pointer to the first occurrence, or NULL if none is found.
`size_t strspn(const char *s1, const char *s2);`	Returns the length of the maximum initial segment of s1 that consists entirely of characters from s2.

Prototype	Description
`char *strstr(const char *s1, const char *s2);`	Returns a pointer to the location of the first occurrence in s1 of the sequence of characters in s2 (excluding the terminating null character); returns NULL if no match is found.
`char *strtok(char *s1, const char *s2);`	This function decomposes the string s1 into separate tokens; the string s2 contains the characters that are recognized as token separators. The function is called sequentially. For the initial call, s1 should point to the string to be separated into tokens. The function locates the first token separator that follows a non-separator character and replaces it with a null character. It returns a pointer to a string holding the first token. If no tokens are found, it returns NULL. To find further tokens in the string, call strtok() again, but with NULL as the first argument. Each subsequent call returns a pointer to the next token or to NULL if no further tokens are found. See the example following this table.
`char * strerror(int errnum);`	Returns a pointer to an implementation-dependent error message string corresponding to the error number stored in errnum.
`int strlen(const char * s);`	Returns the number of characters (excluding the terminating null character) in the string s.

The strtok() function is a bit unusual in how it is used, so here is a short example:

```c
#include <stdio.h>
#include <string.h>

int main(void)
{
    char data[] = "  C is\t  too#much\nfun!";
    const char tokseps[] = " \t\n#"; /* separators */
    char * pt;

    puts(data);
    pt = strtok(data,tokseps);        /* intial call */
    while (pt)                        /* quit on NULL */
    {
        puts (pt);                    /* show token   */
        pt = strtok(NULL, tokseps);   /* next token   */
    }
    return 0;
}
```

Here is the output:

```
C is     too#much
fun!
C
is
too
much
fun!
```

Date and Time: `time.h`

The `time.h` header file defines two macros. The first, also defined in many other header files, is `NULL`, representing the null pointer. The second macro is `CLOCKS_PER_SEC`; dividing the value returned by `clock()` by this macro yields time in seconds.

The header file defines the types listed in Table F.17.

Table F.17   Types defined in `time.h`.

Type	Description
size_t	The integer type returned by the `sizeof` operator.
clock_t	An arithmetic type suitable to represent time.
time_t	An arithmetic type suitable to represent time.
struct tm	A structure type for holding components of calendar time.

The components of the calendar type are referred to as *broken-down time*. Table F.18 lists the required members of a `struct tm` structure.

Table F.18   Members of a `struct tm` structure.

Member	Description
int tm_sec	Seconds after the minute (0–61)
int tm_min	Minutes after the hour (0–59)
int tm_hour	Hours after midnight (0–23)
int tm_mday	Day of the month (0–31)
int tm_mon	Months since January (0–11)
int tm_year	Years since 1900

Member	Description
int tm_wday	Days since Sunday (0–6)
int tm_yday	Days since January 1 (0–365)
int tm_isdst	Daylight Savings Time flag (greater than zero value means DST is in effect; zero means not in effect; negative means information not available)

The term *calendar time* represents the current date and time; for example, it could be the number of seconds elapsed since the first second of 1900. The term *local time* is the calendar time expressed for a local time zone. Table F.19 lists the time functions.

Table F.19   Time functions.

Prototype	Description
clock_t clock(void);	Returns the implementation's best approximation to the processor time elapsed since the program was invoked; divide by CLOCKS_PER_SEC to get the time in seconds; returns (clock_t)(-1) if the time is not available or representable.
double difftime(time_t t1, time_t t0);	Calculates the difference (t1 - t0) between two calendar times, expresses the result in seconds, and returns the result.
time_t mktime(struct tm *tmptr);	Converts the broken-down time in the structure pointed to by tmptr into a calendar time; having the same encoding used by the time() function, the structure is altered in that out-of-range values are adjusted (for example, 2 minutes, 100 seconds becomes 3 minutes, 40 seconds) and tm_wday and tm_yday are set to the values implied by the other members; returns (time_t)(-1) if the calendar time cannot be represented; otherwise, returns the calendar time in time_t format.
time_t time(time_t *ptm)	Returns the current calendar time and also places it in the location pointed to by ptm, providing ptm is not NULL; returns (time_t)(-1) if the calendar time is not available.
char *asctime(const struct tm *tmpt);	Converts the broken-down time in the structure pointed to by tmpt into a string of the form Thu Feb 26 13:14:33 1998\n\0 and returns a pointer to that string.
char *ctime(const time_t *ptm); Wed Aug 11 10:48:24 1999\n\0	Converts the calendar time pointed to by ptm into a string of the form and returns a pointer to that string.

continued on next page

continued from previous page

Prototype	Description
`struct tm *gmtime(const time_t *ptm);`	Converts the calendar time pointed to by `ptm` into a broken-down time, expressed as Coordinated Universal Time (UCT), and returns a pointer to a structure holding that information; returns `NULL` if UTC is not available.
`struct tm *localtime(const time_t *ptm);`	Converts the calendar time pointed to by `ptm` into a broken-down time, expressed as local time; stores a `tm` structure and returns a pointer to that structure.
`size_t strftime(char *s, size_t max, const char *fmt, const struct tm *tmpt);`	Copies string `fmt` to string s, replacing format specifiers (see Table F.20) in `fmt` with appropriate data derived from the contents of the broken-down time structure pointed to by `tmpt`; no more than `max` characters are placed into `s`; the function returns the number of characters placed (excluding the null character); if the resulting string (including null character) is larger than `max` characters, the function returns `0` and the contents of `s` are indeterminate.

Table F.20 shows the format specifiers used by the `strftime()` function. Many replacement values, such as month names, depend on the current locale.

Table F.20   Format specifiers used by the `strftime()` function.

Format Specifier	Replaced By
%a	Locale's abbreviated weekday name
%A	Locale's full weekday name
%b	Locale's abbreviated month name
%B	Locale's full month name
%c	Locale's appropriate date and time designation
%d	Day of the month as a decimal number (01–31)
%H	The hour (24-hour clock) as a decimal number (00–23)
%I	The hour (12-hour clock) as a decimal number (01–12)
%j	The day of the year as a decimal number (001–366)
%m	The month as a decimal number (01–12)
%M	The minute as a decimal number (00–59)
%p	Locale's equivalent of AM/PM for 12-hour clock

Format Specifier	Replaced By
%S	The second as a decimal number (00–61)
%U	Week number of the year, counting Sunday as the first day of week 1 (00–53)
%w	Weekday as a decimal, beginning with Sunday (0–6)
%W	Week number of the year, counting Monday as the first day of week 1 (00–53)
%x	The locale's date representation
%X	The locale's time representation
%y	The year without century as a decimal number (00–99)
%Y	The year with century as a decimal number
%Z	The time zone name or by no characters if the information is not available
%%	% (that is, the percent sign)

DIFFERENCES BETWEEN C AND C++

For the most part, C++ is a superset of C, meaning that a valid C program is also a valid C++ program. The main differences between C++ and C are the many additional features that C++ supports. However, there are a few areas in which the C++ rules are slightly different from the C equivalents. These are the differences that might cause a C program to work a little differently, or perhaps not at all, if you compile it as a C++ program. And they are the differences this appendix discusses. If you compile your C programs using a compiler that does just C++ and not C, you need to know about these differences. Although they affect very few of the examples in this book, the differences can cause some instances of valid C code to lead to error messages if the code is compiled as a C++ program.

Declarations

C requires that all variables other than function parameters be declared at the beginning of a block, that is, just after an opening brace. C++ removes this restriction, and the C++ practice is to declare a variable at the point it first gets a value. C++ even allows you to declare a variable in the initialization slot of a `for` statement. For example, the following code is valid C++:

```
#include <stdio.h>
int main()
{
    puts("Enter a value for n:");
    int n;                        /* valid C++, invalid C */
    scanf("%d", &n);
    for (int i = 0; i < n; i++)   /* valid C++, invalid C */
    {
        puts("Thank you!");
        puts("Enter a word:");
        char word[40];            /* valid C++, invalid C */
        scanf("%s", word);
        printf("%s is ok.\n", word);
    }
    return 0;
}
```

It is not, however, valid C. So if you've found your compiler allows you to write code like the preceding example, it is working in the C++ mode.

C allows you to omit `int` in some declarations; C++ does not. However, omitting `int` in C is considered poor style and is forbidden in C9X. In the following, `const` is interpreted as `const int`, `unsigned` is interpreted as `unsigned int`, and `floobie()` has return type `int`.

```
const que = 88;    /* poor style in C, illegal in C++ */
unsigned jay = 2; /* poor style in C, illegal in C++ */
floobie(double);   /* poor style in C, illegal in C++ */
```

Normally, it is an error to initialize an array using more values than the size of the array. However, C (but not C++) allows one exception. You can initialize an array of `char` to a string literal that is one character longer (counting the null character) than the array. In that case, the null character is not copied, so the array holds characters, but not a string:

```
char rare[3] = "ton";        /* ok C, invalid C++      */
char rare[3] = {'t','o','n'}; /* C, C++ valid equivalent */
```

Function Prototypes

In C++, function prototyping is mandatory, but it is optional in C. This difference shows up if you leave the parentheses empty when declaring a function. In C, empty parentheses mean you are foregoing prototyping, but in C++ they mean the function has no prototypes. That is, in C++, the prototype

```
int slice();
```

means the same as the following:

```
int slice(void);
```

For example, the following sequence is acceptable, if old-fashioned, C but an error in C++:

```
int slice();
int main()
{
...
    slice(20, 50);
...
}
int slice(int a, int b)
{
...
}
```

In C, the compiler assumes you used the older form for declaring functions. In C++, the compiler assumes that `slice()` is the same as `slice(void)` and that you failed to declare the `slice(int, int)` function.

Also, C++ allows you to declare more than one function of the same name, providing they have different argument lists.

Function Definitions

Although this book has used the ANSI C format for function declarations, C still recognizes the old format. C++, however, only recognizes the new format.

```
int twilf(q, n)   /* old-fashioned C, illegal C++ */
int q;            /* declare argument types here  */
int n;
{
    return (q - n) / (q * n);
}
```

Comments

C++ allows comments that begin with // and end with the end of the line:

```
int rank;    // rank goes from 0 (lowest) to 10
```

The C90 standard doesn't allow this comment format, but many compilers do. The C9X proposal recognizes this usage.

char Constants

C treats char constants as type int, and C++ treats them as type char. For instance, consider this statement:

```
char ch = 'A';
```

In C, the constant 'A' is stored in an int-sized chunk of memory; more precisely, the character code is stored in the int. The same numeric value is also stored in the variable ch, but here it occupies just one byte of memory.

C++, on the other hand, uses one byte for 'A' as well as for ch. This distinction doesn't affect any of the examples in this text. However, some C programs do make use of char constants being type int by using character notation to represent integer values. For instance, if a system has a 4-byte int, you can do this in C:

```
int x = 'ABCD';   /* ok in C for 4-byte int but not for C++ */
```

The meaning of 'ABCD' is a 4-byte int in which the first byte stores the character code for the letter A, the second byte stores the character code of B, and so on. Note that 'ABCD' is something quite different from "ABCD". The former is just a funny way of writing an int value, but the latter is a string and corresponds to the address of a 5-byte chunk of memory.

Consider the following code:

```
int x = 'ABCD';
char c = 'ABCD';
printf("%d %d %c %c\n", x, 'ABCD', c, 'ABCD');
```

On our system, it produces this output:

```
1094861636 1094861636 D D
```

This example illustrates that if you treat 'ABCD' as an int, it is a 4-byte integer value, but that if you treat it as type char, the program looks only at the final byte. Attempting to print 'ABCD' by using the %s specifier caused the program to crash on our system, because the numeric value of 'ABCD' (1094861636) was an out-of-bounds address.

The rationale for using values like 'ABCD' is that it provides a means to set each byte in the int independently because each character corresponds exactly to one byte. However, a better approach, because it doesn't depend on particular character codes, is to use hexadecimal values for integer constants, using the fact that each two-digit hexadecimal group corresponds to one byte. Chapter 15, "Bit Fiddling," discusses this technique. (Early versions of C didn't provide hexadecimal notation, which probably is why the multicharacter constant technique developed in the first place.)

The const Modifier

In C, a global const has external linkage, but in C++ it has internal linkage. That is, the C++ declaration

```
const double PI = 3.14159;
```

is equivalent to the C declaration

```
static const double PI = 3.14159;
```

providing both declarations are outside of any function. The C++ rule has the goal of making it simpler to use const in header files. If the constant has internal linkage, then each file that includes the header file gets its own copy of the constant. If a constant has external linkage, then one file has to have a defining declaration and the other files have to have a reference declaration, one that uses the keyword external.

Incidentally, C++ can use the keyword extern to make a const value have external linkage, so both languages can create constants with internal linkage and external linkage. The difference is just in which kind of linkage is used by default.

One additional property of the C++ const is that it can be used to declare an array size:

```
const int ARSIZE = 100;
double loons[ARSIZE];   /* ok in C++, not in C */
```

Structures and Unions

After you declare a structure or union having a tag, you can use the tag as a type name in C++:

```
struct duo
{
    int a;
    int b;
};
struct duo m;  /* valid C, C++ */
duo n;         /* invalid C, valid C++ */
```

As a result, a structure name can conflict with a variable name. For example, the following program compiles as a C program, but it fails as a C++ program because C++ interprets the duo in the printf() statement as a structure type rather than as the external variable:

```
#include <stdio.h>
float duo = 100.3;
int main(void)
{
    struct duo { int a; int b;};
    struct duo y = { 2, 4};
    printf ("%f\n", duo);    /* ok in C, not in C++ */
    return 0;
}
```

In C and in C++, you can declare one structure inside another:

```
struct box
{
    struct point {int x; int y; } upperleft;
    struct point lowerright;
};
```

In C, you can use either structure later, but C++ requires a special notation for the nested structure:

```
struct box ad;      /* valid C, C++          */
struct point dot;   /* valid C, invalid C++ */
box::point dot;     /* invalid C, valid C++ */
```

Enumerations

C++ is stricter about using enumerations than C is. In particular, about the only useful things you can do with an enum variable are assign an enum constant to it and compare it to other values. You can't assign ints to an enum without an explicit type cast, and you can't increment an enum variable.

```
enum sample {sage, thyme, salt, pepper};
enum sample season;
season = sage;            /* ok in C, C++                */
season = 2;               /* warning in C, error in C++ */
season = (enum sample) 3; /* ok in C, C++                */
season++;                 /* ok in C, error in C++       */
```

Also, C++ lets you drop the keyword **enum** when declaring a variable:

```
enum sample {sage, thyme, salt, pepper};
sample season;    /* invalid C, valid C++ */
```

As was the case with structures and unions, this can lead to conflicts if a variable and an **enum** type have the same name.

Pointer Type-Checking

C++ is stricter about pointer assignments than C is. You can't assign a pointer of one type or a numeric value to a pointer of a second type unless you use an explicit type cast.

```
int x;
int * pi;
short *ps;
pi = &x;              /* ok, both type int      */
pi = 0xB8000;         /* ok in C, invalid in C++ */
pi = (int *) 0xB8000; /* ok in C, C++           */
ps = pi;              /* ok in C, invalid in C++ */
ps = (short *) pi;    /* ok in C, C++           */
```

There are a couple of exceptions. In C++, as in C, you can assign a pointer of any type to a pointer-to-**void**, but, unlike C, you cannot assign a pointer-to-**void** to another type unless you use an explicit type cast.

```
int ar[5] = {4, 5, 6,7, 8};
int * pi;
void * pv;
pv = ar;           /* ok in C, C++            */
pi = pv;           /* ok in C, invalid in C++ */
pi = (int * ) pv;  /* ok in C, C++            */
```

The other exception in C++ is that you can assign the address of a derived-class object to a base-class pointer, but that relates to features that don't even exist in C.

APPENDIX H

THE C9X COMMITTEE

The C9X committee is preparing a revised standard for C. The changes from the C90 to the C9X standard are much fewer than the changes from K&R C to the ANSI C90 standard. The two main thrusts are to make the language more international and to fix a few deficiencies in the language. This appendix discusses many of the C9X changes. Keep in mind that at the time of writing, the committee is still working on the new standard and that some of the proposals presented here could very well change before the final standard emerges. This appendix is just a snapshot of the current state of revisions to the C standard.

Types

C9X adds two new types in response to technology growth. Also, it increases support for type portability. That is, it offers portable ways to deal with, say, `int` being different sizes on different platforms.

New Types

C9X adds the `long long` and `unsigned long long` types to the C language. As 64-bit processors begin to move into the mainstream and as storage devices with larger capacities become available, the `long` type, with its guaranteed 32-bit minimum capacity, may no longer be adequate. The `long long` and `unsigned long long` types have the means to store 64-bit values.

Extended Integers: Portable Types

Suppose you have a program that needs a 32-bit integer type. On some systems, `int` will work, but on others, it won't. The `long` type is guaranteed to be at least 32 bits, but that raises the possibility it might be even more than 32 bits. What can you do? You could try to emulate how C handles the return time for the `sizeof` operator. C, recall, uses a `typedef` to define `size_t` as the appropriate integer type for a system. You could do something like this:

```
typedef int int32bit;
```

Your program could then use the `int32bit` type instead of `int`. If you moved to a system that needed a different type, you could just change the `typdef` statement and recompile.

C9X proposes a header file, `inttypes.h`, that takes precisely this approach, using `typedef` to create names that identify types with precise properties. These types are termed *extended integers*.

Exact Width Types

One set of `typedef`s identify types with precise sizes. Table H.1 lists the names and sizes. Note, however, that not all systems may be able to support all the types. For instance, there could be a system for which the smallest usable memory size is 16 bits; such a system would not support the `int8_t` or `uint8_t` types.

Table H.1   Exact width types.

typedef Name	Properties
int8_t	8 bits signed
int16_t	16 bits signed
int32_t	32 bits signed
int64_t	64 bits signed
uint8_t	8 bits unsigned
uint16_t	16 bits unsigned
uint32_t	32 bits unsigned
uint64_t	64 bits unsigned

Minimum Width Types

The minimum width types guarantee a type that is at least a certain number of bits in size. Table H.2 lists the minimum width types. These types always exist. For instance, a system that does not support 8-bit units could define `int_least_8` as a 16-bit type.

Table H.2   Minimum width types.

typedef Name	Properties
int_least8_t	At least 8 bits signed
int_least16_t	At least 16 bits signed
int_least32_t	At least 32 bits signed
int_least64_t	At least 64 bits signed
uint_least8_t	At least 8 bits unsigned

typedef Name	Properties
uint_least16_t	At least 16 bits unsigned
uint_least32_t	At least 32 bits unsigned
uint_least64_t	At least 64 bits unsigned

Fastest Minimum Width Types

For a particular system, some integer representations can be faster than others. For example, int_least16_t might be implemented as short, but the system might do arithmetic faster using type int. So inttypes.h also defines the fastest type for representing at least a certain number of bits. Table H.3 lists the fastest minimum width types. These types always exist. In some cases, there might be no clear-cut choice for fastest; in that case, the system simply specifies one of the choices.

Table H.3   Fastest minimum width types.

typedef Name	Properties
int_fast8_t	At least 8 bits signed
int_fast16_t	At least 16 bits signed
int_fast32_t	At least 32 bits signed
int_fast64_t	At least 64 bits signed
uint_fast8_t	At least 8 bits unsigned
uint_fast16_t	At least 16 bits unsigned
uint_fast32_t	At least 32 bits unsigned
uint_fast64_t	At least 64 bits unsigned

Maximum Width Types

The inttypes.h header file also defines maximum width types. A variable of this type can hold any integer value possible for the system, taking the sign into account. Table H.4 lists the types.

Table H.4   Maximum width types.

typedef Name	Properties
intmax_t	The widest signed type
uintmax_t	The widest unsigned type

Integers That Can Hold Pointer Values

The `inttypes.h` header file also has two integer types, listed in Table H.5, that can hold pointer values accurately. That is, if you assign a type `void *` value to one of these types, and then assign the integer type back to the pointer, no information is lost. Either or both types might not exist.

Table H.5   Integer types for holding pointer values.

typedef Name	Properties
intptr_t	Signed type can hold a pointer value
uintptr_t	Unsigned type can hold a pointer value

Defined Constants

Just as `limits.h` defines constants representing the minimum and maximum values of the fundamental C types, `inttypes.h` defines constants representing limiting values for the types defined in that header file. The constants are named after the type. Take the type name, replace the _t with _MIN or _MAX, and make all the characters uppercase to get the name of the constant representing the minimum or maximum value for the type. For example, the smallest value for the `int32_t` type is `INT32_MIN`, and the largest value for the `uint_fast16_t` type is `UINT_FAST16_MAX`.

Extended Integer Constants

You can indicate a long constant with the L suffix, as in `445566L`. How do you indicate that a constant is type `int32_t`? Use macros defined in `inttypes.h`. For instance, the expression `INT32_C(445566)` expands to a type `int32_t` constant. Essentially, the macro is a type cast to the underlying type, that is, to the fundamental type that represents `int32_t` in a particular implementation.

The macro names are formed by taking the type name, replacing the _t with _C, and making all the letters uppercase. For example, to make `1000` a type `uint_least64_t` constant, use the expression `UINT_LEAST64_C(1000)`.

Reading and Displaying Extended Integers

You can read an unsigned `int` value and display it by using the `%u` specifier, as in the following:

```
unsigned int dogs;
scanf("%u", &dogs);
printf("I count %u dogs.\n", dogs);
```

How can you handle extended integers? For instance, type `uint32_t` might be `unsigned int`, requiring the `%u` specifier, or it might be `unsigned long`, requiring the `%ul` specifier. Once again, `inttypes.h` supplies special macros to facilitate using extended types. Here's how you might use them with the `uint32_t` type:

```
uint32_t dogs;
scanf(SCNu32, &dogs);
printf("I count " PRIu32 "dogs.\n", dogs);
```

The macro expands to a string. For instance, `.\n".` might expand to the string `"%ul"`. C's string concatenation then combines the three strings used by `.\n".` into the single string `"I count %ul dogs.\n"`.

The name of the macro depends on whether it is for the `scanf()` family, in which case the macro begins with `SCN`, or for the `printf()` family, in which case the macro begins with `PRI`.

Next, if it is a `printf()` macro for a signed type, the name uses a `d` or `i` (in honor of the `%d` and `%i` specifiers). Then the macro name ends in uppercase letters and numbers based on the name of the extended type. For instance, the macro for specifying `intmax_t` is `PRIdMAX`. The macro for specifying `int_fast16_t` is `PRIdFAST16`, and so on.

The scheme for unsigned types is similar, except that the letter following the `PRI` is `u` (for the `%u` specifier), `o` (for the `%o` specifier), `x` (for the `%x` specifier) or `X` (for the `%X` specifier). Therefore, to print a type `uint_LEAST16_t` value in base ten, use `PRIuLEAST16`. To print in hex using uppercase letters, use `PRIXLEAST16`.

The macros for input use the same scheme, except that you use `SCN` instead of `PRI` and there is no `X` specifier for input. Therefore, to read a type `int_FAST32_t` value, use the `SCNdFAST32` macro. To read a type `uint_32` value, use `SCNu32`. To read a `uint_32` value that is to be entered in hexadecimal format, use `SCNx32`.

Enhanced Computational Support

Historically, FORTRAN has been the premier language for numerical scientific and engineering computation. C90 brought C computational methods into closer agreement with FORTRAN. For example, the specification of floating-point characteristics used in `float.h` is based on the model developed by the FORTRAN standardization committee. The C9X continues the work of enhancing C's appropriateness for computational work.

The `fenv.h` Header File

The `fenv.h` header file provides a means of interacting with the floating-point environment. That is, it allows you to set floating-point *control mode values* that govern how floating-point calculations take place, and it allows you to determine the value of floating-point *status flags* that report information about the effects of an arithmetic calculation. An example of a control mode setting is specifying the method used to round numbers. An example of a status flag is a flag that is set if an operation produces floating-point overflow.

The status flags and control modes are meaningful only if the hardware supports them. For instance, you can't change the rounding method if the hardware doesn't have that option.

By default, access to the floating-point environment is off. You use a preprocessor directive to turn support on:

```
#pragma STDC FENV_ACCESS ON
```

Support stays on until the program reaches the end of the block containing the pragma, or, if the pragma is external, to the end of the file or translation unit. Or you can use the following directive to turn off support:

```
#pragma STDC FENV_ACCESS OFF
```

This facility is important for those involved in critical floating-point calculations, but of limited interest to the general user, so this appendix doesn't go into the details.

Additions to the `math.h` Library

The C90 math library, for the most part, declares functions with type **double** arguments and type **double** return values, such as the following

```
double sin(double);
double sqrt(double);
```

The C9X library provides type **float** and type **long float** versions of all these functions. These functions use an **f** or an **l** suffix in the name, as follows:

```
float sinf(float);            /* float version of sin()       */
long double sinl(long double);  /* long double version of sin() */
```

Having function families with different levels of precision allows you to choose the most efficient combination of types and functions needed for a particular purpose.

C9X also adds several functions commonly used in scientific, engineering, and mathematical computations. Table H.6 lists the **double** versions for several of the new functions. All have type **float** and type **long double** counterparts, as described previously. In many cases, the functions return values that could be calculated using existing functions, but the new functions do so faster or more accurately. For instance, `log1p(x)` represents the same value as `log(1 + x)`, but `log1p(x)` uses a different algorithm, one that is more accurate for small values of **x**. So you would use the `log()` function for calculations in general, but you would use `log1p()` for small values of **x** if high accuracy were critical. The table refers to **FLT_RADIX**. This constant, defined in **float.h**, is the base used for exponentiation in the internal floating-point representation. The most common value is **2**.

Table H.6   New math library functions.

Prototype	Description
`double exp2(double x);`	Returns 2 to the x power
`double expm1(double x);`	Returns $e^x - 1$
`double logp1(double x);`	Returns $\log(1 + x)$

Prototype	Description
`double log2(double x);`	Returns the base 2 logarithm of x
`double logb(double x);`	Returns the signed exponent of its argument for the underlying base used to represent floating-point values on the system (`FLT_RADIX`)
`double scalbn(double x, int n);`	Returns x × FLT_RADIX^n
`double scalbln(double x, long n);`	Returns x × FLT_RADIX^n
`double ilogb(double x);`	Same as `logb()` except it returns the exponent as an `int`
`double cbrt(double x);`	Returns the cube root of x
`double hypot(double x, double y);`	Returns the square root of the sums of the squares of x and y
`double erf(double x);`	Returns the error function of x
`double erfc(double x);`	Returns the complementary error function of x
`double gamma(double x);`	Returns the gamma function of x
`double lgamma(double x);`	Returns the natural logarithm of the absolute value of the gamma function of x
`double copysign(double x, double y);`	Returns the value of x with the sign of y
`double fdim(double x, double y);`	Returns the absolute value of x − y

In addition to these functions, the math library defines several constants and functions relating to classifying numbers and rounding them. For example, a value can be classified as being infinite, not a number (NaN), normal, subnormal, and true zero. (A *NaN* is a special value indicating that a value is not a number; for example, `asin(2.0)` returns NaN because `asin()` is defined only for arguments in the range -1 to 1. A subnormal number is one whose magnitude is smaller than the smallest value that can be represented to full precision.) There are also specialized comparison functions that behave differently from the standard relational operators when one or more arguments are abnormal values. In short, there is expanded support for detailed control of how floating-point calculations are handled.

Support for Complex Numbers

A *complex number* is a number with a real part and an imaginary part. The real part is an ordinary real number, such as what's represented by the floating-point types. The imaginary part, naturally, is an imaginary number. An imaginary number, in turn, is a multiple of the square root of -1. In mathematics, complex numbers are often written in the form `4.2 + 2.0i`; *i* symbolically represents the square root of -1.

C9X supports three complex types:

- `float complex`
- `double complex`
- `long double complex`

A `float complex` value, for example, would be stored using the same memory layout as a two-element array of `float`, with the real value stored in the first element and the imaginary value in the second element.

C9X implementations may also support three imaginary types:

- `float imaginary`

- `double imaginary`

- `long double imaginary`

You should include the `complex.h` header file before using the keywords `complex` and `imaginary`; the effect of failing to do so is undefined.

Arithmetic operations are defined for complex types following the usual rules of mathematics. For example, the value of `(a+b*I)*(c+d*I)` is `(a*c-b*d)+(b*c+a*d)*I`.

The `complex.h` header file defines some macros and several functions that accept complex numbers and return complex numbers. In particular, the macro `I` represents the square root of -1. It enables you to do the following:

```
double complex c1 = 4.2 + 2.0 * I;
float imaginary c2= -3.0 * I;
```

The `complex.h` header file prototypes several complex functions. Many are complex equivalents of `math.h` functions, using a `c` prefix. For example, `csin()` returns the complex sine of its complex argument. Others relate specifically to the features of complex numbers. For example, `creal()` returns the real part of an complex number, and `cimag()` returns the imaginary part as a real number. That is, given that `z` is type `double complex`, then the following is true:

```
z = creal(z) + cimag(z) * I;
```

If you are familiar with complex numbers and need to use them, you'll want to peruse the contents of `complex.h`. If you use C++, you should be aware that the C++ `complex` header file provides a different way, based on classes, of handling complex numbers than does the C `complex.h` header file.

The `restrict` Keyword

The `restrict` keyword enhances computational support by giving the compiler permission to optimize certain kinds of code. It can be applied only to pointers, and it indicates that a pointer is the sole initial means of accessing a data object. Consider the following:

```
int ar[10];
restrict int * restar = (int *) malloc(10 * sizeof(int));
int * par = ar;
```

Here, the pointer `restar` is the sole initial means of access to the memory allocated by `malloc()`. Therefore, it can be qualified with the keyword `restrict`. The pointer `par`, however, is neither the initial nor the sole means of access to the data in the `ar` array, so it cannot be qualified as `restrict`.

Now consider the following rather artificial example, in which n is an int:

```
for (n = 0; n < 10; n++)
{
    par[n]  += 5;
    restar[n] += 5;
    ar[n]  *= 2;
    par[n]  += 3;
    restar[n] += 3;
}
```

Knowing that restar is the sole initial means of access to the block of data it points to, the compiler can replace the two statements involving restar with a single statement having the same effect:

```
restar[n] += 8;    /* ok replacement */
```

It would be a computational error, however, to condense the two statements involving par to one:

```
par[n] += 8;     / * gives wrong answer */
```

The reason it gives the wrong answer is that the loop uses ar to change the value of the data between the two times par accesses the same data.

Without the restrict keyword, the compiler has to assume the worse case; namely, that some other identifier might have changed the data in between two uses of a pointer. With the restrict keyword used, the compiler is free to look for calculational shortcuts.

You can use the restrict keyword as a qualifier for function parameters that are pointers. This means the compiler can assume that no other identifiers modify the pointed-to data within the body of the function and that the compiler can try optimizations it might not otherwise use. For example, the C library has two functions for copying bytes from one location to another. Under C9X, they have these prototypes:

```
void * memcpy(void * restrict s1, const restrict s2, size_t n);
void * memmove(void * s1, const s2, size_t n);
```

Each copies n bytes from location s2 to location s1. The memcpy() function requires that there be no overlap between the two locations, but memmove() doesn't have that requirement. Declaring s1 and s2 as restrict means each pointer is a sole means of access, so they can't access the same block of data. This matches the requirement that there be no overlap. The memmove() function, which allows overlap, has to be more careful about copying data so that it doesn't overwrite data before it is used.

Wide Character Support

Supporting larger character sets is an important aspect of internationalizing C. C9X provides for a wchar_t type and a host of related functions for dealing with larger character sets.

The stddef.h header file defines wchar_t as an integer type; the exact type is implementation dependent. Its intended use is to hold characters from an extended character set that is a superset of the basic character set. By definition, the `char` type is sufficient to handle the basic character set. The `wchar_t` type may need more bits to handle a greater range of code values. For example, `char` might be an 8-bit byte and `wchar_t` might be a 16-bit `unsigned short`.

Wide-character constants and string literals are indicated with an `L` prefix, and you can use the `%lc` and `%ls` modifiers to display wide-character data:

```
wchar_t wch = L'I';
wchar_t w_arr[20] = L"am wide!";
printf("%lc %ls\n", wch, w_arr);
```

If, for example, `wchar_t` is implemented as a 2-byte unit, then the 1-byte code for `'I'` would be stored in the low-order byte of `wch`. Characters not from the standard set might require both bytes to hold the character code. You could use hexadecimal escape sequences, for example, to indicate characters whose code values exceed the `char` range:

```
wchar_t w = L'\x2f48'; /* 16-bit code value */
```

An array of `wchar_t` values can hold a wide-character string, with each element holding a single wide-character code. A `wchar_t` value with a code value of `0` is the `wchar_t` equivalent of the null character, and it is termed a *null wide character*. It is used to terminate wide-character strings.

You can use the `%lc` and `%ls` specifiers to read wide characters:

```
wchar_t wch;
wchar_t w_arr[20];
puts("Enter your grade:");
scanf("%lc", &wch);
puts("Enter your first name:");
scanff("%ls",w_arr);
```

The `wchar.h` header file offers further wide-character support. In particular, it provides wide-character I/O functions, wide-character conversion functions, and wide-character string manipulation functions. For the most part, they are wide-character equivalents of existing functions. For example, you can use `fwprintf()` and `wprintf()` for output and `fwscanf()` and `wscanf()` for input. The main differences are that these functions require a wide-character control string and they deal with input and output streams of wide characters. For example, the following displays information as a sequence of wide characters:

```
wchar_t * pw = L"Points to a wide-character string";
int dozen = 12;
wprintf(L"Item %d: %ls\n", dozen, pw);
```

Similarly, there are `getwchar()`, `putwchar()`, `fgetws()`, and `fputws()` functions. The header defines a `WEOF` macro that plays the same role that `EOF` does for byte-oriented I/O. It's required to be a value that does not correspond to a valid character. Because it is possible that all values of `wchar_t` type are valid characters, the library defines a `wint_t` type that can encompass all `wchar_t` values plus `WEOF`.

There are equivalents to the `string.h` library functions. For example, `wcscpy(ws2, ws1)` copies the wide-character string pointed to by `ws1` to the wide-character array pointed to by `ws2`. Similarly, there is a `wcscmp()` function for comparing wide strings, and so on.

The `wctype.h` header file adds character-classification functions to the mix. For example, `iswdigit()` returns true if its wide-character argument is a digit, and the `isblank()` function returns true if its argument is a blank. The standard values for a blank are a space, written as `L' '`, and a horizontal tab, written as `L'\t'`.

APPENDIX I

ANSWERS TO THE REVIEW QUESTIONS

Chapter 1

1. A perfectly portable program is one whose source code can, without modification, be compiled to a successful program on a variety of different computer systems.

2. A source code file contains code as written in whatever language the programmer is using. An object code file contains machine language code; it need not be the code for a complete program. An executable file contains the complete code, in machine language, constituting an executable program.

3.   a. Defining program objectives.

     b. Designing the program.

     c. Coding the program.

     d. Compiling the program.

     e. Running the program.

     f. Testing and debugging the program.

     g. Maintaining and modifying the program.

4. A compiler converts source code, such as code in the C language, to machine language code.

5. A linker combines object code from several sources, such as compiled source code and compiled library code, into a single, executable program.

Chapter 2

1. They are called functions.

2. A syntax error is a violation of the rules governing how sentences or programs are put together. Here's an example in English: "Me speak English good." Here's an example in C:

```
printf"Where are the parentheses?";.
```

3. A semantic error is one of meaning. Here's an example in English: "This sentence is excellent Italian." Here's a C example:

```
thrice_n = 3 + n;
```

4. Line 1: Begin the line with a `#`; spell the file `stdio.h`; place the filename within angle brackets.

   Line 2: Use `()`, not `{}`; end comment with `*/`, not `/*`.

   Line 3: Use `{`, not `(`.

   Line 4: Complete the statement with a semicolon.

   Line 5: Mr. I.B.M. got this one (the blank line) right!

   Line 6: Use `=`, not `:=` for assignment. (Apparently, Mr. I.B.M. knows a little Pascal.) Use 52, not 56, weeks per year.

   Line 7: Should be

```
printf("There are %d weeks in a year.\n", s);
```

   Line 9: There isn't a line 9, but there should be, and it should consist of the closing brace, `}`.

   Here's how the code looks after these changes:

```
#include <stdio.h>
int main(void) /* this prints the number of weeks in a year */
{
    int s;

    s = 52;
    printf("There are %d weeks in a year.\n", s);
    return 0;
}
```

5.   a. `Baa Baa Black Sheep.Have you any wool?`

   (Note that there is no space after the period. You could have had a space by using `" Have` instead of `"Have`.)

   b.

```
Begone!
O creature of lard!
```

   (Note that the cursor is left at the end of the second line.)

   c.

```
What?
No/nBonzo?
```

   (Note that the slash (`/`) does not have the same effect as the backslash `\`; it simply prints as a slash.)

   d. `2 + 2 = 4`

(Note how each %d is replaced by the corresponding variable value from the list. Note, too, that + means addition and that calculation can be done inside a `printf()` statement.)

6. `int` and `char` (`main` is a function name, and = is an operator).

7. `printf("There were %d words and %d lines.\n", words, lines);`

8. After line 7, a is 5 and b is 2. After line 8, both a and b are 5. After line 9, both a and b are still 5. Note that a can't be 2 because by the time you say `a = b;`, b has already been changed to 5.

Chapter 3

1.   a. `int`, possibly `short` or `unsigned` or `unsigned short`; population is a whole number.

   b. `float`; it's unlikely the average will be an exact integer. (You could use `double` but don't really need the extra precision.)

   c. `char`.

   d. `int`, possibly `unsigned`.

2. One reason is that `long` may accommodate larger numbers than `int` on your system; another reason is that if you do need to handle larger values, you improve portability by using a type guaranteed to be at least 32 bits on all systems.

3.   a. `char` constant (but stored as type `int`)

   b. `int` constant

   c. `double` constant

   d. `unsigned int` constant, hexadecimal format

   e. `double` constant

4. Line 1: Should be `#include <stdio.h>`.

   Line 2: Should have a pair of parentheses containing `void` following `main`; that is, `main(void)`.

   Line 3: Use `{`, not `(`.

   Line 4: Should be a comma, not a semicolon, between g and h.

   Line 5: Fine.

   Line 6: (blank) Fine.

   Line 7: There should be at least one digit before the e. Either `1e21` or `1.0e21` is okay.

Line 8: Fine.

Line 9: Use }, not).

Missing lines: First, `rate` is never assigned a value. Second, the variable h is never used. Also, the program never informs you of the results of its calculation. Neither of these errors will stop the program from running (although you might be given a warning about the unused variable), but they do detract from its already limited usefulness. Also, there should be a `return` statement at the end.

Here is one possible correct version:

```
#include <stdio.h>
int main(void)
{
    float g, h;
    float tax, rate;

    rate = 0.08;
    g = 1.0e21;
    tax = rate*g;
    h = g + tax;
    printf("You owe $%f plus $%f in taxes for a total of $%f.\n", g,
tax, h);
    return 0;
}
```

5.

	Constant	Type	Specifier
a.	12	int	%d
b.	0X3	unsigned int	%X
c.	'C'	char (really int)	%c
d.	2.34E07	double	%e
e.	'\040'	char (really int)	%c
f.	7.0	double	%f
g.	6L	long	%ld
h.	6.0f	float	%f

6.

	Constant	Type	Specifier
a.	012	unsigned int	%o
b.	2.9e05L	long double	%Le
c.	's'	char (really int)	%c
d.	100000	long	%ld
e.	'\n'	char (really int)	%c
f.	20.0f	float	%f
g.	0x44	unsigned int	%x

7.

```
printf("The odds against the %d were %ld to 1.\n", imate, shot);
printf("A score of %f is not an %c grade.\n", log, grade);
```

8.

```
ch = '\r';
ch = 13;
ch = '\015'
ch = '\xd'
```

9. Line 0: It's better form to have #include <stdio.h>.

Line 1: Use /* and */.

Line 3: int cows, legs;

Line 5: count?\n");

Line 6: %d, not %c

Line 6: &legs

Line 8: %d, not %f

Add a return statement.

Here's one correct version:

```
#include <stdio.h>
int main(void) /* this program is perfect */
{
  int cows, legs;
  printf("How many cow legs did you count?\n");
```

```
        scanf("%d", &legs);
        cows = legs / 4;
        printf("That implies there are %d cows.\n", cows);
        return 0;
     }
```

10.   a. newline character

       b. a slash character

       c. a double quotation mark

       d. a tab character

Chapter 4

1. The program bombs. The first `scanf()` statement reads just your first name, leaving your last name untouched but still stored in the input "buffer." (This buffer is just a temporary storage area used to store the input.) When the next `scanf()` statement comes along looking for your weight, it picks up where the last reading attempt ended, and tries to read your last name as your weight. This frustrates `scanf()`. On the other hand, if you respond to the name request with something like `Lasha 144`, it uses 144 as your weight, even though you typed it before your weight was requested.

2.   a. `He sold the painting for $234.50.`

       b. `Hi!`

(Note: The first character is a character constant, the second is a decimal integer converted to a character, and the third is an ASCII representation of a character constant.)

       c.

```
His Hamlet was funny without being vulgar.
has 42 characters.
```

       d. `Is 1.20e+003 the same as 1201.00?`

3. Use `\"`, as in the following:

```
printf("\"%s\"\nhas %d characters.\n", Q, strlen(Q));
```

4. Here is a corrected version:

```
#include <stdio.h>    /* don't forget this     */
#define B "booboo"    /* add #, quotes         */
#define X 10          /* add #                 */
int main(void)        /* instead of main(int)  */
```

```
{
    int age;
    int xp;            /* declare all variables */
    char name[40];     /* make into an array     */

    printf("Please enter your first name.\n"); /* \n for readability */
    scanf("%s", name);
    printf("All right, %s, what's your age?\n", name); /* %s for
➥string */
    scanf("%d", &age);         /* %d, not %f, &age, not age */
    xp = age + X;
    printf("That's a %s! You must be at least %d.\n", B, xp);
    return 0;                  /* not rerun              */
}
```

5. Recall the `%%` construction for printing `%`.

   ```
   printf("This copy of \"%s\" sells for $%0.2f.\n", BOOK, cost);

   printf("That is %0.0f%% of list.\n", percent);
   ```

6. a. `%d`

   b. `%4X`

   c. `%10.3f`

   d. `%12.2e`

   e. `%-30s`

7. a. `%15lu`

   b. `%#4x`

   c. `%-12.2E`

   d. `%+10.3f`

   e. `%8.8s`

8. a. `%6.4d`

   b. `%*o`

   c. `%2c`

   d. `%+0.2f`

   e. `%-7.5s`

9. a.
   ```
   int dalmations;
       scanf("%d", &dalmations);
   ```

   b.
   ```
   float kgs, share;
       scanf("%f%f", &kgs, &share);
   ```

Note: For input, **e**, **f**, and **g** can be used interchangeably. Also, for all but %c, it makes no difference if you leave spaces between the conversion specifiers.

c.

```
char name[20];
   scanf("%s", name);
```

d.

```
char action[20];
    int value;
    scanf("%s %d", action, &value);
```

e.

```
int value;
    scanf("%*s %d", &value);
```

10. Whitespace consists of spaces, tabs, and newlines; C uses whitespace to separate tokens from one another; scanf() uses whitespace to separate consecutive input items from each other.

11. The substitutions would take place. Unfortunately, the preprocessor cannot discriminate between those parentheses that should be replaced with braces and those that should not. Therefore,

```
#define ( {
#define ) }
int main(void)

(
     printf("Hello, O Great One!\n");
)
<AP>          becomes
int main{void}
{
     printf{"Hello, O Great One!\n"};
}
```

Chapter 5

1.   a. **30**

      b. **27** (not 3). (12 + 6)/(2*3) would give **3**.

      c. **x = 1, y = 1** (integer division)

      d. x = 3 (integer division) and **y = 9**

2.   a. **6** (reduces to **3 + 3.3**)

   b. **52**

   c. **0** (reduces to **0 * 22.0**)

   d. **13** (reduces to **66.0 / 5** or **13.2**, then assigned to **int**)

3. Line 0: Should include **<stdio.h>**.

   Line 3: Should end in a semicolon, not a comma.

   Line 6: The **while** statement sets up an infinite loop because the value of i remains 1 and is always less than **30**. Presumably we meant to write **while(i++ < 8)**.

   Lines 6–8: The indentation implies that we wanted lines 7 and 8 to form a block, but the lack of braces means that the **while** loop includes only line 7. Braces should be added.

   Line 7: Because 1 and i are both integers, the result of the division will be 1 when i is 1, and **0** for all larger values. Using n = **1.0/i;** would cause i to be converted to floating-point before division and would yield non-zero answers.

   Line 8: We omitted a newline character (\n) in the control statement. This causes the numbers to be printed on one line, if possible.

   Line 10: Should be **return 0;**.

   Here is a corrected version:

```
#include <stdio.h>
int main(void)
{
   int i = 1;
   float n;
   printf("Watch out! Here come a bunch of fractions!\n");
   while (i++ < 30)
   {
      n = 1.0/i;
      printf(" %f\n", n);
   }
   printf("That's all, folks!\n");
   return 0;
}
```

4. The main problem lies in the relationship between the test statement (is **sec** greater than 0?) and the **scanf()** statement that fetches the value of **sec**. In particular, the first time the test is made, the program hasn't had a chance to even get a value for **sec**, and the comparison will be made to some garbage value that happens to be at that memory location. One solution, albeit an inelegant one, is to initialize **sec** to, say, 1 so that the test is passed the first time through. This uncovers a second problem.

When you finally type **0** to halt the program, **sec** doesn't get checked until after the loop is finished, and the results for 0 seconds are printed out. What you really want is to have a **scanf()** statement just before the **while** test is made. You can accomplish that by altering the central part of the program to read this way:

```
    scanf("%d", &sec);
while ( sec > 0 ) {
  min = sec/S_TO_M;
  left = sec % S_TO_M;
  printf("%d sec is %d min, %d sec. \n", sec, min, left);
  printf("Next input?\n");
  scanf("%d", &sec);
  }
```

The first time through, the **scanf()** outside the loop is used. Thereafter, the **scanf()** at the end of the loop (and hence just before the loop begins again) is used. This is a common method for handling problems of this sort.

5. Here is the output:

```
%s is a string
 is a string
1
1
2
1
```

Let's explain. The first **printf()** statement is the same as this:

```
printf("%s is a string\n","%s is a string\n");
```

The second print statement first increments **num** to **1** and then prints the value. The third print statement prints **num**, which is **1**, and then increments it to **2**. The fourth print statement prints the current value of **n**, which still is **2**, and then decrements **n** to **1**. The final print statement prints the current value of **n**, which is **1**.

6. Here is the output:

```
DAD:3 3.00
```

The expression **c1** - **c2** has the same value as **'D'** - **'A'**, which in ASCII is **68** - **65**.

7. It prints on one line the digits 1 through 10 in fields that are five columns wide and then starts a new line:

```
    1    2    3    4    5    6    7    8    9   10
```

8. Here is one possibility:

```
#include <stdio.h>
```

```
int main(void)
{
    char c = 'a';
    while (c <= 'g')
        printf("%5c", c++);
    printf("\n");
    return 0;
}
```

9. Here is the output for each example:

    a.   1   2

Note that x is incremented and then compared. The cursor is left on the same line.

    b.

```
101
102
103
104
```

Note that this time x is compared and then incremented. In both this case and in example a., x is incremented before printing takes place. Note, too, that indenting the second printf() statement does not make it part of the while loop. Therefore, it is called only once, after the while loop ends.

    c. stuvw

Here, there is no incrementing until after the first printf().

10. This is an ill-constructed program. Because the while statement doesn't use braces, only the printf() statement is part of the loop, so the program prints the message COMPUTER BYTES DOG indefinitely until you can kill the program.

11.   a. x = x + 10;

    b. x++';   or ++x;   or x = x + 1;

    c. c = 2 * (a + b);

    d. c = a + 2* b;

12.   a. x--';   or --x;   or x = x - 1;

    b. m = n % k;

    c. p = q / (b - a);

    d. x = (a + b) / (c * d);

Chapter 6

1. 2, 7, 70, 64, 8, 2

2. It would produce the following output:

   36 18   9   4   2   1

3. a. x > 5

    b. scanf("%lf",&x) != 1

    c. x == 5

4. a. scanf("%d", &x) == 1

    b. x != 5

    c. x >= 20

5. Line 4: Should be list[10].

    Line 6: Commas should be semicolons.

    Line 6: Range for i should be from 0 to 9, not 1 to 10.

    Line 9: Commas should be semicolons.

    Line 9: >= should be <=. Otherwise, when i is 1, the loop never ends.

    Line 10: There should be another closing brace between lines 9 and 10. One brace closes the compound statement, and one closes the program. In between should be a return 0; line.

    Here's a corrected version:

```
#include <stdio.h>
int main(void)
{                                   /* line 3  */
  int i, j, list[10];               /* line 4  */

  for (i = 0; i <  10;  i++)        /* line 6  */
  {                                 /* line 7  */
      list[i] = 2*i + 3;            /* line 8  */
      for (j = 1; j <= i; j++)      /* line 9  */
          printf(" %d", list[j]);   /* line 10 */
      printf("\n");                 /* line 11 */
  }
  return 0;
}
```

6. Here's one way:

```
#include <stdio.h>
int main(void)
```

```
{
    int col, row;

    for (row = 1; row <= 4; row++)
    {
        for (col = 1; col <= 8; col++)
            printf("$");
        printf("\n");
    }
    return 0;
}
```

7. a. It would produce the following output:

Hi! Hi! Hi! Bye! Bye! Bye! Bye! Bye!

b. It would produce the following output:

ACGM

8. a. It would produce the following output:

Saddle up my char

b. It would produce the following output:

Tbeemf!vq!nz!dibs

c. It would produce the following output:

Saddle up my charg

d. It would produce the following output:

$addle up my char

9. Here is the output we get:

```
11121314
***
1
4
7

***
1 5
2 7
4 9
8 11

***
+++++
++++
+++
++
```

10. a. mint

b. 10 elements

c. type double values

d. Both i. and iii. are correct. In i., mint is the same as &mint[0].

11. Because the first element has index 0, the loop range should be 1 to SIZE - 1, not 1 to SIZE. Making that change, however, causes the first element to be assigned the value 0 instead of 2. So rewrite the loop this way:

```
for (index = 0; index < SIZE; index++)
    by_twos[index] = 2 * (index + 1);
```

Similarly, the limits for the second loop should be changed. Also, an array index should be used with the array name:

```
for( index = 0; index < SIZE; index++)
    printf("%d ", by_twos[index]);
```

One dangerous aspect of bad loop limits is that the program may work; however, because it is placing data where it shouldn't, it might not work at some time in the future, forming sort of a programming time bomb.

12. It should declare the return type as long, and it should have a return statement that returns a long value.

13. Typecasting num to long makes sure the calculation is done as a long calculation, not an int calculation. On a system with a 16-bit int, multiplying two ints produces a result that is truncated to an int before the value is returned, possibly losing data.

```
long square(int num)

{

    return ((long) num) * num;

}
```

14. Here is the output:

```
1: Hi!
k = 1
k is 1 in the loop
Now k is 3
k = 3
k is 3 in the loop
Now k is 5
k = 5
k is 5 in the loop
Now k is 7
k = 7
```

Chapter 7

1. True: b.

2.   a. `number >= 1 && number < 9`

   b. `ch != 'q' && ch != 'k'`

   c. `(number >= 1 && number <= 9) && number != 5`

   d. `!( (number >= 1 && number <= 9) or else number < 1 || number > 9`

3. Line 5: Should be `scanf("%d %d", &weight, &height);`. Don't forget those &s for `scanf()`. Also, this line should be preceded by a line prompting input.

   Line 9: What is meant is (`height < 72 && height > 64`). However, the first part of the expression is unnecessary because height must be less than 72 for the `else if` to be reached in the first place. Therefore, a simple (`height > 64`) will serve.

   Line 11: The condition is redundant; the second subexpression (`weight` not less than or equal to 300) means the same as the first. A simple (`weight > 300`) is all that is needed. But there is more trouble. Line 11 gets attached to the wrong `if`! Clearly, this `else` is meant to go along with line 6. By the most recent `if` rule, however, it will be associated with the `if` of line 9. Therefore, line 11 is reached when `weight` is less than 100 and `height` is 64 or under. This makes it impossible for `weight` to exceed 300 when this statement is reached.

   Lines 7 through 9: Should be enclosed in braces. Then line 11 will become an alternative to line 6, not to line 9.

   Line 12: Simplify to `if (height > 48)`.

   Line 14: This `else` associates with the last `if`, the one on line 12. Enclose lines 12 and 13 in braces to force this `else` to associate with the `if` of line 11. Note that the final message is printed only for those weighing between 100 and 300 pounds.

   Here's a corrected version:

```
#include <stdio.h>
int main(void)                                        /* 1  */
{                                                      /* 2  */
   int weight, height;  /* weight in lbs, height in inches */
                                                       /* 4  */
   printf("Enter your weight in pounds and ");
   printf("your height in inches.\n");
   scanf("%d %d", &weight, &height);                  /* 5  */
   if (weight < 100)                                  /* 6  */
```

```
{
    if (height >= 72)                                   /* 7  */
        printf("You are very tall for your weight.\n");
    else if (height > 64)                               /* 9  */
        printf("You are tall for your weight.\n");
}
else if (weight > 300)                                  /* 11 */
{
    if (height < 48)                                    /* 12 */
        printf(" You are quite short for your weight.\n");
}
else                                                    /* 14 */
    printf("Your weight is ideal.\n");                  /* 15 */
                                                        /* 16 */
    return 0;
}
```

4.   a. 1. The assertion is true, which numerically is a 1.

b. 0. 3 is not less than 2.

c. 1. If the first expression is false, the second is true, and vice versa; just one true expression is needed.

d. 6, because the value of 6 > 2 is 1.

e. 10, because the test condition is true.

f. 0. If x > y is true, the value of the expression is y > x, which is false in that case, or 0. If x > y is false, the value of the expression is x > y, which is false in that case.

5. The program prints the following:

`*#%*#%$#%*#%*#%$#%*#%*#%$#%*#%*#%`

Despite what the indentation suggests, the # is printed during every loop because it is not part of a compound statement.

6. The program prints the following:

```
MerryMerrMerOh no!
MerrMerOh no!
MerOh no!
```

7. The comments on lines 5 through 7 should be terminated with */. The expression 'a' <= ch >= 'z' should be replaced with this:

`ch >= 'a' && ch <= 'z'`

Or, more simply and more portably, include ctype.h and use islower(). Incidentally, 'a' <= ch >= 'z' is valid C; it just doesn't have the right meaning. Because relational operators associate left to right, the expression is interpreted as ('a' <= ch) >= 'z'. The expression in parentheses has the value 1 or 0 (true or false), and this value is checked to see whether it is equal to or greater than the numeric code for 'z'. Neither 0 nor 1 satisfies that test, so the whole expression always evaluates to 0 (false). In the second test expression, ¦¦ should be &&. Also, although !(ch < 'A') is both valid and correct in meaning, ch >= 'A' is simpler. The 'Z' should be followed by two closing parentheses, not one. Again, more simply, use isupper(). The oc++; statement should be preceded by an else. Otherwise, it is incremented every character. The control expression in the printf() call should be enclosed in double quotes.

Here is a corrected version:

```c
#include <stdio.h>
#include <ctype.h>
int main(void)
{
   char ch;
   int lc = 0;      /* lowercase char count */
   int uc = 0;      /* uppercase char count */
   int oc = 0;      /* other char count     */

   while ((ch = getchar()) != '#')
   {
        if (islower(ch))
              lc++;
        else if (isupper(ch))
              uc++;
        else
              oc++;
   }
   printf("%d lowercase, %d uppercase, %d other", lc, uc, oc);
   return 0;
}
```

8. Unhappily, it prints the same line indefinitely:

```
You are 65. Here is your gold watch.
```

The problem is that the line

```
if (age = 65)
```

sets age to 65, which tests as true, every loop cycle.

9. Here is the resulting run using the given input:

```
q
Step 1
Step 2
Step 3
c
Step 1
g
Step 1
Step 3
b
Step 1
Done
```

Note that both b and # terminate the loop, but that entering b elicits the printing of Step 1, and entering # doesn't.

10. Here is one solution:

```c
#include <stdio.h>
int main(void)
{
  char ch;

  while ((ch = getchar()) != '#')
  {
    if (ch != '\n')
    {
        printf("Step 1\n");
        if (ch == 'b')
            break;
        else if (ch != 'c')
        {
            if (ch != 'g')
                printf("Step 2\n");
            printf("Step 3\n");
        }
    }
  }
  printf("Done\n");
  return 0;
}
```

Chapter 8

1. The statement `putchar(getchar());` causes the program to read the next input character and to print it; the return value from `getchar()` is the argument to `putchar()`. No, `getchar(putchar())` is invalid because `getchar()` doesn't use an argument and `putchar()` needs one.

2.   a. Display the H character.

       b. Sound the alert if the system uses ASCII.

       c. Move the cursor to the beginning of the next line.

       d. Backspace.

3. `count <essay >essayct or else count >essayct <essay`

4. Just c. is valid.

5. It's a signal (a special value) returned by `getchar()` and `scanf()` to indicate that they have detected the end of a file.

6.   a. The output is as follows:

    `If you qu`

Note that the character `I` is distinct from the character `i`. Also note that the `i` is not printed because the loop quits upon detecting it.

    b. The output for ASCII is as follows:

`HJacrthjacrt`

The first time through, `ch` has the value `H`. The `ch++` causes the value to be used (printed) and then incremented (to `I`). Then the `++ch` causes the value to be incremented (to `J`) and then used (printed). After that, the next character (`a`) is read, and the process is repeated. An important point to note here is that the incrementations affect the value of `ch` after it has been assigned a value; they don't somehow cause the program to move through the input queue.

7. C's standard I/O library maps diverse file forms to uniform streams that can be handled equivalently.

8. Numeric input skips over spaces and newlines, but character input does not. Suppose you have code like this:

```
int score;
char grade;
printf("Enter the score.\n");
scanf("%s", %score);
printf("Enter the letter grade.\n");
grade = getchar();
```

If you enter **98** for the score, then press the Enter key to send the score to the program, you also sent a newline character, which becomes the next input character and is read into **grade** as the grade value. If you precede character input with numeric input, you should add code to dispose of the newline character before the character input takes place.

Chapter 9

1. A formal argument is a variable that is defined in the function being called. The actual argument is the value appearing in the function call; this value is assigned to the formal argument. You can think of the actual argument as being the value to which the formal argument is initialized when the function is called.

2.   a. `void donut(int n)`

    b. `int gear(int t1, int t2)`

    c. `void stuff_it(double d, double *pd)`

3.   a. `char n_to_char(int n)`

          b. `int digits(double x, int n)`

          c. `int random(void)`

4.

```
int sum(int a, int b)
{
    return a + b;
}
```

5. Replace `int` with `double` throughout:

```
double sum(double a, double b)

{

    return a + b;

}
```

6. This function needs to use pointers:

```
void alter(int * pa, int * pb)
{
    int temp;
    temp = *pa + *pb;
    *pb = *pa - *pb;
    *pa = temp;
}
```

or

```
void alter(int * pa, int * pb)
{
    *pa += *pb;
    *pb = *pa - 2 * *pb;
}
```

7. Yes; num should be declared in the `salami()` argument list, not after the brace. Also, it should be `count++`, not `num++`.

8. Here is one solution:

```
int largest(int a, int b, int c)

{
    int max = a;
    if (b > max)
        max = b;
    if (c > max)
        max = c;
    return max;
}
```

9. Here is the minimal program; the `showmenu()` and `getchoice()` functions are possible solutions to parts a. and b.

```
#include <stdio.h>
void showmenu(void);       /* declare functions used */
int getchoice(int, int);
main()
{
    int res;

    showmenu();
    while ((res = getchoice(1,4)) != 4)
        printf("I like choice %d.\n", res);
    printf("Bye!\n");
    return 0;
}
void showmenu(void)
{
    printf("Please choose one of the following:\n");
    printf("1) copy files          2) move files\n");
    printf("3) remove files        4) quit\n");
    printf("Enter the number of your choice:\n");
}

int getchoice(int low, int high)
{
    int ans;
    scanf("%d", &ans);
    while (ans < low || ans > high)
    {
        printf("%d is not a valid choice; try again\n", ans);
        showmenu();
        scanf("%d", &ans);
    }
    return ans;
}
```

Chapter 10

1. The printout is this:

D D

O O

L L

T T

2. The array `ref` has an external storage class; it is a global variable with external linkage.

3. The array name `ref` points to the first element of the array, the character D. The expression `ref + 1` points to the second element, the character O. The construction `++ref` is not a valid C expression; `ref` is a constant, not a variable.

4. `ptr` points to the first element, and `ptr + 2` points to the third element, which would be the first element of the second row.

    a. 12 and 16

    b. 12 and 14 (just the 12 goes in the first row because of the braces)

5. `ptr` points to the first row and `ptr+1` points to the second row; `*ptr` points to the first element in the first row, and `*(ptr + 1)` points to the first element of the second row.

    a. 12 and 16

    b. 12 and 14 (just the 12 goes in the first row because of the braces)

6.   a. `&grid[22][56]`

    b. `&grid[22][0]` or `grid[22]`

(The latter is the name of a one-dimensional array of 100 elements, hence the address of its first element, which is the element `grid[22][0]`.)

    c. `&grid[0][0]` or `grid[0]` or `(int *) grid`

(Here `grid[0]` is the address of the `int` element `grid[0][0]`, and `grid` is the address of the 100-element array `grid[0]`. The two addresses have the same numeric value but different types; the typecast makes the types the same.)

7.   a. `int digits[10];`

    b. `float rates[6];`

    c. `int mat[3][5];`

    d. `char (*pstr)[20];`

Note

`char *pstr[20];` is incorrect. This would make `pstr` an array of pointers instead of a pointer to an array. In particular, `pstr` would point to a single `char`, the first member of the array; `pstr + 1` would point to the next byte. With the correct declaration, `pstr` is a variable rather than an array name, and `pstr + 1` points 20 bytes beyond the initial byte.

e. `char * psa[20];`. Note that the `[ ]` have higher precedence than `*`, so in the absence of parentheses, the array descriptor is applied first, then the pointer descriptor. Hence, this declaration is the same as `char *(psa[20]);`.

8. a. `int sextet[6] = {1, 2, 4, 8, 16, 32};`

  b. `sextet[2]`

9. 0 through 9

10. a. `rootbeer[2] = value;`

Valid

  b. `scanf("%f", &rootbeer );`

Invalid; `rootbeer` is not a `float`.

  c. `rootbeer = value;`

Invalid; `rootbeer` is not a `float`.

  d. `printf("%f", rootbeer);`

Invalid; `rootbeer` is not a `float`.

  e. `things[4][4] = rootbeer[3];`

Valid

  f. `things[5] = rootbeer;`

Invalid; can't assign arrays.

  g. `pf = value;`

Invalid; `value` is not an address.

  h. `pf = rootbeer;`

Valid

Chapter 11

1. The initialization should include a `'/0'`. Also, pre-ANSI implementations don't allow you to initialize automatic arrays.

2.
```
See you at the snack bar.
ee you at the snack bar.
See you
e you
```

3.

y

my

mmy

ummy

Yummy

4. `I read part of it all the way through.`

5.   a. `Ho Ho Ho!!oH oH oH`

    b. pointer-to-char, that is, `char *`.

    c. The address of the initial H.

    d. `*--pc` means to decrement the pointer by 1 and use the value found there. `--*pc` means to take the value pointed to by `pc` and decrement that value by 1 (for example, H becomes G).

    e. `Ho Ho Ho!!oH oH o`

Note

A null character comes between ! and !, but it produces no printing effect.

    f. `while(*pc)`. Check to see that `pc` does not point to a null character (that is, to the end of the string). The expression uses the value at the pointed-to location.

    `while(pc - str)`. Check to see that `pc` does not point to the same location that `str` does (the beginning of the string). The expression uses the values of the pointers themselves.

    g. After the first `while` loop, `pc` points to the null character. Upon entering the second loop, it is made to point to the storage location before the null character, that is, to the location just before the one that `str` points to. That byte is interpreted as a character and is printed. The pointer then backs up to the preceding byte. The terminating condition (`pc == str`) never occurs, and the process continues until you or the system tire.

    h. `pr()` must be declared in the calling program: `char *pr(char *);`

6. Character variables occupy a byte, but a character constant is stored in an `int`, meaning the `'$'` typically would use 2 or 4 bytes; however, only 1 byte of the `int` is actually used to store the code for `'$'`. The string `"$"` uses 2 bytes: one to hold the code for `'$'`, and one to hold the code for `'\0'`.

7. Here is what you get:

```
How are ya, sweetie? How are ya, sweetie?
Beat the clock.
eat the clock.
Beat the clock. Win a toy.
Beat
chat
hat
at
t
t
at
How are ya, sweetie?
```

8. Here is what you get:

```
faavrhee
*le*on*sm
```

9. Here is one solution:

```
int strlen(const char * s)

{

  int ct = 0;



  while (*s++ != '\0')       /* or while (*s++) */

      ct++;

  return(ct);

}
```

10. Here is one solution:

```
#include <stdio.h>       /* for NULL definition         */
char * strblk(char * string)
{
  while (*string != ' ' && *string != '\0')
     string++;                /* stops at first blank or null */
  if (*string == '\0')
     return NULL;             /* NULL is the null pointer     */
  else
     return string;
}
```

Here is a second solution that prevents the function from modifying the string but that allows the return value to be used to change the string. The expression (char *) string is called "casting away const."

```
#include <stdio.h>        /* for NULL definition       */
char * strblk(const char * string)
{
  while (*string != ' ' && *string != '\0')
    string++;              /* stops at first blank or null */
  if (*string == '\0')
    return NULL;           /* NULL is the null pointer    */
  else
    return (char *) string;
}
```

11. Here is one solution:

```
/* compare.c -- this will work */
#include <stdio.h>
#include <string.h>   /* declares strcmp() */
#include <ctype.h>
#define ANSWER "GRANT"
#define MAX 40
void ToUpper(char * str);
int main(void)
{
    char try[MAX];

    puts("Who is buried in Grant's tomb?");
    gets(try);
    ToUpper(try);
    while (strcmp(try,ANSWER) != 0)
    {
        puts("No, that's wrong. Try again.");
        gets(try);
        ToUpper(try);
    }
    puts("That's right!");
    return 0;
}

void ToUpper(char * str)
{
    while (*str != '\0')
    {
        *str = toupper(*str);
        str++;
    }
}
```

Chapter 12

1. It should have #include <stdio.h> for its file definitions. It should
   declare fp a file pointer: FILE *fp;. The function fopen() requires a
   mode: fopen("gelatin", "w") or perhaps the "a" mode. The order of

the arguments to `fputs()` should be reversed. For clarity, the output string should have a newline because `fputs()` doesn't add one automatically. The `fclose()` function requires a file pointer, not a filename: `fclose(fp);`. Here is a corrected version:

```c
#include <stdio.h>
int main(void)
{
    FILE * fp;
    int k;

    fp = fopen("gelatin", "w");
    for (k = 0; k < 30; k++)
        fputs("Nanette eats gelatin.\n", fp);
    fclose(fp);
    return 0;
}
```

2. It would open, if possible, the file whose name is the first command-line argument, and it would display onscreen each digit character in the file.

3. a. `ch = getc(fp1);`

    b. `fprintf(fp2,"%c"\n",ch);`

    c. `putc(ch,fp2);`

    d. `fclose(fp1); /* close the terky file */`

Note

fp1 is used for input operations because it identifies the file opened in the read mode. Similarly, fp2 was opened in the write mode, so it is used with output functions.

4. Here is one approach:

```c
#include <stdio.h>
#include <stdlib.h>
/* #include <console.h> */   /* for Macs */

int main(int argc,char * argv[])
{
    FILE * fp;
    double n;
    double sum = 0.0;
    int ct = 0;

/*   argc = ccommand(&argv);   */   /* For Macs */
    if (argc == 1)
        fp = stdin;
    else if (argc == 2)
```

```
    {
        if ((fp = fopen(argv[1], "r")) == NULL)
        {
            fprintf(stderr, "Can't open %s\n", argv[1]);
            exit(EXIT_FAILURE);
        }
    }
    else
    {
        fprintf(stderr, "Usage: %s [filename]\n", argv[0]);
        exit(EXIT_FAILURE);
    }
    while (fscanf(fp, "%lf", &n) == 1)
    {
        sum += n;
          ++ct;
    }
    if (ct > 0)
          printf("Average of %d values = %f\n", ct, sum / ct);
    else
          printf("No valid data.\n");

    return 0;
}
```

Macintosh C users, remember to use console.h and ccommand().

5. Here is one approach:

Macintosh C users, remember to use console.h and ccommand().

```
#include <stdio.h>
#include <stdlib.h>
/*  #include <console.h>  */   /* for Mac */
#define BUF 256
int has_ch(char ch, const char * line);
int main(int argc,char * argv[])
{
    FILE * fp;
    char ch;
    char line [BUF];

 /*  argc = ccommand(&argv); */  /* for Mac */
    if (argc != 3)
    {
        printf("Usage: %s character filename\n", argv[0]);
        exit(1);
    }
    ch = argv[1][0];
    if ((fp = fopen(argv[2], "r")) == NULL)
    {
        printf("Can't open %s\n", argv[2]);
        exit(1);
    }
```

```
while (fgets(line,BUF,fp) != NULL)
{
    if (has_ch(ch,line))
        fputs(line,stdout);
}
fclose(fp);
return 0;
}

int has_ch(char ch, const char * line)
{
    while (*line)
        if (ch == *line++)
            return(1);
    return 0;
}
```

The `fgets()` and `fputs()` functions work together because `fgets()` leaves the \n produced by Enter in the string, and `fputs()` does not add a \n the way that `puts()` does.

6. The distinction between a binary file and a text file is a system-dependent difference between file formats. The distinction between a binary stream and a text stream consists of translations performed by the program as it reads or writes streams. (A binary stream has no translations; a text stream may convert newline and other characters.)

7.   a. When 8238201 is saved using `fprintf()`, it's saved as seven characters stored in 7 bytes. When saved using `fwrite()`, it's saved as a 4-byte integer using the binary representation of that numeric value.

     b. No difference; in each case it's saved as a 1-byte binary code.

8. The first is just a shorthand notation for the second; the third writes to the standard error. Normally, the standard error is directed to the same place as the standard output, but the standard error is not affected by standard output redirection.

9. The `"r+"` mode lets you read and write anywhere in a file, so it's best suited. The `"a+"` only lets you append material to the end of the file, and the `"w+"` starts with a clean slate, discarding previous file contents.

Chapter 13

1. The automatic and the static storage classes.

2. The external storage class, the external static storage class, and the static storage class.

3. The external storage class and the external static storage class.

4. One source of inefficiency is that items are often relocated only to be relocated again before the inner loop finishes a cycle. Also, sometimes they actually get moved to positions far worse than the original position. Suppose, for example, that you're sorting the values 2, 10, 14, 8, 6, 19, and 1 in increasing order. At the end of the first inner loop cycle, the 1 and 2 are swapped, positioning the 1 correctly but placing the 2 far from its final position.

5. Replace `array[search] > array[top]` with `array[search] < array[top]`.

6. A string should be stored in a character array, so the array argument should be a pointer to an array of characters; the size of each character array depends on how many characters will be in the hexadecimal number. Let's assume that 20 is sufficient:

```
int getarray(char array[][20], int limit)
```

Because the data type is a string, use the `%s` specifier instead of `%d` for `scanf()` and `printf()`.

You would have to alter the test for a valid number. The new test should examine the string character by character to see whether they are hexadecimal digits; you can apply the `ctype.h` function `isxdigit()` to test each character for that purpose. (If you want to allow for the C-code notation of using a `0x` or `0X` prefix, you'd need to add extra code to check for that.)

7. `daisy` is known to `main()` by default, and to `petal()`, `stem()`, and `root()` because of the extern declaration. The `extern int daisy;` declaration in file 2 makes `daisy` known to all the functions in file 2. The first `lily` is local to `main()`: The reference to `lily` in `petal()` is an error because there is no external `lily` in either file. There is an external static `lily`, but it is known just to functions in the second file. The first external `rose` is known to `root()`, but `stem()` has overridden it with its own local `rose`.

8. Here is the output:

```
color in main() is B
color in first() is R
color in main() is B
color in second() is G
color in main() is G
```

9. a. It tells us that the program will use a variable `plink` that is local to the file containing the function. The first argument to `value_ct()` is a pointer to an integer, presumably the first element of an array

of n members. The important point here is that the program will not be allowed to use the pointer **arr** to modify values in the original array.

b. No. Already **value** and n are copies of original data, so there is no way for the function to alter the corresponding values in the calling program. What these declarations do accomplish is to prevent the function from altering **value** and n within the function. For example, the function couldn't use the expression n++ if n were qualified as **const**.

Chapter 14

1. The proper keyword is **struct**, not **structure**. The template requires either a tag before the opening brace or a variable name after the closing brace. Also, there should be a semicolon after * **togs** and at the end of the template.

2. Here is the output:

```
6 1
22 Spiffo Road
S p
```

3.

```
struct month {

    char name[10];

    char abbrev[4];

    int days;

    int monumb;

};
```

4.

```
struct month months[12] =
{
    {"January", "jan", 31, 1},
    {"February", "feb", 28, 2},
    {"March", "mar", 31, 3},
    {"April", "apr", 30, 4},
    {"May", "may", 31, 5},
    {"June", "jun", 30, 6},
    {"July", "jul", 31, 7},
    {"August", "aug", 31, 8},
```

```
        {"September", "sep", 30, 9},
        {"October", "oct", 31, 10},
        {"November", "nov", 30, 11},
        {"December", "dec", 31, 12}
    };
```

5.

```
extern struct month months[];
int days(int month)
{
    int index, total;

    if (month < 1 || month > 12)
        return(-1);   /* error signal */
    else
    {
        for (index = 0, total = 0; index < month; index ++)
                total += months[index].days;
        return( total);
    }
}
```

Note that index is one less than the month number because arrays start with subscript 0. Therefore, use index < month instead of index <= month.

6. Include string.h to provide strcpy():

```
LENS bigEye[10];
bigEye[2].foclen = 500;
bigEye[2] fstop = 2.0;
strcpy(bigEye[2].brand, "Remarkatar");
```

```
typedef struct lens {      /* lens descriptor */
        float foclen;      /* focal length,mm */
        float fstop;       /* aperture         */
        char brand[30];    /* brand name       */
} LENS;
```

7.   a.

```
6
Arcturan
cturan
```

b. Use the structure name and use the pointer:

```
deb.title.last
```

```
pb->title.last
```

c. Here is one version:

```
#include <stdio.h>
```

```
#include "starfolk.h"   /* make struct defs available */
```

```
void prbem (const struct bem * pbem )
{
    printf("%s %s is a %d-limbed %s.\n", pbem->title.first,
           pbem->title.last, pbem->limbs, pbem->type);
}
```

8. a. willie.born

    b. pt->born

    c. scanf("%d", &willie.born);

    d. scanf("%d", &pt->born);

    e. willie.name.fname[2]

    f. strlen(willie.name.fname) + strlen(willie.name.lname)

9. Here is one possibility:

```
struct car {

       char name[20];

       float hp;

       float epampg;

       float wbase;

       int year;

};
```

10. The function could be set up like this:

```
struct gas {

    float distance;

    float gals;

    float mpg;

};

struct gas mpgs(struct gas trip)

{

  if (trip.gals > 0)

      trip.mpg = trip.distance / trip.gals ;
```

```
       else

           trip.mpg = -1.0;

       return trip;

   }
```

Note that this function cannot directly alter values in the calling program, so you must use the return value to convey the information:

```
struct gas idaho;
idaho = mpgs(idaho);
```

11. `char * (*pfun)(char *, char);`

12.

```
double sum(double, double);
double diff(double, double);
double times(double, double);
double divide(double, double);
double (*pf1[4])(double, double) = {sum, diff, times, divide};
```

Or, more simply, replace the last line of code with these lines:

```
typedef double (*ptype)(double, double);
ptype pf[4] = {sum, diff, times, divide};
```

Chapter 15

1.   a. 00000011

     b. 00001101

     c. 00111011

     d. 01110111

2.   a. 21, 025, 0x15

     b. 85, 0125, 0x55

     c. 76, 0114, 0x4C

     d. 157, 0235, 0x9D

3.   a. 252

     b. 2

     c. 7

     d. 7

e. 5

f. 3

g. 28

4.   a. 255

b. 1 (not false is true)

c. 0

d. 1 (true and true is true)

e. 6

f. 1 (true or true is true)

g. 40

5. In binary, the mask is **1111111**. In decimal, it's **127**. In octal, it's **0177**. In hexadecimal, it's **0x7F**.

6. Both `bitvbal *= 2` and `bitval << 1` double the current value of `bitval`, so they are equivalent. However, `mask += bitval` and `mask |= bitval` have the same effect only if `bitval` and `mask` have no bits set to on in common. For example, 2 ¦ 4 is **6**, but so is 3 ¦ 6.

7.   a.

```
struct tb_drives {
    unsigned int diskdrives  : 2;
    unsigned int             : 1;
    unsigned int cdromdrives : 2;
    unsigned int             : 1;
    unsigned int harddrives  : 2;
};
```

b.

```
struct kb_drives {
    unsigned int harddrives  : 2;
    unsigned int             : 1;
    unsigned int cdromdrives : 2;
    unsigned int             : 1;
    unsigned int diskdrives  : 2;
};
```

Chapter 16

1.   a. `dist = 5280 * miles;` is valid.

b. `plort = 4 * 4 + 4;` is valid. But if the user really wanted 4 * (4 + 4), he or she should have used `#define POD   (FEET + FEET)`.

c. `nex = = 6;;` is valid, but not meaningful. Apparently the user forgot that he or she was writing for the preprocessor, not writing in C.

d. `y = y + 5;` is valid. `berg = berg + 5 * lob;` is valid, but this is probably not the desired result. `est = berg + 5/ y + 5;` is valid, but this is probably not the desired result. `nilp = lob *-berg + 5;` is valid, but this is probably not the desired result.

2. `#define NEW(X) ((X) + 5)`

3. `#define MIN(X,Y) ( (X) < (Y) ? (X) : (Y) )`

4. `#define EVEN_GT(X,Y) ( (X) > (Y) && (X) % 2 == 0 ? 1 : 0 )`

5. `#define PR(X,Y) printf(#X " is %d and " #Y " is %d\n", X,Y)`

Because X and Y are never exposed to any other operations (such as multiplication) in this macro, you don't have to cocoon everything in parentheses.

6.
  a. `#define QUARTERCENTURY 25`

  b. `#define SPACE ' '`

  c. `#define PS() putchar(' ')` or `#define PS() putchar(SPACE)`

  d. `#define BIG(X) ((X) + 3)`

  e. `#define SUMSQ(X,Y) ((X)*(X) + (Y)*(Y))`

7. Try this:

```
#define P(X) printf("name: "#X"; value: %d; address: %p\n", X, &X)
```

Or, if your implementation doesn't recognize the `%p` specification for the address, try `%u` or `%lu`.

8. Use the conditional compilation directives. One way is to use `#ifndef`:

```
#define _SKIP_   /* remove when you don't want to skip code */
#ifndef _SKIP_
     /* code to be skipped */
#endif
```

9.
  a.
```
enum days {sun, mon, tue, wed, thu, fri, sat}; /* 0 - 6 /
enum days {sun = 1, mon, tue, wed, thu, fri, sat}; / 1 - 7 */
```

  b. `enum days visit;`

10. The `argv` argument should be declared as type `char *argv[]`. Command-line arguments are stored as strings, so the program should first convert the string in `argv[1]` to a type `double` value, for example, by using

atof() from the stdlib.h library. The math.h header file should be included for the sqrt() function. The program should check for negative values before taking a square root.

11.   a. The function call should look like this:

```
qsort( (void *)scores, (size_t) 1000, sizeof (double), comp);
```

        b. Here's a suitable comparison function:

```
int comp(const void * p1, const void * p2)
{
    /* need to use pointers to int to access values   */
    const int * a1 = p1; /* a1 is proper pointer type */
    const int * a2 = p2;

    if (*a1 > *a2)
        return -1;
    else if (*a1 == *a2)
        return 0;
    else
        return 1;
}
```

12. The program should include the stdlib.h file, if available, or else declare malloc() or calloc().

```
struct wine * ptrwine;
ptrwine = (struct wine *) calloc(100, sizeof (struct wine));
```

or

```
ptrwine = (struct wine *)
malloc(100 * sizeof (struct wine));
```

Chapter 17

1. Defining a data type consists of deciding how to store the data and of designing a set of functions to manage the data.

2. The list can be traversed in only one direction because each structure contains the address of the next structure, but not of the preceding structure. You could modify the structure definition so that each structure contains two pointers, one to the preceding structure and one to the next structure. The program, of course, would have to assign proper addresses to these pointers each time a new structure is added.

3. An ADT is an abstract data type, a formal definition of the properties of a type and of the operations that can be performed with the type. An ADT should be expressed in general terms, not in terms of some specific computer language or implementation details.

4. Advantages of passing a variable directly: These functions inspect a list or queue, but should not alter them. Passing a list or queue variable directly means the function works with a copy of the original, guaranteeing that the function does not alter the original data. When passing a variable directly, you don't have to remember to use the address operator or a pointer. Disadvantages of passing a variable directly: The program has to allocate enough space to hold the variable, and then copy information from the original to the copy. If the variable is a large structure, using it has a time and space penalty. Advantages of passing the address of a variable: Passing an address and accessing the original data is faster and requires less memory than passing a variable if the variable is a large structure. Disadvantages of passing the address of a variable: You have to remember to use the address operator or a pointer. Under K&R C, the function could inadvertently alter the original data, but you can overcome this objection with the ANSI C **const** qualifier.

5. a.

Type Name:	Stack
Type Properties:	Can hold an ordered sequence of items
Type Operations:	Initialize stack to empty
	Determine whether stack is empty
	Determine whether stack is full
	Add item to top of stack (pushing an item)
	Remove and recover item from top of stack (popping an item)

b. This implements the stack as an array, but that information affects only the structure definition and the details of the function definitions; it doesn't affect the interface described by the function prototypes.

```
/* stack.h -- interface for a stack */

/* INSERT ITEM TYPE HERE */
/* FOR EXAMPLE, typedef int Item; */

#define MAXSTACK 100
typedef enum boolean {False, True} BOOLEAN;

typedef struct stack
{
    Item items[MAXSTACK];    /* holds info              */
    int top;                 /* index of first empty slot */
} Stack;
```

```
/* operation:       initialize the stack                      */
/* precondition:    ps points to a stack                      */
/* postcondition:   stack is initialized to being empty       */
void InitializeStack(Stack * ps);
/* operation:       check if stack is full                    */
/* precondition:    ps points to previously initialized stack */
/* postcondition:   returns True if stack is full, else False */
BOOLEAN FullStack(const Stack * ps);

/* operation:       check if stack is empty                   */
/* precondition:    ps points to previously initialized stack */
/* postcondition:   returns True if stack is empty, else False */
BOOLEAN EmptyStack(const Stack *ps);

/* operation:       push item onto top of stack               */
/* precondition:    ps points to previously initialized stack */
/*                  item is to be placed on top of stack      */
/* postcondition:   if stack is not empty, item is placed at  */
/*                  top of stack and function returns         */
/*                  True; otherwise, stack is unchanged and   */
/*                  function returns False                    */
BOOLEAN Push(Item item, Stack * ps);

/* operation:       remove item from top of stack             */
/* precondition:    ps points to previously initialized stack */
/* postcondition:   if stack is not empty, item at top of     */
/*                  stack is copied to *pitem and deleted from */
/*                  stack, and function returns True; if the  */
/*                  operation empties the stack, the stack is */
/*                  reset to empty. If the stack is empty to  */
/*                  begin with, stack is unchanged and the    */
/*                  function returns False                    */
BOOLEAN Pop(Item *pitem, Stack * ps);
```

6. Maximum number of comparisons required:

Items	Sequential Search	Binary Search
3	3	2
1023	1023	10
65535	65535	16

7. See Figure I.1.

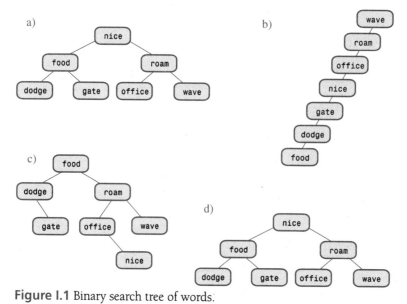

Figure I.1 Binary search tree of words.

8. See Figure I.2.

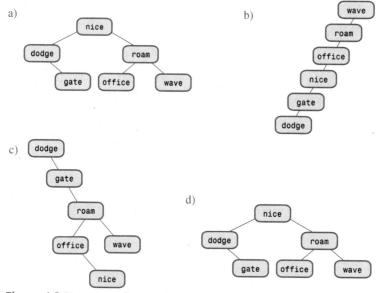

Figure I.2 Binary search tree of words after removal.

INDEX

M

The Waite Group's C++ Primer Plus, Third Edition

The first two editions of *The Waite Group's C++ Primer Plus* are classics that have sold over 75,000 copies and introduced thousands of users to C++. This new edition includes coverage of the Standard Template Library, one of the most significant additions to C++ since the second edition. This edition has also enhanced coverage of the latest object-oriented programming techniques, such as UML, CRC cards, and design patterns. It teaches C++ from the ground up, and makes understanding and experimenting with important object-oriented programming concepts both interesting and manageable. The friendly tone, concise programs, end-of-chapter review exercises, and plentiful illustrations will have readers writing their own programs in no time.

- All the listings and examples have been revised with an emphasis on hands-on learning.
- Guides the reader through complex topics without assuming previous knowledge of C.
- Covers the basics of object-oriented programming for beginners and the essential elements of C++.

$35.00 US, $50.95 CDN   *Beginner—Intermediate*   *Programming*
1-57169-162-6   *850 pp.*

C++ Unleashed

by Jesse Liberty

This book takes experienced C++ programmers to the next level of designing and programming C++ applications. Includes coverage of the most important issues, including namespaces, the STL, object-oriented analysis and design, manipulating data, object persistence and encryption, and distributed computing issues, such as CORBA, COM/DCOM, and Java. Real-world examples and references deliver solutions for everyday programming needs. This book is not focused on any one particular compiler; it's strictly based on the most recent ANSI/ISO C++ standard, so it can be used with any of the C++ compilers on the market, including Microsoft, Borland/Inprise, and others.

$39.99 US, $57.95 CDN   *Intermediate—Advanced*   *Programming*
0-672-31239-5   *800 pp.*

The Waite Group's Object-Oriented Programming in C++, Third Edition

by Robert Lafore

This classic tutorial presents the sophisticated new features of the most current ANSI/ISO C++ standard as they apply to object-oriented programming. Learn the concepts of object-oriented programming and how to use them to create sophisticated, efficient object-oriented applications. This book assumes no C programming experience, but does expect the reader to be familiar with basic programming concepts. Readers get up to speed quickly on emerging new concepts of object-oriented design patterns, CRC modeling, and the new Universal Modeling Language (UML).With this book, you can get up to speed on the latest ANSI/ISO C++ standard and the emerging discipline of object-oriented design and high-level concepts. You can go from simple programming examples straight up to full-fledged object-oriented applications with quick real-world examples, conceptual illustrations, questions, and exercises.

$34.99 USA, $50.95 CDN   *Intermediate*   *Programming*
1-57169-160-X   *850 pp.*

Add to Your Sams Library Today with the Best Books for Programming, Operating Systems, and New Technologies

To order, visit our Web site at www.mcp.com or fax us at

1-800-835-3202

ISBN	Quantity	Description of Item	Unit Cost	Total Cost
1-57169-162-6		The Waite Group's C++ Primer Plus, Third Edition	$35.00	
0-672-31239-5		C++ Unleashed	$39.99	
1-57169-160-X		The Waite Group's Object-Oriented Programming in C++, Third Edition	$34.99	
		Shipping and Handling: See information below.		
		TOTAL		

Shipping and Handling

Standard	$5.00
2nd Day	$10.00
Next Day	$17.50
International	$40.00

201 W. 103rd Street, Indianapolis, Indiana 46290   1-800-835-3202 — FAX

Book ISBN 1-57169-161-8

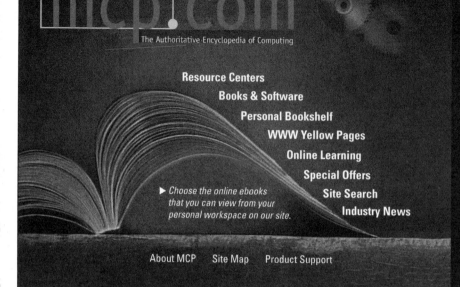